THE WEST YORKSHIRE
REGIMENT IN THE WAR
1914—1918

MILITARY HISTORIES
BY THE SAME AUTHOR

The History of the
2nd DIVISION, 1914-1918

The History of the
62nd (W.R.) DIVISION, 1914-1919
[*Shortly.*]

The History of the
SOMERSET LIGHT INFANTRY,
1914-1918
[*In Preparation.*]

The History of the
MIDDLESEX REGIMENT,
1914-1919
[*In Preparation.*]

The History of the
EAST YORKSHIRE REGIMENT
1914-1918
[*In Preparation.*]

The History of the
30th (HOW.) BATTERY, R.F.A.
1914-1918
[*In Preparation.*]

THE WEST YORKSHIRE REGIMENT IN THE WAR 1914-1918

A HISTORY OF THE 14TH, THE PRINCE OF WALES' OWN (WEST YORKSHIRE REGT.) AND OF ITS SPECIAL RESERVE, TERRITORIAL AND SERVICE BATTNS. IN THE GREAT WAR OF 1914-1918

BY
EVERARD WYRALL

AUTHOR OF "EUROPE IN ARMS: A CONCISE HISTORY OF THE GREAT WAR"; "THE HISTORY OF THE SECOND DIVISION 1914-1918," etc., etc.

VOL. I. 1914—1916.

LONDON
JOHN LANE THE BODLEY HEAD LIMITED, VIGO STREET, W.

Printed and bound by Antony Rowe Ltd, Eastbourne

NEC ASPERA TERRENT

"Namur, 1695," "Tournay," "Corunna,"
"Java," "Waterloo," "Bhurtpore."
"Sevastopol," "New Zealand,"
"Afghanistan, 1879-80,"
"Relief of Ladysmith,"
"South Africa,
1899-1902."

CONTENTS

	PAGE
The First Battalion Embarks for France	1

I.
THE GERMAN INVASION, 1914

Actions on the Aisne Heights	9
The Battle of Armentières	15

II.
TRENCH WARFARE, 1914 - 1916

Trench Warfare, November, 1914—9th March, 1915	29
The Battle of Neuve Chapelle, 10th-13th March, 1915	37
Trench Warfare, 15th March—15th June, 1915	51
The First Attack on Bellewaerde, 16th June, 1915	61

THE DARDANELLES

The Battles of Suvla : Introduction	71
The Landing at Suvla : Capture of Karakol Dagh, 6th-15th August, 1915	75
The Battle of Scimitar Hill, 21st August, 1915	87

FRANCE AND FLANDERS

II.
TRENCH WARFARE, 1914 - 1916—(continued)

Trench Warfare, 1st-31st July, 1915	97
The Actions of Hooge, 9th August, 1915	107
Trench Warfare, 1st-31st August, 1915	113
The Battle of Loos, I., 25th September—8th October, 1915	119
The Battle of Loos, II., Subsidiary	129
Trench Warfare, 1st October—31st December, 1915	133

THE DARDANELLES

Trench Warfare at Suvla and the Evacuation	151

A Note on the Situation at the End of the Year 1915	157

CONTENTS—*continued*

II.

TRENCH WARFARE, 1914 - 1916—(continued)

	PAGE
Trench Warfare, 1st January—31st March, 1916	163
A Minor Enterprise..	183

III.

THE ALLIED OFFENSIVE, 1916

The Battles of the Somme, 1916 : Introduction..	189
The General Attack..	195
The Battle of Albert, 1st-13th July, 1916..	199
The Capture of Fricourt	199
The Attack on Ovillers-la-Boiselle	203
The Attack on Serre and Pendant Copse..	208
The Attack on Thiepval	216
The Next Day—2nd July and after	224
The Capture of Horseshoe Trench	227
The Capture of Bailiff Wood and Contalmaison..	229
The Leipzig Salient..	231
The Battle of Bazentin Ridge, 14th-17th July	235
The Battle of Delville Wood	243
The Attack on Munster Alley	249
The Attack on Lonely Trench	251
The Attack on Thiepval, 3rd September..	255
The Attack on the Wundt Werk	258
The Capture of the Quadrilateral..	264
The Battle of Morval : Capture of Lesbœufs	267
The Battle of Thiepval Ridge	273
The Attack on the Schwaben Redoubt	279
The Battle of Le Transloy Ridge : Capture of Le Sars..	281
The Attack on Mild and Cloudy Trenches, 12th October	284
The Attack on Zenith Trench	290

ILLUSTRATIONS

	PAGE
A Main Street in Armentières	30
The Square, Ypres	56
On the Yser—A deep, fresh shell-hole.	98
"Peace there was none." A Sector in the Ypres Salient after an attack.	104
An Outpost in front of our line in the Ypres Salient	140
Suvla Bay—The afternoon before the evacuation, showing stores accumulated on the beach.	154
"It seemed as if nothing could possibly exist in that inferno" A German trench after the bombardment, 1st July, 1916.	195
At Fricourt—The northern end of the village in July, 1916.	201
"Ovillers lay in the German Second System"—A German trench at Ovillers battered by our Artillery, July, 1916.	205
Longueval Village	243
"An almost unrecognizable mass of tumbled bricks and masonry"—The remains of Thiepval Village, Sept., 1916.	254
Moving up to the Flers Line, September, 1916	261
The Battle of Morval, September, 1916—The Battlefield on the morning of 25th September.	270
Winter on the Somme, 1916—Ammunition for the Front Line, carried up on mules.	300
Panoramic view of Ypres.	304

LIST OF MAPS

	PAGE
The 2nd Battalion's First Sector in France, 1914	29
Trenches of the 1st Battalion, December, 1914	34
The Battle of Neuve Chapelle, 10th-13th March, 1915	48
The Battles of Suvla	92
The Action of Hooge, 9th August, 1915	112
The Battle of Loos, 25th September, 1915	128
Line held by the 49th Division, Winter, 1915-1916	142
A Minor Enterprise	184
The Battle Front on the Somme, 1st July, 1916	196
Trenches of the 23rd Infantry Brigade (8th Division), on 1st July, 1916	206
The Attack on Serre and Pendant Copse, 1st July, 1916. Trenches of the Leeds and Bradford "Pals"	214
The Capture of Horse Shoe Trench, of Bailiff Wood, and Contalmaison	230
The Attack on Thiepval, 3rd September, 1916	256
The Attack on the Wonder Work	260
Battle of Morval : Capture of Lesbœufs	270
The Capture of Stuff Redoubt	276
The Attack on Mild and Cloudy Trenches	286
The Attack on Zenith Trench	294

THE 1st BATTALION EMBARKS FOR FRANCE

ON the outbreak of War in August, 1914, the 14th, The Prince of Wales' Own (West Yorkshire, Regt.) consisted of two Regular Battalions (the 1st and 2nd), two Special Reserve Battalions (the 3rd and 4th) and four Territorial Battalions (the 5th, 6th, 7th and 8th). The 3rd and 4th West Yorks. R. were originally the 2nd West Yorkshires and 4th West Yorks. Militia respectively. The 1st Battalion (contained in the 18th Infantry Brigade of the 6th Division) was stationed at Lichfield; the 2nd Battalion formed part of the garrison at Malta; the 3rd and 4th Battalions were at York. The four Territorial Battalions had their Headquarters as follows: 5th at York, 6th at Bradford and the 7th and 8th ("The Leeds Rifles") at Leeds. The 16th and 17th Infantry Brigades of the 6th Division were at this period in Ireland.

On the 7th of August, the 1st West Yorkshires (as part of the 18th Infantry Brigade) left Lichfield for Dumfermline, arriving on the following day: mobilization was practically complete. On the 13th August, the 18th Infantry Brigade again entrained, this time for Cambridge, where the 6th Division had been ordered to concentrate. Concentration of the Division was completed during the latter days of August, and on the 7th of September, the 18th Infantry Brigade marched to Newmarket and there entrained for Southampton.

The 1st West Yorkshires embarked on the "Cawdor Castle" and sailed at 6-15 a.m. for France, the total strength of the battalion being: Officers, twenty-seven; other ranks, 959; horses, fifty-seven; vehicles seventeen, and bicycles nineteen.

St. Nazaire was reached on the 9th September and disembarkation took place early on the morning of the 10th. By the 12th, the 6th Division was concentrated south of the Marne in billets in the area Coulommiers—Montcerf—Marles—Chaume under the command of Major General T. L. Keir. The 18th Infantry Brigade was commanded by Brig.-General W. M. Congreve, V.C. The 1st West Yorks. Regt. billeted in Croupet, was under the command of Lieut.-Col. F. W. Towsey.

The general situation on the Western Front at the time of the arrival of the 6th Division, south of the Marne, may be summarized briefly. Before the declaration of war, the French scheme of operations ("Plan 17") was based upon the assumption that the Germans would attack across the common frontier, *i.e.*, from Luxembourg to the Swiss Frontier. On this assumption the French General Staff had drawn up plans for an offensive through Alsace and Lorraine.

The German plan (von Schlieffen's) provided not for an offensive along the eastern frontiers of France, but an advance through Belgium and Luxemburg, with five armies, *viz.*, First, Second, Third, Fourth and Fifth (from North to South) pivoting on Thionville: the Sixth and Seventh German armies were to advance against the Moselle, behind Frouard and Meurthe. The right wing of these armies was to advance west of, and round the south of Paris.

The French offensive in Lorraine was duly launched and at first obtained considerable success, but meanwhile the Germans had begun to advance through Belgium in unexpected strength. General Joffre (the French Commander-in-Chief) had therefore to stop his offensive in Lorraine and reinforce the left wing of his armies, the Fifth French Army (Lanrezac) moving north to the triangle Givet—Namur-Charleroi.

The British Expeditionary Force then came into line on the left of the French, along the line of the Mons-Conde Canal, its original area of deployment, the new allied plan, being the envelopment of the German right wing.

The First German Army (von Kluck) was wheeling into line, when the Second German Army (von Bülow) and the Third German Army (von Hausen) attacked the Fifth French Army. Taken in flank by von Hausen as well as heavily attacked on his front by von Bülow, Lanrezac fell back from the line of the Meuse and retired south. His retirement uncovered the right flank of the British Expeditionary Force which now, with both flanks exposed, had to conform to the retrograde movement on its right.

The operations at Mons and Le Cateau and the tortuous days of retreat are already well-known and need not be repeated. Closely followed by the First German Army, and by the Second German Army on its right flank, the British Army, always under orders, retired to a line south of the Marne River.

The success of the German right wing had, however, created delirium at German General Headquarters. Everything had gone according to plan, and might have ended disastrously for the Allies had the enemy possessed sufficient troops on his right wing and followed closely the scheme of von Schlieffen's operations, but the latter was dead and a weaker than he controlled the destinies of the German Armies. The Battle of Guise fought on the 30th August (in which the British Expeditionary Force was not engaged) seems to have impressed the enemy with the idea that the French left might easily be enveloped without continuing the march west and south of Paris. Accordingly the First German Army (having been already weakened by the loss of several divisions transferred elsewhere) under orders from the Supreme Command turned in a south-easterly direction: " the intention is to drive the French in a south-easterly direction from Paris." In this change of direction von Kluck fought three rear-guard actions with the British: one at Néry, another at Crepy and a third at Villers Cotterets, all on 1st September. These actions should have convinced him that the British Expeditionary Force was anything but " out of action." But his march in a south-easterly direction was continued and finally his optimism (and the optimism of German General Headquarters) involved him in difficulties from which he did not escape without heavy losses nor without endangering the whole right wing of the German Armies. For as the British Expeditionary Force lay south of the Marne, with the Sixth French Army on its left and the Fifth French Army (now under d'Esperay) on its right, von Kluck attempted to march across Sir John French's front. It was then that Generals Joffre and French struck hard, throwing von Kluck's right into confusion and forcing him back, from the west upon the Ourcq and from the south upon the River Marne. In this action Gallieni's Sixth French Army, striking from the direction of Paris, was largely responsible for von Kluck's discomfiture. The retirement of the First German Army involved the Second German Army also, which under pressure from d'Esperay's Fifth French Army and Foch's Ninth French Army (on the right of the Fifth) was similarly pressed back upon the Marne. Moreover, as the First and Second German Armies retired northwards an ever-widening gap was uncovered between the inner flanks of both German Armies.

The Battle of the Marne was fought on 7th-10th September, after which the enemy was in full retreat to the line of the Aisne River. He crossed the latter on the 11th, destroying the crossings wherever possible, taking up a position along the northern banks and on the high ground above the river, overlooking the crossings.

On the night of the 11th September, the British Expeditionary Force consisting of five infantry divisions and one infantry brigade (1st, 2nd, 3rd, 4th, 5th Divisions and 19th Infantry Brigade), one

Cavalry Division and one Cavalry Brigade, lay south of the River Aisne; Ist Corps (1st and 2nd Divisions) Beugneux (3 miles west-south-west of Arcy), Bruyeres, south-west to Rocourt, Oulchy le Chateau; IInd Corps (3rd and 5th Divisions) Hartennes, south-east to Grand Rozoy (just west of Beugneux) Oulcay la Ville, Billy sur Ourcq, St. Remy (all just north-west of Oulchy le Chateau); IIIrd Corps (4th Division and 19th Infantry Brigade) La Loge Farm to Chouy; Cavalry Division; Loupeigne (3½ miles north-north-east of Fère en Tardenois), westward to Arcy Ste. Restitue (4½ miles north-north-west of Fère); 3rd and 5th Cavalry Brigades : Parcy Tigny (6½ miles west of Arcy), north to Villemontoire. British General Head Quarters was at Coulommiers On the right was the Fifth French Army, and on the left the Sixth French Army.

It was at this period that the 6th Division arrived south of the Marne.

The Battle of the Aisne (12th-15th August) gave the French and British Armies possession of the River and a footing on the northern banks—but very little more, for the Germans had been able to interpose between the inner flanks of their First and Second Armies, the Seventh German Army, under von Herringen, consisting of the 7th Reserve and XVth Corps, which filled the gap at a critical period.

During the operations on the Aisne the 6th Division began to move forward and after a series of uneventful marches reached Villemontoire on the 16th September, the 16th, 17th and 18th Infantry Brigades billeting in areas mostly south of the town.

I.
THE GERMAN INVASION, 1914

THE BATTLE OF THE AISNE, 1914.
Actions on the Aisne Heights, 20th September.

THE OPERATIONS IN FLANDERS, 1914.
BATTLE OF ARMENTIÈRES: CAPTURE OF METEREN.
14th October—2nd November.

1914

ACTIONS ON THE AISNE HEIGHTS

"ON the 16th, the 6th Division came up into line," said Sir John French in his despatches. "It had been my intention to direct the Ist Corps to attack and seize the enemy's position on the Chemin des Dames, supporting it with this new reinforcement. I hoped from the position thus gained to bring effective fire to bear across the front of the 3rd Division which by securing the advance of the latter, would also take the pressure off the 5th Division and the IIIrd Corps. But any further advance of the Ist Corps would have dangerously exposed my right flank. And, further, I learned from the French Commander-in-Chief that he was strongly reinforcing the Sixth French Army on my left, with the intention of bringing up the Allied left to attack the enemy's flank and thus compel his retirement. I therefore sent the 6th Division to join the IIIrd Corps, with orders to keep it on the south side of the river (Aisne), as it might be available in general reserve."

16TH SEPT.

The position of the British Army on the Aisne at this period was still somewhat insecure. Excepting at Conde, which was still in the possession of the enemy, the crossings of the Aisne from Bourg to the right flank of the Sixth French Army near Soissons, had been won only after hard fighting. The Ist Corps (Sir Douglas Haig) with great gallantry had pushed forward until its right (1st Division) rested on Troyon almost on the Chemin des Dames, and its left (2nd Division) north of Chavonne about Cour de Soupir Fme. The Cavalry Division lay along the Chavonne-Soissons road, between the left of the Ist, and the right of the IInd Corps (Sir H. Smith-Dorrien), the 3rd Division was on the right, north and north-west of Vailly and the 5th Division south of the river opposite Missy and from just west of Missy to St. Marguerite : Conde was in the hands of the enemy and still held out : of the IIIrd Corps (Sir W. P. Pulteney) the 4th Division was at Bray and Venizel, north and south of the Aisne.

The right flank of the Sixth French Army (Gen. Maunoury)

was between Crouay and Braye on Sir John French's left and the Fifth French Army (Gen. D'Esperey) on his right, joining up north-east of Troyon.

The German Armies opposing Generals Maunoury, French and D'Esperey were the First German Army (General von Kluck) from the L'Oise-L'Aisne Canal (IIIrd Corps) to, and turning north through Nampcel: the Seventh German Army (General von Herringen) consisting of the VIIth Reserve Corps and XVth and XIIth Corps, with the right of the former on Braye-en-Laonnois: then the Second German Army (General von Bülow) opposing the bulk of the Fifth French Army. Hostile German Cavalry operated between the Seventh and Second German Armies as well as on the right flank of the First German Army.

17TH/19TH SEPT.

On the 17th, 18th and 19th September the whole of the British line was heavily bombarded. On the 17th, the 1st Division was subjected to a violent infantry attack, but the enemy was everywhere repulsed. On the 18th, these attacks were resumed—still without gain to the enemy. It was on the 18th that General Joffre proposed a new plan to Sir John French. The French Commander-in-Chief had conceived the idea of forming a new Army on the left of his Sixth Army with the intention of turning von Kluck's right flank. Sir John agreed and seeing that the battle must last some days longer until General Joffre had developed his new flank movement, saw also that he must of necessity form a reserve from which he could reinforce any part of his line and at the same time afford the troops engaged in the front-line trenches some measure of relief. Accordingly, he said, " It becomes essential to establish some system of regular relief in the trenches, and I have used the infantry of the 6th Division for this purpose with good results. The relieved brigades were brought back alternately, south of the river, and, with the artillery of the 6th Division, formed a general reserve on which I could rely in case of necessity."

Orders were then issued for the 18th Infantry Brigade to join the 1st Corps.

On the 19th of September the 6th Division was in general reserve in the area Vauxtin-Courcelles-Paars-Bazoches-Quincy—Mont Notre Dame.

At 4 a.m. on the morning of the 19th, in a heavy rain, the 18th Infantry Brigade set out for Bourg, which was reached soon after daylight. Here, at 7 a.m., the Brigade was ordered to take over positions held by the 2nd Infantry Brigade (1st Division) and for part of the day by the 1st Infantry Brigade (1st Division). At 11 p.m. the reliefs were completed.

19TH SEPT. 1ST BATTALION.

The 1st West Yorkshires now held the extreme right of the British line joining up with the left flank of the Fifth French Army, a regiment of Tireulleurs d'Afrique, coloured troops. " A " and " B " Companies under Major A. W. Ingles, were in the firing line which was just south of the Chemin des Dames, from west to east, " C " and " D " Companies were in support trenches echeloned in the right rear of the two forward companies.

The 2nd Durham Light Infantry were on the left of the West Yorkshires, the East Yorks. on the left of the Durhams, in front of Troyon ; and the Sherwood Foresters (2nd Notts. and Derby Regt.) in reserve just in front of the village. Brigade Headquarters were in Troyon.

Enemy snipers opened fire on the West Yorkshiremen before they were properly settled in their trenches, but no infantry attack was made. During the night the battalion improved the trenches and constructed overhead cover. But the trenches were poor, consisting of a series of excavations in the ground. No communication trenches existed and the firing line was connected with the supports by telephone.

The Battalion stood to arms at 3-30 a.m. and shortly afterwards heavy shell fire opened on the French troops on the right flank. About 5 a.m. the enemy launched an infantry attack against the Turcos, who, having lost most of their officers and having suffered heavy casualties during the bombardment, withdrew from their forward trenches towards Paissy, leaving the right flank of the West Yorkshires in the air. An officers' patrol under Lieut. C. T. Meautys was sent out to reconnoitre the right of the battalion, but was fired upon and returned. " D " Company under Capt. Lowe was then ordered to advance and a position was taken up on some open ground facing right, but again rifle fire broke out : it was evident the French had regained their trenches and in the uncertain morning light had mistaken the British troops for the enemy. " D " Company, however retired to its former position. Up to this period the Battalion had suffered several casualties : Lieut. G. V. Naylor Leyland, Royal Horse Guards, temporarily attached, was wounded, one other rank was killed and twenty-six wounded. Lieut. Naylor Leyland died of his wounds on 21st September.

20TH SEPT.

At 8 a.m. heavy rifle-fire was again opened on the West Yorkshires' trenches and Col. Towsey with Lieut. Meautys went forward

20TH SEPT. 1ST BATTALION.

to see what was happening. In going forward Lieut. Meautys was mortally wounded. Once more " D " Company was sent forward to reinforce " A " and " B " Companies in the firing line. Heavy firing continued all the morning and the French on the right of the Battalion again left their trenches. One company of the Royal Sussex Regiment and a squadron of the 18th Hussars were brought up to strengthen the right flank of the battalion. Telephonic communication with the firing line having broken down, touch was possible only by means of runners, but " about 1-30 p.m." the official diary states, " a man ran back from the firing line and reported the companies in front had been captured and the Germans were advancing. From information collected it is certain that the Germans advanced under cover of the white flag on the right flank, and when our men went out to meet them they were surrounded and heavily fired on. Many were killed, a few escaped and eight officers and 436 other ranks were captured. Owing to the retirement of the French the Germans were able to get round our right flank and enfilade us with machine-gun and rifle fire."[1]

The whole affair was a mystery, but it was evident the lost companies had been first tricked and then shot down or taken prisoners.

The C. O., Col. Towsey, was wounded and about 3 p.m. Major Lang went forward to reconnoitre. He signalled the advance and Battalion Headquarters with " C " Company went forward and re-occupied the trenches which had been held by " A " and " B " Companies, having the Durham Light Infantry on their left. This position was maintained until 8 p.m. when Battalion Headquarters and " C " Company were relieved by the Sherwood Foresters. After burying their dead and as far as possible collecting the wounded, all that remained of the Battalion—five officers and 250 other ranks, were ordered into reserve in Troyon.

The official list of casualties was given as follows : seven officers killed (Major A. W. Ingles, Capt. M. Fisher, Capt. J. F. I'Anson, Lieut. W. L. Eliot, Lieut. T. G. Meautys, Lieut. O. C. W. Thompson and 2nd. Lieut. E. W. Wilson), two officers wounded (Lieut.-Col. F. Towsey and Lieut. Pickering); eight officers missing; seventy-one other ranks killed; 110 wounded and 436 missing. Major Ingles was killed whilst gallantly advancing on the trenches captured, with a few men he had collected.

The 20th September was a serious day for the 18th Infantry

[1] Bn. Diary. 1st. W. Yorks. R

Brigade, for the Durham Light Infantry and the East Yorks. also 1ST BATTALION. lost heavily. But the line was maintained, at this period of the Aisne operations a matter of vital importance, for it involved the right flank of the British Expeditionary Force.

On the 21st, Major Lang assumed command of the battalion, 21ST SEPT. which was re-formed into headquarters, C Company and one platoon. On 22nd and 23rd the battalion was in support to the Durham Light Infantry, relieving that battalion in the line on the 24th. Nine more men were killed and two wounded on the 25th, and at 8 p.m. the battalion was relieved and marched back to Pargnan, into Divisional Reserve. On the 27th reinforcements (the first) arrived, *i.e.*, one officer and ninety-six men. At 6 p.m. on the night of the 28th, the battalion again went up into the support trenches north-east of Troyon, having 100 men in the firing line. Two days were thus spent in the trenches, and on the 1st October the battalion was relieved by the Sherwood Foresters and marched into billets at Moulins, arriving at 11 a.m. In the evening, the 18th Infantry Brigade as a whole marched to billets in Vauxtin and Vauberlin.

By the 28th September the newly-formed French Army on the 28TH SEPT. left of the Sixth French Army had begun operations: they were alternately successful and unsuccessful, for the fighting was of a distinctly ding-dong nature. The effect upon the Aisne operations was almost immediate. From the 28th, the enemy's attacks died down: he had been forced to turn his attention to the situation on his extreme right, where the newly-formed French Army had made itself felt with startling suddenness. Indeed, he had withdrawn troops from other portions of his front (the Aisne, Verdun, etc.) in an attempt to outflank the Allies' outflanking movement. In this manner the race to the coast began until finally the Belgian coast was reached, both sides endeavouring to carry out similar plans, and in consequence the operations assumed something of the nature of a running fight until the sea stopped further progress, with the result that both the Allies and the enemy were forced once more to take up positions similar to those on the Aisne before the rush northwards had begun.

Briefly such was the situation: before Sir John French and General Joffre had to abandon their plans for turning the right flank of the enemy, many fierce and bloody engagements were fought, which resulted in the formation of that now famous, but terrible, scene of wholesale slaughter—the Ypres Salient. The reasons which induced the Allies to move the British Expeditionary Force from the

1ST BATTALION.

Aisne were given in Sir John French's despatch dated the 20th November, 1914.[1]

"Early in October a study of the general situation strongly impressed me with the necessity of bringing the greatest possible force to bear in support of the northern flank of the Allies, in order to effectively outflank the enemy and compel him to evacuate his position. At the same time the position on the Aisne as described in the concluding paragraphs of my last despatch appeared to me to warrant withdrawal of the British Forces from the positions they then held. The enemy had been weakened by continual abortive and futile attacks, whilst the fortification of the position had been much improved."

The IInd Corps was the first to move, its destination Abbeville, *en route* to the line Aire-Bethune, where it was ordered to arrive on the 11th October: the IIIrd Corps was then to move and had been ordered to detrain at St. Omer on the 12th: the Ist Corps was to be the last to leave the Aisne, with instructions to detrain at St. Omer on the 19th October.

2ND OCT.

On the 2nd October the 1st West Yorkshires again marched in Brigade to Jury, and *en route* (at Braisne) further re-inforcements, numbering one officer and ninety-two other ranks, joined the battalion: A Company was then reformed. Three days later whilst the battalion was still billeted in Jury, a third party of all ranks, numbering two officers and 326 other ranks, marched into the village and reported their arrival: B Company was reformed. On the 6th October the 18th Infantry Brigade marched to St. Remy—the movement west and north-west from the Aisne had begun.

At St. Sauveur whither the battalion marched *via* Largny, Major Cliffe, with four other officers joined: the strength of the battalion (three Companies, A, B and C) was now thirteen officers and 848 other ranks: thirteen officers and 130 other ranks were still required to bring the battalion up to its war establishment.

9TH OCT.

On the 9th October, the 6th Division entrained at Pont St. Mayence—Languell St. Marie—Le Meux—Compeigne, *en route* (with the IIIrd Corps) for St. Omer.

---

[1] The position was in fact a stale mate. Under the enervating conditions such as prevailed on the Aisne in September, 1914, the *morale* of the finest troops in the world would soon have been in danger. Moreover the Allies in France could not afford to sit down in their trenches whilst the enemy detached portions of his forces in order to send them to Eastern Prussia, where the situation was going not at all favourably for the Germans.

1914
THE BATTLE OF ARMENTIÈRES: CAPTURE OF METEREN

13th October—2nd November, 1914

ON the 8th October, Sir John French visited General Foch (who had been appointed to command the French Forces north of Noyon) at his headquarters at Doullens. There the following scheme of operations was drawn up:

The IInd British Corps was to arrive on the line Aire-Bethune on the 11th October, to connect up with the right of the Tenth French Army then in the vicinity of Bethune. The Corps was then to pivot on the left of the Tenth French Army and to attack in flank the enemy opposing the French.

The Cavalry were to move on the northern flank of the IInd Corps and support its attack until the IIIrd Corps, due to detrain at St. Omer on the 12th, came into line. They were then to clear the front and act on the northern flank of the IIIrd Corps in a similar manner pending the arrival of the Ist Corps.

The 3rd Cavalry Division and the 7th Division under Sir Henry Rawlinson, which were then operating in support of the Belgian Army and assisting its withdrawal from Antwerp, were to co-operate as soon as circumstances would allow.

The IInd Corps (3rd and 5th Divisions) completed its detrainment at Abbeville on the 8th October and, covered by cavalry, moved forward on the 11th, arriving on the line of the Aire-Bethune Canal as ordered.

The 2nd Cavalry Division (General Gough) finding the enemy in possession of some woods north of the Canal, attacked him and drove him eastwards.

The IIIrd Corps (4th and 6th Divisions) reached St. Omer on 13TH OCT. the 11th, and set out eastwards towards Hazebrouck, where it remained during the 12th. On the 13th, the Corps was ordered to advance against the line Armentières-Wytschaete, the line of attack assigned to the Corps.

In this way the Battle of Armentières began.

The official area of the Battle was from Fournes, through Estaires to Hazebrouck Station, thence to Caistre Station and Dranoutre, and the line of the River Douve.

13TH OCT. The enemy opposed the IInd and IIIrd British Corps and Cavalry Corps of two Divisions, with the XIIIth Wurtemburg and the XIXth Saxon Corps which were being pushed forward to the River Lys behind a screen formed by three Cavalry Corps, the Ist, IInd and IVth. These five Corps formed the right wing of the Sixth German Army, the formation of which was: VIIth, XIIIth, XIVth and XIXth Active Corps: Ist, IInd and IVth Reserve Cavalry Corps: 25th and 48th Reserve Divisions: Garde Cavalry Division: Bavarian Cavalry Division: 2nd, 3rd, 4th, 6th, 7th and 9th Cavalry Divisions. A German Cavalry Division at this period included horse artillery batteries, two or three infantry battalions, two or more machine-gun batteries and two or more companies of Cyclists: a Division was therefore a force of all arms, unlike a British Cavalry Division.

On the 12th October, Lille had fallen and the garrison of 4,500 French troops was captured.

On the same day the IInd Corps advanced in line, the right of the 5th Division, connecting up with the left of the French Army north of Annequin, the 3rd Division deploying on the left of the 5th.

In the early hours of the 13th, the IIIrd Corps moved eastwards, an advanced guard occupying the line Strazeele Station—Caestre—St. Sylvestre. The 4th Division was on the left and the 6th Division on the right.

Conneau's French Cavalry operated between the IInd and IIIrd Corps.

The 6th Division having as its first objective the line Vieux Berquin—Merris, moved forward in two columns. The Right Column under Brig. Gen. Congreve, V.C., formed of the 18th Infantry Brigade, XXXVIIIth Brigade R. F. A., 18th Field Ambulance, Cyclists and Engineers, set out at 7-30 a.m. and proceeded to Vieux Berquin, which place was reached about mid-day. Here the Brigade relieved the Queen's Bays and prepared to attack the enemy who was established in Bleu, a small village east of Vieux Berquin. The **1ST BATTALION.** attack was launched at 1-30 p.m., the 1st East Yorks. being on the right of the line, the 1st West Yorkshires in the centre and the 2nd Durham Light Infantry on the left: the Sherwood Foresters were in Brigade Reserve. Bleu was captured about 4-30 p.m., and the battalions then entrenched themselves for the night on the ground won. The attack was made during very misty weather and owing to enfilade fire coming from a small farm south of Bleu, many casualties were suffered, the Brigade losing 120 all ranks—

killed, wounded and missing. The 1st West Yorkshires lost one officer (Major H. T. Cliffe) killed, two officers wounded, nine other ranks killed and thirty-two wounded.

At night the front held by the 18th Infantry Brigade extended from Bleu—Haute Maison to the railway south of Merris.

Meanwhile the main body of the 6th Division had with the 4th Division become involved in an attack for the possession of the line Merris—Meteren—Fontaine Hoek. The 17th Infantry Brigade captured Merris and Oultersteen after stiff fighting, joining up with the left of the 18th Infantry Brigade. The 4th Division captured Fontaine Hoek and the high ground west of Meteren : Meteren itself was captured at midnight.

On the 14th the IIIrd Corps again advanced eastwards.

The 6th Division marched in three columns with the 18th Infantry Brigade as right flank guard. The destination of the Brigade was La Verrier, but its advance was opposed all day by a German rear-guard of cavalry with machine-guns. The 1st West Yorkshires as advanced guard to the Brigade pressed the enemy back, but could not progress further than a line one-third of a mile north of La Verrier : here the battalion remained on outpost duty.

During the day the battalion's losses were 2nd Lieut. J. Carew and one sergeant killed, and 2nd Lieut. Gill and four other ranks wounded. Lieut.-Col. Towsey who had recovered from his wound received on the Aisne, assumed command of the battalion. The 17th Infantry Brigade reached the line Blanche Maison—La Becque : the 19th Infantry Brigade remained in Bailleul with Divisional Headquarters.

The 4th Division at nightfall held the line Bailleul—St. Jans Cappel.

The 15th, 16th and 17th October were days of little interest in the history of the battalion, which marched forward in Brigade and Division as the IIIrd Corps advanced towards the line of the Lys, which the 6th Division crossed on the latter date, at nightfall holding the line Rouge de Bout—Croix Blanche—Bois Grenier (16th Infantry Brigade) Bois Grenier—La Vasee (inclusive, 18th Infantry Brigade) La Vasee—Chapelle D'Armentières (17th Infantry Brigade).

The 4th Division on crossing the Lys on the 17th found Armentières unoccupied and advanced its right flank towards L'Epinette : its left was still on the western banks of the Lys, west of Armentières to Le Gheir.

So far the IIIrd Corps had not experienced much difficulty in advancing. Neither had the IInd Corps, south of the IIIrd, been attacked, but had done all the attacking—the 3rd and 5th Divisions driving back the enemy sometimes at the point of the bayonet. The reason was that on the 14th, the German General Staff ordered the Sixth Army to remain entirely on the defensive along the line Messines, Armentières, La Bassee and to await the attack of the new Fourth German Army against the left flank of the Allies at Ypres. Great store was set on the action of this new Army, the formation of which had been jealously guarded behind a strong screen of cavalry and the IIIrd Reserve Corps thrown across its front in order to prevent detection.

18TH OCT.

But on the 18th October powerful counter-attacks were made against the IInd Corps, whilst the IIIrd Corps, which had been ordered to assist the Cavalry Corps in making good its position on the right bank of the Lys, made little progress, for the German General Staff seems to have realized that the right of the British line was advancing too rapidly and had ordered a more vigorous defence, with counter-attacks if necessary. Moreover the concentration of the new Fourth German Army north, north-east and east of Ypres had begun to relieve Corps and Divisions which were brought south and put into the line against the IInd and IIIrd British Corps.

By the 16th October, the Antwerp Relief Force under Sir Henry Rawlinson, which had been covering the retirement of the Belgian Army, had concluded its withdrawal operations, and the 3rd Cavalry Division (General Byng) and the 7th Division (General Capper) were posted on a line from Zandvoorde, through Gheluvelt to Zonnebeke: the 3rd Cavalry Division acting on the left flank of the 7th Division.

At midnight on the 17th/18th October, the relative positions of the 3rd Corps and the enemy were as follows:

6th Division: 16th Infantry Brigade. Rouge de Bout—Croix Blanche—Bois Grenier.

18th Infantry Brigade. Bois Grenier—La Vesee.

17th Infantry Brigade. La Vesee—La Chapelle d'Armentières.

4th Division: Right near L'Epinette, thence northward across the River Lys to Le Gheir.

On the left flank of the 4th Division the Cavalry Corps operated, whilst French Cavalry under General Conneau filled the gap between the IIIrd and IInd Corps.

Sixth German Army: Radinghem—Prémesques—Pérenchies— Le Temple—Frelinghem, thence along the eastern banks of the Lys to Wervicq.

18TH OCT.

At 1-40 a.m. on the 18th, a reconnaissance in force of the enemy's supposed position was ordered.

The 16th Infantry Brigade in co-operation with the 10th French Cavalry Division was to drive the enemy from the village of Radinghem.

The 18th Infantry Brigade was to reconnoitre in a south-east direction against the line La Vallee—Paradis, with its right on the line Bois Grenier—le Quesne and left on the line of the Boulogne —Lille Road.

The 17th Infantry Brigade was to operate against the line Mt. de Premesques—Perenchies.

Not more than two Infantry Battalions of each Brigade were to be employed in this reconnaissance without reference to Divisional Headquarters.

The 16th Infantry Brigade captured Radinghem, although during its advance of three miles the two attacking battalions (The Buffs and the York and Lancasters) were strongly opposed. At nightfall the Brigade had entrenched a position along the northern outskirts of the Château de Flandres Wood, joining up with the right of the 18th Infantry Brigade at the railway crossing three-quarters of a mile south of La Vallee, and with the left of the French Cavalry at Feterie.

The 18th Infantry Brigade was also successful. The attacking battalions were the 1st East Yorks. and the Durham Light Infantry— the West Yorkshires and the Sherwood Foresters were in reserve. The enemy retired from Paradis as the two battalions advanced, but stoutly opposed further advance. By 5 p.m. however the Durhams on the right had captured Ennetieres, but the East Yorks. found progress difficult owing to the inability of the 17th Infantry Brigade to take Mt. de Prémesques, which gave the enemy an opportunity of enfilading the left flank of the Yorkshiremen. Finally at 5-30 p.m. the Brigade occupied Ennetieres and the west end of Capinghem, but both left and right flanks were out of touch with the 17th and 16th Infantry Brigades respectively.

1ST BATTALION.

The Brigadier then visited Divisional Headquarters and explained his position, and it was decided to retire the centre of the line, hold Ennetieres, and join up with the 17th Infantry Brigade at Mt. de Prémesques and with the 16th Infantry Brigade on the railway

1ST BATTALION.
18TH OCT.

at the bridge south of La Vallee—the latter being held by the 16th Infantry Brigade. During the night the Sherwood Foresters relieved the Durhams and the West Yorkshiremen were put into the centre of the line, as it was too extended for one battalion to hold.

The 17th Infantry Brigade had met with vigorous opposition, and although capturing Prémesque (on its right) was repulsed in its endeavour to capture Pérenchies. At nightfall the line of the Brigade ran right on the Lille-Boulogne Road, just west of Mt. de Premesques, thence through Prémesques village, through Bas Trou to the La Bleue-Halte Road, thence to L'Epinette. At the latter place the 1st Royal Fusiliers (17th Infantry Brigade) joined up with the right of the 4th Division, whose line ran north to 400 yards south of Frélinghein, thence across the River Lys to Le Gheir.

The left of the IIIrd Corps was in touch with Allenby's Cavalry Corps and the right flank with Conneau's French Cavalry.

On the 19th, the 6th Division entrenched the positions won on the previous day, and although the line was heavily shelled only one attack (on the 17th Infantry Brigade) which was unsuccessful, was made.

Col. Towsey of the 1st West Yorks. R. was invalided to England on this day and Major Lang again assumed command of the battalion.

The next two days—the 20th and the 21st of October—were somewhat critical.

20TH OCT.

On the 20th, the enemy who had been gradually concentrating fresh forces attacked all along the line from the Belgian coast to the right of the IInd Corps. His new Fourth German Army had advanced to the attack, which was the signal for simultaneous attacks on the whole front held by the Allies from opposite Bethune to Nieuport in Belgium. This new Army was ordered to break through to Ypres at all costs.

The 6th Division, disposed along a very extended front—five miles—soon found its hold upon the line precarious, and strict injunctions had been issued by Corps Headquarters not to use the reserve battalions. The Division's orders were to maintain its position, but so thin was the line and so heavy the enemy's attacks that it was found impossible to do so.

During the night of 19th/20th there had been a certain amount of firing, but nothing serious happened until 8-40 a.m., when the 18th Infantry Brigade reported the enemy moving in massed formation south and west of Escobecques.

Of the 16th Infantry Brigade, the Buffs alone held Radinghem, the remaining battalions of the Brigade being engaged in preparing a position on the front Bridoux—Le Quesne—Rue du Bois " as a precautionary measure should the remainder of the Division be forced to fall back." During the day the Buffs successfully held on to Radinghem though the village was heavily shelled and strong infantry attacks were launched against it, all of which were repulsed by the devoted Kentishmen. At 10 p.m., however, it was obvious that the enemy was in great strength : the line occupied by the 18th Infantry Brigade had been pierced and Radinghem had to be evacuated and a retirement made to the line Touquet—Le Quesne—Rue du Bois.

20TH OCT.
1ST BATTALION.

The brunt of the attack fell upon the 18th Infantry Brigade at Ennetieres and north and south-west of the village.

Three battalions were in the line—the 1st East Yorks., the 1st West Yorks. R. and the Sherwood Foresters (2nd Notts and Derby) : the Durhams were held in reserve. The East Yorks. appear to have had only one Company in the front line when a heavy attack upon the 17th Infantry Brigade (whose right joined up with the left of the 18th Infantry Brigade) drove in the Lincoln Regiment. The reserve Companies of the East Yorks. were therefore sent up to protect the flank and thus the battalion was minus its supports. At 11 a.m. two Companies of the Durhams were sent up to support the East Yorks. : one advanced to the front line, the other was kept in reserve. In spite of heavy attacks the East Yorks. held their ground with fine tenacity.

The West Yorkshiremen were heavily attacked about 11-30 a.m. and all the battalion's supports were absorbed into the firing line. The battalion was then holding a frontage of 700 yards and its position was no sinecure as may be gathered from the Battalion Diary : " Enemy retired in front of my left and attacked in force in front of my right Company. The Regiment on my right retired to meet a flank attack : enemy occupied Ennetieres. The Regiment on right of 17th Infantry Brigade also retired. Position very precarious : enemy worked round right flank compelling withdrawal of men from left to protect right flank and the latter to be thrown back." The West Yorkshires were in point of fact almost "in the air" and were hard put to it to maintain the position. Nevertheless the battalion *did* hold on and there is but little doubt that the Yorkshiremen helped to save, if it did not of its own gallant efforts save, the line. " The battalion held the line," the Diary states, " and was congratulated by

C

1ST BATTALION.
20TH OCT.

the G. O. C. 6th Division and 18th Infantry Brigade." And a little later: "The Battalion repulsed all attacks which ceased about 4 p.m."

Upon the right flank of the 18th Infantry Brigade, the Sherwood Foresters—who held Ennetieres—disaster had fallen. The gallant Foresters held the salient and Ennetieres, and had a long line to hold. The battalion was continually attacked all the morning, from the direction of Capinghem and Fort Englos and was at the same time heavily shelled. They had repulsed all attacks at this point, but their losses were very heavy, and eventually being too weak to resist the greatly superior forces launched against them, were overwhelmed about 4 p.m., thus giving the enemy possession of the village. "Only the Commanding Officer, Adjutant, Quarter-master and 259 rank and file" said the Diary, "succeeded in escaping."

The 6th Divisional Artillery did good work and gave splendid support to the hard-pressed infantry. Good targets were offered by the enemy who advanced in masses.

The 17th Infantry Brigade on the left flank of the Division and the 18th Infantry Brigade had likewise suffered heavy attacks— the Leinsters (17th Brigade) being pressed back from the village of Prémesques, which was captured by the enemy. The remainder of the line (assisted by the East Yorks.) held its own all day, but at nightfall, owing to the withdrawal of the 18th Infantry Brigade, fell back unmolested to the line Rue du Bois—Pont Egal Fme.— L'Epinette.

Thus at daylight on the 21st, the 6th Division held the line Touquet—Bois Blancs—Le Quesne—La Houssoie—Rue du Bois —Pont Egal Fme., to a point a quarter of a mile west of L'Epinette.

Casualties in the 18th Infantry Brigade on the 20th numbered over 1,000, of which the 1st West Yorks. R. lost four officers and thirty-four other ranks, killed and wounded. Lieut. J. Lawson-Smith was killed: Major G. G. Lang, Capt. E. T. Welchman and Lieut. B. D. Costin were wounded: Capt. Welchman and Lieut. Costin, unfortunately, died of their wounds, the latter on the 24th and the former on the 26th October, 1914.

21ST OCT.

During the whole of the 21st, the Division was shelled, but held to its position. Only on the right of the Division, where the 19th Infantry Brigade had been put in to connect the IIIrd and IInd Corps was the line withdrawn, but this withdrawal did not affect the 6th Division. The right of the 16th Infantry Brigade connected up with the left of the 19th Infantry Brigade about Touquet.

The 1st West Yorks. Regiment which held the line between

Rue du Bois and the Sugar Factory, was withdrawn during the night 21st/22nd into Brigade Reserve in Bois Grenier. _{1ST BATTALION.}

On the 22nd, Lieut.-Col. T. P. Barrington assumed command of the battalion. _{22ND OCT.}

From the 22nd to the 31st October, repeated attempts to break through the greatly extended line of the IIIrd Corps was made by the enemy, but they were unsuccessful. A second line to which a retirement could be made should it become necessary was however dug behind the front line.

The latter days of October, 1914, saw the 1st West Yorkshires once more in the front line trenches where the daily programme seemed to consist of repairing trenches the while the battalion was subjected to sniping and shell-fire.

Reinforcements for the battalion arrived on the 24th and 25th—three officers and 138 other ranks on the former date, and two officers and 153 other ranks on the latter.

The attacks of the IInd and IIIrd Corps south of Ypres had very materially assisted the operations of the Ist Corps and its French and Belgian Allies. The break through to Ypres upon which the German Higher Command had set such store was by the end of October practically frustrated. Though fighting with considerable gallantry, and although his troops advanced singing patriotic songs and with their bands playing, the enemy had been unable to gain anything in the nature of a success and his troops were decimated. The heavy hostile attacks on the 31st October—the most critical day of all—had been successfully repulsed and the enemy denied his objective.

The severe fighting to which the IIIrd Corps had been subjected was fittingly recognized in Sir John French's despatch dated the 20th November, 1914: " I am anxious to bring to special notice the excellent work done throughout this battle by the IIIrd Corps, under General Pulteney's command. Their position in the right central part of my line was of the utmost importance to the general success of the operations. Besides the very undue length of front which the Corps was called upon to cover (some 12 or 13 miles) the position presented many weak spots, and was also astride of the River Lys, the right bank of which from Frélinghein downwards was strongly held by the enemy. It was impossible to provide adequate reserves and the constant work in the trenches tried the endurance of officers and men to the utmost. That the Corps was mainly successful in repulsing the constant attacks, sometimes in great strength, made

1ST BATTALION.

against them by day and by night, is due entirely to the skilful manner in which the Corps was disposed by its Commander, who has told me of the able assistance he has received throughout from his Staff, and the ability and resource displayed by Divisional, Brigade and Regimental leaders in using the ground and the means of defence at their disposal to the very best advantage. The courage, tenacity, endurance and cheerfulness of the men in such unparalleled circumstances is beyond all praise."

II.
TRENCH WARFARE
1914–1916

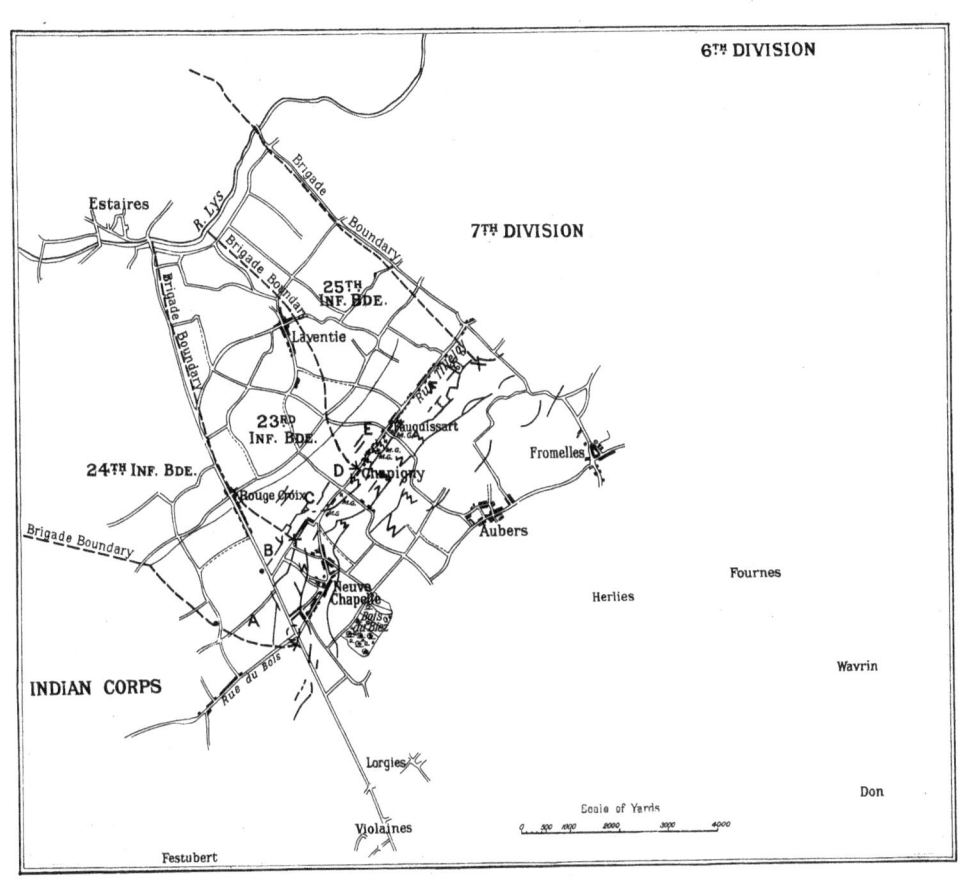

THE 2ND BATTALION'S FIRST SECTOR IN FRANCE, 1914.

TRENCH WARFARE.
   November, 1914—March 9th, 1915.
THE BATTLE OF NEUVE CHAPELLE.
   March 10th—13th, 1915.
TRENCH WARFARE.
   15th March—15th June, 1915.
THE FIRST ATTACK ON BELLEWAERDE.
   16th June, 1915.
TRENCH WARFARE.
   18th—30th June, 1915.
THE DARDANELLES :
  THE BATTLES OF SUVLA.
        6th—21st August.
    THE LANDING AT SUVLA.
        6th—15th August.
    THE BATTLE OF SCIMITAR HILL.
        21st August.
TRENCH WARFARE.
        1st—31st July.
ACTIONS OF HOOGE.
        9th August.
TRENCH WARFARE.
        1st—31st August, 1915.
THE BATTLE OF LOOS.
   25th September—8th October, 1915.
THE BATTLE OF LOOS. II.
   The Actions of Pietre, Bois Grenier, and the Second Attack on Bellewaerde.
TRENCH WARFARE.
   1st October—31st December, 1915.

TRENCH WARFARE
November, 1914—March 9th, 1915

NOVEMBER was a quiet month, for active fighting had for a while almost ceased. The guns, however, were always more or less active, and constant shelling took place though the British Artillery was woefully short of ammunition. Sniping, that deadly form of warfare which claimed many victims, went on day and night, though by his superior marksmanship the British soldier was more than a match for his Teutonic enemy.

The conditions under which the troops lived (or rather existed) and "carried on" were truly appalling. Heavy rains had reduced the trenches to a series of muddy excavations. Rivetting material was unobtainable and in consequence the parapets were so flimsy that men were frequently shot through them. During spells of fine weather they were built up only to be washed down by the first heavy rain. The troops stood knee-deep in mud and water, and wounded men as they fell were often drowned before they could be hauled out of the disgusting slimy mass into which they had fallen. The frail dug-outs were frequently blown to bits by the enemy's heavy shells and by his trench-mortars: even the billets behind the lines were unsafe.

By the middle of November the enemy had spent his fury against Ypres. The last attempt, made by the famous Prussian Guard under the very eyes of the German Kaiser, having failed, he had abandoned the idea of a break through and had settled down for the winter to much the same kind of life he had led on the Aisne, though less comfortable.

On the IInd Corps also attack and counter-attack had for a while ceased.

Both the Allies and the enemy were preparing for the next violent effort.

1ST BATTALION.

Little of outstanding interest seems to have happened to the 1st West Yorkshires during this period, and the Battalion Diaries are barren of anything in the nature of exciting incidents. The battalion led the same kind of life—full of discomforts, wallowing in mud—but the men were wonderfully patient in their intense sufferings and carried on as best they could. During November

1ST BATTALION.

two officers and ninety-nine other ranks arrived from England.

Three officers (two killed and one wounded) and seventy-eight other ranks were the casualties sustained by the battalion during November and December, 1914: they were mostly caused by shell-fire and sniping. The officers killed were Capt. A. R. Loveband (6th December) and Capt. J. K. Clothier (7th December).

17TH—30TH Nov.

From the 17th to 30th November, near Chapelle d'Armentières the battalion had a particularly trying time during which time it was unrelieved. The terrible discomfort of the trenches is told in one of the Battalion Diaries of the 18th Infantry Brigade. "Some of the men's feet were very sore from wet and mud and after getting through communication trenches fully loaded and marching a mile or so to billets, are quite beat——Relieved——In trenches. Only one communication trench, in a ditch 18 in. of water and 6 in. of mud. Men all went in over the ground..Heavy rain. Many sections of trenches flooded. Some of the flooded parts dammed and water localized. No chance of draining. Try digging new trenches, some in front, some behind, but water level everywhere seems about 18 in. below surface. Parapets falling in continually and most of our energy required repairing them, so men spend their time standing in one to two feet of water. Everybody bailing." Again a little later (two days): "Parapet continually falling in. Men employed during day and night digging it out....water in trenches rising steadily....men employed making dams and drains and digging out falls of parapet, etc." The battalion was relieved, but when it got back again into the line it records: "Found trenches wetter than ever."

And to be told that the condition of the enemy's trenches was every bit as bad was poor comfort.

* * * *

2ND BATTALION.

On the outbreak of war, the 2nd Battalion West Yorkshire Regt. was serving at Malta, but was ordered home. On the 14th September the Battalion embarked on *s.s. Galicia*. The boat was afterwards renamed, but was sunk later when acting as a Hospital Ship. On 25th September, the battalion arrived at Southampton and was sent to Hursley Park, Winchester, where the 8th Division was concentrating.

4TH Nov.

On the 4th November the 2nd Battalion (under the command of Lieut.-Col. G. F. Phillips) sailed again from Southampton and with other units arrived at Havre on the 5th. The battalion

A Main Street in Armentières.

disembarked and marched to No. 6 Camp Base. The 6th and 7th were busy days, spent in inspections and making all final arrangements for moving forward to the fighting line. On the 9th the battalion paraded and proceeded in Brigade to Merville, arriving about mid-day, and went into billets near Neuve Berquin. Here the first signs of war were visible, the houses having been badly knocked about by the enemy's shell-fire some weeks previously during the advance of the 6th Division.

The 2nd Devon Regt., 2nd West Yorkshires, 2nd Scottish Rifles, and the 2nd Middlesex Regt. formed the 23rd Infantry Brigade (Brig.-Gen. R. J. Pinney). The 23rd, 24th and 25th Infantry Brigades formed the 8th Division, which was commanded by Major-General F. J. Davies.

On the 11th November the battalion with the Devons marched to Neuve Eglise where they came under orders of the Cavalry Corps. They were joined on the following day by the Scottish Rifles and the Middlesex.

At 11 p.m. on the night of the 13th November the 2nd West Yorkshires had its first experience of trench life, having at that hour completed the relief of the Devons who had gone into the line on the 12th, one mile south-west of Messines, south of the River Douve and just north of Ploegsteert Wood (known in the Army ever afterwards as "Plug Street.") Heavy firing could be heard coming from the direction of Ypres. The night was spent in great discomfort, the trenches in this part of the line being thick in mud. Three men were wounded on the 14th—the first casualties suffered by the battalion. At 6-30 p.m. on the 15th, the Middlesex relieved the 2nd West Yorkshires and the latter marched back to billets in Neuve Eglise—glad to leave the unsavoury trenches behind them.

The 23rd Infantry Brigade left Neuve Eglise on the 17th, and marching to Estaires joined up once more with the Division. The 8th Division on the 16th had assumed command of a Sector of line which extended from just south of the cross-roads (Rue du Bois—Estaires—Violaines Road) south-west of Neuve Chapelle, northeast to the village of Tilleloy. The right flank of the Division (24th Infantry Brigade) joined up with the left of the Indian Corps (just south of the cross-roads) and the left flank (25th Infantry Brigade) with the right of the 7th Division, north of Tilleloy : the 23rd Infantry Brigade held the centre of the line.

From the 18th to the 30th November the battalion spent

alternately three days in the trenches and three in billets. No hostile attacks were made during this period, nor were any attempts made against the enemy's line. Very few casualties were incurred—thirteen in all, mostly from sniping.

1ST DEC.

By the 1st December therefore both the 1st and 2nd Battalions of the West Yorkshires had settled down to trench warfare, which " willy-nilly " had to be endured.

1ST BATTALION.

The 1st Battalion was still alternately in the line at Chapelle d'Armentières and in billets in L'Armee and Armentières, relieving and being relieved by other units of the 18th Infantry Brigade. His Majesty the King accompanied by the Prince of Wales arrived in the billeting area on 2nd December and inspected available troops of the Brigade, amongst which were two Companies of the 1st West Yorks.

On the 8th, Lieut.-Col. F. Towsey again assumed command of the 1st Battalion.

14TH DEC.

A certain amount of excitement occurred on the night of the 14th, during the time the battalion was in billets in Armentières : the enemy shelled the billets from 9 p.m. until 7 a.m. next morning, setting them on fire and clearing out A and B Companies who were billeted in a flax mill. Fifty rifles were destroyed and one man was burned to death. The 16th saw the battalion on the move to Erquinghem where billets were occupied until the 26th, when the Yorkshiremen took over the front line trenches from the Leinsters, east of Armentières. In this unsavoury spot the battalion spent the remainder of 1914.

2ND BATTALION.

The 2nd Battalion, in the meantime, had been involved in active operations undertaken by the 8th Division. The battalion on the 1st December was holding a portion of the line, Pont Logy—Chapigny, three-quarters of a mile north of Neuve Chapelle. Nothing of importance happened during the first seventeen days, though on the 14th, the 23rd Infantry Brigade in addition to its own, took over the line held by the 24th Infantry Brigade, the latter passing into Corps Reserve. On the night of the 17th/18th, the battalion was in billets in Red Barn on the Estaires—La Bassee Road, but at 6-30

18TH DEC.

orders were received stating that at 4-30 p.m. on the 18th an attack was to be made on the German line opposite " C " Section of the Divisional line. This attack was to synchronize with other attacks by the IVth Corps against certain portions of the enemy's trenches, and in conjunction with attacks along the general front of the Allies.

Operation Order No. 18 (23rd Infantry Brigade), issued at noon on the 18th December, contained (besides detailed orders for the attack) the following significant phrase: " With a view to eventually driving the enemy out of Neuve Chapelle, active operations against the enemy's trenches will be undertaken to-night by the 23rd Infantry Brigade."

2ND BATTALION. 18TH DEC.

This was the prologue to the Battle of Neuve Chapelle!

The 2nd Devon Regt. was to make the attack supported by the 2nd West Yorkshires. " As soon as the 2nd Devon Regt. advance out of ' C ' lines, the 2nd West Yorks. Regt. will move forward and occupy these lines, pushing forward at once two Companies to support the 2nd Devon Regt. These two Companies (2nd West Yorks. Regt.) will pick up tools in ' C ' lines and will carry on the work specified." The work specified was as follows: " As soon as the hostile trenches have been gained they will be put in a state of defence, and steps will at once be taken to link up with our existing trenches on the right and left of the trenches taken from the enemy." Bombing parties from the Devons and West Yorkshires were to accompany the assaulting parties. The artillery was ordered to open fire at 4-15 p.m. on the hostile main trenches opposite ' C ' lines, and subsequently shell positions in the rear and on the flanks of the Devons' objective.

At 4-30 p.m. three Companies of the Devons advanced against the enemy's trenches. The left Company got hung up on their own and on the enemy's wire entanglements and suffered very heavily, only a few men reaching their objective. The left-centre Company succeeded in capturing 150 yards of the enemy's trenches, many of the Germans being bayoneted as they came up out of their dug-outs. Lieut. F. J. Harington[1] of the West Yorkshires, who was in charge of the Battalion Bombing party, gallantly bombed a further portion of the enemy's trench which was then occupied by the Devons. The right Company of the Devons did not advance at all. At 5-10 p.m. two Companies of the West Yorkshires with R. E. detachments advanced and began to dig the communication trench from the British line to the saps in the German line. This work proceeded well, and at 9-30 p.m. the 2nd West Yorks. Regt. (as a whole) was ordered to take over the position won by the Devons, who withdrew to their original lines: the two Battalions were then placed under the command of Lieut.-Col. G. F. Phillips, 2nd West Yorks. After the relief was completed the Yorkshiremen set to work to improve the captured trench. But about 8 a.m. on the morning of

[1] The first officer in the Regiment to receive the D.S.O. " immediate award."

2ND BATTALION. 19TH DEC.

the 19th the enemy, using large quantities of bombs, made a strong attack on the West Yorkshiremen, and nearly a whole platoon was immediately knocked out. The hostile bombs were round and fitted with time fuses, they could be thrown a distance of nearly forty yards and were in every way more effective than the old " jam tin " bombs used by the British. The latter were difficult to ignite and invariably failed to carry out their functions at a critical moment. On this occasion they at first refused to ignite, so that in a very little while the battalion having nothing with which to reply to the enemy's bombs was forced back to the original front line of the previous day. The retirement was splendidly assisted by Lieut. Neame, R. E.[1], who stood on the parapet and (after obtaining some fresh bombs) counter-bombed so effectively that he enabled the rest of the Company to retire safely.

Twenty-two unwounded Germans were taken prisoners and approximately a hundred of the enemy killed, but the West Yorkshires lost two officers killed, two wounded and 120 other ranks killed and wounded. Most of these casualties were sustained during the retirement. Lieut. B. H. G. Shaw was killed on the 19th, and Major R. G. Cooper-King died of his wounds on the 20th. The 2nd West Yorkshires were relieved during the evening of the 21st by the 2nd Middlesex and marched back to billets in La Flinque.

1ST AND 2ND BATTALIONS. 25TH DEC.

When Christmas Day, 1914, arrived the 2nd Battalion was less fortunate than the 1st, for whereas the latter spent the day in billets, the former moved back again into the trenches on Christmas Eve, relieving the 2nd Middlesex. A sharp white frost had set in making the trenches dry—" very cold and dry " the 2nd Battalion Diary stated. On Christmas Day hardly a shot was fired by friend or foe, and along the front of the 8th Division British and German troops exchanged greetings : a short unofficial armistice for the purpose of burying the dead was also agreed upon. From Christmas Day until the fall of the year nothing of importance occurred, though on the 29th, the 2nd Battalion had a never-to-be-forgotten first bath at the Divisional Bath House in La Gorgue.

Water from two to six feet in depth stood in the support and communication trenches, and on the 30th December the parapets were again falling in. The horrors of a great campaign are not always caused by shells or bullets !

1915. 1ST JAN.

The New Year arrived without any changes. The 1st Battalion (6th Division) was still in the front line east of Armentières : the

[1] This officer was subsequently awarded the V.C.

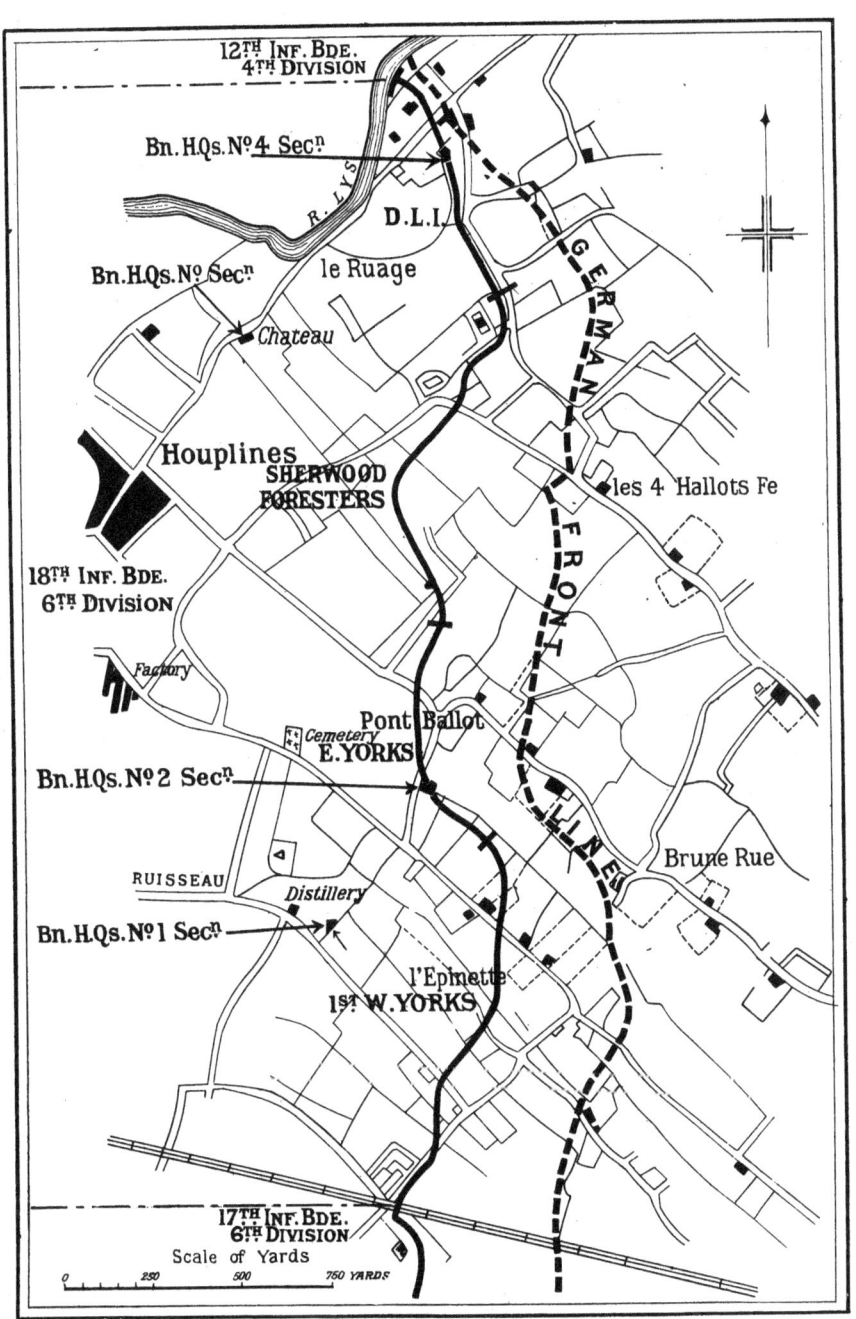

TRENCHES OF THE 1ST BATTALION, DECEMBER, 1914.

2nd Battalion (8th Division) in trenches on the line Pont Logy—Chapigny, three-quarters of a mile north of Neuve Chapelle. Cold and wet weather ushered in 1915, for the River Lys was still in flood, and showed no signs of abating.

* * * *

1ST BATTALION. The January Diary of the 1st Battalion contains little else but the words " In trenches," or " In billets," with an occasional reference to the arrival of drafts from England. Casualties were not numerous, for the enemy was living in no more comfort, and his time also was largely taken up in trying to " keep body and soul " together. The artillery alone seemed to be active: the guns and snipers caused practically all the casualties. It was a dull period, for in the northern part of the line the terrible fighting of October and November round Ypres had somewhat evaporated the enemy's enthusiasm, whilst the Allies were busy recuperating for the next great battle.

2ND BATTALION. In the 8th Division sickness was rife—the flooded nature of the ground and the constant rain creating ravages amongst the troops. The 2nd West Yorkshires had many men evacuated to hospital. Amongst the rank and file of the 23rd Infantry Brigade the casualties suffered from sickness since the 8th Division landed in France—only two months previously—were more than double the numbers sustained in actual warfare. The Brigade had evacuated fourteen officers and 1359 other ranks to hospital from sickness (of which five officers and 338 other ranks were from the 2nd West Yorks. R.): casualties in actual warfare were nine officers killed and thirteen wounded, and 553 other ranks killed, wounded and missing. On the 10th January, Lieut.-Col. G. F. Phillips, commanding the 2nd West Yorkshires was sent to hospital sick, and Capt. P. L. Ingpen took over command of the battalion.

So water-logged was the ground in and about the trenches that the parapets had to be erected on the ground-level, *i.e.*, without digging down. Sand-bags were used for protection, but soon it was found that the enemy's bullets passed through the bags wounding men standing behind them: " At such close range bullets turn over after entering a sand-bag and this causes a large cavity. The next shot which hits the same external sand-bag may come right through the parapet."

18TH JAN. The 23rd Infantry Brigade Grenade Company was formed on the 18th January. One officer, four N. C. O's and twenty-eight men being sent from each battalion. Three days later the Brigade Diary records that "the Grenade Company is now in full swing." It was a very gallant Company and did yeoman service in later and more strenuous days.

The first few days of February promised better weather. Intervals of fine dry sunny hours vastly improved the ground about the trenches: and the spirits of the men rose higher as life became more bearable.

<small>1ST AND 2ND BATTALIONS. FEBRUARY.</small>

No attacks were made either by the 6th or 8th Divisions during February, and in consequence the 1st and 2nd West Yorks. were not involved in active fighting. Nor did the enemy show signs of launching attacks against the line between Armentières and Neuve Chapelle. A few casualties were suffered in both battalions. In the 1st, 2nd. Lieut. Stockdale was wounded on the 7th, and Lieut. B. N. Asprey, Machine Gun Officer, was killed on the 24th. The battalion also lost twenty-one other ranks killed and wounded. Of the 2nd Battalion several more officers were evacuated sick to hospital and eleven other ranks were killed and seventeen wounded. On the 27th, Lieut. J. F. Routledge was awarded the Military Cross for gallantry on the 19th December.

In both Divisional areas work in the trenches was continuous. On the 6th, Divisional front mining had begun. But the 8th Division was more than occupied in keeping the existing defences standing. "There has been no change in the line held by the Division or in the method of holding it, during the month, but working parties have been employed in considerable numbers by day and night in constructing works, fortifying localities behind the trenches and in second and third lines, and the position generally has been strengthened." Fifteen closed works had been constructed just behind the front line trenches and these were subsequently of great value.

1915

THE BATTLE OF NEUVE CHAPELLE
March 10th—13th, 1915

"ABOUT the end of February," said Sir John French in paragraph four of his despatch dated 5th April, 1915, " many vital considerations induced me to believe that a vigorous offensive movement by the Force under my command should be planned and carried out at the earliest possible moment. Amongst the most important reasons which convinced me of this necessity were: The general aspect of the Allied situation throughout Europe, and particularly the marked success of the Russian Army in repelling the violent onslaughts of Marshal von Hindenburg, the apparent weakening of the enemy in my front, and the necessity for assisting our Russian Allies to the utmost by holding as many hostile troops as possible in the Western Theatre, the efforts to this end which were being made by the French Forces at Arras and Champagne, and, perhaps the most weighty consideration of all, the need of fostering the offensive spirit in the troops under my command after the trying and possibly enervating experiences which they had gone through of a severe winter in the trenches."

The plan of operations which arose out of these considerations comprised a main attack by the First Army,[1] with secondary and holding attacks by the Second Army.

The object of the main attack was the capture of the village of Neuve Chapelle and the enemy's position at that point, and the establishment of the British line as far east as possible.

The British line opposite Neuve Chapelle was held by the 8th Division, with the Indian Corps on its right and the 7th Division on its left. The 6th Division was on the left flank of the 7th Division.

The Battle of Neuve Chapelle was the first of several important operations which took place during 1915. Apart from the object and result of the battle, it is of special interest as witnessing the first introduction of intensive bombardments followed by infantry attacks. At Neuve Chapelle, also, the huge 15-in. Howitzer (ever afterwards called "Granny") was first used: it gave the signal for the attack.

In those halycon days before the War, Neuve Chapelle was a quiet country village with walled gardens and orchards. In 1915

---

[1] The First British Army at this period was formed of Ist, IVth and Indian Corps.

it had been altered somewhat by the enemy and adapted for defensive purposes. In the northern portion of the village there was a triangle formed by three roads, along which stood a number of fairly large-sized houses, enclosed with walls, as well as many fruit and vegetable gardens and orchards. The buildings had been put into a state of defence by the enemy, who had mounted machine guns in the houses and cottages and had formed strong points which flanked the approaches to the village.

By his intelligence department the Commander-in-Chief was informed that the enemy's position in this particular part of the line was but lightly held, and that only a few battalions held the village and the vicinity.

Towards the close of February, the General Officers commanding the IVth and Indian Corps were informed of the intended attack and had warned their Divisional Commanders, who in turn had instructed their Brigadiers to prepare for the coming operations.

1ST MARCH.

Accordingly on the 1st March, the 23rd and 25th Infantry Brigades of the 8th Division were withdrawn from the line into reserve, to rest and get fit for the attack. On the 2nd March the 23rd Infantry Brigade was in the Merville area and here for the next few days the 2nd West Yorkshires and their comrades were billeted in farms, cottages and barns—free from the constant strain and wear and tear of trench life. Although the billets were somewhat crowded the men nevertheless rapidly gained in health. This period of training included frequent visits by officers and N. C. O.'s to " B " lines (in front of Neuve Chapelle) for the purpose of reconnoitring the ground over which the attack was to take place.

2ND BATTALION.

8TH MARCH.

On the 8th March, 8th Division Operation Order No. 12 was issued :—

" In accordance with instructions received from the General Officer Commanding First Army, the IVth and Indian Corps will carry out a vigorous attack on the enemy on a date and at an hour to be notified later. The village of Neuve Chapelle will be attacked and captured by assault, after which a further advance will be made to gain the line Aubers—Le Plouich—La Cliqueterie—Ferme—Ligny le Grand.

The attack on the village of Neuve Chapelle will be carried out in two stages by the 8th Division.

First objective : the enemy's front and support trenches opposite ' B ' Lines.

Second objective: eastern edges of Neuve Chapelle village on the right to Orchard No. 6 and the Moated Grange on the left. The point of junction with the Indian Corps will be at the south-east corner of the village. 2ND BATTALION.

For the attack on Neuve Chapelle the artillery of the 7th and 8th Divisions, less the 4·7 Heavy Batteries will be grouped under the orders of the General Officer Commanding 8th Division: the 4·7 Batteries of the 7th and 8th Divisions with certain heavy batteries will form a group under the orders of the First Army.

A similar attack on Neuve Chapelle village will be carried out by the Indian Corps from the south.

The 8th Division will attack with the 23rd and 25th Infantry Brigades in the front line. The dividing line between the two Brigades will be the road 14, 17, 18, 19 and 31, for which the left Brigade will be responsible.

The 24th Infantry Brigade less the 2nd Northampton Regt., the 5th Black Watch and the 4th Cameron Highlanders will be in Divisional Reserve.

Divisional Mounted Troops, 2nd Northampton Regt. and the 4th Cameron Highlanders will hold the trench line 'B,' 'C' 'D.'

The Division will assemble for attack in accordance with the Divisional Instructions herewith:

Right Attack : Commander—G. O. C. 25th Infantry Brigade : 25th Infantry Brigade Mountain Battery (less one section), 2nd Field Company, R. E.
First objective : House at 27 and the trenches immediately west of it, thence the German trenches to the road 14, 17, 18 (exc.):
Second objective : The village.

Left Attack : Commander—G. O. C. 23rd Infantry Brigade : 23rd Infantry Brigade, one section Mountain Battery, 15th Field Company, R. E.
First objective : German trenches 17, 21, to 77.
Second objective : House at 19 and the trench system round it. Orchard No. 6—Moated Grange.

Divisional Reserve—24th Infantry Brigade.

The Infantry of the Divisional Reserve will move forward so as to take the place of the 25th Infantry Brigade in the trenches

2ND BATTALION.

as they are vacated by that Brigade and will remain there under the orders of the General Officer Commanding 8th Division."

The duties of joining up the old British Line with the enemy's front line when captured and taking charge of prisoners were entrusted to the Officer Commanding " B " Lines. The Officer Commanding " C " and " B " Lines was instructed to keep up a heavy rifle fire and machine-gun fire on the enemy's trenches on his front, the moment the artillery bombardment began. Other instructions stated that : " As soon as a body of troops leaves our front line of trenches their places in that trench will be taken up by a supporting body.... as each objective is captured it will at once be placed in a state of defence.... The 21st Infantry Brigade (7th Divisional) will occupy the trenches and breastworks in rear of the left of ' B ' Lines, when they are vacated by the 23rd Infantry Brigade."

The Ist Corps had likewise received orders to support the attack on Neuve Chapelle by delivering a holding attack from Givenchy. Similarly the IIIrd Corps of the Second Army—north of the IVth Corps—had been ordered to co-operate, and 6th Divisional O. O. No. 22 contained the following instructions : " The First and Second Armies will assume the offensive on the 10th March, and on subsequent days. The rôle of the Second Army will be to prevent the enemy from withdrawing from his front any troops for employment against the First Army. With this object the troops of the Division will act as follows : Artillery bombardments will commence at 7-30 a.m. principally directed on Frélinghien, and also on the new German trench east of Pont Baust. General Officers Commanding Brigades will organize fire attacks against the enemy's line by day and night and maintain a state of activity. Sapping and mining operations will be pushed forward vigorously."

On the night 9th/10th March, the 23rd and 25th Infantry Brigades marched from their billets to the rendezvous about one mile in rear of the assembly trenches, and there the men were provided with a hot meal.

10TH MARCH

Soon after 5 a.m. on the 10th the Brigadiers reported to Divisional Headquarters that all troops were in their allotted positions as follows : two battalions of the 25th Infantry Brigade (2nd Royal Berks. on the right, 2nd Lincolns on the left) held the front line from Point 28 to 14 : next (from right to left), two Companies Scottish Rifles (from Point 14-15), one Company Middlesex R. (from Point 15-16), A Company 2nd West Yorks. R. (from Point 16-13). The 25th Infantry Brigade had two battalions in support—2nd

Rifle Brigade (right) and 1st Royal Irish Rifles (left): the 23rd Infantry Brigade, the 2nd Devons in support and the 2nd West Yorks. in reserve with one Company in " C " Lines and three Companies in Rue de Tilleloy, behind breastworks.

2ND BATTALION.
10TH MARCH.

The objectives of the 25th Infantry Brigade were first, Points 69, 46, and second, Points 56, 31.

The objectives of the 23rd Infantry Brigade were first (Scottish Rifles) system of trenches 17-21 inclusive : (2nd Middlesex) system of trenches 21-75-77-20 taking special precautions to secure all trenches bearing to the left. The second objectives were : Scottish Rifles—trench 51-22-52 and posts 18 and 19. The 2nd Devons were to co-operate with the Scottish Rifles in the above attack, by taking Points 78-22. The 2nd Middlesex were given Point 6 and locality ; the battalion was then to extend its left towards Moated Grange. The 2nd West Yorkshires were in Brigade Reserve. " As each system is captured it will be at once placed in a state of defence. Each battalion will move up in succession to the position vacated in the position of assembly by the forward movement of the leading battalions."

The wire in the British front lines had been removed during the night of the 9th/10th by the troops in " B " Lines, and ladders placed in position to enable the assaulting troops to leave their trenches quickly.

After Brigade Headquarters had reported the troops ready in their respective positions, all movement ceased. At 6-15 a.m. a solitary German aeroplane flew low down over the British lines from north to south. At 6-30 a.m. the guns began registering on the enemy's trenches and, as the Diary observes, " from the number of heavy guns which opened it would have been thought that the Germans would have become suspicious that something out of the ordinary was about to happen." At 7-30 a.m. the artillery bombardment opened with a terrific crash ("Granny" was firing for the first time), the "roar of the wire-cutting guns being particularly deafening."

The Germans' reply to the bombardment was insignificant, though there was considerable rifle fire from the enemy's trenches, especially about Point 15.

At 8-5 a.m. the attack was launched, and by 8-15 a.m. the 25th Infantry Brigade had carried the German front-line trenches with but little loss.

The 23rd Infantry Brigade was less fortunate. The 2nd

2ND BATTALION.
10TH MARCH.

Scottish Rifles on the right were subjected to a severe flanking fire coming from the left, but pressing on with great gallantry managed to secure the front line of the enemy's trench from Point 17-74. Heavy losses had however been sustained, "ten of the officers," the Diary states "now lie buried between the British and German trenches." The 2nd Devons were thereupon moved up in support.

The Middlesex, on the left of the Scottish Rifles, were met by a perfect storm of bullets from machine-guns and rifles, as the troops attempted to leave their trenches. The artillery bombardment of the German trenches from Point 15-77 had been ineffective, the wire was uncut and the enemy was entirely unshaken. Three times the battalion made gallant efforts to assault, but on each occasion as the men left their trenches they were mown down by well-directed fire from in front and from the left flank. The British artillery which had bombarded the enemy's position from Point 17-20 was new to the line, having arrived in France only twenty-four hours previously. A further bombardment by batteries familiar with the ground was therefore asked for and soon an extremely accurate and effective fire was being directed upon the enemy's line (20-21) which had proved such a serious obstacle to the Middlesex Regt. The request for the further bombardment was made at 8-58 a.m.

Meanwhile the village had also been subjected to a further bombardment of thirty minutes, and at 8-35 a.m. the 2nd Rifle Brigade (on the right) and the 1st Royal Irish Rifles (on the left) of the 25th Infantry Brigade were bombing their way forward to Points 24-29 and 65-18 respectively. Between 9 and 10 a.m. the Brigade had reached the line 24-29-66-65-18 and shortly after 10 a.m. occupied the line.

Owing to the hold-up of the 23rd Infantry Brigade, the left flank of the 25th Infantry Brigade as it advanced became more and more exposed: the 24th Infantry Brigade was therefore ordered to send one battalion to Point 18 to close the gap between the two Brigades; this was carried out, though the movement was made under heavy rifle and machine-gun fire from Points 85-86.

At 8-30 a.m. the 2nd West Yorkshires had moved up from the Rue du Tilleloy, into the trenches at "E" vacated by the Middlesex. The enemy had by now opened fire with his artillery and in this position the Yorkshiremen had many casualties. About 9-40 a.m. a wounded officer arrived at 23rd Infantry Brigade Headquarters and stated that the Scottish Rifles were holding the line 17-82-21 with difficulty. The 2nd Devons followed a little later by a platoon

The Battle of Neuve Chapelle

of Brigade Bombers and D and C Companies of the 2nd West Yorkshires, under Capt. Francis, were immediately sent forward *via* Sign Post Lane. With these reinforcements the attack made further progress towards Points 41 and 20. "The Artillery shot amazingly well," said the Brigadier. At 11-5 a.m. a message from 8th Division Head Quarters was received saying that the 25th Infantry Brigade had cleared Neuve Chapelle and ordering the 23rd Infantry Brigade to take Points 20-21 and 6 at all costs." Ten minutes later the Brigade Diary relates : " 11-15 a.m. Shelling so good that Germans in front trench (76-7) chucked it and one officer and sixty-four Jägers' hands ' upped ' and came over. 2nd Middlesex occupied German trench."

<small>2ND BATTALION. 10TH MARCH.</small>

Half-an-hour later A and B Companies of the West Yorkshires under Capt. Ingpen, the last reserves of the Brigade, had been put into the line. These two Companies were ordered to make good Point 6 and work towards Point 60, the attack to take place at 12-15 after the artillery had shelled the former point.

Meanwhile Capt. Francis with his two Companies had occupied 18 and was advancing on 22 : he also reported the presence of British troops at 78. Point 19 was next occupied by Capt. Francis and his men.

The guns opened fire on Point 6 and at 12-15 A and B Companies under Capt. Ingpen went forward to the attack which was entirely successful : Point 6 was reported captured at 12-30 p.m. " A " Company then worked towards 60-83 and 60-61-8, all of which approaches were blocked. Unfortunately the British artillery continued firing : the telephone wires had been destroyed and it was difficult to get messages back to the gunners. Points 4 and 5 had been occupied by a few men, but these had to retire, as their own artillery had shelled them out.

At 1-15 p.m. the 23rd Infantry Brigade held the line as follows : 2nd Scottish Rifles, Point 19 : 2nd Devons, Point 18-22 : 2nd West Yorkshires, 22-78-77 : 2nd Middlesex, in support to Point 6 (two Companies of Warwicks of the 24th Infantry Brigade, having relieved the West Yorkshires just after 1 o'clock). Point 60 and 61 and the Moated Grange were held by the 4th Cameron Highlanders, temporarily under the 25th Infantry Brigade. The West Yorkshires finally held the line Point 7-22. The Brigade was now ordered to dig in on the line occupied.

Meanwhile the 25th Infantry Brigade had pushed forward and at 1 p.m. held the line 80-24-49-gardens east of 29-31-55-19 and

2ND BATTALION.
10TH MARCH.

were in touch with the 23rd Infantry Brigade at the latter Point, and with the Garhwal Brigade (Indian Corps) at Point 80.

North and south of the 8th Division (on the 7th Division and Indian Corps front) the attack had met with varying results. The 21st Infantry Brigade (7th Division) on the left flank of the 8th Division had "at first made good progress, but was subsequently held up by machine-gun fire from the houses and from a defended work in the German entrenchments opposite the right of the 22nd Infantry Brigade."

The Garhwal Brigade (Indian Corps) on the right flank of the 25th Infantry Brigade had gone forward with the latter and had carried the German front line: at 1-30 p.m. it held the line immediately south from Point 80.

At 1-30 p.m. the General Officer Commanding 23rd Infantry Brigade received the following message from Divisional Headquarters: "Have you joined up with Moated Grange AAA You can call on Camerons (4th) to assist you AAA I have ordered 24th Infantry Brigade to assemble as rapidly as possible for forward movement AAA You must therefore dispense with battalions of that Brigade and hold line with your Brigade AAA The presence of Brigade (21st) of 7th Division behind your left flank should give you necessary security AAA This Brigade will eventually advance through you."

The 4th Camerons were then ordered to occupy the line 60-61-Moated Grange.

The 24th Infantry Brigade had already begun to assemble when at 3-10 p.m. instructions were received from IVth Corps Headquarters for the 7th and 8th Divisions to advance: "The IVth Corps will move forward from the line captured this morning towards Aubers AAA The 7th Division's first objective—Moulin du Pietre: second objective—Rue d' Enfer. 8th Division's first objective Points 85, 86, 88: second objective Pietre AAA The leading troops of both Divisions will cross the line 1, 2, 3, 4, 54, 34, 31, at 3-30 p.m."

The 25th Infantry Brigade and the artillery were ordered to co-operate with fire on the enemy's position.

Orders for the attack were received by the General Officer Commanding 24th Infantry Brigade at 3-56 p.m., but owing to the great difficulty experienced in re-organizing the troops an advance was not possible until 4-20 p.m. As the right of the Brigade reached 54 heavy fire was opened upon it, coming from Points 85, 86, 94. Progress was slow, the ground being much intersected by ditches and trenches, the former full of water. Eventually the right of the

Brigade reached the line 94-92, the left of the Brigade getting to within 200 yards of the houses at 85-86, where the enemy was found to be occupying a prepared position in considerable strength with machine-guns and was exceedingly active. By this time (it was about 5 p.m.) darkness had already fallen and the 21st Infantry Brigade on the left of the 24th Brigade became mixed up with the latter, which caused some confusion. Further attempts at organizing another advance were fruitless and the troops entrenched themselves for the night with the intention of renewing the attack at daybreak.

2ND BATTALION. 10TH MARCH.

The positions of the 7th and 8th Divisions and the Indian Corps on the night of the 10th March were approximately as follows:
8th Division : 25th Infantry Brigade—80, 50, 31.
24th Infantry Brigade—31, 92, 87.
7th Division : 21st Infantry Brigade, west of 88, 89, north of 90, 92.
8th Division : 23rd Infantry Brigade—68, 67, 48, 18, 22.
7th Division : 22nd Infantry Brigade in line of and in trenches north of the Moated Grange.
7th Division : 20th Infantry Brigade in Corps Reserve.
Indian Corps : in touch with IVth Corps on the line T, P, O, C and B.

There is no doubt that the first attack on the enemy at Neuve Chapelle came in the nature of a surprise. The solitary aeroplane which flew over the British lines in the morning of the 10th March may have given information that the British troops were all lined up for an attack, for a captured German officer stated that he became aware of the concentration of the British troops early in the small hours of the 10th, and immediately asked for artillery support, but was told that it could not be given him excepting under orders from Corps Headquarters. There is also evidence that the German VIIth Corps which held the line in the Neuve Chapelle area was even then in the process of re-organization with the intention of placing fewer troops in the line and adopting a defensive rôle. But it is questionable whether the Neuve Chapelle area was held only by three German battalions: the village was held by the 11th Jäger, but both flanks were held by German Regiments (12th and 16th) each of which consisted of three battalions. Prisoners belonging to the 16th Regiment were captured in Neuve Chapelle, whilst during the day reinforcements from the 13th and 56th Regiments were put into the line. The enemy's chief reserves were, however, at Lille and Salome and during the night 10th/11th March, he moved up the 6th Bavarian Reserve Division (16th, 17th, 20th and 21st Reserve Regts.), as well as a battalion from each of the 139th, 101st, 106th,

2ND BATTALION.

11TH MARCH.

133rd and 179th Regts., *i.e.*, in all reinforcements numbering about seventeen battalions. More guns were also hurriedly brought up.

At 1-30 a.m. on the 11th, " 8th Division Operation Order No. 13 " was issued : " Advance will continue this morning for capture of high ground Le Plouich to La Cliqueterie Fme. AAA Objective of 7th Division will be Aubers and Le Plouich and objective of 8th Division La Cliqueterie Fme. AAA Indian Corps advance simultaneously through Bois du Biez for capture of Ligny le Grand."

The 24th Infantry Brigade was to advance at 7 a.m. : the 23rd Infantry Brigade to hold its front line and in addition to relieve the 25th Infantry Brigade on the line 31, 29, 24, the relief to take place by 6-30 a.m. : the Brigade was then to be in Corps Reserve. The 25th Infantry Brigade when relieved was to assemble in rear of the front line and be prepared to support the attack of the 24th Infantry Brigade.

An artillery bombardment on the houses about 86 was ordered from 6-45 a.m. to 7 a.m.

But in this attack the 2nd West Yorkshires were not involved. The battalion under the command of Capt. Ingpen relieved the Royal Irish Rifles in trenches running from 31, south-west in front of the château (between 31 and 29) with one Company in support on the road in Neuve Chapelle village ready to relieve the Rifle Brigade. The latter, however, owing to congestion in the trenches, did not vacate its position and in consequence the relief did not take place. All day long the West Yorkshires and the whole of the line were heavily shelled, the enemy's newly-arrived guns having opened at dawn with a very heavy bombardment. By 11 o'clock the attacks of the 21st Infantry Brigade and of the Indian Corps had not gone well : the enemy's positions at 85 and 86 and the bridge over the River de Layes, south-east of Point 93 being too strong and well defended. " Owing to the weather conditions, which did not permit of aerial observation, and the fact that nearly all the telephonic communications between the artillery observers and their batteries had been cut, it was impossible to direct the artillery fire with sufficient accuracy. Even when our troops, which were pressing forward, occupied a house here and there, it was not possible to stop our artillery fire and the infantry had to be withdrawn."

The 11th passed without any substantial gain.

12TH MARCH.

At 4 a.m. on the 12th, it was decided to renew the attack during the morning and orders were issued to that effect.

The 7th Division was to assault the houses from Point 103 to

88 exclusive : the 8th Division, the line 98, 95, 93, 85, 86, 88. The 2ND BATTALION. 12TH MARCH.
Indian Corps was again to attack the Bois du Biez when Points 93 and 95 had been captured by the 8th Division.

The 25th Infantry Brigade was to attack 98, 95 and 93 to the road junction 100 yards south-east of 92 (inclusive), troops of the 24th Infantry Brigade south of that road junction to join in the attack; the 24th Infantry Brigade to attack from the left of the 25th Infantry Brigade to 85, 86 and 88 : the 23rd Infantry Brigade was in Corps Reserve.

The attack was timed for 10-30 a.m., preceded by an artillery bombardment beginning at 10 a.m.

But at 8-12 a.m. 8th Division Headquarters received a message from the 24th Infantry Brigade which stated that the enemy had launched a big counter-attack against the line of road between 94 and 92 and the Sherwood Foresters had been forced to retire to its support trenches. The Germans had advanced in considerable force, but as they occupied the position evacuated by the Sherwood Foresters, a heavy enfilade fire was opened by " A " Company[1] 2nd West Yorkshires who held Point 31, with the result that the enemy losing heavily was beaten back.

The timely aid given by the West Yorkshiremen saved the position from capture ! By this time a general hostile attack on the whole line was in progress, but was everywhere repulsed with very heavy loss to the enemy. The attack timed for 10-30 a.m. was postponed for two hours.

At 12-30 p.m. the attack began, but was again held up by the fortified houses at 85 and 86 and the enemy's trenches about 93 and 95.

About 4 o'clock in the afternoon an urgent message was received at Headquarters, 8th Division : " First Army have information enemy in rear line retiring demoralized AAA Cavalry ordered to move on Aubers AAA Sir Douglas Haig orders all troops to push forward at once regardless of enemy's fire AAA All available troops of 23rd and 24th Infantry Brigades will push forward aganist 94, 85, 86 AAA General Pinney as senior Brigadier to command."

In consequence of these orders the 2nd West Yorkshires received instructions at 5-30 p.m. to move with the 2nd Scottish Rifles under the command of Capt. Ingpen (2nd West Yorks. R.) and join up with the Devons on the left, and form the right attack on the first objective—the cross-roads at M35.D7.8 (Point 94) : second objective —Pietre—La Russie Road.

[1] The Coy. Commander (Capt. H. D. Harington) was awarded the D.S.O. " immediate award '

2ND BATTALION.

But to move at once was impossible! The battalions of the 24th Infantry Brigade were much disorganized by their constant attacks and had become intermixed with troops of the 7th Division. Dead and wounded men were everywhere lying in the trenches and vicinity. The ground over which the attack had gone forward was pitted with shell-holes, broken up by ditches full of water, and trenches, difficult to cross. And darkness had almost fallen.

The condition of the gallant fellows who had been fighting and marching to and from the trenches since the early hours of the 10th with practically no respite was by now pitiable. Men fell asleep at every halt, having to be roused by violent means. Many of them could hardly drag their exhausted bodies over the heavy ground. Under such conditions organization for the attack was not easy, and it was 1 a.m. on the 13th before anything like order had been evolved. Even then the 2nd West Yorkshires and the 4th Camerons were not in the position assigned to them.

The West Yorkshires had moved off at 10 p.m., with the Scottish Rifles on their left flank. At 11-30 p.m. the latter reported they were out of touch with the Devons. By 1 a.m. the Yorkshiremen and the Scottish Rifles had lost touch and formed up in the neighbourhood of some houses at Point 31.

Patrols were sent out towards Points 92 and 94 to try and regain connection, but at 3 a.m. these returned, having failed to gain touch. The Yorkshiremen then returned to Neuve Chapelle village and took up a temporary position along road 7—77, where the battalion remained throughout the day of the 13th.

The battalion again moved forward (at 7 p.m.) to take up the line 92—31. This trench was found unoccupied—save by dead bodies. In such sanguinary company, the battalion passed the night, putting out advanced posts in a cottage near Point 92, "The Duck's Bill."

In the meantime at 12 midnight 12/13th, 8th Division Headquarters had ordered all troops to consolidate their positions on the ground held. The final dispositions of the Division was given in that order: "The Division will consolidate itself in its present position, with the Indian Division on its right at 80, and the 7th Division on its left at 88 and strengthened by wire AAA 25th Brigade from 80 to 31 inclusive, 23rd Brigade, with Cameron Highlanders, thence to 88 AAA 24th Brigade will be prepared to withdraw before daylight to positions selected by General Officer Commanding Brigade with area 6, 18, west-ward to Rue Tilleloy, and remain in

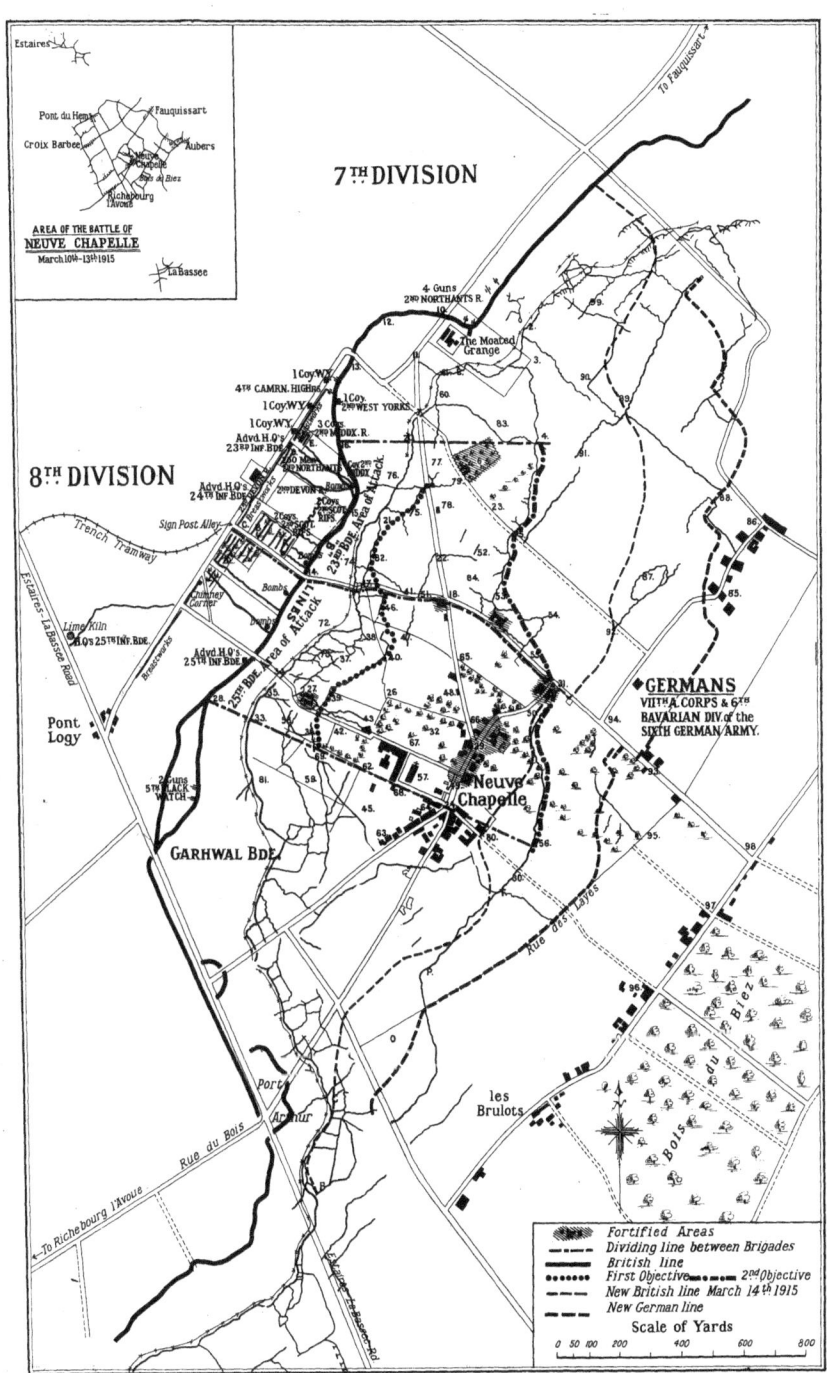

The Battle of Neuve Chapelle, 10th–13th March, 1915.

Divisional Reserve AAA Divisional Headquarters will remain at Red Barn."   2ND BATTALION.

The Battle of Neuve Chapelle was over.

On the 14th, at 9-30 p.m., the 2nd West Yorkshires (in brigade) having been relieved by the 2nd Lincolns marched back into billets near Rouge Croix.   14TH MARCH.

The 8th Division lost 218 officers and 4,387 other ranks killed, wounded and missing. Of this number the 2nd West Yorkshires had two officers killed (Capt. and Adjutant R. A. Colvin on 10th, and 2nd Lieut. Summers-Smith on 11th) and five officers (Capt. S. G. Francis, D.S.O., Capts. A. H. Arnold and C. H. G. Perry, Lieut. T. H. O'B. Horsford and 2nd. Lieut. Kinnell) wounded[1] : fifty-five other ranks were killed, 162 wounded and eighteen missing—a total of seven officers and 242 other ranks.

The subsidiary operations carried out by the Second Army prevented the enemy sending reinforcements to Neuve Chapelle. On the 12th, the 17th Infantry Brigade of the 6th Division captured the village of L'Epinette, east of Armentières, and the adjacent farms. The 18th Infantry Brigade co-operated with fire attacks, but the 1st West Yorkshires were not involved in active operations.   1ST BATTALION.

An offensive further south was also launched by the Ist Corps, against Givenchy. Here the attack was made by the 6th Infantry Brigade of the 2nd Division against 700 yards of the enemy's trenches, and although the attack was repulsed, served its end in that the enemy was unable to send reinforcements from this part of the line northwards to his sorely-pressed forces.

Many valuable lessons were learned at the Battle of Neuve Chapelle—but that which transcended all others was the protection afforded to the infantry by the terrible effects of intensive bombardments.

---

[1] Capts. Arnold and Perry and Lieut. Horsford subsequently died of their wounds. Lieut. Kinnell lost a leg and died in 1918 from effects of his wound.

TRENCH WARFARE

15th March—15th June, 1915

B Y the middle of March, 1915, the weather had improved considerably and work on the trenches continued day and night. The 1st West Yorkshires passed the month in comparative quietude. Reinforcements—three drafts—had arrived to stiffen the ranks of the battalion. These drafts were dispatched from the Reserve Battalions (3rd and 4th West Yorkshires) in England, which served as feeding battalions, not being sent overseas for service abroad. On the 21st, Major T. Barrington left to take over command of the 2nd Battalion (8th Division), and on the following day Major G. G. Lang rejoined. The total casualties for the month were sixteen other ranks killed and fifty-six wounded. [1ST BATTALION.]

Meanwhile the 2nd Battalion (in Brigade) moved forward again into the trenches on the 16th March, taking over old "C" Lines north-west of Neuve Chapelle, relieving the 25th Infantry Brigade. The battalion was relieved on the 22nd, but returned to the line on the 25th, and took over section 5 (east of La Boutille) from the 3rd Canadian Battalion. [2ND BATTALION.]

The 1st of April saw the 1st Battalion in trenches west of Le Touquet, and the 2nd Battalion still in section 5. But the diaries of both battalions for the month of April are barren of interest, nothing happened apparently but the re-building of trenches, tours in and out of the line, sniping and shelling, no attacks were made on or by the enemy. The capture of Hill 60 and the Battles of Gravenstafel Ridge and St. Julien (in The Battles of Ypres, 1915) did not involve either the 6th or 8th Division. [1ST AND 2ND BATTALIONS.]

The two battalions were now within easy reach of one another and on the 10th of the month officers from the 1st visited their comrades of the 2nd Battalion. About the middle of the month also the men of the 2nd Battalion had an uncommon treat: motor-lorries took parties from the battalion into Armentières, where "The Follies" (the 4th Divisional Troupe) were giving shows to crowded houses. This Troupe was the forerunner of many which proved a very great boon throughout the War, helping to dissipate the awful stress of life in the trenches.

On the 12th April, all battalions of the 8th Division who had taken part in the Battle of Neuve Chapelle were inspected by the

Commander-in-Chief, who congratulated then on their fine work.

1/5TH, 1/6TH, 1/7TH, 1/8TH BATTALIONS. 15TH APRIL. Four more Battalions of the Regiment, the 1/5th, 1/6th, 1/7th and 1/8th West Yorks. arrived in France on the 15th. These battalions formed the 1st West Riding Brigade of the 1st West Riding (Territorial) Division. The Brigade was concentrated at Selby on August 10th, 1914, soon after War broke out. The remainder of 1914 and the early months of 1915 were spent in hard training at Strensall and York followed by a period of duty on the Lincolnshire coast until 9th April, when the Brigade moved to Gainsborough. Here busy days were spent preparing for service overseas. The Brigade (in Division) completed concentration at Gainsborough on the 13th April, entrained early on the 14th, and journeying *via* Folkestone reached Boulogne late on the same night. On the following day the Brigade disembarked, and spent the 15th in camp, entraining for Merville on 16th, where the Division was concentrating, Divisional Headquarters having arrived on the 14th.

Each of the four battalions were up to War strength—approximately twenty-seven officers and 913 other ranks. The 1/5th was commanded by Lieut.-Col. C. E. Wood, the 1/6th by Lieut.-Col. H. O. Wade, the 1/7th by Lieut.-Col. A. E. Kirk, and the 1/8th by Lieut.-Col. J. W. Alexander. The West Riding Division was commanded by Major-General T. S. Baldock, the 1st West Riding Brigade by Brigadier General F. A. MacFarlan, the Brigade Major being Capt. T. E. C. Hunt.

Months of somewhat irksome training in England had made all ranks anxious for service overseas, so that it is not unusual to find such expressions in the battalion diaries as the following : " All very keen and cheery and longing for service overseas, and the real thing after eight months of hard training at home."

Many brave souls left England with that great longing—for the " real thing "—in their hearts, but no man ever said that with truth after two or three months in the front-line trenches.

17TH APRIL. By the 17th April, the Division complete was concentrated in the area Merville (1st West Riding Brigade)—Estaires (2nd West Riding Brigade) and Doulieu (3rd West Riding Brigade). Two days later parties of officers and N. C. O.'s were taken round the front line trenches. The four West Yorkshire battalions were attached for instructional purposes to the gallant old 7th Division, the remaining Brigades to the 8th Division. Three days were thus spent in obtaining a first glimpse of trench warfare and then on the 22nd the 1st West Riding Brigade moved into billets in La Gorgue, still attached to the 7th Division, but now an Army Reserve Brigade, with Brigade Head Quarters in Laventie.   1/5TH, 1/6TH 1/7TH, 1/8TH BATTALIONS.

By the 29th April all ranks of the 1/5th West Yorkshires had spent twenty-four hours in the trenches : the 1/7th had completed their first tour by the 28th, but it was not until the 30th that the 1/8th finished their first instruction. Meanwhile on the 27th, the 1/6th Battalion had taken over front-line trenches, one mile east of Laventie from the 2nd Border Regiment (7th Division) for twenty-four hours : thus the 1/6th was the first battalion of the 1st West Riding Brigade to assume sole responsibility for a section of the line. The battalion was relieved at 10 p.m. on the following night by the Rifle Brigade, having suffered seven casualties, all wounded other ranks, no officer being amongst them. The 1/8th Battalion had one man wounded on the 30th, before the battalion was relieved. These were the earliest recorded casualties.   29TH APRIL.

The 1st West Riding Brigade had been " blooded."

From the official diaries it is not possible to gather any impression of what the men felt—how vastly different it was from what the imagination had pictured when in England. An officer in one of these four West Yorkshire Territorial Battalions very well described those first twenty-four hours in the trenches : " When the Battalion took over the line for twenty-four hours at Fauquissart, the absence of all the expected signs of a battle front rather disconcerted our men. They saw no Germans, and had nothing to shoot at except rats. As one of our Sergeants wrote in his diary : ' The veterans of the Border Regiment took their relief as stolidly as woolcombers on the night shift at Isaac Holden's.' No Man's Land was a charming continuation of quiet country scenery, and the dead were hidden in the long grass. This impression of pleasantness of course quickly vanished. During the second night in the line the enemy began shelling—heavily it seemed then. Impossible to describe the first experience of being shelled. The ' old sweats ' of the Border Regiment seemed to ignore shelling."[1]

A Brigade Grenadier Company was formed on the 28th, each battalion furnishing one section. The Company was commanded by Capt. B. S. Bland (1/5th West Yorkshires). On the same day the 1st West Riding Brigade reverted to the West Riding Division, the 7th Division having been ordered further south. The General Officer Commanding (General Baldock) now assumed command

Capt. E. V. Tempest.

of the Fleurbaix Sector (sub-sectors 3, 4, 5 and 6), Divisional Headquarters being at Bac St. Maur.

Meanwhile during the time the four Territorial Battalions of West Yorkshiremen were establishing themselves in France nothing of outstanding interest had happened to the 1st and 2nd Battalions.

1ST BATTALION.

On the 14th, Lieut. Colonel F. W. Towsey, commanding the 1st Battalion, assumed temporary command of the 18th Infantry Brigade owing to the indisposition of Brigadier-General Congreve, V.C.

2ND BATTALION.

On the 20th a conference was held at 23rd Infantry Brigade Headquarters (8th Division) in order to discuss " proposed offensive operations," and a reconnaissance of the ground towards Fromelles was made by the Commanding Officer (Major T. P. Barrington). and officers of the 2nd Battalion.

1ST BATTALION.

Towards the end of April the 1st Battalion (in Brigade) marched to Doulieu where training operations were begun.

An interesting note on the general condition during the first few months of 1915 is given in the private diary of an officer of the West Yorkshire Regiment : " The long period of life in the trenches in the Houpline Sector was one of continual effort to improve the condition of the trenches, though the Sappers were not in a position to give any material. From January to May, 1915, the Battalion was in every trench from Neuve Chapelle to Le Touquet, and although there was no fighting, the wastage from sniping and sickness was great.

" It was during this period however that the *morale* of the battalion was very high, as it was felt that we were gradually able to play the Hun at some of his own games. Our snipers became particularly efficient and many amusing stories will be remembered of Lieut. A——'s efforts to disguise himself as a cabbage or gooseberry tree."

It was also at this period that the battalion (like all others in France) received officers from what appeared to be a General List, and at one time, out of fifteen officers with the battalion, eleven were from units other than the West Yorkshires.

It has been generally admitted that the old Army saved Britain at Mons and the Marne, but a great deal of credit is due to the men of the Special Reserve who formed such a large proportion of the Army during the terrible winters of 1914 and 1915. Many of these men were no longer young and perhaps did not come up to the discipline of the Regular Army, and although they probably groused at their billets, their conduct throughout their hardships in the trenches was a fine example to the New Armies, which followed them.

About the middle of April, General Joffre asked Sir John French to co-operate in an attack which he (the French Commander-in-Chief) proposed to make on the 9th May just north of Arras. Information had been received of the concentration of large hostile forces about Cambrai, St. Quentin and Maubeuge, but the line between Lens and Arras appeared to offer favourable opportunities for an offensive, which would reduce the German salient between Lille and Lens. Sir John French agreed to these proposals and instructed Sir Douglas Haig, commanding the First British Army, to carry out attacks in the neighbourhood of Rouge Banc (north-west of Fromelles) by the IVth Corps, and between Neuve Chapelle and Givenchy by the Ist and Indian Corps. The first of these actions was destined to become known as the Battle of Aubers Ridge, and the second The Battle of Festubert. The Battle of Aubers Ridge consisted of two separate attacks, *i.e.*, the attack at Fromelles and the attack at Rue du Bois : these two attacks took place on the 9th May. The Battle of Festubert extended from 15th to 25th May.

In these two battles, however, the battalions of the West Yorkshire Regiment then in France were not directly involved: the 1st Battalion with other units of the 6th Division and IIIrd Corps co-operated by fire attacks only : the 2nd Battalion, was in 8th Divisional reserve, and the newly arrived 1/5th, 1/6th, 1/7th and 1/8th Battalions, holding the line on the left of the 8th Division assisted, also with fire attacks, for the protection of the flank of that Division as it advanced to the assault on the enemy's trenches. 1ST BATTALION.
2ND BATTALION.
1/5TH, 1/6TH 1/7TH, 1/8TH BATTALIONS.

The attack at Fromelles took place at 5-40 a.m., preceded by an artillery bombardment which began at 5-20 a.m., but the enemy's position was exceptionally strong, the parapets of his trenches varying from 15 to 20 feet thick, provided with " bomb-proofs " capable of keeping out any but the heaviest shells. In rear of the parapet was a second parapet or parados, which the enemy was able to man when (as happened only in a very few places) his front parapet was breached. He also had wired his front with a new kind of barbed wire—very thick which could not be dealt with by the ordinary wire-cutters then issued to the troops. Moreover the fire of the light field guns had had very little effect upon it. The result was failure, though the troops of the Indian Corps and 8th Division fought splendidly and many deeds of gallantry are recorded. The 2nd West Yorkshires were not called upon to cross No Man's Land and remained all day in support. The battalion lost one officer—Lieut. R. J. Legard— who was shot in the head and died of his wounds during the day; 2ND BATTALION. 9TH MAY.

2ND BATTALION. 9TH MAY.
two other ranks killed, and thirteen wounded and three missing.
The inability of the Indian Corps and 8th Division to take the enemy's trenches was a disappointment to the four Territorial Battalions of the West Yorkshires, who in " C," " D " and " E " lines on the left of the 8th Division kept up a brisk fire on the enemy's position, the while waiting orders which never came to go forward. The 1st West Riding Brigade lost a total of forty-three other ranks killed and wounded.

1ST BATTALION.
North of the 8th Division the 1st Battalion West Yorks. R. (6th Division) carried out a fire demonstration, as already stated, but the battalion diary of that date (9th May) contains only four words—"Total casualties, one wounded." In the General Staff Diary 6th Division, however, the following story occurs : "At about 5-45 p.m. the officer-in-charge of the West Yorkshire snipers detected the enemy in the act of carrying out a relief. He extended the range of his two machine guns trained on a post, firing indirect, and also directed the fire of his platoons. Having arranged a code of whistle signals, he returned to his look-out post. On the next appearance of the enemy at the marked spot, he opened fire successfully. When the next party selected a fresh route he re-laid his guns and re-directed the platoon fire. He was rewarded by catching the enemy in a close column of fours. One officer and fourteen men were killed for certain and the estimated casualties were forty or fifty."

14TH—15TH MAY.
Six days later, on the night 14th/15th May, the Battle of Festubert opened, and the 6th, 8th and 49th (formerly the 1st West Riding Division, but re-named on the 12th May) Divisions again co-operated with fire attacks and artillery bombardments on the enemy's trenches, wire and support lines, in order to assist the attacks of the Indian Corps, 2nd and 7th Divisions, further south.

25TH MAY.
By the 25th May, upon which date the Battle of Festubert ended, the French between Arras and Lens had gained ground and captured many prisoners. Neuville St. Vaast, Notre Dame de Lorette and Carnoy had all been occupied and some thousands of Germans taken : the British Army, though suffering heavy losses, had faithfully carried out its *rôle*.

Until the end of May, when the 6th Division marched north to Ypres, trench warfare was much more active along the front held by the Division. Patrol work was carried out nightly, over forty of these parties going out into No Man's Land after dark and obtaining very useful information. Shelling, sniping, bombing, mining and trench-mortar activity were general on both sides—the fine spring weather

The Square, Ypres.

being conducive to these dangerous enterprises. Four other ranks were killed and twenty-eight wounded during the month. On the 27th May, Brigadier-General W. N. Congreve, V.C., commanding 18th Infantry Brigade, assumed command of the 6th Division, Major-General J. L. Keir leaving to take over command of the newly formed VIth Corps.

The 18th Infantry Brigade was relieved in the line on 28th May by troops of the 27th Division, who took over the Le Touquet Houplines Sector from the 6th Division. The 1st West Yorkshires handed over to the Leinsters at 6 p.m. and moved (in Brigade) to Bailleul, a distance of 10 miles. Throughout the 29th, the battalion remained in Bailleul and during the day the whole 18th Infantry Brigade was inspected by Sir John French: "The Field Marshal addressed the Brigade and said he wished to express the greatest admiration for the magnificent work of the Brigade both on the Aisne in September, 1914, and during the very critical days for England when the Brigade assisted in pushing the enemy back and taking up a line between Bethune and Nieuport, and holding the line all through the winter months." 28TH MAY. 1ST BATTALION.

The 30th and 31st were spent in marching north to Ypres and at 10-30 p.m. on the latter date, the 1st West Yorkshires, with the remainder of the 18th Infantry Brigade, arrived at hutments 2,500 yards north-west of the town, being placed in Divisional reserve Brigadier-General S. Ainslie now commanded the Brigade. 31ST MAY.

All ranks were glad to leave the Le Touquet area, though the ill-famed Ypres Salient held out no prospects of more healthy life, for it was at Ypres in April that the enemy first launched his dastardly gas attack. The first sight the battalion had of Ypres was not at all reassuring, for the town was in flames as the troops marched into their billets.

After the fruitless attempts of the 9th May, the 8th Division settled down once more to trench warfare, the increasing activity of the enemy necessitating similar tactics. The diary of the 2nd Battalion West Yorkshires for the 19th May contained the following human touch with the hand of death so close : " Headquarters now full of furniture, and there are windows everywhere. The swallows in the Mess Room are quite tame and their nest is nearly finished." There is little of interest for the remainder of the month, but at the close this sentence occurs : " Heard the 1st Battalion are out of the trenches, to prepare for the next push." Fraternal interest between battalions 2ND BATTALION.

of the same Regiment was a very memorable feature in France and Flanders.

With less than a month's experience of active service conditions the 49th (West Riding) Division was adapting itself admirably to trench warfare. The troops, being Territorials, had less training to undergo than those of the New Armies. They required only the grim realities of war in which to turn their pre-war training to good account, though they found the "real thing" very different from peace warfare. Their first experience of a "trench battle" (on 9th May) in which the Division assisted by fire attacks, had vastly improved their knowledge and understanding, but had not by any means chilled their ardour. "The men are splendid, very cheery and behave like seasoned troops in the trenches" said one of the West Yorkshire diaries. "They feel the strain of night work and fatigue more than regulars, but they are willing to work and obey orders." On the 12th May, the 1/5th West Yorkshires took over a one Company front in "F" lines from the 2nd Battalion West Yorkshires (8th Division), the first instance in the history of the West Yorkshire Regiment of a Territorial Battalion relieving one of its regular Battalions on active service. From the 1st to the 31st May, the battalion had one officer wounded, three other ranks killed and twenty wounded. The 1/6th Battalion was relieved after a ten days' tour in the trenches (from 5th to 15th May) and during that period lost eight other ranks killed and twenty-one wounded. Only two days' respite in billets were allowed, and on the 18th, the battalion again went into the line. Trench work occupied most of the nights, whilst by day a constant watch was maintained upon the enemy's front line. The working parties generally began at 6 p.m., finishing the following day. The following extract shows to what extent this work was necessary: "Drainage attempted. *Note.* Water in Sap 1.R is deep and difficult to drain. 1.S.: Work continued on parapet, parados and dug-outs. 2.P.: Work on parapet, parados and dug-outs continued. Work commenced on defences of saps. Notes on Sap: This is held by six men and one N. C. O. by day, and by one officer and twenty other ranks by night. At present full of water, badly defended and dead not disinfected. Work done by 6 p.m. Dead buried up to a point where Sap held, other dead disinfected as best possible. Sandbags placed so as to prevent garrison being surprised from rear of Sap. Forts 1.B. and 1.C.: general improvements in defences of these forts carried out; communication trenches begun from 1.B. to road

Work was very heavy during the whole tour in the trenches. The total casualties suffered by the 1/6th Battalion in May was one officer wounded, three other ranks killed and thirteen wounded.   1/6TH BATTALION.

The 1/7th West Yorks was the first battalion of the 146th Infantry Brigade to lose an officer killed—2nd Lieut. G. W. Sykes being shot in the trenches on the 25th May.   1/7TH BATTALION. 25TH MAY.

About the middle of the month " German measles " attacked the 1/8th Battalion, and on the 20th, the West Yorkshiremen were isolated in billets, and it was not until ten days later that the men were declared free from infection and were allowed to go into the trenches again.   1/8TH BATTALION.

A re-organization of the First Army took place on the 31st May. The 49th (West Riding) Division came under the orders of the Indian Corps, which was now formed of the 49th, 8th, Lahore and Meerut Divisions. The IVth Corps consisted of the 51st, 7th and Canadian Divisions and the Ist Corps of the 1st, 47th (London) and 2nd Divisions.

The late winter of 1914 and the spring of 1915 had witnessed the arrival in France of many Territorial and New Army Battalions and Divisions, splendid fighting material, though they required training in trench warfare. The period is perhaps better described as one of gestation—pregnant with new ideas and inventions, the results of costly experience gained in warring against an enemy who had anticipated the kind of warfare which might result when the day of the Great War arrived. The treacherous use of asphyxiating gas was no new device, but had been carefully thought out in pre-war days by the German General Staff and used in defiance of the Hague Conventions to which Germany had affixed her signature. But just retribution was not long in falling, though many brave soldiers of the Allies died horrible deaths before the Allied Governments of France and Great Britain decided upon well-merited reprisals.

Hand-grenades, rifle-grenades, trench mortars, howitzers of enormous proportions—all made their appearance early in 1915, though grenades of an improvised pattern had been used on the Aisne in 1914.

At the end of May, 1915, the British Army in France and Flanders was organized and disposed on a line running from a point approximately two miles north of Ypres to one and a half miles south-west of Loos, as follows :

Second Army : VIth Corps—4th, 6th and 28th Divisions.

       Vth Corps—3rd, 3rd Cavalry and 1st Indian Cavalry Divisions.
       IInd Corps—5th, 14th and 46th Divisions.
       IIIrd Corps—48th and 27th Divisions.
       Reserves: Cavalry Corps (less 3rd Cavalry Division), Indian Cavalry Corps (less 1st Indian Cavalry Division), 50th Division and 12th Division (which was then arriving).

First Army: Indian Corps—49th, 8th, Meerut and Lahore Divisions.
       IVth Corps—51st (Highland), 7th and Canadian Divisions.
       Ist Corps—1st, 47th and 2nd Divisions.

1915

THE FIRST ATTACK ON BELLEWAERDE

16th June, 1915

FROM the 1st to the 15th June, nothing of importance happened to the 1st Battalion West Yorkshires. The 6th Division was not involved in the defeat of the enemy's offensive in the Ypres Salient—at Hooge—on the 2nd June. But the guns were never silent, and constant heavy shelling was responsible for almost all the casualties suffered by the West Yorkshiremen. Rain fell heavily about the middle of the month and the Divisional Diaries report: " Trenches in disgusting condition. Communication trenches full of water. Parapets and trenches falling in ": in fact it was January all over again. *1st Battalion.*

On the 16th June, the 3rd Division (Vth Corps) carried out an attack on the Bellewaerde Ridge, east of Ypres. The IInd and VIth Corps delivered holding attacks and were successful in these operations, but of the 6th Division, the 1st West Yorkshires (being one of the flanking battalions to the attack which was going on further south) caught something of the blast of battle. The story is given *in extenso* from the battalion diary : " 16th June. The 3rd Division with the 9th Infantry Brigade on the left attacked the German line immediately on the right of the battalion and in the direction of Bellewaerde Farm. The right of the battalion rested on the railway with two platoons of B Company on the southern side. The battalion with two Companies of Queen's Westminsters and one section of No. 12 Company Royal Engineers under the orders of Lieut.-Col. F. W. Towsey, were ordered to protect the left flank of the 9th Infantry Brigade, and if the attack succeeded to support and assist the attack as opportunity offered." *16th June.*

The artillery bombardment commenced at 2-50 a.m. and ceased at 4-15 a.m., when the 9th Infantry Brigade attacked and took the first and second lines of German trenches, and also part of the third line on a front of 1000 yards. About 200 German prisoners were taken. The Northumberland Fusiliers were unable to take the trenches immediately south of the railway, the artillery not having destroyed the wire in front of these trenches. At about 5 a.m. the enemy commenced to shell our trenches heavily and continued to do so with short intervals throughout the day. The shelling prevented any reinforcements being brought up and also held up the

1ST BATTALION.
16TH JUNE.

attack, compelling the 9th Brigade to retire from the second and third lines of trenches and fall back to the first line of German trenches, which they strengthened and continued to hold.

The battalion was able from its position to assist the attack by rifle and enfilade fire, the machine-guns also getting some excellent targets. Very useful information by Capt. W. T. C. Huffam, commanding C Company, was sent back, which enabled the artillery to prevent the enemy counter-attacking. " During this action," said the official despatches, " the fire of the artillery was most effective, the prisoners testifying to its destructiveness and accuracy. It also prevented the delivery of counter-attacks which were paralysed at the outset."

Capt. Huffam was assisted by two officers' servants, who got across open ground to the artillery with the message, all the communications having been cut by the violent shell-fire. These servants, Lance Cpl. Tyson and Lance Cpl. Wilson, were both mentioned in despatches for their gallantry.

The new stick rifle-grenade was used very successfully on this occasion. The enemy machine-gun was holding up the whole of the line, but Corporal Atkinson placed seven stick-grenades in quick succession into the midst of the hostile gun team and killed them all.

The casualties of the battalion were heavy: The battalion machine-gun officer, 2nd Lieut. O. Tennant was killed, and two other officers were wounded; in other ranks, the battalion lost eight killed, forty-five wounded and two were gassed by gas shells.

Capt. Scott, R.A.M.C. (the Battalion M.O.), Sergt. Baker and the stretcher-bearers rendered invaluable assistance throughout the day and night of the 16th and 17th in helping to evacuate the great number of wounded of the 9th Infantry Brigade, in addition to our own. This work was carried out very often under heavy shell fire.

18TH JUNE. On the 18th, the battalion was relieved by the Buffs at 10 p.m., and marched a distance of seven miles back to a camp in a wood one and a half miles north-west of Vlamertinghe.

1915

TRENCH WARFARE: 18th—30th June

Whilst the 1st Battalion had been engaged in subsidiary actions, the 2nd Battalion and the 1/5th, 1/6th, 1/7th and 1/8th Battalions were enjoying a comparatively quiet time. True, the enemy had been considerably more active with his trench mortars and artillery, but retaliatory measures had quickly dampened his ardour: in particular he objected to the 4-inch Trench Mortar, which usually opened fire at once if he ventured to fire his mortar bombs into the trenches of the battalions. Nothing upset the Germans more than retaliation.

About midnight on the 8th/9th June, the billets occupied by D Company of the 2nd Battalion—a large farm—were accidentally fired and burned to the ground. Fortunately 100 men were away on fatigue duties, but three who were in the farm lost their lives. [2ND BATTALION. 8TH—9TH JUNE.]

The four West Yorkshire Battalions of the 146th Infantry Brigade (49th Division) were gradually settling down. The Brigade (in Division) was not involved in any general attack during June, but gained much experience in trench warfare. The Diaries are full of items which show the alertness of these Territorial Troops. The 1/5th, for instance, from the 6th to the 10th June kept record of the exact number of shells which fell in the trenches of the battalion, whilst the use of a new gun, by the enemy, is also noted: " light shells exploded on the 7th, the ' pip-squeak ' probably." Six days in and six out of the trenches was at this period the rule. On the 18th, the 1/5th Battalion records with evident satisfaction a retaliatory bombardment of the enemy's trenches with " rifle-grenades and ' Archibald ' [1]—very successful, fifteen in trenches or on parapet silenced enemy trench mortars." [1/5TH BATTALION. 6TH—10TH JUNE.]

The diaries of the 1/6th Battalion record that on the 3rd June at 6 p.m. a " Feu du Joie " was fired to celebrate the King's birthday. Strenuous were these days of June, 1915, for working parties were everywhere busy, on parapets and parados and dug-outs. The enemy was apparently similarly employed, in consequence there was not much in the way of trench fighting. The diarist is also concerned over the frequent noise of trains moving at night, there being " no railway shown on the map in this direction." The troops had not then learned to detect the difference between a train and the engines of a Zeppelin airship. [1/6TH BATTALION. 3RD JUNE.]

---

[1] " Archibald " (or " Archie ") was an anti-aircraft gun. The name originated on the Aisne in 1914.

1/7TH BATTALION.
9TH JUNE.

"The accuracy of the howitzer fire on a point so close to our own trenches cheered the men up no end," records the 1/7th Battalion diary on the 9th June. The Bosche had been busy with his trench mortars and nothing was more demoralizing than the arrival of these beastly bombs in the trench, bursting and scattering destruction all round, without immediate retaliation.

1/8TH BATTALION.
3RD JUNE.

The 1/8th Battalion also took part in the King's birthday celebrations, and recorded that the Feu du Joie " caused considerable excitement in the German lines and made them man their parapets and open rapid fire, but this caused no damage. The three cheers brought over a trench-mortar shell which fell short. After this all was quiet."

Little of interest marked the latter half of June. The hot weather had made life much more bearable, though heavy rain and thunderstorms at intervals invariably left the trenches in a sad plight.

1ST BATTALION.
18TH—25TH JUNE.

After the attack of the 16th and 17th June, no operation of importance took place in the Ypres Salient during the remainder of the month. The 1st West Yorkshires remained in camp from the 18th to the 25th, and then relieved the Royal Fusiliers in tents, at 9 p.m., 1500 yards north of La Brique. The 18th Infantry Brigade (6th Division) was distributed as follows : Front line, Sherwood Foresters, Queen's Westminsters, 1st West Yorkshires, East Yorks. In reserve, in Canal Bank, Durham Light Infantry. Brigade Headquarters in Canal Bank. The line extended from and included Wieltje, in a north-westerly direction on a front of 2500 yards.

On the 30th June, Lieut. Melland was killed. Casualties in the 1st Battalion, during June, had been heavy, the intense shelling to which the Ypres Salient was subjected resulting in the loss of 177 other ranks, killed, wounded and missing.

2ND BATTALION.
27TH JUNE.

The principal item of interest in the diaries of the 2nd West Yorkshires and the 23rd Infantry Brigade, is the loss of Brigadier-General R. Pinney, who handed over command of the 23rd Infantry Brigade on the 27th June, and proceeded to England to command a New Army Division. All ranks regretted the departure of General Pinney. He was succeeded by Lieut.-Col. T. E. Clark,[1] Royal Inniskilling Fusiliers.

On the 28th, the 8th Division was transferred to the IIIrd Corps. the Corps having been re-constructed and the areas re-adjusted, The change, however, entailed no move on the part of the Division,

[1] Subsequently became Quarter-Master General.

which still had its Headquarters at Sailly-sur-la-Lys, though the frontage held by the Division was extended to include that previously held by the 49th Division, which was drawn out of the line in order to join the VIth Corps in the Ypres Salient.

The West Riding Division billeted on the night of the 28th in the Fletre area, reaching Proven on the following day, and at nightfall the 1/8th West Yorks. were ordered to proceed to the support of the 11th Infantry Brigade (4th Division) which was in action near Ypres. 1/8TH BATTALION. 28TH JUNE.

Thus five of the six battalions of the West Yorkshire Regiment were now at Ypres, and another—the 10th—was soon to join them. 10TH BATTALION.

THE DARDANELLES

THE BATTLES OF SUVLA: 6th—21st August.
   INTRODUCTION.

THE LANDING AT SUVLA:
   CAPTURE OF KARAKOL DAGH.
   CAPTURE OF CHOCOLATE HILL.
   THE BATTLE OF SCIMITAR HILL.

THE BATTLES OF SUVLA
INTRODUCTION.

ON the 1st July, 1915, the 9th (Service) Battalion West Yorkshire Regt. which had been training at Witley Camp, Godalming, left that place (in Division) for Liverpool. The battalion was contained in the 32nd Infantry Brigade[1], one of the three Infantry Brigades of the 11th Division. The following day, at a strength of 30 officers and 933 other ranks, the Battalion under the command of Lieut-Colonel J. O. B. Minogue, reached Alexandra Docks, and having detrained embarked immediately on the "Aquitania." At 8-30 p.m. on the 3rd July this huge liner, having 6,389 souls aboard, put out to sea escorted by torpedo destroyers, bound for an "unknown destination." Early next morning (at about 5-45 a.m.) when the vessel was off the Scilly Isles the alarm was sounded: an enemy submarine which had not been sighted fired a torpedo at the "Aquitania," which fortunately was taking a zig-zag course at high speed, and in consequence the torpedo missed its mark. Gibraltar was passed at 10-30 a.m. on the morning of the 6th. At sunrise on the morning of the 7th, another dangerous half-hour was experienced: "The alarm sounded and the troops fell in on their boat stations. An enemy submarine had been sighted, she was above water replenishing her fuel from a fuel ship: she was out of range of rifle fire. The submarine was soon left behind. She had not been able to fire at us."

1915.
9TH BATTALION.
1ST JULY.

On the 10th July, very early in the morning, Lemnos Island was sighted (3 a.m.), and four hours later the "Aquitania" dropped her anchor in Mudros Bay. Here all was hurry and bustle, troops arriving and departing, the Bay packed with shipping of all kinds and the Island itself literally "stuffed" with battalions who were destined to take part in that final bid for victory, which has now passed into history under the title of "The Battles of Suvla."[1]

10TH JULY.

To understand this operation in its true relation with the Dardanelles Campaign it is necessary to describe the events which

---

[1]Commanded by Brigadier-General H. Haggard and formed of the 9th West Yorks., 6th Yorkshire Regt., 8th Duke of Wellington's Regt., and 6th York and Lancs. Regt.

9TH BATTALION.

led up to that last splendid, but forlorn, effort which began in the dark hours of the 6th/7th and ended on the 27th of August, 1915.[1] It is necessary also to give some reason why on the early morning of the 10th July, 1915, the 9th (Service) Battalion of the West Yorkshire Regt. found itself aboardship, inside Mudros Bay awaiting orders to disembark.

The Dardanelles campaign has frequently been referred to as " The Great Adventure " : in history it must go down as *the* epic of the Great War, for the Plains of Troy haunted by the ghosts of warriors from whom Thucydides drew his inspiration never witnessed more gallant deeds than were performed by the splendid troops under Sir Ian Hamilton's command :

" All these fought most valiantly, their deeds are immortal."

The position on the Gallipoli Peninsula, which lead up to the Battles of Suvla is well set out in " The Dardanelles "[2] Already early in May, it had become manifest that the campaign undertaken by the Allies in the Gallipoli Peninsula was bound to prove a failure, unless the strength of the Force which had been originally detailed for the the enterprise and which had initiated the venture was to be substantially increased. Foiled as it had been in its attempt to occupy domination over the Narrows of the Dardanelles by a sudden descent upon the enemy's shores, brought to a standstill by a hostile array superior in numbers to itself and better equipped with guns and howitzers, the Expeditionary Army could not hope to accomplish its purpose without considerable reinforcements. If any uncertainty had been entertained on the point after the troops at Helles, although reinforced from Anzac, had been unable to gain more than a few hundred yards by their determined offensive of the 6th/8th May, doubt must have been dispelled by the combat of the 4th of June, and by the stalemate at Anzac following on the great Turkish effort of the 19th May. A good deal of perplexity always existed as to the numerical strength of the Ottoman Army, even if the number of divisions and their approximate distribution in the immediate theatre of operations was usually known. Still it could be foreseen that this Army would grow as time went on and Ottoman resources about the heart of the Empire were developed under German guidance. The Commander-in-Chief was under no illusion as to his prospects. He realized that, as matters stood during May and June, the odds against him were too great to justify his indulging in any hopes of a strategical

[1]The official period of the " Battles of Suvla."
[2]Major-General Sir E. Callwell, C.B.

triumph with the Army at his disposal. So early as the 10th May, he had cabled home asking for two divisions, and a week later, apprised in the meantime that no assistance was to be expected from the Russians, even in the indeterminate shape of threats to Constantinople from across the Black Sea, he followed this message up with another requesting that two additional Army Corps should be sent him."

And in his Despatch dated the 11th December, 1915, Sir Ian Hamilton said : " During June your Lordship[1] became persuaded of the bearing of these facts and I was promised three regular divisions plus the infantry of two Territorial divisions. The advance guard of these troops was due to reach Mudros by the 10th July : by the 10th August their concentration was to be complete."

The 11th Division aboard the " Aquitania " which on the morning of the 10th July had dropped anchor in Mudros Bay was (with the 10th and 13th Divisions) one of the new divisions promised : the 53rd (Welsh) and the 54th (East Anglian) were the two Territorial Divisions.

Four methods of employing these fresh divisions presented themselves to Sir Ian Hamilton : "(a) Every man to be thrown on to the southern sector of the Peninsula to force a way forward to the Narrows ; (b) Disembarkation on the Asiatic side of the Straits followed by a march on Chanak : (c) A landing at Enos or Ebrize for the purpose of seizing the neck of the isthmus at Bulair ; (d) Reinforcement of the Australian and New Zealand Army Corps., combined with a landing at Suvla Bay. Then with one strong push to capture Hill 305, and working from that dominating point, to grip the waist of the Peninsula."

The fourth (d) was deemed the only practicable plan, and with this idea in view the Commander-in-Chief set out to prepare his scheme of operations for the attack. This was

" (I) To break out with a rush from Anzac and cut off the bulk of the Turkish Army from land communication with Constantinople. (II) To gain such a command for my artillery as to cut off the bulk of the Turkish Army from sea traffic whether with Constantinople or Asia. (III) Incidentally, to secure Suvla Bay as a winter base for Anzac and all the troops operating in the northern theatre."

Tactical and strategical diversions had to be made (which were successful in hoodwinking the Turks). But the extraordinary difficulty in concentrating the Force for the operations may be appreciated when it is understood that of the forces to be employed,

[1]The (then) Secretary of State for War—Lord Kitchener.

9TH BATTALION.

part were at Anzac, part at Imbros, part at Mudros and part at Mitylele. "Within the narrow confines of the positions I held on the Peninsula, it was impossible to concentrate even as much as one-third of the fresh troops about to be launched to the attack." Practically every part of the Peninsular was under the eye of the Turk.

Into all the details of that second Homeric attempt to wrest victory from the enemy, it is impossible to go, but that part of it which intimately concerned the 9th (Service) Battalion West Yorkshire Regt., will for generations to come interest the descendants of those brave men.

THE LANDING AT SUVLA: CAPTURE OF KARAKOL DAGH

6th—15th August, 1915

THE diary of the 9th West Yorkshires records that on 1915. 24th July, at Kaphalos Camp, Imbros, Sir Ian Hamilton inspected the Division in which the Battalion was contained, and the Commander-in-Chief subsequently wrote: "Whilst concentrated on the Island of Imbros the spirit and physique of the 11th Division had impressed me very favourably."

On 4th August, 11th Division Headquarters received IXth 4TH AUGUST Corps Orders which contained instructions for the landing at Suvla Bay by the Corps, and for the attack on Sari Bair by the Australian and New Zealand Army Corps. At 8 p.m. on the 5th, the Division issued Operation Order No. 1 to the 32nd, 33rd and 34th Infantry Brigades. The Operation Order so far as it affects the 9th West 9TH Yorkshires (of the 32nd Infantry Brigade) is given in full: BATTALION.

"The main object of the General Officer Commanding Mediterranean Force is to seize a position across the Gallipoli Peninsula from Gaba Tepe to Mados with a protected line of supply from Suvla Bay.

"The following troops under orders of the General Officer Commanding IXth Corps will secure Suvla Bay: 11th Division (less LXth Brigade R.F.A.) to which are attached the IVth Highland Artillery Brigade and one Squadron Motor Machine Guns.

"With this object the 11th Division and attached troops will embark at Imbros at an early date.

"Note. Beach "A" is the N.E. portion of Suvla Bay: Beach "C" is about 900 yards south of Nibrussi Point: Beach "B" NIBRUNESI is immediately south of "C," extending about 1,800 yards.

"Simultaneously with the disembarkation, the General Officer Commanding Australian and New Zealand Corps will make a strong attack so as to capture Sari Bair, drive the troops in a southerly direction and to distract attention from our landing.

"According to information dated 22nd July, the strength of the

9TH BATTALION.

enemy North of Kilid Bahr was then estimated at 30,000, *i.e.*, 12,000 in trenches facing the Anzac position : 18,000 in reserve, mainly about Boghali—Koja Dere—Eski Keui.

" The tasks allotted to the 11th Division are :
To secure the landing in " A," " C," and " B " Beaches.
To secure Suvla Bay for the disembarkation of the 10th Division and stores.
With these objects the General Officer Commanding intends :
To secure his right flank with the 33rd Infantry Brigade, less 2 Battalions.
To seize Lala Baba with the 32nd Infantry Brigade.
To seize Ghazi Baba and Height 10, with the 34th Infantry Brigade,
which will subsequently attack Yilghin Burnu and if possible Ismail Oglu Tepe."

The troops were to be conveyed from Imbros to Suvla in steel-protected oil-propelled lighters (known as the Beetles) in charge of torpedo destroyers : the lighters were to be run ashore and the troops landed.

" Immediately the first troops are landed they will clear the beach and rendezvous about 100 yards east of the landing.

" They will then (I) 34th Infantry Brigade—secure Ghazi Baba with one Battalion, and Height 10 with the other (Battalion). The Ghazi Baba Battalion will then move by Karakol Dagh and Kiritch Tepe Sirt if possible as far as Point 156.

(II) 32nd Infantry Brigade will send a small force to picquet the south shore of the Lake, and with the remainder secure Lala Baba. As soon as Lala Baba is secure the 32nd Infantry Brigade will send out patrols to get in touch with the 34th Infantry Brigade.

This patrol will be followed as soon as possible by the rest of the two Battalions, less sufficient troops to picquet the Lake. A party with picks and shovels must be prepared to improve the passage of the ' Cut ' if necessary.

(III) 33rd Infantry Brigade will take up a line from the right of the landing place to the south-east corner of the Salt Lake."

The troops were to be landed in two trips.

6TH AUGUST

The attack was to be made after dark on the night of the 6th August.

In fighting order, the 9th West Yorkshires with the remaining units of the 32nd Infantry Brigade paraded at 4 p.m. at Imbros

Camp, and marched down to the harbour and embarked on Lighters " K5 " and " K6," leaving Kephalos Bay at 8 p.m.

9TH BATTALION.

All accounts agree that the night was still and dark and that the destroyers and lighters reached their destinations off Suvla, without incident of any kind. " Lighters ran ashore " said the Battalion Diary, " at ' C ' Beach, and the Battalion formed up in support of the 6th Yorkshire Regt. at 10 p.m., advanced in two lines across rough and sandy ground at slow pace in two lines—B and A, and D and C Companies. The Yorkshire Regt. took Lala Baba Hill but lost heavily. The Battalion pushed through in support bayonetting about 10 snipers *en route*. Captain W. B. Hore killed and Lieut. J. W. Worsnop mortally wounded by snipers."

The landings at "C"and "B" beaches were practically unopposed, and the surprise of the Turks was complete. At " A " beach, however, it was found that the shore slope was very gradual, with the result that the lighters grounded about 60 yards from the shore and the troops of the 34th Infantry Brigade had to wade ashore through five feet of water. This not only delayed disembarkation, but gave the Turks time to recover from their surprise. Moreover, the lighters containing the troops of this Brigade came under a crossfire from Hill 10, and Lala Baba and there were casualties.

Detailed accounts of the attack are lacking, and all that can be gathered from the official diaries is that delay took place in the operations. The first lighter containing troops of the 32nd Infantry Brigade (9th West Yorkshires and 6th Yorkshire Regt.) ran ashore soon after 9-30 p.m. on the night of the 6th, and the troops were formed up by 10 p.m. The enemy immediately opened fire from the east. The 6th Yorkshires set out at once for their objective—Lala Baba— followed by the 9th West Yorks. At about midnight, the Commanding Officer of the former battalion reported to Brigade Headquarters that Lala Baba had been captured, but he was unable to proceed further unsupported, as most of his officers had been killed or wounded. The 9th West Yorkshires came up on his right and a little later pushed northwards across the sandy isthmus of the shore of the Salt Lake, where at 7 a.m. they joined up with some troops of the 34th Infantry Brigade (Lancashire Fusiliers) who were then moving forward to attack Hill 10. The two remaining battalions of the 32nd Infantry Brigade (6th York and Lancs. Regt. and 8th Duke of Wellington Regt.) landed about midnight, and at 5 a.m. advanced in close support of the Yorkshires and West Yorkshires across the isthmus north of Lala Baba, towards Hill 10.

7TH AUGUST

9TH
BATTALION.
7TH AUGUST

The capture of Lala Baba by the 6th Yorkshires and the 9th West Yorks. R. was no mean performance seeing that the night was pitch black, the country entirely unknown, and confusion had been caused by the Turks coming right down on to the beach between the advancing troops and their supports, firing on the former from rear as they advanced up the hill towards Lala Baba.

Hill 10 was strongly entrenched and surrounded by land mines, and guns also defended the position, but were withdrawn by the enemy soon after the landings began. The Hill is about 1,000 yards from the shore, almost within rifle-shot of the beach. The Turks here put up a good fight and were able to delay the advance of the 34th and 32nd Infantry Brigades very considerably, the latter having severe casualties. The Manchester Regt. which had landed at the same time as the Lancashire Fusiliers (both battalions belonging to the 34th Infantry Brigade) cleared Ghazi Baba and, advancing gallantly along the ridge towards Karakol Dagh had, when dawn broke, made very considerable headway.

Just after 6 a.m. on the morning of the 7th, Hill 10 was taken, the Turks retiring northwards towards Kiretch Tepe Sirt. The situation of the 11th Division then seems to have been approximately as follows :

32nd Infantry Brigade : 2 Companies, 9th West Yorks. R., 1 Company 6th Yorkshire Regt., 1 Company West Riding Regt. and York and Lancs. Regt. at Lala Baba.

33rd Infantry Brigade : 2 Battalions entrenched from Point 49 (Lala Baba) due east to Punar : 2 Battalions entrenched from south-east corner of Salt Lake to 91 b. 1.

34th Infantry Brigade : 1 Battalion (Manchester Regt.) on the Karakol Ridge, due north of Hill 10, 3 Battalions on or about Hill 10, together with troops of the 32nd Infantry Brigade, *i.e.*, 2 Companies 9th West Yorks. R., 3 Companies 6th Yorkshire Regt., 3 Companies West Ridings.

The 9th West Yorkshires had lost heavily—no less than nine officers being put out of action.

At 6-30 a.m. it was light enough to see and the enemy opened fire with his guns. Hill 10 was shelled heavily and the gorse set on fire.

The retirement of the Turks northwards towards Kiretch Tepe Sirt had drawn the 34th Infantry Brigade from its original objective—Yilghin Burnu (Chocolate Hill). Troops of the 32nd Brigade had attached themselves to the 34th Brigade and at 9 a.m. there was considerable confusion in Brigades and intermixing of battalions.

9TH BATTALION. 7TH AUGUST

In his report on the Suvla Bay operations, both Captain R. Lupton and Captain E. A. T. Dutton of the 9th West Yorkshires were mentioned by the Commanding Officer of the 6th Yorkshire Regt. for their gallantry and determination in leading their men forward.

At dawn the advanced troops of the 10th Division (six battalions), sailed into the Bay: these should have been put ashore at Beach " A," but for some reason were disembarked by lighter at Beach " C," whence they had to march to Hill 10, suffering on the way fatigue and casualties from shell fire, as well as delaying operations.

Thus far the landing at Suvla had been accomplished with great credit to the Navy and the General Headquarters Staff of the M.E.F.

Surprise had been sprung on the Turks, the enemy having no appreciable forces in the northern sector of the Gallipoli Peninsula.

At this period, about 9 a.m. on the morning of the 7th, in the second of the subsidiary attacks, which had taken place at Helles, the southern portion of the Peninsula, the gallant troops of the 29th and 42nd Divisions had at first met with some success, but had later been driven back to their original trenches.

At Anzac, where the main attack was in progress, the Australian and New Zealand Corps with troops of the 10th and 13th Divisions, the 29th Indian Infantry Brigade and 38th Infantry Brigade, had made an appreciable advance and had won Lone Pine, a formidable entrenchment and a decided step on the way across to Maidos : " Table Top " had been captured by General Russell's New Zealanders after extraordinary deeds of gallantry ; Rhododendron Spur, a quarter of a mile short of Chunuk Bair, had been rushed by the 10th Gurkhas and in the words of the Commander-in-Chief " The troops had performed a feat which is without parallel." Just before 5 a.m. on the 7th, Chunuk Bair was occupied.

All eyes were now turned to Suvla. Everything hung upon the rapidity with which the troops of the IXth Corps pressed forward to join hands with the left flank of the Anzac attack. Not unlike Moses viewing the Promised Land from across Jordan, were the eyes of the anxious watchers on Chunuk Bair turned northwards : how soon would they gain touch with General Stopford's men ?

The Battalion Diary of the 9th West Yorks. Regt. for the 7th August is all too short and conveys but little idea of the real situation :
" Saturday, August 7th. After occupying Lala Baba Hill, the Battalion pushed forward across the sandy isthmus and Salt Lake

9TH BATTALION. 7TH AUGUST

and supported the 34th Brigade (Lancashire Fusiliers) in attack on Hill 10, where enemy had strongly entrenched positions surrounded with land mines. Nine officers wounded in assault. Battalion now became rather scattered, some platoons moving North to support 34th Brigade on Kiretch Tepe Sirt, whilst others moved with 34th Brigade and 10th Division to attack Yilghin Burnu (Chocolate Hill). Headquarters (Battalion) went with 34th Brigade. Battalion collected for night and billeted in Turkish Redoubt at Hill 10. Water scarce. Many Turkish rifles and three cases of shell in Redoubt."

The diary of the 32nd Infantry Brigade Headquarters is missing, and of the story of the strenuous days which began on 7th August, only very little can be gathered.

The diary of 11th Division Headquarters stated that about 11 a.m. on the 7th, six battalions of the 10th Division (four of the 31st Infantry Brigade and two of the 30th Infantry Brigade) arrived near Lala Baba and were placed under the orders of the General Officer Commanding 11th Division. These battalions had arrived off " B " beach at dawn.

An attack was then organized on Yilghin Burnu (Chocolate Hill) by the 34th and 32nd Brigades (11th Division), and 31st Brigade (10th Division), under the command of General Sitwell. " The attack moved forward slowly," said the diary. " At 2 p.m. it had only reached Azmak ravine, and orders were then issued by Divisional Headquarters to stop the advance until 5 p.m." Why the advance was stopped at the vital moment is not clear, and will probably remain obscure until the full report and evidence of the Royal Commission on the Dardanelles are published. The enemy was even then hurrying up reinforcements and success hung in the balance. The troops had been fighting all night and were probably exhausted : the scarcity of water had also begun to affect them. They were, however, not opposed by any large force of Turks, the enemy's forces facing the 10th and 11th Divisions being between three and four thousand.

At 5 p.m. the 33rd Infantry Brigade (less two battalions entrenched from the S.E. corner of the Salt Lake to 91. b. 1.) advanced along the northern edges of the Salt Lake, having on the left flank the 31st Brigade, with the West Ridings and York and Lancs. Regt. in support. Four hostile Q. F. guns from ground west of Anafarta Sagir poured shrapnel on to the advancing troops, but were kept down by the guns of the warships in Suvla Bay. At this period the left of the advance was about 105.d.

The first Turkish counter-attack now appears to have been made.

It was against the left flank and drove in the latter as far as Sulajik, 9TH BATTALION. 7TH AUGUST
but did not check the advance. A battery of the LIXth Brigade and the Highland Mountain Brigade opened fire from Lala Baba on the north-western slopes of Yilghin Burnu. The attack reached the lower slopes of the Hill about 7-30 p.m., and at nightfall the trenches here were carried without difficulty. Pushing on up the Hill, the redoubt on the summit was taken by 9 p.m. That night the 11th Division rested on a line as follows: two Battalions of the 33rd Brigade, from the coast to the south-east corner of the Salt Lake: 31st Brigade, with the Lincolns and Border Regt. on Yilghin Burnu and 105. h. 3: 34th Brigade at the "Cut" (the isthmus) about one mile north of Lala Baba, with the Manchesters and Dorsets on the slopes of Kiretch Tepe Sirt: 32nd Infantry Brigade in rear of Hill 10 (between the Hill and the shore).

Late in the evening of the 7th the enemy had withdrawn his guns which had been in action during the day, and contrary to expectations when dawn broke on the 8th, not more than half-a-dozen shells (and these fired from long range guns) dropped into Suvla: nor were there signs of extensive hostile entrenchments. The strength of the enemy lay chiefly in his knowledge of the country, which was of an extraordinarily difficult nature. Thick bushes and scrub abounded on every side and so covered the slopes of the hills that in places men could only move in single file, and then literally had to tear their way through. Under such conditions a small mobile force commanding all the heights was able to keep at bay a much larger concentration of troops.

Of priceless value were the early hours of the 8th August, but it 8TH AUGUST
was 9-45 a.m. before an advance was made. Turkish reinforcements, though on the road, had not arrived and did not arrive until the evening.

The 32nd Infantry Brigade was ordered to advance to the line Sulajik—Anafarta Ova, and at the latter place join up on the left with the 30th Infantry Brigade which held the slopes up the ridge, northwards to Kiretch Tepe Sirt, and on the right with the 31st Brigade and two battalions of the 33rd on Yilghin Burnu. On the left the 30th Brigade could make no headway and was held up. At 11 a.m. the position was roughly as follows: Sherwood Foresters and South Staffords south of the Salt Lake: 31st Brigade Yilghin Burnu: 32nd Brigade continuing the line to about half-way between Sulajik and Anafarta Ova: 33rd Brigade (less two battalions) at Lala Baba in reserve. The 34th Infantry Brigade was presumably still

9TH BATTALION. 8TH AUGUST

about the "Cut." There is nothing in the official diaries to show why the troops made no further advance from this line, but two battalions—the 9th West Yorkshires and the 6th Yorkshire Regt.—apparently made a reconnaissance and succeeded in penetrating to and occupying Hill 70 (Scimitar Hill), and a point nearly as far as Abrikja without meeting with any serious opposition. Three and a half Companies of the 9th West Yorkshires (A, B, C and half of D) reached the latter: a part of Battalion Headquarters was still about 500 yards S.E. of Sulajik and the remaining part with half of D Company and the 6th Yorkshire Regt. near Alibey Chesme.

In the meantime "A" Battery of the LIXth Brigade R.F.A. and a Mountain Artillery Brigade had moved to Yilghin Burnu.

No other advance appears to have been made by the IXth Corps on 8th August, and thus the last opportunity of success was thrown away. Why the 32nd Infantry Brigade as a whole could not have been pushed on further eastwards, thus occupying the high ground, is not clear, for, as already stated, two battalions were actually in occupation of Hill 70 and a point near Abrikja. The occupation of Ismail Oglu Tepe was of paramount importance and does not appear to have been impossible.

In the afternoon the Corps Commander issued orders for an attack to take place on the morning of the 9th. The 11th Division was to advance against the line Ismail Oglu Tepe—Anafarta Sagir. The 33rd Infantry Brigade (less the Sherwood Foresters) and one Battalion of the 31st Infantry Brigade (10th Division) were to attack the line Ismail Oglu Tepe—106 L.W. The 33rd Infantry Brigade was to prolong the line to the left. These orders were however, subsequently altered on the arrival of the Commander-in-Chief M. E. F., who expressed a wish that an advance should be made forthwith in order to secure the high ground before the Turkish reinforcements, which were known to be on the way, arrived. The 32nd Infantry Brigade was in the best position to carry out this attack, the Brigade, according to the General Officer Commanding 11th Division, being then concentrated about Sulajik. The troops were stated to have watered, fed and rested. Orders were immediately issued for an advance, but it was then found that the 32nd Infantry Brigade was not concentrated about Sulajik, for as already stated the 6th Yorks. and the 9th West Yorkshires were even then (6 p.m.) extended in position from Hill 70 to the slopes of Baka Baba, well on the way to Anafarta Sagir. Indeed, to these two battalions belongs the honour of establishing themselves further east during the first attack on Suvla than any other units of the 10th or 11th Divisions, and there is every reason to surmise that had they been supported or their whereabouts known to Brigade Headquarters, and the importance of their position grasped and made use of, the final result of the Battles of Suvla might have been very different. Instead these two battalions never received the orders to concentrate at Sulajik until 5 a.m. on the morning of the 9th—too late. " Orders issued at 20.30 (8-30 p.m.) to concentrate at Sulajik " stated the official diaries " did not reach Battalion (9th West Yorkshires) till 05.00 (5 a.m.) next morning. Situation A, B, C and half of D Companies on Hill 70, and part of Headquarters with 6th Yorkshire Regt. near Alibey Chesme."

<small>9TH BATTALION.</small>

It is as well to let the G. S. Diary of the 11th Division tell its own story of the unsuccessful attack which took place at dawn on the 9th August : " Owing to scattered position of units, 32nd Brigade unable to move until 04.00 (4 a.m.), when East Yorks. Regt., supported by West Riding Regt. and 67th Field Company R.E. moved towards Hill 278. As the East Yorks. Regt. approached top of hill about 05.00 (5 a.m.) Turks counter-attacked and drove column down the slopes, one Company East Yorks. being lost. As West Yorks. Regt. withdrew to their positions to concentrate at Sulajik they were heavily attacked from the direction of Abrikja, 105. K. York and Lancs. Regt. moved up to support them, both battalions compelled to give ground. At 07.45 (7-54 a.m.) 34th Brigade ordered to move forward to support 32nd Brigade. Meanwhile 33rd Brigade attacked north-west slopes of Ismail Oglu Tepe : this attack gained ground and reached following line : 105. O.9—105. P.4—105. K.7, but at 08.00 (8 a.m.) was counter-attacked and forced to give ground. At 09.15 (9-15 a.m.) 2 battalions 53rd Division[1] ordered to support 32nd Brigade, and at 11-30 remaining battalions 159th Brigade moved up to reinforce line."

<small>9TH AUGUST</small>

The 9th West Yorkshires lost heavily. Captain E. Long Price and Captain T. F. Fraser were killed, and six other officers (whose names were not given) were wounded. Part of the Battalion rejoined Battalion Headquarters at Sulajik and part fell back to the second line. Sulajik Farm was then placed in a state of defence. Here the Battalion machine guns under Lieut. Guy did excellent work and created havoc amongst the Turks as they advanced against the Farm. After a while these attacks died down and the 32nd Brigade having

---

[1]The 53rd (Territorial) Division disembarked at Suvla during the night 8th/9th, and early morning of the 9th. The Division had no Artillery.

9TH BATTALION.

been checked in its advance was ordered to consolidate its line and the Farm.

At nightfall on the 9th, the general line ran approximately: Sherwood Foresters (33rd Brigade) Kazlar Chair to 105. X.2.: 31st Brigade Yilghin Burnu; 33rd Brigade (less Sherwood Foresters) with two battalions 53rd Division, from Yilghin Burnu (ecx.) to 105. H.3; 32nd Brigade to 105. B.3 and on to 118. W.7; 34th Brigade less two battalions, to 118. Q.3. Three battalions of the 31st Brigade were ordered to be withdrawn into Corps Reserve at Lala Baba, but only one could be spared from Yilghin Burnu. The 159th Infantry Brigade (53rd Division) was much mixed up with units of the 32nd and 33rd Brigades. The Hereford Regiment was in support of the Sherwood Foresters: the 67th Field Company R.E. at Yilghin Burnu.

The heat throughout the day had been terrific and the troops suffered considerably from thirst, water being very scarce and at times unobtainable.

During the night 9th/10th August, the enemy's snipers were very active and were only kept down by bursts of machine-gun fire from the Farm.

10TH AUGUST

Two attempts were made on the 10th by the 53rd Division, supported by the 11th Division to take the Anafarta Ridge. The first attack failed and the exhausted troops retired at 5 p.m. A second attempt later met with the same result.

All day long the 9th West Yorkshires had held Sulajik Farm and the line of the road for 600 yards running north towards Anafarta Ova. During the day Lieut. Coyne was wounded.

Reinforcements for the Turks were still arriving and apart from his artillery the enemy was by now at least three times stronger than he had been on the 7th August.

11TH AUGUST

On the 11th, the Infantry Brigades of the 54th Division arrived: the Division was not accompanied by its Artillery, which had been left behind in England.

The West Yorkshiremen still held Sulajik Farm and were also supporting the 8th Northumberland Fusiliers and the 11th Manchesters. Hostile sniping at the Farm during the day was heavy, but it was adequately dealt with by the battalion machine gunners. At 7 p.m. the Battalion marched off across the Salt Lake, to Lala Baba, in reserve.

The casualties of the 9th West Yorkshires during the operations from 7th/11th August were very heavy: four officers were killed, six were wounded and missing, and thirteen others wounded. In other ranks the Battalion had lost 46 killed, 61 wounded, 88 wounded and missing, 153 missing. The majority of the " missing and wounded " were afterwards reported as " killed."

9TH BATTALION. 11TH AUGUST

THE BATTLE OF SCIMITAR HILL

FROM the 12th to the 20th August, nothing of outstanding interest happened to the 9th Battalion West Yorkshires. On the 21st, however, the Battalion was again called upon to co-operate in an attack on the enemy. The interim is only very briefly narrated in the Battalion Diary:

1915.
9TH BATTALION.
12TH AUGUST

" Lala Baba : 12th/8/15. 8 p.m. Marched round Salt Lake to Chocolate Hill. In Fort Waller, and relieved 7th Dublin Fusiliers (30th Brigade, 10th Division). Major Wood in command of Fort.

" Fort Waller : 13th/8/15. In front. Shelled at Water Supply. 2 men killed, 2 wounded. Digging and improving trenches all day. Heavy firing at 23.00 (11 p.m.).[1]

" Fort Waller : 14th/8/15. Heavy firing at 03.00 (3 a.m.). Heavy guns on us from Shardagh. 8.2". About 20 shells. 3 killed, 4 wounded.

" Fort Waller : 15th/8/15. Digging hard, line prolonged to right. Colonel Wilson to take over 32nd Brigade. Major W. O. Ward to command 6th Yorkshire Regt. 10th Division attacked Western Ridge and took it. Everyone digging hard. 3 killed, 7 wounded.

" Fort Waller : 16th/8/15. Colonel Minogue (Officer Commanding 9th West Yorks. Regt.) sick. Major A. H. Cuthell took over command. 10th Division did well on left. Artillery drove in centre. Twelve Australian snipers arrive. Second Lieut. H. Farrance aarived from R. Malta Militia.

" Fort Waller : 17th/8/15. Lieut. H. Farrance posted to A Company. Making second line of trenches. General de Lisle[2] and General Hammersley[3] came round. Turned our 18-pounders on to Turkish Redoubt.

[1] " At 16.00 (4 p.m.) 54th and 53rd Divisions moved forward to Kuchuk Anafarta (Ova). Attack progressed, but at 19.00 (7 p.m.) the right appeared to fall back." G. S. Diary, 11th Division. There are no further details of this attack, but the heavy " firing " was probably the guns of both sides engaged in an artillery duel.

[2] Major-General H. de B. De Lisle, who on the 15th took over command of the IXth Corps.

[3] General Officer Commanding 11th Division.

9TH BATTALION.
12TH AUGUST

"Fort Waller: 18/8/15. Still on Chocolate Hill. Shelled every morning and evening. Three Taubes threw bombs. Relieved by 6th Lincolns at 21.00 (9 p.m.). Marched to " C " Beach.

" C " Beach: 19th/8/15. Nothing of importance.

20th/8/15. "Moved at 21.30 (9.30 p.m.) and took over part of Dorset Regiment's trench and old Turk trench, southern slope of Chocolate Hill."

The operations which were to take place on the 21st August were directed chiefly against Ismail Oglu Tepe: " I therefore decided," said Sir Ian Hamilton, " to mass every available man against Ismail Oglu Tepe, a *sine qua non* to my plans, whether as a first step towards clearing the valley, or, if this proved impossible, towards securing Suvla Bay and Anzac Cove from shell fire."

The 2nd Mounted Division, organized as dismounted troops, and 29th Division, were transferred from the southern area of Gallipoli to Suvla. With these new forces and the 10th, 11th, 53rd and 54th Divisions the Commander-in-Chief hoped to break down the resistance of the Turks and gain his objectives.

Briefly, the plan of attack was as follows: The 53rd and 54th Divisions were to hold the enemy from Sulajik to Kiretch Tepe Sirt whilst the 29th and 11th Divisions stormed Ismail Oglu Tepe. Two Brigades, 10th Division and the 2nd Mounted Division, were to be held in Corps Reserve. General Birdwood (Commanding the Australian and New Zealand Corps) was to co-operate from Anzac by sweeping forward his left flank to Susuk Kuyu and Kaiajik Aghala.

The despatches give an interesting description of Ismail Oglu Tepe, the objective: " Ismail Oglu Tepe, as it is called, forms a strong natural barrier against an invader from the Ægean who might wish to march direct against the Anafartas. The hill rises 350 feet from the plain, with steep spurs jutting out to the west and south-west, the whole of it crowned with dense holly oak scrub, so nearly impenetrable that it breaks up an attack and forces troops to move in single file along goat tracks between the bushes. The comparatively small number of guns landed up to date was a weakness, seeing we had now to storm trenches, but the battleships were there to back us, and as the bombardment was limited to a narrow front of a mile it was hoped the troops would find themselves able to carry the trenches and the impetus of the charge would carry them up to the top of the crest. Our chief difficulty lay in the open nature and shallow depth of the ground available for the concentration for attack. The only cover we possessed was the hill Lala Baba, 200 yards from the sea, and Yilghin Burnu half a mile from the Turkish front, the ground between these two being an exposed plain. The 29th Division, which was to make the attack on the left, occupied the front trenches during the preceding night: the 11th Division, which was to attack on the right, occupied the front trenches on the right of Yilghin Burnu."

Of the 11th Division the 32nd and 34th Infantry Brigades were to make the attack, the 33rd Infantry Brigade being held in Divisional reserve, behind the 32nd Brigade.

" Operation Order No. 2 " of the 32nd Infantry Brigade is partly given in order that the operation and attack of the 9th West Yorkshires may be the better understood: " The attack will be preceded by an artillery bombardment beginning at 14.30 (2-30 p.m.). Massed machine guns will open fire from Chocolate Hill at 14.45 (2-45 p.m.). The attack will be launched at 15.05 (3-5 p.m.) precisely.

" The first phase of the attack will be the capture of that part of the Turkish advanced trench which runs north from cross-roads 105. W.2.5., the communication trench from C of Hetman Chair to the slope of Ismail Oglu Tepe, and the trenches round the lower slopes approximately on the line 105. S.7.5. This phase will be a single operation, the troops detailed to assault will not check to reorganize until the second line of trenches is carried. This first phase assault will be carried out by the 6th Yorkshire Regt. on the right, and the 6th York and Lancs. Regt. on the left. The right of the 6th Yorkshire Regt. will direct and will move along the dividing line between 32nd and 34th Infantry Brigades: frontage 150 yards per battalion.

" On the capture of the second line of trenches the two battalions will reorganize as quickly as possible and place the captured trenches in a state of defence.

" At 15.05 precisely, the 8th West Riding Regt. will move forward as quickly as possible from its present position in artillery formation with its right directed on the bend in the telegraph line 105. V..5, and the 9th West Yorks. Regt. will move into the trenches vacated by the 6th York and Lancs. Regt.

" As soon as the head of the 8th West Riding Regt. reaches the line of trenches 105. V.2-5. the 8th West Riding Regt. and the 9th West Yorks. Regt. will move forward, the right of the 8th West Riding Regt. directing and moving along the dividing line between the 32nd and 34th Infantry Brigades: these two battalions will move through the 6th Yorkshire and 6th York and Lancs. Regiments.

9TH BATTALION.

"The 8th West Riding Regt. will assault Knoll 100 (105. U.4-7.) and the 9th West Yorks. Regt. Knoll 100 (105. T.5.). These knolls on being captured will be prepared against counter-attack. The right flank throughout will be guided by the 34th Brigade. The 29th Division will commence the attack as soon as the first line of Turkish trenches is in our hands. The 33rd Brigade will be in reserve behind the 32nd Infantry Brigade...... There will be no cheering and no firing, machine guns will supply the fire......220 rounds per man (will be carried)...... The Hetman Chair position must be taken at all costs, line attack being pushed in after another in quick succession if necessary."

The dividing line between the 32nd and 34th Infantry Brigades ran from the bend in the telegraph line 105. V.5., through the crossroads at 105..W.2-5. to the T of Tike Chesme.

The dividing line between the 11th and 29th Divisions was from the point where the trenches of the 11th Division joined Hill 50 to the gully between Hill 100 and Hill 112.

21ST AUGUST

The official diary of the 32nd Infantry Brigade Headquarters being missing, the narrative of this attack has had to be compiled from battalion diaries. The G. S. Diary of the 11th Division also throws little light upon the operations.

Apparently at 2-30 p.m. the artillery bombardment began, and at 2-45 p.m. the machine guns also opened fire. Seven minutes later (at 2-52 p.m.) the 34th Infantry Brigade on the right of the 32nd Infantry Brigade rushed forward and gained the first line trench of the Turks between Hetman Chair and Aire Kavak practically without loss. But the 32nd Brigade did not advance simultaneously and it was not until 3-7 p.m. that the left of the Brigade went forward to the attack : the right flank started even later. In all probability watches had not been carefully synchronized.

As the 6th York and Lancs. Regt. on the left of the Brigade advanced it bore too much to the left in a north-easterly direction : this drew the 6th Yorkshire Regt. from its line of advance with the result that the line of communication trenches running from the C in Hetman Chair to the slopes of Ismail Oglu Tepe and 400 yards of the enemy's front-line trenches were not attacked at all. The mistake was disastrous. From the trenches not attacked the enemy was able to bring a very heavy frontal and enfilade fire on the advancing troops of the 32nd Infantry Brigade, and very heavy casualties were incurred by the attacking battalions. From the official despatches it is clear that this loss of direction was discovered and a gallant attempt made to attack the vital communication trench from the north-east, but in spite of the troops advancing with great bravery and disregard of life, the original mistake could not be rectified. Some rear waves of the Brigade appear to have kept direction, but these also were decimated by the Turks and only succeeded in reaching some halfway trenches a little in advance of their original line, where, during the night they dug themselves in.

9TH BATTALION.

The 9th West Yorkshires who supported the 6th Yorkshire Regt. and had been ordered to move through the latter when that battalion had secured the Turkish front-line, could not carry out orders. " D Company," said the Battalion Diary " moved forward first as firing line, under Second-Lieut. H. A. Gough, supported by A and B Companies under Major A. H. Cuthell and Second-Lieut. A. B. Gent, with C Company in reserve as third line under Second-Lieut. Walsh. The Battalion moved forward in this order, but owing to regiments in front failing to secure first line of Turkish trenches, were held up and had to dig in. This they did with entrenching tools remaining in position until relieved at night," *i.e.*, on the 22nd.

In the meantime the 33rd Infantry Brigade, sent forward hastily with orders to capture the communication trench, fell into the same error as the 32nd Brigade—part of the Brigade moving north-east and part south-east to Susuk Kuyu.

22ND AUGUST

The 29th Division, attacked Hill 70 (Scimitar Hill) at 3-30 with great dash. One Brigade (the 87th) on the left carried the enemy's trenches on the Hill, but the right Brigade (the 88th) were checked by a raging forest fire. Pressing on, however, the Brigade found it was impossible to advance up the valley between the two spurs (the two Hills—100) owing to the failure of the 32nd Infantry Brigade. Eventually the 88th Brigade was swept down the hill by a galling fire, to a ledge south-west of Scimitar Hill where it found a little cover.

At nightfall the 29th Division was back on its original line.

The attack from Anzac by the New Zealand Mounted Rifles, and British and Indian troops, with the idea of joining up with the IXth Corps at Suvla was a success. On the 21st, an Indian Brigade seized the well at Kabak Kuyu, and by 4-30 p.m. a lodgment had been effected on the slopes of Kaiajik Aghala. At 6 a.m. on the following morning the summit of the latter hill was attacked and eventually appears to have fallen into the hands of the Anzac Corps—a line being entrenched from that place to Susuk Kuyu, where it joined up with the right of the IXth Corps.

The losses of the 9th West Yorks. Regt. on the 21st and 22nd

9TH BATTALION.
22ND AUGUST

were officers: one killed, four wounded; other ranks: 11 killed, 142 wounded, and 43 missing.

On the 22nd, the Battalion, or rather the remnants of it, was relieved and marched back to " C " Beach. Here the roll was called and the strength was found to be (all told) only 4 officers and 196 N.C.O.'s and men. Lieut. C. V. Guy then took charge of the Battalion which was attached to the 6th York and Lancs. Regt., under the command of Colonel Eustace: it became known as " No. 1 Battalion."

Casualties amongst the officers of the Battalion had been very heavy. No less than ten had been killed outright or had died of wounds, and amongst that number were several Regular officers of senior rank. When the " Kitchener " Army was raised on the outbreak of war, these officers who were not serving with their Battalions, *i.e.*, 1st or 2nd, having been seconded for other duties, were posted to the 9th Battalion on its formation, together with two ex-Regular officers of the Regiment, Lieut-Colonel J. O. B. Minogue, the Commanding Officer, and Major R. Isacke. Both these officers who were of long service and were still serving in the Special Reserve of the Regiment were invalided from Gallipoli, and Colonel Minogue shortly afterwards died from the effects of the campaign.

It is easy to be wise after the event, but the policy of sending all these trained officers to a single (and that the first formed) Service Battalion of the Regiment seems open to criticism. It appears that it would have been wiser to have distributed the training experience of these officers among the several Service Battalions of the Regiment which were being raised than to have concentrated it in a single Battalion. The result was that by the time the second Service Battalion (10th) was ready to take the field practically the whole reserve of trained officers of the Regiment had disappeared. Major A. H. Cuthell (killed in action, 22/8/15) belonged to the 2nd Battalion; Captain C. E. Long-Price (killed in action, 7/8/15) to the 1st Battalion; Major M. D. Wood (died of wounds, 22/8/15); and Captain A. Geary-Smith (killed in action, 7/8/15) were other Regular officers. The remaining officers on the casualty list were Captain T. F. Fraser (killed in action, 11/8/15); Captain R. Lupton (died of wounds, 22/8/15); Lieut. H. Curtis (killed in action, 7/8/15); Lieut. E. Worsnop (died of wounds, 22/8/15); Lieut. F. E. Gent (killed in action, 7/8/15); and Second-Lieut. J. A. C. Spencer (killed in action, 9/8/15).

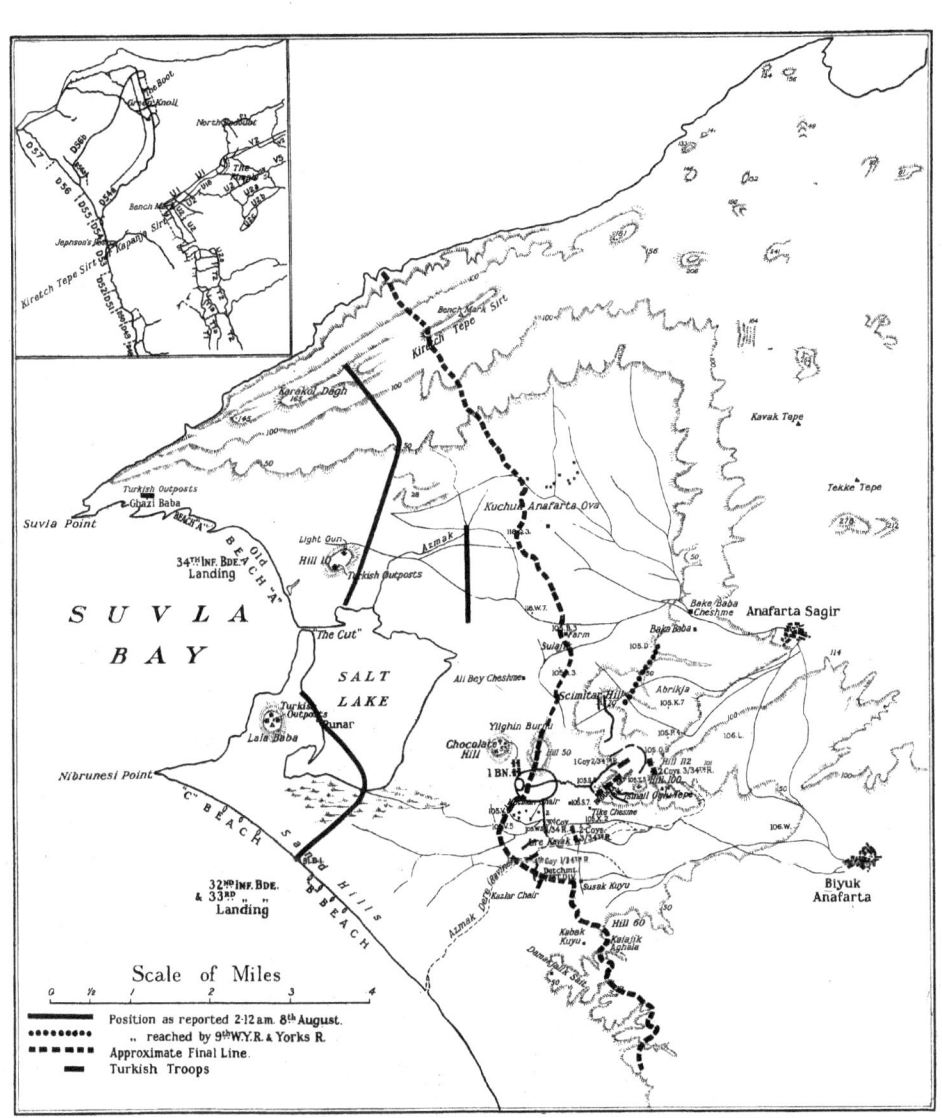

THE BATTLES OF SUVLA.

Throughout August the position at Suvla Bay remained stationary. Nothing of importance happened. From 26th to the 30th, the Battalion was again in the fire trenches on the northern slopes of Kizla Dagli—"improving trenches," but on the 31st was relieved by the 6th York and Lancs. and marched back to support trenches. Only two casualties (two other ranks wounded) are recorded in the Diary for this period. 9TH BATTALION. 31ST AUGUST

After the attack of 21st August the only other " battle incident " recorded in the despatches, was one which took place on 27th August, when Hill 60 was attacked and during the next forty-eight hours was, after desperate fighting by the Anzacs, finally captured: "This gave us complete command of the under-feature, an outlook over the Anafarta Sagir valley, and safer lateral communication between Anzac and Suvla Bay."

FRANCE AND FLANDERS
TRENCH WARFARE, 1915

TRENCH WARFARE
1st—31st July, 1915

SINCE the First Attack on Bellewaerde, by the Vth Corps, east of Ypres on the 16th June, no other assault on the German trenches had been made: neither had the enemy's infantry attacked the British positions in the Salient. Shell fire was always more or less vigorous, and constant work and vigilance by the troops in the front lines were necessary in order to maintain their trenches in a complete state of defence.

By the 1st of July the wet weather of June had changed to oppressive heat. The 1st Battalion West Yorks. R. (18th Infantry Brigade, 6th Division) was in trenches north-east of Ypres and came in for a gas bombardment. Enemy snipers were busy, but these having been located were dealt with by the Divisional Artillery. [1ST BATTALION. 1ST JULY.]

A forward post in front of the Battalion trenches formed a bone of contention between the Yorkshiremen and the Germans. Each night Captain Costin (A Company) took a party of bombers out and by effective bombing kept the enemy at bay and denied him the possession of the coveted post. In this little affair no casualties were sustained, and the men " behaved with great coolness and fortitude." German aeroplanes were very active, flying low over the trenches and dropping bombs, and affording the troops excitement and innumerable opportunities in which to test their marksmanship with the rifle.

Relief came at 10 p.m. on the 4th, when the Battalion marched back to dug-outs on the Canal Bank, in a position to hold the second line if necessary: here the Battalion remained until the 14th, when it was relieved by the Sherwood Foresters and proceeded to hutments in the old camp in the Woods a mile and a half north-west of Vlametinghe. [4TH JULY.]

The 49th (West Riding) Division though now in the Ypres area had not as yet taken over a front-line sector. Only the 1/8th West Yorkshires of the 146th Infantry Brigade had been sent forward to the Ypres Canal in support of the 11th Infantry Brigade (4th Division). The 1st of July, therefore, still found the Division (less the 1/8th West Yorks. R.) in, and in the neighbourhood of, Proven. Here the Army Commander, General Sir H. Plumer, inspected the 146th Brigade in their billets, the Corps Commander, Sir John Keir, inspecting the men on the following day. [1/5TH, 1/6TH 1/7TH, 1/8TH BATTALION. 1ST JULY.]

4TH JULY.

On the 4th July, the 1/6th West Yorkshires were sent up to the Canal Bank in support of the 12th Infantry Brigade (4th Division), the 1/5th and 1/7th Battalions still remaining in Proven. But a move was imminent, for on the same evening the Brigade Major, Signalling Officer, four Company Commanders and four Platoon Commanders, all of the 146th Brigade, visited Headquarters of the 12th Brigade to make final arrangements for taking over that part of the front-line.

6TH JULY.

A small operation on a German salient in the line between Boesinghe and Ypres, was carried out on the 6th July by the 11th Infantry Brigade. The result was the capture of 500 yards of the enemy's front-line trenches. The 1/8th West Yorkshires (still with the 11th Brigade) in reserve, were not called upon during the action, but in the evening the Battalion provided large working parties, which were sent up to the captured trenches, and assisted in putting them into a state of defence.

During the day the enemy's guns were very active and the 1/6th West Yorkshires, on the Canal Bank, had sixteen casualties, all wounded by shrapnel.

7TH JULY.

On the 7th, the 49th (West Riding) Division relieved the 4th Division, the 146th Infantry Brigade (less the 1/6th and 1/8th West Yorks. R.), taking over from the 12th Infantry Brigade: the relief was completed without incident. The position occupied was a line of trenches about two miles north-east of Ypres, which the 1/5th and 1/7th West Yorkshires took over from troops of the 4th Division. During the evening the 1/6th and 1/8th Battalions reverted to their Brigade, one Company of the former moving up into the second line trenches and three Companies remaining on the Canal Bank: the 1/8th Battalion, however, moved back to the Château des Trois Tours, just north of Brielen Village. On the 8th and 9th the 147th and 148th Brigades of the West Riding Division relieved the 10th and 11th Brigades of the 4th Division respectively. The 49th Division was thus firmly established in the Ypres Salient, with the 6th Division on its right and French troops on its left.

The Division was now to feel the difference between the comparative quietude in that part of the line south of Armentières which it had vacated, and the troublous, noisy Ypres Salient. For no sooner was it settled in the line than the enemy began a heavy bombardment of the front line and support trenches. The change is very apparent from the diaries of the West Yorkshire Battalions. Gas shells, rifle-grenades and those noxious projectiles " whiz-bangs" are all recorded in the diary of the 1/5th West Yorkshires from 9th

ON THE YSER: A DEEP, FRESH SHELL-HOLE.

to 14th July. On the 11th, four other ranks were killed and eleven wounded: during the next day two more were killed and fifteen wounded. But by this time the Battalion bombers had got to work, and the enemy's activity slackened considerably. Hales' bombs, and the 56-lb. trench mortars had a most wholesome effect, aided by the 15 and 18-pounders, and howitzers, which retaliated whenever the hostile guns opened fire. [1/5TH, 1/6TH, 1/7TH, 1/8TH BATTALIONS.]

At 10 p.m. on the 10th the enemy massed, and attacked and captured two lines of trenches from the 148th Infantry Brigade, on the left of the 146th, but after an hour's bombardment, the K.O.Y.L.I. counter-attacked and regained all which had been temporarily lost. The 1/6th West Yorkshires in reserve on the Canal Bank were shelled with gas shells. The 1/7th in line with the 1/5th evidently caught the full blast of the gas shells, for fourteen men were sent to hospital suffering from the effects of the fumes and " gas hung about the trenches for a considerable time." Again on the 13th, the whole line was severely bombarded with mixed projectiles, including gas shells, and more casualties were suffered by the Yorkshiremen. [10TH JULY.]

Even the 1/8th West Yorks. R., then in Divisional Reserve had gas casualties. The battalion had furnished large working parties for completing the defensive arrangements round the Château des Trois Tours when shells fell round about the Château. Four other ranks were wounded and eighteeen had to be sent off to hospital suffering from gas poisoning.

During the night of the 13th, the 1/6th relieved the 1/5th, and the 1/8th the 1/7th in the front line. And the diary of the 1/8th West Yorkshires contains an interesting item written on the 14th: " For the third time since joining the Expeditionary Force we have five battalions of the West Yorkshire Regt. together, the first occasion being the 9th May, when the 6th, 8th, 7th, 5th and 2nd Battalions were in the front line side by side as named from right to left north of Neuve Chapelle. The next occasion was when the four Territorial Battalions were beside the 2nd Battalion at Le Troy." [13TH JULY. 2ND BATTALION.]

On the date on which this entry in the Diary appears, the 1st Battalion West Yorks. R. (6th Division) held the trenches next to the 1/8th Battalion, the two battalions joining up at Algerian Cottage.

The reliefs had been carried out only under great difficulties, for, during the evening of the 13th, the enemy put down an especially heavy bombardment, using large quantities of gas shells. Over seventy men were sent down suffering from gas. Both the British and French guns retaliated and at one time as many as 160 guns were in action against the enemy. This intense retaliation soon cooled the ardour of the enemy's artillery, whose fire very considerably decreased, and the delayed reliefs were proceeded with.

* * * *

10TH BATTALION. 13TH JULY.
At 11 p.m. on the night of the 13th July, another Battalion the 10th of the West Yorkshire Regt. arrived off the coast of France.

The 10th Battalion West Yorks. Regt. was contained in the 50th Infantry Brigade of the 17th Division, and was commanded by Lieut.-Colonel H. K. Umfreville. The 50th Infantry Brigade (commanded by Brig.-General L. Banon) was formed of the 10th West Yorks. R., 7th East Yorks., 7th Yorks. Regt. and 6th Battalion Dorset Regt. The two other Brigades of the 17th Division were the 51st and 52nd. It was a New Army Division. The General Officer Commanding was Major-General T. D. Pilcher.

On the morning of the 14th, disembarkation was begun and at 3-30 in the afternoon the Battalion left Boulogne by rail for the Lumbres area, arriving at 10 p.m. Here the troops were detrained and marched to Ouve—Wirquin: Brigade Headquarters were in Elnes, and Divisional Headquarters in Lumbres.

18TH JULY.
From the 14th to the 17th inclusive, the Battalion remained in billets, but on the 18th marched (in Division) to the Arques—Hazebrouck—Blaringhem area. The 10th West Yorkshires were billeted in the town of Arques. The following morning at 8-45, the Battalion set out for Steenwoorde, arriving at 3-30 p.m.—a long march. Another two days' rest, however, gave the troops an opportunity of getting used to the rough roads of Northern France. From Steenwoorde the Battalion (in Brigade) set out for La Clytte at 8 p.m. on the 22nd, arriving at the hutments at the latter place in the early hours of the 23rd. The 17th Division was now in the Dickebusch area (between two and three miles south-west of Ypres) under the Vth Corps.

24TH JULY.
Instruction in trench warfare began almost immediately. At 8 a.m. on the 24th, A Company of the 10th West Yorkshires with two machine guns marched off to the trenches of the 6th Sherwood Foresters (46th Division) : at 8 p.m., two platoons of B Company followed by two more platoons of the same Company at 8 p.m. on the 25th went into " J " trenches. Thence onward until the night of the 28th, the Battalion received its first introduction to life in the trenches. On this date also the Battalion suffered its first loss, Private Hall died of wounds received on the 26th.

A Bombing Instructional School was started on the 29th.

On the 31st July orders were issued to the 50th Infantry Brigade to proceed to a position about a thousand yards north of Dickebusch, preparatory to taking over the front line trenches of the 7th Infantry Brigade (3rd Division) on the night of August 2nd/3rd.

★ ★ ★ ★

Meanwhile, south of the troubled Ypres Salient, the 2nd Battalion West Yorks. R. (8th Division) were enjoying a comparatively quiet period. No attack had been made on or by the enemy. Throughout the whole of July work on the trenches, the rebuilding and revetment of parapets, in fixing new and stronger wire entanglements, cutting the thick grass which grew in No Man's Land, just in front of the trenches, and in constructing new shelters and dug-outs, occupied the troops by day and night.

The Battalion was in Brigade Reserve on 1st July, billeted in the Rue du Bois. Battalion Headquarters were in a quiet farm, and the Companies were fairly well housed with the exception of A Company which was at Croix Marechal, in support of the left Battalion, in No. 4 Section. On the night of the 7th, the Battalion relieved the 2nd Devons in the line. Two nights later a patrol went out across No Man's Land, and bumped into a hostile party engaged in similar work. A fight ensued, in which one man of A Company was hit and taken prisoner: several casualties were inflicted on the enemy and the patrol returned. After six days in the trenches, most of which were spent in digging, the Battalion was relieved by the Devons, but was back again in the front line on the 19th. On the following day the Battalion Diary records: " Trench-Mortar Battery was introduced into the lines. This is a small gun which can fit complete into a box of about eight cubic feet and is made by Vickers. It throws a bomb of 30 lbs. over a distance of 350 yards (maximum range). Lieut. Ruttledge was detailed for this command with 20 men from the Companies, as well as a few R.G.A. gunners." Two days later the gun was in action: " Trench-Mortar Section made excellent use of the new weapon and the enemy gave no trouble." The month closed as quietly as it had begun.

The 8th Divisional Intelligence Reports mostly contain the phrases " Enemy quiet " or " Enemy very quiet " and his attitude may be explained by a little incident which took place on the 3rd July :

"No. 2 Section report German heard playing on a cornet and afterwards shouting in English, 'If you wont shoot I will play to you again,' our reply was a burst of machine-gun fire."

It was a lull before the storm which was to burst during the early autumn of 1915.

On the 19th July the IIIrd Corps was reconstituted and under the new organization consisted of the 8th and 27th Divisions and the 19th Infantry Brigade, the latter being placed under the command of the former Division.

* * * *

1ST BATTALION.

East of Ypres during the latter half of July, a new enemy device —liquid fire—was employed against the gallant defenders of the Salient. Neither the 6th nor the 49th Divisions were involved in this dastardly attack, though the 1st Battalion West Yorks. was on the left flank of the 14th Division into whose trenches the liquid fire was projected.

15TH—25TH JULY.

From the 15th to the 25th inclusive, the 1st Battalion was partly in Old Camp north-west of Vlamertinghe, or in the support trenches in the neighbourhood of Ypres. The Battalion went into the front line on the left of the 14th Division, south of Potijze during the evening of the 26th the relief being completed by 9-30 p.m. Three days of shelling, sniping and trench mortar fighting resulted in the loss of four other ranks killed and eight wounded. But the diaries record (with evident gratification) the ascendancy which at this time had been gained over the enemy's snipers.

30TH JULY.

At 3-30 a.m. on the morning of the 30th the enemy, after projecting (by means of strong jets) burning liquid into the trenches of the 14th Division along the Menin Road, carried several lines of trenches belonging to that Division. The surprise and confusion caused by this fresh example of the enemy's disregard of the rules of civilized warfare were responsible for the loss of the position. Heavy shelling continued throughout the day, the 1st West Yorks. R., lying next to the 14th Division and along the northern flank, coming in for a good deal of attention. The Battalion, however, lost only a few men, and was asked to assist in a counter-attack organized by the 14th Division. A bombing party from A Company under Captain Costin, which had already done good work in demonstrating against the enemy's line in the early morning, was again organized ready to assist the Division on on the right. The counter-attack by the Division was held up and the West Yorkshire bombers were not called upon. A second attack by the enemy which took place on the morning of the 31st was repulsed with heavy losses to the attackers. In this attack the trenches of the West Yorkshiremen were again deluged with shells, but the Battalion escaped serious losses. <small>1ST BATTALION</small>

During the latter half of July, the 49th Division, on the left of the 6th Division, had suffered heavy losses from the enemy's guns. The latter had discovered an excellent target in the Trois Tours Château, and on this spot at all hours he placed salvoes of shrapnel or "H. E." until at last Corps Headquarters ordered the evacuation of the house. But before this was done, the General Officer Commanding, General Baldock, was wounded (on the 16th) in the head by a splinter. There was no quietude in the terrible Salient. If the guns were silent it boded no good, some fresh scheme was afoot by either side. To the new-comer that never-ceasing scream of shells and the roar of the guns was an awesome and terrifying thing. The Canal Banks and the front line trenches were always marks for the enemy's gunners, just as the British artilleryman had marked down certain targets in the hostile lines which were regularly bombarded and blown to atoms. Retaliation shoots were often indulged in, and how the enemy hated it! The Germans had a wholesome dread of such measures. The West Riding Division had also largely reduced to impotence the activities of the enemy's snipers.

On the night of the 14th, the right of the 146th Infantry Brigade still rested on Algerian Farm, but on the left the Brigade line was extended, the 1/8th West Yorkshires taking over another 100 yards of trenches. The 1/6th Battalion was in the front line with the 1/8th and the 1/5th and 1/7th Battalions were in reserve and support respectively. <small>1/5TH, 1/6TH 1/7TH, 1/8TH BATTALIONS. 14TH JULY.</small>

In the early hours of the 15th, Second-Lieut. Wilkinson and Riflemen Clough and Mudd of the 1/8th Battalion went out on patrol. The enemy opened fire and Mudd fell shot through the chest. His cries brought heavy fire from the enemy; nevertheless, Lieut Wilkinson and Clough picked the wounded man up and carried him back towards their trenches. But before they were able to pass through the barbed wire Clough had to enter the trenches and get a pair of wire cutters with which he returned to Lieut. Wilkinson. A gap was then cut in the wire and the wounded man brought in. During all this while the enemy continued to fire on Mudd's two rescuers, who for their gallantry were subsequently rewarded. This was by no means an uncommon instance of the close comradeship between officers and their men, who were always ready to take risks and sacrifice themselves, if needs be, one for the other.

1/5TH, 1/6TH 1/7TH, 1/8TH BATTALION. On the 16th the 1/8th Battalion was heavily shelled and during the bombardment Lieut C. Hartnell was killed—the first officer casualty in the Battalion since its arrival in France. The 1/8th Battalion was relieved by the 1/7th on the night of the 19th, when the 1/6th Battalion was also relieved by the 1/5th. The 1/6th had suffered fourteen casualties (all wounded) during the five days' tour. The guns were hardly ever silent, and even when they did cease fire, the intervals were broken by the heavy explosion of trench mortar bombs, " whiz-bangs," rifle and hand-grenades. Peace there was none! The Ypres Salient was to know no rest for three years and more, until the bare gaunt walls of the beautiful Cloth Hall stood stark and naked to mark the holocaust for all the world to see.

25TH JULY. The 1/6th went into the trenches on the night of the 25th, and during the way up Lieut. E. Myers was wounded in the thigh by a sniper's bullet. From 10 a.m. to 1 p.m. on the 27th, the Battalion was heavily shelled, the enemy firing trench-mortar bombs, aerial torpedoes and " Pom Poms." Six men were wounded and four buried, but were dug out. The Divisional artillery eventually reduced the enemy's activity.

30TH JULY. On the 30th July, a chance and somewhat amusing patrol encounter out in No Man's Land ended successfully for the West Yorkshiremen. About 9-30 p.m. Second-Lieut. Will and No. 1960 Rifleman Brooke, of the 1/8th Battalion went out in front of the line for the purpose of repairing the wire which had been cut during the day by the enemy's shell fire. They had already begun work when distinct sounds of movement accompanied by a low whistle were heard close by. Lieut. Will replied with a similar whistle, and two men stood up a little way beyond the wire. Thinking they belonged to his Battalion Lieut. Will spoke to them, but getting no reply and being unarmed, he pointed his finger at them and shouted " hands up." Whereupon the men, who were Bavarians, at once held a white handkerchief above their heads in token of surrender. The officer and Rifleman Brooke then advanced and after taking away their arms marched the two men into the Battalion's trenches. The men, who belonged to the 281st I. Regt., were at once sent off to Brigade Headquarters, where useful information was obtained from them. The

"Peace, There was None." A sector in the Ypres Salient after an attack.

Divisional Commander congratulated the Battalion on this capture, as identifications were badly needed.

The 1/8th Battalion was relieved by the 1/7th on the 31st, and moved back to dug-outs west of the ill-starred Château des Trois Tours, into Divisional Reserve. The 1/6th Battalion was relieved on the same night by the 1/5th and took over dug-outs from the 1/7th on the Canal Bank, one mile north of Ypres.[1]

---

[1] The casualties of the 1/5th, 1/6th, 1/7th and 1/8th West Yorkshires during July numbered: 1/5th—eight other ranks killed, thirty-three wounded; 1/6th—two officers wounded, one other ranks killed and fifty wounded; 1/7th—one officer killed, one officer and seventeen other ranks wounded; 1/8th—one officer killed, four other ranks wounded. About fifty other ranks from all four battalions were sent to hospital suffering from gas poisoning.

THE ACTIONS OF HOOGE

THE General Staff Diary, 6th Division for 1st August, 1915, contains the following entry: " On the night of the 31st July, an order was issued from the VIth Corps that the 6th Division was to be relieved from its position in the line on a future day, by a Division to be furnished by the Second Army. On being relieved the 6th Division was to carry out an attack to regain the Hooge position. The 14th Division to strengthen the position they were holding."

1ST AUGUST

On receipt of this warning, 6th Divisional Headquarters issued orders to the 18th Infantry Brigade to hand over its front to the 9th Infantry Brigade (3rd Division) on the night of the 2nd/3rd August. The 17th Infantry Brigade was also informed that it would be relieved during the night of the 3rd/4th August, by the 7th Infantry Brigade (also of the 3rd Division.)

The 1st Battalion West Yorks. Regt. was in the front line trenches south of Potijze, having relieved the East Yorks. on the 26th July. Heavy hostile shelling again broke out on the morning of the 1st August, and although the 14th Division (on the right of the 6th Division) suffered most, a large number of shells fell in the sub-sector held by the 18th Infantry Brigade. The Battalion bombers of the 1st West Yorkshires were in action during the day, seven of them being placed in vital positions on the railway, whilst nine more had been lent to the Rifle Brigade (of the 42nd Infantry Brigade) on the right of the Yorkshiremen. In the latter position the bombers were in forward saps, opposite German saps. Here they remained all day, having a strenuous time in preventing the enemy from working in his saps. At one period a shell burst near one of the saps held by the West Yorkshiremen, burying two of the bombers, but they were promptly dug out and found to be uninjured. Throughout the night of the 1st/2nd August, until the afternoon of the latter date, the gallant bombers stuck to their post with fine tenacity. They were then relieved and returned to their own battalion.

1ST. BATTALION.

During the night (at 11 p.m.) of the 2nd/3rd August, the 18th Infantry Brigade was relieved by the 9th Infantry Brigade and moved back to billets in Poperinghe. And on the 3rd, the whole of the

3RD AUGUST

1ST BATTALION.

6th Division was withdrawn from the line in order to prepare for the attack on Hooge.

The timely assistance lent by the Battalion bombers of the 1st West Yorks. R. to the 42nd Infantry Brigade on the 1st, was acknowledged in a telegram from the Brigadier received on the 4th by the Battalion Headquarters in Poperinghe : " On the 1st the West Yorkshires were good enough to lend a party of bombers to us, to replace casualties. I am most grateful for such prompt assistance and I hope you will convey my warmest thanks to the Battalion."

The enemy shelled Poperinghe during the afternoon of the 5th, and in all fifty shells fell in the town. One struck a house in which a number of men of the West Yorks. Regt. were billeted, wounding four. There was no safety, front or back areas, in the Ypres Salient!

Several hours later the 18th Infantry Brigade (less the 1st West Yorks. R.) moved forward and took over the trenches of the 43rd and 139th Infantry Brigades (14th and 46th Divisions respectively). Lieut.-Colonel Towsey, 1st West Yorks. Regt. had during the day taken over command of the Brigade, as Brigadier-General Ainslie was too ill to assume command of the Brigade on going into the front line. Major Lang then assumed temporary command of the West Yorkshires.

Throughout the 6th, 7th and 8th, the enemy continued to shell the front line very heavily : the British artillery retaliated with marked effect. Zouave and Sanctuary Woods, the trenches crossing and north and south of, the Ypres—Menin Road were heavily pounded, and by the 8th were very crumbled. The attack, at first ordered for the 8th, had been postponed until 3-15 a.m. on the morning of the 9th.

Two Brigades of the 6th Division had been detailed for the operations, *i.e.*, the 16th and 18th; the 17th Infantry Brigade was held in reserve. At midnight, the positions of the attacking troops were as follows : 18th Infantry Brigade : Front line—Durham Light Infantry in Sanctuary Wood ; in support—Sherwood Foresters also in Sanctuary Wood ; East Yorks. in Zouave Wood ; Queen's Westminsters (T.F.) in Maple Copse, and the 1st West Yorks. R. on the Ramparts, Ypres. The 16th Infantry Brigade was on the left of the 18th Brigade and had disposed the K. S. L. I. on the right, the York and Lancs. Regt. on the left, with the Buffs in support and the Leicesters in reserve.

The objective to be captured was the high ground north of the Crater and in the direction of Q.19. and P.7., and to consolidate a line through the Stables and Q.14. towards Q.19.

On the right the Durham Light Infantry had been ordered to attack from Sanctuary Wood with the right of the Battalion on G.1, G.2. and G.3., and their left on The Strand. The first objective of the attack was the establishment of a line continuing G.3., across the Menin Road, north of the houses (exclusive). As the attack progressed the troops were ordered to work down G.7., G.8., and Bond Street towards Old Bond Street and meet the troops of the 16th Infantry Brigade advancing from the West. *1ST BATTALION.*

The left attack was to advance from the line G.10. and S.3a., with its right on Old Bond Street: its first objective was the line—Crater (inclusive) to Q.20 (inclusive) thence to Q.19 and P.7. where the line would be consolidated. During the advance the troops on the left attack were ordered to work east down Bond Street, G.8. and G.7. to meet the troops of the 18th Infantry Brigade.

The 6th Division was therefore to launch two attacks, one north and the other east.

The right attack was very difficult, for here the Durhams not only had the enemy on their front, but on their right rear: the enemy's guns on the high ground south of Sanctuary Wood were able to pour a particularly severe fire on the rear of the attacking troops. To add to the difficulties the latter were new to the ground, and the area in which they were to assemble was very cramped.

As already stated, the artillery preparation had been continuous for some days, but at 2-45 a.m. on the 9th, the bombardment became intense, and in accordance with programme, was maintained until 3-15 a.m. Every British gun in the area poured shell into and on to the German trenches, tearing great gaps in the parapets and flinging the wire entanglements far and wide. The mangled remains of Germans were tossed into the air, and the whole position to be attacked seemed for ever changing its appearance. *9TH AUGUST*

At 3-5 a.m. the assaulting troops left their trenches and removed their own wire entanglements which had been previously loosened. They then moved slowly forward until at 3-15 a.m. when the guns lifted. At that hour they dashed forward and jumped into the enemy's trenches, or rather into what remained of them. The dazed occupants either surrendered or were bayoneted immediately, and within ten minutes the German line on the front of the right attack was in the possession of the 18th Infantry Brigade.

The left of the attack succeeded in establishing itself almost immediately in the deep trenches running from Q.20. to the Crater, and bombers were at once sent out towards P.7 and P.6., which were

1ST BATTALION.

blocked. The enemy's guns however, had by now found the range of G.1., G.2., and G.3., where the Sherwood Foresters in close support of the Durhams had moved up. Heavy losses were now sustained, the enfilade fire from the south causing many casualties. As the day wore on this fire increased in violence, and at 4-30 p.m. the Foresters were driven out of their position, the Durhams still remaining in somewhat isolated parties in the Hooge Stables and Crater, and towards G.3. The West Yorkshires and the Royal Fusiliers were thereupon ordered up to relieve the battalion which had suffered most. The Queen's Westminsters succeeded in occupying G.1., G.2. and and G.3., with posts, and the West Yorkshiremen had by nightfall established a line of posts and machine guns in Bond Street. Captain Palmes (1st West Yorks. Regt.) and some men of D Company were later highly commended by the General Officer Commanding for wiring their part of the line under very heavy fire.

During the evening, however, it was decided to evacuate part of the line about the Crater and to the right of the latter. The troops were therefore withdrawn from these positions, not without considerable heartburning, for the possession had cost the battalion dear. The day's casualties had been heavy (about 150), but in view of the success of the operations, capture of prisoners and severe losses inflicted on the enemy, they were not excessive. The hostile trenches when taken were full of dead and wounded Germans.

When the British troops set to work to reverse the parapets they found that many of the enemy's dead had been built into them, and under the circumstances consolidation was anything but an easy matter.

The whole attack was well planned and carried out and the brilliant re-capture of the trenches lost in July brought the 6th Division many congratulations from the Army and Corps Commanders. Colonel Towsey (temporarily commanding 18th Infantry Brigade) and the General Officer Commanding 16th Infantry Brigade were also congratulated by the General Officer Commanding 6th Division.

10TH AUGUST

On the 10th consolidation was continued, but was much hampered all day by heavy hostile shelling. As early as 3 a.m. the German guns opened fire, and again at 9 a.m., continuing intermittently throughout the day.

Near the Stables a party of the Durham Light Infantry still maintained their ground with the utmost gallantry. At dusk the West Yorkshiremen took over the high ground between the Crater and the Stables. As darkness fell the work of putting the new position into a better state of defence was begun in earnest.   1ST BATTALION.

The 1st West Yorkshires were then ordered to send out a party to re-occupy the Stables which had been evacuated. Lieut. A. H. Daly with twelve men from B Company crept out for the purpose of reaching the Stables, but was unfortunately wounded, and he and his party were forced to return. Lieut. J. H. Trafford Rawson then went out with a party, but he also was unable to reach the objective before dawn, and was obliged to return, several of his party having been wounded. Throughout the night stretcher parties furnished by the Battalion were busy searching the ground for wounded, and collecting the casualties. In the early morning of the 11th, Captain M. B. B.   11TH AUGUST
Riall, whilst out with a working party, was wounded.

Consolidation was continued during the day. A reconnaissance of the ground to the Stables was carried out by Lieut. W. Barwiss, who obtained useful information : no enemy was found on the ridge of Hooge. Another officer of the Battalion (Lieut. H. D. Chamier), was wounded by shrapnel during the morning.

Later, Lieut. Bastow with a party of twelve men from A Company made another attempt to occupy the post in the Stables. The attempt was successful, but on reaching the Stables the post was found to be non-existent, and for twenty-four hours the party was obliged to remain in the Crater   On the 12th, Lieut. Bastow and his party   12TH AUGUST
were relieved by Captain Palmes and twelve men of D Company, and on the following night (at about midnight), the whole battalion was relieved by the Rifle Brigade and marched back to Ypres, billeting in houses near the Water Works. The 1st West Yorkshires were now in support.

The enemy made no attempt to re-capture the lost trenches though he shelled the whole front line heavily.

From the 9th to the 13th inclusive, the casualties of the 1st West Yorks. R. were three officers wounded, four other ranks killed, twenty-eight wounded and two missing. The whole battalion was employed in the night of the 14th, 15th and 16th, in digging communication trenches.

Brigadier-General R. J. Bridgeford took over command of the 18th Infantry Brigade on the 16th, and Colonel Towsey returned to his Battalion.

At 3 a.m. on the 17th, the Battalion was relieved by the East   17TH AUGUST
Yorks., and taken back to Poperinghe in motor buses and billeted in farms. The strenuous work of the last few days had exhausted the

1ST BATTALION.

men, who were glad to be out of the line in reserve once more. On the 19th an unfortunate bomb accident resulted in the death of one man and the wounding of four others.

21ST AUGUST

The VIth Corps Commander (Lieut.-General Sir J. L. Keir) addressed the Battalion on parade on the 21st, and said : " He wished to convey his thanks to the Battalion for the splendid work done during the recent operations at Hooge. The satisfactory work done during these operations had caused congratulatory messages to be sent to him, not only from Sir Herbert Plumer, Commanding Second Army, but also from Sir John French, and he wished to convey his personal thanks to the Battalion for their splendid behaviour and hard work. He was pleased to say he had another Yorkshire Division (the 49th) in his Corps and no one had come out better during the War than the Yorkshiremen. The 6th Division had always upheld the honour of the British Army in all the hard fighting that had taken place previously, and he was quite sure they would do so in the future."

---

[1] Battalion Diary, 1st Bn. West Yorkshire Regt.

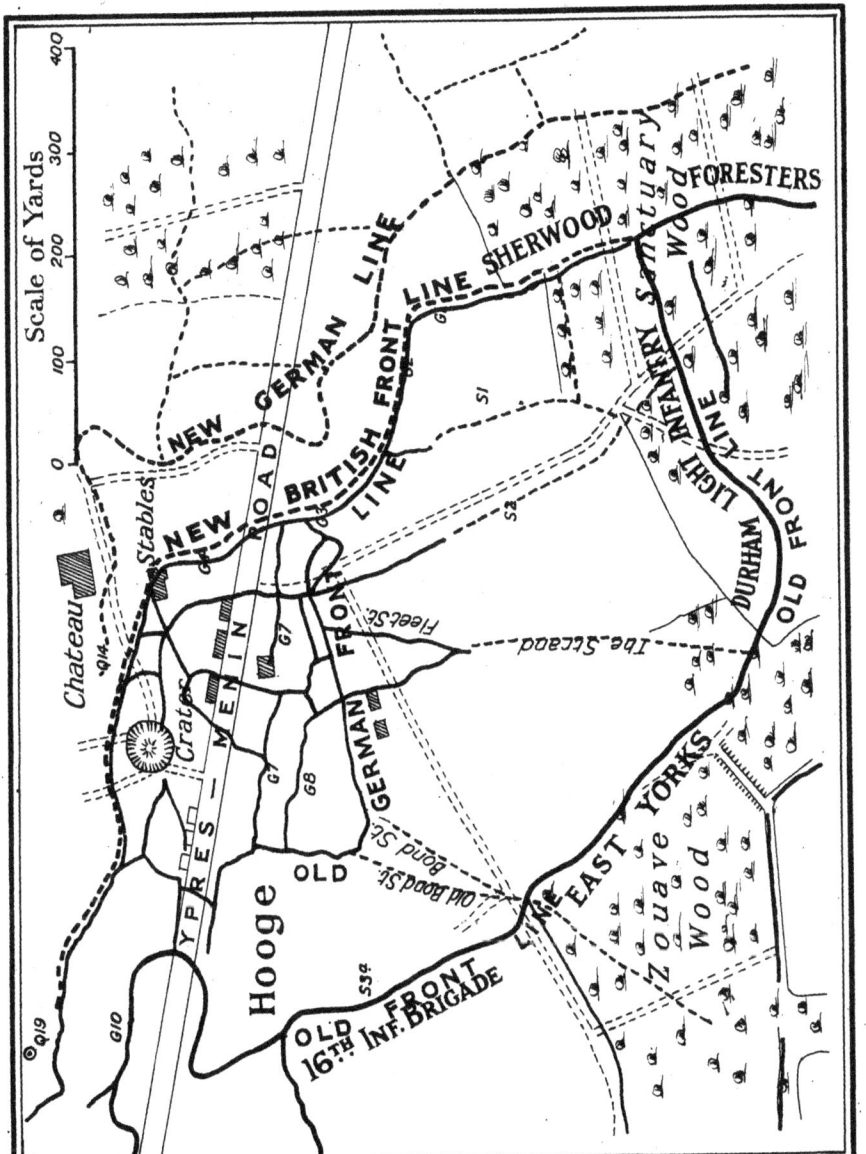

THE ACTIONS OF HOOGE, 9TH AUGUST, 1915.

TRENCH WARFARE

1st—31st August, 1915.

NORTH and south of the 6th Division, the 49th (W. R.) and the 17th Divisions, respectively, co-operated with fire attacks and artillery bombardments in the successful operations at Hooge.

The 49th Divisional Artillery, north and north-east of Ypres assisted by the 45th French Divisional Artillery and "Heavies," opened fire at 6-30 p.m. on the 8th in order to divert the attention of the enemy from the preparations for the attack by the 6th Division timed for 3-30 on the following morning. Heavy rifle fire was also brought to bear on the enemy's front line trenches and approaches, and continued until darkness fell, a further burst of gun-fire being opened at 12-45 a.m. on the 9th. And, as only to be expected, the enemy's guns were also busy with retaliation shoots. Turco Farm held by the 1/5th West Yorkshires was probably the most unhealthy spot in the whole Divisional front line, and here the Battalion was kept continually on the alert. Dug-outs were blown in and parapets wrecked, necessitating heavy work. The Canal Bank regularly received a good deal of attention from the enemy's artillery, frequent attempts being made to break the dams and flood the country: and constant vigilance was necessary. On the 8th, the dam *was* breached, but promptly repaired and little damage resulted. 8TH AUGUST. 1/5TH BATTALION.

After the successful attack at Hooge the enemy's guns up and down the line seemed more active than ever. On the 11th, an unfortunate cavalry regiment—the 9th Lancers—billeted in a Wood just behind the line had thirty-one casualties from a single salvoe. A post at No Man's Cottage held by the 1/6th West Yorkshires was also badly knocked about, the enemy's trench mortars plastering the position with bombs. But the battalion revenged itself upon the enemy, for several Germans fell to the West Yorkshiremen's snipers —a good day's work at a difficult and highly dangerous task. 1/6TH BATTALION.

The 49th Division had now been in France a little over four months and had done well. Its steadiness in the trenches had won the approval of Corps and Army Commanders: its peace training had borne excellent fruit and when on the last day of August, Lord Scarborough and General Mends arrived on a visit and went round the Divisional area they congratulated the General Officer Commanding, the Brigadiers and Battalion Commanders on the reputation they had gained whereby they had most worthily upheld the honour of the West Riding Territorials.

* * * * *

10TH BATTALION.
The 10th Battalion West Yorks. Regt. (50th Infantry Brigade, 17th Division), which on the 31st July was just north of Dickebusch, marched in Brigade on the night of the 1st/2nd August to the 3rd Division area. The latter on this date was holding the line from the Vierstraat—Wytschaete Road (O.12.c.) to near Verbranden Molen (I.34.b.), the 9th Infantry Brigade being on the right, the 7th Infantry Brigade in the centre and the 8th Infantry Brigade on the left. The 50th Infantry Brigade had been ordered to relieve the 7th Brigade in the centre sub-sector.

2ND AUGUST.
On the 2nd August, at 2-30 p.m., eight officers and eight sergeants of the 10th West Yorks. visited the trenches of the Honourable Artillery Company (7th Brigade) whom the West Yorkshiremen were to relieve, and at 8 o'clock that night the Battalion began the relief, which was completed by 2 a.m. without incident. B Company settled down in Q.2., C Company in Q.3 and A and D Companies in Scottish Wood.

But trouble was early afoot. Shortly after the relief had been completed 2nd Lieut. Howe was wounded, the first officer casualty suffered by the 10th Battalion. Then about 10-45 a.m. the enemy began to shell the trenches though on the Divisional Artillery opening fire the German guns ceased. Twenty-five minutes later there was a sudden roar, and a column of earth shot up into the sky—the enemy had exploded a mine near B Company. Another officer, Lieut. Maidlow, and four other ranks were wounded, but the exploded mine did more damage to the enemy than to the West Yorkshiremen, for two Germans were killed. A German tunic was also blown into the British trenches which furnished a much-needed identification. The front-line parapets in Q.2. were partly damaged, but were soon repaired on the arrival of a couple of hundred sandbags which had been despatched as soon as the explosion had taken place.

After this sudden burst of activity the situation seems to have been "all quiet" and from the 4th to the 8th August the West Yorkshiremen had a comparatively uneventful time. Periodically, however, aerial torpedoes, "whiz-bangs," and other objectionable missiles were fired by the enemy.

On the 9th the 17th Division co-operated in the Actions of Hooge by fire attacks and bombardments. the 10th West Yorkshires and flanking battalions firing heavy bursts of rifle fire, each lasting three minutes. 9TH AUGUST. 10TH BATTALION.

The Battalion was relieved on the night of the 13th/14th by the Border Regt., and marched back to La Clytte, where twelve days were spent in training in bombing, sniping, physical drill and route-marching, interspersed with sports during the daytime, and at night concerts and visits to " Troupes " which had begun to make their appearance behind the trenches, in the " rest " areas in France and Flanders.

On the 26th August the West Yorkshiremen marched out of La Clytte for " P " trenches relieving the Border Regt. The relief was completed by 11-20 a.m., Battalion Headquarters being at Wiltshire Farm, which according to the Battalion Diary was a " damnable place." There were others ! 26TH AUGUST

But the month closed quietly, for since the operations at Hooge, on the whole British Front in France and Flanders little happened of interest, though behind the front line preparations for operations on a large scale were being made.

★ ★ ★ ★

The 8th Division, south of the 49th, 6th and 17th Divisions, was likewise experiencing (and benefiting by) a quiet spell. The 2nd Battalion West Yorkshires on the 1st August was in billets in the Rue du Bruges, Battalion Headquarters being in Rue Quesnoy. Eight days in and eight out of the front line was the rule at this period. Trench mortar activity and sniping occupied the troops in the front line during the daylight hours, and at night time patrols went out into No Man's Land : constant vigilance was necessary. Weird and thrilling were the experiences men went through out in that dread space between the two lines of opposing trenches. Ghastly indeed were the weapons used—bludgeons, daggers, knuckle-dusters and many other more or less " unofficial armaments "—for the great thing was to kill or capture, without firing shots from rifle or revolver. 2ND BATTALION. 1ST AUGUST.

Out of the line, work on the communication and support trenches absorbed large working parties and the West Yorkshiremen, in their particular part of the line, put in much useful though very hard work building and re-building the defences.

No infantry attacks were made on or by the enemy. The

2ND BATTALION.

summer of 1915 will always be remembered (in France and Flanders at least) as a period of training and preparation. Large numbers of troops belonging to the New Armies (Kitchener's) were arriving, and had to be given their first introduction to trench warfare. They were fortunate in arriving in dry weather, thus at the very outset avoiding the terrible hardships through which the gallant fellows, who held on with marvellous tenacity and courage to the front line during the winter of 1914 and the early spring of 1915, had to pass.

One incident of particular interest to West Yorkshiremen took place during the early days of August. On the 7th, H.R.H. the Prince of Wales paid an informal visit to the 23rd Infantry Brigade Headquarters. His Royal Highness was taken by the Brigadier to see the 2nd Battalion West Yorkshire Regt., and was introduced to some of the officers and senior N. C. O.'s. This Royal visit was very much appreciated by all ranks of " The Prince of Wales's Own."

7TH AUGUST.

A somewhat stormy reception greeted the Battalion on the 24th, when, just after it had relieved the 2nd Middlesex, the enemy sent over a large number of trench-mortar bombs, killing one man and wounding five others : retaliation effectively put an end to the enemy's activity.

Behind the lines much had been done to give the men some relief from the constant strain through which they passed when in the forward trenches, and the Battalion Diary of the 2nd Battalion West Yorkshires for August, 1915, contains such entries as " Sailly Empire opened for the first time " : " Boxing Competition, A Company *v.* Machine Guns " : " Concert in B Company " : " B Company boxed D Company in the evening " : " Divisional Band performed for the first time " : " Divisional Horse Show."

Laughter and tears, comedy and tragedy were very close together in those days. A man might indeed go off to Sailly Empire where for a brief space he would forget the horrors of War, but on coming out would find his platoon or company detailed for the relief of a sub-sector of the front line. In the darkness with his comrades he would pick his way carefully towards the front line, and soon would be standing on " sentry go," gazing over the parapet across No Man's Land towards the enemy's lines. Of a sudden the dark night would be illuminated by the flash of trench mortars, and bombs would begin to drop on the parapet or into the trench, and he who but a few hours before had sat laughing in Sailly Empire had passed beyond the necessity of soothing his tortured mind with ephemeral things. For days and nights on end the official diaries might indeed report "The attitude of the enemy was normal" or "situation quiet," but even quietude was a menace.

There was no rest, though all was still. That long period of comparative quietude during the summer of 1915 was pregnant with death and destruction, for the brains of the greatest scientists in the world were bent upon the invention and construction of deadly weapons with which to gain the mastery.

* * * *

During August yet another Battalion of the West Yorkshire Regiment—the 11th (Service)—arrived in France. This Battalion formed part of the 69th Infantry Brigade of the 23rd Division— a New Army Division. On the 20th August, the 11th Battalion was in England, at Bramshott, training with its Brigade and Division when orders were received for the 23rd to hold itself in readiness to proceed overseas. Within the next few days Divisional Headquarters left Bramshott and, on the 26th, began to arrive in its concentration area in France. The 11th West Yorkshires had embarked at Southampton on the previous day and disembarked on the 26th at Le Havre, proceeding to Rest Camp, No. 2. On the 27th, the Battalion entrained and arrived at Watten at 9 a.m. on the 28th. Here the West Yorkshiremen detrained and marched to the Bayengham area, where the 69th Brigade was billeted. The Brigade was formed of the 8th and 9th Battalions of the Yorkshire Regt., 10th Battalion West Riding Regt., and the 11th Battalion West Yorkshire Regt., and was commanded by Brigadier-General F. S. Derham. The 23rd Division was under the Command of Major-General J. M. Babington.

11TH BATTALION.

20TH AUGUST

* * * *

"Until the last week in September," said Sir John French in his despatches, "there was relative quiet along the whole of the British line, except at those points where the normal conditions of existence comprised occasional shelling or constant mine and bomb warfare. In these trying forms of encounter all ranks have constantly shown the greatest enterprise and courage, and have consistently maintained the upper hand."

The early days of September were accompanied by heavy downpours of rain and once again the trenches became quagmires, feet deep in viscous mud and water.

On the 9th, to the joy of all ranks, the 146th Infantry Brigade of the 49th Division was relieved, the 5th, 6th, 7th and 8th West

9TH SEPT.

1/5TH, 1/6TH
1/7TH, 1/8TH
BATTALIONS.
Yorkshires spending the next twelve days back in the rest area. It was the first relief from the line for so many days which had fallen to these West Yorkshire Territorials since their arrival in France, and the change was very much appreciated. In between the hours of drill and training, the men were able to indulge in games and other pastimes, whilst at night the 6th Divisional Troupe drew crowded houses. So for a little while the men forgot the awfulness of the front-line trenches in the indulgence of such harmless anodynes as " Sister Susie," " If you were the Only girl in the World " and other popular ditties.

THE BATTLE OF LOOS
25th September—8th October, 1915

THE desperate struggle, called by the Germans "The Battle of Loos and Hulluch," which began in the early hours of the 25th September, 1915, was the first offensive on a large scale delivered by the Allies in combination since the Battle of the Aisne, 1914. Only one Battalion of the West Yorkshire Regt. — the 12th Battalion contained in the 21st Division — took part in the main operations, though some of the remaining Battalions then in France and Flanders were concerned in the subsidiary Actions of Pietre, Action of Bois Grenier, and the Second Attack on Bellewaerde—all north of the La Bassee Canal.

The summer of 1915 had been spent by the Allies and the enemy in preparing for operations on a much larger scale than had hitherto been attempted. Sir John French and General Joffre, the Allied Commanders-in-Chief, after a careful survey of the whole line, had based their plans on concerted action. "It was arranged," said Sir John, "that we should make a combined attack from certain points of the Allied line, during the last week in September."

There were to be two offensives, one east and west of Rheims by the Fourth, Eleventh, Third and Fifth French Armies, and another north and south of Arras by the First British and the Tenth French Armies: the Second British Army and the Indian Corps were to carry out subsidiary attacks north of the La Bassée Canal and in the neighbourhood of Ypres. The Third British Army was to undertake operations along its front between Monchy, south-west of Arras, and the Somme.

The intentions of the Allied Commanders were:
  I.—To break the enemy's front;
  II.—Prevent him re-establishing his line;
  III.—To defeat decisively his divided forces.

On the British front the main attack was to take place between Givenchy (just north of the La Bassée Canal) and the Double Crassier, south-west of the mining town of Loos.

Three Corps had been detailed for the offensive. The Ist Corps (General Gough) consisting of the 2nd, 9th and 7th Divisions:

the IVth Corps (General Rawlinson) formed of the 1st, 15th (Scottish) and the 47th (London) Divisions : and the XIth Corps (General Haking) made up of the newly-formed Guards Division and two New Army Divisions, the 21st and the 24th. The British and Indian Cavalry Corps were at St. Pol and Doullens respectively with orders to advance through the gaps in the enemy's line if circumstances permitted.

Of the Ist Corps, the 2nd Division was disposed north (as far as Givenchy) and south of the La Bassee Canal; the 9th Division was on the right on the 2nd, opposite Fosse 8 ; the 7th Division came next, between the right flank of the 9th, and the Hulluch—Vermelles Road.

The left Division of the IVth Corps (1st Division) joined up with the right Division of the Ist Corps, *i.e.*, the 7th : the 15th Division on the right of the 1st and the 47th Division on the right of the 15th completed the IVth Corps line.

The Guards Division of the XIth Corps was at Lillers, west of Bethune : the 21st Division was north-west of Beuvry and the 24th Division just west of Nœux-les-Mines.

These dispositions are as shown by the official documents, on the morning of the 25th September, when the attack was launched. And they are important, for the XIth Corps formed Sir John French's reserves.

The First British Army was opposed by part of the Sixth German Army.

The objective of the First British Army was the line, Henin—Lietard—Carvin, the line of advance, between the La Bassée Canal and Lens.

For the first time in the War the Allies were to use asphyxiating gas : the enemy having attempted by this treacherous means to gain an advantage was now to be hoist with his own petard.

The lessons learnt at Neuve Chapelle had been assimilated and certain innovations were to be made, principally dealing with the Artillery. A great number of guns had been massed behind the First Army front and these were to fire modified barrages. At Neuve Chapelle the barrage had been first introduced in the form of concentrated fire on certain points—there were no " lifts." But now (at Loos) the lifting barrage was to be tried.[1]

---

[1] This should not be confused with the " rolling " (or creeping) barrage—first introduced during the Somme Battles of 1916. At Loos the " lifts " were definite.

The preliminary Bombardment began on the morning of the 21st September. On the night of the 24th/25th, Zero hour was fixed for 6 a.m. north of the Canal and 6-30 a.m. between the La Bassee Canal and Lens, on the 25th. At 5-45 a.m. the guns were to open on the enemy's trenches and at 5-50 a.m. gas was to be discharged.

At dawn on the 25th rain fell heavily. The wind was negligible and what there was of it was unfavourable for gas operations: but the projection was ordered to take place. After five minutes' intense artillery fire, during which light and heavy guns pounded the enemy's trenches, the gas cylinders discharged their deadly fumes. Immediately north and south of the Canal, along the front of the 2nd Division, the dense clouds hung about the British trenches, causing serious casualties amongst the troops waiting for the order to " go over." The enemy appeared quite unaffected. Several attempts by this gallant Division to advance were swept away and so little was the enemy affected by the gas that his troops stood up on their fire-steps and shot down the British soldiers as they advanced. Farther south the gas was likewise a failure. *25TH SEPT.*

On the right of the 2nd Division, the 9th, 7th, 1st, 15th and 47th Divisions made splendid progress, the whole German front line from the right flank of the first named Division (approximately Fosse 8) to Loos inclusive, falling into the hands of the First British Army. South of Loos the French also made fine progress between Angres and Souchez, and near Perthe, north-east of Rheims.

It was not, however, until the night of the 25th/26th, when after hard fighting in which the troops of the Ist and IVth Corps had been heavily counter-attacked and forced back from some advanced positions won in the morning and reserves were necessary, that the 21st Division in which the 12th Battalion of the West Yorkshire Regt. was contained, was ordered up into the front line. *12TH BATTALION.*

The 21st and 24th Divisions of the XIth Corps had been placed at the disposal of the General Officer Commanding First Army at 9-30 a.m., but at that hour they were some distance behind the line and it was late on the night of the 25th before they were in position. They were both New Army Divisions. The 21st had only arrived in France on the 10th September and had never held a front-line sector, much less taken part in major operations. The Division was Commanded by Major-General G. T. Forestier-Walker, its Infantry Brigades were numbered 62nd, 63rd and 64th. The 12th Battalion West Yorkshires was brigaded with the 8th Lincoln, 8th Somerset

12TH BATTALION.

L. I. and 10th York and Lancs. Regt. in the 63rd Brigade. Brigadier-General H. T. Nickalls commanded the Brigade and Lieut.-Col. R. A. C. L. Leggett the West Yorkshiremen.

The Division had concentrated in the Watten area on the 13th September, parties of officers, N.C.O.'s and men proceeding to Nieppe and Armentières for a tour of twenty-four hours in the trenches. For a week the Division remained at Watten, but on the 20th received orders to proceed on the night of the 20th/21st south, by road, to an area south-east of Lillers.

In view of subsequent events it is important to note that from the night of the 20th/21st and throughout the following days and nights until it went into the line north of Loos, the 21st Division was marching to the battle area, billeting and bivouacking *en route*, that as a whole the Division had had no practical experience of warfare in France.

With their Brigade the 12th West Yorkshires left the Watten area at 7 p.m. on the night of the 20th : Wardrecques was reached at 1 a.m. on the 21st where the Battalion bivouacked. St Hilaire-Cottes and Auchel were reached on the nights of 22nd and 23rd respectively.[1] The next day's march is thus described in the Battalion diary : " Marched from Auchel about 7 p.m., 24/9/15, bivouacked near cross-roads, south of Houchin, and a mile-and-a-half west of Nœux-les-Mines,[2] about 1 a.m. 25/9/15, ready to be put into the battle, timed to begin at dawn. Orders have now arrived and we are falling in to march into fight. Everybody wet through from lying in the rain."

The Battalion moved in Brigade.

No time is given in the Battalion diary when the " fall in " took place, but the next entry states : " Marched from last bivouac west of Nœux-les-Mines about 11 a.m., Saturday, 25/9/15, through Nœux-les-Mines, along the road to Mazingarbe. Turned left at first road junction on north side and along that road to bivouac for about an hour at first cross-roads. Thence marched to Noyelles-les Vermelles, thence through Philosophe along Lens road till about dark we passed Puits No. 7, of Fosse No. 7 de Béthune, where we lay down in close column on the north side of the road.[3] About eight

---

[1] These marches were of the following (approximate) distances :—
20/21st Sept., Watten to Wardrecques—10 miles.
21/22nd Sept., Wardrecques to St. Hilaire-Cottes—15 miles.
22/23rd Sept., St. Hilaire-Cottes to Auchel—11 miles.
[2] Distance, about 15 miles.
[3] Distance, about 10 miles.

or half-past (everybody wet through) we moved along the Lens road till we crossed our (old) front-line trenches, crossed the (old) German front-line trenches, and turned along the first road to the left (the Grenay-Benifontaine road unmetalled) till we came to the north-west corner of Loos.... The battalion moved off along north of the La Bassée Road about ten o'clock p.m. as far as point 69. in G.23.d.[1]
.... There it faced east in column of companies in line of platoons in fours and after midnight marched to the strip of wood running north-east and south-west in H. 25.a. Arrived there about 3 a.m., 25/9/15. The formation was (now) changed to column of half-companies in line and the Battalion passed the north-east corner of the Wood, crossed the road Lens—Cité St. Elie and took up a position, three Companies extended in (the) front line and one Company extended in support in rear, relieving some Northamptons of the 15th Division[2] which had won the ground that far during the day. Brigade Headquaters were in a Red House at the edge of the road just east of the strip of wood before mentioned."

During the while the 21st Division was moving forward to the front line heavy fighting had been continuous. The Lens—La Bassée road had been reached and was in places held by the First British Army. East of Loos around Hill 70, west of Cité St. Elie at the Quarries, and again north-west about the Dump and Fosse 8, the fighting was still of a very desperate nature. At 5·15 p.m. on the 25th, Ist Corps Headquarters had issued an official " Situation Report." In this report the positions of the Ist and IVth Corps were given: " Situation on IVth Corps front as follows: right, secured on Double Crassier, thence south of Loos Chalk Pit to Hill 70 inclusive. The line runs thence northwards to include Puits 14 Bis and German trenches immediately south and west of Hulluch, but Hulluch is not in our hands: enemy is reported to be making strenuous efforts to recapture Hill 70. Situation on Ist Corps front as follows: right of 7th Division about 1300 yards north of cross-roads H.7.c.5.2. along road to same cross-roads, thence due west to G.12.b. 4.4., along Gun Trench to Point 39. north of road and the Quarries: 9th Division reported to be holding Pekin Trench from cross-roads G.6.b.5.2. to A.3.0.—A.7.4.—Fosse 8, back to our old front line on Vermelles—Auchy road."[1]

[1] Map reference: France 36c. 1/40,000.

[2] There were no Northamptons in the 15th Division: they belonged to the 2nd Infantry Brigade, 1st Division.

12TH BATTALION.

But when the 21st Division had come into the line about midnight on the 25th, almost all of Hill 70 had been lost again : only a footing on the western slopes remained in the hands of the 15th Division.

The situation on the IVth Corps front is very tersely given in the official despatches : " On the IVth Corps front, attacks on Hulluch and on the Redoubt on the east side of Hill 70 were put in operation, but were anticipated by the enemy organizing a very strong offensive from that direction. These attacks drove in the advanced troops of the 21st and 24th Divisions which were then moving forward to attack."

The " advanced troops " of the 21st Division were the four battalions of the 63rd Infantry Brigade, of which the 12th Battalion West Yorkshires held the most forward position : both the 62nd (right) and the 64th (left) Infantry Brigades were thrown back, with the result that the 63rd Brigade offered a vulnerable point of attack, a point of which the enemy took full advantage. But as the interest in this attack is purely Regimental the report contained in the Battalion diary of the 12th West Yorks. Regt. is given in full, for it contains certain reasonable statements of the cause of the subsequent retirement : " When daylight came the position was found to be rather curious. The order had been that the Brigade should take up a line running north and south just east of the road Lens—Cité

26TH SEPT. St. Elie and from thence begin to advance eastwards at 7 a.m. (26th). Daylight found a position taken up, beginning with the left, west of the road at a point in H.19.c. Crossing the road before it came to the Red House and then beginning with the left of the 12th West Yorks. (our battalion) it suddenly went east, south-east by east to the salient, into the Bois Hugo in H.26.a. where the right of our battalion front line found itself digging rifle pits in the open about twenty yards from the edge of the wood which ran along part of its front, while the right flank of the line was about twenty yards from the edge of the wood where it ran back south-west to the road behind. Our line from left to right was B, A and C Companies with a bend to the front : while D Company in support was nearly parallel with the road behind and 150 to 200 yards in front of it. But here again the right-hand man of the line was about twenty yards from the flanking wood. On the right of the West Yorkshires it was understood that the Lincolns were in position refused all day along the edge of the Bois Hugo. It was in fact as if the Brigade had worked too much to its right and so had been compressed out of shape by the pressure on its right of the Division (15th) which was in front of Hill 70. A Scottish Regiment, either Camerons or Cameronians, was in possession of Puits No. 14 Bis, and our 62nd Infantry Brigade had been lent to the same Division for a fresh attempt on Hill 70. It must have been the knowledge of all these troops on the south side of the wood (Bois Hugo) which influenced the Battalion Commander and prevented him extending his line into the wood and so protecting his own flank with his own men. No attempt was made to straighten out the Brigade line, possibly because the order had come that the line would advance at 11 a.m. and it was thought that it could be straightened then. Meanwhile the men were trying to dig themselves in with their entrenching tools.

"The position began to be more or less shelled at daylight and enemy snipers began to be effective shortly afterwards: there had been some blind shelling during the night. At some time after 9 a.m. Commanding Officer was hit by three shrapnel bullets in the left shoulder and was carried off. Major J. H. Jacques then took command. An order which had been passed along for Company Commanders brought up Captain Matthew, commanding B Company on the left in time to find Major Jacques carrying on, Battalion Headquarters being at the edge of the wood in front of the right flank of D Company and in rear of the right flank of C Company: Battalion Headquarters were then, at least, on the right flank of the Battalion, a position probably induced by the fact that the battalion was facing north-east. The sun could not be seen and no one thought of taking out a compass, being altogether under the impression that they were facing east, in which case Battalion Headquarters were pretty well where any staff officer would naturally look for them.

"Things began to happen swiftly. The firing grew heavier. The Scottish regiment retired for some reason from Puits 14 Bis. Two of the battalion machine guns in position on the left flank of C Company, found a target in a body of Germans who came out in the open in front of them and only about a dozen of these escaped by bolting into the wood. One of the guns jammed. Captain Branch continued working the other when some men of the Brigade ran into the right of our line from the south side of the wood, and a sudden order to retire, which cannot quite be accounted for, began on our right and passed along the line to the left. The men began retiring, the Brigadier was killed in rallying some of the men. Many of the officers were knocked over at the same time, including Major Jacques, Captain Jacques, Captain and Adjutant Vann and others.

12TH BATTALION.

Captain Branch tried to stop the Germans who were pressing on out of the wood on the right, by getting into a shell-hole with his gun and firing while his ammunition lasted. Captain Matthew kept some hold on B Company and brought them back in something like shape : Lieut. Dunbar and Lieut. Vann being conspicuous in correcting the error and rallying the men, the retirement being north-westward. About now the line was more or less re-formed and the re-advance began. It reached D Company's rifle pits, but could get no further and eventually from lack of officers and N. C. O.'s the Battalion had to retire again, in company with the rest of the Brigade. Major Bullock marched the men back to Philosophe and they were then bivouacked on the south-west side of the road at Noyelles-les-Vermelles, in a ploughed field. At dark as good a meal as could be got was served out to them. Rain came down very heavily just afterwards, the men had practically all lost their packs and overcoats, the transport had been mostly destroyed by shells and there was very little recovery possible for the men that night."

Apart from that sudden order passed along the line, there was no ostensible reason for the first retirement : the troops were dug in and their flanks (so they at least believed) were secure. Under such conditions men do not voluntarily leave their trenches. Throughout the War sudden orders to retire emanated from *somewhere*—whence no one ever found out, or rather were discovered later to have been false when the mischief had been done. More than once they were shouted by the enemy's troops in close proximity to the British trenches. On that Sunday morning in September, 1915, the troops were in such a " jumpy " condition through want of food and experience in actual warfare that if they had retired without orders, it might have been forgiven them. Hunger and thirst and physical exhaustion have throughout the ages beaten brave men in battle and have affected their *morale:* the nations show it in their histories.

The condition of the 12th Battalion West Yorkshires (which really was the condition of all troops of the 63rd Brigade, if not the whole of the 21st Division) is well described in the concluding paragraphs of the Battalion diary dealing with the Battle of Loos : " Certain points should be borne in mind. The men had breakfast in the wet bivouac on Saturday morning and the cookers were set going for the midday meal. A certain amount of rations were carried on the men, one M. (meat) and V. (vegetable) to three men and of course the iron ration. Next day's rations had been brought up but had, to be left because there was no means of carrying it, the supply wagons having been taken away. From the time of leaving the bivouac the men received no more food till Sunday night. The hot meal in the cookers for Saturday noon was never served out and most of the men, practically all, obeyed the order not to touch the iron ration till ordered by an officer : an order which no officer gave as far as can be gathered. The packs were wet and heavy, the men wet through. The worst was the thirst. The men had always been able to get liquids when they wanted them and suddenly had to go without from Saturday midday till the ration next day, while carrying a wet pack and 220 rounds of ammunition. The packs were only taken off once, from bivouac to battle, and then for one hour only when the Battalion lay down in the dark on the north side of the wood between Puits No. 7 and our front-line trenches. During all the rest of the time the word had been " We are going on at any minute. It is only a check, not a halt."

It is impossible to state why this New Army Division—the 21st —was put into the front line of battle without any experience whatsoever of war in France. Up and down the British line there were many other Divisions which might have been employed in the Battle of Loos in place of these New Army formations. The work demanded of troops flung into the line after the first attack had been made was often of a much more severe nature than the initial attack at Zero hour. It invariably happened that after the first assault the enemy's resistance hardened considerably and certainly his gun fire was always heavier. Why then employ troops lacking the necessary training (and certainly the necessary experience) in the following up of initial attacks ?

The Battalion Diary of the 12th West Yorkshires records that " Many gallant actions were done, and the names of Captain Matthew, Lieuts. Dunbar and Vann and Sergeant McLoriman were sent in for awards. The transport officer, Lieut. Barret (ably assisted by Quarter-master Lieut. Woodmore) was also commended for good work. The transport was caught by a storm of shells about 9-40 a.m. on Saturday and practically wiped out.

Severe casualties were suffered by the Battalion—16 officers and 300 ranks, killed and wounded. Four officers (Major J. H. Jacques, Capt. and Adjutant A. H. A. Vann, Captain A. Jacques and Captain W. J. G. Norris) were killed, and twelve wounded, including the Commanding Officer, Lieut.-Col. R. A. C. L. Leggett and Major Bullock.

12TH BATTALION. 28TH SEPT.

On the 27th September, the 63rd Infantry Brigade bivouacked half-a-mile north-west of Noyelles-les-Vermelles where it remained until the evening of the 28th. At 4 p.m. on the latter date Major A. O. Vaughan, 14th Northumberland Fusiliers, assumed command of the 12th Battalion West Yorkshires.

So far as the Battle of Loos was concerned the 21st Division did not again enter into the fight, having been ordered to move back and refit after relief by the Guards Division.

North of the main operations, *i.e.*, north of Givenchy, subsidiary actions by certain Divisions containing battalions of the West Yorkshire Regt. had taken place on the 25th and 26th September. These attacks were made for the purpose of holding the enemy to his ground, and to prevent him sending reinforcements further south to the scene of the main operations.

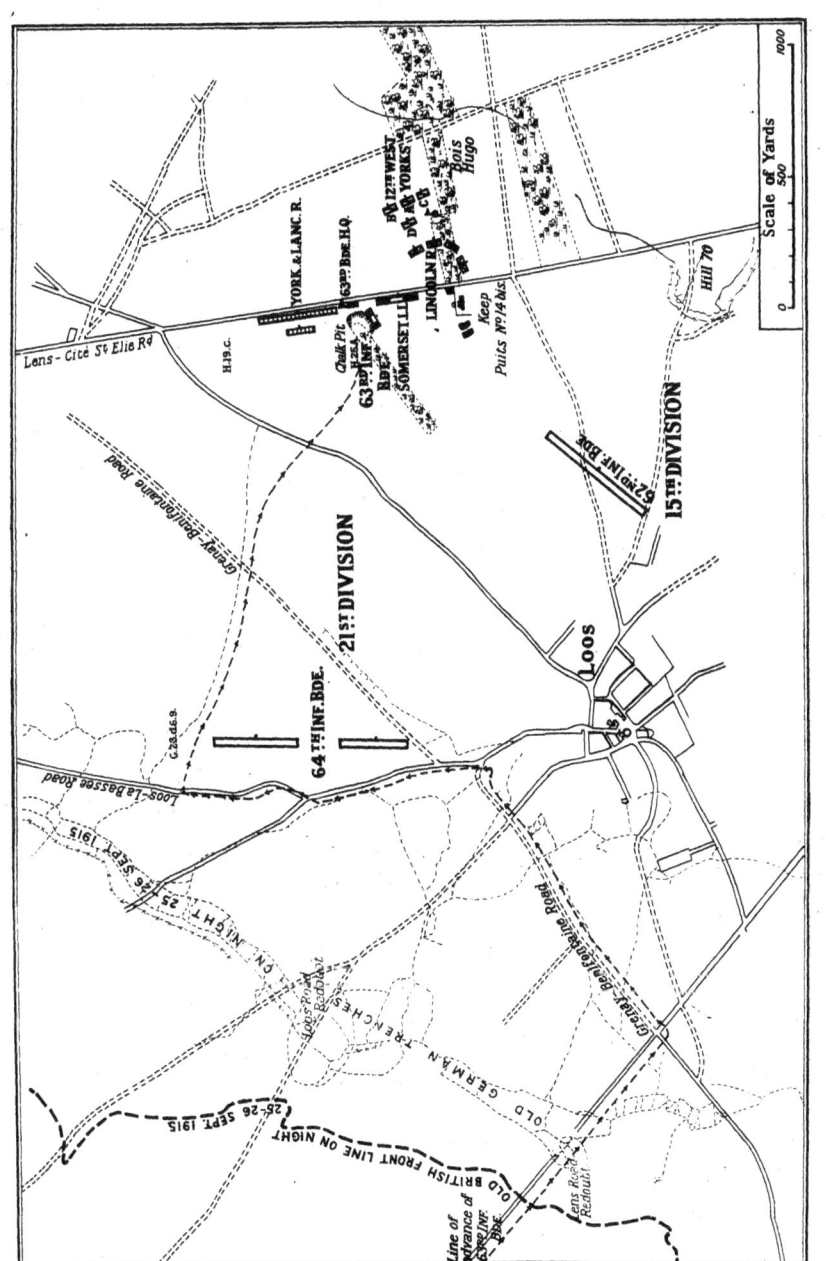

The Battle of Loos, 25th September, 1915.

THE BATTLE OF LOOS
II.
Subsidiary: The Actions of Pietre and of Bois Grenier, and the Second Attack on Bellewaerde

THE 8th Division of the IIIrd Corps and the Meerut Division of the Indian Corps were principally engaged in the Action of Pietre. But of the first-named Division only the 25th Infantry Brigade had been detailed for the assault, the 24th Brigade was in support, and the 23rd Brigade in Divisional reserve: the 2nd Battalion West Yorkshire R. therefore, saw little of the attack, though the battalion " stood to arms " all day in anticipation of being moved forward to join in the operations. The support and reserve Brigades were only to be employed to exploit any success gained. The attack was at first successful, some hundreds of yards of the enemy's front and second line trenches being captured after heavy and gallant fighting by the troops of the 25th Brigade. Later in the day, however, owing to very strong enemy counter-attacks the positions won had to be evacuated. Throughout the attack the 2nd West Yorkshires remained in reserve in an orchard in the Rue Biache, the battalion's position of assembly, taken up on the previous night just before midnight. Here at 1 a.m. on the 25th September the men were served out with hot stew from the cookers. The attack took place at 4-30 a.m. from Bridoux and Well Farm salients. Throughout the day the 23rd Brigade escaped hostile shelling and at night temporary billets were found for the men, heavy rain having set in.

25TH SEPT.

2ND BATTALION.

On the left of the 8th Division, the 23rd Division which had arrived in France towards the end of August, was holding a sector of the line from La Chapelle d'Armentières—Wez Macquart Road to approximately the Fme. Grande Flamengrie, and co-operated in the Action of Bois Grenier by fire attacks. The Division heavily bombarded the enemy's trenches at 4-32 a.m., and at 5-56 a.m. put down a smoke barrage along the whole Divisional sector. Between 8 and 9 a.m. an aeroplane report stated that the enemy was hurrying troops overland with considerable horse and motor transport towards

11TH BATTALION.

Ennetières and Lomme, east of the Divisional sector. Bursts of rifle, machine-gun and artillery fire were kept up during the night of the 25th/26th. But the 11th West Yorkshires in the 69th Infantry Brigade were out of the line on the 25th. The battalion was in billets in the Rue Dulettre and stood to arms all day, but was not called upon. On the previous day the West Yorkshiremen had suffered their first casualty, a private being killed by shrapnel whilst on sentry duty. The Battalion moved into the front line on the night of the 26th, and took over trenches Nos. 52, 53, 54 and S-54 from the 10th West Riding Regt.

10TH BATTALION.

The 17th Division just south of the Ypres—Comines Canal co-operated with fire attacks also, the 10th West Yorkshires of the 50th Infantry Brigade opening rapid rifle fire at Zero hour and at intervals throughout the day, but no infantry attacks were launched.

In the Second Army's attack on Bellewaerde, a simulated gas attack was made by the 6th Division in order to assist the 14th and 3rd Divisions who were carrying out the operations. The attack, like those at Pietre and Bois Grenier, was subsidiary to the main operations at Loos.

1ST BATTALION.

The 1st Battalion West Yorkshires were then holding the line about Wieltje, having relieved the Leicester's on the 15th of the month. The 6th Division had been ordered to assist the attacks of the 14th and 3rd Divisions by a bombardment on selected points in the enemy's lines, wire-cutting, and (as already stated) by the simulation of a gas attack by means of smoke clouds maintained for thirty minutes along the Divisional front.

At 4-20 a.m. the attack was launched upon the enemy's trenches, from east of Sanctuary Wood (3rd Div.) to Bellewaerde Farm (14th Div.). The morning was heavy with mist and the machine gunners and infantry of the 6th Division waiting to open fire were unable to find targets.

The West Yorkshiremen hurled their smoke grenades over towards the enemy's trenches, which had the desired effect. The Germans were obviously alarmed and immediately lighted fires of shavings on their parapets, which method they had adopted as a means of counteracting asphyxiating gas : they also threw petrol bombs and directed a heavy fire on the trenches of the Division, but made no infantry attack.

" Nothing can be seen of the attack on our right (14th Div.), and nothing is known of its progress until 5-20 a.m. when it is reported that the left Battalion of the attack (Rifle Brigade of 42nd Infantry

Brigade) had captured the trenches aimed at. About 9 a.m. it is reported that the 42nd Infantry Brigade had captured the enemy's trenches up to Bellewaerde Farm, that the 3rd Division had captured trenches south of Hooge, but nothing is known of the fighting about Hooge itself. There is a certain amount of shelling on our trenches about Crump Farm and Warwick Farm but nothing serious. Subsequently during the afternoon we hear that the 14th Division had been heavily counter-attacked and was back again in its original trenches."[1] Very heavy hostile artillery fire had compelled the 14th and 3rd Divisions to retire from the positions they had so gallantly won and at nightfall the attacking troops had had to retire. Two German officers and 138 other ranks were captured.

North of the 6th Division the 49th (West Riding) Division carried out similar demonstrations and the Divisional Artillery co-operating with a number of French batteries obtained excellent results. But no infantry attacks were made, either on or by, the Division, and the four West Yorkshire Battalions of the 146th Infantry Brigade had a generally quiet day.

A small incident, the outcome of the successful operations at Loos and on the French front, is related in the diary of the 1/5th West Yorkshires on the 27th September. The battalion had put up a notice board informing the enemy that the Allies, during the Battle of Loos, had captured fifty guns and 2,800 prisoners. The enemy first opened with a heavy bombardment of the Yorkshiremen's trenches, and then at 9-55 a.m. an angry party of Germans numbering ten men and one officer rushed across No Man's Land and tore down the notice. Then jumping into a sap thay knifed a bomber and withdrew, but in withdrawing three of them were shot down.

1/5TH BATTALION. 27TH SEPT.

---

[1] Diary of 18th Infantry Brigade Headquarters.

TRENCH WARFARE
1st October—31st December, 1915

ON the morning of the 1st October, 1915, there were 1ST OCT. ten Battalions of the West Yorkshire Regt. overseas engaged in active warfare. Nine of these were on the Western Front in France or Flanders, the tenth battalion was engaged in the Dardanelles Campaign. The 1st Battalion was in the Ypres Salient, with three Companies in support on the Canal Bank and one Company in the Potijze Defended Post: the 2nd Battalion was immediately south of the Bois Grenier Sector (south of Armentières) billeted in the Rue du Quesnoy, relieving later in the day the 2nd Scottish Rifles in the front line between Mine Avenue and the Western Convent Wall. Of the four Battalions forming the 146th Infantry Brigade of the 49th Division, the 1/6th and the 1/8th occupied the front line between the Morteldje Estaminet and Wyatts Lane, north and north-east of Ypres; the 1/5th was in support and the 1/7th in Divisional Reserve in Coppernolle. The 9th Battalion (in the Dardanelles) was occupying a precarious position in Suvla Bay: the 10th Battalion held the front line south-east of Dead Dog Farm in the St. Eloi Sector, south of Ypres. The 11th Battalion was in the trenches in the Bois Grenier Sector, south of Armentières. Only one Battalion—the 12th—was not in a front-line sector and that Battalion on 1st October was marching (in Division) from Rely to Thiennes *en route* for Hazebrouck area where the 21st Division had been ordered to refit and recuperate.

ALL BATTALIONS.

After the Battle of Loos and the subsequent Actions of the Hohenzollern Redoubt, the general situation was one of preparation for the next offensive. Although a considerable portion of the enemy's line between the La Bassée Canal and Lens had been captured the intentions of the Allied Commanders had not been realized—the enemy had re-established his line. The Battle had also brought into prominence the absolute necessity of training the New Armies in actual warfare before further operations on a large scale could be undertaken. Their Home training was as good as could be expected, but it lacked the essential experience in front-line fighting. Moreover, training in the conduct of operations involving the handling of large numbers of Divisions was necessary amongst the Staff. This had been amply demonstrated at Loos, when night fell on the 25th September, for liaison work had gone to pieces during the Battle; there were Battalions out of touch with their Brigade Head Quarters and Brigades out of touch with Divisional Headquarters whilst, in some instances, communication between Divisions and Corps broke down completely. Lack of experience in the handling of enormous forces of men was general amongst both the Allied Armies and the Armies of the Central Powers : but more especially in the British Army. Staff work during the Battle of Loos was very poor and there is no reason why it should not now be admitted. No one was to blame, for the British Army, compared with the great conscript Armies of the Continental Powers, was in pre-War days but a small force, though very highly trained and perfect in discipline. The immediate need, therefore, was to train the new troops and the Staff, and with this idea preparations were made after Loos to fit the British Army on the Western Front for the coming operations of 1916.

Rumours were afloat of a German offensive at Verdun, but it did not materialize during 1915.

The Battle of Loos will, however, always be remembered as the first operation on a large scale in which the Allied Armies co-operated after the line from Alsace to the North Sea became stabilized in 1914.

With their comrades the various Battalions of the West Yorkshire Regt. began early in October to settle down to a period of trench-warfare, spending their periodical " rests " out of the line in hard training and in fitting themselves for the next great battle which every one felt was coming, but (with the exception of General Headquarters) none knew the hour or day.

The 1st and 2nd Battalions of the Regiment were now seasoned warriors : they had been largely reinforced from the 3rd and 4th Reserve Battalions, kept behind in England. The 1/5th, 1/6th, 1/7th and 1/8th, being Territorial Troops, their pre-war training had taught them much which the 9th, 10th, 11th and 12th, being New Army Battalions, had to learn. Moreover, trench warfare was yet in its infancy, for the Mills Hand-Grenade had not as yet been issued to the troops, the anti-gas apparatus was still in its experimental stages and raids on the enemy's trenches were not the scientifically prepared operations they assumed at later periods ; while by far the most important thing of all—an intelligent use of the rifle had yet to be mastered by the new troops. And all these things had to be taught and learned in the midst of conditions which defy adequate description. Only the 1st and 2nd Battalions had so far spent a winter in the trenches, the remaining Battalions had yet to drink the cup of bitter agony: to know the awfulness of days and nights spent in the midst of mud and filth, the while the enemy's shells, rifle and machine-gun bullets took toll of men and changed the face of peaceful earth to a hell of fury and a wilderness of desolation the like the world had never seen. To their everlasting glory let it be said that these new troops played well the part of British soldiers, maintained to the full the splendid traditions of that grand old Army which alas! had almost disappeared, leaving comparatively few survivors behind to impart its knowledge, its spirit, its discipline to those who came after, to " carry on."

It is not surprising, therefore, that the diaries of those Battalions, who were experiencing for the first time all the rigours of life in the trenches, should record in no uncertain tones their disgust at the havoc wrought by the inclement weather and the advent of winter.

South of Armentières, the 2nd and 11th Battalions were in normally quiet sectors, where the enemy seemed bent upon improving his position and preparing for the winter, rather than in waging constant and worrying trench-warfare upon opponents whose retaliatory measures had already begun to inspire him with wholesome dread.

But in the Ypres Salient there was no peace. At all times of the day and night shells shrieked overhead, machine-gun and rifle bullets and trench-mortar bombs whizzed through the air: and Death stalked grimly along the front-lines, through the communication trenches and even in the " rest " area about Poperinghe.

Men of the 49th Division especially, never forgot their first view of the Town of Ypres—that of a flaming mass of battered wood, stone and masonry. And that first impression was not belied in all the weary months the Division spent in the Salient.

In October, 1915, the 49th Division held the extreme flank of the British Army in France and Flanders, having on its left French troops and on its right the 6th Division. The boundary line between the left flank of the Division and the French troops was very close to the enemy's trenches and was a most unsavoury spot. It was thus described by an officer of the 1/6th Battalion West Yorks. Regt., which Battalion had taken over the Pilkem trenches (as they were called) on the 20th September: " This sector was probably the most dangerous on the front: some of the trenches had been captured from the Germans in July and were in a very broken-up condition. For three

1/6TH BATTALION.

weeks the Battalion remained in this sector with the exception of two short periods of five days each in support. Owing to the discomforts of the line, reliefs were carried out every four instead of every six days, and were often extremely unpleasant and dangerous. With ominous accuracy the enemy seemed to time his bombardment with the hour of relief. . . On the extreme left of the Pilkem sector was the International Trench, where our men were within twenty to thirty yards of the enemy, and where outposts passed some anxious hours. In many ways trenches so close to the enemy had compensations. There was an entire freedom from artillery fire, as no gunner, English or German, would risk killing his own men. Heavy trench-mortar fire, was also absent as there was not sufficient margin of safety. But bombs were so easily lobbed over at that convenient range of twenty yards that during bombing " stunts " the trenches became intolerable and casualties certain. The German bombs at this time were better made than ours, and they had a more plentiful supply. Our Mills Hand-Grenades were not yet in use, and we had to rely on the " Gas-Pipe " bomb, French " Pear " bombs, and Hale's Hand-Grenades—less serviceable and more dangerous to use. At night, the tension, was extreme, as a distance of thirty yards was rushed in as many seconds. Wiring was of course impossible at such proximity to the enemy, and rudely made *chevaux de frise* were pushed out from the trenches over the parapet. . . The enemy took nothing lying down, and invariably retaliated if one of our platoons became demonstrative, very often an innocent platoon which had arrived just in time to receive the reward of their comrades' pugnacity. If we sniped a German we were certain to receive a shower of rifle-grenades or bombs to remind us someone " over yonder " had noticed our little effort. No quietness, no time for sleep, even if one could sleep in trenches without dug-outs, up to the knees in water, where hot food was impossible and where drinking water was often taken from the shell-holes and was powerfully dosed with chloride of lime."

1/6TH BATTALION.

4TH OCT.

It is clear from the diaries of the Division that the bad weather had already set in when October began, for on the 4th one diarist records " Trenches collapsing in many places." On this date also there was considerable liveliness along the Divisional front. The enemy's activity seems to have been directed principally against the 1/6th West Yorkshires in the Pilkem Trenches. A German bombing party of eight men engaged the bombers of the left Company of the Battalion and a regular duel ensued. The enemy also fired a number of large trench-mortar bombs (known as "Rum jars") which fell behind the front-line trenches. The Yorkshiremen thereupon signalled to the gunners, who opened "retaliation" fire with field guns and howitzers. No infantry attacks followed, and eventually the situation quieted down. Again on the 11th and 12th of October bombing duels took place. On the former date the enemy began hurling grenades into the Yorkshiremen's trenches just after midnight, but on this occasion the latter throwing two bombs to one, soon forced the enemy to cease fire. At 12 noon, the enemy opened fire with light and heavy trench mortars, until he was again silenced by rifle grenades and trench mortar bombs. "Bombing duel between our left Company and enemy" records the Battalion Diary, "we got the upper hand and silenced the enemy's bombers."

These little affairs were typical of the continuous warfare at all times in the Salient.

On the 14th the 146th Infantry Brigade, *i.e.*, the four West Yorkshire Battalions, of the 49th Division moved back to Coppernolle, into Divisional Reserve. On the 27th, His Majesty the King inspected troops in the Salient, all Divisions of the VIth Corps sending representative parties to the parade.

14TH OCT.

Just south of the 49th Division, the 1st Battalion West Yorks. R. (6th Division) on the 1st October was in support along the Canal Bank with one Company in the Potijze Defended Post. A few days later the trenches on the southern side of the Potijze Road, which the Battalion had taken over from the Leinsters, was heavily bombarded and three other ranks were killed and sixteen wounded. During October the casualties of the Battalion were one officer wounded, twelve other ranks killed and forty-six wounded.

1ST BATTALION.

Changes in the formation of the 6th Division and 18th Infantry Brigade took place during the month. The 17th Infantry Brigade, which had landed in France in 1914 with the Division, was replaced by the 71st Brigade from the 24th Division : the Sherwood Foresters of the 18th Brigade were transferred to the 71st Brigade and were replaced by the 11th Essex Regiment. These changes were in accordance with orders which had been issued to brigade battalions of the New Army with troops of the old Army, and for Brigades of the former to be exchanged into and with similar formations of the Divisions of the Army which had formed the original British Expeditionary Force.

The months of October and November and the early part of December passed without any operations of an important nature taking place between the La Bassée Canal and Armentières, and the latter place and the northern flanks of the Ypres Salient. South of the La Bassée Canal, however, during October, the Hohenzollern Redoubt was the scene of bitter fighting, but it was localized, and it was not until December that the diaries of the West Yorkshire Battalions contain anything abnormal.

It was, however, during this period of comparative inaction that the West Yorkshire Regt. won its first Victoria Cross.[1] The coveted honour was gained by a young Territorial Corporal of B Company of the 1/6th Battalion, 49th Division—Corporal S. Meekosha. On November 19th a party of about twenty N. C. O.'s and men were holding an isolated section of trench at The Pump Room, when the enemy suddenly put down one of his violent bombardments. Six of the platoon were killed and seven wounded, while all the remainder were more or less buried. When all the senior N. C. O.'s had been either killed or wounded, Corporal Meekosha at once took command, sent a runner for assistance and in spite of no less than ten more big shells falling within twenty yards of him, continued to dig out the wounded and killed men in full view of the enemy, and at close range from the German trenches. By his promptitude and magnificent courage and determination he saved at least four lives.

On the 19th December a gas attack of a violent nature was launched by the enemy in the Ypres Salient. The attack was preceded on the 17th by a particularly heavy bombardment, but the 18th was a quiet day, and at nightfall there was an ominous stillness across No Man's Land.

The 49th Division seems to have suffered most, for the 6th Division on the right had comparatively few casualties.

At midnight on the 18th/19th December, the 146th Infantry Brigade was disposed in the following positions : the 1/5th Battalion West Yorkshires, the right-front battalion of the 49th Division, held D. 19—D. 20, with A Company on the Canal Bank, B Company in the Pump Room and Clifford's Tower, C Company at La Belle Alliance, and D Company in the front-line trenches—D. 19—D. 20 : the 1/6th Battalion was on the immediate left of the 1/5th and held sectors D. 21—D. 23 : the 1/7th was in support, and the 1/8th in Divisional Reserve.

The 1st Battalion West Yorkshires (6th Division) was in support on the Canal Bank and the Diary of the 1/5th Battalion records the fact that their comrades of the Regular Army were beside them

[1] *London Gazette*, 22nd Jan., 1916.

during the early hours of the morning when the gas clouds floated across No Man's Land, and throughout the remainder of the day.

Since the enemy had first used asphyxiating gas on April 22nd, all troops in the front line had been ordered to watch closely the direction of the wind, and for any signs which might denote an impending gas attack. And for some days before the 19th December, there had been certain indications that such an attack would be launched at no distant date. But great improvements had been made in anti-gas apparatus, and whereas after the initial attack in the Spring, improvised masks saturated with a comparatively weak concentration of pure chlorine had been used, the new " P.H." mask had now been issued to the men, providing protection not only against chlorine, but phosgene also.

The issue of these new masks gave rise to an amusing story :

A certain G.O.C. asked one of his Battalion Commanders if all the latter's men had masks, and on being told they had, the General said he would go round the line on the following morning and inspect the men.

The next morning the G.O.C. followed by the Battalion Commander entered the front-line trenches, and asked the first man he met if he had his respirator.

" No, Sir," replied the man.

The General, annoyed, turned to the next man and addressed a similar question to him, receiving a similar reply.

Very angry, the G.O.C. turned to the Battalion Commander : " I thought you said all your men had respirators ? " Now as the Battalion Commander on the previous day had inspected every man's mask he was extremely puzzled, and was about to reply when a sergeant standing near saluting, suggested he should ask the men.

" Yes ! of course," replied the General. Whereupon the sergeant turned to the men : " 'Ave yer got yer muzzles," he said in a contemptuous tone, to which the men replied : " Yus ! " It is not recorded what the General said as he continued his inspection.

As already stated, two days previous to the gas attack on the 19th, the enemy's bombardment was unusually heavy. All along the line the trenches were badly damaged and shelters blown in. An officer's dug-out in the sector held by the 1/6th Battalion was demolished and two officers wounded. A platoon of C Company of the same Battalion was reduced to seven men, and rows of front-line trenches very soon resembled a series of shell holes. The 18th was a quiet day, hardly a shell was fired : " The enemy's artillery was not

1/5TH BATTALIONS.

so active," said the diary of the 1/5th Battalion. "Seeing that the day has been fine, it is somewhat unusual."

When night fell an eerie stillness charged the atmosphere with that sense of coming danger so often experienced on the battlefield. An ominous silence across No Man's Land, a sudden change in the direction of the wind to N.E., and warnings from prisoners that at the first opportunity the enemy intended "gassing" the British front lines, turned suspicion to certainty, and all ranks were ordered to be prepared, gas masks were examined and kept ready at hand.

19TH DEC.

Throughout the night nothing untoward happened, both sides were apparently hard at work repairing trenches. No Verey lights burst in the air and to all intents and purposes everything was normal. But suddenly in the early hours of the 19th, red lights flared out in the dark skies, and a terrifying hiss was heard from across No Man's Land.

1/5TH BATTALION.

"About 4-50 a.m. the sentries in D.20 heard a shout which was immediately followed by the firing of coloured rockets, all along the German line. These seemed to be the signal for the gas to be turned on, for the hiss of escaping gas was heard most distinctly, and as a dense white vapour it was soon blown across to our own trenches by the prevailing N.E. wind. Warning was at once sent to Headquarters by telephone and by runners, and this message was the only one that was got through by wire from D.20, as the terrific bombardment delivered by the Germans immediately after the gas had got into our trenches, cut the wire. In D.19 and 20, as well as at The Willows, prompt measures were taken to meet the gas which got to Headquarters at La Belle Alliance by 5-15 a.m. Communication was kept up with Brigade Headquarters throughout the attack which lasted about an hour, but the Company on the Canal Bank was cut off immediately notification had been got through to them. The enemy did not take any advantage of the gas, for beyond three small parties which were caught between the lines by our machine-guns and rifle fire, no advance was made by the Germans, who kept up a heavy bombardment all day. This shelling was responded to by our own guns and considerable damage was done to the enemy's front trenches.

"Over eighty casualties were reported at night, chiefly gassing, and some fine work was done by stretcher-bearers and others in bringing them in. Owing to serious effect of the gas upon officers and men of C Company, the ordinary relief was altered. C Company went to Canal Bank, A Company to D.19 and 20, and D Company was brought to La Belle Alliance. This relief and the removal of the

An Outpost in front of our Line in the Ypres Salient.

casualties to the Dressing Station on the Canal Bank was carried out under great difficulties, for the whole area was heavily shelled. Lieut. Walker after being gassed at La Belle Alliance, so far recovered as to enable him to go with his Company to Canal Bank, where he was killed, as he sat in his dug-out, by a shell. Captain Lansdale and Second Lieut. Griffiths and Second Lieut. Casebourne, were also sent to Hospital."[1]

The casualties of the 1/6th Battalion were about 100, of which eighteen were killed by shell-fire. The Battalion Diary contains only a very brief account of the gas attack, but a private account (from which the following quotation is taken) shows something of what happened along the front of the Battalion: "Gas was hurled over in bombs and shells of all calibres, in addition to the cylinders. In Brigade Headquarters two miles from the front line, on the Canal Bank, the message was put through to the Division only one minute before all signal lines were down under the heavy shelling. The Canal Bank was bombarded heavily, and the 1/7th Battalion, ordered to move from Elverdinghe up to close support near Bridge 4, was fortunate to escape without many casualties. Thanks to the promptitude of the Staffs concerned, our guns got to work almost immediately, and as a good supply of ammunition was available they made a magnificent field day of it. The French 75s.[2] joined in and swept the German parapets with a hail of shells which gladdened the heart of every Tommy in the front line, who was firing his rifle till the barrel was almost red hot. The enemy gas shelling began in earnest about half-an-hour after the cylinder gas was let off, and the shower of these deadly shells coming through the darkness like rockets and exploding with a dull splash added a new horror to the scene. Men in some cases were gassed by them before they had realized what kind of shells they were, or had adjusted their helmets. Everyone stuck to his post, however. There were no stragglers that day from the 49th Division. Instead of the enemy finding a trench full of the gassed and dead, and a clear way to the Canal, he was checkmated before he left his own trenches, and a few enemy parties who got on to their parapets melted away before the storm of our bullets and shells. The cylinder gas came over for about forty or fifty minutes, and the concentrated enemy bombardment lasted about an hour. At 7 a.m. all was comparatively quiet and remained so till 2-30 p.m., when a

[1] Diary of the 1/5th Bn. West Yorkshire Regt.
[2] On the left of the 49th Division.

heavy bombardment with H.E.'s began and continued intermittently till 3 a.m. next morning. By that time, however, the Battalion had been relieved by the 1/7th West Yorkshires and had moved to support on the Canal Bank. Throughout that night the sky was one great glare like a vast electric light, and the atmosphere was laden with a choking, sickly heaviness."[1]

1/7TH BATTALION.

In moving up to the relief of the 1/6th Battalion the 1/7th had marvellous good luck, for not a single shell fell on the road the Battalion passed along, in spite of the fact that two hostile observation balloons and four enemy aeroplanes were " up " at the time. The ground mist mercifully shielded the men from the enemy's observers. The 2nd Sherwood Foresters and a Battalion of York and Lancs. Regt. marching a little later along the same road were heavily shelled and suffered many casualties: the mist had lifted.

The splendid spirit of the troops had averted disaster: " Not a single man moved back," said a battalion diary, " and the general request from the men to their officers was to be allowed to go forward. It seems a pity that the German infantry did not come forward to get what was ready for them."

Thus, so far as the 49th Division was concerned, ended the heaviest gas attack experienced by the troops of the Division.

Along the front of the 18th Infantry Brigade, 6th Division (on the right of the 49th), most of the gas floated down from the north and was not discharged from opposite the Brigade. The 1st Battalion West Yorks R.was on the Canal Bank, and "stood to" during the attack which was felt far behind the front line trenches. At 7 a.m. the Battalion, under orders, sent B Company to the Ramparts near the Menin Gate, and A Company to the Reserve Trenches, Kaaie Salient. The former Company had eleven casualties during the move, but only two men of A were knocked out. At about 10 a.m. B Company was withdrawn from the Menin Gate and returned to the Canal Bank. During the evening Ypres and all its defences were heavily shelled and two dug-outs of D Company were blown in —eighteen men becoming casualties. During the 19th, the 1st Battalion lost eleven other ranks killed and twenty-five wounded, and several men suffering from gas poisoning.

1ST BATTALION.

The German gas attack of the 19th December was exceptionally heavy, and though it is doubtful whether (as some authorities asserted) it was the strongest concentration of phosgene cylinder gas used by the enemy during the whole war, some idea of its virulence may be

[1] Captain E. V. Tempest, D.S.O., M.C.

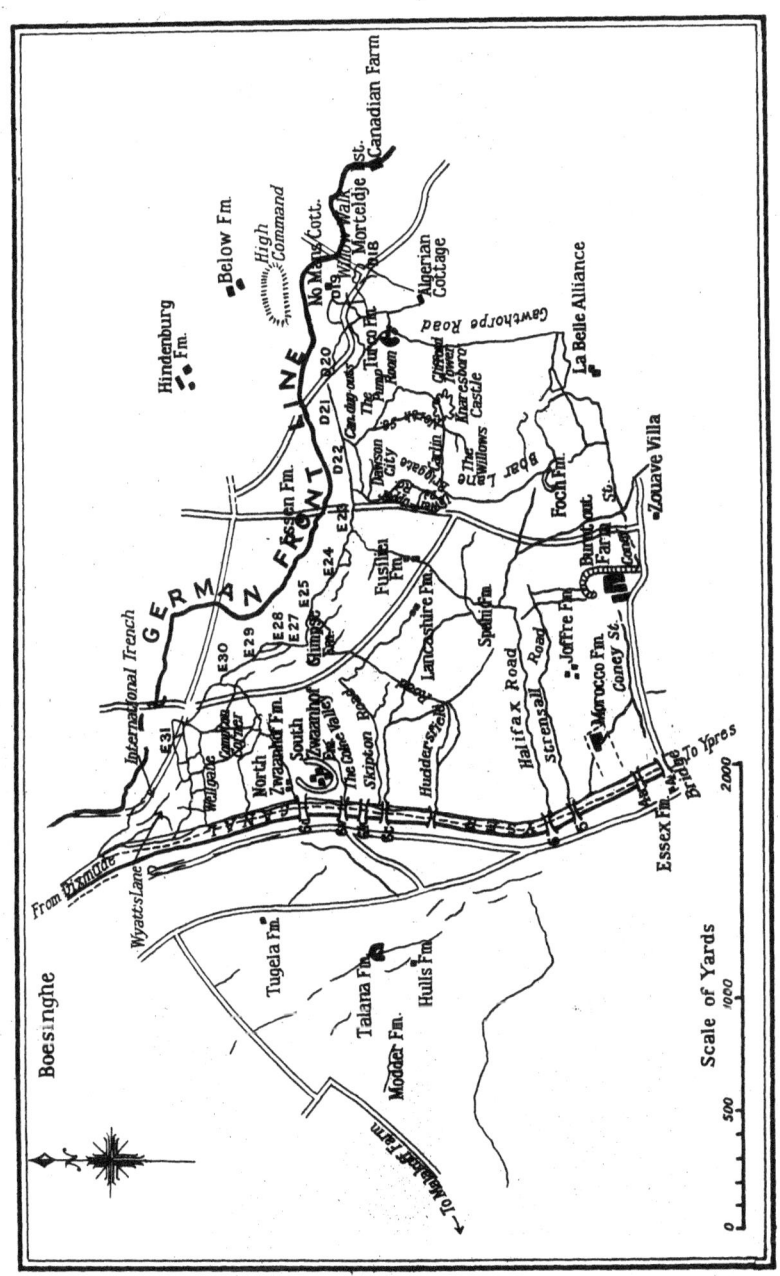

LINE HELD BY THE 49TH DIVISION, WINTER, 1915-1916.

gathered from the fact that Canadians on parade at Bailleul, twelve miles away, felt the effects. Nevertheless, it was a failure, and not a yard of ground was lost by the gallant fellows who held the Ypres Salient.

The two other Battalion of the West Yorkshire Regt.—the 10th and 12th—in the Salient, were not seriously affected by the gas attack.

10TH BATTALION.

The 10th Battalion (17th Division) had moved up to the Hooge Sector towards the end of October and at once began to experience the terrible conditions prevailing in the front line : " The trenches taken over were in a very bad condition. They had all suffered heavily from both our own and the enemy's shell fire during the fighting between the end of July and the 25th September. Several trenches had been entirely destroyed and in the support and reserve lines it had not been possible to reconstruct them. North of the Menin Road the trenches varied from 80-20 yards distant from the enemy's front trenches. The large crater blown up on June 10th, when the 3rd Division attacked, is 80 feet across and 40 deep. The inside has been constantly shelled and some hundreds of men are buried in it. On the line south of the Menin Road there is a gap of 200 feet between C.1 and C.3 trenches. It has never been possible to reconstruct the intervening trench C.2 as it is constantly destroyed by enemy shell fire. Zouave Wood is a mass of debris and broken trees. The enemy opposite are Wurtemburgers and regiments from Alsace. They appear to have little enterprise, but the whole line is subjected to enfilade fire and north of the Menin Road to reserve hostile gun fire."[1]

1ST NOV.

On 1st November, the Battalion was relieved by the 6th Dorsets and marched back to the Rest Camp, where several days were spent in cleaning up and in training. The remainder of the month was spent by the Battalion alternately in the front-line trenches at Hooge, on the Ypres Ramparts, and in the Rest Camp, York Huts and Dragon Huts. Casualties were not heavy, but the conditions under which the men existed and carried on their work, were appalling. " Up to the waist in water," reported the Battalion Diary on the 10th. And from the sounds of pumping and splashing about across No Man's Land, it was evident that the enemy's trenches were in no better condition. To know this was grim satisfaction to the British troops ; it certainly helped to keep them cheerful, for they had much of this sort of life before them. From the 1st to 10th December, the

10TH BATTALION.

---

[1] Diary of 50th Infantry Brigade, 17th Division.

Battalion (in Brigade) was in Divisional Reserve in York Huts, moving during the evening of the latter date back again to the Hooge trenches. The Yorkshiremen were relieved on the 14th, and when the German gas attack was launched were in Busseboom Camp, where the Battalion stood to arms all day.

14TH DEC.

On the 28th December a small bombing duel took place between the enemy and the West Yorkshiremen, who had moved back into the front line on the 26th. During the night the enemy was heard getting out of his trenches opposite Hooge. A patrol went out under Second-Lieut. Smith, 10th West Yorkshires, and a fight ensued between the two parties. Three times the enemy attacked Lieut. Smith and his men, but each time was driven off. The trench mortars, both of the 50th and 51st Brigades, then joined in and plastered the enemy's trenches with bombs, badly damaging them. The patrol returned safely after a reconnaissance of the enemy's wire had been made.

12TH BATTALION.

The 12th Battalion, since the Battle of Loos, had been reorganized. From Rely, it had marched (in Brigade) by successive stages *via* Thiennes, Borre, Strazeele and Bailleul to Armentières. *En route*, the Battalion was reinforced by officers and men from the 3rd Reserve Battalion in England. Armentières was reached about 7 p.m. on the 25th October. Here the Battalion billeted and remained training and gaining experience in trench warfare in the front line held by the 150th Infantry Brigade of the 50th Division. The 1st November still found the Battalion billeted in Armentières. On the 3rd, Lieut.-Col. C. H. Campbell (Queen's Own Cameron Highlanders) arrived and assumed command of the Battalion. Eight days later, Colonel Campbell was informed that his Battalion would be transferred on the 21st to the 3rd Division, in accordance with the new scheme under which units of Kitchener's Army were to be interchanged with units of the old Regular Army.

1ST NOV.

The Battalion marched out of Armentières on the 15th, arriving at Bailleul at 12 noon. The following morning the Battalion was again on the march to join the 9th Infantry Brigade (Brigadier-General W. Douglas Smith) of the 3rd Division, then at Winnezeele. At 2-30 p.m. the West Yorkshiremen marched into the village and went into billets.

Their new comrades of the 9th Brigade were the 1st Northumberland Fusiliers, 4th Royal Fusiliers, 1st Royal Scots and 10th Liverpool Scottish; thus the 12th West Yorkshires formed the fifth battalion of the Brigade. Three days later, the G.O.C., Major-General Haldane, inspected the Battalion.

Early on the morning of the 21st, the 12th West Yorkshires moved to Poperinghe, arriving at 3 p.m. Another march on the 22nd brought the Battalion to Dickebusch, where the West Yorkshiremen remained in Brigade Reserve, the 9th Brigade having relieved the 72nd Brigade of the 24th Division in the St. Eloi Sector—a section of the line running approximately from just north-east of Triangular Wood, south-west to where the Diependaalbeek cut across the British lines. A few days later the Brigade was relieved and with the Liverpool Scottish and the Royal Scots the West Yorkshiremen marched to Reninghelst, the two remaining Battalions of the 9th going on to Poperinghe. A drenching rain was falling and the going very heavy, and the 12th West Yorkshires reached their Camp, very done, but cheerful. " This Camp can at present be best described as tents and a few wooden huts, eking out a miserable existence in a sea of mud."[1]

All ranks set to work immediately to try and make the Camp habitable, as the weather conditions prevented adequate training being carried out: it is impossible to drill troops in a sea of mud ! So the best had to be made of the prevailing conditions.

On the 6th December, the 9th Brigade moved south-west again, 6TH DEC. relieving the 8th Brigade in the front line trenches. During this tour (from the 7th to the 13th) the enemy was comparatively quiet, which, considering the amount of work to be carried out in front of, and on the parapets, was fortunate. Two officers were wounded during this tour—Lieut. I. Gorbutt (badly wounded when returning from patrol work) and Second-Lieut. H. M. Cook, who was hit by a shell splinter when in the support trenches. One other rank was killed and five wounded.

By the end of December the Battalion had vastly improved (by hard training in the hardest school of all—experience) in its knowledge of trench warfare. The officers had greatly benefited from courses at the Second Army School and 3rd Divisional Grenade School at Terdeghem and Reninghelst, whilst the courses of instruction given at the Officers' School at Poperinghe were extremely helpful.

Little more than a few weeks had passed since the 11th Battalion 11TH West Yorkshires, with the 23rd Division, had landed in France, and, BATTALION. when towards the end of September, the Division took over the Bois Grenier Sector the winter had not properly set in, though heavy rains had begun to turn the trenches into mud alleys. In this

[1] Diary, 12th Bn. West Yorkshire Regt.

particular sector of the line, the enemy was not very active and the West Yorkshiremen, new to trench warfare, had little difficulty in pursuing their training and initiation into the actualties of the somewhat theoretical instruction imparted to them in England. Shelling and trench-mortar activity was sporadic. Working parties of both sides, who at night carried on their dangerous duties out in No Man's Land, afforded targets for the machine-gunners and snipers, but, speaking generally or rather comparatively, the days and nights passed quietly. The constant unrest, heavy shelling, the ceaseless bombing and almost continuous crackle of rifles and " tack-tack-tack " of machine-guns, which went on in the Ypres Salient was practically unknown in this sector south of Armentières. The months of October, November and December thus slipped away and although the trenches were deep in mud and water and the conditions far from inviting, casualties were light and the enemy made no attacks. The Battalion lost only three other ranks killed and thirteen wounded in November, and seven other ranks wounded during December. Billeting areas, when out of the line, were generally in the Rue de Lattrée or Fort Rompu.

On the 19th December, 1915, Sir John French handed over Command of the British Forces in France and Flanders to Sir Douglas Haig, and returned to England.

2ND BATTALION.

Until the last week in November, the 8th Division held the Sector immediately on the right of the 23rd Division : thus the 2nd Battalion West Yorkshires were very close to their comrades of the 12th Battalion. In this sector of the line also comparative quietude reigned. The trenches best known to the 2nd Battalion during this period were those between Mine Avenue and the Convent Wall. The trenches here grew more unbearable as the winter advanced ; falling parapets and blocked communication trenches are frequently referred to in the Battalion Diaries : the rest can be better imagined than described.

19TH Nov.

The Battalion, however, was in luck's way, for on the 19th November, it moved out of the front line into Brigade Reserve, and on the 23rd, the 23rd Infantry Brigade passed into Divisional Reserve. On the following day the whole Division moved out of the line into Corps Reserve between Vieux Berquin and Sec Bois, *en route* for Morbecque. From the 1st to the 19th December the Battalion (in Division) was in training, and resting, and on the 20th took part in First Army Divisional exercises, marching *via* Sercus, Lynde-Wardrecques to billets in Ecques. Early the following morning a

20TH DEC.

march towards Thérouanne and Radinghem was begun with the 2nd West Yorkshires as advanced guard, the latter place being reached about 6 p.m., when the West Yorkshiremen went into billets for the night. The return to Morbecques *via* Matringhem and Blaringhem was accomplished in less than a two days' march, the Battalion going into billets in the town at twelve noon on the 23rd December. These marching exercises were extremely beneficial to the troops, for, after protracted periods in the trenches, a good healthy march worked wonders. At first foot troubles were frequent, and the continued marching was very fatiguing, but recovery was speedy and combined with the relief from the hazardous and trying life in the front line, the spirits of the men rose rapidly. During the three days' manœuvres from 20th to the 23rd, although the troops on the 22nd marched twenty-one miles, the diary of the 2nd Battalion records (with pardonable pride) that " no man fell out on the line of march "—a very creditable performance.

From the 24th to the 31st, the 8th Division remained in the Morbecques area, training hard. It was the longest period the 2nd Battalion West Yorks. R. had had out of the line since it arrived in France in September, 1914.

THE DARDANELLES.

TRENCH WARFARE AT SUVLA AND THE EVACUATION

19th—20th December, 1915

BY the 1st September, the situation at Suvla Bay, had assumed the character of a stalemate. Without reinforcements (or of such a nature as to be almost negligible) and little ammunition, it was impossible to do anything more than consolidate the position won and nibble away at the enemy's front line, in the hope of gradually pressing him back and taking his positions further south, in rear.

The severe nature of the casualties suffered by the original landing force now began to make itself felt. On the 1st September, the whole of the 32nd Infantry Brigade (11th Division) could muster only nineteen officers and 1163 other ranks. To this number the 9th Battalion West Yorks. R. could contribute only four officers and 185 other ranks.

1ST SEPT.

9TH BATTALION.

After the attacks of the 27th and 29th August, trench warfare set in. The 32nd Brigade held the left sub-sector of the Suvla Bay defences. The right of the Brigade was on a pathway just below Jephson's Post and the left on the seashore at 135 N.6. : the 9th West Yorkshires were in support when September opened, digging dug-outs and generally improving the position which, as will be seen from the following description, was no sinecure : " During the last few days the infantry of the (11th) Division has been engaged in establishing itself in its new position on the left of the IXth Corps, the extreme left resting on the Gulf of Saros. The position lies on both sides of a steep rocky ridge, part of which was occupied on the 7th August by the 11th Manchester Regt.—Karakol Dagh and Kiretch Tepe Sirt. The highest part of the Ridge, known as Jephson's Post, lies about fifty yards west of the Bench Mark on our maps. The right sector of the line extends from the left of the 29th Division at 135.z.5. to Jephson's Post inclusive : the left sector runs almost due north to the sea. The Turks at present hold the Bench Mark and the eastern peak of the ridge known as The Pimple. To the south their position runs from the Bench Mark about parallel to our own : on the north there is no extension to the sea and the

9TH BATTALION.

line appears to be drawn back along the crest to The Pimple. From the high ground to the east, as well as from The Pimple, the enemy can overlook all our movements, and can make our position very uncomfortable. For this reason it is important that the 11th Division should gain complete possession of the Kiritch Tepe Sirt as soon as possible. At present (1st September) it is not in a condition to do so. Losses have been heavy, especially in officers. Reinforcements are badly needed and time to reorganize is required. At present Brigades consist of two amalgamated battalions only.

"Meanwhile efforts are being made to improve our communications with the beach (at present all rations and water are carried up by hand) and to fixing and developing our wire, water supply, sinking wells, etc. All this work, in addition to work in the trenches is very heavy, makes great demands upon the men who are already rather run down as the result of their recent exertions, and sickness—chiefly diarrhœa, in a more or less aggravated form, is very prevalent. In the front line the G.O.C. intends to push his left forward as far as possible along the sea so as to bring us more or less parallel to the Bench Mark—Pimple line. When this is done, battalions brought approximately up to strength and communications developed, we may again be in a position to assume the offensive. A beginning has already been made by the nightly patrol to the Green Knoll."[1]

One of the most demoralizing things in trench warfare is the knowledge that your position is overlooked by the enemy, and as the patrol reports stated, with the exception of Jephson's Post on a line with the Bench Mark, the Turkish positions were situated on higher ground than the British trenches. The remedy lay partly in making deeply-dug trenches and dug-outs : also in effective artillery fire.

So, to the digging of deep trenches and dug-outs the troops turned their attention, whilst at night patrols went out towards the enemy's positions and generally found him engaged in similar work, for the Turk was none too sure of himself, even though he had German officers to direct him. Snipers were the greatest danger and claimed many victims. The cunning Turk was especially good at this kind of warfare and his disguises were many and effective.

2ND SEPT.

Late in the evening of the 2nd September, the enemy opened fire with his artillery on Jephson's Post (32nd Infantry Brigade) and the trenches running to the south of it, held by the 33rd Infantry Brigade. This was followed first by heavy rifle fire and later by a

[1] G. S. Diary, 11th Division.

half-hearted infantry attack on the right sub-sector. But it was swept away and not a Turk reached the British trenches. Two destroyers, out at sea, flashed a search-light on to the enemy's trenches and a few well-directed shells reduced him to silence. Heavy sniping on both sides, followed this abortive attack, until 8-45 p.m., when all was again quiet.

9TH BATTALION.

The 34th Infantry Brigade relieved the 32nd Brigade on the 4th, and the West Yorkshiremen (in Brigade) marched back down the slopes of the Hill to the Rest Camp. On the 7th, the G.O.C. Division inspected the Battalion and on the same day a draft of ninety-eight N.C.O.'s and men arrived from England. For eight days the Battalion was "resting" on the beach, but on the 12th moved back again into the line on the right of Jephson's Post, relieving the 6th Lincolns. The remainder of the month was spent similarly. On the 22nd September, Major R. Isacke, 3rd West Yorks. Regt. arrived and assumed command of the 9th Battalion, which owing to the arrival of more reinforcements gradually increased in numbers until by the 30th, all four Companies had been re-formed with a total strength of nineteen officers and 824 other ranks.

22ND SEPT.

A new Brigadier—Brigadier-General A. C. Dallas—had also arrived during the month to command the 32nd Infantry Brigade.

Casualties, killed, wounded and missing, were light, the 9th West Yorkshires losing only two other ranks killed and twelve wounded for the whole month. But against this small number there were seventy-one cases of sickness in the Battalion: sick cases in all battalions far out-numbering the casualties inflicted by the enemy.

The hard work, the training in trench warfare, the constant vigilance necessary, and above all, the gradual acclimatization of the troops to the peculiar conditions of the Gallipoli Peninsula had improved the troops out of all semblance to the somewhat raw battalions which had landed at Suvla, on August 7th, and on the days following. "The 11th Division promises to be as fine a unit as any in the Army, once they get their gaps filled in," said the Commander-in-Chief, Sir Ian Hamilton, in the middle of September. As in many other gallant battalions the gaps in the ranks of the 9th West Yorks. Regt. were filled, but no more, for reinforcements stopped early in October; the disastrous policy of evacuation had begun to fill the minds of all but the gallant fellows on the spot.

Little more remains to be told. The diary of the 9th West Yorkshires for October contains few variations from the words

9TH BATTALION.

"Nothing of importance." Of discomfort there was much, but it was no more intense than in France or Flanders. If sickness, the activities of snipers and enemy shells took toll of the brave troops who held the slopes of the bare rugged hills of Gallipoli, were not similar conditions, many times intensified, being suffered *for the second winter* along the Western Front? Yet all these things were urged as reasons for evacuation. The strategical value of "holding" the Turks in Gallipoli seems to have been put aside as of no account.

Throughout October the ordinary routine of trench warfare was carried out under varying conditions. No infantry attacks were made either by the British or Turks. Snipers claimed many victims, but sickness was again responsible for the largest number of casualties.[1]

13TH OCT. On the 13th, an unlucky shell caused the death of Second-Lieut. P. R. Anderson, 9th West Yorkshires and one other rank, besides wounding thirteen more of the battalion. On the 17th Sir Ian Hamilton, the Commander-in-Chief handed over command of the Gallipoli Peninsula to Sir Charles Monro, and proceeded to England.

Strenuous work on the defences and the gradual pushing forward of posts marked the activities of the troops during November, for although the evacuation had already been decided upon the men had to be kept employed, as it was obviously necessary not to give the enemy an inkling of what was to happen. On the 11th November,

11TH NOV. Capt. A. M. Phillips was killed in Jephson's Post by shell fire. A heavy storm broke over the Peninsula on 26th November, damaging the trenches and causing great discomfort.[2]

Early in December, preparations were pushed forward to evacuate the Peninsula, and on the 18th, an advanced party of the 9th West Yorkshires, with other troops embarked on a lighter at 11-30 p.m., and were taken off to H.M.S. *Magnificent*, lying in Suvla Bay. The Battleship then set sail for Kephalos. On the following evening a second party of the 9th West Yorks. R. and other troops left the trenches stealthily, and marched down to West Beach, where they embarked at 10-30 p.m. on H.M.T.S. *Redbreast*.

The last party to leave Suvla was formed of A and C Companies of the West Yorkshires: "C Company held posts behind the 3rd Line of defence" said the Battalion diary, "and A Company, the Keep. This party being the last to leave Suvla. No casualties." But it

---

[1] Casualties of 9th West Yorkshires for October: one officer and ten other ranks killed, thirty-five other ranks wounded.

[2] Casualties during November were one officer and fourteen other ranks killed, twenty-nine other ranks wounded.

SUVLA BAY: THE AFTERNOON BEFORE THE EVACUATION, SHOWING STORES ACCUMULATED ON THE BEACH.

To face p. 154.

was not until 5-15 a.m. on the 20th that this last party embarked on "K" lighters and arrived at Kephalos at 8 a.m.

9TH BATTALION.

Thus ended a brilliantly conceived operation, fraught with great opportunities which were there for the taking, ended, alas! in failure. If there is such a thing as a glorious failure the Gallipoli Campaign must come under that heading. No troops in any theatre of War wherein British soldiers were to be found, displayed more valour or dogged perseverance under the most extraordinary difficulties than the gallant fellows who clung tenaciously to the fringe of the Gallipoli Peninsula. The evacuation was an altogether extraordinary performance, the many ruses adopted for deceiving the enemy being entirely successful.

After landing at Kephalos, the 9th Battalion West Yorks. R. spent the remainder of December on the Island, camped out in tents.

A NOTE ON THE SITUATION AT THE END OF THE YEAR 1915

IT is unnecessary, and indeed inexpedient, here to enter into a discussion of the cumulative effect of the operations by the Allies during 1915, but from the German point of view it is evident that the Battles of that year had seriously disorganized the enemy's plans. "We had been compelled to abandon our intentions " said the Chief of the German Imperial Staff (then von Falkenhyn) " of conducting the operations in the West in such a way that the French and English would lose all hope of changing the situation in their favour before France bled to death ....We had therefore been compelled, so far as the Western Theatre was concerned, to be satisfied with holding the line we had won."

But by the end of 1915 both the Allies and the enemy had formulated plans for the coming year. So far as the Allies were concerned their intentions for 1916 are summarized in Sir Douglas Haig's despatches dated 23rd December, 1916 : " The principle of an offensive campaign during the summer of 1916 had already been decided upon by all the Allies. The various possible alternatives on the Western Front had been studied and discussed by General Joffre and myself and we were in complete agreement as to the front to be attacked by the combined French and British Armies." And a footnote to the Despatch adds : " The choice of front for the Allied offensive was governed by the consideration that neither the French nor ourselves were at the moment deemed strong enough to undertake unaided an offensive on a really large scale. It was therefore necessary to deliver a combined attack."

The German plans, however, contained no intention of an attack upon the British, other than purely local actions of a small nature. For the enemy was under no delusion as to the fighting power and strength of Sir Douglas Haig's troops. In all enemy reports at this period it is interesting to note the constant reiteration of Great Britain as the principal foe. And it is not surprising to find von Falkenhyn in a report written at Christmas, 1915, saying : " We must equally discountenance any attempt to attack the British sector with comparatively inadequate means. We could only approve that course if we could give such an attack an objective within reasonable reach. *There is no such objective.* Our goal would have to be nothing less than to drive the English completely from the Continent and force the French behind the Somme. If that object at least were not attained, the attack would have been purposeless. But even if it is reached, our ultimate aim will not yet have been secured, because England may be trusted not to give up even then, and further, France herself would not have been very hard hit."

Of Great Britain's Allies, von Falkenhyn conceived that France had been weakened almost to the limit of military and economic endeavour, Russia, though not completely overthrown, had been so shattered that she could never recover her old strength, Serbia had been destroyed, and Italy deprived of her " Brigands' intentions " : only Great Britain stood in the way and for the moment she was too powerful to attack. What then remained to be done ? The answer is given by von Falkenhyn himself : " The upshot of this discussion is that the attempt to seek a decision by an attack on the English Front in the West cannot be recommended, though an opportunity of doing so may arise in a counter-attack. In view of our feelings for our arch enemy in this war that is certainly distressing, but it can be endured if we realize that for England the campaign on the Continent of Europe with her own troops is at bottom a side show. Her real weapons here are the French, Russian and Italian Armies. If we put these Armies out of the War, England is left to face us alone, and it is difficult to believe that in such circumstances her lust for our destruction would not fail her. It is true there would be no certainty that she would give up, but there is a strong probability."

So that was the enemy's intentions : to destroy utterly Great Britain's Allies in order that his " arch enemy," isolated, would be forced to capitulate. To that end France was to be attacked at Verdun, Russia left for the time to " stew in her own juice " for her " internal troubles will compel her to give in within a relatively short period." Italy was to be left to the Austro-Hungarian Army for she " is that one of our enemies whose internal conditions will soon make her further active participation in the war impossible, provided the Austro-Hungarian Army continues to do its duty at all."

That von Falkenhyn's extraordinary optimism in this report was totally at variance with the true facts is shown by the outcome of the operations which took place during the summer of 1916.

The front selected by Generals Joffre and French to be the scene of the operations of 1916 was south of Arras along the Somme. With that offensive in view a new British Army—the Fourth—was to be formed and for that purpose many divisions serving as far north as Ypres were to be withdrawn and sent south to take part in the great battle which had been planned. Thus it came about that early in the year 1916 various divisions were pulled out of the front line to refit and reorganize, and to perfect their training. Meanwhile, though some of the divisions were moved early down to the Somme area[1], trench warfare went on unceasingly and numerous local actions took place, which, from a Regimental point of view, cannot be overlooked.

---

[1] The 49th Division left Calais on the 1st February and on the 2nd reached Sailly-sur-Somme.

TRENCH WARFARE.
1st Jan.—31st March, 1916.
A MINOR ENTERPRISE.

1916

TRENCH WARFARE.
1st Jan.—31st March, 1916.

"AT 11 o'clock on the 31st, (German midnight) our guns gave the Germans ten minutes intense bombardment, and again when at midnight the New Year came in, to make sure of his getting our New Year Greetings."

* * * *

1ST JAN. On the 1st January, 1916, there were nine battalions of the West Yorkshire Regt. in France and Flanders, one at Kephalos (in the Mediterranean) withdrawn from the Gallipoli Peninsular, and three in Egypt. Of the two regular battalions the 1st. (Lieut.-Col. G. G. Lang) was in A.5., A.3., X.2 and X.3 trenches in the St. Jean's sector of the Ypres Salient: the 2nd Battalion (Lieut.-Col. Barrington) was resting and training in Brigade and Division in General Headquarter Reserve in the Morbecque—Blaringham area—the 8th Division being still out of the line when the New Year came in. The four first-line Territorial Battalions, 1/5th (Lieut.-Col. C. E. Wood), 1/6th (Lieut.-Col. G. W. Knowles), 1/7th (Lieut.-Col. A. E. Kirk) and 1/8th (Lieut.-Col. E. K. Clark). of the 146th Brigade, 49th Division were also in billets, the 1/5th and 1/7th in Wormhout, and the 1/6th and 1/8th in Houtkerque, the Division having been redrawn from the line to refit and train. The 9th (S) Battalion (Lieut.-Col. R. Isacke) with the 32nd Infantry Brigade of the 11th Division was still awaiting orders at Kephalos in the Mediterranean, after a strenuous period of five months on the Gallipoli Peninsular. The 10th (S) Battalion (Lieut.-Col. W. M. Edwards) saw the New Year in, in dug-outs at Kruissart, the 17th Division (in which it was contained) at this period holding the line south of Ypres. The 23rd Division was in the front line south of Armentières and here the 11th (S) Battalion (Lieut.-Col. F. W. Evatt) of the 69th Brigade were in trenches I. 26—5———1.20, 1 and 2 and 1.21, 1 and 2. The 12th (S) Battalion (Lieut.-Col. C. H. Campbell) contained in the 9th Infantry Brigade, 3rd Division was in " J " Camp, Reninghelst, resting, the Division being still in the St. Eloi Sector.

JANUARY.

Three more battalions, the 15th (Leeds Pals—Lieut.-Col. S. C. Taylor); the 16th (1st Bradford Pals—Lieut.-Col. W. M. Goodwyn) and the 18th (2nd Bradford Pals—Lieut.-Col. E. C. H. Kennard) of the 93rd Infantry Brigade, 31st Division were carrying out patrol and guard duties in Egypt along the Banks of the Suez Canal. Several more battalions were in training in England.

Although along the British front, the opening months of 1916 were bare of operations on a large scale the year was destined to be one of considerable importance and very heavy fighting. Sir Douglas Haig, who had succeeded Sir John French in Command of the British troops in France and Flanders, on 19th December, 1915, said in his first despatch dated 19th May, 1916: "On the Western front no action on a large scale such as that at Verdun,[1] has been fought during the first five months, nevertheless our troops have been far from idle or inactive. Although the struggle, in a general sense has not been intense, it has been everywhere continuous, and there have been many sharp local actions."

In only two of these local actions—at the Bluff and at St. Eloi were battalions of the West Yorkshire Regt. in any way concerned.

The maintenance and repair of the defences amidst all the discomfort of winter went on without cessation. The inclement weather brought the floods and these, combined with the enemy's shells and bombs, destroyed trenches and dug-outs and communications, and all such damage had constantly to be made good promptly under fire and almost entirely by night. The guns were practically never silent, and the sharp crack of the sniper's rifle was heard at all hours. In No Man's Land, patrols carried out their arduous duties, frequently encountering parties of the enemy: then followed the inevitable bombing fight. Mining and counter-mining with its consequent heavy strain on the nerves went on unceasingly. There were no general actions it is true, but nevertheless the great fight went on day and night, above ground and below it. And of all this minor warfare raids on the enemy's trenches were the most exciting. They gave to the full, opportunities of displaying those qualities of skill, daring and gallantry which have always been an inherent part of the British soldier. The initiative in these raids was taken by British troops and on the whole it was held by them: many successful raids were, however, made by the enemy.

1ST BATTALION.

A careful survey of the diary kept by the 1st Battalion West Yorks. R. for the first month of 1916 reveals nothing of outstanding

[1] The German attack on Verdun began on 21st February, 1916.

importance. The awful unrest of the Ypres Salient had by this time become proverbial. The battalion spent its unenviable existence either in the front line trenches of the St. Julien Sector, along the banks of the Yser Canal, or in billets in Poperinghe. The Adjutant, Captain F. A. W. Armitage was wounded on the 23rd January, the enemy's snipers on that day claiming one killed and five wounded. And a week later Second-Lieut. J. Parish, whilst out on patrol became a " missing " casualty. On the 12th February, the enemy attacked the 14th and 20th Divisions and the French troops north of Potizje[1] and although the Battalion was not involved the West Yorkshiremen came in for a hot gruelling from the enemy's guns, which caught the left of the 6th Divisional front. Again on the 13th and 14th, the enemy's artillery was very active. Casualties for the three days in the 1st Battalion numbered eight other ranks killed and forty-four wounded. On the 14th, the enemy had attacked The Bluff, a narrow ridge some thirty to forty feet high, covered with the poor remnants of trees, on the northern banks of the Ypres—Comines Canal. The ridge formed a feature of the flat wooded country at the southern head of the Ypres Salient, and ran through British territory almost into the German lines. A heavy bombardment of Hooge and Railway Wood began at 3-45 p.m. increasing in intensity. About 5-30 p.m. S.O.S. rockets were sent up from Hooge. A mine was blown by the enemy about the same hour at Railway Wood : the 18th Infantry Brigade (6th Division) promptly occupied the near lip of the crater formed. Heavy shelling was continuous all along the southern side of the Salient and appeared to be very intense just south of St. Eloi. About 3 a.m. Vth Corps Headquarters reported that the enemy had attacked and had captured 600 yards of trenches and in spite of counter-attacks still held on to his gains. The attack had fallen on the 17th Division, then holding the St. Eloi Sector.

Violent shell fire continued to characterize the whole of February, though no attacks were made on the 6th Division.

On the 2nd March, the 17th Division attacked The Bluff and re-took it, together with five German officers and 251 other ranks. In this attack the 6th Division co-operated, the West Yorkshiremen who were then in the front line trenches opening rapid rifle fire while the attack was proceeding. Two weeks later (on the 16th March) the Battalion left the trenches and marched to billets in

---

[1] On the 4th February, the 6th Division was transferred to the XIVth Corps which had taken over command of the Ypres Salient.

M

16TH MARCH Poperinghe, for a week's rest. The 6th Division was to be relieved by the Guards Division and then proceed to the Rest Area for a months rest and training. The 23rd of the month saw the 1st West Yorkshires (in Brigade) *en route* for Calais, where a tent camp had been established four miles from the town. Rumour was already busy as to the destination of the Division when the month was over and all things pointed to a move south: there were hopes that it would be to a " quiet " sector. Beyond the havoc caused by a violent gale which broke over the camp and wrecked many tents, there was little excitement, only the usual round of life out of the line—cleaning up, re-organizing, training and hard work by day and an uncomfortable existence in tents at night.

10TH JAN.
2ND BATTALION.
On the 10th January, the 2nd Battalion West Yorks. Regt. (8th Division) was still in billets in the Morbecque area: the Division was in Corps Reserve. Rest and regular training combined with sports had done the men a vast amount of good, for the rigours of trench life tried even the hardiest constitutions. But on the 11th, the Battalion (in Brigade) marched to Neuve Berquin, and on the following day reached billets at the Sailly Cross Roads (in the Sailly area), the 23rd Infantry Brigade having been detailed as Divisional Reserve. On the 12th, the G.O.C. 8th Division (Major-General Hudson) took over command of the right sector of the IIIrd. Corps front—Fleurbaix-Bois Grenier.

18TH JAN. The 2nd Battalion was in fine fettle when on 18th January it marched once more into No. 5 trenches and relieved the 2nd Lincolns. During the period in rest and training when many long route marches were made the 2nd Battalion West Yorkshire Regt. was the only battalion of the 23rd Infantry Brigade which had got through without a single man falling out. The men were no strangers to the sector of trenches into which they now moved—Convent Wall to Well Farm Salient (exclusive). No changes had taken place in the front system which consisted of front-line trenches, support trenches with dug-outs and reserve trenches and defended posts. The Divisional front line consisted almost entirely of breastworks, these being an average of 250 yards distance from the German lines. Tours in the trenches lasted four days, with an alternate four days out of the front line.

1ST FEB. On the 1st and 2nd February, the Battalion was in Brigade Reserve, moving on the following day to Cul de Sac Farm, in Divisional Reserve. Several days were spent in supplying working parties, but on the 14th, the Battalion moved to Estaires. Battalion Headquarters were established at the Hotel de Ville, and here for the first time since the arrival of the Battalion in France an Officers' Mess for the whole Battalion was established.   2ND BATTALION.

The 23rd Infantry Brigade relieved the Welsh Guards (Guards Division) in the front line on the night of the 15th, the 2nd West Yorkshires taking over a portion of old "F" Lines—Fauquissart, being in rear of the centre of the frontage (about a mile in length). All three Brigades of the 8th Division were now in the line, and the Brigadiers had been warned not to expect any rest in Divisional Reserve for at least six weeks. The prospect was by no means pleasing yet only one little adventure befel the West Yorkshiremen and is recorded in the diaries. On the night of the 26th, a patrol crossed No Man's Land and bombed a German working party. The enemy evidently much annoyed tried to surround the patrol, but after considerable excitement the latter regained its own trenches in safety.   15TH FEB.   26TH FEB.

On the 22nd March, the Battalion left the front line trenches in the Laventie Sector for the last time, for the IIIrd Corps had received orders to move south to join the Fourth Army east of Amiens. The 8th Division was to move on the 26th, 27th and 28th, the 23rd Brigade being ordered to move to Sailly on the 26th, to Calonne on the 27th, and entrain on the 28th. The Brigade was relieved by the 105th Brigade on the 26th, and went into billets in Sailly as ordered. The next morning, led by the drums, the Battalion marched to near Merville, arriving at Calonne at 12-30 p.m. The Battalion's last impressions of Merville were not pleasant, for on the march to the station rain fell heavily and the roads were in an appalling state so that all ranks were not sorry to tumble into the train as quickly as possible. The next morning (29th) the Battalion reached Longueau, two miles south-east of Amiens and detrained immediately. "We halted within a mile of the station," recorded the Battalion diary, "and had breakfast. Moved off at 11-20 a.m. through Amiens to St. Vaast—ten miles. Drums were a great help and played well. The country here is very open and undulating with extensive cultivation and villages three miles apart. No intermediate houses as in the district around Laventie. The cottages are all small, no large farms, and charming people. Weather continued perfect.... The men stood the march well."   22ND MARCH.   29TH MARCH.

The country through which the Battalion had just passed and the village in which it was now billeted had not yet suffered from the ravages of War. For the Somme Battles had not yet turned these fair fields of Picardy into desolate wastes, nor the cottages of the peasants and farmers into mere tumbled masses of stone and blackened ruins. Fair indeed, was the first view the West Yorkshiremen had of the future battlefield of Picardy, reminding them somewhat of their own county in England. All was, as yet, comparative peace and quietude, but not far distant was the time when the Battalion was to look back on the time spent in the old Laventie Sector as a period almost beyond belief.

31ST MARCH. By the last day of March, 8th Divisional Headquarters and 25th Infantry Brigade were settled at Flesselles, 23rd Brigade at Bourdon and the 70th Brigade at Vignacourt. The 2nd West Yorkshires were at St. Vaast, seven miles from Amiens.

The 2nd Battalion however, was not the first of the Regiment to move south to Picardy, for the four Territorial Battalions of the 146th Brigade, 49th Division, had after a month of training, entrained at Calais on 1st February, arriving at Amiens on the following day.

1ST JAN.
1/5TH, 1/6TH
1/7TH, 1/8TH
BATTALIONS.
The 1st of January, 1916, had found the 1/5th and 1/7th West Yorkshires billeted in Wormhoudt, and the 1/6th and 1/8th Battalions at Houtkerque, for the 49th Division was out of the front line enjoying a well-earned rest. About the middle of the month all four battalions marched to camp near Calais in order to complete their training. Lewis guns were for the first time issued to the

29TH JAN. Battalions and on the 29th, the 146th Brigade Machine-Gun Company was formed. During this period a new G.O.C. arrived—Brigadier-General M. D. Goring-Jones to command the 146th Brigade, *vice* Brigadier-General F. A. MacFarlan. The loss of General Macfarlan was keenly felt by all ranks, for his fine soldierly qualities, his interest and care of his officers and men had endeared him to all ranks of the 146th Infantry Brigade.

1ST FEB. As already stated the Brigade (in Division) entrained at Calais (at Fontinettes Triage, a small station near the town) on the 1st February, and set out for an "unknown destination." On the previous day the Second Army Commander (General Sir H. Plumer) had sent the 49th Division a farewell message in which he said: "I should like to say how sorry I am that you are leaving the Second Army. I cannot expect you to share my regret. No one, so far as I know, has felt any deep regret at quitting the Ypres Salient. But while you will not regret your change of scene, when you look back at the time you have spent up here, notwithstanding the arduous time you have gone through, notwithstanding the losses of your comrades which we all deplore, you will, I know, have some pleasant memories to carry with you of your comrades of the Second Army."

True words indeed, but just then with all the dull misery and terrible conditions of the trenches of the Salient fresh in their minds, both officers and men of the Division felt that *anywhere* and *any place* was preferable. Thiepval was unbeknown to them then! {1/5TH, 1/6TH, 1/7TH, 1/8TH BATTALIONS.}

By the time the train had left Calais the " unknown destination " had partly leaked out and the men knew they were going south to the Somme, a portion of the front hitherto known as a " quiet sector." Some months later, after the Somme Battles had begun General Plumer's words were remembered.

Very early on the morning of the 2nd February, the 146th Infantry Brigade arrived at Longeau station, a place as already stated, very near Amiens. Detraining began immediately and very soon the four Battalions of West Yorkshiremen were on the march to Ailly-sur-Somme, a small manufacturing town on the southern banks of the river. Hour after hour, tired and hungry officers and men tramped along the dark roads and about 6 a.m. Ailly was reached, where it was learned that the billets were scattered over a wide area. Picardy, with its rolling plains, dotted here and there with farmhouses and peasants' cottages, is not unlike certain parts of Yorkshire, and the men were greatly cheered by the sight of the smiling country which could be seen and appreciated with the coming of daylight. A few hours later the Brigade was concentrated in the Ailly area, the 1/5th and 1/6th West Yorkshires were billeted in the town and the 1/7th and 1/8th Battalions in Fourdrinoy. {2ND FEB.}

For several days the troops " carried on " with their programme of " resting and training," during which time the two remaining Brigades of the 49th Division arrived from Flanders. After the dreary monotony of the Ypres Salient those first few days on the Somme were very much appreciated. The town of Amiens provided a certain amount of entertainment for those who could get there; in the billeting areas entertainments were fairly plentiful and the prices reasonable—the native of Picardy being a good type of Frenchman. On the whole the Somme was a very pleasant change from the battered and churned-up area about Ypres.

On the 5th, the 49th Division had made all arrangements to take over a sector of the line from the 32nd Division, the relief to begin on the night of 12th. Accordingly, on the 10th, the Division began to move forward. The 146th Infantry Brigade, which had been detailed to take over the left sub-sector of the Thiepval sector from the 96th Infantry Brigade (32nd Division), set out from Ailly on the 10th and, marching *via* Rubempré and Bouzincourt, reached {5TH FEB.}

12TH FEB. Martinsart on 12th, where two Battalions—1/6th and 1/8th West Yorkshires went into the front line trenches, the 1/7th and 1/5th Battalions remaining in support and reserve respectively.

The new sector of the line taken over by the 146th Infantry Brigade ran east of Thiepval Wood; this was G.2 sub-sector. South of G.2. the line ran east again from Authuille, *i.e.*, G.1 sub-sector held by 148th Infantry Brigade. Authuille was, however, only 700 yards from the front line and, as was only to be expected, was a shambles.

As the West Yorkshiremen filed into the trenches—1/6th on the right and 1/8th on the left—they were greatly surprised to find how deep, dry, well revetted and comfortable (comparatively) they were compared with the flimsy substitutes for trenches which they had not long left behind up north. The 1/6th occupied the line from Hamilton Avenue to Hammerhead Sap inclusive[1]; the 1/8th Battalion was along the northern and eastern edges of Thiepval Wood, having the River Ancre on the left flank. The 36th (Ulster) Division was on the left of the 49th (West Riding) Division.

Intense cold weather and frequent heavy falls of snow spread a regular epidemic of trench feet, for the trenches, though well-dug and dry, nevertheless lacked deep dug-outs in which the men could shelter. The line was held very thinly and after a three-hours bout on sentry, often in a blinding snow storm, a man came off duty more dead than alive. The most unpleasant feature of the new sector was the frequency with which the enemy " plomped " his trench-mortar shells into the British trenches. There was one huge mortar, throwing an enormous minenwerfer bomb, weighing 140 lbs., active near Hamilton Avenue. As the bomb appeared in the air it looked like a huge cigar and when it exploded there appeared a mine crater 29TH FEB. big enough to engulf a house. On the 29th February one of these " rum jars " (as the bombs were called) fell at the head of a com-
1/5TH munication trench, where a platoon of the 1/5th West Yorkshires
BATTALION. had arrived to take over a section of the line; the whole platoon became casualties. Retaliation often drew heavy fire though the enemy was not allowed to shell the British trenches with impunity.

1/6TH "The 1/6th Battalion had suffered frequent trench-mortar
BATTALION. bombardments and had only been able to obtain feeble artillery retaliation, when a trench-mortar enthusiast ' fra' Scotland ' went round the Battalion front trying to choose an emplacement for his engine. Each company was very pleased to see him and anxious

---

[1] The morning after the line had been taken over, considerable astonishment was caused in the 1/6th Battalion by the platoon holding Hammerhead Sap hearing some Germans across No Man's Land shout out, " Hullo, West Yorkshires ! "

that he should fire off all rounds possible, but they were even more anxious that he should not fire his 'beastly engine' on their own company front, as the enemy was sure to retaliate. The trench-mortar enthusiast informed B Company Headquarters that he had received instructions to 'settle down' on their front, saying affectionately 'Wait till I fire my little football.' Everyone got on the fire-step to watch 'his little football' throw the enemy's parapet about the field. The football flew splendidly and fell right on top of what we thought was a German dug-out. Prolonged silence; a dud! the next—a dud! The third and last made amends, exploding magnificently, but the stick of the 'football' flew back to our line, nearly wounding the Company Sergeant-Major. Our Trench Mortar rations for that day were three shells."[1]

No tactical incident of importance took place during February or the early days of March, and, during the first week of the latter the 49th Division was relieved by the 36th (Ulster) Division and passed out of the front line into Corps Reserve.

On the 8th March, Divisional Headquarters were at Senlis and 146th Infantry Brigade, with 1/5th and 1/7th West Yorkshires at Harponville and the 1/6th and 1/8th at Varennes. The battalions changed their billeting area about the middle of March, for large working parties had to be found each day and the troops were located as near their work as possible. Up and down the line preparations for the Somme Battles had begun and the construction of new roads, light railways, hutments, camps, etc., claimed the attention of all divisions not in the front line. Training also had to be carried out and new-comers from Home put through a first apprenticeship in the rear area, before going into the line. 8TH MARCH. 1/5TH, 1/7TH BATTALIONS. 1/6TH, 1/8TH BATTALIONS.

On the 31st March, Divisional Headquarters were at Naours, the 1/8th West Yorkshires were at Behencourt, 1/6th Battalion at Senlis (two companies) and Bouzincourt (two companies), 1/7th Fréchencourt and 1/8th at Bavelincourt. 31ST MARCH. 9TH BATTALION.

The 9th Battalion West Yorkshires (in Brigade) sailed from Mudros on 4th February, and on the 7th arrived at Alexandria, in Egypt. There the Battalion disembarked and marched to Sidi Bishr Camp. About the middle of March a move was made from Sidi Bishr to El Ferdan, on the Suez Canal, where the end of the month still found the Battalion training and carrying out guard duties. 4TH FEB. 31ST MARCH.

The Brigade Diary of the 50th Infantry Brigade (17th Division) 10TH BATTALION.

[1] Capt. E. V. Tempest, D.S.O., M.C., 1/6th Battalion West Yorkshires.

1ST JAN.	in which the 10th Battalion West Yorkshires was contained records little of interest for January, 1916. And, so far as the Battalion was concerned, it was out of the line the whole month, passing the first four days between dug-outs at Kruisstraat and work on the communications and roads, which always had to be maintained in fair condition. The 17th Division was relieved by the 24th Division
7TH JAN.	on the 7th and gradually, by marches, the former moved back to the new area Audruicq—Salperwick—Aiquines; Divisional Headquarters were at Tilques. No military operations took place, the time was spent in training—steady drill, marching and the training of Grenadiers forming the key note of this period out of the line. Towards the end of the month Brigade Field days took place. Until
5TH FEB.	5th February the 10th West Yorkshires were training at Ruminghem, but on that date preparations were made by the 17th Division for moving up to the front line and taking over the St. Eloi sector, held by the 3rd Division. By the evening of the 7th, the 10th West
7TH FEB.	Yorkshires were back again in Reninghelst, furnishing working parties and straightening up New Camp. One officer per company made a preliminary tour of the trenches on 11th and 12th, as the Battalion was due to march into the front line on the night 14th/15th.
12TH FEB.	On the 12th, however, the enemy had attacked the left of the British front line north of Pilkem and the 50th Infantry Brigade (being then in Divisional Reserve) was held in readiness to move at half-an-hour's notice, but was not called upon.
13TH FEB.	The 13th was a quiet day. All arrangements had been made by the Brigade to move up into the front line on the following night; meanwhile the Machine-Gun sections and battalion bombers of the 9th Northumberland Fusiliers and 12th Manchester Regt. were due to be relieved on the night 13th/14th by similar units of the 10th West Yorkshire and 7th Yorkshire Regiments. These reliefs duly took place. But during the 14th the left-sector of the Divisional front (*i.e.* about the Bluff) was heavily shelled and the 51st Infantry Brigade, holding the line, asked for retaliation which was given.
14TH FEB.	At 5-25 p.m., when the 10th West Yorkshires and 7th Yorkshires were actually moving up to take over, the enemy blew a mine under trench 31, after a particularly heavy and accurate bombardment of the trenches north of the Comines Canal. Under cover of a barrage the Germans swarmed over the *débris* of the blown-up trench and succeeded in capturing some of the British trenches in the vicinity of the Bluff. The relief which was about to take place was immediately suspended; the 10th West Yorkshires were then in General

Headquarter lines when the relief was held up. Other reliefs, taking place along the line, were also cancelled and all units ordered to "stand fast." 10TH BATTALION.

From all reports, it appears that the 10th West Yorkshires were finally collected in Scottish Wood in Divisional Reserve by 3-30 a.m. on the 15th; that later (about 6-15) "A" Company went off to Voormezeele to unload bombs from a broken-down lorry and carried them up to the 10th Lancashire Fusiliers, who were wanting them; this Company was afterwards attached to the 10th Lancashire Fusiliers; "B" Company, at 6-43 a.m. went forward to support the same Battalion. Only two companies ("C" and "D") and half the Machine-Gun Section now remained in Scottish Wood in Divisional Reserve. The remainder of the Machine-gun Section and the Battalion Bombing Platoon were attached to the 9th Northumberland Fusiliers. All attempts to recapture the Bluff had failed and the 16th and 17th were comparatively quiet days, the enemy consolidating and reinforcing his newly-gained trenches, the British guns maintaining a slow barrage on the old German line opposite the Divisional Sector. 15TH FEB.

About mid-day on the 17th, A and B Companies of the 10th West Yorkshires were returned to the Battalion and joined up with C and D in Scottish Wood; the Machine-Gun Section and Bombing Platoon also rejoined the Battalion. 17TH FEB.

In the evening, at 6 p.m., the Battalion proceeded to relieve the 10th Lancashire Fusiliers. A and B Companies went into the front line and C and D Companies remained in support, with Battalion Headquarters at the Spoil Heap, on the southern bank of the Comines—Ypres Canal. From now onwards until the end of February (indeed until the 2nd March, when the 3rd and 17th Divisions re-captured the Bluff and a part of the German line) there was continual unrest; heavy bombardments, bombing attacks and the ceaseless activities of machine-guns and snipers kept all ranks of both Divisions and also the enemy, continuously on the alert.[1] On the 28th the 50th Infantry Brigade Diary contains the following note :—" 10th West Yorkshire's Intelligence Officer has sent in reports of considerable value as to the enemy's works on the Bluff, which has enabled the artillery to destroy them. This officer, and the Intelligence Officer of the 7th Yorkshires, also discovered some 2ND MARCH

---

[1] Casualties of the 10th West Yorkshires for February were :—One officer wounded, six other ranks killed, twenty-two wounded and eight missing.

enemy strong points opposite the trenches held by their Regiments. These are being destroyed by the siege battery."

On the 1st March, the British artillery poured a continual storm of shells on to the Bluff and the attack took place at 4-30 a.m. on 2nd with complete success. The 10th West Yorkshires did not take part in the attack, but from 5-30 a.m. till noon came in for a terrible gruelling from the enemy's guns. One Section of trench " V.28 " was completely demolished and by evening the Spoil Heap (Battalion Headquarters) practically ceased to exist. The Battalion's casualties this day were 120.

11TH—12TH MARCH.

On the night 11th/12th the 50th Infantry Brigade was relieved by 8th Infantry Brigade (3rd Division). The 17th Division had been transferred to the IIIrd Corps and was due to move south to

18TH MARCH.

relieve the 21st Division in the Armentières Area on 18th March, which relief was duly carried out, the Divisional Headquarters

29TH MARCH.

being established in the town. On the 29th, the 10th West Yorkshires moved up to the front line trenches, relieving the 10th Lancashire Fusiliers, as right battalion of the left sub-sector, Armentières Sector. The 30th and 31st March were quiet days.

11TH BATTALION.

By the time the 10th West Yorkshires had arrived in the Armentières Sector, the 11th Battalion of the Regiment (23rd Division) which had held the Bois Grenier Sector (immediately south of Armentières) had gone south.

1ST JAN.

The 11th Battalion West Yorkshire Regt. on 1st January, 1916, was in the front line, holding the trench system from I.26-5 to I.21-2 (the left flank of the left sub-sector of the Bois Grenier Sector).

The New Year had hardly dawned (Zero hour was 12-15 a.m.) when the 23rd Division made two raids on the enemy's trenches and, although the 11th West Yorkshires were not involved, the raids being made from other portions along the Divisional front, the enemy's retaliation was heavy and the Battalion suffered the loss of one officer killed (Captain A. C. Whitaker), another officer wounded, two other ranks killed and six wounded. The remainder of the month

4TH FEB.

passed quietly. On 4th February the Battalion moved out of Rue de Lettrée (the reserve billets) to the right sub-sector, and took over a portion of the line from I.31-1 to I.31-5, in front of Bois Grenier. Four days later after a period during which sniping was the chief form of activity, the 11th West Yorkshires were relieved by the Durham Light Infantry and marched (in Brigade) back to billets in Rue Dormoire, near Fort Rampu. Towards the end of February, the 23rd Division was relieved in the line and moved south to the

Bruay area, the relief being completed by 29th February. The Division was now in the IVth Corps area. The 11th West Yorkshires were billeted at Haillicourt. *11TH BATTALION. 29TH FEB.*

On 1st March, the 23rd Division received orders from IVth Corps Headquarters to relieve the 17th French Division from the Souchez River as far as (opposite) Boyeau d'l'Ersatz, the relief to begin on 7th and finished by 10 a.m. on the 8th March. The 69th Infantry Brigade was detailed to take over the front line from the French, with 24th Infantry Brigade in support and 68th Brigade in Divisional Reserve. *1ST MARCH.*

The 11th West Yorkshires were ordered to relieve a French regiment in the right sub-sector of the Carency Sector and for this purpose marched off to billets at Grande Servains on the 6th.

In very bad weather, having to traverse very long communication trenches carrying heavy loads, the West Yorkshiremen relieved the Frenchmen on the evening of 7th. Very slow and tedious was that relief and it will be remembered by many. *7TH MARCH.*

The Souchez Sector was an extremely uncomfortable part of the line. The enemy's trenches were generally sited on higher ground and from the Vimy Ridge he commanded extensive views over the Allied lines. The position of the Battalion was therefore unenviable. The whole line was in a very bad state of repair and the left Battalion of the Brigade front was inaccessible by day and connected by short lengths of shallow trenches. Through the night 7th/8th the enemy showed but few signs of activity, but when daylight dawned on the 8th, his guns opened fire and all day long intermittent shelling with trench mortars, shrapnel and 5.9s demonstrated to the new comers in the Souchez Sector that their life was going to be a much more strenuous affair than it had been along the Bois Grenier front. On the 10th the Battalion was relieved by the 2nd Worcesters and returned to their billets in Grande Servins. The 23rd Division was relieved in the Carency Sector on the 12th by the 47th (London) Division. On the 13th, the 11th West Yorkshires changed their billeting area to Collonne Ricquart. In the latter place four days were spent in training and then on the 18th the West Yorkshiremen marched to Hersin, as the 23rd Division had been ordered to relieve the 2nd Division in the left sector (Angres Sector) of the IVth Corps Front. *10TH MARCH.*

The 11th West Yorkshires relieved the 17th Royal Fusiliers of the 2nd Division in the Angres Sector on the 19th, the Battalion being right Battalion of the Centre Brigade. Shelling and counter- *19TH MARCH.*

shelling, duels between hostile rifle-grenadiers and the Divisional trench mortars took place at all times. These conditions continued to the 31st March, when the 11th West Yorkshires were still holding the front line. The casualties of the Battalion for March were Captain H. H. Hill (died of wounds), one officer wounded, two other ranks killed and eighteen wounded.

12TH BATTALION.
It is rather a strange coincidence that for several months only one battalion of the West Yorkshire Regt.—the 12th (9th Infantry Brigade, 3rd Division)—makes any mention in the Battalion War Diary of a raid on the enemy's trenches.

1ST JAN.
When the New Year dawned the 12th West Yorkshires were resting in "J" Camp, Reninghelst, the 9th Infantry Brigade being then out of the line. (The 3rd Division at this period was holding

4TH JAN.
the St. Eloi Sector). On the 4th January, the 9th Infantry Brigade relieved the 8th Infantry Brigade, the 12th West Yorkshires relieving the 8th East Yorks. Regiment. Apparently, at this period, the system was, a week in and a week out of the front line, for it was not until the 11th that the Battalion was relieved by the 8th East Yorkshires and marched back to Dickebusch, into Brigade Reserve. These seven days were evidently of a strenuous nature, for the Battalion Diary has the following entry :—" During this tour of duty excellent work was done by the Battalion in building, strengthening and repairing parapets, parados and traverses, all of which were badly needed to strengthen the line. The Major-General, commanding the Division, instructed the C. O. to express in the Battalion Orders, " how pleased he was with the work done." Men found relief from the terrible strain of trench warfare in hard work ; there was nothing like it as a means of getting rid of that lurking fear of mutilation or death. Even out of the line work on the trenches proceeded, for the Battalion, when " resting," furnished daily working parties, amounting approximately to six officers and 450 N. C. O.'s and men. These parties usually left Dickebusch between 4 and 6 a.m. and returned any time between 10 p.m. and 1 a.m. the following morning.

18TH JAN.
On the 18th the Battalion was back again in the front line trenches and it was during this tour (18th—25th), on the night of

24TH JAN.
24th January, that the West Yorkshiremen raided the enemy's trenches.[1]

---

[1] Battalion Order of the 17th January, 1916, contained the following note :—
"The Mudlarks."
" Opening performance Wednesday, January 19th, 1916, 5-30 p.m. in the tent behind Y.M.C.A. Hut, and thereafter daily (Sundays excepted) at the same hour. Prices of admission, Officers, one franc ; first front row, fifty centimes, remainder, twenty-five centimes (two for half-a-franc)."

Many attempts had already been made to cross No Man's Land and enter the German trenches, but the enemy was extremely alert; neither friend nor foe ever seemed to sleep in the Ypres Salient! Frequent patrols sent out were invariably discovered by the enemy long before they reached his wire and a storm of machine-gun and rifle bullets swept No Man's Land until it was more or less clear. The main object of these patrols was to secure identifications.

But on this particular night the patrols set out early, soon after 6 p.m., before the moon had risen. Each patrol consisted of two officers and fifteen N. C. O.'s and men. The left was led by Lieut. A. J. Vann and Second-Lieut. J. Conchar, the right by Second-Lieuts. J. L. Barritt and H. S. Wooler.

Shortly after 6 p.m. both patrols (the left from P.1 and the right from P.4 trenches) left their trenches and crept across No Man's Land towards the enemy's front line. Both parties succeeded in doing this undiscovered and with wire cutters forced a way through the enemy's entanglements and reached the hostile parapets. Here, unfortunately, the left patrol was discovered. The enemy's trench was strongly held and the patrol could do no more than throw bombs into the trenches, now crowded with startled Germans, and then retire. Both officers of this patrol were wounded, one on the enemy's parapet and the other by a stray bullet, just as the patrol was about to enter its own lines, but no other casualties were suffered.

The adventures of the right patrol were, however, much more exciting; the patrol had, like the left patrol, reached the enemy's parapet, but it was *not* discovered. The trench appeared empty, but not far off a German sentry was on guard at the junction of a small sap. Taking a sergeant with them the two officers of the patrol crossed the enemy's trench and, crawling behind the parados, gradually drew near to the place where the solitary sentry stood, all unaware of the fate soon to overtake him. The sap over which he stood guard ran out to a small bombing post, held by two German bombers. A few seconds later a revolver was presented at the German's head and he was ordered to keep quiet. He resisted, there was a snap, the revolver had missed fire. A grim struggle then took place, during which an attempt to throttle the man quietly failed and as he still persisted and was successful in raising the alarm, he had to be killed. From all directions Germans now came hurrying down the trench and the patrol was forced to retire. Before retiring, however, the patrol successfully bombed the enemy, killing several, including the two German bombers at the end of the sap. Owing

12TH BATTALION. 24TH JAN.	to the depth of the trench, however, the patrol was unable to get the dead man out and it was thus impossible to obtain an identification. The right patrol had one casualty—an N. C. O. wounded.
	On the 25th, the Battalion was relieved by the East Yorks. and marched, by companies, back to the rest camp at Reninghelst.¹
7TH FEB.	The 3rd Division was relieved by the 17th Division during the first week of February, and on the 7th the 12th West Yorkshires marched out of the camp at Reninghelst *en route* to Godesweld, where the Battalion entrained and arrived at St. Omer at 10-30 p.m. Very early the next morning (4 a.m.) the Battalion went into billets at Recques. The billets were very good and the men were soon
4TH MARCH.	comfortably settled in. From 8th February until the 4th March the West Yorkshiremen (with other battalions of the 3rd Division) were
5TH MARCH.	engaged in training and when on the 5th the Battalion marched out of Recques and entrained at Audruick for Poperinghe, there was but little doubt but that the month's rest had very greatly benefited the men.
	On reaching Poperinghe the Battalion marched to " B " Camp at Reninghelst (where 3rd Divisional Headquarters were established). The Camp was very crowded and wet, and the men were not sorry when during the 6th they moved into the trenches, relieving the 13th
6TH MARCH.	King's at Kingsway. The 12th West Yorkshires were now temporarily under the 76th Infantry Brigade. Their Diary for the 6th March concludes with the following terse, but businesslike statement : " worked very hard on the front line, making recently-won trenches on the Bluff strong and habitable. Casualties slight." Nothing of importance happened during the next four days and on the 10 h the Battalion was relieved by the 1st Gordons and marched into camp at Dickebusch. The Battalion was split up during the next tour in the trenches, two companies marching off to Kingsway on
13TH MARCH.	13th to relieve the 1st Gordons, the remaining two companies staying behind in camp until 15th, when they proceeded to Voormezeele under the 8th Infantry Brigade. On this same day the G. O. C. Division, again congratulated the Battalion on the good work carried out in the recently captured trenches on the Bluff. The two companies at Voormezeele had a very strenuous time supplying working
24TH MARCH.	parties ; but the Battalion was once more concentrated on 24th, and on the following day relieved the 8th East Yorks. in " P " Trenches (St. Eloi Sector).

¹ Casualties for the month of January were officers—two wounded ; other ranks—two killed, ten wounded.

Orders had been issued and preparations made for an attack to take place on 27th March, with the object of " straightening out the line at St. Eloi and cutting away the small German salient, which encroached on the semi-circle of the British line in the Ypres Salient to a depth of about 100 yards, on a front of some 600 yards."[1]

12TH BATTALION. 27TH MARCH.

The 12th West Yorkshires (Lieut.-Col. R. A. C. L. Leggatt) were not detailed as attacking troops, the attack being carried out by the 1st Northumberland Fusiliers (right) and 4th Royal Fusiliers (left). The West Yorkshiremen, however, were in support of the 1st Northumberland Fusiliers and their part in the attack was to set to work, immediately the six mines had been exploded on the craters thus formed, reclaiming trenches and consolidating the line. The work of consolidation was carried out under terrible conditions; the enemy's shell fire was very heavy, his snipers were busy and his machine guns extremely active. The communication trenches were full of mud and water, the men being frequently immersed up to their waists.

Heavy casualties on 27th and 28th were sustained by the Battalion; two officers were killed (Second-Lieuts. C. B. Underhill and H. S. Wooler, died of wounds on 28th) and six were wounded (Major A. S. Mathews, Capts. R. S. Vardy and A. J. Vann, Second-Lieuts. G. Smith, F. W. Rycroft and F. Welch). In other ranks the Battalion lost eight killed, seventy wounded and seventeen missing. On 29th the Battalion, less one company, which remained in " P " Sector was relieved by Canadian troops and marched (in Brigade) back to Reninghelst. The 31st March saw the Battalion back again in " T " Trench. That all ranks had come through the ordeal splendidly was shown in a report which the O.C. 1st Northumberland Fusiliers, forwarded to 9th Brigade Headquarters on the work carried out by the 12th West Yorkshires. " I wish to report for the information of the G.O.C. the valuable support given to this battalion during the recent operations by the Commanding Officer and all ranks of the 12th Battalion West Yorks. Regt. The men attached to this Battalion for carrying and other duties, carried out their duties under fire with coolness, determination and devotion. All ranks worked equally well and I am unable to single out any special names for reward or distinction. At a critical period in the operations the Commanding Officer placed two bombing squads at my disposal, but these were not required. The assistance given throughout the day by this Battalion was of the greatest help to me."

29TH MARCH.

[1] Official description of the Actions of St. Eloi Craters, 27th March—16th April.

17TH BATTALION.

      In the meantime four more battalions of the West Yorkshire Regiment had landed in France. The first of these to arrive was the 17th (Service), contained in the 106th Infantry Brigade (35th Division). The battalion was raised in December, 1914, and had moved about successively from Leeds to Ilkley, thence to Skipton, Morham, Chiseldon, Perham Downs and Larkhill, thence back again to Perham Downs (Salisbury). From the latter place 35th Division H. Qs. and 104th Infantry Brigade set out for Southampton on 29th January, the remaining brigades of the Division followed, the 106th entraining at Perham on 31st and, on reaching Southampton, embarking immediately.

31ST JAN.

      The 17th (Service) Battalion West Yorkshires was commanded by Lieut.-Col. F. N. J. Atkinson; the 106th Infantry Brigade by Brigadier-General H. O. Donnell.[1]

      After a smooth crossing, Havre was reached on 1st February, and here the troops disembarked and marched to camp at Harfleur. A somewhat cheerless night was passed in tents and on the following day the Battalion, with transport, marched back to Havre and there entrained, arriving on 3rd and detraining again at Blendeques, whence the Battalion (in Brigade) marched to Campagne and went into billets. The whole of the 106th Infantry Brigade was now concentrated in the Wardrecques—Racquingham—Campagne area, where the next five days were spent in completing equipment and training.

3RD FEB.

9TH FEB.

      On 9th, the 106th Infantry Brigade marched from Wardrecques to new billets at Bueseghem and Thiennes, the battalion being inspected on the road by Sir Douglas Haig and H.R.H. Prince Arthur of Connaught. The 17th West Yorkshires were at Bueseghem. Here nine days were spent in getting ready for a first visit to the front line—the 35th Division, being at that period in Divisional Reserve in the XIth Corps (Lieut.-General R. C. B. Haking, K.C.B.). On the 18th the troops again marched out of billets and proceeded to Les Lauriers and Merville; the West Yorkshiremen were billeted in the latter town. Two days later the Battalion, on being attached to the 19th Division for training in trench warfare, marched from Merville to La Gorgue. W and Z Companies went into billets in Riez—Bailleul and Pont du Hem respectively and X and Y Companies into the trenches; X Company was attached to the 9th Royal Welsh Fusiliers and Y Company to the 9th Welsh Regiment. The two

18TH FEB.

[1] It is interesting to recall that General O'Donnell was himself a West Yorkshireman, who had served all his service with the Regiment, and had commanded the 2nd Battalion from 1907 to 1911.

companies were in the trenches by 9 p.m. on 20th; at 10-45 p.m. the Battalion suffered its first casualty in Flanders—Pte. Caxton, X Company, being shot through the head by a machine-gun bullet. ^{17TH BATTALION. 20TH FEB.}

The portion of the line held by the 9th Royal Welsh Fusiliers and the 9th Welsh Regiment (to which X and Y Companies were attached) was the sector N.E. of Neuve Chapelle and opposite the Aubers Ridge. The line between Armentières and Festubert seems to have been a regular training ground for the West Yorkshire Regiment—for here many battalions received their first initiation in and introduction to, trench warfare.

On the night 21st/22nd W Company (attached to the 9th Cheshires) relieved the 9th Royal Welsh Fusiliers and X Company in the front line and, on the morning of the 22nd, the 6th Wiltshires, accompanied by Z Company, relieved the 9th Welsh Regiment and Y Company. The two relieved companies marched back to billets— X to Riez Bailleul and Y to Pont du Hem. ^{21ST—22ND FEB.}

For several days instruction in trench warfare continued, but on 27th and 28th all four companies of the 17th West Yorkshires were returned to the 35th Division; the Battalion's casualties had been two other ranks killed and two wounded. ^{27TH—28TH FEB.}

On the 7th March, the 35th Division took over from the 19th Division the La Quinque Rue—Plum Street front of the XIth Corps, a frontage of about 2,750 yards. The 106th relieved the 57th Infantry Brigade in the left sector, Sign Post Lane—Erith Post, the 17th West Yorkshires holding the left sub-sector and the 17th Royal Scots the right. ^{7TH MARCH.}

The 17th West Yorkshires found that they had the 2nd Battalion of the Regiment (in the 8th Division) on their left. The relief was completed by 7-30 p.m., but, owing to the snow, no patrols were sent out. From the Battalion Diary for March and from the Intelligence Reports sent into Brigade Headquarters, a strenuous period of trench life was passed by the West Yorkshiremen during their first month in the trenches. There were no attacks on, or by, the enemy and no patrol encounters, but the amount of work performed and the inclement weather, which ranged from anything included under the headings of " fine " to " bitterly cold " and " snow," the activities of enemy snipers and the keen endeavours of the men to get the better of the enemy's marksmen, the constant bombardment by the trench mortars and artillery and the retaliation by hostile guns, all helped to give the new-comers a first impression of trench life, which they would never lose. At the close of the month, on

31ST MARCH. the 31st, the 17th West Yorkshires were relieved by the 19th Durham Light Infantry and marched back to Fleurbaix and went into billets and posts in and around the village. Major Gill was wounded on this day by a rifle grenade.

Meanwhile three more battalions of the Regiment had arrived and disembarked at Marseilles from Egypt.

15TH, 16TH AND 18TH BATTALIONS. These three Battalions, 15th (Leeds Pals), 16th (1st Bradford Pals) and 18th (2nd Bradford Pals), with the 18th Durham Light Infantry, formed the 93rd Infantry Brigade of the 31st Division. All these Battalions had been raised in 1914, and until early in December, 1915, were training in England, finishing up, as many battalions finished, on Salisbury Plain. On 5th December, the Division set sail for Egypt and landed at Port Said on the 21st of the month. *En route*, one of the boats in the convoy, between Gibraltar and Malta, rammed and sank an empty French transport; whilst off Cyprus, two German submarines were encountered, but successfully eluded. The remainder of December, January and February were spent along the banks of the Suez Canal, where there was much work to be done in outpost duties and in constructing a line of trenches to protect the northern caravan route from Palestine.

1ST MARCH. But on 1st March the Division set sail from Port Said, arriving at Marseilles on 7th and 8th of the month.

From Marseilles the Division moved north towards the British battlefront, detraining at Abbeville, where three weeks were spent in re-equipping the troops, getting acclimatized to France after the warmth of Egypt and generally in getting fit and training for the front line.

Towards the end of March the 31st Division marched into the trenches in the Beaumont Hamel sector, relieving the 36th (Ulster)

29TH MARCH. Division. On 29th, the 15th West Yorkshires (Lieut.-Col. S. C. Taylor) took over the right sub-sector of the Brigade (93rd) front line from the 9th Royal Irish Rifles, *i.e.*, from Hawthorn Ridge to Q.4.b central. The 16th (Major H. H. Kennedy) and 18th (Lieut.-Col. E. C. Kennard) Battalions moved to Beauquesne on the same day.

15TH BATTALION. The trenches taken over by the 15th West Yorkshires lay about 800 yards east, south-east of Auchonvillers. At the railway crossing south-west of the village, guides from the 36th Division met the Battalion and the relief began. Two Companies—C and D were placed in the front line, with B Company in support and A Company in reserve in Auchonvillers. The relief began at 7 p.m. and was completed by 9-25 p.m. Nothing of importance happened on the 30th and 31st March, and the situation is generally described in the diaries as "normal."

<small>31ST MARCH.</small>

A Minor Enterprise.

Only one small action—a minor enterprise it was called in official language—of special interest to the Regiment, took place during the three months which intervened between the 31st March and the 30th June, the day preceding the opening of the Battles of the Somme, 1916. Those three months were spent in a combination of active trench warfare, and busy preparations for the Allied Offensives of 1916, originally designed to begin in June, but postponed later until the 1st July.

The minor enterprise in question was carried out by the 1st Battalion West Yorkshire Regt. (18th Infantry Brigade, 6th Division), which was then in Brigade Reserve along the banks of the Yser Canal, north of Ypres. The 18th Infantry Brigade, which was holding the left sub-sector of the 6th Divisional Sector, had received orders on the 27th May, "to seize," during the night of the 3rd/4th June, and hold, old British trenches from C.13 b.6.6. to C.7.d.3.4., which had been previously evacuated by another division and was now lighty held by the Germans. The Brigadier selected the 1st Battalion West Yorkshire Regt. for this enterprise. The C.O. (Lieut.-Col. G. G. Lang) decided to carry this out with C Company, made up to 200 strong from D Company—and to wire the front with forty other ranks from B Company—this Company also to provide carriers for stores to consolidate and twenty-five men of D Company (under Second-Lieut. E. J. Rendall) to fill sand-bags, the night previous to the enterprise. A Company was kept intact in battalion reserve.

<small>1ST BATTALION.</small>

"Close reconnaissance of the position, which was in parts 450 yards from the trenches held by the Brigade, were started nightly from 29th May. The first two nights No. 9728 Lance-Sergeant Ward reconnoitred with an N. C. O.'s patrol. On the following night officers patrols went out. Each platoon commander reconnoitred the sector his platoon was to seize and the company commanders the whole ground gradually."

The attack was organized in four parties, each party having a sector of the Old British Trenches. Zero hour was 9-30 p.m. on the night 3/4th June.

<small>3RD—4TH JUNE.</small>

By 11-15 p.m. all four parties had reached their objectives.

1ST BATTALION.

The enemy was occupying a position in the centre of the Old British Trenches, but retired on the approach of the West Yorkshiremen. "It was not possible," said the Battalion Diary, "to wire just in front of Point 98 in the German line, eighty yards away, owing to the deadly fire from machine guns and rifles at this close range. The parapet opposite this front had been obliterated for a distance of thirty yards by our own heavy shells during the afternoon, which had also smashed Point 98 out of recognition. At 12 midnight we were able to inform the 18th Infantry Brigade Headquarters that the position was captured and consolidation had commenced. The only resistance met with was in the right and left sectors, but the rifle and machine-gun fire throughout the night was most deadly, especially in the gap in the right sector. Here Second-Lieut. C. T. K. Newton, platoon commander, was immediately killed and No. 7197 Sergeant F. Coles, C Company's bombing sergeant, was seriously wounded and there was slight confusion. Second-Lieut. W. K. Marshall came over from the other side of the gap and reorganized the platoon. Casualties were as follows :—Killed—Second-Lieut. C. T. K. Newton, five sergeants and five other ranks ; Wounded—two sergeants, twenty-four other ranks. This list includes five sergeants killed and two sergeants wounded, a very heavy percentage and one we could ill afford. At the beginning of the war all these sergeants were privates and had worked their way up by hard work and merit. The Battalion was kept in the line until further orders, to consolidate the positions won."[1]

B Company (under Capt. B. Corp) who was responsible for wiring the captured positions, did its work splendidly. As the Battalion Diary records, owing to the very heavy machine-gun and rifle fire at close range, from Point 98, it was impossible to wire the right of the Old British Trench, but the whole of the objective, excepting this small space was wired.

The Battalion was heartily congratulated on the results of this enterprise by the Brigade, Division, Corps and Army Commanders. The Second Army Commander sent the following message :—" The Army Commander desires me to say that he considers that the operations were well planned and carried out and he will be glad if you will express his appreciation to the 6th Division, G.O.C., 18th Infantry Brigade and the 1st Battalion West Yorkshire Regiment.

---

[1] Battalion Diary, 1st Battalion West Yorkshire Regiment.

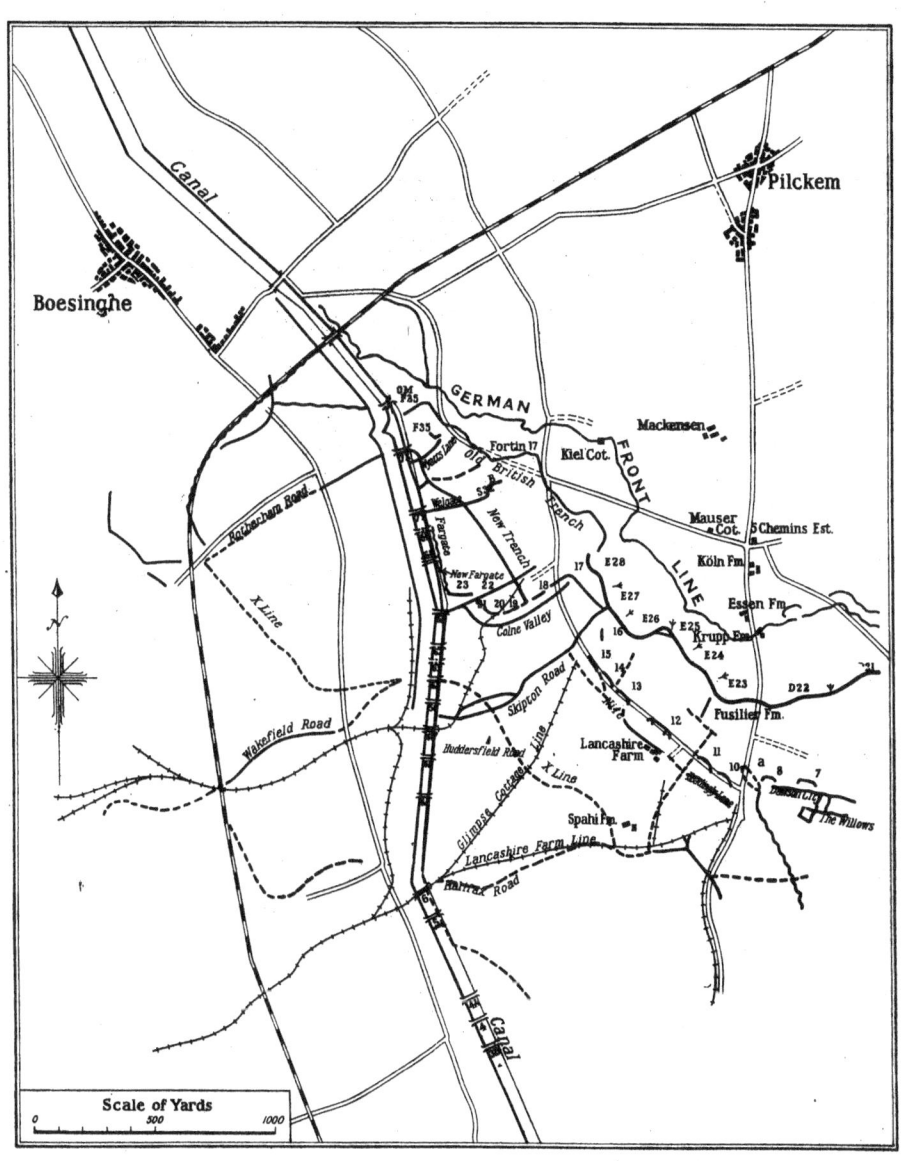

A MINOR ENTERPRISE.

To face p. 184.

III.

THE ALLIED OFFENSIVE, 1916.

OPERATIONS ON THE SOMME,
1st July—18th November, 1916.
The Battles of the Somme, 1916.

Introduction.
The General Attack—1st July, 1916.
The Battle of Albert, 1st—13th July:
    The Capture of Fricourt.
    The Attack on Ovillers-la-Boisselle,
    The Attack on Serre and Pendant Copse
    The Attack on Thiepval, 1st July.
    The next day—2nd July—and after.
    The Capture of Horseshoe Trench.
    The Capture of Bailiff Wood and Contalmaison.
    The Leipzig Salient.

The Battle of Bazentin Ridge; 14th—17th July:
    The Capture of Bazentin-le-Grand and Longueval.

The Battle of Delville Wood; 15th July—3rd September
    The Attack on Munster Alley, 2nd August.
    The Attack on Lonely Trench, 17th August.
    The Attack on Thiepval, 3rd September.
    The Attack on Wundt Work, 14th September.

The Battle of Flers Courcelette; 15th—22nd September
    Capture of The Quadrilateral, 18th September.

The Battle of Morval; 25th—28th September:
    Capture of Les Bœufs.

The Battle of Thiepval Ridge; 26th—28th September:
    Attack on the Stuff Redoubt.
    Attack on the Schwaben Redoubt.

The Battle of Le Transloy Ridge; 1st—18th October:
    Attack on Mild and Cloudy Trenches.
    Attack on Zenith Trench.

THE BATTLES OF THE SOMME, 1916.
Introduction.

NO one who lived in England during the early Summer of 1916, will ever forget the wave of expectancy which swept over the United Kingdom, when reports of the opening of the Somme Battles of that year first reached the country; whilst those who had their habitations along the South Coast from Southampton to Dover will for ever remember the boom of the guns which passed across the English Channel, from the shell-torn area between the Somme and the Ancre Rivers, when the preliminary bombardment opened towards the end of June.

When 1916 dawned, an offensive campaign had already been decided upon by the Allies, and the area of attack selected. A combined attack was necessary, inasmuch that neither Sir Douglas Haig nor General Joffre deemed themselves strong enough to attack the enemy unaided; preparations were being made all through the latter part of the winter of 1915-1916, and the Spring and early Summer of 1916, only the date was unfixed, in order that the Allies might postpone the attack as long as possible, consistent with safety and the needs of the general situation.

" Subject to the necessity for commencing operations before the summer was too far advanced, and with due regard to the general situation," said Sir Douglas Haig," I desired to postpone my attack as long as possible. The British Armies were growing in numbers and the supply of ammunition was steadily increasing. Moreover, a very large proportion of the officers and men under my command were still far from being fully trained and the longer the attack could be deferred, the more efficient they would become. On the other hand the Germans were continuing to press their attacks at Verdun, and both there and on the Italian front, where the Austrian offensive[1] was gaining ground, it was evident that the strain might become too great to be borne, unless timely action was taken to relieve it. . .
. . .By the end of May the pressure of the enemy on the Italian front assumed such serious proportions that the Russian campaign

[1] The Austrian offensive in the Trentino took place on 14th May, and by the end of the month had reached Arsiero and Asiago.

was opened early in June and the brilliant successes[1] gained by our Allies against the Austrians at once caused a movement of German troops from the Western to the Eastern front. This, however, did not lessen the pressure on Verdun. The heroic defence of our French Allies had already gained many weeks of inestimable value and had caused the enemy very heavy losses, but the strain continued to increase. In view, therefore, of the situation in the various theatres of war, it was eventually agreed between General Joffre and myself that the combined French and British offensive should not be postponed beyond the end of June."

" The objects of that offensive were threefold :—
(1) To relieve the pressure on Verdun.
(2) To assist our Allies in the other theatres of war by stopping any further transfer of German troops from the Western front.
(3) To wear down the strength of the forces opposed to us."

During the Spring months, Sir Douglas Haig had gradually moved divisions from other and more active sectors of the British front, down to the (then) comparatively quiet sector between the Somme and the Ancre, and northwards from the latter river to Gommecourt. And as these divisions arrived they were set to work to make all the necessary preparations for the coming offensive, which being of a very elaborate nature, took a considerable time to complete.

Up to that period no such extensive preparations for battle had taken place either in France or Flanders. Within easy distance from the front line huge stocks of ammunition and stores of all kinds had to be accumulated. The collection and carrying forward of these could only be carried out after many miles of new railways and trench tramways had been built. All roads in rear of the British front were repaired and made fit to bear the constant heavy traffic which would have to pass over them ; many other new roads were made, whilst across the neighbouring valleys, of which there were many, long causeways were constructed. Below ground a great number of additional dug-outs, for the shelter of troops, for use as dressing stations or magazines, for the storage of ammunition, food, water and engineering material, had to be provided. Miles of deep communication trenches, trenches for telephone wires, assembly and assault trenches, had to be dug ; and numerous gun emplacements

---

[1] On the Galician front, the Russians, under Brussilov, had captured Lutsk and Czernovitz from the Austrians.

and observation posts built. Over one hundred and twenty miles of water mains had to be made.

The troops upon whom all these heavy labours fell, and who not only had to perform them but, in addition, " carry on " with trench warfare and the ordinary maintenance of existing defences, bore everything, as the Official Despatches state—" with a cheerfulness beyong all praise."

Neither were those who were to conduct the operations under any illusions as to the strength of the enemy's positions to be attacked ; for the latter were of a very formidable character. The whole terrain of the battlefield-to-be was admirably suited to the requirements of a vigorous defence such as the enemy might be expected to put up; whose positions were " Situated on a high undulating tract of ground, which rises to more than 500 feet above sea level, and forms the watershed between the Somme on the one side and the rivers of south-western Belgium on the other. On the southern face of this watershed, the general trend of which is from east-south-east to west-north-west, the ground falls in a series of long irregular spurs and deep depressions to the valley of the Somme. Well down the forward slopes of this face, the enemy's first system of defence, starting from the Somme near Curlu, ran northwards for 3,000 yards, then westwards for 7,000 yards to near Fricourt, where it turned nearly due north, forming a great salient angle in the enemy's line.

" Some 10,000 yards north of Fricourt the trenches crossed the River Ancre, a tributary of the Somme, and still running northwards, passed over the summit of the watershed, about Hebuturne and Gommecourt, and thence down its northern spurs to Arras.

" On the 20,000 yards front, between the Somme and the Ancre, the enemy had a strong second system of defences, sited generally on or near the southern crest of the highest part of the watershed at an average distance of from 3,000 to 5,000 yards behind his front system of trenches.

" In and between these two systems of defence, the numerous woods and villages had been turned into veritable fortresses. Practically every house in the villages of Picardy had its large cellar, and these the enemy had supplemented by deeply-dug and well-constructed dug-outs, connected up by passages as far down as thirty feet below ground level. The salients in the enemy's front line, were in reality self-contained forts, protected mostly by mine-fields. Strong redoubts and concrete machine-gun emplacements commanded No Man's Land."

In short, the enemy's defences formed not merely a series of defensive lines, but one huge composite system of enormous depth and strength.

During the final preparations for the offensive, the enemy twice endeavoured to interfere with Sir Douglas Haig's plans; on 21st May he attacked on the Vimy ridge, south and south-east from Souchez, and although he obtained a small success and added a little more ground to his front line, his gain was of no military or tactical importance. On the 2nd June he attacked the Canadians between Mount Sorrell and Hooge, and penetrated to a depth of 700 yards, but on the 13th, in a counter-attack, the Canadians regained all the lost ground. Neither of these attacks delayed preparations for the Somme Battles.

As already stated the divisions which were to take part in this great offensive were gradually brought down to the Somme area in the early months of the year. Several of these divisions contained battalions of the West Yorkshire Regt. and the Somme Battles of 1916 are especially interesting to the Regiment for, all up and down the line between Maricourt in the south and Gommecourt in the north, Battalions of the Regiment went forward with their divisions in one concerted operation; this was the first occasion on which they had done this.

Although the arrival in the Somme areas of some of these battalions with their divisions has already been recorded, the situation of the Regiment as a whole (*i.e.* the various battalions then in France and Flanders forming the Regiment) on " Y " day, 30th June, the day before the opening of the offensive on July 1st, 1916, is interesting and gives a clearer view of the part played by the Regiment in the opening moves of the Somme Battles, a part be it said, of great glory and gallantry but also, of great loss. Victory was purchased dearly in those days, and often for every yard of ground won, a hundred brave men lost their lives.

At nightfall on the 30th June, the British divisions in line from Maricourt to Hebuterne, *i.e.* from right to left, were :—30th, just north of Maricourt; 18th south-west of Montauban; 7th south of Mametz; 21st, west of Fricourt; 34th, west and also just south of La Boisselle; 8th, immediately west of Ovillers-la-Boisselle; 32nd, west of Thiepval; 36th, west of St. Pierre-Divion; 25th, from Mary Redan (on the left flank of the 36th) to just south of a point where Watling Street cuts the British Line, west of the village of Beaumont Hamel; 4th, Redan Ridge to a point west of Ten Tree

Alley; 31st, from opposite Ten Tree Alley to John Copse. Such were the British divisions in line as given in the Official Despatches. But to the 21st Division had been added a brigade of the 17th Division— the 50th—in which the 10th Battalion West Yorkshire Regiment was contained, and the four battalions of the West Yorkshire Regiment in the 49th Division, were, with 146th Infantry Brigade Headquarters in Aveluy Wood, for the purpose of supporting the attack of the 36th (Ulster) Division. And therefore from right to left (south to north) the battalions of the West Yorkshire Regiment actually on the Somme, which took part in the operations on the 1st July were the 10th (50th Infantry Brigade, 17th Division), 2nd (23rd Infantry Brigade, 8th Division), 5th, 6th, 7th and 8th (146th Infantry Brigade, 49th Division), 21st (Pioneers—in the 4th Division), 15th, 16th and 18th Battalions (93rd Infantry Brigade, 31st Division); the 3rd Division (then in the Audricques area in Belgium, and in which the 12th Battalion was contained), was under orders to entrain for the Somme on 1st July; the 23rd Division (containing 11th West Yorkshires—69th Infantry Brigade) was in the Coisy area, just north of Amiens ready to join in the battle. Of the remaining battalions of the Regiment in France and Flanders, the 1st Battalion (18th Infantry Brigade, 6th Division) was still in the Ypres Salient, and the 17th Battalion (106th Infantry Brigade, 35th Division), in the Festubert area. The 9th Battalion (32nd Infantry Brigade, 11th Division) was then actually on the sea between Egypt and Marseilles, *en route* for France.

It is remarkable that between the opening of the Somme Battles, 1916, on 1st July, and the final struggle (the Battle of the Ancre in November), every battalion[1] of the West Yorkshire Regiment in France and Flanders was involved in the operations.

Artillery action began on 24th June on which date the guns were engaged in wire cutting, the bombardment of trench systems and fortified localities, registration, bombardment of billets, and, at night, the shelling of all communications. The enemy's retaliation was generally described as " feeble."

Every day the enemy's trench systems were pounded, every night when his front-line troops were likely to be relieved, his communication trenches were bombarded,[2] gas was also discharged and

---

[1] There were fifteen battalions.

[2] No less than 1,513 guns and howitzers were used in the preliminary bombardment on the 1st July, one field or heavy gun to every twenty yards of front attacked. Between 24th June and 1st July, the total number of rounds of artillery ammunition fired was 1,627,824.

mines exploded. Raids and active patrol work kept G.H.Q. informed of the enemy's dispositions.

During the night, 30th June/1st July, all attacking troops moved up to their assembly positions without incident.

Zero hour was at 7-30 a.m. on the 1st July.

"IT SEEMED AS IF NOTHING COULD POSSIBLY EXIST IN THAT INFERNO."—*p*. 196.
A GERMAN TRENCH AFTER THE BOMBARDMENT, 1ST JULY, 1916.

THE GENERAL ATTACK.

THROUGHOUT the night of 30th June the artillery bombardment continued with unabated intensity. At 6-25 a.m. on 1st July a concentrated bombardment started all along the line. Guns, hitherto silent, opened fire, and added their roar to the infernal din of that final hour of preparation before the infantry attack.

30TH JUNE.

1ST JULY.

The morning was bright but a haze hung over the battlefield, clearing a little later. At 7-27 a.m. the Stokes mortars opened with an intense bombardment of the enemy's front-line trenches and between that time and 7-30 a.m. various mines were exploded beneath he German front-line system.

To the British troops, waiting in their assembly positions for the guns to lift from the enemy's front trenches, it seemed as if nothing could possibly exist in that inferno. Clouds of earth shot into the air, and trench boards and the mangled remains of men were flung about in horrid confusion; the crash of the guns almost deafened the troops waiting to rush across No Man's Land, whilst the " rat-tat-tat " of machine guns began to add its ominous sound to the frightful row created by both British and hostile artillery. For the enemy had by this time put down a very heavy barrage which, in one part at least of the British front line, had swept the assembly trenches level with the ground.

At 7-30 a.m. the guns lifted from the enemy's front-line trenches, and the infantry all along the line swarmed across No Man's Land towards the battered hostile trenches.

Half-an-hour later (at 8-0 a.m.) reports began to reach Army Headquarters of progress made. Of the XIIIth Corps (30th and 18th Divisions) the 18th Division was well across the German front-line system; the whole of the IIIrd Corps (34th and 8th Divisions) were in the German second line; the 32nd Division and the 36th (Ulster) Division of the Xth Corps were in the enemy's front line, and first and support lines all along, respectively; the whole of the VIIIth Corps (29th, 4th and 31st Divisions) had overrun the whole German first line, on the Corps front south of Beaumont Hamel to Serre.

Yet another half-hour (8-30 a.m.), and the situation, as known at A.H.Q., was :—XIIIth Corps—the 21st Infantry Brigade (30th Division) had reached Alt Alley, and the 89th Brigade of the same

1ST JULY. division was in German Wood; the 54th Infantry Brigade (18th Division) had passed over Emden Trench—" number of prisoners unknown but surrendering freely "; XVth Corps—two battalions of the 7th Division had reached their objective, *i.e.* " defence flank behind Bois Français, also southern edge of Mametz "; IIIrd Corps —no further report; Xth Corps—the 36th Division in, all along the enemy's reserve line and the 109th Infantry Brigade had captured Schwaben Redoubt; VIIIth Corps—no further report.

All appeared to be going well. But soon after 9-0 a.m. reports began to arrive of divisions being held up (Xth and VIIIth Corps), and (a little later) that a small German counter-attack had retaken a lost trench (XVth Corps area). Next, about noon, the 29th Division (VIIIth Corps) reported " enemy has retaken front line and cut off troops who got through." Therefore it became evident that only on the southern flanks of the British line had any real progress been made.

" On our right our troops met with immediate success," said Sir Douglas Haig, " and rapid progress was made. Before mid-day Montauban had been carried by the 30th Division, and shortly afterwards the Briqueterie to the east, and the whole of the ridge to west of the village was in our hands (18th Division). Opposite Mametz part of our assembly trenches had been practically levelled by the enemy's artillery, making it necessary for our infantry (7th Division) to advance to the attack across 400 yards of open ground. None the less they forced their way into Mametz and reached their objective in the valley, having first thrown out a defensive flank towards Fricourt on their left. At the same time the enemy's trenches were entered by the 21st Division north of Fricourt[1] so that the enemy's garrison in that village was pressed on three sides. Further north, though the villages of La Boisselle and Ovillers, for the time being, resisted our attack, our troops (34th and 8th Divisions) drove deeply into the German lines on the flanks of these strongholds, and from Theipval the work, known as the Leipzig Salient was stormed by the 32nd Division and severe fighting[2] took place for the possession of the village, and its defences. Here, and north of the valley of the Ancre as far as Serre, on the left flank of our attack, our initial successes were not sustained. Striking progress was made at many points and parties of troops penetrated the enemy's positions to the outer defences of Grandcourt (36th Division) and also to Pendent

---

[1] The 50th Infantry Brigade (17th Division) was attached to the 21st Division.
[2] The 146th Infantry Brigade of the 49th Division assisted in this attack.

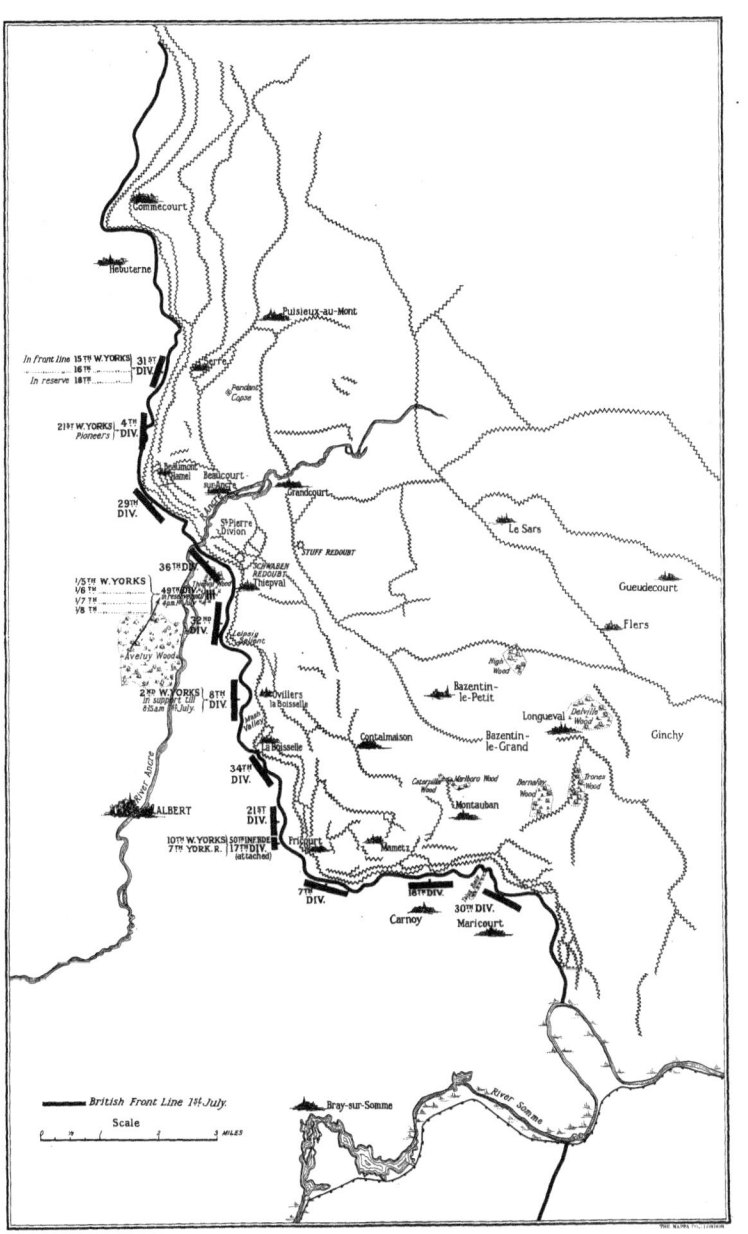

THE BATTLE FRONT ON THE SOMME, 1ST JULY, 1916.

Copse (4th Division) and Serre (31st Division); but the enemy's continued resistance at Thiepval and Beaumont Hamel (29th Division) made it impossible to forward reinforcements and ammunition and, in spite of their gallant efforts, our troops were forced to withdraw during the night to their own lines. The subsidiary attack at Gommecourt, also forced its way into the enemy's positions, but there met with such vigorous opposition that as soon as it was considered that the attack had fulfilled its object, our troops were withdrawn.[1]

The foregoing description of the general attack is given in order that the actions of the several battalions of the West Yorkshire Regiment operating with their divisions on the first day of the Battle, may be more clearly understood. No less than ten Battalions of the Regiment were in action on the 1st July.

THE BATTLE OF ALBERT (1st-13th July), 1916.[1]

ON that sunny morning of July, 1916, taking the 1ST JULY. battle line from south to north, *i.e.*, from right to left the battalions of the Regiment actually in the front line at " Zero " hour were 10th West Yorkshires (50th Infantry Brigade, 17th Division, attached to 21st Division, XVth Corps), commanded by Lieut.-Col. A. Dickson, west of Fricourt; the 15th (Major R. B. Neill), and the 16th (Major G. S. Guyon, commanding), battalions of the 93rd Infantry Brigade, 31st Division in the vicinity of Serre. The battalions in support were the 2nd West Yorkshires (Lieut.-Col. Hume Spry, D.S.O.), 23rd Infantry Brigade, 8th Division, west of Ovillers, and the 18th West Yorkshires (Lieut.-Col. M. N. Kennard), 93rd Infantry Brigade, 31st Division. The 2nd Battalion went into action at 8-25 a.m., and the 18th Battalion about 8-40 a.m.

The four Territorial Battalions—1/5th (Lieut.-Col. C. E. Wood), 1/6th (Lieut.-Col. H. O. Wade), 1/7th (Lieut.-Col. A. E. Kirk), and 1/8th (Lieut.-Col. J. W. Alexander), forming the 146th Infantry Brigade (49th Division) were with their Division in Aveluy Wood, in Reserve, and did not take part in the battle until 4-0 p.m.

The 21st (Pioneer) Battalion (Lieut.-Col. Sir E. H. St. L. Clarke, commanding) of the 4th Division, whose Headquarters were at Bertrancourt, had five officers and 198 other ranks at work in the trenches on July 1st, but on the following day (2nd) apparently took part in the Battle, for the Battalion Diary for that date records the fact that D Company and three platoons of B Company (nine officers and 296 other ranks) were " engaged with 4th Division attack."

The Capture of Fricourt.

With the captures of Montauban and Mametz, which took place on 1st July, the West Yorkshire Regiment was connected only so far

---

[1] The Official Despatches divide the Somme Battles of 1916 into three distinct phases :—
(i) The over-running of the German Entrenched Positions.
(ii) The Struggle for the Ridge.
(iii) The Exploitation of Success.
But this division is inconvenient for the Histories of *Units* ; the Report of the Battles Nomenclature Committee is therefore followed. The Report divides the Battle of Albert (1st—13th July) as follows :—The Capture of Montauban, The Capture of Mametz, The Capture of Fricourt, the Capture of Contalmaison, and the Capture of La Boisselle ; with the subsidiary Attack on the Gommecourt Salient—1st July.

10TH BATTALION.

1ST JULY.

as "concerted action" was concerned. But in the following operations which resulted in the capture of Fricourt, one battalion was actively engaged.

This Battalion—the 10th West Yorkshires (in Brigade and Division)—had left the Armentières sector on 12th May, and after a period of "intensive training" at Bayenghem, moved south during the second week in June to join the Fourth Army. On the 12th the Battalion (with 50th Infantry Brigade) arrived at Bussy; the 51st Infantry Brigade was at Allonville and Cardonette and the 52nd Infantry Brigade at Coisy and Poulainville. On the 13th the 50th Infantry Brigade relieved a brigade of the 7th Division in the trenches, but the 10th West Yorkshires did not go into the line, and on subsequent days marched to Bois de Tailles, Mericourt and Heilly. Whilst at the latter place, a Rest Camp, the Battalion with the remainder of the 50th Infantry Brigade was (on 26th June) placed under the orders of the 21st Division.

The *rôle* of the 50th Infantry Brigade in the Battle of Albert is thus aptly described in the G.S. Diary of the 17th Division :—
" As Fricourt Village and Wood had been excluded from attack in the first phase of operations, it was decided to cover the right flank of the 21st Division, by occupying the north edge of Fricourt Village as far as Red Cottage and Lonely Copse. This attack was allotted to the 50th Infantry Brigade, which was therefore detached and placed under the orders of the G.O.C., 21st Division, and under his orders this Brigade took over the trenches opposite Fricourt Village, with instructions to advance against their objective at 7-30 a.m. on the 1st July."

The attacks of the 21st Division, on the left, and 7th Division on the right of the 50th Infantry Brigade, were to converge near the north-east end of Fricourt Wood. The former Division faced east and the latter north, but although the left flank of the 7th Division was protected by the lie of the ground, the right of the 21st was dangerously exposed and open to enfilade fire. To cover this flank two battalions of the 50th Infantry Brigade were put into the line—the 7th Yorkshire Regiment (right) and the 10th West Yorkshire Regiment (left) with orders, the first to make a frontal attack on the village, the second, to form a defensive flank to protect the right of the 21st Division.

The 7th Yorkshire Regiment held the Battalion front line from the Cemetery to opposite " German Tambour "; thence the 10th West Yorkshires carried the line as far as the apex of " Purfleet."

At Fricourt: The Northern End of the Village in July, 1916.

Battalion Orders of the 10th West Yorkshires contained the following instructions :—" The 7th Yorkshire Regiment will assault on a front from the Wing Corner to south side of German Tambour in conjunction with the 22nd Brigade on the right, with the following objectives : (1) Of clearing up to the eastern edge of Fricourt Village from Well Lane to Cottage Trench and Cottage Trench to Willow Avenue, there joining with the 22nd Brigade (7th Division). On reaching this objective the Battalion will re-organize with the object of (2) Clearing Fricourt Wood as far as Willow Trench and the track leading N.N.E. to X.28.C.8.0. as soon as the barrage on the west front of Fricourt Wood lifts (*i.e.* 2nd Zero plus fifteen minutes from S.W. edge of wood and 2nd Zero plus one hour forty-five minutes from a parallel line 150 yards back from edge of wood).

" The 10th West Yorkshire Regiment will co-operate with the 7th Yorkshire Regiment against both objectives.

" The boundary between the two battalions will be—
(1) Through Fricourt Village :—The line of trenches running from the junction of Hare Lane and Red Trench to Well Lane at F.3.b. central,
(2) Through Fricourt Wood :—Roughly the line of clearing running N.E. through the middle of the wood."

The West Yorkshiremen were to attack in four waves. The Battalion bombers were to work down all trenches until touch with the clearing parties of the 7th Yorkshire Regiment had been obtained. In the following order the Companies were to go forward—A, D, C and B.

At 7 a.m. when the bombardment had reached its greatest fury, the two battalions were formed up in their assembly positions, all ready to advance. Half-an-hour later the guns lifted from the enemy's front line trenches and the infantry swept forward. The two leading companies of the West Yorkshires got across No Man's Land with but few casualties for, between the lifting of the British barrage and the advance of the leading companies of the British infantry, the enemy had not sufficient time to mount his machine guns and get them into action. And yet the creeping barrage (as such) was, at this date, unknown.[1] The barrage consisted of a series of definite lifts, and in consequence the assaulting infantry were unable to keep close up to the zone of fire. It was not until a few weeks later that the lessons of the " creeping barrage " and the effectiveness of keeping as close as possible on the heels of it, was insisted upon, with excellent results.

[1] The " Creeping Barrage " was introduced on the 15th September, 1916.

10TH BATTALION. 1ST JULY.

In consequence, in many places up and down the battle front on July 1st, the assaulting infantry were not close enough to the barrage, which gave time to the enemy's troops to come up out of their deep dug-outs, after the barrage had lifted and meet the assaulting troops.

As already stated the two leading companies of West Yorkshiremen got across No Man's Land and into Konig Trench where they gallantly pressed forward to their objective, the northern edge of Fricourt Village. But the artillery fire which should have covered their right, keeping the enemy below in his dug-outs, until the assault of the 7th Yorkshire Regiment had taken place, was not sufficient protection to the right flank of the two companies, nor did it prevent the enemy swarming up from his underground defences in large numbers. The third and fourth companies, led by Lieut.-Col. Dickson and his second-in-command, Major J. Knott, had attempted to cross No Man's Land in order to support the first and second companies, but as they left their trenches a murderous machine-gun and rifle fire swept the leading ranks away, killing both the C.O. and his second-in-command and practically annihilating the whole of the third and fourth companies. For the enemy had by then had time to mount his machine guns. Only a very few men got across into Konig Trench, and these gallantly remained there until withdrawn.

Survivors of the two leading companies, who crawled back to their own lines after dark on the 1st July, stated that, receiving no support and practically surrounded, they fought the enemy until utterly exhausted. In endeavouring to maintain their position they became divided into small groups and these, becoming isolated, were wiped out by the enemy.

Strenuous efforts made by other battalions of the 50th Infantry Brigade to reach the gallant West Yorkshiremen were made by the 7th East Yorkshire and 7th Yorkshire Regiments, who again attacked at 7-30 p.m., but the same murderous fire swept the attack away. In three minutes only, the 7th Yorkshire Regiment lost thirteen officers and 300 men.

" Thus six hours' fruitless fighting had destroyed one battalion completely and the larger part of two others. And of what magnificent stuff had they proved themselves to be ! Each line, with the fate of those in front terribly evident to their eyes, mounted the parapet, and stepped forward to face the same storm of bullets and to be mown down in the same pitiless fashion."[1]

The Battalion Diary of the 10th West Yorkshires thus describes

---

[1] " History of the 50th Infantry Brigade."

the operations of that day of disaster :—" At 7-30 a.m. the Battalion took part in the general assault. . . .On the right was the 7th Division, and on the left the 21st Division. The Battalion assaulted in four waves. Two lines got through the German positions to the fourth line (of the objective) and were cut off, the attack on our left having failed. Casualties were very heavy, chiefly caused by machine guns which enfiladed our left flank, and were so deadly that the third and fourth lines failed to get across No Man's Land. Twenty-two officers casualties, including Lieut.-Col. Dickson and Major J. Knott—second-in-command (both killed)—and approximately 750 other ranks. The Battalion was then withdrawn to Ville.

10TH BATTALION. 1ST JULY.

At 4 a.m. on the 2nd July, the 50th Infantry Brigade was relieved and marched to Ville and Meaulte.

During the night, 1st/2nd July, the enemy evacuated Fricourt, leaving rearguards behind; the village was taken by the 17th Division which had taken over the front held by the unfortunate 50th Infantry Brigade.

Meanwhile, north of the attack on Fricourt by the 50th Infantry Brigade, La Boisselle had been assaulted by the 34th Division and Ovillers-la-Boisselle by the 8th Division and, although on 1st July both villages resisted these attacks, " Our troops," the Official Despatch stated, " drove deeply into the German Lines on the flanks of these strongholds, and so paved the way for their capture later."

The Attack on Ovillers-la-Boisselle.

Briefly the scheme of attack drawn up by the IIIrd Corps (8th, 34th and 19th Divisions) was to attack on a two-division front—34th on the right and 8th on the left, the enemy's positions from X.20.d.9.3. to R.31.d.9.0. The objective of the Corps was the line Acid Drop Copse (inclusive), The Cutting, eastern outskirts of Pozières to about R.28.C.2.0. The objective of the 8th Division was the line X.5.C.O.5.—the village of Pozèires—R.28.C.2.0. The 19th Division was in Corps Reserve.

The 8th Division was to attack with all three brigades in line, 23rd Infantry Brigade on the right, 25th Infantry Brigade centre, and 70th Infantry Brigade on the left.

Each Infantry Brigade was to have two battalions in the front line, one in support and one in reserve.

The 23rd Infantry Brigade disposed the 2nd Battalion Middlesex Regiment on the right and the 2nd Battalion Devon Regiment on the

2ND BATTALION.

2ND BATTALION.
1ST JULY.

left; the 2nd Battalion West Yorkshire Regiment was battalion in support[1] and the 2nd Battalion Scottish Rifles was in reserve.

The 2nd West Yorkshires (Lieut.-Col. Hume Spry, D.S.O.) had moved into the assembly trenches at 6 a.m. on the 27th June, taking up position in the support trenches. Zero hour had been originally fixed for 29th June, but about 6 p.m. on 28th, probably on account of the weather, the attack was postponed until the 1st July.

That last short period in the assembly trenches before the assault was one of strenuous labour and anxiety. Two patrols which the Battalion sent out on the night of 28th, reported the enemy's wire to be " more or less intact " and the gunners were asked to do all that was possible to break down the entanglements. The following entries in the Battalion Diary for 29th and 30th June are not without interest :—

29th June : In the Trenches : Enemy's retaliation to our bombardment slacked off. During the night a new assembly trench was commenced parallel to and 100 yards from, Border St., by fifty men of A and B Companies, under Major A. M. Boyall, who became a casualty prior to work commencing. The 2nd Battalion Devonshire Regiment relieved C and D Companies in the front line and Ryecroft Street. D Company withdrew to Hodder St. when relieved and C Company to Ribble St. Casualties during the day were two.

30th June : Enemy retaliation to our bombardment was very

---

[1] The period between the 1st April (on which date the 2nd West Yorkshires left St. Vaast and moved forward to take their place in the line), and the opening of the Somme Battles, 1916, was one of preparation. On the 2nd April, the Battalion marched to Albert, the troops being "very fit and marching well." On the 4th the Battalion left Albert and relieved the 2nd K.O.Y.L.I. and 11th Border Regiment in the trenches east of Becourt. The first entry in the Battalion Diary after its arrival in the Somme trenches states :—Trenches, 5th April : Found a different enemy to the quieter VII Bavarians to whom we were accustomed in the Sailly area. Enemy very active with rifle grenades (time fuses) canisters (oil cans filled with H.E.), and trench mortars. Very little material protection was found available and it was two days before any rifle grenades could be obtained. The supply became more regular after the second night, and vigorous retaliation was carried out, with rifle grenades chiefly. Two trench mortars were brought into the line on the last night (8th). The Battalion was not accustomed to such activity. . . .The work was of a very different nature to the old breastwork-deep chalk trenches, making digging difficult, and the burst of a shell more widely felt. The wire in front of the trenches was very old and scarce and the enemy had the upper hand certainly in the siting of trenches. The left Company (D) had a bad time, there being several large mine-craters immediately in front of an occupied almost indiscernible front line. Deep dug-outs holding as many as thirty men were near to us, and the cooking was done in Trench Headquarters."

But the Battalion was relieved on the 9th April, and in a little while settled down to the changed conditions.

On the 10th, Lieut.-Col. Hume Spry joined the Battalion from 30th Division, to command vice Col. Barrington, who left to command the 118th Infantry Brigade.

Throughout May and June trench warfare continued of a more or less vigorous nature. The Battalion formed a permanent raiding party consisting of two officers and sixty-two other ranks, under the command of Lieut. Alexander. Working parties were busy at all times getting ready for the coming offensive, and on the 20th June, the Battalion Diary contained the following entry :—" Special Order received from the Brigadier thanking all ranks for the good work done, and the cheerfulness with which it had been done, during the past fortnight of continual working parties."

Looking back over the War Diaries of that period (and indeed, of all periods), that splendid spirit of cheerfulness, so dominant a character of the British soldier, is constantly evident.

"Ovillers Lay in the German Second System."—p. 205.
A German Trench at Ovillers Battered by our Artillery July, 1916.

slight. The battalion remained in its assembly positions. During the night ladders were finally pegged in position and numbered by D Company. Sixteen men with wire cutters from A and B Companies finally removed the wire from the front of Ryecroft St. Twenty-five men from each company, under selected officers, completed the new assembly trench in rear of Border St. Capt. P. Y. Harkness, second-in-command, reported the work completed at 1 a.m., July 1st.

Thus all was ready. The 2nd Battalion Middlesex Regiment, on the right, and the 2nd Battalion Devonshire Regiment, on the left, were to go forward in four waves, supported by the 2nd Battalion West Yorkshire Regiment. The Middlesex and Devons were to make good the first and second objectives. The West Yorkshiremen, with orders to move from their assembly trenches when the enemy's front line had been captured, were to go through the two attacking battalions and capture and consolidate the third objective, the capture of the village of Pozières was allotted to the Battalion as a special task. The 2nd Battalion Scottish Rifles (in Brigade Reserve) was to follow the 2nd West Yorkshires.

The positions of all four companies of the 2nd West Yorkshires at Zero hour is thus given in the Battalion Diary :—" Positions of companies in assembly trenches : In Houghton Street from Port Louis Street to junction with Hodder Street, companies in the following order—from the right, facing the enemy D Company ; in the centre A Company, on the left B Company ; in Hodder Street C Company.

On the right of the 23rd Infantry Brigade was the 102nd Infantry Brigade (34th Division) and on the left, the 25th Infantry Brigade.

Between Maricourt and Serre there does not seem to have been a more difficult part at which to attack the enemy than that which faced the 23rd Infantry Brigade, on that misty July morning. A careful study of the terrain of the battlefield will reveal the fact that La Boisselle was built upon the forward slopes of a hill ; then came a valley, gradually rising towards the north-east to the slopes of another hill, upon which the village of Ovillers was sited. La Boisselle was protected by a powerful system of trenches and Ovillers lay in the German second system. The valley between the two villages cut right across No Man's Land, which here was wider than almost any other part of the dread space between the opposing trenches along the whole front of the Somme battle line. It is well that the terrain should be clearly understood.

2ND BATTALION. 1ST JULY.

As the Battalion Diary stated, everything was ready by 1 a.m. on the morning of 1st July, and there remained only the long wait until 7-30 a.m.—Zero hour. At 5-30 a.m. the Battalion (twenty-one officers and 702 bayonets) breakfasted. An hour later the hurricane bombardment began and was immediately replied to by the enemy's guns, which at this period put down a light barrage of " 5.9's " at the rate of one shell per minute.

Shortly before zero hour, the Middlesex and Devons left their assembly positions and began to crawl across No Man's Land, towards the German front-line trenches. A storm of bullets from machine guns and rifles met their advance, much of the fire being in enfilade from the direction of La Boisselle and Ovillers. The space to be crossed was anything between 500 and 700 yards, a terribly long distance when the advance had to be made through a perfect hail of bullets. Moreover the enemy began to speed up his barrage and soon four shells per minute were falling in No Man's Land and on the British trenches beyond. At 7-27 and 7-28 a.m. respectively, to the roar of the guns were added loud explosions as the ground heaved and two mines were exploded under the La Boisselle Salient.

At 7-30 a.m. the barrage lifted and the Middlesex and Devons rushed towards the enemy's trenches. The first three waves of both battalions were shot to pieces. Of the first wave only a few gallant survivors reached the German front line, some men of the Middlesex crossing the enmy's front line and getting actually as far as his second line ; they were never seen again.

On the right of the 23rd Infantry Brigade, a similar fate had met the 102nd Infantry Brigade (34th Division), both attacking battalions being practically wiped out ; on the left the 25th Infantry Brigade had been not more fortunate.

B Company (Capt. H. Freeman) of the 2nd West Yorkshires was apparently the first to go forward in support of the Middlesex, a company of which battalion had left Ryecroft Street about 7-35 a.m. A Company (Capt. J. F. Routledge) followed B at about 7-52 a.m., the Company being delayed three minutes by the fall of two heavy shells into the entrance of Ryecroft, putting fifteen men of the Company out of action. " The fine way in which the right of this Company swung forward so as to correct the misalignment of Ryecroft Street to the general direction of the attack was very noticeable."[1]

Capt. P. Y. Harkness, second-in-command of the Battalion, who led these two companies forward, had received orders not to proceed

---

[1] Battalion Diary, 2nd Battalion West Yorkshire Regiment.

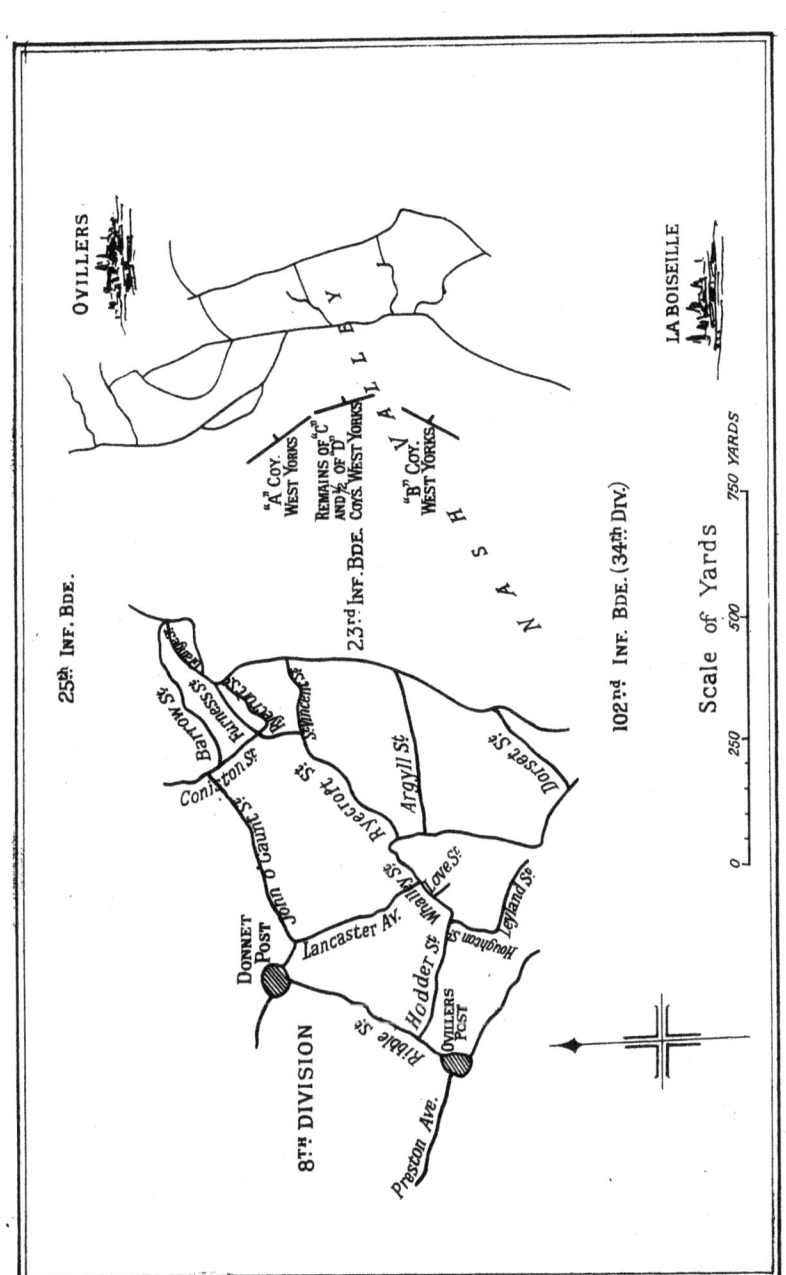

TRENCHES OF THE 23RD INF. BDE. (8TH DIVISION) ON 1ST JULY, 1916.

beyond the Battalion front trench until Ovillers had been made good, or unless asked for support by the leading battalions, *i.e.* Middlesex and Devons. As A Company followed B, D Company began to file into Ryecroft Street. By now the enemy had placed a sharp barrage of shrapnel along the whole length of Ryecroft Street which, with Whalley Street, was in a terrible condition. The broken state of the former affected the advance of D Company, the head of which advanced out of the trench before reaching the further end of it.

2ND BATTALION. 1ST JULY.

At 8 a.m. a message reached Battalion Headquarters from the Brigade that the enemy's front line had not been forced and C Company was ordered to delay its advance out of Ryecroft Street. But about 8-23 a.m., as the nerve-racking "rat-tat-tat" of the enemy's machine guns, from across No Man's Land, seemed to have died down C Company was ordered to advance and a message " all clear " was sent back to Brigade Headquarters. Misled by the quietude of the enemy's machine guns, Battalion Headquarters moved forward at the same time as C Company, for the purpose of passing through Ovillers up to the head of the Battalion, in accordance with pre-arranged plans.

On reaching the front-line trenches, however, the reason hostile machine-gun fire had died down was at once apparent ; all movement in No Man's Land had ceased. The intervening space—that dread space of dead land—was littered with motionless forms. The head of B Company had apparently penetrated the enemy's trenches about X.14 a.3.5. : their helmets could be seen on the parapet and still and inert bodies hung over the enemy's wire. All was comparatively silent and the survivors of the Company lay close in shell holes in front of the battered entanglements ; D Company and half of C Company being in the gap between the Middlesex and Devons ; on the left of D and C, A Company—or all that remained of it—lay crouching in shell holes or as close to Mother Earth as was possible. On the parapet of the enemy's trenches could be seen the bodies of West Yorkshiremen, intermingled with those of men of the Middlesex and Devon Regiments. All were still, dead and living alike, for any movement instantly brought down a hail of machine-gun and rifle bullets. Capt. P. Y. Harkness, second-in-command, Capt. J. F. Routledge (commanding A Company) and four other officers had been killed, nine officers had been wounded, one of whom died later of his wounds. Of twenty-one officers and 702 other ranks, who had breakfasted that morning, only five officers and 212 men came out of action.

2ND BATTALION. 1ST JULY.

There is little more to be told. At about 10-30 a.m. orders were issued from Brigade Headquarters that no further advance was to be made. During the day many wounded men crawled back to the old British lines and, late that night—at 10-30 p.m.—two officers patrols, under Second-Lieutenants G. Phillips and F. H. Matheson, crept out and down the battle front line, shouting to such men who could, to crawl back.

The failure of the attack was due to the numerous machine guns, cunningly placed in deep emplacements and tunnels on the slopes of the hill on the La Boisselle side of the valley, which swept with a terrible enfilade fire the whole of the Brigade attack. The West Yorkshiremen alone had 280 casualties between Ryecroft Street and the front line trench, at least seventy-five per cent. of these being due to the enemy's machine-gun fire; of these casualties 200 were in C and D Companies, the last Companies to go over. Of very gallant B Company, which had supported the Middlesex in that Battalion's attack, and penetrated through the enemy's trenches, only 23 out of 169 came out of action.

"The Battalion as a whole," said the Diary, "accurately carried out their orders to the best of their ability under the conditions which obtained."

Of that there is no doubt.

2ND JULY.

The 8th Division was relieved on the night, 1st/2nd July, by the 12th Division; the 2nd West Yorkshires (in Brigade) marched back to Millencourt, where the survivors of the Battalion bivouacked. At 4 p.m. on the 2nd July the 23rd Brigade (in Division) entrained at Millencourt, detraining at Ailly-sur-Somme, and marched into billets in Yzeux and La Chaussée, south of the Somme.

It was not until 3rd and 4th July that the reduction of La Boisselle took place and not until 7th July that a footing was obtained in Ovillers. On the 11th, Contalmaison was captured.

The Attack on Serre and Pendent Copse.

1ST JULY.

Serre, Pendent Copse and Ten Tree Alley, south of the River Ancre, were places destined to become known to many battalions of the West Yorkshire Regiment. And it was in front of Serre from that curious line of clumps of trees, shown in the maps as Matthew

Copse, Mark Copse, Luke Copse and John Copse (from right to left) that the 31st Division attacked on 1st July.¹

2ND BATTALION. 1ST JULY.

The VIIth Corps, to which the 31st Division belonged, consisted of the 29th, 4th and 31st Divisions, in line from right to left, and the 48th Division in Corps Reserve. The frontage of attack allotted to this Corps extended from Mary Redan, a point some 1,200 yards directly south of the village of Beaumont Hamel to John Copse in the British Line, just north-west of Serre.

The plan of attack issued by 31st Divisional Headquarters was on a two-brigade front—93rd Infantry Brigade on the right, 94th Infantry Brigade on the left; the 92nd Infantry Brigade was in reserve. The two assaulting Brigades were each to attack with two battalions, another battalion in support and a fourth battalion in reserve.

The 15th (Leeds Pals) West Yorkshires, under Major R. B. Neill, at Zero hour (7-30 a.m.) were to assault the enemy's trenches facing the 93rd Brigade front, from opposite Matthew Copse, to approximately where Ten Tree Alley cut into the Sunken Road running south-west from the village of Serre.

15TH BATTALION.

The Leeds Pals were ordered to assault the first three lines of the enemy's trenches and establish themselves in the fourth line, *i.e.* the first objective, the advance to be made on a two-company front, each company on a front of two platoons. Having captured the first objective, four strong posts were to be established.

At 7-40 a.m. the 16th (1st Bradford Pals) West Yorkshires, under Major H. H. Kennedy, were to move forward in the same formation and, passing through the Leeds Pals, were to capture the second and third objectives. One company of the 18th D.L.I. was attached to the 1st Bradford Pals, with the special object of capturing Pendent Copse and establishing there a strong point.

16TH BATTALION.

As soon as the 1st Bradford Pals had passed on to the third

---

¹ The 31st Division, after landing in France from Egypt early in March, had been railed north direct to the Somme Area, and by the end of the month had become sufficiently acclimatized to take its place in the trenches. The three West Yorkshire Battalions in the Division—the 15th (Leeds Pals), 16th (1st Bradford Pals), and the 18th (2nd Bradford Pals), with the 18th D.L.I. formed the 93rd Infantry Brigade.

The first sector occupied was Beaumont Hamel, a by no means salubrious spot for any battalion newly-arrived in France to see trench warfare in all its discomfort. Little happened during April, May and June, but the usual round of vigilance by day, patrolling by night when in the trenches, and work on the defences and preparations for the Somme Battles when out of the line. The 93rd Infantry Brigade lost its Brigadier (Brig.-General N. B. Kirk) who died on 12th May, Brig.-General J. D. Ingles assuming command of the Brigade on 17th May. On 19th June, the Brigade moved to Gézaincourt to undergo a course of special training for the coming offensive, returning to Bus on the 25th. On the afternoon before the 93rd Infantry Brigade moved up to the assembly trenches, the VIIIth Corps Commander (Sir A. Hunter-Weston) addressed the Brigades in stirring words. The Battalion Diary contains the following words on 30th June :—" Here ends the War Diary for June 1916, on the eve of the greatest battle of modern times; everyone is confident of victory."

1ST JULY. objective, the Leeds Pals were to push forward two companies to occupy the second objective.

18TH BATTALION. At 9-30 a.m. the 18th (2nd Bradford Pals) West Yorkshires under Lieut.-Col. E. C. Kennard, were to advance through the first and second objectives, and assemble in rear of Pendent Trench for an advance on the final objective, which was to take place at 11 a.m.

Briefly such was the plan of attack to be carried out by the 93rd Infantry Brigade. The 94th Infantry Brigade was on the left and the 4th Division on the right of the 93rd Brigade.

When the preliminary bombardment opened along the whole front from Maricourt to Serre on 24th June, the enemy's retaliation south of the Ancre had not been very marked, but north of that River, his guns replied vigorously and on the very first day of the bombardment the front line battalion reported "active enemy retaliation." On the 25th hostile shell fire was "intense," on the 26th heavy shelling of the whole front line, including canister bombs and rifle grenades was reported; by the 27th the trenches of the front line were in a very bad condition owing to rain and shelling. Throughout the 28th, 29th and 30th the enemy's guns continued to reply vigorously to the British guns, though the steady bombardment by the latter never ceased and the front line trenches and No Man's Land were gradually assuming the appearance of a shambles, and great gaps in the enemy's wire were becoming more evident.

29TH—30TH JUNE. On the night of the 29th/30th June the 18th Battalion (2nd Bradford Pals) made a raid on the enemy's trenches for the purpose of obtaining identifications and observing the state of his wire and defences. The raiding party was commanded by Lieut. M. Clough, and consisted of four officers and thirty-eight other ranks.

The party started out at 12-28 a.m., picking its way slowly and gingerly across No Man's Land between mines, shell holes and craters. Flares sent up from the enemy's trenches assisted the West Yorkshiremen's advance and when within twenty-five to thirty yards of the hostile lines, showers of bombs met them. Next a single green rocket broke out in the dark sky above the raiders and a barrage of hand grenades was fired in front of Lieut. Clough and his party and a trench-mortar and artillery barrage behind them. The enemy's trenches were full of troops and, as there was no possibility of effecting an entry or of obtaining a prisoner, the signal to retire was given. But valuable information of the condition of the enemy's 18TH BATTALION. defences was obtained. "The trenches," said Lieut. Clough in his report, "seemed fairly knocked about and the wire was cut where we were, in sufficient quantity to allow of the passage of troops. Their trenches seemed very full of men and apparently very deep."[1]

During the late afternoon of the 30th, a message from General Hunter-Weston (Commander of the VIIIth Corps) was circulated to all ranks of the 31st Division:—"My greetings to every officer, N.C.O. and man of the 31st Division in the coming battle. Stick it out, push on, each to his objective, and you will win a glorious victory and make a name in history. I rejoice to be associated with you, as your Corps Commander."

The assaulting troops moved up from Bus to their assembly 15TH BATTALION. positions during the night, 30th June/1st July. The 15th Battalion 1ST JULY. (Leeds Pals) had an unlucky start. The Battalion paraded at 5-30 p.m. and just before moving off from Bus, two bombs fell on D Company, killing one and wounding fourteen other ranks. The march to the assembly trenches was trying in the extreme, but eventually the Battalion reached its allotted positions, C and D Companies in the front line, A and B Companies in the second line. 16TH BATTALION. The 16th Battalion (1st Bradford Pals) paraded at 6-30 p.m. and marched *via* Colmagies to the assembly trenches. In Colmagies the Battalion was served with a very welcome hot meal and shortly before 10 p.m. again moved forward in small parties along the communication trenches—"outward bound." The 18th Battalion (2nd Bradford Pals) left Bus about 8-45 p.m. and were in position 18TH BATTALION. in their support trenches by 4-30 a.m.

At 4-15 a.m. the 31st Division despatched the following report to VIIIth Corps Headquarters:—"Exceptionally quiet night in forward trenches AAA Front Line shelled slightly AAA Villages of Courcelles and Colincamps shelled between 10 and 11 p.m. AAA Bus Wood and vicinity shelled between 12-30 and 2-30 a.m. and again at 3-30 and still continues AAA Assembly almost complete."

The 93rd Infantry Brigade reported all troops assembled in their positions at 4-40 a.m. At that hour the Germans were shelling the front line and there had been about twenty casualties; the 92nd Infantry Brigade (in reserve) reported assembly complete at 4-50 a.m. and the 94th Infantry Brigade at 5 a.m. At 6 a.m., a thick haze

---

[1] Casualties in this raid were:—Killed, Lieut. F. Watson 2nd Lieut. J. W. Worsnop; wounded, Lieut. M. Clough; other ranks, nine killed, eighteen wounded (of whom two died of wounds later).

1ST JULY.

hung over the battlefield. At 6-20 a.m. both the 93rd and 94th Infantry Brigades were asked if they were satisfied that their own wire (to admit the troops through) had been cut, to which both Brigades replied—"perfectly." Just before seven (at 6-53 a.m.) the 93rd Infantry Brigade reported the loss of one officer wounded three other ranks killed and twenty-six wounded. A minute later the Brigade reported that the enemy had put down a light barrage on the front line and Sackville Street. By ten minutes past seven, the enemy's shells had begun to fall heavily in the right sector of the Divisional front (93rd Infantry Brigade). Hostile shells now began to fall on Matthew Copse and Bleneau at the rate of ten per minute. Meanwhile the British guns had, at 6-30 a.m. begun an intense bombardment of the objectives and back areas. The air was now full of shrieking and bursting shells and trench mortar bombs hurtled through the misty morning, exploding with a roar. The din was truly appalling! The final half-hour before the troops went over the top was made awful by the firing of a Stokes-mortar barrage from the front line and four front saps, which had been run out into No Man's Land and a heavy artillery barrage of H.E. shells which fell as far west as the trenches where the 16th West Yorkshires were waiting in rear of the 15th Battalion.

15TH BATTALION.

It was during this final period of very heavy shell fire that the leading waves went over the parapet—at 7-20 a.m.—forming up in No Man's Land preparatory to the attack. At once the enemy manned his front line trenches and opened a heavy rifle and machine-gun fire on the troops as they advanced. Terrible casualties were suffered by the 15th Battalion (Leeds Pals), ere ever the Battalion attacked the enemy's trenches, eleven officers being killed and eleven wounded, while the losses in other ranks were very severe. When Zero arrived ten minutes later, and the British guns lifted for the troops to assault the enemy's trenches but a remnant of the 15th West Yorkshires remained. The C.O.—Major R. B. Neill—was now out of action, having been wounded twice, his adjutant—Capt. S. T. A. Neil— had been killed, and No Man's Land was a shambles of dead and dying men. The first wave of the Battalion was practically swept away and of the second wave few men succeeded in reaching the forming-up tape. Of the Leeds Pals, who left the front line, none returned who had advanced more than 100 yards beyond their own wire. Of those assembled in Leeds Trench, none were known to have got 40 yards beyond the parapet.

Only from the Diary of the 93rd Infantry Brigade Headquarters, 1st July, is it possible to follow the collective actions of the three West Yorkshire battalions on that day of disaster. And the story, briefly told, is as follows :—" At 7-30 a.m. the 15th West Yorkshires had been almost wiped out, though the rear platoons continued to advance from Leeds Trench. At 7-35 a.m. the leading platoon of the 16th Battalion[1] and D Company of the Durham Light Infantry, left their assembly trenches and advanced as far as Leeds Trench. Before reaching the latter they came under heavy fire and had many casualties. The enemy's barrage was by now very heavy both on the front-line trenches and on Leeds Trench, where the communication trenches, Flag, Bleneau, Grey and Warley, had been badly knocked about as far as the line of Monk Trench. More cheerful reports were received about 8 o'clock when news reached Brigade Headquarters that on the left and right of the 93rd Brigade British troops were in and over the enemy's front line. Major G. S. Guyon, O.C., 16th West Yorkshires, was reported wounded at 8-15 a.m. At 8-26 a.m. Sap A was blown in. Here, Second-Lieut. S. F. Bobby, in command of a Light Trench-Mortar battery, was killed and his guns put out of action. The next report in the Brigade Diary stated that the O.C., 16th West Yorkshires (Major Guyon), was reported killed and nine of the officers were casualties and the advance of that Battalion held up also.

16TH BATTALION.

The first line trenches of the Brigade were now crowded with the survivors of both the 15th and 16th Battalions, while dead and wounded men were everywhere. This crowding of the front line, unavoidable, as practically all the officers had been put out of action and orders were unobtainable, entailed still further casualties from the enemy's barrage. " As far as is known," said Brigade Headquarters, " none of the 16th West Yorkshires advanced beyond our wire and none of D Company, 18th Durham Light Infantry, more than twenty yards beyond."

A message had been sent to the 18th West Yorkshires stating that the 16th Battalion had been held up and ordering the C.O. to go to Sap A and investigate the situation. The C.O.—Lieut.-Col. E. C. Kennard—accordingly went forward, but was killed by shell fire before he reached the Sap.

18TH BATTALION.

The 18th West Yorkshires (2nd Bradford Pals) left their assembly trenches about 8-40 a.m., but between their own trenches and the

---

[1] Extract from the Diary of the 16th Battalion :—" 7-30 a.m. The infantry assault commenced, but owing to the large number of casualties, including the loss of all officers, no detailed narrative is possible."

P

**18TH BATTALION.
1ST JULY.**

front line, the Battalion had to pass through an intense barrage of shrapnel and H.E. and casualties were very heavy. The Adjutant (Capt. F. F. Williams) and the O.C., A Company (Capt. C. H. C. Keevel), were wounded almost at the outset and many other officers became casualties. The majority of these casualties occurred between Leeds Trench and the wire along the Brigade's front line and were chiefly due to machine-gun fire from front and flank. Three very heavy barrage lines had also to be traversed. For a time the first and second lines were vacated and the 2nd Bradford Pals, in retiring through the trenches, were broken up into small parties.

There is little need to follow the tale of disaster further; the attack of the 93rd Infantry Brigade was definitely held up and during the afternoon (at 3-5 p.m.) orders were received at Brigade Headquarters to re-organize the line and adopt a purely defensive attitude. When night fell on the 1st July, the strength of the 93rd Infantry Brigade was approximately 1,000 of all ranks, that of the 94th Infantry Brigade 836, including reinforcements.

15TH BATTALION.

16TH BATTALION.

18TH BATTALION.

The Leeds Pals (15th West Yorkshires) had lost twenty-four officers and 504 other ranks, their C.O. was wounded and command of the Battalion had been taken over by Major J. C. Hartley. Only forty-seven of the Battalion answered roll call. Of the 1st Bradford Pals (16th Battalion), twenty-two officers, including the C.O. and Adjutant killed and all company commanders, and 515 other ranks were in the list of killed, wounded and missing. The 2nd Bradford Pals (18th Battalion) also lost their C.O. (succeeded later in the day by Major H. F. C. Carter), besides thirteen more officers and 400 other ranks, killed wounded and missing. At 8-45 p.m. that night the 2nd Bradford Pals (the strongest of the three West Yorkshire Battalions) numbered only six officers and 120 other ranks, though before the evening of 2nd July the ranks had been swelled by stragglers and others coming in, to seven officers and 170 other ranks.

On the left of the 93rd Infantry Brigade, the 94th Brigade, after making slight progress (troops of the Brigade had been reported in Serre Village and Munich Trench) had fallen back to its original starting point, and no portion of the enemy's positions remained in its possession.

On the right of the 93rd Infantry Brigade, the right flank of the attack of the 4th Division had reached the Red Line, but being unsupported north and south had, during the night, 1st/2nd July, to fall back to its original front line.

21ST BATTALION.

The 21st West Yorkshires (Lieut.-Col. Sir E. H. St. L. Clarke,

THE ATTACK ON SERRE AND PENDANT COPSE, 1ST JULY, 1916.
TRENCHES OF THE LEEDS AND BRADFORD "PALS."

commanding)—Pioneers—were with the 4th Division in this attack and, from the Battalion Diary, apparently took part in the operation, but the Battalion Diaries for the 1st and 2nd July contain only the following entries :— 21ST BATTALION. 1ST JULY.

"Bertrancourt, July 1st. C Company—five officers and 198 men in trenches. Heavy bombardment. Camp shelled without direct result. First day of Battle of the Somme.

"2nd July. A and B still in trenches. C Company still in trenches. B Company and three platoons of B—nine officers and 296 other ranks engaged with 4th Division attack. One officer wounded and two other ranks killed—nine other ranks wounded." The following account was, however, related by an officer of the Pioneer Battalion :

"The task assigned to the 21st was to follow the attack with communication trenches across No Man's Land. Tunnels had been prepared under the front line and the forward communication trenches sited. The 4th Division quickly gained its objective and A Company of the 21st under Captain Noon, with Captain Boulnois as his second-in-command, proceeded to the tunnels and began work. Owing to the failure of the attacks on Serre and Beaumont Hamel the German machine guns came into action again and a deadly cross-fire was kept up on the 4th Division front. No work was possible, and the Division had to make its way back, losing very heavily in this retirement. A counter-attack was expected and A Company was put in a support trench and afterwards, for a time, in the front line. The anticipated German attack did not materialize and after being in the trenches for two days, the Company rejoined Headquarters of the Battalion, which was then employed clearing the battlefield, forward trenches and No Man's Land of dead and bringing in the bodies for burial, a very trying experience for a battalion just out from England. It gained considerable praise from the Divisional Commander for this work, which was well carried out."

The actions of five battalions (10th, 2nd, 15th, 16th and 18th) of the West Yorkshire Regiment, which took part in the initial attack on 1st July, have now been described, and brief reference has been made to the Pioneer (21st) Battalion. It remains to describe the operations of the four battalions of the Regiment (5th, 6th, 7th and 8th West Yorkshires) contained in the 146th Infantry Brigade of the 49th Division, which, waiting all day until 4 p.m., were called upon to support the attacks of the 36th and 32nd Divisions. 1/5TH, 1/6TH 1/7TH, 1/8TH BATTALIONS.

The Attack on Thiepval.

1ST JULY.

On the morning of 1st July the Xth Corps consisted of the 32nd Division, on the right, and the 36th (Ulster) Division on the left; the 49th (W.R.) Division in support in Aveluy Wood, and the 25th Division in reserve.

The task of the Xth Corps was to capture Thiepval and its defences, including the Leipzig Salient, on the right, and St. Pierre-Divion and the Schwaben Redoubt on the left. The Corps front extended from the right of the 29th Division (VIIIth Corps) at Mary Redan north-west of the River Ancre to the north-east corner of Authuille Wood, just south of the Leipzig Redoubt. And no portion of the German line from Maricourt to Serre was stronger than this sector of the battle front. From the right of the Corps boundary to the southern banks of the River Ancre was a maze of trenches, literally stuffed with machine guns. The first, second and third German lines were each protected by powerful belts of wire, and though these had been torn and flung about in confusion by the preliminary bombardment, which began on 24th June, they still presented formidable obstacles. In front of Thiepval, which was sited upon high ground, a maze of trenches protected all approaches to the village. And in these trenches countless machine guns commanded No Man's Land in front and north and south. The Leipzig Salient had a powerful redoubt; a little further north was the "Wunderwerk," another point of considerable strength; north of Thiepval, in the German Third Line was the Schwaben Redoubt and, finally, on the southern banks of the Ancre, was St. Pierre-Divion, protected on the right by the River and in front by four lines of trenches. Behind these defences were a number of communication trenches leading back to rear lines, these also being protected by powerful belts of wire. North of the Ancre, opposite the left flank of the 108th Infantry Brigade (36th Division) there were three lines of trenches, all well protected. The final objective of the Corps was the German Line which ran east of the last system of German trenches, south of Grandcourt to about 500 yards due east of Mouquet Farm.

From the Schwaben Redoubt, the enemy commanded the whole of the Ancre trenches and the bridges over the River; his machine guns were everywhere sited to search not only the British front line, but also the approaches to it. Thus it will be seen that the 32nd and 36th Divisions had no light task before them.

On the night 30th June/1st July, the 49th Division[1] moved forward to Aveluy Wood in readiness to support the attack of the 32nd and 36th Divisions. No definite orders had been issued to the 49th Division, for the action of the latter depended entirely upon the measure of success obtained by the two attacking divisions. But it was expected that the West Riding Division would go into action somewhere about the Green Line, *i.e.* the third objective.

All night long the British guns boomed with unstinted fury, during which the 32nd and 36th Divisions formed up in their assembly trenches. The 49th Division lay close in Aveluy Wood, suffering but few casualties. At 6-30 a.m. the final hour of " intense " fire began, and batteries hitherto silent added their voices to the roar of a thousand guns. At 7-30 a.m. the leading waves of the assaulting divisions " went over the top." Thereafter for a little while there was no news. Then about 8-58 a.m., Headquarters 146th Infantry Brigade (Brig.-General M. D. Goring-Jones) received orders to cross the River Ancre and take up its position in the assembly trenches in Thiepval Wood, lately vacated by troops of the two attacking divisions. These orders were the outcome of a warning received at Headquarters 49th Division from Xth Corps Headquarters " to move a brigade into Thiepval Wood in readiness to support the right of the 36th Division, or the left of the 32nd Division, as required." The 5th and 6th Battalions West Yorkshire Regiment (under the command of Lieut.-Col. C. E. Wood and Lieut.-Col. H. O. Wade, respectively) moved off along the railway and crossed the Ancre by the southern Causeway—the Passerelle de Magenta—

[1] The Division had had a long rest out of the front line at Vignacourt, training and getting ready for the Somme offensive. About the middle of June a move, in stages, was made towards the front line. An officer of one of the West Yorkshire battalions which had reached Puchevillers gives the following vivid sketch of life behind the front line before the offensive began :—
" The period at Puchevillers was the final calm before the storm. No one could overlook the signs of the approaching conflict. The most patent reminder was the enormous Casualty Clearing Station which had been built within three miles walk of the Camp. For weeks this Casualty Clearing Station had been accumulating stretchers and other paraphernalia, and during the ten days the Battalion remained at Puchevillers, men walked up every evening to watch the Casualty Clearing Station orderlies working overtime digging graves. The Battalion was used to speculate as to which of the new recruits would fill them ! Another portent was the enormous new railway siding, with scores of thousands of shells of all calibres. An even more ominous sign was the entire absence of parades at Puchevillers. ' Enjoy yourselves,' said the Colonel, and the implication was that we should not have much opportunity for enjoyment in the future. Vignacourt days had been altogether ' too good.' ' They're fattening us up for the slaughter,' the men said. And ' so they were,' and everyone, in spite of the prospect, seemed to enjoy the process. The Camp in the Puchevillers Orchard was a very lively place, games and horseplay of every variety. . . . Some of the men brought out ' knuckle dusters' and knives and any other murderous implements which they thought would help them to give a good account of themselves in the coming battle. A few people wore ' safety waistcoats ' of steel, and other protections, but these expedients were not generally approved. ' If your turn comes, you can't do nothink to get out of it,' said the Philosopher of the Battalion, and the men preferred to take their chances all together, and with rather a fine unselfishness, would have refused protection which everyone else could not equally have enjoyed. The men were as eager to attack on July 1st as they had been to come out to France, fifteen months before." Capt. E. V. Tempest, D.S.O., M.C

1ST JULY.
1/7TH AND 1/8TH BATTALIONS.

to the assembly trenches in the southern portion of Thiepval Wood. The 7th and 8th Battalions West Yorkshire Regiment (commanded by Lieut-Col. A. E. Kirk and Lieut.-Col. J. W. Alexander) crossed by the Hamel Bridge.

All four Battalions got across the Ancre and into Thiepval Wood with but four casualties, though the two Causeways were under machine-gun fire from Thiepval. The positions taken up were just east of the star cross roads towards the Thiepval edge of the Wood—the 1/5th, on the right, the 1/6th, on the left, the 1/7th in support, and the 1/8th in reserve.

The Brigade Diary reports that all battalions were in position by 2-15 p.m. on the afternoon of the 1st July.

The situation along the Xth Corps front, after the initial attack at 7-30 a.m. is difficult to follow. But at noon the Corps reported that the 32nd Division was still held up south of Thiepval in the enemy's lines about the " Wunderwerk " and Lemberg Trench, and two battalions of the 14th Infantry Brigade had been ordered to advance up Mab Valley and take the enemy in flank and rear. In Thiepval itself the situation was still obscure. Fighting still continued in the village, the enemy using machine guns. A battalion of the 96th Infantry Brigade had been ordered to go round the north of the village. The 36th Division was holding and consolidating the Blue Line from R.20.C.7.4. to R.13.d.9.9. This implied that the Schwaben Redoubt had been captured. Across the Ancre, the left Brigade (the 106th) of the 36th Division was advancing towards Beaucourt Station, though the enemy was still reported to be in occupation of his line opposite Mary Redan.

At 2-30 p.m. the Corps report stated :—" Position at Thiepval is still obscure. It is now going to be re-bombarded and attacked from the front. A part of the 146th Infantry Brigade will assist the 32nd Division in this attack."

1/5TH AND 1/6TH BATTALIONS.

Almost every moment expecting the receipt of orders to cross No Man's Land and go through to the third objective and the line south of Grandcourt, the West Yorkshiremen lay in their trenches full of excitement. The 1/5th and 1/6th had reached their assembly positions in Thiepval Wood about 11-30 a.m., and for three hours all was obscure in front of them. The roar and din of the battle came to them as they lay waiting to go forward. Only one conclusion could be drawn, that the blow had not fallen as heavily against the foe as had been expected. Else had they been, ere this, east of the Blue Line, consolidating the Third (the Green) Line.

Orders for the Attack

Shortly before 2-30 p.m. Brigade Headquarters received a message from the Division, ordering the 1/5th and 1/6th Battalions to each send out an officers' patrol to reconnoitre, with a view to attacking Thiepval Village. The next message received at Brigade Headquarters from the Division, was for the 146th Infantry Brigade to attack Thiepval Village. The C.O.'s of the battalions were hurriedly sent for and were given verbal orders :—" They were told," said the report, " they had just, and only just, time to carry them out." The orders were as follows :—" The Brigade will attack Thiepval Village from the west at 4 p.m. exactly. Preliminary bombardment will be carried out from 3-30 to 4 p.m. One battalion from another front (32nd Division) will be ordered to co-operate from the north.

" Attack will be carried out as follows :—Front line, 1/5th Battalion West Yorkshire Regiment on right, and 1/6th Battalion on the left, 1/8th Battalion in support, 1/7th Battalion in Brigade Reserve. Frontage of attack 600 yards. 1/5th Battalion and 1/6th Battalion, each on a frontage of 300 yards. Dividing line between battalions is due east and north through Cross Roads in centre of Thiepval.

Brigade Headquarters will remain at Belfast City (Thiepval Wood) during operations. O.C., Signals, will arrange a system of runners to follow attacking troops and send back by relays or otherwise direct to Brigade Headquarters."

The above orders (written) were issued at 3-30 p.m.

The time for preparation was scant indeed. No time for consultation between C.O. and Company Commanders, nor between Company Commanders and Platoon Commanders and N.C.O.'s. Very few of the officers or men had anything but the vaguest idea in which direction Thiepval Village lay. The reconnoitring patrols which had left shortly before had not yet returned, and preliminary reconnaissance was out of the question. One thing only dominated the minds of all—Thiepval had not, after all, fallen, and it had to be captured!

As soon as the C.O.'s returned to the Battalions, the latter were ordered to advance at once.

The guns had already opened fire at 3-30 p.m. and were pounding the hostile front lines and Thiepval, but down in his deep dug-outs the enemy suffered few casualties, though heavy howitzer shells fell into his trenches and toppled the already crumbled buildings of the village still closer to the ground.

The 1/5th were unavoidably late in starting, and at 4 p.m., when

1ST JULY.
1/6TH
BATTALION.

the guns lifted from the enemy's front system, the 1/6th Battalion went over the parapet alone. Already, when crossing the valley between the high ground from Thiepval Wood and the front line, the Battalion had suffered casualties. It was here, that about 3·45 p.m., the Battalion Medical Officer (Capt. A. Hamilton) and Colonel Wade were wounded, and the Signalling Officer (Lieut. N. Dodd) killed. "The last glimpse some of the Battalion had of the Colonel," said one of the 1/6th officers, "was seeing him running to overtake the Battalion before it went over the top, minus one puttee, with his leg tied up and the end of the bandage flapping behind him[1]."

C and D Companies of the 1/6th went over the parapet together. It is a misnomer to say they attacked Thiepval, for not a man got more than a hundred yards across No Man's Land. One platoon commander (Second-Lieut. S. Hickson) of C Company, with many men of his platoon following, rushed forward a dozen yards and then looking round, saw no one behind him, all had fallen, killed or wounded. A minute later he, himself, was dangerously wounded and dropped into a shell hole. Both Company Commanders, Capt. Fawcett (C) and Capt. Heselton (D) became casualties. "The men dropped down in rows, and platoons of the other companies following behind remained in our lines, as to do anything else was suicide. It is impossible to describe the angry despair which filled every man at this unspeakable moment."

Against the storm of machine-gun and rifle bullets which swept every corner of No Man's Land, a division could not have done more than these two fine companies of the 1/6th attempted to do. "It was a gallant attack," said the Brigade Diary, "but could not succeed from the first." The enemy's parapet was alive with machine guns; the preliminary bombardment had indeed battered his trenches, but had in no way caused or prevented his troops from manning the ruins and meeting the advancing West Yorkshiremen with a murderous fire. Again and again attempts were made to climb the parapets and advance, but all in vain, those who succeeded in reaching No Man's Land only added their bodies to the pile of dead and dying.

The 1/6th was the only Battalion of the 146th Infantry Brigade which succeeded in obeying the orders to advance, with what result has been described—every third man in the Battalion had become a casualty—the results were nil!

Soon after the attack had started the 146th Infantry Brigade was

---

[1] Major C. E. Scott assumed command of the 1/6th Battalion on July 2nd *vice* Lieut.-Col. H. O. Wade, wounded. Lieut.-Col. C. E. Scott was wounded later in July, in the Leipzig Salient and died of wounds on 9th August, 1916.

The Capture of Horse Shoe Trench, of Bailiff Wood, and of Contalmaison.

ordered to place two battalions at the disposal of the 36th Division to reinforce the garrison at the Schwaben Redoubt, but at that period it was obviously impossible to carry out the orders for the 1/6th was then making its gallant, but vain, effort; the 1/5th was on the way the 1/8th waiting in support and a part of the 1/7th (the reserve battalion) had been despatched to Paisley Avenue and Authuille to fetch up ammunition which was badly needed. A little later the 146th Infantry Brigade was ordered to place two battalions at the disposal of the 32nd Division. 1ST JULY.
1/5TH, 1/6TH
1/7TH, 1/8TH
BATTALIONS.

Eventually the 1/7th Battalion was ordered up to assist the 32nd Division; the 1/6th had also received the same order, but this order was subject to the collection of sufficient men of the battalion to form an efficient reinforcement, and only the 1/7th was able to proceed. The 1/5th and two companies of the 1/8th were ordered up to the Schwaben Redoubt to "make good and consolidate," but it was not until much later that they were able to go forward to the Redoubt, and then they found that previous to their arrival, three companies of the 1/7th Battalion had also been sent to the Redoubt.

From this time onward what exactly happened cannot be gathered from the Brigade or Battalion Diaries. A later entry in the Brigade Diary stated that about 8-30 p.m., one company of the 1/7th and one company of the 1/8th West Yorkshires were sent over to the German lines to form a defensive flank, facing north, to cover the operations at Fort Schwaben (Schwaben Redoubt) and to reinforce the 107th Brigade, already there. 1/7TH AND 1/8TH BATTALIONS.

The same Diary stated also :—" Exactly what happened at Fort Schwaben in the general confusion and darkness it is only possible to draw conclusions. There were a good many casualties in both officers and men and eventually the 5th West Yorkshires and the companies of the 7th and 8th West Yorkshires withdrew." There is evidence, however, that Lieut.-Col. Wood, Major Thompson, Lieut. and Adjutant Casebourne, Lieut. Jameson and Second-Lieuts. A. B. Lee, Dresser and Clough, with a small party of the 1/5th Battalion reached the Redoubt, the remainder of the Battalion moving to Johnstone's Post. 1/5TH, 1/7TH AND 1/8TH BATTALIONS.

Moreover, the 1/7th must have been engaged with the enemy, for it was in the enemy's trenches near Thiepval that Corporal George Sanders of the Battalion gained for the Regiment the second Victoria Cross awarded to it during the War. The official story was subsequently given thus in the London Gazette of 9th September, 1916 :— 1/7TH BATTALION.

" No. 3203 Corporal George Sanders, 1/7th Battalion West Yorkshire

1ST JULY.
1/7TH
BATTALION.

Regiment, Territorial Force: For most conspicuous bravery. After an advance into the enemy's trenches he found himself isolated with a party of thirty men. He organized his defence, detailed a bombing party and impressed on his men that his and their duty was to hold the position at all costs. Next morning (2nd July) he drove off an attack of the enemy and rescued some prisoners who had fallen into their hands. Later two strong bombing attacks were beaten off. On the following day he was relieved after showing the greatest courage, determination and good leadership during thirty-six hours under very trying conditions. All this time his party was without food and water, having given all their water to the wounded during the first night. After the relieving force was fully established he brought his party, nineteen strong, back to our trenches."

1ST AND 2ND
JULY.

The night of 1st/2nd July, was a horrible nightmare. Thiepval Wood was a veritable inferno. Before the attack in the early morning the Wood had been thick with trees providing ample cover, but all day long it had been pounded and lashed by H.E. and shrapnel, and when night fell, broken branches littered the ground, gaunt stumps stood naked to the skies, shorn of their beauty; the damp and churned up ground beneath reeked with gas fumes, so that men moving in the darkness and wearing their gas masks, stumbled about in vain efforts to find their units and their whereabouts. The front line trenches and many communication trenches were thick with lost and weary men, who waited for daylight in order to find their whereabouts. The dead lay everywhere and the wounded in hundreds, waiting to be evacuated. The scene at Paisley Dump was horrible in the extreme:—" As one approached Paisely Dump one became aware of noise—a noise inhuman. A wail as of enormous wet fingers on an enormous glass; a wail that rose and fell, interminable, unbearable. Then suddenly one became aware whence that wail came. All along the muddy roadway they lay—the wounded; hundreds of them; brown blanket shapes; some shouting, some moaning, some singing in delirium, some quite still."

It was warfare in its most ghastly, horrible and damnable form, but warfare of necessity; the strategical demands could not be ignored. What had the gallant Frenchmen suffered at Verdun, where the enemy had made terrific efforts to break the Allied line, and was within an ace of succeeding? The Somme—Verdun, they could not be separated! Strategically they were bound together.

It was unfortunate that the ten battalions of the West Yorkshire Regiment, in line on the 1st July, should have been engaged only

along those parts of the battle front, where the attacks were un- <small>1ST AND 2ND</small>
successful, for the impressions gained were those of bitter failure[1]. <small>JULY.</small>
The immediate success and rapid progress of the attack on the right
had not been repeated on the left. The Bapaume—Albert Road was
roughly the dividing line between success and failure. North of the
road the enemy's defences were of a very powerful nature, whilst
along the whole front, the deep dug-outs, many of them concrete, in
which his troops sheltered during the heavy bombardments, were a
surprise to General Rawlinson's divisions. In spite of the very heavy
shell fire[3] to which the German trenches and positions were subjected,
in spite of the fact that above ground enormous damage had been
done to the enemy's defences, those deep dug-outs sheltered his troops
and prevented him suffering thousands of casualties. For as soon
as the bombardments started the Germans betook themselves to
these shelters, often thirty feet below ground, coming up when the
guns had lifted in time to mount their machine guns and meet the
advancing British infantry; it was not till later that the enormous
importance of assaulting troops keeping close on the heels of the
barrage was appreciated.

The enemy, however, all along the line, in spite of the partial
failure of the initial attack, had been badly shaken and, after careful
consideration of all facts, Sir Douglas Haig decided to "carry on."
The decision to continue was given thus in the Commander-in-
Chief's own words:—" In view of the general situation at the end of
the first day's operations, I decided that the best course was to press
forward on a front extending from our junction with the French to a
point half-way between La Boisselle and Contalmaison, and to limit
the offensive on our left for the present to a slow and methodical
advance. North of the Ancre such preparations were made as would
hold the enemy to his positions, and enable the attack to be resumed
there later, if desirable, in order that General Sir Henry Rawlinson
might be left free to concentrate his attention on the portions of the
front where the attack was to be pushed home. I also decided to

[1] So far as can be ascertained from the official diaries, the casualties suffered by the ten battalions of the West Yorkshire Regiment on the 1st July, the first day of the Somme Battles of 1916, were in killed, wounded and missing:—2nd Battalion (8th Division), Officers—sixteen, Other Ranks—490; 1/5th Battalion (49th Division), Officers—three, Other Ranks—58; 1/6th Battalion (49th Division), Officers—fourteen, Other Ranks—250[2]; 1/7th Battalion (49th Division), unobtainable; 1/8th Battalion (49th Division), unobtainable; 10th Battalion (17th Division), Officers—twenty-two, Other Ranks—750; 15th Battalion (31st Division), Officers—twenty-four, Other Ranks—514; 16th Battalion (31st Division), Officers—ten, Other Ranks—313; 18th Battalion (31st Division), Officers—sixteen, Other Ranks—400; 21st Battalion Pioneers (4th Division), Officers, one, Other Ranks—eleven. Total, Officers—106; Other Ranks—2,786.

[2] These casualties were for 1st *and* 2nd July.

[3] The Artillery Ammunition Expenditure on 1st July, 1916, was 376,280 rounds.

1ST AND 2ND JULY.	place the operations against the front La Boisselle to Serre under the command of General Sir Hubert de la P. Gough, to whom I accordingly allotted the two northern Corps[1] of Sir Henry Rawlinson's Army. My instructions to Sir Hubert Gough were that his Army was to maintain a steady pressure on the front from La Boisselle to the Serre Road, and to act as a pivot on which our line would swing as our attacks on his right made progress towards the north. During the succeeding days the attack was continued on these lines."

The agonizing hours of the night 1st/2nd July crept on, and almost imperceptibly the first day merged into the second. There is a sense of comfort, of comparative safety, in daylight, which the dark hours of night deny, when the phantoms of fear and suspicion are abroad and are distorted into horrible thoughts and visions. And there was none of the many thousands who held the front line trenches on 1st July who had not had his vision of horror. For, up to that period, the Battles of the Somme, 1916, were the largest of any operations in which the British Army had taken part. " The greatest battle in the world's history," one official Diary had described it. The Diarist may be forgiven for not knowing what was to come after !

The next day—the 2nd July and after.

2ND JULY.	When dawn of the 2nd July stole across the sky, the beginning of another day of torment faced the survivors of those gallant Battalions of West Yorkshiremen.
2ND AND 10TH BATTALIONS.	Battered and broken, but with a spirit which refused to be depressed, the remnants of the 2nd and 10th Battalions (in division and in brigade respectively) had been withdrawn from the line opposite Ovillers and Fricourt.
1/5TH, 1/6TH 1/7TH, 1/8TH BATTALIONS.	The positions of the four Battalions of the 146th Infantry Brigade (49th Division) are given thus in the divisional diary :— " The 5th and 6th West Yorkshires are attached to the 32nd Division, of these three weak companies of the 6th are in the line facing Thiepval. The 5th, who were sent last night to reinforce the 107th Infantry Brigade (36th Division) in Schwaben Redoubt, are being collected near Johnstone's Post. The 7th and 8th are under the 36th Division. They are much scattered, some in the front line and some behind."

Of the 93rd Infantry Brigade (31st Division) the 15th West

---

[1] Designation—The Reserve Army : Xth and VIIIth Corps from right to left.

Yorkshires[1] were in Legend; the 16th West Yorkshires (strength five officers and 155 other ranks, including reinforcements) were in Dunmow; the 18th Battalion (strength seven officers and 170 other ranks, including reinforcements) were in Languard. _{2ND JULY. 15TH, 16TH AND 18TH BATTALIONS.}

About 8-30 in the morning the Corps Commander (Sir Aylmer Hunter-Weston) sent the following message to the 31st Division :—
" Well done, my comrades of the 31st Division. Your discipline and determination were magnificent, and it was bad luck alone that has temporarily robbed you of success."

A mournful day of collecting the wounded and burying the dead and trying to reorganize their scattered ranks, was spent by the Leeds and Bradford Pals. A comparatively quiet day was a boon for which all were thankful, no attack being made from the front of the 93rd Infantry Brigade, throughout the 2nd July.

At Thiepval the situation was still obscure, and in the early hours of the 2nd July neither 146th Brigade Headquarters nor 49th Divisional Headquarters were quite certain of the exact whereabouts of the West Yorkshire battalions. The 1/5th, which had been reported as attached to the 36th Division, was holding Schwaben Redoubt, but only a small party of officers (including Lieut.-Col. Wood) and men were in the stronghold; the remainder of the Battalion was at Johnstone's Post. Throughout the 2nd, the 36th Division claimed the services of the companies at Johnstone's Post, so that all day the 1/5th Battalion may be said to have been engaged in furnishing carrying parties for the Ulstermen. Shell fire was again heavy and the 1/5th lost Major F. C. Thompson (missing) and three officers killed (including the Adjutant, Lieut. Canbourne), three officers wounded and three other ranks killed and fifty wounded. _{1/5TH BATTALION}

The 1/6th Battalion (all that was left of it) again went through a day of agony. The Battalion held the front line opposite Thiepval, with three weak companies. The trenches were packed, the fire bays in places sheltering as many as a dozen men. Grimly they held to the battered trenches, into which every now and then, the enemy's big shells fell, spreading death and destruction. The line resembled a shambles. " For hours," said an officer of the Battalion, " sweating, praying, cursing, we worked at the heaps of stark and mangled bodies. Men did astonishing things, at which one did not wonder till after. Here is an instance of fortitude. A man had his right arm and leg torn off clean. His left hand wandered over his chest to the pulp _{1/6TH BATTALION.}

---

[1] Strength not given, but the Battalion had lost twenty-four officers and 504 other ranks, and was practically non-existent. A private diary stated that only forty-seven answered " roll call."

2ND JULY.

where his right shoulder had been. 'My God,' he said, 'I've lost my arm.' The hand crept down to the stump of the right thigh. 'Is that off too?' he asked. I nodded. It was impossible to move him at that time. For five hours he lay there fully conscious and smoking cigarettes. When at last we tried to carry him out the stretcher stuck in the front traverse. We got him on a ground sheet and struggled on. But our strength was gone; we could not hold his weight. 'Drag me,' he suggested then, and we dragged him along the floor of the trench to the medical dug-out."

1/7TH AND 1/8TH BATTALIONS.

The 1/7th and 1/8th Battalions were also with the 36th Division. Two companies—A and B—had been gradually withdrawn from the front line trenches in the wood and assembled in trenches near Gordon Castle; C and D Companies remaining in the front line. Both the 1/7th and 1/8th Battalions passed through a day of horrors. But relief came at last, when during the evening of 2nd, the whole Brigade was drawn out of the line to the Assembly Trenches (A) in Aveluy Wood.

Utterly exhausted and worn, with their ranks terribly thinned, the West Yorkshiremen, on reaching Aveluy Wood, bivouacked for the night. Some of the Companies, however, were not " in " until dawn. " I found myself leaning on a rifle," said a man of the 1/6th Battalion, " staring stupidly on the forty exhausted men who slept around me. It did not occur to me to lie down until someone pushed me into a bed of ferns. There were flowers among the ferns and my last thought was a dull wonder that there could still be flowers in the world."

10TH BATTALION.

Along the whole front of the Battle during the 2nd July, the capture of Fricourt and Fricourt Wood and the farm to the north of it by the 17th Division, was the only notable achievement. But, as already shown, the 10th West Yorkshires (of the 50th Infantry Brigade, 17th Division) were not in these attacks.

Strong enemy counter-attacks on the Briqueterie and on Montauban had been repulsed.

North of the Ancre no attacks had been launched, on or by the enemy, only south of the River was the struggle continued, the Germans contesting every yard of ground.

3RD—4TH JULY.

On the 3rd and 4th July, the village of Bernafay and Caterpillar Wood were captured and the British Line had been pushed forward to the railway north of Mametz. The reduction of La Boiselle was also completed, after hard fighting.

Fresh divisions had come up into the line, whilst those who had taken part in the initial attack were withdrawn for a period, to rest and refit. Amongst the new divisions which replaced their exhausted comrades and carried on the Battle were the 23rd ("in" on July 3rd) and 3rd ("in" on the 8th July); both these divisions took over the front line trenches for the first time in the Somme Battles, on the dates given.

The 11th Battalion West Yorkshire Regiment (Lieut.-Col. Barker, commanding) belonged to the 23rd Division and the 12th Battalion West Yorkshire Regiment (Major W. O. Oswald, commanding) to the 3rd Division. 11TH AND 12TH BATTALIONS.

From the 1st April until the end of May the 11th West Yorkshires were in and out of the Ancres Sector, in front of Souchez. June 1st found the Battalion in billets and training near Hersin, and it was not until the end of the month (on 24th) that the 23rd Division, as a whole, entrained for Longeau, from which place a move was made towards the scene of the Somme Battles. On the last day of June, the 11th Battalion was at Coisy, billeted in the village with 69th Infantry Brigade Head Quarters (23rd Division). 11TH BATTALION. 1ST APRIL— 30TH JUNE.

The 23rd Division had been ordered to move on the night of 1st July to the Baizieux area. At 9-30 a.m. on the morning of 3rd July, the Division received orders from IIIrd Corps Headquarters to place one brigade at the disposal of the 34th Division, then holding the line opposite and south-east of La Boisselle. The 69th Infantry Brigade was detailed. During the day the Brigade moved forward and occupied the line Usna Hill—Tara Hill—Bécourt Wood. 1ST JULY.

At 5-30 p.m. the Brigade was ordered to take over the front line trenches held by troops of the 101st and 102nd Infantry Brigades (34th Division). The line extended from the northern edge of Round Wood (X.21.d.5.6.), thence along the trenches running north-west (including Scots Redoubt) to X.21.a.0.6. Two battalions were to hold the front line—11th West Yorkshires on the right, and 9th Yorkshire Regiment, on the left, the two remaining battalions of the Brigade in reserve on the Usna—Tara—Bécourt Line.

The Capture of Horseshoe Trench.

In darkness and under shell fire, each man carrying three days' rations, the Battalions set out to take over the line. The West Yorkshiremen relieved the 16th Royal Scots in Scots Redoubt and the adjacent trenches, the relief being completed at 11-30 p.m. On 11TH BATTALION. 3RD—4TH JULY.

11TH BATTALION.

the morning of the 4th July the 9th Yorkshire Regiment began bombing operations, and by 9-30 a.m. had made progress. The 11th West Yorkshires joined in but the attack does not seem to have been very successful, for although the Battalion reached its objective, it was forced to relinquish the position gained. " Attacked the enemy's lines during the afternoon and obtained our objective. We were forced to retire, so fell back on our own lines."[1] Constant bombing attacks by both sides took place during the remainder of the day, and on the night of the 4th/5th, but no important alteration of the line took place.

4TH—5TH JULY.

5TH JULY.

The 69th Brigade had received orders to capture Horseshoe Trench on the 5th, Zero hour being fixed for 4 a.m. The attack was to be made by the 10th West Riding Regiment, the objectives Point X.21.b.5.6., through Point 74. Orders to 11th West Yorkshires to co-operate from Point 35 did not reach that Battalion, but none the less the gallant West Yorkshiremen attacked, and by 6-45 a.m. reports were sent back that the Battalion held Points 35 and 56. For two hours the 11th stuck to the positions gained, but under heavy bombing attacks were forced to retire in the face of a fierce counter-attack. By 10-25 the 11th West Yorkshires were back in Scots Redoubt, where they entirely held their own after being reinforced by one company and one Lewis gun from the 10th West Riding Regiment. The latter Battalion had also been pressed back and by 10-55 a.m. held Point 33 only.

Throughout the day incessant bombing attacks by and on the enemy took place. The confused fighting in unknown and broken trenches, in very wet weather tried the men to the very utmost, but they stuck it grandly.

A second attack across the open by the 9th and 8th Battalions Yorkshire Regiment, sent up to relieve the 11th West Yorkshires and 10th West Riding Regiment was ordered for 6 p.m. But before the relief took place, and before Zero hour arrived, at about 4-30 p.m., the 11th West Yorkshires, with the 10th West Ridings again made local attacks on the enemy. Horseshoe Trench was stormed and over eighty Germans surrendered. On the left the 9th Yorkshires, advancing across the open completed the demoralization of the enemy, who surrendered freely, and over a hundred more prisoners and several machine guns were taken.

The whole of Horseshoe Trench was now rapidly occupied, and

[1] Battalion Diary, 11th Battalion West Yorkshire Regiment.

cleared of the enemy by 7 p.m. By 10 p.m. the whole line 74-56-00-79 to just west of 49 were in possession of the 69th Brigade. A detached post was pushed out to the Triangle, and held during the night.

The 11th West Yorkshires on relief by the 8th Yorkshire Regiment marched back to bivouacs in Bécourt Wood. "The perseverance and tenacity shown by the 11th West Yorkshire Regiment, and by the 10th West Riding Regiment in their ultimately successful efforts to gain ground, displayed very high qualities and both Battalions, though exhausted physically, were in the highest spirits, and full of devotion up to the time of their relief."[1]

On the 8th July, the 69th Infantry Brigade (less 10th West Riding Regiment, placed at the disposal of the 24th Infantry Brigade), marched to billets and bivouacs in Albert and, during the 9th, " stood fast," the battalions parading for " cleaning up."

The Brigade had, however, been warned that it was to attack and capture Contalmaison on 10th, and on the morning of that day, at 11 a.m., moved off independently to positions of readiness for the attack.

The Capture of Bailiff Wood and Contalmaison.

Bailiff Wood lay due west of the village of Contalmaison and, during the 7th and 8th July, gallant efforts had been made by the 24th and 68th Infantry Brigades of the 23rd Division to capture both places. The village had indeed been entered but, under the enemy's barrage of great intensity and the fire of countless machine guns in Bailiff Wood, in Contalmaison itself, and at the northern end of Quadrangle Trench, the two Brigades were forced to retire. Ground had, however, been won.

On the morning of the 10th July, the position of the 23rd Division was approximately as follows:—the 24th and 68th Infantry Brigades were at the southern and western approaches to Contalmaison village, and the 69th Infantry Brigade was preparing to pass between them to the assault. Early in the afternoon the latter Brigade was drawn up in two extended lines behind Bailiff Wood, the first line consisting of two companies of the 11th West Yorkshires, the second, of the 9th Yorkshire Regiment, and the 8th Yorkshires were about 500 yards in rear. The remaining companies of the 11th West Yorkshires were in reserve around Scots Redoubt. The attack as

[1] 69th Infantry Brigade Diary—July, 1916.

11TH BATTALION. 10TH JULY.

planned consisted of two operations—the capture of Bailiff Wood and the trenches to the north of it, which flanked the approaches to Contalmaison from the west; and the main attack on the village, with the line of trenches just west of it.

The actual disposition of the 69th Infantry Brigade at Zero hour was:—two companies 11th West Yorkshires (under Lieut.-Col. Barker) from about X.15.b.7.2. to X.15.d.9.7.; 9th Yorkshire Regiment from about X.15.a.8.0. (exc.) to about X.15.d.3.2.; 8th Yorkshire Regiment from about X.15.d.3.2. to X.21.b.5.6.

Two companies 11th West Yorkshire Regiment in reserve between Scots Redoubt and Point X.21.b.5.6.

The West Yorkshiremen were to attack Bailiff Wood at 4-30 p.m., and twenty minutes later the 9th and 8th Yorkshire Regiment were to assault the trenches west of Contalmaison.

The bombardment and barrage began at 4 p.m. On the latter lifting at 4-30 p.m., the assault on Bailiff Wood began. The two companies of West Yorkshiremen, in four waves per company, followed by " searching " and consolidating parties, left their forming-up line and advanced in quick time in extended order on Bailiff Wood. Ten minutes before the assault the enemy counter-attacked Points 46 and 65 from the north, but machine guns previously placed in position, broke up the attack with heavy loss.

The Artillery barrage had been very effective, and large parties of the enemy were seen running northwards from Contalmaison. Posts which had been placed about Bailiff Wood kept the enemy under heavy machine-gun fire as the West Yorkshiremen advanced, materially assisting the task of the latter. Considerable opposition was however, experienced, but Colonel Barker's two companies were not to be denied, and the Wood was occupied. The next movement was to wheel northwards from the eastern exits of the Wood, and capture the trench running east and west, from Point 26 to 13. This was carried out with great dash and, although the enemy again counter-attacked, Lewis guns and machine-gun fire broke up all attempts to eject the West Yorkshiremen from their new positions. At 4-50 p.m., especially, the enemy attempted a bombing attack from the east along the trenches north of Bailiff Wood, but was driven off.

At 4-50 p.m. the main attack began, the guns lifting from the trenches west of the village to 200 yards further east. With great gallantry the 9th and 8th Yorkshire Regiments pressed forward, though the enemy's machine guns caused heavy casualties. The success on the northern flank of Colonel Barker's two companies of

West Yorkshiremen, relieved the pressure, however, on the 9th Yorkshire Regiment, who, fighting their way forward, pushed through the village, the 9th wheeling north and forming up eventually in the north-west corner of the village with the 11th West Yorkshires. Here, at Point 25, the latter Battalion had formed a strong point with a block and two Lewis guns. The 8th Yorkshire Regiment, on the right, had a very severe task, as the enemy had mounted many machine guns to repel the attack which he knew would be made. But nothing could stem the dash of the Yorkshiremen, and soon Contalmaison was in the hands of the 69th Infantry Brigade. {11TH BATTALION. 10TH JULY.}

The 11th West Yorkshires did not stay long in the line they had captured, for shortly afterwards they were relieved by the Cameron Highlanders, and withdrawn to Albert during the 11th July.

The two reserve companies of 11th West Yorkshires in and about Scots Redoubt, moved forward on the successful assault of Contalmaison, with ammunition and materials, as reinforcements. Major Hudson was in charge of these companies and with great skill and intrepidity led his men through a very heavy barrage, which the enemy had put down, without the loss of a single man. They were joined by the 10th West Riding Regiment and the two battalions, though much exhausted, set to work to place the village in a state of defence.

The whole attack had gone well and the congratulations which were afterwards showered upon the 69th Brigade, and the battalions which had taken part in the operations, were well deserved.[1] Over 280 prisoners and nine machine guns were taken.

On the 11th the two companies of West Yorkshiremen, who had gone up to the village as reinforcements, were relieved and rejoined their battalion in Bécourt Wood. The Battalion in this and the actions of 4th and 5th July had lost sixteen officers and about 350 men.

The 69th Brigade was relieved by the 1st Brigade (1st Division) at 1-20 a.m. on the 12th, and marched to bivouacs near Albert, moving later in the day to billets in Franvillers. {12TH JULY.}

The Leipzig Salient.

During the fight for Horseshoe Trench and Contalmaison, the 1/5th, 1/6th, 1/7th and 1/8th West Yorkshires of the 49th Division {1/5TH, 1/6TH, 1/7TH, 1/8TH BATTALIONS. 7TH JULY.}

---

[1] "The G.O.C., the Division cannot allow the action of the 69th Brigade on July 10th, to pass without special recognition. Nothing could have exceeded the steadiness and gallantry with which they carried out the attack and bore themselves in the hard fighting that followed. The example of gallantry and devotion to duty they set calls for the highest admiration and the Division is proud to possess such gallant comrades in their ranks." Special Order of the Day by Major-General J. M. Babington, C.B., C.M.G., 11th July, 1916.

7TH JULY.

had, on the 7th July, moved forward for the second time into the troubled area about Thiepval. The Leipzig Salient was the portion of the line now allotted to the 146th Infantry Brigade.

It will be remembered that after the opening phase of the Somme Battles, 1916, on 1st July, the two northern corps of the Fourth Army had been transferred to the Reserve (Fifth Army), the latter receiving instructions to contain the enemy by maintaining a steady pressure on the front from La Boisselle to Serre. There was strong evidence that the *morale* of the enemy had been badly shaken, his lines being in a state bordering on chaos. Under these circumstances the continuance of attacks by the Fourth Army and the maintenance of steady pressure by the Reserve Army might be expected to produce the desired results.

And so, north of La Boisselle, steady pressure, or the " nibbling process," had already begun when the 146th Infantry Brigade was ordered back into the front line trenches.

1/8TH BATTALION.
1/5TH BATTALION.

The new front to be taken over by the Brigade extended from Mersey Street (just west of The Nab) to Thiepval Avenue. The 1/8th West Yorkshires were to hold the right sub-sector from Mersey Street to Oban Avenue, and the 1/5th Battalion from Oban Avenue to Thiepval Avenue, both inclusive. The 1/5th was to hold the front on a two-company basis, the remaining companies in Authuille defences.

1/6TH AND 1/7TH BATTALIONS.

The 1/6th and 1/7th Battalions were ordered to remain in B Group Assembly trenches in Aveluy Wood during the night 7th/8th, and on the following morning the 1/7th Battalion was to take over the Leipzig Salient from the 8th Loyal North Lancashires.

The relief of the 25th Division was to be completed on the 8th.

7TH/8TH JULY.
1/8TH BATTALION.
1/5TH BATTALION.

Throughout the night 7th/8th—a cold night of incessant rain—the four battalions of West Yorkshiremen moved forward to take over the sector. The 1/8th duly relieved the 10th Cheshire Regiment in the right, and the 1/5th, the other battalion of the 25th Division, in the left sub-sectors.

1/7TH BATTALION.
1/6TH BATTALION.

Very early in the morning, the 1/7th completed the relief of the Loyal North Lancashires in the Leipzig Salient, while the 1/6th moved up to " Quarry Dug-out " on the Aveluy—Authuille Road, relieving the remnants of the 3rd Worcester Regiment. " These men had been in the line continuously since July 1st, and were in a state of extreme exhaustion. They were asleep and crowded together in the small stuffy dug-outs. It was almost impossible to wake them. Only one officer was left, and he roundly declared that he would not disturb his men 'for any damned battalion in the British Army!" 8TH JULY. Who could blame him! "There were about eighty of them, all that was left of his battalion. They marched off at noon, covered with mud and blood, and decorated with German helmets and bayonets and other souvenirs of the Leipzig Salient."[1]

Throughout the day the shelling on both sides was heavy, snipers were busy, and bursts of machine-gun fire every now and then added their din to the roar of the artillery. There was but one order—to hold on; and to the battalion in the Leipzig Salient—to hold the Salient "at all costs." For the Salient was of great military importance. Its high elevation provided a fine field of view over the German lines and from Moquet Farm to Pozières any movement of the enemy could be observed and machine-gun fire brought to bear on him from "N" and "K" Saps, to which the West Yorkshiremen clung with great tenacity.

From the 8th to the 15th the 1/8th Battalion records that it "took part in demonstrations connected with this operation." The Diary of the 1/5th, covering the same period, records principally "Repair of trenches," with daily list of casualties suffered—three officers wounded; twelve other ranks killed and fifty-six wounded for the period. 1/8TH BATTALION. 1/5TH BATTALION. 8TH—15TH JULY.

On the 9th the 1/6th Battalion filed into the trenches in the Salient, and relieved the 1/7th, the latter marching back to the Bluff, Authuille. Heavy shelling on the 10th and 11th kept the 1/6th Battalion constantly on the alert: "The 1/7th Battalion had very little to hand over except thousands of Mills bombs, S.A.A. and the curiosities of the place, such as corpses, German rifles, bayonets and gas masks." On the 13th (at 1 a.m.) the enemy made an attack on the 1/6th, but was repulsed. On the night 12th/13th the 1/7th again took over the Salient and the 1/6th moved back to dug-outs at the South Bluff, Authuille. 1/6TH BATTALION. 9TH JULY. 13TH JULY. 1/7TH BATTALION.

The Battle of Albert ended on the 13th July, and by that date practically the whole of the enemy's front system of defences from east of Montauban to Ovillers-la-Boisselle were in the hands of British troops. The enemy had done his best to render this system impregnable. The villages captured were all most elaborately defended; the enemy's deep dug-outs of immense strength admirably protected his troops from the intense shell fire of light and heavy guns, which had poured concentrated fire upon the German trenches,

[1] The Official Despatches do not mention that a permanent footing was obtained in the Leipzig Salient on 1st July, but from various diaries it seems certain that a foothold was obtained and *held* in this portion of the German line on the first day of the Battle of Albert (1st—13th July).

1/7TH BATTALION. 13TH JULY.

in many places levelling them to the ground, but the underground defences remained.

Both sides had suffered very heavy casualties, but, as has already been pointed out, the Battle was not without favourable results—the enemy's *morale* had been badly shaken and the " wearing out " tactics had begun to show signs of success, for the pressure on Verdun—a highly necessary outcome of the operations—had to be relieved.

THE BATTLE OF BAZENTIN RIDGE:
14th—17th July.
1. The Capture of Bazentin-le-Grand and Longueval.

THE line reached by the British attacks from 1st to 13th July (inclusive) ran from just north-west of Hardicourt, thence northwards to Trones Wood, where a portion of the eastern, the whole of the southern and half of the western edges of the Wood were held. From Trones Wood the line gradually sloped south-west to the northern exits of Bernafay Wood, thence round the northern and western edge of Montauban, rising again in a snake-like line (the shape of Caterpillar Wood) to the eastern and northern outskirts of Mametz Wood, then almost direct north, north of the village of Contalmaison, round Contalmaison Wood, joining up with the old British line, north-west of Ovillers-la-Boisselle.

It will be seen from the map that both the operations which began on 14th July and ended on 17th July were directed against the Bazentin Ridge, lying roughly between Bazentin-le-Grand and Longueval. There was a break along the Ridge, in the German Second Line defence system, and it is obvious that the attack was designed for the purpose of penetrating this gap in the enemy's defences, then by turning north-west and south-east exploit the successes gained. The attack would have to cross the valley between Trones Wood and Mametz Wood and storm the slopes which led up to the Ridge; it was not an easy proposition. 14TH JULY.

In the interval between the 1st and 13th July, the enemy had no doubt dug trenches along the Ridge and had erected belts of wire entanglements sufficient to hold up the advance of troops, unless previously cut by shell fire.

Artillery preparations began on 11th July; the guns bombarded heavily the whole of the line to be assaulted, and especially the villages of Bazentin-le-Petit, Bazentin-le-Grand and Longueval. The positions already won offered facilities for enfilading the enemy's lines, and these were exploited to the fullest advantage.

The divisions detailed to take part in the operations, from right to left:—18th (West of Trones Wood), 9th (North-east of

Montauban), 3rd (Caterpillar Wood), 7th (East of Mametz Wood), 21st (north-west corner of Mametz Wood), 1st, north-east, and 34th north-west of Contalmaison.

The 3rd Division occupied almost the centre of the attack and, with the 9th Division, had a great deal of hard and desperate fighting, the enemy's resistance between Longueval and Bazentin being particularly stubborn.

In this fighting the 12th Battalion West Yorkshire Regt. (9th Infantry Brigade, 3rd Division) took a prominent part.

As early as the 20th March, the 3rd Division had begun to train for the "approaching offensive," but the move south to the Somme area did not take place until the 1st July. In the meantime the Division continued to relieve and be relieved, by various divisions in the St. Eloi Sector, Kemmel Defences, and the line east of Bailleul, and it was not until 17th June that the Division entrained, at 9 a.m., for Audricqs where, until the 30th of that month, training and final preparations were made for the coming operations. By that time the "Somme Battles" had acquired an evil reputation; it was said that a subaltern's life down south was worth only about a week's purchase; and the stories of awesome bombardments, the like of which had never been witnessed, made hideous the days and nights. Nevertheless all ranks were keen and entrainment orders were welcome.

The 12th West Yorkshires were now commanded by Major W. O. Oswald, Lieut.-Col. Leggett having been appointed to command the Second Army School of Instruction. The Battalion, since the St. Eloi actions, had passed a comparatively quiet existence, the dull monotony of trench warfare being relieved only by tours out of the line in reserve.

On the 1st July, the Battalion, in Brigade, entrained at Audricqs for Doullens and, on detrainment at the latter place, marched to Bernaville, where a day's rest afforded all ranks opportunities for making final preparations. On the 3rd, the Battalion marched to Vignacourt, on the 4th to Poulainville, on the 5th to La Houssaye and on the 6th to Morlancourt. The 3rd Division was now in reserve in the Somme Area and ready to move up to the front line. At 4-30 p.m. on the afternoon of the 6th, orders were received from 3rd Divisional Headquarters: the 8th Infantry Brigade was to relieve the 53rd Infantry Brigade (18th Division) in the right sub-sector of the line on the night 7th/8th; the 9th Infantry Brigade was to relieve the 54th Infantry Brigade in the left sub-sector on the night 8th/9th, while the 76th Infantry Brigade was to relieve the 27th Infantry Brigade of the 9th Division on the right of the 8th Infantry Brigade. The relief of the 53rd Infantry Brigade by the 8th Brigade was duly carried out on the night 7th/8th.

12TH BATTALION.

At 10-15 a.m. on the 8th, the 9th Infantry Brigade Column, led by the 13th King's R. set out from Morlancourt. The 12th West Yorkshires followed at 12-15 p.m., and the remaining battalions and Brigade Headquarters at various times until 4-15 p.m. When darkness fell on the 8th, the 13th King's R. took over the front line of the left sub-sector, the 12th West Yorkshires being in support in the Triangle, the old German Front Line system.

8TH JULY.

The new line of the 3rd Division ran from the Montauban—Longueval Road (inclusive to 9th Division) along Montauban Alley, thence westward including almost the whole of Caterpillar Wood; there was a deep pocket between Montauban village and Caterpillar Wood. Marlboro' Wood was also held by the Division.

With the exception of the 13th King's R., holding the front line trenches, the 12th West Yorkshires and other units of the 9th Infantry Brigade were employed in forming a main Brigade Dump at The Loop.

After dark, the Brigade Staff, with C.O.'s and Company Commanders of each unit (in particular of the King's R. and 12th West Yorkshires, the two battalions detailed for the attack on 14th) proceeded to reconnoitre the ground over which the assault was to take place. On the 10th and 11th similar reconnaissances were carried out.

The 12th West Yorkshires relieved the 13th King's in the front line on the night of 10th/11th. On the 11th the Devons, of the 7th Division, relieved the West Yorkshiremen, the latter battalion returning to The Loop, with the exception of one company in Montauban, two platoons in Marlboro' Wood and one platoon in Caterpillar Wood. The Battalion Diary of the 12th records the first casualty on the Somme—Lieut. E. A. Courthope being wounded.

11TH JULY.

Divisional Operation Orders were issued on the 13th. Briefly the plan of attack to be carried out by the 3rd Division was as follows: under cover of darkness, an approach from the Montauban Ridge was to be made to a line roughly 250 yards from the enemy's front line of wire, where the troops would be deployed for the attack. The 8th Infantry Brigade on the right and the 9th on the left were to attack, each brigade having two assaulting battalions ("New Army battalions," the Divisional narrative states), with a battalion in

12TH BATTALION. 13TH JULY.

support and another in reserve. The assaulting battalions were to attack in four lines, the supporting battalions being in similar formation in rear. The 9th Division was attacking on the right and the 7th Division on the left of the 3rd.

The objective of the Division was the enemy's second line from just east of the communication trench between S.16.b.6.5 and S.16.b.5.2 to S.15.a.2.1 and the village of Bazentin-le-Grand.

On the 9th Infantry Brigade front, the 13th King's R. was to attack on the right and the 12th West Yorkshires on the left.

The task set the 12th West Yorkshires was by no means light. The Battalion had (*i*.) to capture and consolidate the enemy support line from S.15.a.3.3 (*ii*.) To establish a defensive line from road junction at north-east corner of Bazentin-le-Grand Wood, along track or ditch to road junction S.15.a.9.9 exclusive (*iii*.) to construct strong points at (*a*) S.15.C.5.7; (*b*) S.15.C.2.4 at elbow of trench (*c*) S.15.a.3.1; (*iv*.) to keep in touch with and assist the attack of the 20th Infantry Brigade (7th Division) on their left.

Zero hour was to be at 3-25 a.m. on the 14th.

At 9-45 p.m. on 13th markers were sent out to mark out a track for units proceeding to positions for attack. Previously, after darkness had fallen, the troops of both Brigades, who were to assault the enemy's positions, assembled in Caterpillar Valley; only one man was wounded during the operation.

14TH JULY.

By 10-30 p.m., under cover of a screen of picquets, which had been established within 200 yards of the German trenches, the 8th and 9th Brigades advanced in line of companies, in fours, at 100 yards interval. The line of deployment was marked by the Sunken Road parallel with, and 250 yards from, the German trenches and, by 1.45 a.m., all four battalions forming the assault were digging cover in the positions allotted to them. No casualties were suffered during these operations. About midnight three Prussian deserters had given themselves up to the outposts of the 12th West Yorkshires. No sooner were the troops in position, than carrying parties waiting at the dumps in rear, began to move stores and ammunition up to the forward dumps behind each assaulting battalion; this procedure continued until 3 a.m.

Meanwhile the assaulting and supporting battalions of the 8th Infantry Brigade had begun creeping forward and by 3-15 a m. the leading line was only about 120 yards from the German trenches. The 9th Infantry Brigade, being nearer the enemy's positions, began this operation at 3-20 a.m. At that hour also an intense bombardment of the German front line began and unfortunately several casualties were caused by " short " shells.

12TH BATTALION.
14TH JULY.

The move forward towards the enemy's trenches was undiscovered and was a highly creditable performance.

As Zero hour approached there was great excitement amongst the attacking troops, for no one knew for certain whether the enemy was prepared or whether the attack (as planned) would be a complete surprise.

At 3-25 a.m. the guns lifted from the enemy's wire and front line to the support trenches and the assaulting troops jumped to their feet and advanced at quick time towards their objectives.

On the right the 8th Infantry Brigade came up against strong belts of wire, which had not been properly cut, and although desperate and gallant efforts were made to get through, only small parties managed to get into the German first line, the majority of the troops of the two assaulting battalions taking cover in shell holes, whence the Lewis guns fired on the German trenches, or fell back taking whatever natural cover offered itself.

Meanwhile the 9th Infantry Brigade had progressed in its forward movement. The 13th King's (right) crossing the rise in front of the enemy's wire came under heavy machine-gun fire from the first trench and Bazentin-le-Grand, and also a certain amount of hostile shell fire, but the wire in front of the Battalion had been well cut and the trench was quickly reached and captured. The King's then pushed on immediately to the second line (or where it was presumed to be) but it had been utterly obliterated by the British Artillery and was non-existent. Heavy machine-gun fire was now opened from the village and the communication trench joining the first and second German lines, which formed the dividing line between the 9th and 8th Infantry Brigades. A considerable number of men of the King's fought their way into the village, where they came under their own artillery fire; what happened to them is not recorded. By 4-15 a.m. the machine guns of the King's R. were in position in the German front line, and the enemy's fire from the communication trench was kept down.

On the left of the King's the 12th West Yorkshires were making good progress, though the existence of a gap between their right and the left of the King's, who had lost heavily, held the Battalion back. By 4-30 a.m., however, Major Oswald had sent back a report to Brigade Headquarters that his Battalion had not only gained all

12TH
BATTALION.
14TH JULY.

its objectives in the front line but a part of the German second line as well. He stated also that his casualties were heavy and appealed for reinforcements. Three companies of the 1st Northumberland Fusiliers were therefore sent forward to strengthen the attack. Ten minutes later the West Yorkshiremen reported that they were in the second line and were experiencing little or no opposition. At 5-26 another report reached Brigade Headquarters stating that Major Oswald's Battalion had gained all objectives.

The Northumberland Fusiliers had reinforced the 13th King's and 12th West Yorkshires each with one company, the third company remaining in the Sunken Road.

Stokes guns now opened on Bazentin-le-Grand, and with the assistance of the Northumberland Fusiliers the village was cleared of the enemy. Considerable machine-gun and rifle fire from Bazentin-le-Grand Wood and from the village had for a while caused the 12th West Yorkshires considerable trouble and losses, but as the 7th Division, on the left of the Battalion, advanced, fire from these two places ceased. By 6-30 a.m. both the German second line and the village were captured and the West Yorkshiremen, assisted by the Northumberland Fusiliers, were in possession of their allotted portion of Bazentin-le-Grand, *i.e.*, the north-west corner of the village. A counter-attack on the 13th King's was repulsed with considerable loss to the enemy.

Just before 9 a.m. British Cavalry passed through and advanced towards High Wood, capturing a few prisoners.

From 8-55 a.m. onwards until noon, the positions gained were in process of consolidation, but the 8th Infantry Brigade, on the right of the 3rd Division front, was still in difficulty. However, after further artillery preparation and vigorous attacks by bombers, the trenches, which had held up the advance of the Brigade, were taken, and consolidation of the whole front was rapidly begun.

Turning to the Battalion Diary of the 12th West Yorkshires, there is little in it not hitherto explained. But the concluding part describes the wounding of its gallant Commanding Officer :—" The battalion carried out the tasks allotted to it and during the day worked hard at consolidation. About 7 p.m., the C.O., Major W. O. Oswald, who had returned to Battalion Headquarters to rest, was hit by a piece of the driving band off one of our own shells, also Second-Lieut. W. Murrell. Major Thomson was wired for and he arrived to take over command."

The Battalion's losses on the 14th July, were six officers killed and seven wounded, including Major Oswald, who unfortunately died of his wounds on 16th July. In other ranks the Battalion lost forty-six killed, 170 wounded and twenty-four missing. <small>12TH BATTALION. 14TH JULY.</small>

Elsewhere along the whole front attacked the enemy's trenches had been overrun by troops of the 18th, 9th, 7th, 21st, 1st and 34th Divisions, from right to left; it will be remembered the 3rd Division operated between the 9th and 7th Divisions. The 18th cleared the whole of Trones Wood; the 9th had captured Longueval; the success of the attack of the 3rd has already been recorded; Bazentin-le-Grand Wood and the village of Bazentin-le-Petit had been taken by the 7th Division; the 21st cleared Bazentin-le-Petit Wood; the 1st had gained ground west of the latter wood and posts had been established immediately south of Pozières by the 34th Division.

From the 15th to the 18th the 9th Infantry Brigade made no attack, the time being spent in consolidating the positions won on 14th. Heavy shelling caused a great deal of work and the garrison of Bazentin-le-Grand had to be thinned out to minimize the danger. On the 18th, the 12th West Yorkshires had a particularly bad time. The enemy's bombardment of the second line completely levelled the trenches. One officer and twenty other ranks were killed and wounded and a party of 200 men of the Royal Fusiliers had to be sent up to assist in rebuilding the damaged trenches. <small>15TH—18TH JULY.</small>

The 9th Infantry Brigade was relieved by the 23rd Infantry Brigade on the 19th July, and marched back to bivouacs east of Talus Boise. At 6 p.m. on the 18th the 3rd Division had side-stepped and had relieved the 26th Infantry Brigade of the 9th Division in order to continue the Battle of Delville Wood which began on 15th July.

The German counter-attack on Delville Wood was launched during the afternoon of the 18th July, and, as Sir Douglas Haig stated :—

"This enemy attack on Delville Wood marked the commencement of the long, closely-contested struggle which was not finally decided in our favour till the fall of Guillemont on the 3rd September."

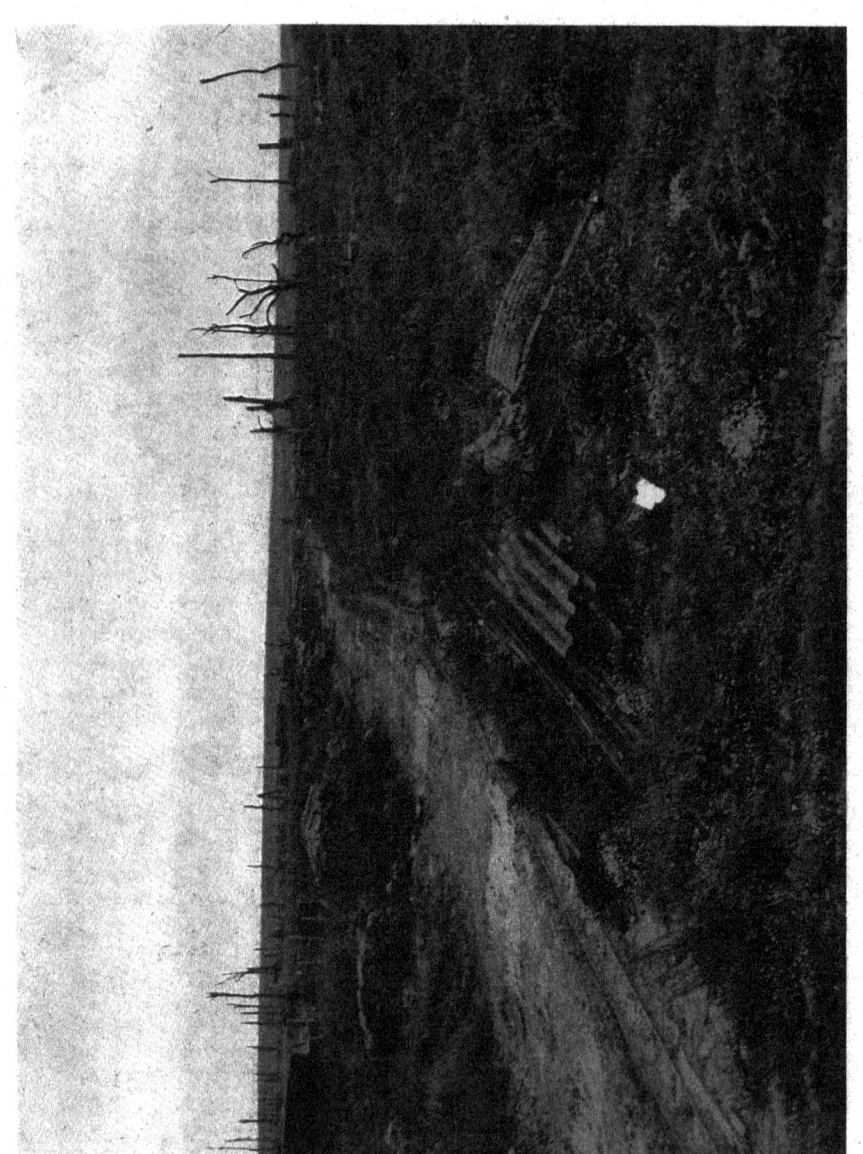

LONGUEVAL VILLAGE.

THE BATTLE OF DELVILLE WOOD.

OF the numerous operations included under the general heading of the Battles of the Somme, 1916, it would be difficult to select one in which attacks and counter-attacks took place more frequently before the final capture of the objective than the Battle of Delville Wood. For seven weeks that desperate and bloody struggle waged with the utmost fury, and when at last it remained definitely in British hands the wood itself was but a patch of tree stumps, the churned-up ground soaked with the blood of many brave men and planted thickly with their mangled bodies. To one Brigade, at least—the South African—of the 9th Division, the very name of Delville Wood conjures up memories of glorious fighting and brave deeds but also of terrible losses.

Exactly how much of the Wood was captured by the 9th Division in the first attack on 15th July it is difficult to say, but in his narrative of the operations of the 3rd Division the G.O.C. stated :—" On the 17th July, I was directed to clear the enemy from the northern edge of Longueval and the north-west corner of Delville Wood, the operation to be carried out on the following morning," *i.e.* the 18th. This attack took place at 3-45 a.m. on the 18th and was completely 18TH JULY. successful, with the exception of the capture of two German strong points north of Longueval village. " The line taken up therefore ran along the north-west edge of Delville Wood, through the north of the village and along the avenue to the west." Beginning at 9 a.m. the Germans began shelling the wood and village and all day long poured a veritable storm of shells of all calibre into these two places. At 4-30 p.m. the enemy counter-attacked and the northern half of the village and wood being untenable, the remnants of the troops who had so gallantly won these posts in the early morning were withdrawn. On the night of 19th July, the G.O.C. 3rd Division, was again ordered " to undertake the recapture of Longueval Village and Delville Wood, the southern portions of which only were in the hands of the 9th Division and ourselves." The 9th Division then held from the southern exits of Delville Wood, northwards to Princes Street, a ride running east and west, through the centre of the Wood.

20TH JULY.

22ND JULY.

12TH
BATTALON.
23RD JUILY.

17TH
BATTALION.
23RD JULY.

12TH
BATTALION.

The attack took place at 3-35 a.m. on the 20th, the 3rd Division having taken over a portion of the front from the 9th Division, as already stated. The attack failed to make any apparent progress, nevertheless a continuation of the operation was ordered. On the night of the 20th, the 3rd Division relieved portions of the 9th and 18th Divisions, holding ground in Delville Wood and about Waterlot Farm. From the latter place, on 22nd, the 8th Infantry Brigade made an attempt to reach the railway north of Guillemont, with the object of facilitating an attack later by the 30th Division against the village. Only slight progress, about half-way between Waterlot Farm and the railway, was made.

The operation against Guillemont had been fixed for the 23rd. On that date also an attack to secure Longueval Village and Delville Wood, by a mixed brigade composed of units of the 9th and 70th Infantry Brigades (3rd Division), was to be carried out.

Unfortunately the attack of the 30th Division, against Guillemont, lost direction and failed, so that the operations of the 8th Infantry Brigade, north of the village, also came to naught, the troops having to retire to their jumping-off places.

For the northern attack on Longueval Village and Delville Wood the troops were concentrated by 2-30 a.m. The 1st Northumberland Fusiliers, 13th King's and 12th West Yorkshires were in Pont Street; the 8th K.O.R.L. in the German front line, west of Longueval; two companies of the 17th West Yorkshires (attached from 106th Infantry Brigade, 35th Division) were in trenches immediately south of Montauban, the remainder of the latter Battalion being in Silesia Support and Silesia Trench. On the left of the 3rd Division, the 5th Division was to attack the enemy's line north of Longueval Village.

From the 19th July, until 9-30 p.m. on the 22nd, the 12th West Yorkshires had been out of the line resting and training at Talus Boise. The Battalion had been warned during the day that it would probably be required for another attack and the men were therefore ordered to rest as much as possible. About 10 p.m. the Battalion received orders to march in fifteen minutes and, meeting guides at Montauban, would take up their assembly positions in Pont Street. On the way up the troops ran into a heavy hostile barrage and fifteen casualties were caused amongst the Lewis gunners and bombers. On arrival at Montauban the Battalion was led on to Longueval and finally formed up for the attack in the Sunken Road west of the village.

At 3-35 a.m. the artillery had been ordered to open " intense fire " on the enemy's positions, but as one diary reports :—" very little artillery fire, however, was observed " ; the lack of it naturally affected the subsequent attack. *12TH BATTALION. 23RD JULY.*

At 3-40 a.m. the assault was launched and from the very beginning of the attack heavy machine-gun fire met the troops as they rushed forward, and caused very heavy casualties among them. At 7-25 a.m. the right company of the 1st Northumberland Fusiliers was repulsed, being held up in the village ; no news was received of the other companies ; the 12th West Yorkshires were reported in Delville Wood ; but apparently they had been held up along Piccadilly. The western portion of Longueval Village was now an inferno, Pont Street being very heavily shelled. The enemy's barrage prevented communication with Brigade and Divisional Headquarters. The attack of the 5th Division on High Wood and on the immediate left of the 3rd Division had failed and nothing could be done but withdraw the Northumberland Fusiliers, West Yorkshiremen and the King's to Pont Street.

The attempt to retake Longueval and Delville Wood had again failed, not for want of gallantry, but because it so often happened that if one part of the line failed the remainder made no progress. The failure of the 5th Division, the want of time for careful reconnaissance of the ground over which the attack was to be made, and previous heavy losses by the troops engaged, all contributed to the lack of success.

The 12th West Yorkshires lost four officers killed, four officers wounded and 155 other ranks killed, wounded and missing. At 6-30 p.m. on 23rd, the West Yorkshiremen and King's were withdrawn to Montauban Alley.

The 17th West Yorkshires, who had been attached to the 3rd Division for this operation, did not go into action, though they came under heavy shell fire and had casualties. *17TH BATTALION.*

The Battalion had but recently arrived in the Somme Area. On the 1st April, the 35th Division (in which the Battalion was contained) held the line south of Armentières ; the Battalion was at Fleurbaix. There was little doing in this part of the line in the summer of 1916. On the 4th April, the 17th West Yorkshires were at Neuf Berquin, on the 8th a move was made to Estaires and on the 12th the Battalion again went into the trenches, moving out again on the 16th to Croix Barbée. Then followed a period of moves to the following places :—Les Lobes (21st), Richbourg (10th May),

R

St.Vaast (19th), Festubert (20th); June 1st found the Battalion still at Festubert, but on the 28th it marched to Béthune, where orders were received by the 35th Division to be prepared to move at any time. The Battalion (in Brigade) entrained at Chocques on July 2nd, and on the 3rd arrived at Frevant, where the troops detrained and marched to billets in Souich; the 106th Infantry Brigade (35th Division) was now attached to XIIIth Corps of the Reserve Army. After a day in billets the journey was continued south *via* Bois du Warnimont and Varennes to Bresle, and when the operations of the 14th July began, the 17th West Yorkshires (in Brigade) were on the march to Talus Boise, where the Battalion bivouacked by the roadside, ready to move up to the front when the 35th Division went into the line. During the afternoon and evening of the 14th, working parties from the Battalion loaded trench mortar bombs at Carnoy. On the night of the 15th a working party of 200 men was sent forward to Bernafay Wood, with the object of burying cable, but owing to heavy hostile shelling little work was done; the Battalion had several casualties. Orders for an attack on Ginchy by the 106th Brigade were cancelled and the West Yorkshiremen again furnished working parties to convey ammunition to the 106th Infantry Brigade forward dumps. Another attempt on the night of 17th to bury cable in Bernfay Wood was again stopped owing to heavy shelling; the Battalion lost one officer wounded, four other ranks killed and several wounded. In the morning the C.O. 17th Battalion West Yorkshires (Lieut.-Col. F. N. J. Atkinson) and company commanders reconnoitred Delville Wood and Ginchy.

On 18th the 17th West Yorkshires were placed under the orders of the 26th Infantry Brigade (9th Division) and marched to South Trench, *i.e.* the old German line south of Montauban. Some shelling throughout the night gave the men an exceedingly uncomfortable time, but the expected order to move forward did not arrive and on the following morning (19th) two companies (Y and Z) of the Battalion were attached to the 9th Seaforths of the 8th Infantry Brigade (3rd Division) for the purpose of consolidating Montauban. During work the O.C. Z Company was wounded by shrapnel. These two companies returned to bivouacs in Caftet Wood on the night 19th/20th. Meanwhile three platoons of W Company had been lent to the 27th Infantry Brigade (9th Division) and carried lights, flares and wire up to South Street, Delville Wood.

Salvage work and the burial of dead left lying about in the neighbourhood of South Trench occupied W and X Companies most of the day, and in the evening Y and Z Companies were recalled from Caftet Wood. The Battalion was by this time under the orders of the 53rd Infantry Brigade (18th Division). At 3 a.m. (on 21st) the Battalion was relieved by a battalion of Shropshires and marched back to Caftet Wood,[1] arriving about 5 a.m. The 106th Infantry Brigade had done no fighting since it went forward on the 15th, but between that date and 20th it had lost two officers and 183 other ranks. It is possible to judge from these casualties the exceedingly uncomfortable conditions prevailing *behind* the front line. On this date Capt. S. Huffam, 17th West Yorkshires, took over temporary command of the 19th Durham Light Infantry, the C.O. of which had been injured and evacuated sick.

17TH BATTALION.
21ST JULY.

At about 8 p.m. on the 22nd the Battalion again moved up to the advanced trenches south-west of Montauban, W Company going forward to a position in Montauban Alley. The West Yorkshiremen were now under the orders of the 9th Division for the attack on Longueval and Delville Wood, which was to take place early next morning.

22ND JULY.

At 10 a.m. on the 23rd, X Company went forward to South Trench, but heavy shelling compelled the company to evacuate the trench and, about mid-day, X Company joined W in Montauban Alley. These two companies were used during the day as working parties, W Company carrying ammunition and X carrying wire to the front-line trenches in Delville Wood.

23RD JULY.

Orders were received on the 24th for the Battalion to move off and take up a position north-east of Bernafay Wood. Less sixty-five men employed at 106th Infantry Brigade Forward Dump the West Yorkshiremen took over a cummunication trench north-east of the wood. Hostile shell fire again caused the Battalion "comparatively heavy" casualties and at 9 p.m. orders to "stand to" were issued, as a German attack was expected. An outpost line was manned during the night but no attack was made. In the very early hours of the 25th—1-15 a.m.—the 106th Infantry Brigade, less the 17th West Yorkshires and 17th Royal Scots, marched off to Caterpillar Valley. More salvage work and the burying of dead kept the Battalion busy during the 25th, and at 8 p.m., through a heavy barrage of gas and tear shells, during which gas helmets had to be worn, the tired-out West Yorkshiremen marched back to Caftet Wood.

24TH JULY.

25TH JULY.

The next morning the G.O.C., 35th Division, ordered a message of congratulation and thanks to be sent to the 106th Infantry Brigade

---

[1] Caftet Wood was on the south-western outskirts of Carnoy.

17TH BATTALION.

for "the hard and good work" it had performed since the 15th. It was well deserved, for of all trying work that of continually moving about over heavily-shelled areas, suffering casualties, though unable to retaliate in any way, was most difficult and imposed a very heavy strain on all ranks.

29TH JULY.

Finally, on 29th, at 7-30 p.m., the 17th West Yorkshires moved up to Dublin Trench, in reserve to 89th Infantry Brigade, the right Brigade of 30th Division, which had been ordered to attack south of Guillemont on the following morning. Continuous preparations were made through the night 29th/30th and, although the Battalion was heavily shelled with gas and tear shells, only five casualties were suffered. The attack of the 30th Division failed and the Battalion,

31ST JULY.

on being relieved at 4-30 a.m. on the morning of 31st July, marched back, in Brigade, to Caftet Wood, thence to Sand Pit Valley, arriving at 8-30 p.m. at the latter place. The whole of the 35th Division had now been relieved and was in Sand Pit Alley.

The casualties of the 17th West Yorkshires since the 13th July are given in the Battalion Diary as ten officers and 304 other ranks, an exceedingly high percentage, as the Battalion made no attacks on the enemy, neither was it attacked directly. In the one operation on the 30th, during which the Battalion was in reserve, it had earned the commendations of the G.O.C., 106th Infantry Brigade (Brigadier-General H. O'Donnell)—" I consider that the O.C., 17th West Yorkshires, did well in firstly proceeding himself to the front line trench before Zero hour and, secondly, in pushing his battalion through the troops in front of him, and occupying the front line at a time when it would otherwise have been left vacant ; more especially as his battalion had, during the early hours of the morning, suffered from the effects of gas shells."

The 104th and 105th Infantry Brigades of the 35th Division seem to have had incessant fighting, but from the foregoing record of the movements of the 106th Infantry Brigade it will be seen that the latter had a particularly disappointing time in being attached to several different Brigades of at least four other divisions.

" On the 27th July the remainder of Delville Wood was recovered by the 2nd Division and, two days later, the northern portions of Longueval and the orchards were cleared by the 5th Division, after severe fighting."[1]

During the month of August attacks on, or by, the enemy were, to a certain extent, localized either at Delville Wood or between

---

[1] Official Despatches.

Bazentin-le-Petit and Thiepval. No opportunity was lost by British or French troops, whenever a chance offered itself, to gain ground or improve their positions.

So far as the West Yorkshire Regiment was concerned, the first of these opportunities occurred early in August when the 11th Battalion (23rd Division) took part in an attack on Munster Alley. 11TH BATTALION.

After the capture of Contalmaison the 23rd Division went into Corps Reserve (on 21st July), the 11th West Yorkshires marching to Millencourt. On 25th and 26th the Division moved back again into the line, relieving the 1st Division in the IIIrd Corps area, but it was not until the 28th that the West Yorkshiremen relieved the 13th Durham Light Infantry in Contalmaison. From the 29th July to 1st August the Battalion spent a most uncomfortable time in the village, heavy enemy shelling characterizing the tour. The 2nd, 3rd and 4th August were spent in Albert, but on the 5th the Battalion (in Brigade) again moved back to Contalmaison, relieving the 10th Northumberland Fusiliers. The line taken over by the 69th Infantry Brigade (from the 68th Infantry Brigade) extended from Munster Alley to Gloster Alley. 28TH JULY. 5TH AUG.

The Attack on Munster Alley.

The attack on Munster Alley began on 29th July, and was continued on 4th and 6th August, but not until the third attack did the 11th Battalion West Yorkshire Regt. take an active part in the operations.

The point of attack was the junction of Torr Trench and Munster Alley, the latter being an important point in the enemy's communications with Martinpuich.

At 4-15 p.m. picked bombers from the 8th Yorkshire Regt. after previous artillery bombardment, having orders to carry and hold the junction of Torr Trench and Munster, and to establish double blocks in each trench at least fifty yards beyond the junction, rushed forward to the attack. The enemy was encountered near the junction, but was at once driven back and followed 150 yards beyond the junction. Two prisoners were taken and a number of Germans killed. Heavy opposition was then encountered and the leading party, when endeavouring to make a block, was driven back twenty yards. Here another block was made and eventually two others farther back. During all this time heavy shell fire continued 6TH AUG.

and counter-attacks were made by the enemy, but the gallant Yorkshiremen held their position. Two Lewis guns were then brought up to cover Munster Alley and Torr Trench, but the latter had been completely blown out of existence by the Divisional Artillery.

At 9 p.m. the 8th Yorkshire Regt., who for five hours had been bombing and attacking continuously, was relieved by part of the 11th West Yorkshires. The latter Battalion was counter-attacked immediately by the enemy, but the attack was bloodily repulsed. All through the night the enemy continued his efforts to retake the lost ground, but in vain. No part of the trench was lost and heavy casualties were inflicted on the enemy by bombs and Lewis guns. Altogether from twenty to thirty prisoners were taken, but many of them were killed by German shell and rifle fire while being passed back. On the left of the West Yorkshires, an Australian Brigade lent very great assistance by supplying bombs of which large numbers were required.

By this time Torr Trench, Munster Alley and the surrounding ground were hardly recognizable. Shell fire had tumbled and blown the defences to bits and all around lay German dead. In many places the bodies were half buried and trodden under foot during the progress of the attack.

Towards morning (7th) the heavy hostile shelling died down and during the day the 8th Yorkshires and 11th West Yorkshires were relieved by the remaining portion of the West Yorkshiremen and three companies of the 9th Yorkshire Regt. On the 8th August the 69th Infantry Brigade was relieved by the 45th Brigade (of the 15th Division), the latter having taken over the sector from the 23rd Division. The 11th West Yorkshires moved back from Contalmaison to Bresle, billeting in the village. In his subsequent report of the attack on Munster Alley the G.O.C., 69th Infantry Brigade (Brigadier-General Lambert), said :—" Much credit is also due to the 11th West Yorkshire Regiment and other troops under Lieut.-Col. Barker for the skilful manner in which fresh men were brought up to relieve exhausted troops, to carry up bombs, ammunition and food and to defeat constant counter-attacks which continued throughout the night."

From Bresle the 11th West Yorkshires moved to Bellancourt. On the 13th, the 23rd Division entrained for Fletre (to join the Vth Corps), the West Yorkshires arriving and detraining at Bailleul at 9-30 a.m. on the 14th August. Thereafter the Battalion moved in successive stages to Mount Kokereele, Steenwerke, Romarin,

Creslow and Lewisham Lodge; at the latter place the Battalion was in support of the front-line trenches. [12TH BATTALION.]

The next operation, of a minor character, in which West Yorkshiremen were engaged, was an attack of the 3rd Division on Lonely Trench, on the 17th August. The 12th West Yorkshires, of the 9th Infantry Brigade, 3rd Division, after the only partially successful attacks of the 3rd and 5th Divisions on Delville Wood in the third week of July, had returned on 24th to Montauban Alley. From the latter place the West Yorkshiremen moved back to Sand Pits, near Meaulte, thence to Ville-sur-Ancre where, until the 12th August, the Battalion rested, reorganized and trained. On the 12th the 9th Brigade, as a whole, moved back to the Sand Pits, near Meaulte, and on the 14th paraded and marched to Carnoy, to billets. On the 15th all officers reconnoitred the trenches south of Guillemont and at 4 p.m. D Company moved forward to Maltz Horn Trench. [15TH AUG.] Heavy shelling caught the West Yorkshiremen who, in a few minutes, suffered the loss of ten other ranks wounded and one missing. At 6-30 a.m. on the 16th the remainder of the Battalion paraded and marched off independently to Maltz Horn Trench, where Battalion Headquarters with A and C Companies were placed, with B in Swainson Trench and D in Jackson Trench. The 9th Brigade generally was acting in support of the Royal Fusiliers, holding T Trench to the Barrier. Again the Battalion suffered casualties from heavy shelling, one officer sustaining shell shock and one other rank killed, fourteen wounded and one missing.

Late on the 17th, orders were received to prepare to make another attack on Lonely Trench. The previous attack launched at 5-30 p.m. on the 16th had failed. Zero hour was 10 p.m. [17TH AUG.]

In conjunction with other officers Major Thomson (commanding 12th Battalion West Yorkshires) reconnoitred the positions to be attacked.

The Attack on Lonely Trench.

This attack, in which the 12th West Yorkshires took part, was, like other minor local operations, designed to improve the position of the general British line.

The 3rd Division had relieved the 55th Division in the line on the night 14th/15th and had taken over responsibility for the capture not only of Lonely Trench but of Cochrane Alley also,

12TH BATTALION. 17TH AUG.

which the 55th Division had been ordered to capture on the 14th, handing it over after consolidation to the relieving (3rd) Division.

In the attack at 5-30 p.m. on the 16th, Cochrane Alley was captured but Lonely Trench was not, and a continuation of the operation was ordered to take place on 17th.

"It was clear that Lonely Trench had proved a much more formidable obstacle than had been anticipated, that it was strongly held by infantry and machine guns and had been protected by wire. The trench had a low command, was irregularly sited, difficult to observe and could not, in its most important parts, be bombarded by our heavy artillery without clearing our front line."

A surprise attack at night, with bayonet and bomb, was decided upon.

The assault was to be delivered by the 10th Royal Welsh Fusiliers on the right and the 12th West Yorkshires on the left, the assaulting companies of each battalion to move at dusk on the 17th to the assembly trenches and immediately it was dark to a line previously taped out in front of the first line trenches. All were to be in position by 9 p.m. The 24th Division on the left and French troops on the right of the 3rd Division, were to make simultaneous attacks.

The 12th West Yorkshires were formed up by 9-30 p.m. as arranged, but the 10th Royal Welsh Fusiliers were delayed by shell fire and were late in getting into position. Meanwhile, fearing that something serious had happened to the Welsh Fusiliers, the O.C., 12th West Yorkshires, withdrew his two companies (A and C) to the assembly trenches. Just before Zero hour the O.C., 10th Royal Welsh Fusiliers came to Major Thomson and said that his men were advancing. The two assaulting companies of West Yorkshiremen were at once ordered to advance from the assembly trenches. Thus an irregular advance was made and although the artillery bombardment had certainly damaged the enemy's position, an intense machine-gun fire met the West Yorkshiremen and Welsh Fusiliers as they advanced across No Man's Land. Although the attack advanced within a few yards of the hostile trenches, the latter were not penetrated.

18TH AUG.

At 4 a.m. on the 18th the attack was again renewed. But on this occasion machine-gun and rifle fire was even heavier than on the previous occasion and again the attack failed. For this attack A and C Companies of the West Yorkshires were reinforced by B Company; D being in support.

At 11 a.m. the 12th West Yorkshires were relieved by the 1st

Thiepval Again

Northumberland Fusiliers and marched back to Silesia Trench, north-east of Talus Boise. The Battalion had suffered heavy casualties in these two attacks. In the first Second-Lieut. W. I. Hogben was killed, three officers were wounded and one officer sustained shell shock; fifteen other ranks were killed, 135 wounded and eleven missing. In the second attack Lieut. E. C. Squires and Second-Lieut. J. R. Macguire were killed, seventeen other ranks were wounded and twenty were missing. _{12TH BATTALION.}

Lonely Trench finally passed into the possession of the 3rd Division about 6-30 p.m. on the 19th August, and the same night the 35th Division took over the line, the relief being completed by 6-30 a.m. on the morning of 20th. _{19TH AUG.}

In successive stages the 12th West Yorkshires, in Brigade and Division, moved from the Somme area, northwards, and at the end of August the 9th Infantry Brigade occupied the area Marles-les-Mines—Lapugnoy, the Battalion being billeted at the latter village. On the 31st August, the 3rd Division took over the Hulluch section from the 8th Division, the latter side-stepping to the right of the 3rd Division; the 40th Division was on the left. _{31ST AUG.}

September was destined to be a troubled month in the Somme Battles of 1916, for whereas, as already stated, August had witnessed a certain number of localized operations, there now came a period of general activity along the whole line. No less than five fresh battles were fought during the month, whilst the struggles for the Pozières Ridge and Delville Wood still continued.

But it is to the stormy Thiepval sector, where battalions of the West Yorkshire Regiment were still in line, that the story turns next; to the Leipzig Salient, to which the 1/5th, 1/6th, 1/7th and 1/8th Battalions of the 146th Infantry Brigade, with other battalions of the 49th Division, serving turn and turn about, in the front line and reserve trenches, clung with great tenacity. _{1/5TH, 1/6TH 1/7TH, 1/8TH BATTALIONS.}

About the middle of July the fury of the enemy knew no abatement. The West Yorkshiremen were then holding the Leipzig Salient and trenches just north of the Nab (from Mersey Street) to Thiepval Avenue. Early on the 15th July a vicious attack on the 1/6th Battalion, with bombs and liquid fire, began at 4 a.m. but was beaten off. The troops behaved splendidly and there was no loss of *morale*, or anything like the confusion the enemy hoped to produce, by his devilish methods of making warfare. The Stokes mortars did well on that day and took heavy toll of the enemy. On the 16th the 1/8th repulsed a heavy bombing attack. The 1/8th _{1/6TH BATTALION. 15TH JULY.}

1/8TH BATTALION. 20TH JULY.

attacked the enemy on the 20th, the Germans retaliating on the 21st. On the latter occasion the enemy penetrated the trenches of the 146th Infantry Brigade, but was immediately ejected. Later in the day the Brigade was relieved by the 148th Brigade, though the 1/6th and 1/8th were left in the line under the 148th. On the 3rd August the 146th Brigade again took over the front line from the 148th Brigade, *i.e.*, from the old German line opposite The Nab to Thiepval Avenue.

3RD AUG.

1/5TH, 1/6TH 1/7TH, 1/8TH BATTALIONS.

The 1/7th went into the Leipzig Salient, the 1/8th the trenches on the right and 1/6th those on the left of the Salient; the 1/5th were in reserve. Little happened during the early part of the month but continual shelling and occasional bombing attacks. On the 18th, the 25th Division relieved the 49th, the 146th Infantry Brigade marching out to the Lielvillers—Acheux Wood area. Then followed a week of training for the attack. The Brigade moved back into the line on 26th, when the 1/7th Battalion West Yorkshires once more marched into Thiepval Avenue, the 1/5th and 1/8th continuing the line northwards to the River Ancre. This northern part of the Thiepval sector was not quite unknown to the 146th Infantry Brigade, whose activities (and sufferings), however, had been mostly confined to sectors south of the village or immediately west of it. The fighting strength of all four battalions of the West Yorkshire Regt. at this date was as follows :—1/5th twenty officers and 438 other ranks; 1/6th twenty-one officers and 620 other ranks; 1/7th twelve officers and 529 other ranks; 1/8th twenty-five officers and 591 other ranks. Even of these small numbers only about 50 per cent. were Yorkshiremen, for the reinforcements which had arrived to partly fill the depleted ranks of the four battalions were from many other units. Thus the old Territorial Brigade had largely lost its original character. But none the less these reinforcements were good stout fellows.

Towards the end of August it had been decided to make another attack on Thiepval, or perhaps it would be more correct to say, on the ruins of Thiepval, for by this date the village had become an almost unrecognizable mass of tumbled bricks and masonry. The attack was to be made by the 39th and 49th Divisions, north and south of the Ancre respectively.

The 146th Infantry Brigade was to capture the German front and second lines, approximately from the Pope's Nose to the mound running directly north-east from Peterhead Sap. The 1/6th West Yorkshires were to attack on the right, the 1/8th on the left, with

"AN ALMOST UNRECOGNISABLE MASS OF TUMBLED BRICKS AND MASONRY."—p. 254.
THE REMAINS OF THIEPVAL VILLAGE, SEPTEMBER, 1916.

one company of the 1/5th in the old British line and three companies in Gordon Castle; the 1/7th were to remain in the assembly trenches in Aveluy Wood, in reserve. Each attacking battalion was to have one and a half companies in the front line and one and a half companies in the second line.

1/5TH, 1/6TH 1/7TH, 1/8TH BATTALIONS.

The 147th Brigade was attacking on the right of the 146th, and the 39th Division was no the left of the 49th.

But instead of the attacking battalions being kept out of the line to rest and get as fit as possible, every available man was engaged in carrying ammunition and reserve rations to the forward dumps in Elgin Avenue and the parallels. It was a two hours march up to these dumps and almost always had to be carried out under shell fire and of course always at night. Those who were not engaged in carrying duties were digging trenches. The consequence was that at dawn each day the men were so exhausted that they could hardly stand. In view of the results of the attack this should be borne in mind.

The Attack on Thiepval—3rd September.

The operations had been originally designed to take place on the 31st August, but were postponed, on the 30th, until 3rd September. Zero hour was 5-10 a.m.

3RD SEPT.

At 2 a.m. on the morning of the 3rd September, the troops began to take up their final positions. D Company of the 1/5th crossed the Ancre and put out eight posts in front of the parallels to cover the movements of the 1/6th and 1/8th Battalions *into* the parallels; A, B and C Companies of the 1/5th remaining at Gordon Castle. The 1/6th marching *via* Sandy Avenue, and the 1/8th *via* Cromarty Avenue, crossed the Ancre and moved up to their respective positions, each battalion leaving three companies in the parallels.

The whole movement was made without incident, the enemy being very quiet. The night was very dark, which fully accounted for the troops reaching their assembly positions without drawing the enemy's shell fire. By 5 a.m. the Division had been informed that the 146th Infantry Brigade was in position ready for the attack. At that hour the artillery barrage began and fell promptly and accurately on the German trenches. But the enemy was on the alert. The troops were already lined up within forty yards of the barrage when the latter lifted and the hour of assault arrived. Steadily the

1/5TH, 1/6TH 1/7TH, 1/8TH BATTALIONS. 3RD SEPT.
men went forward. The enemy's barrage opened three minutes after Zero hour and, although the first wave of West Yorkshiremen suffered little from it, the second wave, on leaving the first parallel and crossing the sunken road, were badly caught in the zone of fire. The second line group, consisting of the machine gunners, trench mortars, carrying parties, etc., were so badly cut up that they were unable to advance and the remnants never crossed No Man's Land.

Meanwhile the first wave had reached the enemy's front line with only few casualties, and for a little while it really seemed as if the attack was going to succeed. Then suddenly the enemy's machine-guns from the Pope's Nose, on the immediate right front

1/6TH BATTALION.
of the 1/6th Battalion, opened a terribly accurate enfilade fire and casualties at once became very heavy. A number of men pushed forward and entered the enemy's trenches, but the impetus of the attack had been stayed.

1/8TH BATTALION.
At 7·4 a.m. the 1/8th Battalion reported that their two companies—A and C—had been counter-attacked and driven out of the German line and had retired to the second parallel. Six minutes later the 1/6th also reported a hostile counter-attack, which had driven the last survivors of the West Yorkshiremen out of the

1/5TH BATTALION.
enemy's line and back to their original position. At 8 a.m. the 1/5th West Yorkshires relieved the 1/6th Battalion.

The attack of the 146th Infantry Brigade was practically over by 7 a.m. On the right of the Brigade the 4th and 5th West Ridings of the 147th Infantry Brigade had won forward, but the former (the battalion on the right of the 1/6th West Yorkshires) had failed to take the Pope's Nose (one of its objectives). It was this strong point, with its enfilade machine-gun fire, which not only broke up the attack of the West Yorkshiremen, but also that of the West Riding battalions.

From a German account of the action it is evident the enemy also had considerable losses and, as his report stated :—" In the whole sector all traces of trenches and fire steps had vanished. There is nothing left but a confused mass of shell holes and the wretched remnants of wire entanglements."

On the left of the 49th Division, the 39th Division had also failed to obtain a permanent footing in the enemy's trenches and had retired to the " O.B.L."

1/5TH, 1/6TH 1/7TH, 1/8TH BATTALIONS.
At 7·40 p.m. on the 3rd September, orders for the relief of the 146th Infantry Brigade by the 148th Infantry Brigade were issued and, on relief, the 1/5th and 1/7th Battalions West Yorkshire Regt.

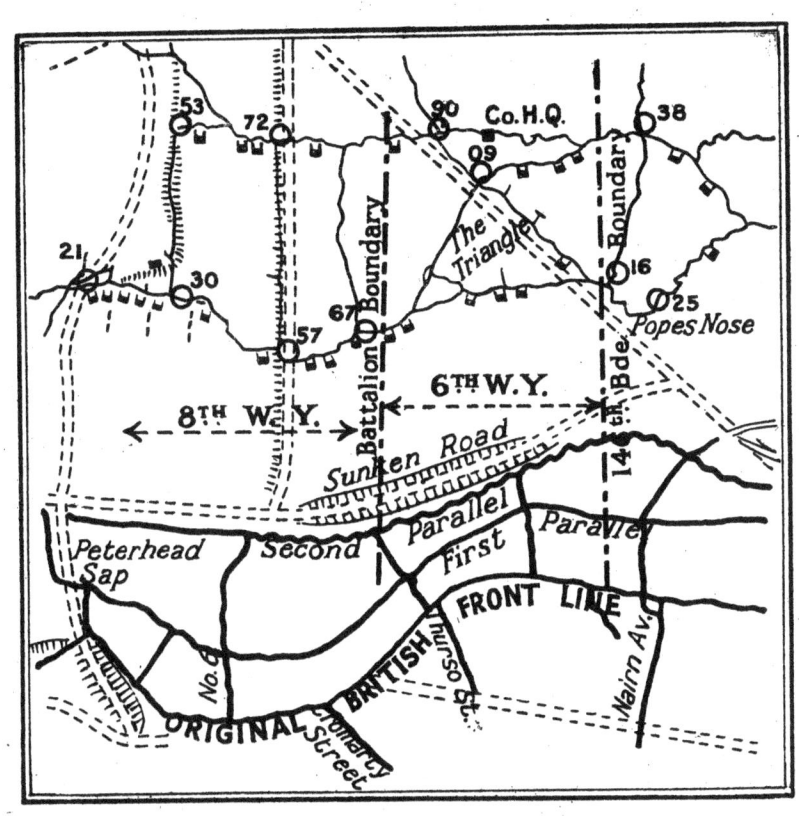

THE ATTACK ON THIEPVAL, 3RD SEPTEMBER, 1916.

were located in Malincourt Wood and the 1/6th and 1/8th Battalions in Forceville with Brigade Headquarters.

The casualties were heavy :—1/6th Battalion six officers and 235 other ranks; 1/8th, nine officers and 294 other ranks; 1/5th, six officers and 103 other ranks.

There is no doubt that the exhausted state of the men was a very large factor in the failure of this attack. Always willing the men did all that was possible, but they were utterly worn out and quite unfit to attack when Zero hour arrived, and that parties of them, even under those conditions, should have obtained a footing in the enemy's trenches was an eloquent tribute to their fighting qualities.

A few days later (on 14th September), south-east of Thiepval, an attack took place on the Wundt Werk (Wonder Work) by the 9th Battalion West Yorkshire Regt. of the 32nd Infantry Brigade, 11th Division. It was the first operation of any importance undertaken by the 11th Division since its arrival in France. 9th Battalion. 14th Sept.

The 11th Division landed at Marseilles from Egypt on the 1st July—the first day of the Somme Battles. On leaving Egypt the strength of the 9th West Yorkshires (Lieut.-Col. J. O. B. Minogue) was thirty-nine officers and 1,096 other ranks. The Battalion was fortunate in landing in France in the midst of summer weather, and its first introduction to the trenches was not attended by the discomforts which always characterized winter in the front-line areas.

On the 4th July, the 9th West Yorkshires arrived at St. Pol and on detraining marched to Croisette, where for several days the battalion remained in billets. On the 9th a move was made to Averboignt and, on the following day, to Agnez-les-Duisans, four miles west of Arras. The 11th Division was now in the VIth Corps Area, the 32nd Infantry Brigade being attached to the 35th Division for instruction in trench warfare. The period of instruction was, however, short, for on the 16th the 32nd Brigade relieved the 166th Infantry Brigade, 55th Division, in the line (east of Daneville) though it was not until the end of July that the 9th West Yorkshires marched, for the first time, into the front line trenches. The Battalion was then at Daneville, but marched out of the village at 9-30 p.m. on the 31st, relieving the 6th Battalion Yorkshire Regt. in " G " Sector. The relief was carried out quickly and without incident, and was completed by 1-30 a.m. on the morning of 1st August. The Battalion Diary records that " the first night in the trenches

9TH BATTALION.

was very quiet." The first casualties were suffered on 1st August—one other rank being killed and four wounded.

Very little of importance happened to the Battalion during August. The enemy's activity with trench mortars and rifle grenades caused a number of casualties, but no attacks were made by or on the Battalion. On the 16th Lieut.-Col. Minogue relinquished command of the Battalion, which was taken over temporarily by Capt. K. E. S. Stewart, until the arrival of Major C. L. Estridge (6th Battalion E. Yorkshire Regt.) on the 21st August. On that day the Battalion marched to Simencourt and Manin, billeting in the latter village. The 32nd Brigade now occupied the Givenchy-le-Noble area, where the units of the Brigade set to work to prepare for offensive operations. The training programme included drill, bayonet-fighting, bomb throwing and rapid wiring; all officers were trained to use the Lewis gun; specialists were trained in all the above. The total strength of the 9th West Yorkshires was now twenty-one officers and 747 other ranks, but towards the end of the month it had risen to thirty-two officers and 810 other ranks.

On the 2nd September, the 32nd Infantry Brigade (in Division) began to move southwards to the Somme area and by the 4th the Brigade was located in the Arqueves area, under orders to relieve the 75th Infantry Brigade of the 25th Division in the Leipzig Salient.

7TH SEPT. The relief took place early on the morning of 7th September, when the 9th West Yorkshire and 8th Duke of Wellington's Regiments took over the Salient from the 10th Cheshire and 8th Border Regiments (25th Division). The 32nd Infantry Brigade thus held the left of the 11th Division line, the 33rd Infantry Brigade was on the right and the 34th Brigade in reserve. It will be remembered that the 148th Infantry Brigade (49th Division) was then holding the Thiepval Sector on the left of the 11th Division.

8TH SEPT. On the 8th the Battalion had to undergo its introduction to the enemy's activity. Heavy hostile shelling knocked down the parapets of the trenches, but the West Yorkshiremen were soon hard at work repairing the damage done. Four men killed and nine wounded were the first day's casualties in the Salient. The Battalion was relieved on the 10th at 6 a.m. and marched back to Crucifix Corner, in reserve.

The Attack on the Wundt Werk.

The 9th West Yorkshires had been three days in reserve, when on the morning of the 14th September the Battalion again took over the front line trenches from the 6th York and Lancaster Regiment.

9TH BATTALION. 14TH SEPT.

In his official despatches Sir Douglas Haig stated that from about the middle of September the time was approaching when the capture of the Thiepval defences would be distinctly necessary. In the meantime other minor actions had to be undertaken and the way prepared for larger operations to follow. The completion of the capture of the Leipzig Salient was almost the last of these minor operations and for this purpose an attack to take place on the evening of 14th September (before the Battle of Flers-Courcelette began on the following day—15th Sept.) on Turk Street and the Wundt Werk had been planned and was to be carried out by the 32nd Infantry Brigade of the 11th Division.

On the morning of the 14th therefore after the reliefs had been completed, the 8th Duke of Wellington's being on the right and the 9th West Yorkshires on the left, the 32nd Infantry Brigade stood ready waiting for Zero hour, which had been fixed for 6-30 p.m. Each battalion was disposed on a two-company frontage, with one company in support and one company in reserve. The attacking companies were to go forward in two waves. Each wave consisted of a platoon with its complement of bombers. The first waves were to push on to the final objective, dropping " care takers " in Turk Street; the first wave was the " clearing up " party. Of the 9th West Yorkshires D Company was the right attacking company and C Company the left. Two platoons of B Company were to clear Prince Street, by bombing, and protect C Company's flank, the remaining two platoons of B were in support to D and C Companies. A Company was in battalion reserve.

For both attacking battalions Turk Street was the first and the Wundt Werk the final objectives. On the left of the West Yorkshiremen the 6th Yorkshire Regiment was to carry out a bombing demonstration.

The move up to Hindenburg Trench, from which the attack was to set out, was carried out subsequently through desultory shelling and, unfortunately, Lieut. C. B. Robinson was killed.

During the day the following message was received from IInd Corps Headquarters :—" Identifications along IInd Corps front are urgently required by Reserve Army within the next forty-eight hours. Especially between Thiepval and Moquet Farm. Endeavours should be made to obtain them."

At 6-28 p.m. the first waves left Hindenburg Trench and began

9TH BATTALION. 14TH SEPT.

to form up in No Man's Land. The offensive was greeted by spasmodic firing from Turk Street. Hostile green lights went up and a machine-gun began to bark from the enemy's trenches.

Two minutes later (at 6-30 p.m.) the intense bombardment began and a perfect tornado of shell fell upon the enemy's positions, smashing his trenches and creating wholesale destruction. The artillery bombardment was very heavy and was carried out by a part of the IInd Corps "Heavies," three French 75 batteries, the 11th Divisional Artillery and portions of the 25th and 48th Divisional Artillery. In addition, Stokes mortars and machine-guns added to the volume of fire which swept the enemy's positions.

The hostile machine gun which had opened fire just before the bombardment began fired only a few rounds and was not heard again! The troops stood and watched the bombardment and its terrific results and as the guns lifted were almost immediately afterwards into the enemy's trenches or all that remained of them. "Doubtless," said the Battalion Diary of the 9th Battalion West Yorkshire Regiment " we lost men from our own shells owing to the closeness of the bombardment to which they advanced," which means that the troops had been well drilled in the necessity for keeping close on the heels of the barrage. For a little later the Diary states :—" We certainly did not suffer from rifle or machine-gun fire."

The enemy had by now put down a heavy barrage, which " was very effective and caused practically all our casualties." But nothing could hold up the attack. Turk Street fell at once and the waves swept on towards the Wundt Werk, which fell with as complete a success as the first objective.

Consolidation was begun immediately. Only two officers (Captain O. Y. Goy and Second-Lieut. N. T. Hartley) reached the final objective and both these were wounded, " but they pluckily carried on."

The 8th Duke of Wellington's, on the right, had progressed equally well, only the 6th Yorkshire Regiment, on the left, being hung up in their bombing demonstration, which witnessed the last of their gallant Colonel.

15TH SEPT.

Throughout the night and through the 15th consolidation proceeded and on the night of the latter the 1/7th Duke of Wellington's Regiment of the 49th Division relieved the 9th West Yorkshires, who marched back to the dug-outs at ill-famed Crucifix Corner.

The casualties of the Battalion were heavy. The strength of

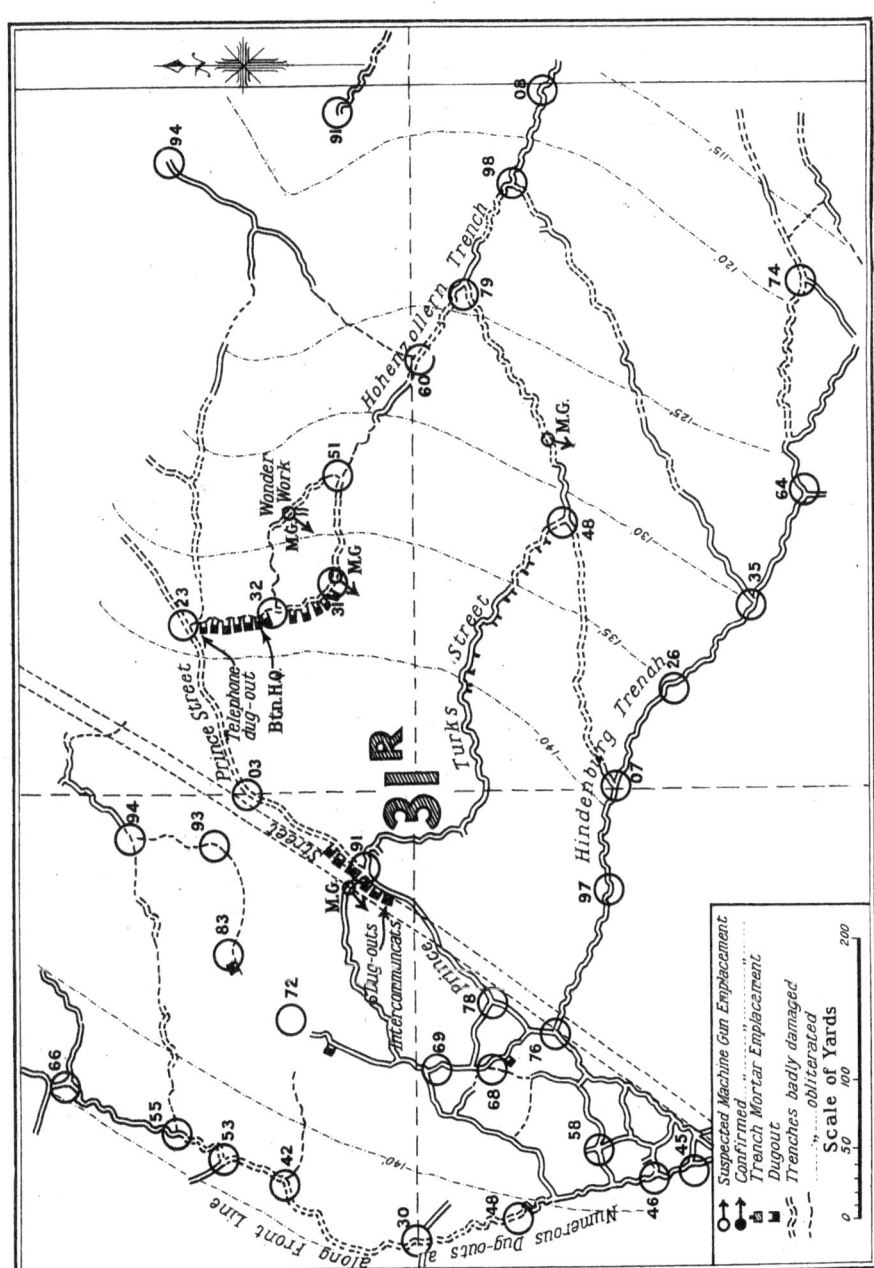

THE ATTACK ON THE WONDER WORK.

Moving up to the Flers Line, September, 1916.

To face p. 261.

the 9th West Yorkshires on going into action had been twenty officers and 780 other ranks, but of this number eight officers were killed and four wounded. In N. C. O.'s and other ranks the Battalion lost thirty-three killed, 240 wounded and thirty-three missing.

_{9TH BATTALION.}

Thus the first action of any importance in which the 9th West Yorkshires took part, after their arrival in France, cost the Battalion twelve officers and 306 other ranks. About 100 prisoners were taken and the necessary identifications obtained.

On the 16th the Battalion (in Brigade) marched back to Hedauville for a well-deserved rest.

_{16TH SEPT.}

Meanwhile, as the 9th Battalion West Yorkshire Regiment was marching away to their rest billets, on the 15th September, the Battle of Flers-Courcellette had opened. This operation will be long remembered, not only on account of the successes gained, but because "Tanks" were first used. The delight of the British "Tommy" and the terror of the Boche, on the appearance of this new weapon, are amongst the immortal things of the war.

The intentions of the Commander-in-Chief in the Battle of Flers-Courcelette were well outlined in the official despatches :—
" The general plan for the combined Allied attacks, which were opened on the 15th September, was to pivot on the high ground south of the Ancre, and north of the Achiet—Bapaume Road, while the Fourth Army devoted its whole effort to the rearmost of the enemy's original systems of defence, between Morval and Le Sars. Should our success in this direction warrant it, I made arrangements to enable me to extend the left of the attack to embrace the villages of Martinpuich and Courcelette. As soon as our advance on this front had reached the Morval Line, the time would have arrived to bring forward my left across the Thiepval Ridge. Meanwhile, on my right our Allies arranged to continue the line of advance, in close co-operation with me, from the Somme to the slopes above Combles, but directing their main effort northwards against the village of Rancourt and Fregicourt, so as to complete the isolation of Combles and open the way for their attack upon Sailly-Saillisel."

_{15TH SEPT.}

The Order of Battle of the Fourth Army, which was to carry out the attack, shows three corps, from right to left—XIVth (56th, 6th and Guards Divisions)—XVth (14th, 41st and New Zealand Divisions) and IIIrd (47th, 50th and 15th Divisions)[1] in the front line on the morning of 15th September. But with only one division

---

[1] Reserves not stated in official despatches.

S

1ST BATTALION.

—the 6th—is this story concerned, for that Division contained the senior battalion (1st) of the West Yorkshire Regiment.

After the successful minor enterprise of the 3rd June, the 1st West Yorkshires were relieved on the 15th by a battalion of Guards, the Guards Division having taken over the front held by the 6th Division. The latter moved back to the Esquelbec area and, on the 30th the 1st Battalion was in billets in Bollezeele. On 1st July it moved to Houtkerque and on the following day to that very familiar and unpleasant spot—"L" Camp at Poperinghe. Nearly a fortnight was spent in training and on the 14th the Battalion was inspected by the Corps Commander, who warmly congratulated the C.O. on the smart turn out of the men and their drill.

A few days later, front-line trenches in the Ypres Salient were taken over, the 6th Division having relieved the 20th Division on the 14th.

During this tour the enemy was not very active; his exertions were all centred farther south in the Somme area, where he was hard put to it to maintain his line. The 6th Division was relieved by the 29th Division on the night 1st/2nd August, and, on the 2nd entrained for Doullens, where the Division was to join the Reserve Army on the Somme. On 3rd the 1st West Yorkshires reached Orville, Acheux on the 4th, and Mailly Maillet on the 6th, taking over trenches from the 3rd Worcestershire Regiment of the 25th Division, the 6th Division occupying a frontage of 2,500 yards of line from the River Ancre to the junction of Broadway and the front line, just south of Hawthorne Ridge (Q. 10.b.2.2). On the 7th, the first day in the trenches, on the Somme, the Battalion lost two other ranks killed and ten wounded, including one officer wounded. The guns were active and were engaged in wire-cutting operations. On the 9th a battalion of the Buffs relieved the West Yorkshiremen, who marched back to billets in Englebelmer. Until the 18th August the Battalion remained in billets, furnishing large parties of officers and men each day for digging and carrying purposes. A further tour in the front line began on 19th and ended on the 26th, when the Battalion marched out of the trenches to camp at Bertrancourt. The 6th Division had been relieved by the 39th Division. The weeks spent in the trenches north of the Ancre had been busy, preparing for an attack, which was at one time to be carried out by the 6th Division. On the 28th the Division was located in the Vth Corps area, moving on the following day to the Xth Corps area—Fesselles—Vignacourt—Naours. The 18th Infantry Brigade was at

7TH AUG.

29TH AUG.

Vignacourt, where the 1st West Yorkshires were billeted. For a few days a general "clean-up" and training occupied the men and it was not until 6th September, that the 18th Infantry Brigade (in Division) moved south to the XIVth Corps area, just north of the Somme. The 7th September found the 1st West Yorkshires at Vaux-en-Somme, Brigade Headquarters being at Corbie and 6th Divisional Headquarters at Forked Tree Camp on the Bray—Albert Road. _{1ST BATTALION. 6TH SEPT.}

While the Division was still in reserve the Battle of Ginchy took place, in which the 56th and 16th Divisions took part.

On the morning of the 10th September, the 6th Division received orders to take over a portion of the 56th and Guards Division front, and, on the night of 11th/12th went into the line east of Guillemont. The position in the front line was very obscure and on the afternoon of 12th the Division was ordered to clear up the situation on its front and occupy the Quadrilateral by the night of the 14th, with a view to taking part in the advance on Morval on the 15th, when the general attack was taking place. _{11TH/12TH SEPT.}

The 6th Division had no light task; nothing was known of the German positions south-east of Ginchy and the trenches running thence northwards, and the positions taken up by the 71st and 16th Infantry Brigades of the Division formed a curious semi-circle facing north. The 71st Brigade, however, during the 13th and night of the 13th/14th pushed its way through and dug itself in opposite the Quadrilateral.

The preliminary bombardment for the Battle of Flers-Courcelette had begun on the 12th, but owing to the difficulty in obtaining any reliable information of the enemy's trenches (the bad weather preventing the taking of aerial photographs) the hostile trenches were not adequately shelled and on the 14th were still insufficiently reduced. But the general attack could not be postponed. In consequence, when on the morning of the 15th the 71st and 16th Infantry Brigades of the 6th Division, attacked the Quadrilateral and the trenches running north of it, the assaulting troops were held up by strong uncut wire and heavy machine-gun, rifle and artillery fire. On the left, however, the divisions were successful in reaching their first objectives. Along the whole front of attack from just west of Ginchy and north-west to Courcelette the general attack had made excellent progress; Flers, Martinpuich and Courcelette had fallen to the Fourth Army and only the right flank was held up. _{15TH SEPT.}

As it was necessary to drive the enemy from his positions in

1ST BATTALION.

16TH SEPT.

front of the 6th Division, the 18th Infantry Brigade, which during the attacks of the 71st and 16th Infantry Brigades had been in Divisional Reserve, was ordered to rush both flanks of the positions from north and south, at 7-30 p.m. that same night.

The distribution of the 18th Infantry Brigade at dawn on the 16th was as follows :—11th Essex and 1st West Yorkshires near Chimpanzee Trench ; 14th Durham Light Infantry in trenches and shell holes between Ginchy and Leuze Wood ; 2nd Durham Light Infantry in, and near, the trenches won during the night (the northern end of Straight Trench).

Throughout daylight on the 16th, the 2nd Durham Light Infantry and the 16th and 71st Infantry Brigades endeavoured to improve their positions. The Guards Division, on the left of the 6th Division, supported by the 20th Division, attacked Les Bœufs and reached their objectives just west of the village, but failed to enter the village.

During the evening the enemy put down a heavy barrage on the line Ginchy—Leuze Wood, and counter-attacked the 20th Division, on the left of the 6th. The attack was repulsed. But the G.O.C., 18th Infantry Brigade, received orders to move at once to take over the left sector of the 6th Divisional front and relieve the 71st Infantry Brigade during the night 16th/17th. The 1st West Yorkshires were sent up to dig themselves in on a line 130—200 yards west of Straight Trench, taking over from troops of the 71st Brigade. This was done by 3 a.m. on the morning of the 17th. The 14th Durham Light Infantry were then ordered to get into touch with the right of the West Yorkshiremen. The trenches of the 2nd Durham Light Infantry were also taken over by the 1st West Yorkshires.

The Capture of the Quadrilateral.

17TH SEPT.

The 18th Infantry Brigade received warning on the morning of the 17th September to attack and capture the Quadrilateral and the German trenches running northwards from it, on the 18th. Preparations were at once taken in hand and the necessary orders issued. The 14th D.L.I. was to attack on the right, and the 1st West Yorkshires (Lieut.-Col. G. G. Lang) on the left. The 16th Infantry Brigade on the right and 20th Division on the left of the 18th Infantry Brigade were to attack simultaneously. Zero was fixed for 5-50 a.m., and at that hour D Company of the West Yorkshires (Capt. G. N.

Stockdale) began a bombing attack up the trenches towards the Quadrilateral. B and C Companies (Capt. B. Corp and Capt. J. H. E. Trafford-Rawson respectively) attacked frontally across the open, but were met by very heavy machine-gun and rifle fire, which caused so many casualties that a temporary withdrawal to the starting point was made. At Zero plus ten minutes, two platoons of A Company advanced to a quarry, 250 yards in front of the Quadrilateral and dug in. By 6-10 a.m. D Company had captured a strong point and bombing up the trench met the 14th D.L.I. At this moment B and C Companies, having been reorganized, again advanced and joined up with the Durhams on the right and A Company on the left. At 6-15 a.m. consolidation began. Half an hour later the situation was :—A Company was strongly established with one Lewis gun and two platoons at a strong point, 250 yards in front of the strong point in the Quadrilateral (at about T.15 central). Patrols pushed out had obtained touch with the 20th Division. The left flank of the West Yorkshires was covered by two machine guns. D Company had consolidated, and was making four strong points.

Thus the whole of the Quadrilateral, which had for some days defied capture, was captured in less than an hour, reflecting great credit on the 1st Battalion West Yorkshire Regiment and 14th D.L.I. The weather was atrocious. Heavy rain fell all day and there was a high wind : and aeroplanes could not go up to observe. The ground had become thick in mud, cross country tracks being impassable for wheeled traffic, and all roads were deep in mud and water.

The 1st Battalion captured, during the day, one trench mortar, one machine gun and 100 wounded and unwounded prisoners.

Casualties were especially heavy : Capt. B. Corp (commanding B Company) and Capt. J. H. E. Trafford-Rawson (commanding C Company), Second-Lieuts. C. S. Gell, and P. S. L. Green, and ten other ranks were killed ; four officers and ninety-three other ranks were wounded and thirty-eight missing.

During the night of 18th/19th, the 5th Division relieved the 6th Division ; the 1st West Yorkshires were relieved at 2 a.m., and marched back to Morval, proceeding later on in the day to Meaulte where the 18th Infantry Brigade went into billets. As the troops marched into the village they were seen to be caked in mud from head to foot. Major H. M. Dillon had now taken over command of the 1st Battalion, Lieut.-Col. G. G. Lang having been evacuated to hospital.

The capture of the Quadrilateral on the 18th September was but a minor action in the major operation—the Battle of Flers-Courcelette, which, however, did not end until 22nd September. But before the latter date arrived, certain reserve divisions had been drawn back again into the battle line. Amongst these was the 23rd Division.

11TH BATTALION.

After the attack on Munster Alley the 23rd Division had been relieved in the line, and had gone north, taking over trenches in the Plugsteert area. Here the 11th Battalion West Yorkshire Regiment (69th Infantry Brigade) went into the trenches in Hope Street on 3rd September, but were relieved on the following day. A few days

10TH SEPT.

later (on 10th) the 23rd Division again entrained for the Somme area, arriving at Longeau on the 11th. The 69th Infantry Brigade spent the 12th, 13th and 14th in billets in Hennencourt Wood. On the 15th the Brigade marched to Millencourt and three days later moved up into the front line, taking over the trenches of the 44th Infantry Brigade, 15th Division, which the 23rd Division was relieving in the line. The 11th West Yorkshires, however, moved up into Martinpuich, relieving troops of the 46th Infantry Brigade.

Three uneventful days were spent in Posh Alley, Gunpit Road and Factory Line, and on the 22nd the Battalion marched back to bivouacs at Willow Patch, near Round Wood. Three more days in Round Wood and a move on the 26th to Gourlay Support trenches, where four days were occupied chiefly in work of all kinds, closed the month of September so far as it concerned the 11th Battalion West Yorkshire Regiment.

THE BATTLE OF MORVAL:
Capture of Lesbœufs.

AFTER the successful Battle of Flers-Courcelette (which included the capture of Martinpuich), which began on 15th and ended on 22nd of September, operations had been hindered by bad weather. But on the 25th the advance was again renewed and a general attack was launched by the Allies between the Somme and Martinpuich. " The objectives on the British front included the villages of Morval (5th Division), Lesbœufs (6th Division and Guards Division) and Gueudecourt (21st Division), a belt of country about 1,000 yards deep, curving round the north of Flers to a point midway between that village and Martinpuich (55th, New Zealand, and 1st Divisions)."

The 6th Division was in the Treux area when, on the 20th September, orders were received to move back into the front line west of Lesbœufs, between the 5th Division (right) and the Guards Division (left).

On the morning of the 21st the 16th and 18th Infantry Brigades, 21ST SEPT. moved up to the vicinity of the Briqueterie and a little later began the relief of the 1st Guards Brigade, opposite Lesbœufs. The 16th Infantry Brigade took over the right sub-sector and the 2nd D.L.I. (right) and 13th Essex (left) the front allotted to the 18th Infantry Brigade. The positions were somewhat extraordinary as the trenches on both flanks of the 16th and 18th Infantry Brigades were still in the occupation of the enemy. The 1st Battalion West Yorkshire Regiment and 14th D.L.I. were in reserve, the former occupying reserve trenches between Trones Wood and Guillemont. The march up, owing to the terrible state of the roads and tracks was very difficult, and the men arrived very tired after their six miles' walk, but on the following day, being still in reserve, were able to obtain some measure of rest. This was important for, on the 25th, the Battalion was to attack Lesbœufs, the second objective allotted to the West Yorkshiremen.[1]

[1] As detailed Operation Orders, which were evidently issued by 18th Infantry Brigade Headquarters, were not with the Diaries, the story is taken from the narrative in both the Battalion and Brigade Diaries.

1ST. BATTALION. 24TH SEPT.

At 7 a.m. on the 24th September, a steady bombardment of the enemy's positions in and about Lesbœufs, and the whole line, was begun and continued all day until 6-30 p.m., when the usual night firing operations were resumed.

Zero was 12-35 p.m. on the 25th September, and there was to be no intense fire prior to Zero hour.

25TH SEPT.

At 6-30 a.m. on the morning of the 25th September, the artillery again opened a very heavy bombardment of the enemy's positions, under cover of which the troops moved up to their assembly positions and awaited the arrival of Zero hour.

Punctually at 12-35 p.m. the 2nd D.L.I. (on the right) and 13th Essex (on the left) went forward to the attack, with orders to halt on the line of the first objective, in order that the 1st West Yorkshires might go through them and attack the second objective. The latter Battalion had, during the morning, moved up to the assembly trenches, some distance behind the front line.

At 1-35 p.m. the West Yorkshiremen started out from the assembly trenches, reports having come in of the successful advance of the two attacking battalions. The first line (Green Line), was reached at 1-50 p.m., and here the Battalion awaited orders to advance on the second objective. These orders came at 2-15 p.m., when the Battalion, on a two-company frontage, went forward to the attack.

The Sunken Road in front of Lesbœufs was reached at 2-30 p.m., about five minutes before the creeping barrage, 150 yards in front of the Sunken Road, was due to lift. At this point, touch was gained on the right with the 16th Infantry Brigade, and on the left with the 1st Guards Brigade. There was very little fighting, the bombardment having demoralized the enemy to such an extent that he could only put up a weak resistance. In the Sunken Road, however, were numerous dug-outs, still undamaged, and from these many Germans emerged and surrendered.

Five minutes later, at 2-35 p.m., the barrage lifted, and A and D Companies of the 1st West Yorkshires, followed closely by C Company in support, and in conjunction with the 16th Infantry Brigade on the right, and the Guards on the left, advanced straight on to Lesbœufs.

On reaching the village several Germans offered resistance, but these were quickly overpowered and the Battalion pressed on. Lesbœufs had suffered terribly from shell fire. Most of the houses and cottages had been entirely wrecked, piles of *débris* blocked the streets and roads. Even the cellars beneath the houses, which usually were most difficult to demolish, were mostly blown in. There was, however, plenty of cover, had the enemy been minded to use it.

Advancing rapidly A and D Companies of the 1st West Yorkshires passed through the village to a sunken road on the far side of it. C Company followed more slowly, being engaged in systematically searching the ruined houses and cellars for lurking enemy, for the Germans had an ugly method of lying hidden until an attack had passed and then emerging and taking the attack in rear, with rifle, bomb and machine gun.

A and D Companies reached the sunken road on the far side of Lesbœufs at 2-50 p.m., but the creeping barrage was still only a little way off and did not lift until 3-5 p.m. At that hour, however, the two companies advanced fifty yards beyond the sunken road and dug in. C Company's bombers were still busy, the remainder of the company, therefore, joined A and D Companies. Just before 4 p.m. the enemy opened a very heavy bombardment with " 5·9's," and casualties became serious. But in spite of its losses, the Battalion carried out its work of consolidation.

Two sections of Sappers were sent up at 6-30 p.m. with orders to build strong points and, at 7 p.m., B Company, 1st West Yorkshires, which had been in reserve all day, was sent forward to supply the garrisons.

Until 1 p.m. on the 26th September, the Battalion occupied the following positions :—all four companies were in the Blue Line; B holding strong points ; D, C, and A in line from right to left, the right and left flanks being in touch with the 16th Infantry Brigade and Guards respectively.

Patrols were sent out during this period and kept the ground, up to within 400 yards of the new front line, under close observation.

The whole attack had gone splendidly, and the men worked like Trojans to consolidate their gains : the trenches were completely dug by 7 p.m. on the 25th, and were wired by 11 p.m. the same night.[1]

Desultory sniping took place during the night, and small parties of Germans were observed between 700 and 800 yards away, but the only time that hostile troops appeared in large numbers was at 6 a.m. on the 26th, but these were quickly dispersed.

During the morning of the 26th, the following wires were received at 1st Battalion Headquarters :—" Best congratulations from

---

[1] Lieut. E. N. Chart and 2nd Lieut. W. H. Bore, and eighteen other ranks were killed, four officers and seventy-seven other ranks wounded, and fifteen other ranks were missing.

1ST BATTALION. 26TH SEPT.

us all on your splendid achievement," G.O.C. 18th Infantry Brigade. " Hearty thanks, sincere congratulations to you all. A very fine achievement splendidly executed." Cavan, XIVth Corps Commander."

At 12-15 p.m. instructions were received from Brigade Headquarters, stating that, under cover of a creeping barrage, beginning at 1 p.m., a succession of strong posts were to be made in a line 200 yards in advance of the Blue Line. Similar posts on both flanks were to be constructed by the 16th Infantry Brigade and the Guards. At 1 p.m., B Company of the 1st West Yorkshires, moved out to make these strong points. A heavy machine-gun fire met the men as they moved forward, but in spite of it some old gun positions were occupied, the enemy in them being killed. These points were about the distance named in Brigade orders, *i.e.*, 200 yards from the Blue Line.

A very heavy hostile fire was now directed on these new posts, but B Company held its ground until 10 p.m., having been reinforced two hours earlier by A Company; the latter were replaced by a company of the 11th Essex Regiment.

But apparently orders to the 16th Infantry Brigade had miscarried and A and B Companies of the West Yorkshires were, therefore, isolated with their flanks quite unprotected. An effort was made to form defensive flanks, but the position was most disquieting and at 10 p.m. Brigade Headquarters ordered the two companies back to the Blue Line.

27TH SEPT.

At 7-15 a.m. on the 27th September, the Battalion was relieved by the 14th D.L.I., and marched back to its original assembly trenches, occupied before the attack, on 25th. Here the West Yorkshiremen remained until 3 p.m. on the 28th, when the Battalion (in Brigade) marched back to bivouacs, arriving at 5 p.m. and, during the concluding days of September to Meaulte and Ville-sur-Ancre. The 6th Division was relieved by the 20th Division on 30th September, command of the front line trenches being taken over by the G.O.C., 20th Division, on the morning of 1st October.[1] The Battle of Morval was a great success. With the exception of Gueudecourt and Combles (which fell on the 26th) all the objectives were captured, with large numbers of prisoners and much material and on the evening

---

[1] The 1st Battalion West Yorkshire Regiment lost heavily during September, 1916, the casualty rolls contained in the 18th Infantry Brigade Diary give the following figures :—Officers, seventeen; other ranks—305, killed, wounded and missing.

The total losses of the 18th Infantry Brigade were :—Fifty-seven officers, and 1,171 other ranks, killed wounded and missing.

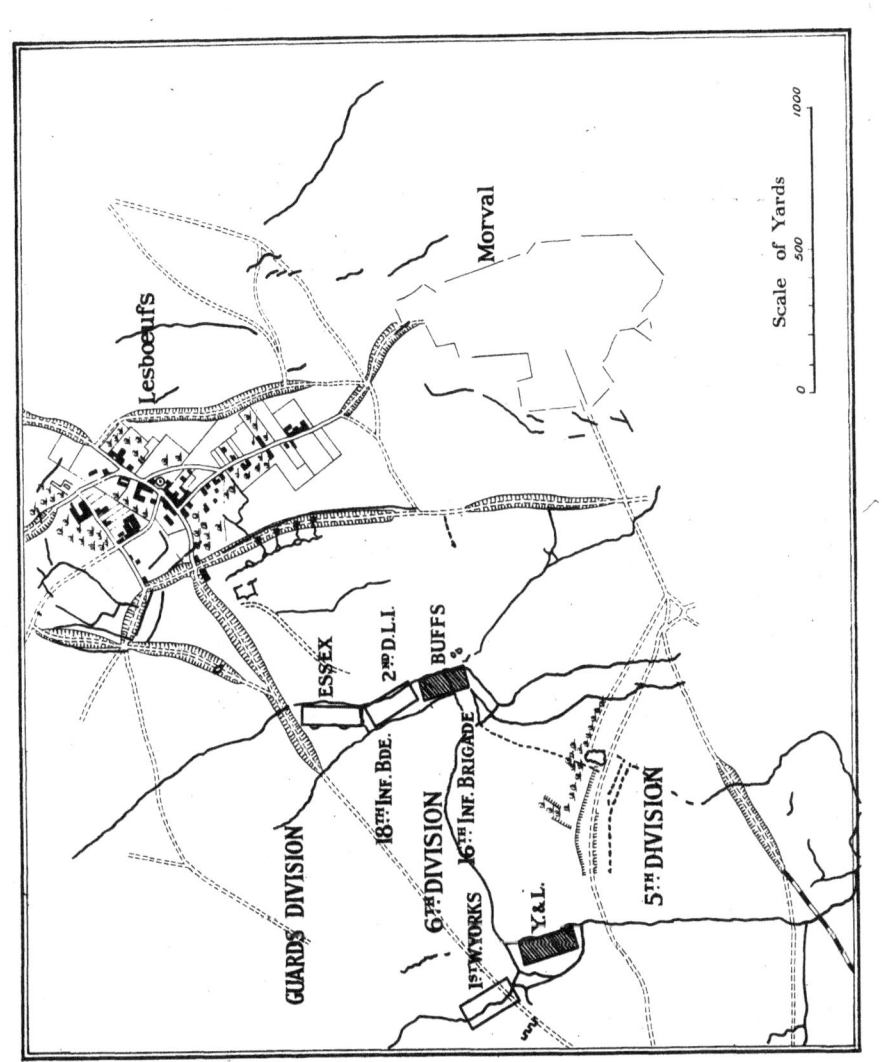

The Battle of Morval; Capture of Lesbœufs.

To face p. 270.

The Battle of Morval, September, 1916.
THE BATTLEFIELD ON THE MORNING OF 25TH SEPTEMBER.

of the 26th the line ran approximately from north-east of Combles, thence round the eastern and northern exits of Gueudecourt to north of Martinpuich, thence round the eastern outskirts of Courcelette to just north-west of Thiepval. For while the Battle of Morval had been proceeding, Thiepval, after many attempts, had at last fallen into British hands.

1ST BATTALION.

THE BATTLE OF THIEPVAL RIDGE.

AT the close of the first day of the Battle of Morval (25th September) the operations of the Fourth Army had been so successful that Sir Douglas Haig deemed it advisable to attack Thiepval, with the object of bringing the left flank of the Fourth Army into line with the advance of the right. Moreover, the establishment of the left flank on the ridge above the village would be of considerable tactical value in future operations. 25TH SEPT.

The objective of this new attack consisted of the whole of the high ground still remaining in the possession of the enemy, extending over a front of some 3,000 yards north and east of Thiepval, and including in addition to that fortress the Zollern Redoubt, the Stuff Redoubt and the Schwaben Redoubt, with the connecting system of trenches.

Four divisions were to be employed in this operation, 2nd Canadian Division, 1st Canadian Division, 11th Division and 18th Division, in the order given from right to left. The 49th Division, which had so often attacked Thiepval and whose dead lay thick around the ruins of the village, in the German trenches in front of it and out in No Man's Land, was not destined to take part, as a whole, in the final capture, but one brigade (146th), which had been left in the sector when the 18th Division had relieved the 49th Division on 25th September lent valuable assistance during the attack.

The line of attack was from the north-west corner of Courcelette to the north-west of Thiepval.

The attack was launched at 12-25 p.m. on the 26th September, before the enemy had been given time to recover from the blow struck by the Fourth Army, east of the Bapaume—Albert Road, and was another brilliant success. The 2nd and 1st Canadian Divisions reached their objectives without great difficulty, but in Thiepval and the strong works north of the village, the enemy's resistance was more desperate. The 33rd and 34th Infantry Brigades of the 11th Division, carried Moquet Farm and, pushing on, entered the Zollern Redoubt, which was stormed and consolidated. On the left of the 11th Division, the 18th Division, greatly assisted by tanks, 26TH SEPT.

27TH SEPT.

9TH BATTALION.

established a footing in Thiepval and, although all day long fierce fighting for the possession of the village took place, by 8-30 a.m. on the 27th, the whole of it had passed into the hands of the Division.

It was on the 27th September that the 32nd Infantry Brigade, then lying in Divisional Reserve about Crucifix Corner, received orders at 8-45 a.m. to hold two battalions in readiness to support the 34th Infantry Brigade. At 10 a.m. the two battalions—9th West Yorkshires and the 6th Yorkshire Regiment—were to move up to the trenches in close support. The West Yorkshires to occupy trenches from R.27.d.9.3 to R.27.d.1.2, the old front line trench running through Moquet Farm and the newly-dug support trench in rear of it ; the 6th Yorkshire Regiment to occupy Ration Trench and trenches immediately in rear.

By 2 p.m. the leading companies of the 9th West Yorkshires had reached the Quarry, about 300 yards south-west of the Farm, the order of companies being—B, C, D, A.

Meanwhile the 32nd Infantry Brigade had been ordered to attack (through the 34th Infantry Brigade) the line Hessian Trench —Stuff Redoubt, " clearing up on the way."

Preliminary orders for this attack were received at Brigade Headquarters at 12-15 p.m. The two battalions were then *en route* to the trenches and the Brigadier set out to the Quarry in order to give verbal instructions concerning the attack to the C. O.'s of the 9th West Yorkshire and 6th Yorkshire Regiments.

These instructions were received by the West Yorkshires at 2-30 p.m., the Battalion being ordered to " attack the line point 99-Hessian Trench to Point 97, with the right of the Battalion on Point 99, in touch with the 1st Canadian Division, and the left, in touch with the 6th Yorkshire Regiment at Point 97 in Stuff Redoubt. The barrage was to begin at 3 p.m. and lift beyond objectives at 3-8 p.m. Positions of assembly, the line Zollern Trench, 1,000 yards east of the Quarry."

Apparently C and D Companies could not be informed in time of the impending attack, and only A and B Companies received the necessary instructions : A forming up on the right and B on the left. C Company was to be in support on the line Point 52 right, Chalk Pit left, and D in reserve in High Trench.

A message, saying that the attack had been postponed reached Brigade Headquarters at 2-30 p.m., on receipt of which a runner was despatched to the 9th West Yorkshires and 6th Yorkshire Regiment informing them of the postponement of the attack.

This message did not reach the West Yorkshiremen, who had begun their advance from High Trench at 2-57 p.m. A and B Companies had, however, moved forward, when C and D Companies, on the left, seeing the advance, went forward also in line with A and B, D Company remaining on the left flank of the Battalion.

9TH BATTALION. 27TH SEPT.

On leaving the line Point 52—Row of Apple Trees, the Battalion came under very heavy indirect machine-gun fire, while the enemy's artillery shelled the advance, but fortunately casualties were not heavy and, with great gallantry, the West Yorkshiremen pushed on to their objective. That they were alone in the attack did not deter them; for the 6th Yorkshire Regiment had been stopped in time.

About the Zollern Redoubt, however, great masses of barbed wire and a somewhat confusing system of trenches caused loss of direction and, instead of arriving at Hessian Trench, the Battalion entered the Stuff Redoubt and captured it; the time was 3-15 p.m. The gallant West Yorkshiremen immediately set to work to consolidate their gains, for the enemy was on both flanks and their position in the Redoubt was anything but a sinecure.

At 4 p.m. the 6th Yorkshires advanced on Hessian Trench West, which they captured, together with eighty prisoners and two machine-guns. A part of the Battalion had, however, advanced on the Stuff Redoubt and were surprised to find that it was already held by the 9th West Yorkshires.

As the two Battalions in the Redoubt were now somewhat mixed, a Composite Force was formed and Captain White of the 6th Yorkshire Regiment took command.

At 8-45 p.m. on the 27th, the position, as reported to Brigade Headquarters was :—" the Yorkshire Regiment were holding Hessian Trench West from R.20.d.9.1. to R.21.C.4.5. and that a mixed force of West Yorkshires and Yorkshires were holding R.21.c.1.8 to R.21.c.8.7, latter point exclusive, where much fighting was going on."

From the above report it seems clear that the 6th Yorkshire Regiment during its advance at 4 p.m. captured eighty prisoners in Hessian Trench and that the enemy had by this time partly worked round the left flank of the 9th West Yorkshires holding the Stuff Redoubt, but there is no record to this effect.

During the night 27th/28th, two companies of 8th Duke of Wellington's Regiment were sent up to reinforce the 9th West

Yorkshires and 6th Yorkshire Regiment, one company to each Battalion. These two companies were placed in Zollern Trench.

Efforts made by the West Yorkshiremen, assisted by the Duke of Wellington's Regiment to bomb eastwards and gain touch with the Canadians did not meet with any success.

On the 28th at 6 p.m., the 8th Duke of Wellington's were ordered to attack the line Point 99 to Point 97, their left resting on the Stuff Redoubt. The Composite Force in the Redoubt (9th West Yorkshires and 6th Yorkshire Regiment) was ordered to co-operate by advancing simultaneously with the attack on Hessian Trench and seizing the eastern edge of the Redoubt. But, owing to congestion in the trenches, not all of the Duke of Wellington's Regiment detailed for the attack reached the assembly positions in time, and the attack had to be postponed. Unfortunately it was impossible to inform the Composite Force, in the Stuff Redoubt, of the postponement of the attack and therefore, as arranged, the garrison of the Redoubt attacked the eastern edge at 6 p.m.

Again the West Yorkshiremen were successful and with the 6th Yorkshires drove the enemy from his position and captured the whole of the eastern edge of the Redoubt. Very gallantly the Yorkshiremen had fought the enemy, suffering many casualties, but inflicting still more on the enemy. But finally bombs ran short and with no support, they had to fall back to their original positions.

The night of the 28th/29th passed quietly.

At noon on the 29th, the 6th York and Lancaster Regiment was ordered to attack and consolidate Hessian Trench. The staunch garrison in the Stuff Redoubt were again ordered to co-operate by another attack on the eastern edge of the Redoubt.

The York and Lancasters succeeded in gaining touch with the Canadians at Point 99 and also captured 400 yards (to R.21.d. 3.8) of the Hessian Trench, running westwards towards the Stuff Redoubt. But there a gap existed between R.21.d.3.8 and thirty yards west of Point 87. This portion of the Hessian Trench, not captured, as will be seen by the map, was fed by a communication trench and was constantly reinforced by the enemy.

The West Yorkshiremen and 6th Yorkshires meanwhile had again captured the eastern edge of the Stuff Redoubt and again had to evacuate the position owing to a shortage of bombs and ammunition. This was sheer bad luck, for all ranks had fought most valiantly and although the enemy pressed very hard the Yorkshiremen could

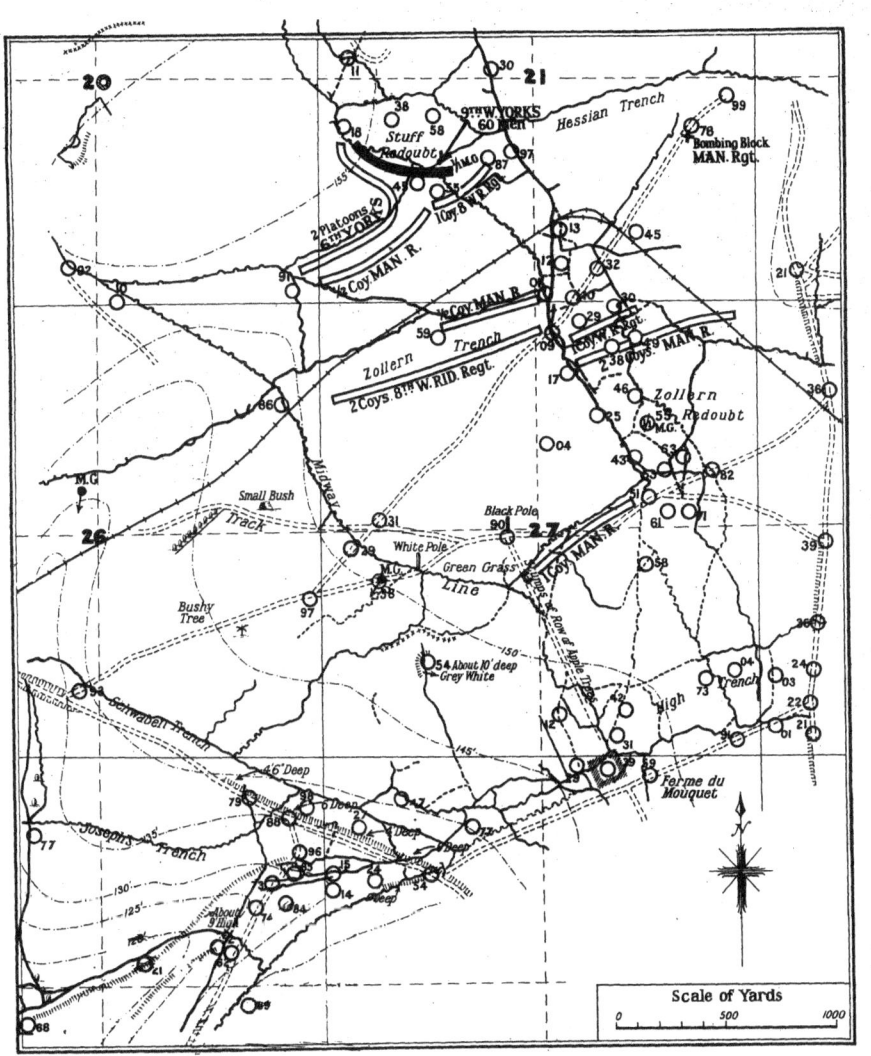

THE CAPTURE OF STUFF REDOUBT.

To face p. 276.

have held the sap head had they not run short of munitions. Touch was now lost with the York and Lancasters on the right.

9TH BATTALION.

Emboldened, no doubt, by this slight success, the Germans, towards evening, counter-attacked heavily, but were bloodily repulsed, without regaining a foot of the ground they had lost earlier in the day.

The remainder of the 29th and all next day up to 4 p.m. passed fairly quietly and the enemy made no infantry attack though his artillery shelled the position held by the Yorkshiremen.

29TH/30TH SEPT.

At 4 p.m., however, three separate bombing attacks to close the gap between the eastern edge of Hessian Trench and the Stuff Redoubt were successful and the whole line was then consolidated. The garrison of the Stuff Redoubt and the York and Lancasters carried out these attacks which resulted in touch being obtained between all units. Throughout the whole of this operation the enemy's continued shell fire on the northern end of Zollern Redoubt made communication extremely difficult. Moreover, enemy troops still clung to the trench running from R.21.d.1.3 to R.31.d.9.7.

The worn-out garrison of the Stuff Redoubt was relieved on the night of 30th Sept./1st October by troops of the 25th Division and all that remained of the gallant 9th West Yorkshires trudged wearily back, battered but triumphant, to Varennes.

30TH SEPT./ 1ST. OCT.

"Of the four Companies," said the Battalion Diary, "(less two platoons) of the Battalion that had attacked and occupied the Redoubt on 27th, only one officer and twenty-four other ranks answered 'roll call' on the morning of the 1st October."

Numerous congratulatory messages to the Battalion on its very gallant behaviour, in spite of great losses, were received from the Army, the Corps and Divisional Commanders. At 11 a.m. the Battalion embarked on buses for Beaumetz to recuperate and refit.

1ST OCT.

The 9th West Yorkshires had lost in the capture of the Stuff Redoubt two officers killed, eleven officers wounded and twenty-eight other ranks killed, 177 wounded and fifty-nine missing. The Battalion on the morning of 15th September, had gone into action with a strength of twenty officers and 780 other ranks. During the capture of the Wunter Werk on that date the casualties were eight officers killed, four officers wounded, thirty-three other ranks killed, 240 wounded and thirty-three missing. The Battalion's total casualties were thus twenty-five officers and 650 other ranks.

As already stated, the 49th Division, which had so valiantly striven to capture Thiepval on previous occasions, was not in the

T

attack, though battalions of the West Yorkshire Regiment (of the 146th Infantry Brigade) lent valuable assistance. For, when the 49th Division was relieved by the 18th Division on the 25th September, the 146th Infantry Brigade was left behind in the line, under the command of the G.O.C., 18th Division.

The 1/7th West Yorkshires held the line from Thiepval Avenue to Union Street, 1/8th Battalion from Union Street to the Ancre; the 1/6th were in support and the 1/5th in Brigade Reserve in Martinsart Wood.

On the morning of 26th, the 54th Infantry Brigade (18th Division) attacked and captured Thiepval, the 146th Infantry Brigade still continuing to hold its line, covering the village during the operations.

The 1/5th West Yorkshires were placed at the disposal of the 54th Infantry Brigade (18th Division) and "stood by" all day, but were not called upon. In the evening the 1/6th Battalion was sent across to Thiepval Château, where the men were employed in digging a strong point. Much assistance was given to the 18th Division by the 146th Infantry Brigade by the sending out of two officers' patrols, who returned with valuable information. Observation Posts, manned by officers of the West Yorkshires, were established along the 146th Infantry Brigade front, in the front line trenches, and these also proved valuable in obtaining information of the progress of the 54th Infantry Brigade through Thiepval and of the character of the fighting during the day. At 2 a.m. on the 27th the 1/5th Battalion was ordered up to the trenches between the Leipzig Salient and Thiepval Village, in close support of the 7th Battalion Bedfordshire Regiment, which had been ordered to attack the Schwaben Redoubt. The Battalion was in position at about 6 a.m. The formation for the attack was "Company behind company in the open, under cover of shell holes, each company having a frontage of 250 yards and being 150 yards behind the last wave of the Bedfords. The right of the front company rested on the Thiepval Château, the left near the old German front line; and the company faced the Redoubt."

At 3 p.m. in the afternoon the 1/5th West Yorkshires were ordered to form up by 4 p.m. ready to attack at 5 p.m. In full view of the Schwaben Redoubt and under considerable shell and rifle fire, this difficult operation was carried out, the men moving to their positions with fine steadiness. The attack was, however, cancelled and a retirement had to be made to the point of deployment, during which the Battalion suffered about sixteen casualties. Shortly afterwards a heavy hostile barrage fell on the front of Thiepval Village. During the night 27th/28th the Battalion was again ordered to form up for the attack, the movement to be completed by 6-30 a.m. on the 28th.[1] In the dark the companies moved off and by 6-27 a.m. every man was in his place, without attracting the notice of the enemy, whose guns were silent. Zero hour was not until 1 p.m. All the morning the four companies lay out in the open, practically undisturbed—a fine test of discipline and courage.

1/5TH BATTALION.

28TH SEPT.

The Attack on the Schwaben Redoubt.

At Zero hour the Bedfords attacked, the 1/5th West Yorkshires in line of sections at 150 yards distance, following the last wave of the former Battalion. A Company of the West Yorkshiremen led, followed by C, then D, and finally B Company. On reaching the line of the Château, B Company lay down in reserve. Colonel Bousfield (commanding 1/5th West Yorkshires) reported:—" It is not easy to unravel exactly what happened between Zero hour and our men reaching the final objective about 1-45 p.m." But apparently the German strength was greater on the left of the attack than on the right and the bulk of the troops were therefore drawn off towards the former. For on the left lay the German trenches, whereas on the right the advance was over open ground.

On the left much confused fighting in the front line and second line and communication trenches took place, in which the 1/5th Battalion became involved immediately. Hand-to-hand fighting was frequent and the clearing-out of the dug-outs still further broke up the formation of the three companies which early became a part of the main advance. Co-operation between the Bedfords and West Yorkshiremen seems to have been excellent, for the battalions pushed on up the hill towards the Redoubt, the final objective being reached by both units. Where the Bedfords pushed forward in sufficient strength the West Yorkshires remained in close support and where there were gaps the West Yorkshiremen stepped into the breaches and filled them up.

Both battalions had lost heavily and when the first objective was reached the West Yorkshiremen had only two officers left, one of whom held a line in close support, with men from all three

---

[1] The 1/5th Battalion was still attached to the 54th Infantry Brigade.

1/5TH BATTALION. 28TH SEPT. companies. A detachment from this party reinforced, with bombers and Lewis guns, the men fighting in the German front line towards the Ancre.

Consolidation was begun and the reserve Company (B) of the West Yorkshires was moved up to the right flank, which at this period was thinly held and " in the air."

29TH SEPT. With the exception of sixty-two other ranks and one officer, left in the line, the 1/5th West Yorkshires and the Bedfords were relieved by the West Kents before dawn on the 29th. The West Yorkshires moved back to North Bluff, Authuille, and later to Martinsart Wood.

The general situation is thus described in the Official Despatches :—" Schwaben Redoubt was assaulted during the operations of the 28th September (18th Division) and in spite of counter-attacks, delivered by strong enemy reinforcements, we captured the whole of the southern part of the Redoubt and pushed out patrols to the northern face and towards St. Pierre-Division."

The small party of West Yorkshiremen left behind most worthily maintained the reputation of the Regiment. These men fought for thirty hours without food or rest and acquitted themselves magnificently.[1]

30TH SEPT. On the 30th the Battalion marched to Halloy with the three other battalions forming the 146th Infantry Brigade.

Thus Thiepval had fallen—fallen to troops of another Division, though the 49th had striven most valiantly for its possession. It might almost be said that during the strenuous fighting in front of the village, since the 1st July, the old 49th (West Riding Territorial) Division, had become reconstituted, for the reinforcements poured in to replace the awful toll of casualties were drawn from at least twenty other units, not of the County.

---

[1] In the attack on the Schwaben Redoubt the 1/5th West Yorkshires lost Capt. P. Mandeville; 2nd Lieuts. E. W. Lee and W. Barraclough, and seventy-six other ranks, killed; seven officers and eighty-seven other ranks, wounded.
   Brigadier-General Shoubridge (G.O.C., 54th Infantry Brigade), writing afterwards to Col. Bousfield, said : " The 54th Brigade will never forget the advance of the 1/5th West Yorkshire Regiment on that day."

THE BATTLE OF LE TRANSLOY RIDGE:
Capture of Le Sars.

BY the end of September, practically the whole of the high ground between the British line from Morval to the Ancre, with the exception of that just north and north-east of Thiepval, had been wrested from the enemy, and already Sir Douglas Haig's troops were on the downward slopes towards the valley stretching north-west from Le Transloy towards Irles. The possession of Sailly-Saillisel and the Le Transloy Ridges was, however, necessary not only to rob the enemy of his observation over the Combles Valley, but to facilitate the Allied scheme of operations, which, if events went well, included an advance to, and capture of, the enemy's last system of defences in front of Le Transloy and Beaulencourt, south of Bapaume and west of Lafont Wood. In order to facilitate the attack on Sailly-Saillisel, the village of Morval had been handed over to the French at the end of September.

On the 1st October, the Fourth Army attacked Flers Trench, 1ST. OCT. south-east, west and W.N.W. of Eaucourt l'Abbaye to north-east of Destremont Farm. In this attack, the 23rd Division took part, though the 69th Infantry Brigade was not involved, the operation being carried out by the 70th Infantry Brigade. The 69th Brigade 11TH was still in Martinpuich, the 11th West Yorkshires holding trenches BATTALION. near the ruined village. By the evening of 3rd October, the whole of 3RD OCT. Eaucourt l'Abbaye was in the hands of the Fourth Army. Meanwhile, on the 2nd, the 69th Infantry Brigade had relieved the 70th Brigade in the line.

On the 4th, the 11th West Yorkshires moved up from Martin- 4TH OCT. puich to trenches towards Le Sars, and shortly after 6 p.m. on the same day, the 10th West Ridings and the 8th Yorkshire Regiment attacked the Second Flers Line, west and south (respectively) of the Bapaume Road.

Wet and stormy weather had already interfered with the main operations, and the trenches were in a terrible state. Hostile shell fire had blown the hastily constructed defences to pieces, and what

11TH BATTALION. 4TH OCT.

little protection remained was fast being washed away by the incessant rain. Sleep was impossible, and the men were much exhausted. The battalions in reserve were little better off: they had no cover from shell fire or weather, and had to furnish large carrying parties day and night to maintain a constant supply of food, water, bombs, ammunition and other stores, all of which had to be carried long distances.

When, therefore, during the evening of the 5th October, the 11th West Yorkshires relieved the 10th West Ridings, and the 9th Yorkshires the 8th Yorkshires, in the front line, the relief took place under the worst possible conditions.

5TH/6TH OCT.

Throughout the night of the 5th/6th, and all the following day the enemy's shell fire was particularly heavy. The front line, rear lines and Brigade Headquarters were constantly under fire, and casualties were considerable. The weather had, however, shown some slight improvement and the main attack of the Fourth Army on Le Transloy Ridges (previously postponed) was definitely ordered to take place on the 7th.

The capture of Le Sars was the task allotted to the 23rd Division, and for the attack the Division disposed the 68th Infantry Brigade on the right, and the 69th Infantry Brigade on the left. The dividing line between Brigades was from M.21.d.8.5. through the cross roads in Le Sars.

7TH OCT.

Of the 69th Infantry Brigade, the 9th Yorkshire Regiment on the right, and the 11th West Yorkshires[1] on the left, were to attack the southern parts of Le Sars, and the Second Flers Line, west of the Bapaume Road, respectively. The 68th Brigade, on the right, was to carry the enemy's trench system about the Sunken Road, and the northern half of the village. The 47th Division was attacking on the right of the 23rd Division.

The operation was by no means easy, for whereas the First and Second Flers Lines, south-east of and up to the Bapaume Road were held by the Division, only the First Flers Line north-west of the road was held. It was the latter line from which the West Yorkshiremen, at Zero plus twenty minutes, were to attack the Second Flers Line, North-west of the Bapaume Road, in flank.

Zero hour, for the whole attack along the Fourth Army front, was 1-45 p.m., and at that hour the bombardment of the enemy's lines, which had been continuous from 3-35 p.m. on the 6th, lifted.

---

[1] The Battalion record of the capture of Le Sars is as follows:—" October 7th—2-10 p.m. Battalion attacked trenches to the left of Le Sars. Objective gained and held. Losses heavy—eight officers and 217 other ranks."

Le Sars and the Flers Line

On the right, the 68th Brigade advanced rapidly, but just before reaching the Sunken Road, was enfiladed by machine-gun fire from Le Sars, which was maintained until the 9th Yorkshire Regiment (on the right of the 69th Brigade) had taken the lower portion of the village.

11TH BATTALION 7TH OCT.

The 9th Yorkshire Regiment, at Zero hour, however, had followed quickly on the heels of the barrage, so closely indeed, that an officer and some men were killed by British shells at the cross roads of the village. The enemy attempted to man his machine guns, but the latter were bombed, and other Germans coming up out of their dug-outs were bayoneted. Fierce hand-to-hand fighting took place at the cross roads, and here the occupants of a strong point, who refused to surrender, were killed. The machine-guns which were enfilading the left of the 68th Infantry Brigade, were now bombed and captured by the latter Brigade. Much hand-to-hand fighting took place before the southern part of the village was captured, but the troops of both the 68th and 69th Brigades fought splendidly, and soon the former Brigade set out to clear the northern portions of the village, while the 9th Yorkshires of the 69th Brigade pressed eastwards to clear the enemy out of the system of trenches north-west of the Bapaume Road.

Meanwhile, on the left of Le Sars, the 11th West Yorkshires (Lieut.-Col. Barker) had moved to the assault at 2·5 p.m., but were at once met by a heavy rifle and machine-gun fire from both the front and left flanks: the enemy's artillery also shelled the area over which the attack was going forward. This bombardment had, unfortunately, caught the two supporting companies of West Yorkshiremen who, five minutes earlier (2 p.m.), had endeavoured to cross from Destremont Farm to the First Flers Line. Of these two companies, only two unwounded officers and thirty other ranks reached the Flers front line.

The first attack on the Second Flers Line was unsuccessful. A bombing attack was then launched. From Le Sars, along the Second Flers Line, bombing parties pushed westwards and drove the enemy out of 50 yards of his trenches. Other bombing parties tried to bomb northwards up the two communication trenches between the First and Second Flers Lines. After a further attempt, in which the 9th Yorkshires, now holding the village, co-operated, the enemy was driven from his position. His troops streamed back from the Second Flers Line across the open and were caught by Lewis-gun fire, which killed or wounded some seventy or eighty Germans. Lieut.

11TH BATTALION.
7TH OCT.

R. E. Hobday captured a German corporal and compelled him to go with him to collect his men and make them surrender; over 100 Germans were taken. Twenty more were chased by a subaltern of the 69th Machine Gun Company, and surrendered. A Company of 10th West Ridings, which had been placed at the disposal of Col. Barker, now came up, and entering Flers support line drove the enemy before them into the arms of other troops, or they were shot down in the open. Gradually the whole battalion of West Ridings was absorbed into the front line, the 11th West Yorkshires being very weak, having lost a large number of men. Finally, the village of Le Sars and the trenches won were consolidated and, during the evening, strong points were established by the 69th Brigade, trenches were improved or dug, and communication joined up with the 68th Brigade.

8TH OCT.

At 4-50 a.m. on the morning of the 8th, the Quarry and the remainder of the Flers front and support lines were attacked and captured, but it is not clear from the reports whether the 11th West Yorkshires were engaged in this attack. The Battalion was relieved on the 8th by the Cameron Highlanders of the 15th Division, which had been sent up to take over the front held by the 23rd Division. The West Yorkshiremen bivouacked that night in Round Wood, and on the following day marched to billets in Albert. The capture of Le Sars, and a considerable portion of the enemy's line, east and north-east of Gueudecourt, were the principal gains of the Fourth Army on the 7th and 8th October.

12TH OCT.

On the 12th, the 69th Brigade, with the 70th Brigade, entrained at Albert for the Xth Corps area, and the former, after considerable delay *en route*, arrived at Houpoutre on the 15th, where the units detrained and marched to billets in Poperinghe. The 23rd Division was now in the Ypres area, with some months of trench warfare before it. From this period onward, until the end of the year, nothing of importance happened to the 11th West Yorkshires. The round of tours in the trenches, or in support, or reserve, were not marked by any attack on, or by, the enemy.

The Attack on Mild and Cloudy Trenches— 12th October.

The operations of the 7th and 8th October, though successful, had not resulted in the gain of positions from which observation of the Le Transloy line could be obtained. This was absolutely necessary before operations against the Le Transloy line could be undertaken. With this idea in view, orders were issued by Fourth Army Headquarters to continue the attack on the 12th October, simultaneously with an attack by the Sixth French Army (on the right of the Fourth British Army) in the direction of Sailly-Saillisel.

The Fourth Army attack was to be made with three corps—XIVth, XVth and IIIrd (from right to left in the order given). The XIVth Corps was to attack with the 4th Division on the right and the 6th Division on the left. Thus the 1st and the 21st Battalions of the West Yorkshire Regiment were concerned in the attack, the former as one of the assaulting battalions of the 6th Division, the latter as Pioneers of the 4th Division. 1ST AND 21ST BATTALIONS.

From the 1st to the 6th October, the 1st West Yorkshires (in Brigade) remained at Ville-sur-Ancre, training and getting ready for the next operation. On the latter date, the 18th Infantry Brigade received orders to move on the following day to the Citadel area, preparatory to moving up into the front line. On the 8th, the Brigade took over the trenches in front of Gueudecourt from the 20th Division—the 2nd Durham Light Infantry and 11th Essex occupying the right and left sub-sectors respectively. The 1st West Yorkshires were in support in Needle Trench, west of the village, and the 14th Durham Light Infantry were in Brigade Reserve. The front line was reorganized on the 9th, when the 71st Infantry Brigade moved up a battalion to the front line trenches, relieving the 2nd Durham Light Infantry. All three Infantry Brigades of the 6th Division now held the front line, *i.e.*, 16th on the right, 71st in the centre and 18th on the left. 1ST. BATTALION. 6TH OCT. 8TH OCT.

At 9 p.m. on the 10th, the 1st West Yorkshires set out to relieve the 11th Essex in a portion of Cloudy and Rainbow Trenches. The relief took five hours to complete, the front line being, not only heavily shelled by the enemy, but of a very irregular nature. Cloudy Trench was held partly by the 6th Division, and partly by the enemy. 10TH OCT.

Orders for the general attack on the 12th October were issued during the previous day. At 7 a.m. on the 11th, the guns began the preliminary bombardment, which ceased at 5 p.m., opening again on the 12th at 7 a.m. until Zero hour—2-5 p.m.

The attack was of a complicated character; only the 16th and 18th Infantry Brigades of the 6th Division were to assault the enemy's trenches, the 71st Brigade being already on the line of the Army Objective Line. Thus, the front of the 6th Division formed a salient, 11TH OCT.

1ST BATTALION.

with the 4th Division on the right, and the 12th Division on the left, thrown back some distance in an irregular and sketchy front line.

The 1st West Yorkshires (on the right) and the 14th Durham Light Infantry (left) were to carry out the attack by the 18th Infantry Brigade.

11TH/12TH OCT.

During the night, 11th/12th the West Yorkshiremen, and the 14th D.L.I., moved up to their assembly positions, the former in Shine Trench, and a portion of Cloudy Trench, the Durhams in Bordon. The West Yorkshiremen were to attack Mild and Cloudy Trenches at Zero plus twenty, when the Durhams, attacking at Zero, had carried the outer portion of Rainbow Trench, and had come up on the left of the former Battalion. "The defences to be dealt with in this task," said the G.S. Diary of the 6th Division, "were a series of disconnected trenches, over most of which observation was difficult; no air photographs had been taken on the 11th and the morning of the 12th was dull with low clouds."

At Zero hour (2-5 p.m.) the bombardment ceased, and the creeping barrage began to move forward. On the right, the 4th Division gained its first objective, but the 16th Infantry Brigade (6th Division) after gallantly advancing 150 yards was held up by long distance machine-gun fire. The 14th Durham Light Infantry (18th Infantry Brigade) advanced and gained the outer portion of Rainbow Trench, gaining touch with the right battalion of the 12th Division. The Durhams then pressed on northwards, joining up with the left of the West Yorkshires, just east of the Sunken Road. The two battalions now moved forward to the attack on Mild and Cloudy Trenches. The 1st West Yorkshires had disposed their companies as follows :—C Company on the right, D Company on the left, with one Company in support, and one in reserve.

12TH OCT.

Previous to the attack, and while waiting for the Durhams to come up on their left, the West Yorkshires had gone through a terrible experience. Not only were they under heavy fire from the German artillery, but also from the British guns, which, owing to a mistake had directed their fire on the trenches in which the assaulting troops were assembled. On leaving their trenches they were met by intense machine-gun fire, coming both from the front and flank. The enemy had moved up fresh troops to meet the attack, which he judged rightly, owing to the preparatory bombardment, was imminent. Twice the gallant West Yorkshiremen tried to get forward. C Company on the right, tried to turn the enemy out of Cloudy Trench, but the Germans were in great strength, and the attack failed. D

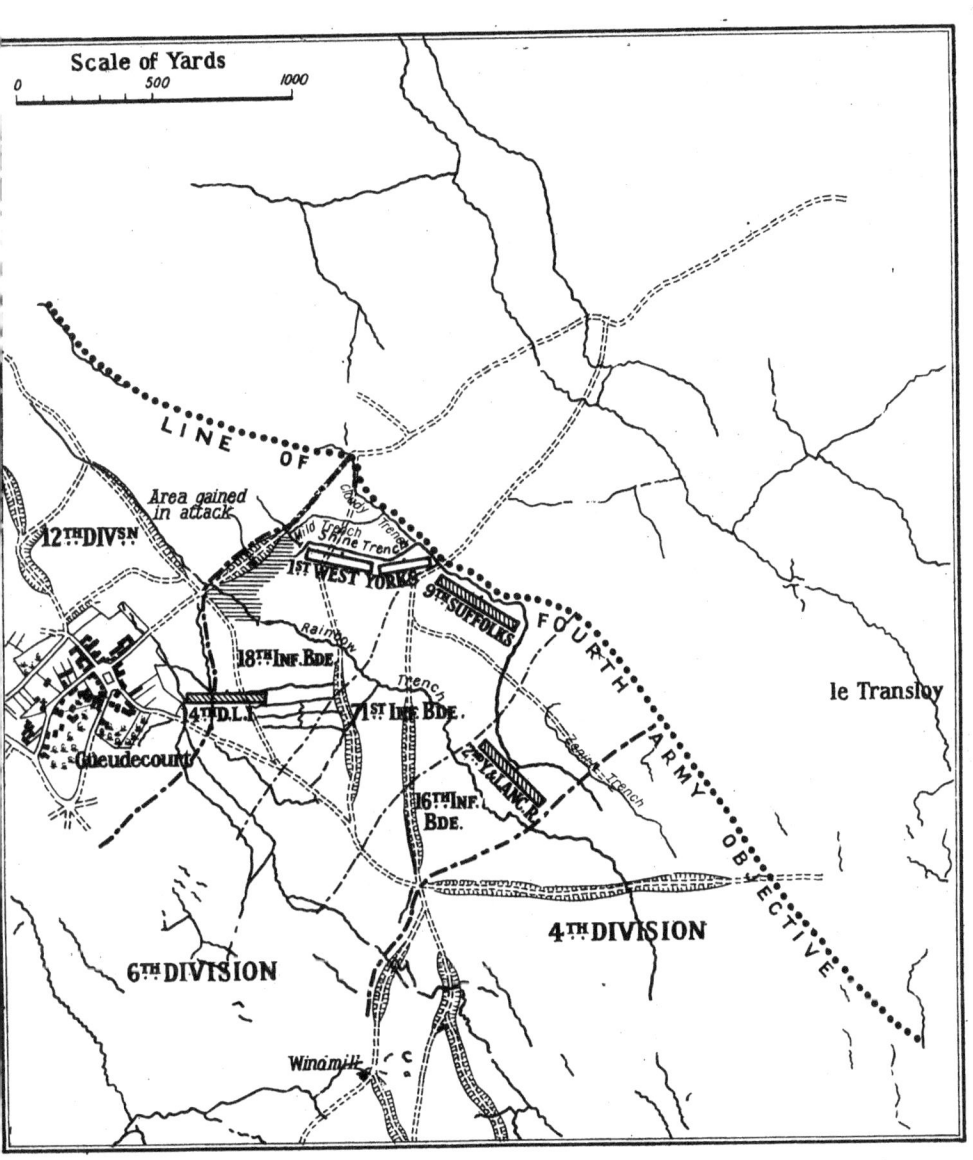

THE ATTACK ON MILD AND CLOUDY TRENCHES.

Company had no sooner set foot outside its own trenches than de- 1ST
vastating rifle and machine-gun fire compelled a withdrawal to the BATTALION.
original starting point. At 3-55 p.m., 6th Divisional Headquarters 12TH OCT.
received a report, forwarded by Headquarters, 18th Infantry
Brigade, from the O.C., 1st West Yorkshires :—" Impossible to
advance against concentrated machine-gun and rifle fire. Hold part
of Cloudy Trench on my right, otherwise in original position. Fire of
every description very heavy at present." Finally, the West Yorkshiremen and Durhams were ordered to consolidate their positions
as strongly as possible, the latter Battalion to form a defensive flank as
touch on the left had not been maintained with the 12th Division.

The 1st Battalion West Yorkshires lost in this attack two officers,
wounded, twenty-four other ranks killed, seventy-one wounded and
ten missing. An appreciative letter from the G.O.C., 18th Infantry
Brigade (General Bridgford) was received by the C.O. of the 1st
West Yorkshires :—" Your Battalion had a most exasperating time
up in the line. Great credit is due to you all for carrying on so well
under such disadvantageous circumstances."

The Battalion was relieved during the night of the 13th October 13TH OCT.
by the 2nd Durham Light Infantry, and marched back to
bivouacs in Trones Wood, where the 14th was spent in reserve
in cheerless surroundings. At 7 p.m. on the 15th, the Battalion 15TH OCT.
again went up to the front line, taking over a portion of Shine
Trench and portions of Cloudy and Rainbow Trenches ; but
this was a short tour, the 9th Norfolks marching in to relieve
the West Yorkshiremen during the night of the 16th. Another
officer was wounded during the day, and four other ranks were
killed, sixteen wounded and one missing.

This was the last tour served by the 1st Battalion West Yorkshire
Regiment in the front line trenches in the Somme area in 1916.
The 18th Infantry Brigade, as a whole, was relieved on the night
16th/17th, and moved back to Trones Wood, thence later to the 16TH OCT.
Citadel area, well pleased to leave the Somme battlefield behind. The
relief of the 6th Division was completed on the night of 19th/20th
October, the 24th and 25th Infantry Brigades of the 8th Division
relieving the 71st and 16th Infantry Brigades. A few days later the
Division, as a whole, was on the way north to the Béthune sector,
where on the last day of the month, Divisional Headquarters and
16th Infantry Brigade were in Béthune, 71st Infantry Brigade in
Fouquereuil, Annezin and Fouquieres and the 18th Infantry Brigade
in La Beuvrière and Marles-les-Mines. The 1st West Yorkshires

were billeted in La Beuvrière. Before the West Yorkshiremen left the Somme, the Battalion was visited by H.R.H. the Prince of Wales, who inspected the N.C.O.'s and men and, in kindly words, congratulated officers and other ranks who had been awarded decorations during the recent operations. These visits from His Royal Highness were rare, but they were greatly appreciated.

21ST BATTALION. 12TH OCT. To return to the 12th October, *i.e.*, the operations of the 4th Division, on the right of the 6th Division. The 21st West Yorkshires —Pioneers of the 4th Division—had but recently returned to this Division having, on 26th September, been lent to the C.E., XIVth Corps who, so far as can be ascertained from the official diaries, had formed a " XIVth Corps Pioneer Group." On the 21st July— after the first three weeks of the Somme operations—the 4th Division had entrained at Doullens and Candas for the Ypres sector, and on the 25th the 21st West Yorkshires were billeted in Poperinghe.

It is an eloquent tribute to the Pioneers of all divisions, that the diaries of the latter constantly refer, without exception, to the work carried out by these gallant fellows. Seldom the glories of battle fell to the Pioneers—their work at all times in consolidating ground taken from the enemy was of a most dangerous nature. For no sooner did the enemy lose ground to the British, than he at once turned his guns on to the lost trenches, and lucky indeed were the Pioneers if they escaped without loss.

For several months after their arrival in the Ypres area, the 21st West Yorkshires were engaged on work in the trenches, and on the roads in that troubled sector. The Pilkem road was one of the unhealthy spots in the Salient, and here the Pioneers were constantly at work repairing the damage done by the enemy's shells. The trenches north of Bridge " B " (on the Yser Canal) was another undesirable spot. Lancashire Farm, Ritz Street, Fort Street and Kirby Street, were all scenes of the Pioneers' activities. It was in the latter trenches—Kirby Street—on 26th August, while an officer and fifty men of C Company were at work, making a deep living trench with dug-outs, that the enemy suddenly opened a very heavy bombardment on the front line. Half-an-hour later the bombardment was lifted on to Kirby Street, where the Pioneers were at work. In a very little while the trenches were wrecked in three places for a length of 50 yards, rendering reconstruction almost impossible. Two men were killed, and fourteen wounded in this bombardment.

Towards the end of August, heavy rain set in, with its immediate result—parapets fell down, the trenches became quagmires and the pioneers were kept continually at work draining and rebuilding the dilapidated defences.

On the 2nd September, the Battalion Diary contained the following entry :—"B and D Companies moved from Belgian Infantry Barracks to other billets in Ypres. One platoon occupied part of the Cloth Hall, the rest of B Company the church of a convent. D Company partly in cellars, partly in the hall of a convent. These billets being very much exposed had to be protected with heavy shell-proof covers, on which a proportion of both companies was engaged during the whole time they remained in Ypres. By the time they left, very good and safe shell-proof billets had been made, and the surroundings were clean and wholesome." A and C Companies seem to have been engaged mostly in Barnsley (Canal) Road, Halifax and Huddersfield communication trenches, and in Threadneedle Street and Gowthorpe Road. On the 16th September, work was stopped, and the 21st West Yorkshires concentrated with the 4th Division. On the following day the Pioneers (with the Division), were *en route* for the Somme. Longeau was reached on the 18th, where the Division detrained. On the 30th the Battalion was in Citadel Camp, and remained there for several days when, on the 8th of October, the Pioneers were returned to their Division, and moved forward with the latter towards the front line.

A very strenuous period was now before the Pioneers. Three weeks of terrific warfare, during which the opposing forces used prodigious quantities of shell, had turned the once-beautiful Somme Valley into nothing more or less than one huge mud patch, gaping with great shell holes and craters, in many places foul with the stench of decaying bodies, almost impassable in daylight, and a death trap at night. Amidst such surroundings the Pioneers came back from that other place of torture—the Ypres Salient—to dig and burrow in the ground and provide shelter for the nerve-wracked infantry.

On the 10th the 21st West Yorkshires relieved the Cheshire Pioneer Battalion in camp near Briqueterie, and were put to work almost immediately on the roads. The 11th was spent in this manner.

10TH OCT.

On the 12th, when the XIVth Corps attacked, A and B Companies of the Pioneers moved up to the trenches, A Company to help the Durham R.E., and B to assist the 9th Field Company in consolidating the ground, after the assault had taken place. The attack was only partially successful, but there is no mention of the

12TH OCT.

21ST.
BATTALION.
12TH OCT.

exact portion of ground gained, which the Pioneers helped to consolidate. The Battalion Diary has the following entry:—" An attack by the 10th and 12th Brigades (4th Division) took place this afternoon, to establish a line in advance of existing position, but was not entirely successful. The work done by the Companies was to consolidate the portion of position gained."[1]

23RD OCT.

Until the 23rd October, the Pioneer Battalion (21st West Yorkshires) continued to labour in the front line trenches and vicinity, suffering casualties and generally leading a strenuous and very uncomfortable existence. Casualties amongst officers and other ranks were numerous. Captain E. Boulnois was killed and Captain G. S. Noon severely wounded on 22nd. Captain H. B. Adamson died on 30th of wounds received on 21st October. It was with thankfulness that the Battalion arrived in Citadel Camp on the 24th. November was spent at Fresne and Pierrecourt.

The Attack on Zenith Trench, 23rd—26th October.

After the 18th October, the attack on Le Transloy defences assumed the nature of local attempts to gain ground and push the line forward, and no sooner had the 8th Division relieved the 6th, than immediate plans were formulated to turn the enemy out of the salient formed, west of Le Transloy, by Eclipse and Zenith Trenches.

21ST OCT.

On the 21st October, the 23rd Infantry Brigade (8th Division) took over the left sub-sector of the 4th Division sector, the front line of which consisted of Spectrum Trench. All three Brigades of the former Division were now in the front line.

2ND
BATTALION.

After the terrible experiences through which the 8th Division had passed from the 1st and 2nd July, the Division, as a whole, was transferred to the 1st Corps, First Army area, entraining at Longeau on the 6th and 7th and reaching Bruay, the reserve area of the Army, on the 8th, the 2nd West Yorkshires going into billets at Maisnil.

After a few days' rest and reorganization the 8th Division moved forward and relieved the 39th Division in the Cuinchy sector, the 23rd Infantry Brigade taking over the sub-sector from Boyeau 1 to the La Bassée Canal; the 2nd West Yorkshires were in support in the village line. Several weeks of active trench warfare were now before the Division.

[1] The gain of the XIVth Corps (4th and 6th Divisions) of the Fourth Army on 12th October, was officially given as follows:—" 4th Division advanced to T.5.d.2.9 on the extreme right, a post being established and touch with the French obtained at that point. The whole of Spectrum was taken, and a small advance was made on the extreme left, troops having dug in between Zenith and Misty Trenches; 6th Division captured a portion of Rainbow; no other advance was made."

On the 22nd July, the 2nd West Yorkshires moved up to the front line, relieving the 2nd Devons from Boyeau 20 (exclusive) to Boyeau 36 (inclusive). The position occupied by the Battalion was one which permitted little peace by day or by night. The opposing trenches were very close together and throughout the night continual bombing, the firing of rifle grenades and trench mortar activity kept the men on the alert. The daylight hours were, however, fairly quiet, partly because the trenches being so close together, both sides kept well down behind their parapets. Between 23rd and 29th July, two mines were exploded by the enemy opposite the Battalion's trenches, but did little damage. On the 30th (at 2 a.m.) the Battalion was raided. Under cover of a thick mist and a sharp bombardment ending in a barrage, two strong parties of the enemy attacked B Company's front line trench between Boyeau 30 and 31, held by No. 5 and No. 6 Platoons. Captain L. D. Gordon-Alexander was at the time commanding B Company. Warning reached No. 5 Platoon (Lieut. S. Rogerson) from a wiring party at work out in No Man's Land, when the enemy approached. By sustained rifle fire and bomb-throwing this Platoon successfully beat off the attack of one party of the enemy. But No. 6 Platoon was less fortunate, not having received warning of the attack. Along the Platoon's frontage was a sap-head (No. 6) containing four men and another man was on his way up to the sap. The enemy, about thirty strong, first captured the sap-head and then jumped into the main trench. Lieut. A. H. Daly, commanding No. 6 Platoon, threw a bomb at the Germans and emptied his revolver into them and the Platoon set to work to eject the enemy. This was done without sustaining any casualties, neither was the enemy able to do any damage, his object being undoubtedly to destroy mine-heads, as he left behind charges of perdite. Near No. 6 sap-head, in No Man's Land were found, many articles, such as caps, revolvers, bombs, equipment, etc. There were also other grim indications of the fight put up by the small but gallant garrison of the sap-head before the men were overpowered by superior numbers, several arms and fingers being found in the vicinity of the sap-head.

On the 12th August, the enemy again raided the West Yorkshiremen. The Battalion was now in the Hohenzollern sector, holding the front line from Boyeau 101 to 109. The enemy had been active since the Battalion came into the line on the 7th August, and two officers and several other ranks had already been wounded. At 8-10 p.m. on the night of the 12th the enemy opened a very heavy

2ND BATTALION.

bombardment of the front line and support trenches, the bombardment becoming more intense as it proceeded. For an hour the enemy's guns gave the Battalion's trenches a very bad time and in many places the defences were entirely flattened out. Under cover of the bombardment a strong hostile raiding party advanced against the battered defences of the West Yorkshiremen and attempted to enter what remained of the trenches. A Company, on the right, met his advance with Lewis-gun fire and, with the exception of a few men who managed to penetrate the line between A and D Companies, where the line had been completely flattened out, beat off the attack. The few Germans, who penetrated the line, were immediately ejected, leaving seven killed and wounded behind them. A Company lost eight and D Company fourteen other ranks, killed, wounded and missing. Seven men of the latter Company were buried in a deep dug-out which had been blown in by shell fire.

Little of interest (so far as trench warfare is concerned) happened to the Battalion during the remainder of August. On the 22nd of the month, Lieut.-Col. L. Hume-Spry, D.S.O., left the 2nd West Yorks Regiment and was succeeded by Major J. L. Jack, 2nd Scottish Rifles, who assumed command of the Battalion.

The 1st September saw the Battalion marching out of billets in Fouquières to relieve the 2nd Rifle Brigade in the front line of the Quarries sector. Up to the 12th, everything was very quiet in the line, but that the enemy was very much on the alert may be gathered from the following note in the Battalion Diary of the above date :—
" Last night one or two of the enemy with incredible audacity crept through our wire and shell holes and shot two sentries behind our parapet."

A gallant but futile attempt (owing to the extraordinary strength of the enemy's wire) to raid the hostile trenches was made by two officers and twenty-four other ranks on the night of the 15th September. The raiding party left the trenches at 9-20 p.m. on the 15th, and did not return until 1-30 a.m. on the 16th. Two men were wounded and the Battalion Diary states that " The pertinacity of Second-Lieut. Smailes and his party was admirable and this officer and Second-Lieut. Fisher and Sergeant W. R. Mellor behaved most pluckily in getting Private Standish (one of the wounded men) back."

The remainder of September and the early part of October (until 11th) passed without anything abnormal happening to the Battalion, which now occupied the Hulluch sector. Considerable annoyance was, however, caused the West Yorkshiremen by the enemy's use of a particularly vicious implement of warfare—the air dart. On the 9th, 10th and 11th October, these darts fell on the trenches of the Battalion and caused many casualties. On 12th, however, the Battalion was relieved for the last time in the Hulluch sector and marched to La Bouverie. During the three months (from 15th July to 12th October) the 2nd West Yorkshires had been engaged in trench warfare. Seventy days out of ninety had been spent either in the front-line or support trenches.

At 4 p.m. on the 14th, the Battalion marched, in Brigade, to Chocques and there entrained for Longpré, detraining at the latter place at midnight on 15th, and marching to billets in Fontaine-sur-Somme. The 8th Division was now transferred from the Ist Corps, First Army, to the Xth Corps of the Fourth Army. Another march of four miles, on the 12th, brought the Battalion, in Brigade, to Sorel, where French motor buses carried the West Yorkshiremen as far as Buire-sur-l'Ancre. Another march of two miles and the Battalion reached Meaulte in the XIVth Corps area, where two days were spent in training. On 20th, at 5 a.m., a miserably cold and wet morning, the Battalion began to move forward to the line, nearly six miles to Camp "D" in Bernafay Wood. The nearer the Battalion got to the front line the more the awful conditions under which men fought and existed became apparent. Day and night fatigue parties were found by the Battalion on the 21st and, finally, on the 22nd, the Battalion went forward to Windmill and Shin trenches, in support. Throughout the night until about 4 a.m. on the 23rd, the Battalion was on fatigue duty and, unfortunately, whilst with a carrying party, Second-Lieut. G. Smailes was killed by hostile shell fire. "He had performed some excellent patrols in the Loos Salient," said the Battalion Diary, "and was a most gallant and promising officer."

At 2-30 p.m. on the 23rd October, the 8th Division attacked Zenith Trench. On the 21st, the 23rd Infantry Brigade had (as already stated) taken over the left sub-sector of the 4th Division sector, the front line of which consisted of Spectrum Trench—all three brigades of the 8th Division being then in the front line, which ran (from right to left) Spectrum Trench (23rd Brigade), Gusty and Misty Trenches (25th Brigade), a portion of Cloudy Trench with the Salient in front of it, and Shine Trench (24th Brigade).

Spectrum Trench was held by the 2nd Scottish Rifles, on the right, and the 2nd Middlesex, on the left, the 2nd West Yorkshires

2ND BATTALION. 23RD OCT.

were in support in Windmill Trench and Shine Alley; the fourth battalion of the 23rd Brigade—the Devons—was in reserve in Sap and Punch Trenches. These were the dispositions prior to the attack.

At 2-30 p.m. the assault took place, the Scottish Rifles and Middlesex with great gallantry advancing close behind the barrage, stormed Zenith Trench along the Brigade front. The Scottish Rifles were, at first, checked by machine-gun fire, which caused many casualties, but, being reinforced, gained their first objective, capturing twenty-five prisoners. The Middlesex also captured the enemy's trenches on their front, with few casualties, and inflicted heavy losses on the enemy. At 3 p.m. both Battalions advanced from Zenith Trench and established themselves on a line from 100 to 150 yards in front, occupying Orion. At 3-15 p.m. and again at 4-15 p.m. the enemy counter-attacked, but was repulsed.

Meanwhile the 2nd West Yorkshires had been waiting in Windmill and Shine Alley Trenches expecting orders to go forward. The enemy's barrage, which fell almost immediately the assault took place, was severe and swept the front-line and support trenches with increasing fury; telegraph wires were cut, communication trenches and cable wires were blown to atoms and it was only with the greatest difficulty, that any reports of what was going on in the front line could be obtained. Shortly after 3 p.m. Major Jack (commanding 2nd West Yorkshires) was ordered to send up one company to occupy the old front line, now empty and vacated by the 2nd Scottish Rifles. A Company (Capt. Palmes) was selected and, in line of platoons in file, the Company set out on its perilous undertaking. This advance to the " O.B.L." (Spectrum Trench) had to be made across open ground, on which the enemy's barrage was falling heavily. Before the Company reached Spectrum Trench fifteen other ranks had become casualties. At 5 p.m. C Company (Second-Lieut. Cowdray) proceeded, in similar manner, to the old line held by the Middlesex, but by this hour the enemy shelling had died down and no casualties were suffered by the second company.

Between 6 and 7 p.m. the enemy heavily barraged Orion, which had to be evacuated by the Scottish Rifles, who retired to Zenith. Orders were then given to Major Jack to organize a strong bombing party, to push forward to the Sunken Road south of Orion, and be prepared to retake the latter Trench. But this attack was eventually cancelled by Corps Headquarters and the 23rd Infantry Brigade ordered to consolidate its ground. On the front of the 23rd

THE ATTACK ON ZENITH TRENCH.

Infantry Brigade no appreciable advance had been made, whereas the 24th Infantry Brigade (on the left) had captured a small portion of Mild Trench and had connected it up with Shine Trench by the communication trenches. *2ND BATTALION. 23RD OCT.*

All night long the work of consolidation was pushed forward with great energy, the Division having ordered all units in the front and support lines to make their positions secure before daylight on 24th.

When dawn broke on the 24th A and C Companies of the West Yorkshires were still in Spectrum Trench, and B and D Companies in Windmill Trench. With daylight came the inevitable never-ceasing shelling, and during the day the West Yorkshiremen suffered twenty more casualties. At night all four companies of the Battalion relieved the 2nd Scottish Rifles, A Company taking over the right, C the left, whilst B and D remained in support. *24TH OCT.*

Operations on the 25th October, consisted, during the day, in improving the forward line and at night in patrol work. A patrol of the 2nd West Yorkshires, consisting of Second-Lieut. Peters and three other ranks, went out and worked gradually towards Orion. This small patrol bumped into a party of fifteen Germans, who had lost their way and, on being summoned to surrender, gave themselves up and were marched back to the West Yorkshire's trenches. *25TH OCT.*

Casualties had again been heavy from shell fire; Second-Lieut. T. S. E. John Littlejohn was killed and another officer was wounded; seven other ranks also were killed, twenty-one wounded and thirteen were missing. The Battalion also, unfortunately, lost its Medical Officer—Capt. B. J. L. Fayle, R.A.M.C., who was killed instantaneously by a shell whilst tending wounded men in the trenches. "No words," said the Battalion Diary, " can convey any appreciation of his tireless and brave devotion to duty."

An entry in the Battalion Diary on 26th October, adequately sums up the situation in the front line during the time the Battalion was in occupation :—" Weather continues bad. Casualties about thirty, chiefly to carrying parties, but also due to enemy's shelling on trenches. Patrolling proceeded with each night, often under sharp fire from enemy snipers and work of consolidation also continues ; the trenches, bad to begin with, suffered seriously from shell fire." *26TH OCT.*

On the night of 29th/30th, the Battalion was relieved by the 10th West Yorkshires of the 50th Infantry Brigade, 17th Division, which had been ordered up to take over the line held by the 8th Division. The relief was completed by 6-30 a.m. on the latter date *10TH BATTALION. 29TH/30TH OCT.*

2ND BATTALION.
30TH OCT.

and, in a pouring rain, the 2nd Battalion marched back to Carnoy—" to find the accommodation not ready, but completed at night fall."

"The Battalion," said Major Jack, the Commanding Officer, in his report on this tour in the line, "when it went into action—actual fighting men—on 22nd, and including officers, but not including officers and other ranks on transport or left in camp as reinforcements, was 437 strong. Between 22nd and 30th the casualties were six officers (including one officer attached 23rd Trench Mortars, *i.e.*, Lieut. N. Bastow, killed on 23rd) and 214 other ranks. A and C Companies only lost about fifteen casualties advancing to front line on 25th. B and D Companies suffered most in the trenches, whilst carrying parties of all companies and Headquarters suffered severely. All the stretcher bearers and orderlies worked with the greatest gallantry and had to traverse ground continually swept by heavy shell fire. Battalion Headquarters in a Sunken Road well marked by the enemy's artillery, also suffered severely and was continually shelled both by 5·9's and shrapnel, whilst the routes both to rear and to the front, particularly the former, were very exposed and dangerous."

4TH NOV.

Six none too comfortable days were spent by the 2nd West Yorkshires (and the 8th Division generally) out of the line, the Battalion being, until the 3rd November, billeted in Meaulte. On the 4th, a move was made to Citadel, whence, on the morning of 7th, the West Yorkshiremen again marched up to Bernafay Shelters (in Brigade Reserve), the 23rd Infantry Brigade having relieved the 19th Infantry Brigade (33rd Division) in the left sector of the Lesbœufs sector, on the immediate right of the line previously held in October. The march to Bernafay took place under the worst possible conditions. Rain fell in torrents and when the Battalion reached the wretched shelters, situated between Bernafay and Trones Woods, the men had to wait in the open until the "mudholes" (they were very little else) were vacated by the out-going unit.

10TH NOV.

The Battalion relieved the 2nd Devons after dusk on the 10th, B Company taking over the right front in Autumn Trench, A Company the centre and D the left front, partly in Summer Trench, C Company was in support in Dewdrop. These trenches were directly in front of Lesbœufs, they were much exposed and afforded little protection. The enemy's main Le Transloy line was only about 800 yards in front, with numerous and hard-to-locate posts and machine guns in shell holes. Small lengths of the enemy's trenches ran right up to the front-line trenches of the sector.

At 11 p.m. an officers' patrol went out into No Man's Land 2ND for the purpose of reconnoitring a Sunken Road, which lay in front BATTALION. of, and ran south through, Summer Trench. Second-Lieut. V. L. Pimm was in charge of the patrol, which pushed forward 150 yards up the road without encountering the enemy. On returning, however, the patrol was fired on from the direction of Pollux Trench and Lieut. Pimm was missing when the party re-entered Summer Trench. Another officer, Second-Lieut. A. E. P. Skett, gallantly went out to search for the missing officer, but was killed soon after he had gone over the parapet. Seven other casualties were suffered by the Battalion that night.

For several days the 2nd West Yorkshires lived in what was aptly described by an officer, who was present with another unit as " concentrated misery," but relief came on the 13th, when the 13TH Nov. Battalion marched back to Briqueterie Camp. From the latter Camp the Battalion (in Brigade) moved to Citadel and six days later both the 23rd and 25th Infantry Brigades entrained at Grove Town and Edgehill Stations, respectively, for Oisemont; the 8th Division was at last to be given a rest. By 21st November, all units of the Division were located in the Belloy St. Leonard area, the 2nd West Yorkshires being billeted in Le Fay. Here, until the 26th December, 26TH DEC. the Battalion remained, training and re-fitting, until the rest period came to a close. On the 27th, the Battalion, in brigade, entrained at Oisemont and journeyed again to the Somme area, arriving in camp about two miles north-east of Sailly Laurette. Here a day 29TH DEC. was spent in hutments. On the 29th, the Battalion paraded and marched up to Priez Farm, the 23rd Infantry Brigade having taken over the Priez sector from the 11th Infantry Brigade, 4th Division. On the 20th, the 25th Brigade came into the line on the left of the 23rd Brigade, taking over the Saillisel sector from the 10th Infantry, Brigade. On the last day of the year the G.O.C., 8th Divison, assumed command of the line.

The 2nd West Yorkshires were in support in Priez Farm, the 31ST DEC. Battalion begin in poor shelters on the side of a hill.

The last of the Battles of the Somme, 1916, *i.e.*, the Battle of the Ancre, opened on the 13th, and concluded on the 18th November. 12TH BATTALION. In this operation, although the 3rd and 31st Divisions were in the 15TH, 16TH line, the 12th West Yorkshires contained in the former, and the 15th, AND 18TH 16th and 18th West Yorkshires of the 31st Division, did not take any BATTALIONS. important part in the Battle.

The 12th West Yorkshires, after the attack on Lonely Trench,

12TH BATTALION.	had left the Somme area and had taken over the Hulluch sector between Loos and the La Bassée Canal, where the whole of September was spent in and out of the front line, in comparative quietude. Early in October, the 3rd Division entrained at St. Pol, for the
8TH OCT.	northern sector of the Somme Battlefield and, on the 8th of the month the 12th West Yorkshires relieved the 17th R. Fusiliers of the 2nd Division, in the front line trenches west of Serre; the 3rd Division was now on the left of the 2nd Division. October and the first few days of November passed without anything happening of more than normal trench warfare, though preparations were being made for the Battle which, originally designed for October, had again and again to be postponed owing to the persistent bad weather. The West Yorkshiremen practised the attack and generally prepared for the coming operations, but when at last the attack was definitely
13TH NOV.	fixed for (and took place on) 13th November, the 8th and 76th Brigades of the 3rd Division were the attacking units, and the 9th Infantry Brigade was in Divisional Reserve. The 12th West Yorkshires, however, marched to Colincamps to await orders for the attack and were moved up to Euston Dump, which, the Battalion Diary states, was "a very unhealthy spot," but later moved back to Colincamps, without being actively engaged. And it was not until the 19th (when the Battle was over) that the Battalion once more took over its old line of trenches from the R. W. Fusiliers and K.O.R.L. Regiments in front of Serre. Heavy shelling while in the line and finding large working parties when out of it, sums up the activities of the Battalion during the remainder of the year, the last
31ST DEC.	days of which saw the Battalion in billets in Louvencourt.
15TH, 16TH AND 18TH BATTALIONS.	The three West Yorkshire Battalions of the 31st Division, *i.e.*, the 15th (Leeds Pals), the 16th (1st Bradford Pals) and 18th (2nd Bradford Pals), had also spent a comparatively quiet period from 27th July to the end of September in the trenches at Neuve Chapelle, Festubert and Givenchy. On the 3rd October the 31st Division was relieved in the line and moved to Béthune, the 16th and 18th West Yorkshires going into billets in the town, the 15th Battalion to
6TH OCT.	Gorre. On the 6th, the 93rd Infantry Brigade was collected in the Busnes area and, on the following day entrained at Lillers for Doullens. From the latter place the Brigade marched to the Thievres area, the 18th West Yorkshires being billeted in the village, and the 15th and 16th Battalions in Famechon.
21ST OCT.	The 31st Division had already taken over the Hebuterne sector, when on 21st October the 93rd Infantry Brigade relieved the 92nd

Brigade (in the Hebuterne sector) from John Copse to the Sunken Road in K.17.a.; the 16th West Yorkshires taking over the right sub-sector, and the 18th Battalion the left; the 15th Battalion was in the right support sector. _{15TH, 16TH AND 18TH BATTALIONS}

Artillery and trench-mortar activity by both sides was the principal feature of this tour in the trenches, though several raids on the enemy's trenches were made by the Leeds and Bradford Pals. The 16th Battalion sent out raiding parties on 23rd and 27th; the 18th sent out a fighting patrol on night of 24th/25th and, during a reconnaissance within ten yards of the enemy's parapet, Second-Lieut. D. A. Gill was unfortunately killed. The 15th Battalion made two raids on the enemy's trenches, one on the 26th and the on the 28th. On the 30th the 93rd Infantry Brigade was relieved by the 94th Brigade, and marched back to Couin—Thievres and Coigneux. _{30TH OCT.}

"From the 20th to the 30th," records the 93rd Infantry Brigade Diary, "when in the line in the Helvert sector, all ranks had had an arduous time. Constant rain had made the trenches into a very bad state, and the work in preparation for an offensive has entailed very heavy labour which has often been carried out under difficult conditions. Owing to heavy shelling, constant clearing of our own trenches for our own Heavy Artillery and heavy trench mortars to fire, and to some extent also the liberal use by the enemy of ' tear ' and gas shells, has delayed work. Owing to large drafts the percentage of young and inexperienced men is high, very many of them having had only a few weeks' training."

The next tour in the front line began on 7th November, when the 93rd Brigade moved back into the Hebuterne sector and when, on 13th of the month, the Battle of the Ancre opened, the 16th West Yorkshires were holding the right sub-sector with the 18th Battalion on the left. The 93rd Infantry Brigade, however, made no attack on the enemy, heavy shelling characterizing the day's operations in the Hebuterne sector. The West Yorkshiremen suffered fifty-five casualties, killed and wounded, during the day. On the following day, the Brigade was again relieved, and to the end of the year the never-ending round of tours in the front line, and general training when in reserve, kept all ranks busy and in comparatively good health. On the last day of December, the 15th West Yorkshires were in Autheux (two companies) and St. Leger (two companies), and the 16th West Yorkshires in Coigneux, and the 18th Battalion occupied Hebuterne Keep and Sailly-au-Bois. _{7TH Nov.} _{31ST DEC.}

1/5TH, 1/6TH 1/7TH, 1/8TH BATTALIONS.	While the Leeds and Bradford Pals of the 31st Division were holding the Hebuterne sector, the four Territorial Battalions of the West Yorkshire Regiment, *i.e.*, 1/5th, 1/6th, 1/7th and 1/8th of the 146th Infantry Brigade, 49th Division, were holding a line north of the village, about five kilometres from Gommecourt to Monchy-au-Bois, known as the Fonquevillers—Hannescamps sector. At the the end of September, when the 49th Division left the Thiepval sector, the 146th Infantry Brigade concentrated in the Warluzel area, about two or three miles north of the main Doullens—Arras Road.
18TH OCT.	On the 18th October the Brigade took over the Fonquevillers—Hannescamps sector, which was held by three battalions in the front line, and one in Brigade Reserve in Bienvillers. The line was thinly held, one battalion having a frontage of at least 1,000 yards.
	The trench system in this part of the line was extremely complicated, and gave rise to much amusement and bad language. Relief and ration parties lost themselves in the maze of trenches and, as one officer said, " A visit to a strange part of the line was an adventure. You never knew exactly where you would come out."
24TH OCT.	On the 24th, however, the Brigade front was shortened, and ran from La Brazelle Road to Hannescamps, two battalions holding the front line. All three Brigades of the 49th Division were now in the front line—the 148th right, 147th centre, and 146th on the left. The remainder of October passed without anything happening, but the usual conditions of trench warfare.
13TH NOV.	On the 13th November, during the early stages of the Battle of the Ancre, farther south, the 49th Division assisted by " fire demonstration," but otherwise did not join in the general attack. Thence onwards to the end of November, and the early days of December, the West Yorkshiremen spent a comparatively quiet time. Trench warfare was always of an uncomfortable nature, and there is little need to labour the point. Between the 4th and 6th December, the
31ST DEC.	146th Brigade was relieved and, from the 8th to the 31st of the month the 1/5th and 1/7th Battalions, West Yorkshires, were at Bouque Maison, and the 1/6th and 1/8th Battalions at Le Souich. Brigade Headquarters were also at the latter place.[1]
9TH BATTALION. 1ST OCT.	The remnants of the 9th Battalion West Yorkshires (11th Division), after their terrible fighting at the Stuff Redoubt, had at 5 p.m. on the 1st October marched from Varennes to Acheaux Junction and entrained for Candas. At midnight, the latter place

---

[1] On the 6th October, Lieut.-Colonel H. O. Wade rejoined the 1/6th Battalion West Yorkshire Regiment, and Lieut.-Colonel R. A. Hudson, the 1/8th Battalion. 2nd Lieut. Treleavan (1/6th West Yorkshires) was killed on 23rd November.

WINTER ON THE SOMME, 1916.
AMMUNITION FOR THE FRONT LINE, CARRIED UP ON MULES.

To face p. 300.

was reached, whence the West Yorkshiremen embussed to Beaumetz, and there billeted. On the 7th of the month the Battalion was inspected and congratulated on its fine fighting by the Corps Commander.

9TH BATTALION.

Until the 13th November, the Battalion remained at Beaumetz training and reorganizing. Drafts of officers and men arrived, and by the 14th, when the West Yorkshiremen marched out of Beaumetz, for Pernois, the strength of the Battalion had been brought up to twenty-eight officers and 715 other ranks. At the end of October, Lieut.-Col. C. L. Estridge, having been appointed to command the 11th Division School of Instruction, handed over command of the Battalion to Major F. P. Worsley.

13TH Nov.

On the 28th November, the 9th West Yorkshires moved up from Englebelmer to reserve trenches in the Beaumont Hamel sector, just west of Beaucourt Station. In this sector, amidst all the cheerless surroundings which prevailed in that part of the line, the West Yorkshiremen spent the whole of December, the 31st finding the Battalion in dug-outs near Beaucourt.

28TH Nov.

31ST DEC.

When, on the 29th October, the 10th West Yorkshires (17th Division) moved up to the trenches N. of Lesbœufs, and relieved the 2nd Battalion of the Regiment (8th Division), the conditions in that part of the line were appalling. An officer of the 50th Infantry Brigade Headquarters described the relief in the following vivid terms:— " The leading battalions of the 50th Infantry Brigade, (which included the 10th West Yorkshires) moved from Mansell Copse straight to the front line. The going was very bad, traffic congestion and control regulations separated the Lewis-gun limbers from their companies, and from Ginchy onwards the way lay across a filthy wilderness of shell holes and sloppy mud, which grew worse nearer the front. Outgoing battalions (2nd West Yorkshires and other battalions of the 23rd Infantry Brigade) were in a state of utter exhaustion, having been engaged in costly local attacks, and there was the utmost difficulty in effecting a relief with incoming troops, themselves in great distress. This relief, the hardest ever done by the Brigade, was not carried through till 6-30 a.m., and daylight revealed the full beastliness of the surroundings. If the mud of the (Ypres) Salient had been bad, this was even worse; trenches deemed impossible there, were here the normal places of habitation. The mire in the front lines *was hip deep, and could only be dealt with by hand;* neither spades nor scoops were of any use. Men became

10TH BATTALION. 29TH OCT.

imprisoned and could not be released, in some cases for over twenty-four hours. Hot drinks depended on a precarious and improvised supply of 'Tommy Cookers.' With power of physical resistance lowered by exposure, the fight against trench feet became more difficult and many of the new drafts were not hardened. The trenches themselves were a maze and the line intricate; men of different units and even strange divisions, hopelessly lost, were adopted for the night until they could be sent off by daylight."[1]

Under these awful conditions, with brief respites of relief and rest, the 10th West Yorkshires spent the remainder of the year. No attack was made by the Battalion during this period, but casualties from shell fire, and ever-active hostile snipers, were many. From 29th October to 11th November, the Battalion suffered 170 casualties, including one officer killed, (Second-Lieut. I. P. Waterhouse, by a sniper on 8th November), and one missing. On the 11th December, Lieut.-Col. G. H. Soames left the Battalion, handing over command to Major P. R. Simner of the 9th Duke of Wellington's R. The 50th Brigade also had a new Commander, Brigadier-General Yatman assuming command on 5th December. On the 31st December, the Battalion was relieved in the line by the 7th East Yorkshires, and marched back to Camp 22 on the Carnoy—Montauban Road.

Trench warfare of a more or less strenuous nature had occupied the 17th Battalion of the West Yorkshire Regiment (35th Division) from the middle of September, for the Division, after leaving the Somme area at the end of August, had entrained north for the Arras sector of the line. The normal round of life in the front line, in support or reserve, was unrelieved by attacks on or by the enemy and, on 31st December, the 17th West Yorkshires were in billets in Ternas.

It is impossible to follow one Battalion of the West Yorkshire Regiment—the 22nd (Labour) Battalion—through the Somme Battles of 1916. That the Battalion worked with the XIVth and XVth Corps is evident from the War Diary. Also it is clear from the location of the West Yorkshires, that this work was of a strenuous and dangerous nature, for the 22nd saw service in and about Montauban, Guillemont, Bazentin and Longueval—all scenes of very heavy fighting, and on which the enemy's shells fell night and day, after the ruined villages had passed into the possession of British troops.

The Battalion Diary of 28th October contained the following entry:—" Letter of appreciation from Lieut.-Col. R. B. Fife

[1] "History of the 50th Infantry Brigade."

for valuable assistance rendered in feeding the guns." It is a pity more details are not available. On the 5th November, Lieut.-Col. J. S. S. Stewart, arrived, and took over command of the Battalion *vice* Lieut.-Col. H. S. Atkinson, who had returned to England to take up another appointment. From the 10th to the 31st December, the 22nd West Yorkshires were at work at Albert Station.

The Battles of the Somme, 1916, have been described by some writers as if they were something in the nature of a series of disastrous operations. But looked at impartially, weighing the objects of the Battles against the results, there is no doubt that they achieved the intentions of the Commander-in-Chief. The pressure at Verdun *had* been relieved; the enemy's strength *had* been largely worn down, and he *had* been prevented from sending reinforcements to other fronts. As Sir Douglas Haig said in his despatches, dealing with the operations from 1st July, 1916, to the end of that year :—" Any one of these three results is in itself sufficient to justify the Somme Battles. The attainment of all three of them affords ample compensation for the splendid efforts of our troops, and for the sacrifices made by ourselves and our Allies."

The casualties of the British Army were enormous, so were those suffered by the enemy, whose weakness was so dangerous that, early in 1917, he was forced to shorten his front, and beat a retreat to the Hindenburg Line.

END OF VOLUME I.

PANORAMIC VIEW OF YPRES.

THE PRINCE OF WALES'S OWN (WEST YORKS. REGT.)

CASUALTIES
AUGUST 1914 TO DECEMBER 1916

OFFICERS.

(The Theatre of War is France and Flanders unless otherwise indicated).
"k" = killed in action. "d" = died of wounds. "d.h." = died, home.

NOTE.—Small number before name denotes Battalion.

21 Adamson, Henry Bardell, Capt. (Tp.), d., 30/10/16.
13 Adlington, Ernest Mason, 2/Lt. (Tp.), k., 14/9/16 (att. 9th Bn.).
18 Akam, James Rhodes, Lt., k., 1/7/16.
10 Allen, Humphrey Decius, T/Lt., k., 1/7/16.
10 Anderson, Archibald Joseph, Capt. (Tp.), k., 1/7/16.
13 Anderson, Percival Robert, 2/Lt. (Tp.), k., 12/10/15.
14 Andrews, Hector George Robert Frank, Lt., k., 28/6/15.
15 Appelbee, Thomas, 2/Lt. (Tp.), k., 20/8/16.
12 Appleyard, Harry Elston, 2/Lt. (Tp.), k., 14/7/16.
2 Arnold, Alfred Huntriss, Capt., d., 30/12/16.
Asprey, Bernard Noel, Lt., k., 24/2/15.
4 Bailey, Cecil Arthur, Lt., k., 5/5/15 (att. 2nd W. Riding R.).
3 Bastow, Norman, Lt., k., 23/10/16 (att. 23 Trench Mortar Battery).
12 Beaumont, Leslie, 2/Lt. (Tp.), k., 17/8/16.
9 Benn, Alfred Maurice, Lt., k., 27/9/16.
Bennett, Alfred Charles, D.S.O., Lt.-Col., died, 16/1/15.
10 Berkley, John Humphrey, Capt., d., 8/4/16.
15 Bickersteth, Stanley Morris, Lt. (Tp.), k., 1/7/16.
10 Blackburn, Geoffrey Gaskell, Capt. (Tp.), k., 1/7/16.
10 Blatherwick, Robert Hugh, 2/Lt., k , 1/7/16.
15 Booth, Major William, 2/Lt. (Tp.), k., 1/7/16.
9 Boston, Lawrence, T/Lt., died, 6/5/16.
21 Boulnois, Edmund, T/Capt., k., 23/10/16.
19 Bowman, William Powell, Lt., k., 17/10/16 (att. R.F.C.).
4 Brooks, Leslie, Lt., k., 25/9/15 (att. Lincs. Regt.).
2 Brophy, Ernest Gordon, 2/Lt. (Tp.), k., 1/7/16.
1 Brotherton, Vincent, 2/Lt. (Tp.), d., 14/10/16.
1 Burke, Martin, 2/Lt.. k., 18/9/16.
11 Busher, Charles Joseph, T/Lt., d., 30/1/16.
2 Campbell, Robert Alexander Rankine, 2/Lt., k., 1/7/16.
Carew, Jasper, 2/Lt., k., 14/10/14.
4 Chalcraft, George Arthur, Lt., d., 7/5/15 (att. 2nd Bn. W. Rid. Regt.).
1 Chart, Eric Nye Lt., k., 25/9/16.
2 Cholmeley, Eric Randolph, Lt., k., 1/7/16.
1 Clayton, George, 2/Lt., d., 24/10/16 (and R.F.C., 11 Sqd.).
3 Cliff, Herbert Theodore, Major, k., 13/10/14
16 Clough, Alan, T/Capt., k., 7/12/16.
Clothier, John Keith, Capt., k., 7/12/14.
18 Colley, Harold, 2/Lt., k., 1/7/16.
Colvin, Robert Alexander, Capt., k., 10/3/15.
Consterdine, Arthur Edward, T/Capt., k., 26/12/16 (att. 9th Bn.)
Cooper-King, Reginald Garret, Major, d . 20/12/14.
1 Corp, Benjamin, M.C., T/Capt., k., 18/9/16.
Costin, Bruce Duffus, Lt., T/Capt., d., 24/10/14.

17 Crawford, Alexander Basil, Capt. (Tp.), k., 10/5/16.
18 Cross, Ronald Sydney, Capt. (Tp.), k., 27/7/16.
9 Curtis, Horace, Lt., k., 7/8/15.
9 Cuthell. Algernon Hubert, T/Maj., k., 22/8/15.
1 Davies, Harold Blakeney, 2/Lt., k., 23/4/16.
9 Davison, Charles William Joseph, 2/Lt. (Tp.), k., 14/9/16.
13 Davison, Henry James Goddard, 2/Lt. (Tp.), k., 4/6/15 (att. 3 Lan. Fusrs.).
13 Dawson, Leonard, 2/Lt. (Tp.), k., 4/6/15 (att. Lan. Fusrs.).
3 Day, Samuel Albert, 2/Lt. k., 10/11/16 (att. 15th Bn.).
18 Derwent, Robert Ivor, 2/Lt. (Tp.), k., 1/7/16.
14 Deverell, Richard Seddon, 2/Lt. (Tp.), died, 4/11/16 (att. 15th Bn.).
15 De Pledge, Edward Karl, T/Capt., k., 3/6/16
Dore, William Hayward, 2/Lt., k., 25/9/16.
11 Doyle, Edward Percival, 2 /Lt. (Tp.), d., 5/7/16.
Eliot, William Lawrence, Lt., k., 20/9/14.
13 English, Eric, 2/Lt. (Tp.), k., 7/8/15 (att. Man. Regt.).
3 Evans, Rupert Ancrum, 2/Lt., died, 25/1/16.
15 Everitt, John Paxman, T/2/Lt., k., 1/7/16.
9 Evers, Bertram Saxelbys, T/Capt., k., 14/9/16.
14 Field, Edwin Arthur, (Tp.), k., 14/9/16 (att. 9th Bn.).
14 Fippard, Richard Clift, Capt. (Tp.), k., 4/6/15 (att. Lan. Fus.).
Fisher, Mortimer, Capt., k., 20/9/14.
18 Foizey, Harold Egbert, Lt. (Tp.), k., 1/7/16.
15 Foster, Leonard, 2/Lt. (Tp.), d., 17/8/16.
9 Fraser, Thomas Francis, Capt. (Tp.), k., 7-11/8/15.
4 Freeman, Frederick John, 2/Lt., d., 3/7/16 (att. 2nd Bn. W. Yorks. Regt.).
13 Fyffe, John James, Temp. 2/Lt., k., 14/9/16.
9 Geary-Smith, Alexander. Capt., k., 7/8/15.
1 Gell, Christopher Stowell, 2/Lt., k., 18/9/16.
9 Gent, Frank Ernest, Lt., k., 7/8/15.
12 Gibbon, Oliver Vernon, T/2/Lt., k., 3/4/16.
18 Gill, Daniel, T/2/Lt., k., 24/10/16.
15 Glenn, Archibald Patrick, T/2/Lt., k , 14/9/16.
4 Green, Philip Louis Samuel, 2/Lt., k., 18/9/16 (att. 1st Bn.).
14 Hall, M. E. A., 2/Lt., died, 27/3/15.
2 Harkness, Percy Yarborough, Capt., k., 1/7/16.
4 Harris, Reginald William, T/Lt., k., 3/9/16 (and Z1, T.M.B.).
11 Haselden, Edgar Adolphus, T/Capt., d., 9/7/16.
10 Henderson, William Lewis, T/Capt., d., 3/5/16.
13 Hicking, Francis Joseph, 2/Lt. (Tp.), k , 1/7/16 (att. 1st Bn.).

11 Hill, Henry Hamp, T/Capt., d., 8/3/16.
17 Hitchen, Stanley Lucas, Temp. 2/Lt., k., 6/6/16.
12 Hogben, William Iggulden, 2/Lt., k., 18/8/16.
Horsford, Thomas Herbert O'Bryan, Lt., d., 14/3/15.
18 Hummel, Raymond, T/2/Lt., k., 19/5/16.
15 Humphries, Thomas, 2/Lt. (Temp.)., k., 1/7/16.
18 Humphries, Walter Rawleigh, 2/Lt. (Tp.), k., 27/7/16.
16 Hyde, Charles Stuart, T/2/Lt., k., 1/7/16.
3 I'Anson, John Francis, Capt., k., 20/9/14.
10 Ibbitson, William Beveridge, T/2/Lt., k., 1/7/16.
Ingles, Alexander Wigton, Major. k., 20/9/14.
15 James, Clement Wilbraham, 2/Lt., k., 1/7/16.
12 Jaques, Arthur, Capt. (Tp.), k., 27/9/15.
12 Jaques, Joseph Hodgson, Major k., 27/9/15.
11 Jaye, Harold Conway, T/2/Lt., d., 9/7/15
14 Jennings, Basil Spencer, 2/Lt. (Tp.), d., 7/11/15 (att. 6th).
13 Jones, Robert Henry, T/2/Lt., k., 29/9/16 (att. 18th Bn.).
10 Keighley, William Munkley, T/Lt., k 1/7/16.
18 Kennard, Maurice Nicholl, T/Lt.-Col., k., 1/7/16.
13 Kent, William James, Capt., k., 7/8/15 (att. Manch. Regt.).
10 Knott, James Leadbitter, D.S.O., T/Major, k., 1/7/16.
Lawson-Smith, John., Lt., k., 20/10/14.
16 Laxton, Reginald Earl, T/2/Lt., k., 10/6/16.
Legard, Reginald John, Lt., d., 9/5/15.
15 Lintott, Evelyn Henry, T/Lt., k., 1/7/16.
2 Littlejohn, John, T/2/Lt., k., 26/10/16.
15 Liversidge, Albert, T./2/Lt., d., 2/7/16.
9 Long-Price, Cecil Evelyn, Capt., k., 7/8/15.
Loveband, Arthur Reginald, T/Capt., k., 6/12/14.
9 Lupton, Reginald, T/Capt., d., 22/8/15.
14 Macdonnell, Francis William Joseph, T/Major, died, 4/10/15 (att. 9th Bn.).
3 Maguire, John Reginald, T/2/Lt., k., 18/8/16 (att. 12th Bn.).
13 Maitland, Arthur Dudley, T/Lt., k., 1/7/16.
1 Marten, Charles Peter, T/Lt.-Col., k., 15/9/16.
2 Maude, Robert Henry Ernest, 2/Lt., died, 12/9/16 (Gar. Bn., att. 3rd N. Staff.).
11 Maufe, Statham Broadbent, T/Major, d., 5/7/16.
Meautys, Thomas Gilliat, Lt., k., 26/9/14.
11 Mills, George Charles, 2/Lt., k., 10/7/16.
3 Minogue, John O'Brien (C.M.G.), Lt.-Col., died, 26/10/16 (att. 9th Bn.).
1 Morkill, Ronald Falshaw, Lt., killed, 23/6/15 (att. R.F.C.).
12 Morland, Leonard Mark, T/Lt., d., 3/5/16.
15 Neil, Stanley Thomas Arthur, T/Capt., k., 1/7/16.
16 Newlands, Sydney Barron, T/2/Lt., k., 1/7/16.
4 Newman, Vernon William, 2/Lt. (T/Capt.), k., 25/9/15 (att. 1st N. Lancs.).
1 Newton, Charles Thomas Kemp, 2/Lt., k., 3/6/16.
12 Norris, William James George, Capt., k., 25/9/15.
18 Nowell, Francis Percival, T/2/Lt., d., 2/7/16.

15 O'Land, Valentine, T/2/Lt., k., 1/7/16.
12 Oliver, Cyril Francis Harrison, T/Capt., k., 14/7/16.
12 Osborne, Hugh Corry, T/2/Lt., k., 23/7/16.
13 Parker, Edward Thompson, 2/Lt. (Tp.), k., 4/6/15 (att. 1st Bn. Lan. Fus.).
9 Pearkes, Andre Mellard, Capt., k., 7/8/15.
14 Pennington, William Henry, 2/Lt., died, 2/3/15.
12 Perham, Edgar, T/Capt., k., 23/7/16.
2 Perkins, George, 2/Lt., (Tp.), k., 1/7/16.
2 Perry, George Herbert Gresley, Lt. (T/Capt.) d., 15/3/15.
13 Pierce, Ronald Hugh MacGregor, T/2/Lt., k., 14/9/16.
2 Pimm, Victor Lionel, 2/Lt., k., 10/11/16.
16 Pringle, Robert William Hay, T/Capt., k., 1/7/16.
16 Ransome, Cecil Talbot. T/Lt., k., 1/7/16.
10 Ratcliffe, Alfred Victor, T/Lt., k., 1/7/16.
15 Rayner, Roy Balfour Hodgson, T/Lt., d., 24/5/16.
10 Reynolds, Victor Eustace, T/Capt., k., 4/5/16.
10 Richardson, Arthur Douglas, 2/Lt., died, 12/1/15.
13 Robinson, Cecil Beaumout, T/Lt., k., 14/9/16 (att. 9th Bn.).
16 Robinson, John Holdsworth, 2/Lt., k., 1/7/16.
17 Roscoe, E., 2/Lt., died, 26/6/15.
16 Russell, Henry, Capt. (Tp.), d., 10/6/16.
2 Ruttledge, John Forrest, T/Capt., k., 1/7/16.
15 Saunders, Charles, T/2/Lt., k., 1/7/16.
12 Scarr, Reginald Graham, T/2/Lt., k., 14/7/16.
12 Sewill, Arnold Waterlow, T/2/Lt., k., 23/7/16.
10 Shann, John Webster, Lt. (Tp.), k., 1/7/16.
3 Sharp, Cyril Robert, Capt. (Tp.), k., 14/7/16.
Shaw, Bernard Henry Gilbert, Lt., k., 18/12/14.
12 Shaw, Sydney Thomas, T/2/Lt., d., 11/5/16 (att. 10th Bn.).
2 Skett, Arthur Edwin Pye, 2/Lt., k., 11/11/16
4 Slade, Charles Godfrey Mitford, Major, k., 8/11/14 (att. N. Lancs. R.).
2 Smailes, George, T/2/Lt., k., 22/10/16.
4 Smart, George Henry, Capt., k., 22/12/14. (att. N. Lancs. R.).
16 Smith, Donald, Temp. Capt., k., 1/7/16.
1 Smith, Frederick William, Temp. Capt., k., 25/4/16.
9 Spencer, John Aldersley Craven, 2/Lt., k., 9/8/15.
12 Squires, Edward Constable, M.C., Temp. Capt., k., 18/8/16.
12 Stananought, Richard Frederick, T/Lt. and Adjt., d., 5/9/16.
16 Stead, Ralph, 2/Lt. (Tp.), k., 1/7/16.
17 Stead, Willie Wouldhave, Temp./Lt., k., 25/8/16.
9 Surtees, William Beverley, Temp. Capt., d., 28/9/16.
16 Sutcliffe, Robert, 2/Lt., d., 5/7/16.
16 Symonds, Frank James, Temp. 2/Lt., k., 1/7/16.
1 Taylor, Charles Edward, Lt., k., 1/11/15.
10 Taylor, Charles Harry, 2/Lt., drowned, 17/11/15.
12 Taylor, Francis Galloway, 2/Lt., k., 23/7/16
Tennant, Oswald Moncreiff, 2/Lt., k., 16/6/15.

Thompson, Offley Charles Wycliffe, Lt., k., 20/9/14.
15 Tolson, Robert Huntries, 2/Lt., k., 1/7/16.
12 Townsend, John, Temp. 2/Lt., k., 14/9/16 att.(9 Bn.).
1 Trafford-Rawson, John Henry Edmund, Temp Capt., k., 18/9/16.
12 Turner, Herbert Norman, Temp. Lt., k., 14/7/16.
13 Tweedale, Eric, 2/Lt. (Tp.), k., 1/7/16 (att. 16 Bn.).
12 Underhill, Charles Bertram, Lt. (Tp.), k., 27/3/16.
12 Vann, Arthur Harrison Allard, Capt. and Adjt., k., 25/9/15.
15 Vause, John Gilbert, Lt. (Tp.), k., 1/7/16.
18 Walton, Francis John George, 2/Lt. (Tp.), k., 1/7/16.
15 Wardle, James Kenneth, Temp. Lt., d., 30/4/16.
4 Warren, Fred Langford, 2/Lt., k., 1/7/16 (att. 2 Bn.).
10 Waterhouse, Irvin Preston, Temp. 2/Lt., k., 8/11/16.
18 Watson, Frank, Lt., k., 1/7/16 (att. 93 T.M.B.).
13 Webster, Michael Harold, Lt. (Tp.), k., 1/7/16 (att. 16 Bn.).
1 Welchman, Edward Theodore, D.S.O., Capt., d., 26/10/14.
11 Whitaker, Arthur Cecil, Temp. Capt., k., 1/1/16.
15 Whitaker, George Clifford, Temp. Capt., k., 1/7/16.
11 Whitby, Harry Alden, Temp. Capt., k., 10/7/16.
4 Wilkinson, W. S., 2/Lt., died, 6/9/15.
15 Willey, Thomas Arthur Raymond Robert Ellicott, Temp. 2/Lt., k., 1/7/16.
Wilson, Eric Western, 2/Lt., k., 20/9/14.
4 Winch, Edmond Arthur, 2/Lt., k., 19/10/15 (att. 2 Bn.).
11 Winser, Frederick Herbert, Temp. 2/Lt., k., 7/10/16.
9 Wood, Maxmilian David Francis, Major, d., 22/8/15.
12 Wooler, Charles Armytage, 2/Lt. (Tp.), d., 20/7/16.
12 Wooler, Herbert Sykes, Temp. 2/Lt., d., 28/3/16.
9 Worsnop, Edgar, Temp. Lt., d., 7/8/15.
18 Worsnop, John William, 2/Lt., k., 30/6/16

5th BATTALION (Territorial).

Allen, Richard Gerrard Ross, Capt. (Act.), k. 16/11/16 (R.F.C.).
Barraclough, William, 2/Lt., k., 28/9/16.
Gaunt, Edward, 2/Lt., d., 28/9/16.
Goodwill, Cyril, 2/Lt., k., 3/9/16.
Irish, Edward, 2/Lt., k., 20/6/15.
Jameson, James Leslie, Lt., k., 2/7/16.
Lee, Arthur Basil, 2/Lt., k., 2/7/16.
Lee, Ernest William, 2/Lt., k., 28/9/16.
Mandeville, Pierce, Capt., k., 28/9/16.
Prest, William Charles Seagar, 2/Lt., k., 17/8/16.
Thompson, Frederick Charles, Major, k., 1/3/16.
Treleaven, Noel Houghton, 2/Lt., k., 23/11/16.
Walker, John Chinnery, 2/Lt., k., 19-20/12/15.
Watson, Alfred Charles, Capt., k., 3/9/16.

6th BATTALION (Territorial).

Dodd, Neville, 2/Lt., k., 1/7/16.
Gibson, Alwyn Morland, 2/Lt., d., 27/9/16.
Harper, Clarence Rucil, 2/Lt., k., 15/7/16.
Heaton, Stanley Tomlinson, 2/Lt., k., 27/9/16.
Higgins, Cuthbert George, 2/Lt., d., 1/7/16.
Mitchell, Charles Henry, 2/Lt., k., 3-4/9/16.
Moore, Richard, 2/Lt., k., 15/7/16.
Oddy, James Leslie, Capt., d., 3/9/16.
Scott, Charles Edward, Lt.-Col., d., 9/8/16.
Senior, Walter Talbot, 2/Lt., k., 3/9/16.
Storey, Harrison Leetham, 2/Lt., d., 12/9/16.
Strachan, David Livingston, Capt., died. 29/12/16.
Turner, Ernest Arthur, Lt., k., 3/9/16.

7th BATTALION (Leeds Rifles) (Territorial).

Brannigan, Ernest Edward, 2/Lt., k., 3/9/16.
Briggs, Richard Stanley, Lt., k., 29/7/15.
Calvert, Reginald Cullen, Capt., d., 15/7/16.
Coy, Alfred Reginald, 2/Lt., k., 2/7/16.
Harrison, Edgar Brooks, 2/Lt., d., 28/9/16.
Leresche, Alfred Sunderland, 2/Lt., k., 3/9/16.
Lupton, Maurice, Capt., k., 19/6/15.
Salter, Robert, Capt., k., 26/8/16.
Stewart, John Charles Miller, 2/Lt., k., 3/7/16 (and R.F.C.).
Sykes, Gerald Wolriche, 2/Lt., k., 25/5/15.
Tarr, William, Lt., k., 31/10/15.
Wilson, Norman, Lt., k., 14/7/16.
Wyllie, Hugh Alexander, 2/Lt., k., 3/9/16.

8th BATTALION (Leeds Rifles) (Territorial).

Bottomley, John Cecil, 2/Lt., k., 3/9/16.
Hartnell, Cuthbert, Lt., A/Capt., k., 16/7/15.
Hess, Arthur Frank, Major d., 14/7/16.
Hossell, Leslie Cartmell, Capt., k., 8/8/16.
Ives, Kenneth Hill, 2/Lt., died, 9/12/14.
Middleton, Reginald, 2/Lt., k., 3/9/16.
Pearson, Sydney James, Capt., d., 15/8/16.
Penny, George, 2/Lt., k., 3/9/16.
Sissons, Roland Edward, Lt., k., 2/6/16.
Stimpson, John Crockett, 2/Lt., k., 2/7/16.
Vause, Thomas Christopher, 2/Lt., k., 3/9/16.
Ward, George Cecil, 2/Lt., k., 2/7/16.
Will, George Kennedy, Lt., d., 11/9/16 (in German hands).

SOLDIERS.

DEPOT.

Bowling, Norman, 3/9077, Pte., d.h., 17/3/16.
Hanton, Harry, 3/9825, Pte., d.h., 18/9/14.
Hartley, Joseph, 39001, Pte., d.h., 10/11/16.
Keeley, John, 19387, Pte., d.h., 15/5/15.
Knox, Joseph Tait, 17120, A/Cpl., d.h., 2/1/16.
Middleton, Herbert, 13044, Pte., d.h., 16/7/16.
Myhill, Walter, 7787, Pte., d.h., 13/8/14.
Pickersgill, William, 4/8102, Pte., d.h., 26/7/16.
Scholefield, George Laybourne, 18643, Pte., d.h., 12/10/16.
Teale, Joseph, 3/9629, Pte., d.h., 14/10/14.
Taylor, Alfred, 18039, Pte., d.h., 27/5/16.
Wade, Robert, 13304, Pte., d.h., 12/9/14.

1st BATTALION.

(The Theatre of War is France and Flanders unless otherwise indicated).
" k." .. killed in action.   " d." .. died of wounds.   " d.h." .. died, home.

Addy, Fred, 7746, Pte., k., 20/9/14.
Aisbitt, Albert, 6723, Pte., k., 20/1/15.
Albin, Thomas, 3/8658, Pte., k., 28/7/15.
Alderson, Cyril Laverick, 15/1787, Pte., k., 12/10/16.
Alderwick, Richard, 3/9232, Pte., k., 11/8/15.
Allgood, Harry, 8108, Pte., k., 20/9/14.
Allinson, Robert Henry, 9873, Pte., k., 20/9/14.
Allison, James, 4/7036, Sgt., d., 4/8/15.
Allman, Thomas, 17935, Pte., k., 13/10/15.
Anderson, Harry, 16332, Pte., d., 22/2/16.
Anstead, Henry, 8524, L/Cpl., k. (accidentally), 18/8/15, D.C.M.
Appleby, Harry, 7236, L/Cpl., k., 20/9/14.
Appleby, William, 4/8256, Pte., k., 12/10/16.
Arch, Thomas, 7494, Pte., d., 29/6/15.
Archer, Mark, 6605, Pte., k., 20/9/14.
Armitage, Joseph, 12231, Pte., k., 13/6/16.
Arnold, Joseph John, 9854, Pte., d., 19/2/16.
Ashton, Edward Charles, 8502, Sgt., d., 5/10/14.
Ashton, John, 18955, Pte., k., 2/3/16.
Atkinson, Isaac, 4/7882, Pte., k., 20/10/15.
Baker, George Edward, 7877, Pte., k., 13/11/14.
Balme, Harry, 203634, Pte., k., 20/7/16, formerly 14869, West Riding Regt.
Banks, Arthur, 6740, L/Cpl., k., 22/9/14.
Barnfed, John, 9922, Pte., k., 13/10/14.
Barraclough, Herbert, 9258, A/Sgt., k., 18/9/16.
Barratt, Walter William, 3/9191, Pte., d., 9/11/14.
Barrett, Frank, 34084, Pte., k., 19/10/16.
Bateman, William, 7124, Pte., k., 21/10/14.
Bates, John, 8479, L/Cpl., k., 20/9/14.
Batt, Robert, 3/9475, Sgt, d., 22/7/15.
Bedford, Horace Henry, 7622, Sgt., k., 20/9/14.
Bee, Herbert, 24430, Pte., d., 13/10/16.
Beeston, Albert, 15726, Pte., k., 14/2/16.
Bell, George, 3/9599, Pte., k., 14/2/16.
Bell, James William, 3/10007, Pte., d., 6/5/15.
Bellinger, Reuben, 8380, L/Cpl., k., 20/9/14.
Bemrose, Thomas, 7521, Pte., d., 23/9/14.
Bennison, Harry, 7534, Pte., k., 16/9/15.
Bentley, Charles Aris, 8261, Sgt., k., 14/10/14.
Benton, Hubert, 15804, Pte., d., 25/6/16.
Beresford, Robert, 3/8872, Pte., d., 22/2/15.
Berry, Thomas, 3/9372, Pte., d., 13/4/15.
Binns, George William, 8121, Pte., k., 20/9/14.
Birkby, John William, 9871, Pte., d., 7/1/15.
Blocksidge, James, 7112, Sgt., k., 4/4/15.
Blyth, Peter, 8565, Pte., k., 12/10/16.
Boldison, Mark, 7524, A/Cpl., k., 12/10/16.
Booth, Herbert, 3/8852, Pte., k., 28/3/15.
Bott, James, 3/9476 Pte., d., 23/2/15.
Boyington, Fred, 7797, Pte., k., 20/9/14.
Bradley, Arthur, 7375, A/Sgt., k., 18/9/16.
Bradshaw, George, 18093, L/Cpl., d.h., 2/11/16.
Bramley, Arthur, 12108, Pte., k., 18/9/16.
Brewster, William, 17171, Pte., k., 7/6/16.
Bridger, Walter Charles, 9666, Pte., k., 25/9/14.
Briers, Sidney, 8501, Pte., k., 20/9/14.
Briggs, Charles, 6479, Pte., k., 20/9/14.
Briggs, Maurice, 34040, Pte., k., 19/10/16.
Briggs, Thomas, 7787, Pte., k., 3/3/15.
Brightmore, Edward John Henry, 9828, Pte., k., 20/9/14.
Broadley, Albert, 10090, Pte., k., 13/10/14.
Broadley, William, 3/7930, A/Sgt., d., 31/7/15.
Brough, Gilbert Charles, 17683, L/Cpl., k., 7/8/16.
Brown, Charles William, 5328, Pte., k., 13/10/14.
Brown, John Edwin, 3/8962, Pte., d., 23/1/15.
Brown, Percy, 3961, Pte., d., 20/9/14.
Brown, Thomas, 10074, Pte., k., 25/9/14.
Broxson, Thomas, 4/7912, Pte., d., 6/7/15.
Brumfitt, Ernest, 22207, Pte., k., 13/10/16.
Buckley, Fred, 7385, L/Cpl., k., 20/9/14.
Budd, Alfred, 5604, Pte., d.h., 11/2/16.
Bullock, Ernest Edward, 10080, Pte., k., 20/9/14.
Bunting, John Henry, 8153, Pte., k., 20/9/14.
Burke, Thomas, 4/7077, Pte., k., 16/12/15.
Burton, Robert, 6692, Pte., k., 20/9/14.
Butt, Edward, 18512, Pte., k., 18/9/16.
Buttress, Samuel, 3/10257, L/Cpl., d., 15/4/16
Cairns, Robert Harry, 6078, C.S.M., k., 21/2/16
Capstick, William, 13861, Pte., k., 16/10/16.
Carroll, John, 7486, Cpl., k., 18/9/16, M.M.
Carroll, John, 9872. Pte., d., 23/5/15
Carter, Charles, 4107, C.S.M., k., 20/9/14.
Carter, Ernest, 7875, Pte., k., 19/12/15.
Cawkwell, Alfred Edward, 7154, Pte., k., 20/9/14.
Chadwick, Frederick, 8932, Sgt., d.h., 26/10/14.
Chadwick, Herbert, 8133, L/Cpl., k., 12/10/16.
Chapman, Alfred, 21104, Pte., k., 2/3/16.
Charlesworth, James Arthur, 34082, Pte., k., 19/10/16.
Clark, Harry, 11648, Pte., k., 16/10/16.
Clark, John Edward, 4/6748, Pte., k., 18/9/16.
Clarke, John, 17248, Pte., k., 11/2/16.
Clarke, Michael, 3/9116, L/Cpl., k., 10/8/15.
Clarkson, Fred, 9891, Pte., k., 19/12/15.
Clarkson, George, 17238, Pte., d. at sea, 17/11/15.
Clayton, George Willie, 15/1447, Pte., k., 3/11/16.
Clayton, James William, 17281, Pte., k., 14/6/16.
Clayton, William, 17778, Pte., k., 11/8/15.

The Prince of Wales's Own (West Yorks. Regt.)—Casualties

Cleasby, Robert, 7602, Pte., k., 22/9/14.
Cockerill, William, 3/21113, Pte., k., 2/3/16.
Coleman, William, 21406, Pte., d., 4/6/16.
Collins, John, 7472, Pte., k., 31/7/15.
Collins, John, 6558, Pte., k., 19/12/15.
Common, Robert, 4/8606, Pte., d., 31/7/15.
Conlon, Robert Ernest, 21482, Pte., k., 12/10/16
Connell, James Edward, 22257, Pte., k., 30/12/15.
Cook, Charles Frederick, 8270, Pte., k., 27/3/15.
Cooksey, Thomas Henry, 9616, Drmr., k., 18/11/14.
Cooper, Edmund Charles, 23283, L/Cpl., k., 18/9/16.
Copeland, Frank, 5861, L/Cpl., k., 20/9/14.
Costello, James, 10176, Pte., k., 15/10/15.
Coulson, Joseph 16414, Pte., k., 25/1/16.
Coulthard, George Henry, 5821, Cpl., k., 1/11/14.
Cousins, Percy, 29402, Pte., k., 12/10/16.
Couves, Percy, 10166, Pte., k., 12/10/16.
Cowan, James, 3/7529, Pte., k., 20/10/14.
Cowsill, John, 22309, Pte., k., 12/10/16.
Cox, Joseph, 6733, Pte., k., 20/9/14.
Crampton, Edward, 3/9574, Pte., k., 5/9/15.
Cranfield, George, 9835, L/Cpl., d., 31/1/15.
Craven, Herbert, 9702, L/Cpl., k., 17/8/16.
Croft, Albert, 7610, Pte., k., 20/9/14.
Cronin, Thomas, 22452, Pte., k., 25/9/16.
Crookes, Ernest, 3/10120, Pte., drowned, 7/3/15.
Crookston, William, 3/9589, Pte., k., 2/10/15.
Croxton, Ivan Lewin, 10165, Pte., k., 13/10/14.
Cruddes, Robert, 12534, Pte., d., 18/9/16.
Cunningham, Fred, 8079, Cpl., k., 20/9/14.
Cunningham, Joseph, 22282, Pte., k., 14/2/16.
Currell, John Thomas, 9783, Pte., k., 25/9/16.
Curry, Robert 3/7597, Pte., k., 18/4/15.
Dalby, Albert, 6186, Pte., k., 5/2/15.
Dalton, Edwin 5779, C.S.M., k., 25/9/16.
Dalton, Patrick, 6646, Pte., d., 10/11/14.
Davison, John Henry 4/8615, Pte., d., 21/2/16.
Davison, Thomas Charles, 9083, Sgt., k., 15/9/16.
Dawson, William, 6324, Sgt., k., 16/10/16.
Dearlove, Edward Albert, 3/7509, Pte., k., 11/11/14.
Devine, Hugh, 15807, Pte. d., 29/9/16.
Dickinson, William Henry, 3/9879, L/Cpl., k., 14/3/15.
Dixon, Benjamin, 27193, Pte., k., 15/9/16.
Dixon, Henry 7122, Pte., d., 21/2/15.
Dixon, Robert, 4/7695, Pte., k., 25/9/16.
Dobson, Benjamin, 17266, L/Cpl., k., 25/4/16.
Donnelly, Thomas, 10857, Pte., k., 9/8/15.
Drake, Vincent William, 8463, Pte., d., 22/9/14.
Duckworth, Herbert, 6219, Pte., d.h., 20/10/15.
Dunbar, Arthur, 19343, Pte., d h., 20/11/16.
Dunn, Frederick, 24910, Pte., k., 8/9/16.
Dyson, Harry Fryer, 3/7527, Sgt., k., 18/9/16
Eardley, David, 18263, L/Cpl., k., 18/9/16.
Eastwood, Charles, 4/8015, Pte., k., 30/7/15.
Eastwood, Tom, 15/1511, Pte., k., 25/9/16.
Egan, Harry, 5596, Pte., d., 5/8/15.
Eldrett, Emanuel, 10051 L/Cpl., k., 6/6/15.
Ellerbeck, Walter, 25067, Pte., d., 6/9/16.
Elliott, Walter, 3/10029, Pte., d., 26/6/15.
Ellis, John, 7265, Pte., k., 20/9/14.
Ellis, Joseph, 7860, Pte., k., 20/9/14.
Emmott, James William, 19158, Pte., k., 7/8/16.
Emmott, Walter, 6223, Pte., k., 3/3/16.
Etherington, William, 8010, Pte., k., 20/9/14.
Evans, Charles Edward, 8408, A/Sgt., k., 19/8/16.
Eyles, Alfred Henry, 4249, Cpl., k., 20/9/14.

Fairbrother, Arthur, 3/7510, A/Sgt., d., 27/9/16.
Farrar, Thomas Mawson, 27163, Pte., k., 11/9/16.
Fell, John William, 24026, Pte. k., 12/10/16.
Fenby, Thomas Paul, 15/1298, Pte., k., 16/5/16.
Ferguson, Ralph, 3/8910, Pte., d., 19/6/15.
Firth, John, 7522, A/Sgt., k., 4/6/16, D.C.M.
Fishwick, Walter, 9648, Pte., k., 11/10/15.
Fitzgerald, James, 7286, Pte., k., 13/10/14.
Flanagan, John, 4/8632, Pte., d., 29/3/15.
Flanagan, Thomas Edward, 4/7449, L/Sgt., d., 12/7/15.
Forder, Sydney Henry, 10663, L/Cpl., d., 19/12/15.
Foreman, Charles, 6684, L/Cpl., d., 30/7/15.
Form, William, 4/8120, A/Cpl., k., 22/12/16.
Forster, William, 3/9560, Pte., k., 23/1/16.
Fossey, Robert, 15/1702, Pte., d., 22/5/16.
Foster, Tom, 3/9245, Pte., k., 14/3/15.
Gadsby, Joseph, 3/8553, Pte., k., 20/4/15.
Gale, Charles, 7972, Pte., k., 11/10/15.
Galinsky, Harry, 29459, Pte., k., 12/10/16.
Gallacher, Michael, 17799, Pte., k., 26/9/16.
Gallagher, Thomas, 3/8988, Pte., k., 14/3/15.
Galloway, Theodore, 8260, L/Cpl. k., 26/4/15.
Ganley, Thomas, 7513, Pte., d., 31/7/15.
Gannon, John Edward, 6209, Pte., k., 12/10/14.
Garnett, Frank, 17774, Pte., d., 21/11/15.
Gavaghan, James, 3/8833, Pte., k., 10/8/16.
Gavins, Joseph, 9791, L/Cpl., k., 19/12/15.
Gerrard, John, 4/8540, Pte., k., 28/7/15.
Gibson, John Henry, 4/7064, Pte., k., 27/10/15.
Gill, Arthur, 18317, Pte., d., 21/12/15.
Gill, John Henry, 3/9812, Pte., d , 3/5/15.
Gill, Joseph, 18957, A/Cpl., k., 14/8/16.
Gillespie, William, 3/8931, Pte., k., 26/3/15.
Gillies, Harry, 9797, Pte., k., 16/6/15.
Glover, Arthur, 3/9380, L/Cpl., k., 30/6/15.
Goodhall, Robert, 7798, Pte., k., 20/10/14.
Gospel, Fred, 3/9621, L/Cpl., d.h., 31/7/16.
Gracie, William James, 4/8696, Pte., k., 25/9/16.
Gray, Percy, 24337 Pte., k., 18/9/16.
Grayson, Thomas, 9618, Pte., k., 13/10/14.
Green, Joseph, 3/9274, Pte., k., 4/1/15.
Greensmith, Turner, 4/8205, Pte., d., 17/8/15.
Greenwood, Alfred, 7180, Pte., k., 20/9/14.
Greenwood, Herbert, 3/8249, Pte. d., 16/2/15.
Greenwood, John, 3/8284, Pte., k., 20/1/16.
Gregory, Alfred, 9846, Pte., d.h., 24/4/15.
Gregory, Donald James Herbert, 5554, Pte., k., 20/10/14.
Greig, Adam, 3/8667, Pte., k., 16/10/16.
Grindrod, Harold, 9154, L/Cpl., k., 27/8/16.
Gurden, Alfred, 8082, Pte., d., 1/10/14.
Guthrie, James, 10061, Pte., k., 20/12/15.
Gwilliams, William Arthur, 3/7768, Pte., d., 13/8/15.
Hainsworth, Arthur, 8618, Pte., k., 25/9/14.
Hall, Frederick, 4/8288, L/Cpl., d., 11/11/15.
Hamilton, John Alexander, 9931, L/Cpl., k., 20/9/14.
Haney, Peter, 9754, L/Cpl., k., 20/9/14.
Hardisty, Harry, 19756, Pte., k., 16/10/15.
Hardwick, James, 9494, Cpl., k., 1/3/16.
Hardy, James, 4/6990, Pte., k., 15/9/16.
Hargrave, Herbert, 3/8407, Pte., k., 21/10/14.
Harney, Thomas, 20086, Pte., k., 25/9/16, formerly 13254, 4th Hussars, M.M.
Harrison, Lewis, 4/8306, Pte., k., 18/9/16.
Harrison, Thomas, 3/9058, Pte., d., 27/2/15.
Hart, Thomas, 4/8407, Pte., k., 17/6/15.
Hart, Thomas, 3/8514, Pte., k., 12/10/16

Harvey, Ephraim Edward, 21280, Pte., k., 13/2/16.
Harvey, George, 9331, Sgt., k., 6/6/16.
Head, Reginald, 9326, Pte., d., 19/12/15.
Heald, Joshua, 9815, Pte., d., 25/10/15.
Heald, Walter, 6707, Pte., d., 24/10/14.
Hemsworth, Frank, 9869, Pte., k., 20/9/14.
Hennigan, Joseph, 3/6985, A/Cpl., k., 19/11/14.
Henry, Edward, 8173, Pte., d., 18/2/15.
Hetherington, Milton 3/8990, Pte., k., 16/6/15.
Hewett, Frederick David Arthur, 10060, Pte., k., 20/9/14.
Hewitt, Tom, 11726, Pte., k., 12/10/16.
Higgins, John Arthur, 19693, Pte., k., 4/6/16.
Hildree, James, 7498, Pte., d., 15/5/15.
Hill, Andrew, 6571, Pte., k., 20/9/14.
Hill, Charles Albert Willmotte, 9824, Pte., k., 15/9/16.
Hill, John Butler, 7150, A/Cpl. k., 18/9/16.
Hill, James, 3/9474, Pte., k., 17/9/16.
Hilliers, Henry, 9893, Pte., k., 11/10/15.
Hilton, George Henry, 9711, Pte., k., 16/6/15.
Himsworth, Charles Edward, 19679, Pte., k., 26/8/16.
Hinchliffe, Ernest, 7899, Pte., d., 22/9/14.
Hitchings, Robert, 3/8637, Sgt., k., 4/6/16.
Hobson, Joseph, 6010, Pte., k. 14/3/15.
Hodgson Frederick James, 9459, L/Cpl., d., 26/9/14.
Hogg, Harry, 10006, Pte., k., 30/11/14.
Holdsworth, Joseph, 9695, Pte., d. 18/6/15.
Holgate, Arthur, 34870, Pte., k., 11/12/16.
Holland, Christopher, 3/7566, Pte., k., 28/10/14
Holliday, George Riley 24488, L/Cpl., d., 24/10/16.
Hollin, Harry, 22256, Pte., k., 15/9/16.
Hollingworth, Joseph, 18930, Pte., k., 25/9/16.
Holman, Robert, 4/7968, Pte., k., 15/9/16.
Holmes, George William, 16355, Pte., k., 18/9/16.
Holmes, Joseph, 6127, A/C.S.M., k., 12/10/16.
Holmes, William, 9508, Pte., d.h., 1/11/15.
Holt, Richard, 4/6841, Pte., d., 26/7/15.
Hood, William Henry, 3/10123 Pte., k., 24/8/15.
Hooligan, John, 7647, Pte., k., 20/9/14.
Hopkins, James, 7512, Pte., d., 22/10/14.
Horne, Elijah, 22148, Pte., k., 25/9/16.
Horton, Reuben, 3/9465, Pte., k., 30/1/15.
Howard, Thomas, 3/9622, Pte., k., 12/10/16.
Howell, Charles, 3/9833, A/Sgt., k., 10/4/15.
Howes, Louis, 8869, Pte., k., 16/10/16.
Howley, Daniel, 7556, Sgt., d., 26/4/15.
Hudson, John, 7353, Pte., k., 20/9/14.
Hudson, James, 9714, Pte., d., 26/9/14.
Hudson, John Thomas, 10007, Pte., 20/9/14.
Hull, William John, 22421, Pte., d., 8/6/16.
Hunter Harry, 3/8321, Pte., d., 18/6/15.
Hunter, John, 6089, Sgt., d., 4/6/16.
Hutchinson, Samuel, 9975, Pte., k., 20/9/14.
Ineson, Ben, 4/8254, Pte., k., 28/3/15.
Ingle, Frank, 4/7557, Pte., d., 14/6/16.
Jackson, Arthur, 3/10214, Pte., k., 12/10/16.
Jackson, Fred, 17150, L/Cpl., k., 4/5/16.
Jackson, George Barber, 3/9594, Pte., k., 16/3/16.
Jackson, Percival, 3/8970, Pte., k., 4/3/15.
Jacobson, Abe, 31876, Pte., k., 22/12/16.
Jefferson, Frank, 7757, Pte., k., 13/10/15.
Johnson, Arthur, 3/9735, A/Sgt., k., 29/6/15.
Johnson, Albert, 9776, Pte., k., 10/8/15.
Johnson, Arthur, 17147, Pte., k., 18/9/16.
Johnson, Arthur, 32756, Pte., k., 23/12/16.
Johnson, Henry Edward, 9985, L/Sgt., k., 25/9/16.
Johnson, James, 4/8383, Pte., d., 29/4/16.
Johnson, John Henry, 21516, Pte., d., 26/9/16.
Jones, Bert, 3/20153, Pte., k., 25/9/16, formerly 21007, Hussars of the Line.
Jones, Charles, 3/8355, Pte., k., 28/11/14.
Jones, Fred, 20248, Pte., k., 12/10/16, formerly 30367, K.O.Y.L.I.
Kane, William James, 8406, Pte., k., 20/9/14.
Kay, Ernest, 3/8490, Pte., k., 11/10/15.
Kay, William, 7998, Sgt., k., 20/9/14.
Kaye, Joshua, 3/8281, Pte., k., 16/6/15.
Keen, George Albert Undy, 4/7988, Pte., k., 18/9/16.
Keens, Albert, 24320, Pte., k., 15/9/16.
Keighley, Abednego, 27173, Pte., k., 18/9/16.
Kemp, Wilfred, 11657, Pte., k., 3/5/16.
Kendrew, Joseph, 19437, Pte., d., 10/9/16.
Kennalley, James, 4/8474, Pte., k., 6/10/15.
Kent, Edward, 8774, Sgt., k., 11/2/16.
Kent, Fred, 7345, L/Cpl., d., 31/3/15.
King, Arthur, 10216, Pte., k., 29/12/14.
King, John, 9972, Pte., k., 19/12/15.
Kitson Herbert, 17730, Pte. k., 16/3/16.
Kitson, Henry, 19081, Pte., k., 18/9/16.
Knott, George, 7349, Pte., d., 25/9/14.
Laird, George, 13/8622, Pte., k., 31/10/14.
Lamb, Maurice William, 3/8236, Sgt., k., 4/6/16.
Larty, Henry Thomas, 9948, Pte., d., 28/9/14.
Larvin, John, 3/8873, Pte., d., 11/1/15.
Lavender, Alfred Patrick, 13955, Pte. k. 25/9/16.
Lawrence, Gilbert, 9807, A/Cpl., k. 3/9/16.
Lee, Edward, 8003, Pte., k., 18/9/16.
Lemm, James, 7665, Pte., d.h., 19/10/14.
Lennahan, Arthur, 10950, Pte., k., 15/5/16.
Leonard, Patrick, 3/8118, Pte., k., 14/2/15.
Liddle, Edward, 4/6999, Pte., k., 30/7/15.
Lievesley, William, 10168, Pte., d., 29/9/16.
Limbert, James 3/8018, Pte., d., 19/6/15.
Lindley, Harry, 3/9672, Pte., k., 2/3/15.
Lindsay, Thomas, 4/7811, Pte., k., 9/1/16.
Linfoot, William, 3/7954, d., 24/1/16.
Lister, Joseph Exley, 3/8521, Pte., k., 20/9/15
Little, George, 29507, Pte., k., 12/10/16.
Lofthouse, Alfred, 16260, Pte., k., 25/9/16.
Lynn, Martin, 8318, A/Cpl., k., 15/9/16.
Lyson, Thomas Henry, 7653, Pte., k., 25/9/14.
Macheil, John, 7713, Sgt., d., 30/9/14.
Main, Thomas, 4/8645, Pte., k., 21/4/16.
Manby, James, 6615, Pte., d., 7/10/14.
Mangan, John James, 6679, L/Cpl., k., 28/10/14.
Manley, James, 3/10163, Pte., k., 14/8/16.
Manning, James, 7792, Pte., k., 25/9/14.
Marlow, David, 35060, Pte., d., 23/12/16.
Marsden, Charles, 4/7264, Pte., k., 18/9/16.
Marshall, Frank, 21372, Pte., k., 4/6/16.
Marshall, Herbert, 8160, Pte., k., 20/9/14.
Marshall, Philip Messenger, 3/8906, Pte., d., 15/3/15.
Marshall, Samuel, 4/8489, Pte., k., 19/12/15.
Marston, Herbert, 21371, Pte., k., 14/8/16.
Martin, George, 8409, Pte., k., 20/9/14.
Martin, Joseph, 19524, Pte., d., 28/9/16.
Massey, Robert, 8007, Pte., k., 20/9/14.
Mather, Ralph Burdon, 3/9055, Pte., k., 19/10/15.
Matthews, Thomas, 10151, L/Cpl., k., 25/9/14.
Maunders, Sidney, 10221, Pte., d., 4/7/15.
May, John William, 21087, L/Cpl., d., 15/8/16.
Mercer, Alfred, 22267, L/Cpl., k., 27/5/16.
Milner, Charles, 4/7902, Pte., k., 2/4/15.
Missett, John Edward, 7479, Pte., k., 20/9/14.
Missett, James, 6564, C/Sgt., d., 20/9/14.

The Prince of Wales's Own (West Yorks. Regt.)—Casualties 313

Mitchell, Andrew David, 9596, Pte., k., 22/9/14.
Mitchell, Herbert, 3/7543, Pte., k., 30/10/14.
Mitchell, John Willie, 6178, Pte., k., 18/9/16.
Mitchelson, Harry, 22290, Pte., d.h., 11/12/16.
Molloy, Arthur, 9882, L/Cpl., k., 18/9/16.
Moore, Edward, 3/9036, Pte., d., 22/4/16.
Moore, Frederick, 23552, L/Cpl., k., 4/6/16.
Morley, Fred, 3/7816, Pte., k., 29/6/15.
Morley, James, 4/8094, Pte., d., 18/6/15.
Morrell, George, 7324, Pte., k., 22/9/14.
Morris, Richard, 3/10387, L/Cpl., k., 18/9/16.
Morrison, Thomas, 14463, A/Sgt., k., 18/9/16.
Mortimer, Fred, 24345, Pte., d., 19/9/16.
Mountain, Lewis, 8073, Pte., k., 29/12/14.
Muckles, Bertie, 3/8584, Pte., k., 19/12/15.
Mumby, William, 8138, A/Sgt., k., 31/12/14.
Munroe, Patrick, 3/9130, L/Cpl., k., 5/6/16/
Murgatroyd, Sam, 17704, Pte., k., 25/9/16.
Murphy, Edward, 3/9297, L/Cpl., k., 25/4/16.
Murray, David, 12537, Pte., d., 25/9/15.
Murray, William, 22364, Pte., k., 3/5/16.
McCann, John William, 3/7654, Pte., k., 16/10/16.
McCarthy, Owen, 23600, Pte., d., 21/9/16.
McDermott, Edward, 3/9382, L/Cpl., d.h. 27/10/15.
McDonald, George, 40074, Pte., d., 10/10/16, formerly 20935, Durham L.I.
McDonald, Michael, 7901, Pte., k., 13/10/14.
McDonald, Thomas, 5958, Pte., k., 20/11/14.
McGregor, Frank, 7173, Pte., d., 20/9/14.
McKenzie, William, 8197, Pte., d., 6/6/16.
McLean, John, 8027, Pte., k., 13/10/14.
McMullen, Patrick, 7243, Pte., k., 14/10/14.
McNulty, William Henry, 8118, L/Cpl., k., 20/9/14.
McPherson, William Littlejohn, 7810, L/Cpl., k., 19/12/15.
Neary, William Joseph, 3/9136, Pte., k., 16/6/15.
Newell, Albert, 8208, Pte., k., 20/9/14.
Newing, Jonathan, 3/9480, Pte., k., 28/10/14.
Newman, William, 10739, Pte., k., 26/4/16.
Newton, George, 4/8223, L/Cpl., k., 18/9/16.
Nicholson, Thomas, 3/7887, Pte., k., 20/10/14.
Nixon, Edmund, 20130, L/Cpl., k., 12/10/16, formerly 22882, 20th Hussars.
Nunns, Sam, 3/8238, Pte., k., 22/2/15.
Nutter, Ernest Alfred, 8124, Cpl., k., 22/2/16
Oates, George Arthur, 8670, Pte., k., 11/3/15.
O'Brien, Alexander, 3/8158, Pte., k., 12/10/16.
Ogden, William, 9529, Pte., d., 26/9/14.
Oliver, Albert Edward, 10033, Pte., k., 14/2/16.
O'Neill, William, 3/8263, Pte., d., 26/10/14.
Ormsby, John, 7796, L/Cpl., 22/9/14.
Padden, John, 4/6876, Sgt., k., 4/11/15.
Page, William, 15184, Pte., k., 29/7/15.
Pannett, Arthur, 15/1428, L/Cpl., k., 12/10/16.
Pannett, Arthur, 17777, Pte., k., 14/3/15.
Parker, Charles, 8882, L/Cpl., k., 14/2/16.
Parker, Robert Winder, 9420, Pte., k., 20/9/14.
Parker, Thomas, 9999, Pte., k., 2/4/15.
Parkin, Harry, 7509, Pte., k., 20/9/14.
Parrsloe, William, 8275, Pte., k., 20/9/14.
Paul, Thomas, 15/1757, Pte., d., 1/10/16.
Peake, George, 7924, Bdsmn., k., 25/9/14.
Peel, James William, 14822, Pte., d., 27/10/15.
Pegg, John Richard, 3/7873, Pte., k., 10/12/14.
Pemberton, Harry, 6458. Pte., d., 23/10/14.
Pert, Edward, 8421, Pte., d., 26/9/14.
Perry, William, 10541, Pte., k., 13/2/16.
Pestell, Percy, 8971, Cpl., d., 27/9/14.
Pickard, Francis George, 5713, L/Sgt. k., 20/9/14.

Picken, Walter, 20093, L/Cpl., k., 12/10/16, formerly 15761, Hussars.
Pickering, Joseph, 4/5726, Pte., k., 18/9/16.
Pickles, Thomas, 10147, Pte., d., 21/12/15.
Pilkington, Thomas, 15/1429, Pte., d.h., 3/9/16.
Pine, Thomas, 18192, Pte., k., 18/9/16.
Pond, William Henry, 7785, Pte., k., 20/9/14.
Porter, Edward, 7697, Pte., k., 20/9/14.
Potter, David, 7771, Pte., k., 29/10/14.
Powell, John William, 6653, d., 4/5/15.
Power, Joseph, 6708, Pte., k., 20/9/14.
Pratt, George William, 7636, Pte., k., 20/9/14.
Pratt, Robert, 10050, A/Sgt., d., 11/6/16, D.C.M.
Priestley Bert, 7123, Pte., k., 20/9/14.
Prince, Peter, 3/8183, Pte., k., 18/9/16.
Prior, John, 3/8085, Pte., d., 19/3/15.
Prudhoe, John, 3/8987, Pte., k., 4/5/15.
Purver, Harry, 6729, Pte., k., 13/10/15.
Quaid, Charles, 23611, Pte., d., 20/10/16, formerly 6524, Dublin Fusiliers.
Queenan, Thomas, 9958, L/Sgt., k., 4/6/16.
Quinn, John, 6608, Pte., k., 18/10/14.
Radford, William Edward, 7121, Pte., k., 22/9/14.
Raistrick, Ernest, 22050, Pte., d.h., 20/9/16.
Ratliff, Arthur Henry, 9333, Cpl., k., 20/9/14.
Raw, Robert, 5440, Pte., k., 16/6/15.
Rayner, Fred, 13127, Cpl., k., 12/10/16.
Rayner, James, 3/8763, Pte., k., 12/8/15.
Rayner, Sam, 5586, Pte., k., 30/6/15.
Reddington, Anthony, 18405, Pte., k., 14/8/16.
Redfern, Thomas Joseph, 6184, A/C.S.M., k., 3/7/15.
Reed, Harry, 9924, L/Cpl., k., 12/10/16.
Reynold, Ernest, 7253, Pte., k., 12/10/16.
Rhodes, John William, 18958, Pte., d., 2/12/15.
Richardson, Frank, 6522, Pte., k., 3/5/15.
Richardson, William, 8045, Pte., d., 25/9/14.
Riley, John Thomas, 7425, Pte., k., 20/9/14.
Roberts, Charles Henry, 9507, L/Cpl., k., 20/10/14.
Roberts, Herbert, 9750, Cpl., k., 20/9/14.
Robinson, George, 3881, L/Cpl., k., 26/11/14.
Robson, Ernest Lindsay, 6480, Pte., k., 20/9/14.
Robson, Frank, 4/7779, Pte., k., 11/10/16.
Roe, Charles Blyton, 7515, Pte., k., 20/9/14.
Roe, Ernest Victor, 7885, Pte., k., 20/9/14.
Rooke, Arthur Eustace, 8168, Pte., k., 20/9/14.
Roper, William, 3/8572, Pte., d., 17/9/16.
Rosenbloom, Abraham, 29528, Pte., k., 12/10/16.
Royston, James, 4/7211, Pte., k., 14/5/15.
Rumble, Alfred, 15573, Pte., k., 13/2/16.
Ryan, Joseph, 20/132, Pte., k., 24/12/16.
Ryan, Roger, 9822, L/Cpl., k., 25/9/16.
Ryan, William, 3/8054, Pte., k., 14/11/14.
Sanders, James, 15/1765, Pte., k., 13/10/16.
Sanderson, Samuel, 7656, Pte., k., 20/9/14.
Sandiforth, Arthur, 7938, Pte., k., 20/9/14.
Saville, Fred, 7127, Pte., k., 17/9/16.
Saynor, George Arthur, 9930, Pte., k., 13/8/16.
Scaife, Robert, 7992, Pte., d., 23/11/14.
Schofield, William, 7918, Pte., k., 25/9/14.
Scott, Hauxby, 10386, Pte., d., 1/10/16.
Scott, James Stanley, 3/8605, Pte., d., 12/2/16
Selby, Thomas, 7551, Pte., k., 30/6/15.
Shaw, Albert, 7691, Pte. k., 20/9/14.
Shaw James, 8015, L/Cpl., k., 25/9/16.
Shearon, James Edward, 4/7964, Pte., k., 18/9/16.
Sheldon, Arthur, 12364, L/Cpl., k., 25/9/16.
Shepherd, Albert, 8317, Pte., k., 20/9/16.
Siddons, Joseph Robert, 4/8655, Pte., k., 12/10/16.

The Prince of Wales's Own (West Yorks. Regt.)—Casualties

Sillence, Walter Edward, 20028, Cpl., d., 24/2/16, formerly 16454, 12th Res. Cav. Regt.
Simmonds, Harry, 7518, Pte., k., 20/9/14.
Simpson, Bernard, 22253, Pte., k., 12/10/16.
Simpson, Emanuel, 4/8193, Pte., k., 9/10/16.
Simpson, Ernest William, 10749, Pte., k., 28/9/16.
Skellorn, Horace, 9947, Pte., d., 15/10/14.
Skirrow, John, 3/8360, Pte., d., 27/11/14.
Slack, Thomas, 4/8580, Cpl., k., 29/1/15.
Slater, William Henry, 9452, Pte., k., 20/9/14
Smiles, James, 6056, Pte., d., 18/2/15.
Smith, Albert Edward, 15241, Pte., k., 4/3/16.
Smith, Arthur, 3/8789, Pte., d., 28/6/15.
Smith, Edward, 19870, Pte., k., 12/10/16.
Smith, Fred, 3/9025, Pte., k., 18/9/16.
Smith, George, 7809, L/Cpl., k., 19/12/15.
Smith, Henry Thomas, 8069, C.S.M., k., 16/3/16.
Smith, Robert, 7125 Pte., k., 20/9/14.
Smith, Samuel, 9798, Pte., k., 28/12/14.
Smith, William, 6081, Pte., k., 9/12/14.
Smith, William Henry, 7136, Pte. k. 16/6/15.
Snow Frank, 3/8708, Pte., k., 25/3/15.
Snowdon, John Robert, 9840, L/Cpl., d., 6/10/14.
Soakell, John, 7658, Pte. k. 20/9/14.
Sowden, Fred, 5475, Pte., k., 20/9/14.
Sowden, William Thomas, 22318, Pte., k., 12/10/16.
Spicer, Alfred John, 7453, L/Cpl., k., 3/5/15.
Spurway, Charles Henry, 4/7734, L/Cpl., d.h., 26/6/15.
Stead, Ernest, 7268, Pte., k., 20/9/14.
Stembridge, Harry, 3/8711, L/Cpl., d., 29/4/15.
Sterling, William, 3/9097, Pte., d., 14/3/15.
Stimpson, George Thomas Christmas, 9204, Pte., k., 18/9/16.
Straits, John 4/8589, Pte., k., 19/12/15.
Stuteley, Charles, 9588, L/Cpl., k., 22/9/14.
Surplice, William Alfred, 4/8211, Pte., d., 28/9/16.
Swales, Herbert, 5754, L/Sgt., k., 31/8/15.
Tallant, Charlie, 17722, Pte., k., 30/12/15.
Tanner, George William, 13227, Pte., k., 25/9/16.
Tate, Thomas Scrutton, 3/9093, Pte., k., 23/9/15.
Taylor, Frank Allen, 3/8926, Pte k., 30/6/15.
Taylor, Harry, 24284, Pte., k., 25/9/16.
Taylor, Harry, 6620, Pte., k., 20/9/14.
Taylor, Jack, 3/8721, Pte., k., 12/10/16.
Taylor, Joseph Roberts, 6696, A/C.Q.M.S., k., 20/7/16.
Taylor, William, 3/9970, Pte., k., 16/2/15.
Teale, Albert, 9544, Pte., d., 6/11/14.
Tempest, Samuel, 8815, Sgt., k., 10/8/15.
Temple, Edwin, 17817, Pte., k., 11/8/15.
Temple, Thomas Whitfield, 9836, Pte., d.h., 13/3/15.
Thackray, William, 8434, L/Cpl., k., 20/9/14.
Thomas, Harold, 15/1549, Pte., k., 27/5/16.
Thompson, Edward, 17971, Sgt., k., 25/9/16.
Thompson, Howard, 23291, Pte., k., 18/9/16.
Thorley, George, 9739, L/Cpl., k., 20/10/14.
Thorpe, John Henry, 6576, Pte., k., 20/9/14.
Thrall, Benjamin, 7722, Pte., k., 15/11/14.
Todd, William Lindsay, 3/7753, Pte., k., 13/10/14.
Tomlinson, John, 19251, L/Cpl., d., 7/6/15.
Tomlinson, William, 7727, Pte., k., 22/9/14.
Townrow, Bertie William, 9988, Pte., k., 20/9/14.

Tucker, George, 5261, L/Cpl., d., 28/10/14.
Turner, Albert Ernest, 21058, Pte., k., 12/10/16.
Turner, Thomas 6482, L/Cpl., d., 7/10/16.
Twigg, Arthur, 4/8488, Pte., k., 11/6/15.
Tyreman, Tom Wheatley, 10118, Pte., k., 12/10/16.
Tyson, James Henry, 4172, Sgt., k., 4/6/16.
Vasey, Joseph, 3/7553, Pte., k., 20/10/14.
Vincent, Walter William, 4/7447, Pte., k., 27/5/15.
Vollans, James Reginald, 15490, L/Cpl., d., 27/9/16, M.M.
Wadsworth, Herbert, 7761, Pte., k., 20/9/14.
Walker, Frederick, 9795, Sgt., k., 19/12/15.
Walker, John William, 17791, Pte., k., 10/1/16.
Walker, William, 6690, Pte., k., 18/11/14.
Walsh, Charles, 4/8032, Pte., k., 30/7/15.
Walton, Joseph, 19376, Cpl., k., 25/9/16.
Wandless, Robert, 14699, Pte., k., 30/7/15.
Ward, Arthur 8675, L/Cpl., d., 17/9/16.
Ward Arthur, 18367, Pte., d., 14/3/16.
Ward, George, 7750, Pte., k., 20/9/14.
Ward, James, 4/7990, Pte., d., 6/10/15.
Ward, John Thomas, 22479, Pte., d., 23/7/16.
Ward, Walter Charles, 9953, L/Cpl., k., 20/9/14.
Warne, Charles, 17283, Pte., k., 17/9/16.
Warner, George, 7363, L/Cpl., k., 20/9/14.
Waterson, John Edward, 3/10373, Pte., k., 12/10/16.
Watkinson, Robert, 7911, Pte., k., 22/9/14.
Watson George, 9704, Pte., d., 22/8/15.
Watson, George William, 17693, Pte., k., 4/6/16.
Watson, Herbert, 6413, Pte., k., 15/12/14.
Watson, Sydney, 6568, Pte., k., 10/3/15.
Watts, Charles, 10174, L/Cpl., k., 14/3/15.
Webster, Henry, 24340, Pte., k., 18/9/16.
Wells, Arthur Henry, 3/9685, Pte., d.h., 14/4/15.
Wells, John Henry, 17952, Pte., d., 11/10/16.
West, Fred, 5773, Pte., k., 30/12/14.
Westcott, George, 8127, Sgt., k., 20/9/14.
Westerman, Arthur, 8117, Pte., k., 14/2/16.
Wheeler, Albert Howard, 3/8429, Pte., k., 13/10/14.
Whitaker, Sidney, 4/8545, Pte., d., 29/7/15.
Whittaker, Harold, 9818, L/Cpl., d., 14/10/16.
White, Charles, 5942, Pte., k., 27/10/15.
White, William, 3/8482, Pte., k., 2/11/14.
Whitham, Milton, 19238, A/Cpl., k., 12/10/16.
Whittlestone, Walter, 15177, Pte., k. 29/1/15.
Whomack, Israel, 17692, Pte., k., 12/10/16.
Wilcock, Arthur, 17831, Pte., d.h., 2/11/16.
Wilford, William Henry, 18504, Pte., d., 13/10/16.
Wilkinson, Charles, 3/9270, Pte., d., 5/5/16.
Wilkinson, Fred, 3/9554, Pte., k., 14/3/15.
Wilkinson, Sydney, 4/7694, A/Cpl., k., 13/10/16.
Wilkinson, William, 5978, Pte., k., 22/9/14.
Williams, Smithson, 8067, Pte., k., 20/10/14.
Williams, William, 9005, Pte., k., 28/7/15.
Williams William 9655, A/Cpl., k., 25/9/16.
Williamson, William, 7328, Pte., d., 24/9/14.
Wilson, George, 4668, Dmr., k., 20/9/14.
Wilson, Harry, 24550, Pte., d., 16/9/16.
Wilson, John William, 16335, Pte., k., 11/10/16.
Wilson, Samuel James, 3/8309, Pte., k., 17/11/15.
Winkle, Robert, 9691, Pte., k., 13/10/14.
Winn, Thomas, 9817, Pte., d., 29/6/15.
Winterburn, Herbert, 27031, Pte., k., 18/9/16.
Wisbey, George, 19163, Pte., k., 12/10/16.
Witty, Herbert, 22367, Pte., k., 14/8/16.

The Prince of Wales's Own (West Yorks. Regt.)—Casualties 315

Wood, Ephraim, 21227, Pte., d., 25/9/16.
Wood, Willie, 16372, Pte., k., 18/9/16.
Woodhead, Herbert, 4/7574, L/Sgt., d., 21/7/16.
Woodley, William, 9720, Sgt., d., 14/2/16.

Wybrew, Frank, 10622, Pte., k., 18/9/16.
Yearby, Richard, 7309, Pte., k., 18/10/15.
Young, Eric Norman, 23626, Pte., k., 12/10/16.
Young, William, 7508, Pte., k., 20/9/14.

1st GARRISON BATTALION

Calverley, Fred, 24819, Pte., d. at sea, 27/4/16.
Power, Thomas, 23177, Pte., d. Malta, 5/1/16, formerly 9333, Yorkshire Regt.

Warwick, William, 22987, L/Cpl., d., 14/5/16, formerly 15595, West Riding Regt.
Wright, Frank, 24398, Pte., d. Malta, 8/9/16.

2nd BATTALION.

Adams, James, 3/10032, Pte., d., 11/3/15.
Adamson, Robert, 10158, L/Cpl., k., 1/7/16.
Airlie, James, 24436, Pte., k., 1/7/16.
Alderthay, David, 12371, Pte., k., 1/7/16.
Aldrich, Sidney, 9167, L/Cpl., k., 19/12/14.
Allinson, Willie, 21986, Pte., k., 2/9/16.
Archibald, William, 3/9047, L/Cpl., d.h., 13/9/16.
Armitage, William, 24459, Pte., k., 23/10/16.
Armstrong, John Robert, 4/8595, Pte., k., 8/8/16.
Arrowsmith, George, 8998, Pte., d., 9/5/15.
Arthur, James, 4/7626, Pte., k., 13/3/15.
Asdale, Robert, 3/8755, Pte., k., 1/7/16.
Atkin, Bernard Willis, 7205, Sgt., k., 7/4/16.
Atkinson, Harry, 9877, Pte,, k., 23/10/16.
Atkinson, Tom, 25457, Pte., k., 14/7/16.
Ayton, Robert Christopher, 9441, Pte., d., 19/12/14.
Backhouse, Thomas, 8903, L/Cpl., k., 1/7/16.
Bailey, Arthur, 8911, Pte., k., 26/10/16.
Bailey, Horace, 3/9162, Pte., k., 23/10/15.
Baines, Bernard, 23630, Pte., k., 1/7/16.
Baker, Major, 8830, Pte., k., 19/12/14.
Balme, Percy, 28075, Pte., k., 22/10/16.
Banner, James, 3/8451, Pte., d., 16/7/16.
Barclay, Thomas James, 8183, L/Cpl., k., 21/11/14.
Barclay, Sydney Herbert, 7117, Bndsmn, k., 19/12/14.
Barker, Archibald, 4/8503, Pte., d., 3/7/16.
Barnwell, Philip, 9888, Pte., k., 11/3/15.
Barrett, Frederick Charles, 4/7203, L/Cpl., k. (accident), 9/6/15.
Bates, William, 9089, L/Cpl., k., 23/7/15.
Bax, Gordon, 32199, Pte., k., 28/10/16.
Baylis, Albert James Thomas, 8322, Sgt., k., 19/12/14.
Beecroft, Albert John, 9172, Cpl., k., 18/3/15.
Bell, Charles Herbert, 17103, Pte., d.h., 23/7/16.
Bell, John James, 8004, Pte., k., 19/12/14.
Bell, Lionel, 24195, Pte., k., 11/9/16.
Bell, William, 8818, Pte., k., 12/3/15.
Bennett, Dan, 9049, Pte., k., 26/10/16.
Benson, Daniel Leo, 9338, Pte., k., 11/2/15.
Berrill, Harry, 4/7893, Pte., k., 2/10/15.
Berry, Harold, 13211, Pte., k., 1/7/16.
Bickerdike, Walter, 4/8249, Pte., k., 14/5/16.
Bird, Robert, 19423, Pte., k., 6/3/16.
Bird, Thomas George, 8996, Pte., d.h., 27/5/15.
Birkhead, Joseph, 24202, Pte., k., 14/8/16.
Bisson, Charles, 8601, L/Cpl., d., 11/3/15.
Blackburn, Edwin, 9282, Pte., k., 19/12/14.
Blackburn, John, 10230, Pte., d., 13/3/15.
Blackburn, Wilfred, 25443, Pte., k., 1/9/16.
Blacker, William Henry, 3/9862, Pte., k., 6/4/15.
Blakeborough, Ernest, 28998, Pte., k., 26/10/16.
Blakeley, John William, 8480, L/Cpl., d., 11/12/14.

Boland, Joseph, 3/7352, Pte., k., 25/10/16.
Bowyer, George, 4/8453, Pte., k., 1/7/16.
Bradley, Fred, 11318, Pte., k., 25/10/16.
Bramhall, George Emanuel, 17666, Pte., d.h., 26/11/16.
Brannan, Nicholas, 3/9312, Pte., k., 19/12/14.
Branton, Noel Francis, 14308, Pte., k., 25/1/15.
Brigham, John William, 8609, L/Cpl., k., 18/12/14.
Broadbent, Thomas Henry, 22436, Pte., k., 24/10/16.
Broadbent, William, 8788, A/Cpl., k., 1/7/16.
Broadhead, Charles, 4/7069, Pte., k., 14/5/16.
Brogden, Joseph, 3/9243, Pte., k., 22/10/15.
Brown, Frederick, 23590, Pte., k., 29/6/16.
Brown, Herbert, 4/8062, Pte., k., 1/7/16.
Brown, James, 3/9147, Pte., k., 24/2/15.
Browne, John Clifford, 24478, Pte., k., 13/8/16.
Buckley, Ernest, 12393, Pte., d., 9/10/15.
Bullough, Albert, 4/8189 Pte. k. 12/8/15.
Burling Albert, 8947, L/Cpl., d., 19/12/14.
Burnell, Fred, 8448, Pte., k., 11/3/15.
Burnet, John William, 9962, Pte., k., 12/3/15.
Burnett, Thomas Edward, 8441, L/Sgt., k., 1/7/16.
Bush, Edwin, 35656, Pte., k., 11/11/16.
Butcher, Albert, 9595, L/Cpl., k., 11/3/15.
Caller, James Alfred, 8697, Cpl., k., 1/7/16.
Carnall, Albert Edward, 19054, Pte., k., 1/7/16.
Carr, Jerry, 4/6838, Pte., d., 14/8/16.
Carr, John, 4/8463, Pte., d., 26/4/15.
Carroll, James, 9084, Pte., k., 25/10/16.
Case, William John, 9788, Pte., k., 19/12/14.
Casey, John, 7762, Pte., d., 18/1/16, formerly 6177, Northumberland Fusiliers.
Chamberlain, Joseph, 8906, Sgt., k., 28/10/16.
Chapman, John, 4/8611, L/Cpl., k., 1/7/16.
Chappell, William, 4/7920, Pte., d., 10/3/15.
Child, Clifford, 9990, Pte., k., 1/7/16.
Child, William, 23650, Pte., d., 2/7/17.
Chilvers, John, 9462, Pte., k., 19/12/14.
Clark, Ernest Albert, 9981, Pte., d., 20/1/15.
Clark, Leonard, 29103, Pte., k., 25/10/16.
Clark, Thomas, 15452, Pte., d.h., 29/5/15.
Clarke, Alfred, 3/10227, Pte., k., 1/7/16.
Clarke, Benjamin, 9589, Pte., k., 21/10/16.
Clarke, George, 3/9326, Pte., k., 12/3/15.
Clarke, George Frederick, 8375, Sgt., d., 19/3/16.
Clarkson, Henry, 22193, Pte., k., 1/7/16.
Clarkson, John, 4/8374, L/Cpl., k., 11/3/15.
Clayton, Fred, 25367, Pte., k., 25/8/16.
Clayton, George William, 28856, Pte., d., 30/10/16.
Clibbens, William, 9680, L/Cpl., k., 1/7/16.
Cliffe, Joseph, 10161, Pte., k., 1/7/16.
Cliffe, Sam, 4/7724, Pte., k., 25/10/16.
Clissold, Herbert, 9614, Drmr., d., 15/4/15.
Cockburn, James Richard, 3/9204, Pte., d., 8/4/16.

Colley, George, 4/7532, L/Cpl., k., 1/7/16.
Collier, Edward, 15/1583, Cpl., k., 26/10/16.
Collins, William Albert, 8443, Pte., k., 19/12/14.
Conmy, Robert, 23588, Pte., d., 4/7/16.
Cooper, Ernest, 30840, Pte., d.h., 18/4/16, formerly 9220, South Staffs Regt.
Cottage, Frank, 8905, Pte., k., 19/12/14.
Cox, Harry, 3/8556, Pte., k., 19/12/14.
Crane, John, 23562, Pte., k., 10/10/16.
Craven, Albert, 25366, Pte., d., 17/7/16.
Craven, John, 7270, Pte., k., 20/1/15.
Craven, Joseph Edmund, 7896, Pte., k., 12/3/15.
Crispin, Thomas, 9105, A/Cpl., k., 12/3/15.
Croft, Thomas Albert, 8180, Sgt., k., 10/3/15.
Crossley, Francis, 28345, Pte., k., 25/10/16.
Crossley, John Starmond, 27932, Pte., k., 28/10/16.
Crowther, Charles, 9307, Pte., k., 19/12/14.
Cummings, John, 4/8419, Pte., k., 9/6/15.
Curtis, Louis Richard, 3/9365, L/Cpl., k., 10/3/15.
Cushnie, John, 1145, Pte., k., 1/7/16.
Dale, George, 9748, Pte., d., 28/11/14.
Daly, William, 9476, Pte., k., 8/4/16.
Davis, John Henry, 4/7059, Pte., k., 13/3/15.
Day, Ernest Alfred, 9185, L/Cpl., k., 18/12/14.
Dayes, George William, 11728, Pte., k., 1/7/16.
Delaney, Thomas, 15874, Sgt., k., 1/2/15.
Dennis, Edward Henry, 8975, Sgt., k., 1/7/16.
Dennison, Charles Edward, 19306, Pte., k., 1/7/16.
Derbyshire, William, 62307, Pte., k., 24/4/16.
Dickinson, Harry, 4/8239, Pte., k., 1/7/16.
Dickinson, Joseph Bradley, 3/8615, Pte., k., 13/1/15.
Dobson, Mark, 3/10012, Pte., k., 3/4/15.
Dodgson, George Greenwood, 28029, Pte., k. 25/10/16.
Dolan, Albert, 3/9173, Pte., k., 1/7/16.
Donovan, Michael, 3/7774, Pte., k., 19/12/14.
Dorsey, Patrick, 4/7787, Pte., k., 7/4/16.
Dove, George Herbert, 8489, L/Cpl., d. 3/7/16, D.C.M.
Downing, Tom, 8861, Pte., d., 11/3/15.
Doyle, Joseph, 4/8359, Pte., d., 10/4/16.
Draper, William Cornelius, 15509, L/Cpl. k., 1/7/16.
Drury, Harry, 27995, Pte., k., 26/10/16.
Dryden, John, 8876, Pte., k., 19/12/14.
Dunn, Percy, 3/9035, Cpl., k., 1/7/16.
Ealand, James, 15/1658, Pte., k., 26/10/16.
Eastwood, Charlie, 4/7668, Pte., k., 10/3/15.
Eastwood, Harold, 29014, Pte., k., 28/10/16.
Eastwood, Isaac 3/9548, Cpl., d., 27/9/15.
Elkins, David, 3/8974, Pte., k., 19/12/14.
Elvin, Ernest, 9226, Sgt., k., 10/11/16.
Fairchild, George, 10114, Pte., k. 11/3/15.
Farr, Edward, 17096, Pte., k., 24/10/16.
Farrar, Edgar, 4/7600, Pte., d., 19/5/16.
Fearnhead, James Henry, 9814, L/Cpl., k., 2/12/14.
Firth, John, 9532, Pte., k., 18/1/15.
Fishburn, Albert, 25935, L/Cpl., k., 25/10/16.
Fitzgerald, James Patrick, 7920, A/Cpl., k., 10/3/15.
Fleming, Thomas, 4/8553, Pte., k., 18/10/15.
Flint, John, 10183, Pte., d., 8/3/15.
Flynn, Thomas, 3/9059, Pte., k., 25/3/18.
Foggin, George Prest, 15237, Pte., k., 11/3/15.
Foster, Arthur, 10128, Pte., k., 6/1/15.
Fowler, Alfred, 8412, Pte., k., 1/7/16.
Freeman, George, 8506, Sgt., d., 30/10/16.
Fryer, Percy, 8969, Pte., k., 10/3/15.
Gallagher, William, 4/8164, Pte., k., 16/6/15.

Gallantree, Arthur William, 9503, Pte., k. 11/3/15.
Galloway, Herbert, 9355, L/Cpl., k., 19/12/14.
Gibson, George, 4/8543, Pte., k., 1/7/16.
Gibson James, 40068, Pte., k., 25/10/16, formerly 22370, Durham L.I.
Gibson, Thomas, 40093, Pte., k., 24/10/16, formerly 23526, Durham L.I.
Gill, Fred, 10013, Pte., k., 9/5/15.
Gill, John Robert, 3/9415, Pte., d., 12/12/14.
Gittings, Thomas, 3/10254, Pte., d., 8/3/15.
Glazier, William, 8497, Bndsmn., k., 12/1/15.
Goddard, Ernest, 5396, Sgt., d., 12/3/15.
Goff, Sidney Albert, 9180, Sgt., d., 9/2/15.
Good, John, 9102, Pte., k., 11/3/15.
Goodhall, William, 8949, Pte., k., 10/3/15.
Goulder, Frederick, 3/8552, Pte., d., 19/12/14.
Graham, George, 3/9769, Pte., k., 26/1/15.
Graham, Percy William, 9200, A/Cpl., k., 10/3/15.
Grant, Harold Joseph, 4/8105, Pte., k., 1/7/16.
Gray, Ernest, 3/9339, Pte., k., 25/6/15.
Green, William Oliver, 3/9069, Pte., d., 14/8/15.
Gregory, Thomas, 3/9354, Pte., k., 10/31/5.
Guthrie, Fred, 17176, Pte., k., 25/10/16.
Hague, Arthur, 4/8487, Pte., k., 30/6/16.
Hanley, William Edward, 10101 Pte., k., 1/7/16.
Hardcastle, James, 9280, Pte., k., 1/7/16.
Hardcastle, Percy, 17132, Pte., k., 11/3/15.
Hardy, John, 21416, Pte., k., 1/7/16.
Hare, William Henry, 29031, Pte., k., 26/10/16.
Harland, Albert, 17091, Pte., k., 1/7/16.
Harris, George Thomas, 4/8009, Pte. k., 11/6/15.
Harrod, James, 4/7095, Pte., k., 1/9/15.
Hart, Albert Robert, 8511, L/Cpl., k., 10/3/15.
Harvey, John Alexander, 8953, L/Cpl., k., 14/3/15.
Hayward, Lewis, 3/8398, Pte., k., 1/7/16.
Heaton, Lambert, 4/8202, Pte., d., 9/6/15.
Helm, Joseph, 9800, L/Cpl., k., 1/7/16.
Helm, William Robert, 9350, Pte., k., 27/12/14.
Hicks, James George Charles, 11716, Pte., k., 3/11/15.
Hill, Edward, 17758, Pte., k., 9/7/15.
Hill John 9109, Pte., k., 26/12/14.
Hindley, Charles, 9279, Pte., k., 5/2/15.
Hoban, Thomas Patrick, 8687, Pte., d., 25/3/15.
Hobson, Charles 8706, Pte., d., 4/2/15.
Hodgson, Thomas, 17796, Pte., k., 23/10/15.
Hoitt, Sidney, 8616, Sgt., k., 1/7/16.
Holdsworth, Leslie, 9299, Pte., k., 1/7/16.
Holmes, Henry Horace, 4/7745, Pte., d., 4/7/16.
Hood, Herbert, 3/9217, Pte., k., 11/3/15.
Hooley, Arthur, 12484, Pte., k., 1/7/16.
Hopkins, Joseph Henry, 24487, Pte., k., 1/7/16.
Horner, George Oswald, 28841, Pte., k., 25/10/16.
Horner, Septimus, 22069, Pte., d., 12/2/16.
Huckin, William, 8377, Pte., k., 12/3/15.
Hudson, James, 8/9698, Pte., k., 9/7/15.
Hullah, Frederick, 23534, Pte., d., 1/7/16.
Hunt, Henry Charles, 8282, Pte., k., 26/5/15.
Hunter, Charles Sidney, 8205, Pte., d., 25/12/14, formerly 4681, Scots Guards.
Hunter, Herbert, 25032, Pte., k., 12/8/16.
Hunter, Robert, 7824, Pte., d., 17/7/16.
Hunter, William Napier, 3/9140, Pte., d., 2/7/16.
Hurd, William Charles, 10134, Pte., k., 9/5/15, formerly 13901, Middlesex Regt.
Hurley James William Thomas, 16329, Pte., k., 18/3/15.

The Prince of Wales's Own (West Yorks. Regt.)—Casualties 317

Husthwaite, Thomas, 3/10060, Sgt., k., 1/7/16.
Ibbetson, George, 24021, Pte., k., 1/7/16.
Jackson, Albert, 3/8798, Pte., k., 1/7/16.
Jackson, Richard, 9709, Pte., k., 18/7/15.
Jackson, Thomas, 6083, C.S.M., k., 26/1/15.
Jefferson, John, 9013, L/Cpl., k., 1/7/16.
Jennings, Matthew, 9313, Sgt., d., 19/5/16.
Jobling, Joseph, 8125, Pte., d., 30/10/16.
Johnson, Ernest, 8757, Pte., d., 19/12/14.
Johnson, Frederick Walter, 9161, Cpl., k. 1/7/16.
Johnson, Harold 9076, Pte., d., 28/3/15.
Johnson, George Henry, 8104, Pte., k., 12/3/15.
Johnson, Jim, 18326, L/Cpl., k., 26/10/16.
Johnson, William, 4/7848, Pte., k., 13/9/16.
Johnston, James, 3/9137, Pte., k., 10/3/15
Jones, Ernest, 23602, Pte., k., 1/7/16.
Jowett, Arthur, 7269, Pte., k., 1/7/16.
Kaigg, Richard, 3/7769, Pte., k., 19/12/14.
Kearney, John William, 10275, Pte., k., 11/9/16.
Kellett, Arthur, 28109, Pte., k., 28/10/16.
Kellett, Harry, 23312, Pte., k., 1/7/16.
Kellett, John William, 24420, Pte., k., 1/7/16.
Kelly, Alfred Fitzroy, 9292, L/Cpl., k., 24/10/16.
Kelly, Lawrence, 10404, Pte., k., 1/7/16.
Kelsey, John William, 11672, L/Cpl., k., 11/9/16.
Kemp, James, 6505, L/Cpl. k., 20/9/14.
Kendall, Joseph, 13/8642, Pte., k., 26/7/16.
Kent, Charles, 3/8694, Pte., k., 10/3/15.
Kent, Ernest, 11530, Pte., k., 6/6/16.
Kerr, William, 3/8633, Pte., d.h., 15/4/16.
Kettlewell, John William, 8945, Pte., d., 13/3/15.
Kettley, Joseph, 15967, Pte., k., 1/7/16.
Kinder, Albert, 10014, Pte., k., 24/7/15.
King, William, 20249, Pte., d., 18/11/16.
Kirby, Tom, 28790, Pte., d., 27/10/16.
Kirkwood, James William, 3/9265, Pte., k., 1/7/16.
Knaggs, Charles William, 23331, Pte., d., 11/7/16.
Lackenby, William, 3/8927, Pte., k., 12/3/15.
Lang, Patrick, 3/9257, Pte., k., 19/12/14.
Leaf, Christopher, 25003, Pte., k., 14/7/16.
Lee, Daniel Walter 11929, Pte., k., 1/7/16.
Leeming Charles Henry 10054, Pte., k., 8/8/16.
Leeming, James, 23632, Pte., k., 1/7/16.
Leithead, Robert, 9115, Pte., k., 19/12/14.
Lewis, Alfred, 9044, L/Cpl., k., 7/4/16.
Lewis, James, 9477, Pte., k., 13/3/15.
Lewis, Richard John, 8612, Pte., k., 19/12/14.
Liddle, Ralph, 4/7615, Pte., k., 1/6/15.
Lightfoot, Albert, 4/7907, Pte., k., 1/7/16.
Limbert, George, 4/7636, L/Cpl., k., 25/10/16.
Lindsley, Thomas, 7719, Pte., d., 7/9/15.
Livingstone, Andrew, 4/8272, L/Cpl., k., 1/7/16.
Lockwood, William, 28593, Pte., d., 11/10/16.
Lomax, Henry, 8569, L/Sgt., k., 19/12/14.
Lowrey, Michael, 9097, Pte., k., 19/10/15.
Luders, George, 8500, Pte., k., 11/3/15.
Lund, William, 16314, L/Cpl., k., 27/10/16.
Lynch, John David, 3/9038, Pte., k., 24/10/16.
Mackay, William, 17825, Sgt., k., 1/7/16.
Mackwell, Frank, 22122, Pte., d., 2/7/16.
Maclaughlan, John, 7688, Pte., k., 5/2/15.
Manning, Patrick, 3/8832, Pte., d., 21/12/14.
Mansfield, John, 9742, Pte., k., 1/7/16.
Mansfield, Sidney Albert, 9740, Pte., k., 10/3/15.
Marriott, John Albert, 9015, Pte., k., 19/12/14.
Marshall, Leonard, 21232, Pte., k., 24/4/16.

Martin, Thomas, 9889, Pte., k., 19/12/14.
Mason, Albert, 11673, Pte., k., 1/7/16.
Mason, Christopher, 4/8270, Pte., d., 23/11/15.
Mather, Edward, 9601, Sgt., k., 11/11/16.
May, Alfred 4/8220, L/Cpl., k., 1/7/16.
Mead, Thomas, 4/8446, L/Cpl., k., 21/10/15.
Megginson, Harold, 23550, Pte., k., 1/7/16.
Mehrten, William Henry, 9789, Pte., d., 29/12/14.
Mercer, John Herbert, 31990, Pte., d., 9/11/16.
Miller, Arthur James, 9405, L/Cpl., k., 10/3/15.
Milner, James, 8482, Cpl., k., 19/12/14.
Milner, Matthew, 28932, Pte., d., 23/10/16.
Mincher, John, 45420, Pte., d.h., 19/9/16, formerly 3/17848, North Staffs. Regt.
Mitchell, Herbert, 24474, Pte., k., 1/7/16.
Moffett, Arthur, 3/8591, Pte., k., 10/3/15.
Morgan, Llewellyn, 10124, Pte., k., 10/11/16.
Morley, Clifford, 3/8456, Pte., k., 1/7/16.
Morrell, Fred, 24355, Pte., d., 7/7/16.
Morrell, John, 8373, Pte., k., 28/10/16.
Morton, Edward, 4/8572, Pte., d., 11/11/15.
Morton, John, 22472, Pte., k., 1/7/16.
Morton, Lawrence, 8722, Sgt., k., 27/6/16.
Murphy, James, 5133, Pte., d., 12/3/15.
Murray, James, 9114, Pte., k., 10/3/15.
McBarron, John, 3/8920, Pte., k., 6/4/15.
McCall, Peter, 10714, Pte., d., 22/7/15.
McCammon, George, 8979, Pte., d., 12/3/15.
McCarthy, Patrick, 4/8089, Pte., d., 2/7/16.
McDonagh, Patrick, 22262, Pte., d., 16/8/16.
McGowan, John, 7212, L/Cpl., d., 16/5/15.
MacGregor, George, 8721, Sgt., k., 19/12/14.
McCrae, Robert, 3/9607, Pte., k., 1/7/16.
Nacey, James Joseph, 7465, L/Cpl., k., 19/12/14.
Naylor, Abraham, 29538, Pte., d., 28/10/16.
Newby, Joseph, 19415, Pte., k., 1/7/16.
Newton, Albert, 32185, Pte., k., 26/10/16.
Nicholson, William, 9676, Pte., k., 15/12/14.
Norton, Clifford Vincent, 23643, Pte., k., 1/7/16.
Nottingham, Benjamin, 3/10359, Pte., k., 1/7/16.
Nye, Alexander, 12196, Pte., k., 14/6/15.
O'Brian, Joseph, 17149, Pte., k., 11/9/16.
O'Rourke, Christopher, 9525, Pte., k., 19/12/14.
Outhwaite, Joseph, 10303, Pte., d. at sea, 17/3/15.
Oxley, Thomas William, 19111, Pte., k., 1/7/16.
Parr, Richard, 8619, Pte., k., 25/1/15.
Parrott, John Robert, 4/7519, Pte., d., 13/9/16.
Parry, William, 10723, Pte., k., 13/6/15.
Paterson, James, 10294, Pte., k., 1/7/16.
Pattison, John, 9301, Pte., k., 1/4/15.
Pearson, Edwin, 17272, Pte., k., 25/8/15.
Peel, Thomas, 3/8328, Pte., k., 11/3/15.
Perrin, Henry George Edwin, 8330, Sgt., k., 10/3/15.
Pickering, Harold, 23549, Pte., k., 1/7/16.
Pitcher, Percival James, 32606, Pte., d., 22/10/16.
Pitts, Albert, 3/8563, Pte., k., 19/12/14.
Plummer, William, 3/9608, Pte., k., 12/3/15.
Poole, John, 3/8625, Pte., k., 19/12/14.
Pope, Joseph Arthur, 8590, Pte., k., 10/3/15.
Powell, Charles, 3/9403, Pte., k., 31/12/14.
Power, Francis, 5257, Pte., d., 10/3/15.
Prest, Edgar, 4/8246, Pte., k., 24/7/16.
Priestley, Harry Jeffrey, 28800, Pte., k., 28/10/16.
Proctor, Albert, 24452, Pte., k., 1/7/16.
Proctor, Herbert, 29098, Pte., k., 28/10/16.
Pryce, George, 4/7286, Pte., k., 1/7/16.

Pugh, Edwin, 4/8381, Pte., d., 14/12/16.
Quinn, James, 3/8764, Pte., d.h., 30/3/15.
Quinn, Thomas, 10227, Pte., k., 19/12/14.
Quinn, Thomas Henry, 3/10332, Pte., d., 31/1/15.
Race, Ernest, 29151, Pte., k., 25/10/16.
Ragsdale, George, 8671, Pte., k., 19/12/14.
Rainey, John Clifford, 25166, L/Cpl., d., 6/9/16.
Rawson, James Symes, 10229, Pte., k., 12/3/15.
Rayner, Edward John, 9198, Pte., k., 12/3/15.
Reavey, James, 3/8706, Pte., d., 15/6/15.
Redding, Edwin, 4/8016, Pte., k., 1/7/16.
Redmond, William, 8245, Pte., d.h., 3/2/16.
Reed, Charles, 8242, L/Cpl., k., 1/7/16.
Regan, Charles, 4/7661. Pte., k., 1/7/16.
Reid, Squire, 22283, Pte., k., 12/8/16.
Retford, Albert, 8782, Pte., k., 1/7/16.
Revell, Albert, 4/7691, L/Cpl., k., 22/4/15.
Reynolds, Charles, 25214, Pte., d., 9/8/16.
Richardson, Ernest, 24465, L/Cpl., k., 1/7/16.
Richardson, Frederick William, 3/10173, Pte., k., 10/3/15.
Richardson, Herbert, 24434, Pte., k., 1/7/16.
Richmond, William, 9538, Pte., d., 19/12/14.
Roberts, James, 9153, Pte., d., 18/8/16.
Roberts, Robert, 10145, Pte., d., 2/7/16.
Roberts, William Andrew, 9078, Pte., d.h., 12/2/16.
Robinson, Albert Gilbert, 10342, Pte., d., 16/1/15.
Robinson, Joseph Alfred, 29121, Pte., d., 17/11/16.
Rodgers, Charles, 7533, Sgt., d.h., 26/5/15.
Rook, Ernest William, 8771, Pte., d., 11/7/16.
Roseman, Myer, 9269, Pte., k., 12/3/15.
Roundhill, John, 10105, Pte., d., 26/3/15.
Rourke, Francis, 8229, L/Cpl. k., 10/10/16.
Rowan, Michael, 8660, L/Cpl. k., 25/10/16.
Rowe, John Edward, 4/8248, Pte., d., 6/7/16.
Ruffle, Benjamin, 9041, Sgt., k., 19/12/14.
Sanderson, Thomas, 16352, Pte., k., 4/11/15.
Sansom, George, 3/8846, Pte., k., 18/3/15.
Saunders, Arthur William, 9211, Pte., d., 4/5/16.
Schofield, Harold, 4/7620, Pte., k., 13/8/15.
Scott, Alfred, 19439, Pte., k., 24/10/16.
Scott, Herbert, 12002, Pte., k., 2/11/16.
Scott, John William, 4/8548, Pte., k., 25/10/16.
Scott, William, 10077, Pte., d., 12/3/15.
Scrace, John, 9713, Cpl., k., 12/11/16.
Seaman, Arthur, 4/7539, Pte., d., 9/4/16.
Seddon, Fred, 25160, Pte., d.h., 23/7/16.
Sharood, Frederick, 8337, L/Cpl., k., 11/3/15.
Shelton, Ernest, 3/9747, Pte., k., 6/2/15.
Shepherd, George, 3/10025, Pte., k., 19/11/14.
Shippen, Tom, 8572, L/Cpl., d., 20/12/14.
Shipton, Harry, 9834, Drmr., d., 22/8/16.
Shortell, Ernest, 4/7722, Pte., k., 1/7/16.
Simpkin, Raymond Alick Risley, 9162, A/Sgt., d., 5/5/16.
Skeet, Leonard, 9166, Cpl., k., 1/7/16.
Slater, Joseph, 4/7961, L/Cpl., k., 1/7/16.
Smallwood, Alfred, 12836, L/Cpl., k., 1/7/16.
Smith, Albert, 9638, Pte., k., 19/12/14.
Smith, Harold Arthur, 9357, L/Cpl., k., 19/11/14.
Smith, John, 4/7499, Pte., k., 1/7/16.
Smith, John, 9385, L/Cpl., k., 28/10/16.
Smith, John, 11504, Pte., k., 26/10/16.
Smith, Thomas, 4/8035, Pte., k., 10/3/15.
Smith, William Joe, 17137, L/Cpl., k., 1/7/16.
Smithson, Charles, 22250, Pte., k., 18/2/16.
Smithson, Joe, 21428, Pte., k., 14/5/16.
Southall, George, 3/9419, Pte., k., 1/7/16.

Southwood, Sidney, 7209, Pte., d., 12/3/15.
Speight, John, 25536, Pte., k., 11/10/16.
Spence, Edward, 11668, Pte., k., 1/7/16.
Spence, George, 3/9955, Pte., k., 3/10/15.
Spencer, Edwin Bernard, 9862, Pte., k., 19/12/14.
Springham, John William, 10012, L/Cpl., k., 25/10/16.
Sprod, Alfred Bray, 8709, Pte., k., 11/3/15.
Stamp, William Norman, 40058, Pte., d., 10/10/16.
Standing, Greenwood James, 28427, Pte., k., 26/10/16.
Standish, Charles, 4/8636, Pte., d., 16/9/16.
Steeden, John, 8781, Pte., k., 10/3/15.
Stephenson, Tom, 8827, Pte., d., 14/3/16.
Steven, Thomas, 8458, L/Cpl., k., 11/8/15.
Stevens, George Henry, 8539, Pte., k., 11/3/15.
Storey, William, 8290, Pte., k., 10/7/15.
Sunderland, Alfred, 5597, L/Cpl., k., 1/2/15.
Sykes, Willie, 32194, Pte., k., 26/10/16.
Tadwell, Alfred, 5954, Pte., k., 1/7/16.
Taylor, George, 4/8206, Pte., k., 1/7/16.
Taylor, Herbert, 3/9677, Pte., k., 25/9/15.
Taylor, James, 7919, Pte., k., 6/4/16.
Taylor, Nelson, 9838, Pte., d., 19/12/14.
Taylor, Robert Heslop, 40083, Pte., d., 28/10/16.
Teal, Joseph Thomas, 9559, Pte., k., 18/12/14.
Tennyson, Richard Alfred, 9512, Pte., k., 28/6/16.
Thackray, Thomas, 28901, Pte., k., 28/10/16.
Thackwray, Joseph, 9369, L/Cpl., k., 1/7/16.
Thompson, Frank, 21112, Pte., k., 23/10/16.
Thompson, George, 4/8247, Pte., d., 23/5/15.
Thompson, James, 29082, Pte., k., 24/10/16.
Thompson, Joseph, 12131, Pte., k., 23/5/15.
Thompson, William Bentley, 28106, Pte., k., 26/10/16.
Thorley, Thomas William, 8636, Pte., d., 26/4/16.
Thorpe, Thomas William, 23774, Pte., k., 1/7/16.
Todd, Albert, 31850, Pte., k., 26/10/16.
Tomlinson, James, 3/9968, Pte., d., 11/3/15.
Townsley, Robert, 4/8292, Pte., d., 13/7/16.
Toyne, Alfred, 32144, Pte., k., 25/10/16.
Turner, Martin, 4/8465, Pte., k., 25/9/15.
Turner, Sam, 4/7417, Pte., d., 3/7/16.
Umpleby, Charles Kenyon, 11516, Pte., d., 2/7/16.
Umpleby, William, 3/9227, L/Cpl., k., 23/10/16.
Upton, Alfred, 23624, Pte., k., 19/7/16.
Varley, William, 8858, Cpl., k., 1/7/16.
Verity, Alfred, 24362, Pte., k., 28/10/16.
Vickers, Ernest, 8174, L/Cpl., k., 19/12/14.
Wade, Harry, 24461, Pte., d., 12/9/16.
Wake, Vincent, 23616, Pte., d.h., 12/8/16.
Walker, Alfred, 4/8429, Pte., k., 25/10/16.
Walker, Herbert, 23766, Pte., k., 26/10/16.
Walker, Moses, 8793, Pte., k., 14/7/16.
Wallace, John Patrick, 9250, Pte., k., 18/8/16.
Waller, Ralph, 9510, Drmr., d., 22/11/14.
Walsh, Edward, 4/7643, Pte., d., 18/8/16.
Ward, John, 8891, L/Cpl., k., 10/3/15.
Ward, Samuel, 32000, Pte., k., 25/10/16.
Watson, Cornelius Herbert, 19799, Pte., k., 1/7/16.
Watson, Harold, 4/8276, L/Cpl., k., 24/10/16.
Watson, Henry, 3/10295, Pte., k., 12/9/16.
Watson, John William, 15179, Pte., k., 6/4/15.
Webster, John William, 24014, Pte., k., 1/7/16.
Weldon, Ernest, 3/10340, Pte., d.h., 27/3/15.
West, Arthur, 8861, Pte., d.h., 26/5/16.

The Prince of Wales's Own (West Yorks. Regt.)—Casualties

Westerman, Tom, 8886, Pte., k., 1/7/16.
Wheelhouse, Thomas William, 9492, Pte., k., 10/3/15.
Whelan, Bartly, 8986, L/Cpl., k., 11/5/15.
Whitaker, Ernest, 10177, L/Cpl., k., 1/7/16.
White, Frederick William, 8447, Pte., k., 24/7/16.
White, George, 8644, Pte., k., 10/3/15.
White, Joe, 24000, Pte., k., 1/7/16.
White, John, 9879, Pte., k., 26/10/16.
Whiteley, John Appleby, 9920, Pte., k., 22/4/15.
Whitfield, Bateson, 10905, Pte., k., 6/6/16.
Whiting, Joseph, 15500, Pte., k., 13/3/16.
Widdas, George, 21352, Pte., d., 10/6/16.
Wigglesworth, Fred, 22195, Pte., d., 6/7/16.
Wilkins, William Frederick, 9302, Pte., k., 19/12/14.
Wilkinson, Ernest, 28999, Pte., d., 27/10/16. formerly 6/11093, East Yorks. Regt.
Willis, David, 3/8177, Pte., k., 1/7/16.
Wilson, Emmanuel, 3/8804, Pte., k., 11/3/15.
Wilson, Harry, 8576, Pte., k., 10/3/15.
Wilson, James, 3/7703, Pte., k., 26/10/16.

Wiltshire, Albert Edward, 5897, Cpl., k., 28/10/16.
Winteringham, Richard Henry, 4/7836, Pte., k., 12/8/16.
Wolstenholme, William, 19044, L/Cpl., k., 19/6/16.
Wood, George, 9689, Pte., k., 19/12/14.
Wood, Hollings, 3/9392, Pte., d.h., 29/3/15.
Wood, James Roland, 12259, Pte., d., 19/5/15.
Wood, John William, 3/9974, Pte., d., 7/6/16.
Woodhead, George, 8437, Pte., k., 5/2/15.
Woodhead, Richard, 10084, Pte., k., 25/1/15.
Wortley, Edward, 8540, Drmr., d., 14/11/14.
Wrather, Ernest Lawrence, 8746, Pte., k., 23/2/15.
Wrigglesworth, James, 4/8137, Pte., k., 26/10/16.
Wright, Harry, 24476, Pte., k., 1/7/16.
Wright, Isaac, 8835, Pte., k., 1/3/15.
Wrigley, Thomas, 15581, Pte., k., 25/4/16.
Young, Harry, 3/9357, Pte., k., 1/12/14.
Young, Thomas, 8060, Pte., k., 12/12/14.

2nd HOME SERVICE BATTALION

Appleby, Joseph, 30820, Pte., d.h., 2/12/16. formerly 6798, South Staffs Regt.
Bruce, James, 4/8466, Pte., d.h., 1/9/16.

Heale, Ernest, 31016, Pte., d.h., 9/6/16, formerly 11958, West Riding Regt.
Wade, Daniel, 31117, A/Sgt., d.h., 30/10/16, formerly 10588, North Staffs Regt.

3rd BATTALION

Almond, Henry, 3/9845, Pte., d.h., 8/6/15.
Birch, Ernest, 26495, Pte., d.h., 19/5/16.
Bishop, George, 23566, Pte., d.h., 26/12/15.
Bower, William Harbron, 19354, Pte., drowned (accidentally), h., 16/6/15.
Burnd, John William, 3/8853, Pte., d.h., 29/8/14.
Clark, Osmond, 33342, Pte., d.h., 1/7/16.
Cobb, William, 19207, Pte., d.h., 30/6/15.
Donohue, William, 3/8159, Pte., k., 15/1/15.
Fowler, Albert, 26724, Pte., d.h., 7/4/16.
Frost, James Henry, 8835, C.Q.M.S., d.h., 6/5/16.
Hartley, Herbert, 3/9774, Pte., d.h., 8/10/14.
Hewitt, Bartholomew, 3/9073, Pte., d.h., 4/9/15.
Howes, Frederick William, 20224, Pte., d.h., 2/7/16.

Keith, John, 17086, Pte., d.h., 30/12/14.
Lacey, Charles, 21094, Pte., d.h., 25/4/16.
Lock, William Arthur, 32826, Pte., d.h., 21/11/16.
Naylor, Edward, 32349, Pte., d.h., 29/11/16.
Nightingale, Joseph, 3/10348, Pte., d.h., 17/12/14.
Oakes, Frank, 26335, Pte., d.h., 17/3/16.
Pickles, Arthur, 7468, A/Sgt., d.h., 14/5/15.
Ruston, John, 2577, Pte., d.h., 7/1/16.
Shepherd, George Edward, 22175, Pte., d.h., 24/11/15.
Smith, Arthur, 16365, Pte., d.h., 28/7/16.
Summers, John, 6725, Pte., d.h., 2/11/14.
Waite, William, 19262, A/Cpl., d.h., 16/5/15.
Walker, Fred, 5417, A/C.Q.M.S., d.h., 7/12/15.
Watson, Thomas, 3/8165, Pte., d.h., 26/10/14.

4th BATTALION

Bramley, George, 7287, Sgt., d.h., 13/9/15.
Budd, John, 4/8517, Pte., d.h., 25/1/15.
Ellis, George Henry, 34389, Pte., d.h., 10/12/16.
Fenton, John Robert, 27871, Pte., d.h., 19/12/16.
Gee, Samuel Thomas, 11488, L/Cpl., d.h., 20/8/15.
Hall, Herbert, 4/8362, Pte., k. (accident) h., 27/2/15.
Hertel, Stanley, 3/10326, Pte., d.h., 20/11/14.
Leatham, George William, 25656, Pte., d.h., 5/5/16.

Mullen, William Robert Mackie, 19681, Pte., d.h., 16/1/16.
Mulligan, James, 27876, Pte., d.h., 20/7/16.
Newstead, Thomas, 34418, Pte., d.h., 23/8/16.
North, Arthur, 19733, Pte., d.h., 2/6/16.
Penrose, William Henry, 4/8428, Cpl., d.h., 5/5/15.
Thornhill, Arthur William, 25650, Pte., d.h., 16/3/16.
Wells, Bertie, 4/8063, Pte., d.h., 12/3/15.
Yarborough, Thomas William, 37173, Pte., d.h., 17/12/16.

5th RESERVE BATTALION

Kelly, Michael, 8091, Pte., d.h., 28/12/16.

Mackley, William, 2069, Pte., d.h., 31/3/16.

1/5th BATTALION

Abrams, Ernest, 1159, Pte., k., 5/9/15.
Anderson, Robert William, 1846, C.S.M., d., 17/10/16.
Anderson, Thomas Henry, 5914, Pte., k., 28/9/16, formerly 255, Northumbrian Cyclist Corps.
Andrews, John Martin, 5903, L/Cpl., k., 28/9/16, formerly 133, Northumbrian Cyclist Corps.
Armitage, Frank, 202992, Pte., k., 28/9/16, formerly 14/366, York & Lancaster Regt.
Atkinson, James, 288, Sgt., k., 18/11/15.
Baines, Benjamin, 2123, Pte., d., 27/12/15.
Baker, Edward Arthur, 2301, Cpl., k., 5/8/15.
Bamford, John, 203144, Pte., k., 28/9/16, formerly 12653, West Riding Regt.
Barber, Henry, 2167, L/Cpl., d., 4/9/16.
Barker, Edward, 201509, Pte., k., 3/9/16.
Barnes, Fred, 22684, Pte., k., 28/7/16, formerly 1219, York & Lancs. Regt.
Barrett, Robert, 2253, A/Cpl., k., 28/8/16.
Barron, James William, 1198, L/Cpl., k., 3/9/16.
Batters, Sydney Harold, 1099, L/Sgt., k., 9/5/15.
Bean, Fred, 2359, Pte., d., 31/7/15.
Bedell, Ernest Luford, 372, Cpl., d., 18/12/15.
Bennett, H., 202226, Pte., k., 3/9/16.
Bentley, Wilfred, 5625, Pte., d., 29/9/16, formerly 48, Northumbrian Cycle Corps.
Bickerdike, George, 5053, Pte., k., 28/9/16.
Bishop, Charles, 2576, Pte., k., 13/7/15.
Boldison, Arthur, 540, L/Sgt., k., 14/7/16, M.M.
Bonnett, Harry, 4770, Pte., k., 3/9/16.
Boothman, Albert, 19520, Pte., k., 15/7/16.
Boothman, William, 3880, Pte., k., 28/9/16.
Borrows, John Robert, 203632, Pte., k., 1/7/16, formerly 12214, Yorks Regt.
Bracewell, Leonard Luke, 1467, Drmr., k., 29/12/15.
Bradley, George Albert, 4900, Pte., k., 3/9/16.
Bradley, Horace Ferdinand Banton, 456, Pte., k., 21/7/15.
Bradley, Sidney, 22780, Pte., d., 5/7/16 formerly 15255, West Riding Regt.
Braithwaite, James Ellis, 4697, Pte., d., 4/10/16.
Broadbent, Hugh, 1769, Pte., k., 14/11/15.
Broader, Robert Kirk, 3267, Pte., k., 15/7/16.
Brown, Bernard, 5829, Pte., k., 27/9/16 formerly 4749, West Riding Regt.
Brown, Ernest, 3939, Pte., k., 28/8/16.
Brown, John, 2187, Pte., k., 10/7/15.
Buckborrough, Edwin, 2565, Pte., d., 20/12/15.
Buckle, Leonard, 2819, L/Cpl., k., 3/9/16.
Buckle, Thomas Henry, 2109, Pte., d.h., 6/12/15.
Buller, William, 21870, Pte., k., 15/7/16.
Bullock, Herbert, 203635, Pte., k., 1/7/16.
Cahill, James, 2608, Pte., k., 19/12/15.
Cahill, Joseph, 1066, Pte., k., 18/6/16.
Calpin, James, 201510, Pte., k., 28/9/16.
Calvert, Herbert, 2701, Pte., k., 2/8/15.
Carney, Thomas, 6428, Pte., d., 5/9/16, formerly 13866, West Riding Regt.
Carrack, Herbert, 200078, Pte., k., 28/9/16.
Carslake, George, 20110, Pte., k., 15/7/16, formerly 13664, 12th Res. Cav. Regt.
Carter, Joseph, 202976, Pte., k., 28/9/16.
Cartmel, George Mounsey, 2170, Pte., k., 24/12/15.
Carver, Robert William, 203623, Pte., k., 3/7/16.
Castle, John George, 2375, Pte., k., 21/7/15.
Chapelow, Charles Henry, 23052, Pte., k., 9/7/16, formerly 9/14107, East Yorks Regt.
Clark, Alfred, 2687, Pte., d., 27/1/16.
Clark, Henry, 27227, Pte., k., 15/7/16, formerly 13/1361, East Yorks Regt.
Coleman, Thomas, 2290, Pte., d., 22/6/15.
Connell, Gilbert, 2387, Pte., k., 21/7/15.
Cousins, Robert, 1821, Pte., d., 20/12/15.
Crofts, Alfred, 3860, Pte., k., 20/7/16.
Crow, Herbert Sidney, 202236, Pte., k., 3/9/16.
Crowe, Gilbert Baldwin, 1693, Pte., k., 3/9/16.
Crust, William, 2143, L/Cpl., k., 3/9/16.
Currell, James Richard, 2588, Pte., d., 10/7/16, M.M.
Cussins, Cecil, 3557, Pte., k., 20/7/16.
Cutler, Joseph, 23112, Pte., k., 9/7/16.
Dalby, Alfred, 2987, Pte., k., 20/2/16.
Daniel, Robert, 1850, Pte., k., 19/12/15.
Davies, Edward, 202294, Pte., k., 3/9/16.
Dawes, Frederick, 1310, Pte., d., 15/7/16.
Dawson, Fred, 5584, A/L/Cpl., k., 28/9/16.
Dawson, Walter, 2235, Pte., d., 20/12/15.
Day, Arnold Ellis, 2088, L/Cpl., k., 13/7/15.
Deans, Harold, 2127, Pte., k., 5/8/15.
DeMersy, Daniel, 201553, Pte., k., 3/9/16.
Dixon, Edward, 202856, Pte., k., 28/9/16.
Dormand, Alfred, 5909, L/Cpl., d., 28/9/16, formerly 291, Northumbrian Div. Cyclist Corps.
Drury, James, 1374, Pte., k., 15/11/15.
Dunn, Frank, 2423, Pte., k., 3/9/16.
Elsworth, George, 1986, Cpl., d., 20/6/15
Elsworth, Samuel, 202306, Pte., k., 3/9/16.
Exelby, George Harry, 2236, Pte., k., 19/5/15.
Exelby, John Henry, 1204, C.S.M., k., 1/10/16.
Fairburn, Wilfred, 5503, Pte., k., 15/7/16, formerly 9098, West Riding Regt.
Farmery, Frederick Ernest, 3237, Pte., d., 15/10/16.
Fenton, John William, 3194, Pte., k., 3/9/16
Ferguson, William, 1870, Cpl., d., 7/1/16.
Field, Harold, 1306, Pte., d., 27/5/15.
Flint, James, 202166, Pte., k., 3/9/16.
Foster, Arthur, 202221, Pte., k., 3/9/16.
Fox, Walter, 200976, Pte., k., 28/9/16.
Francis, Thomas, 7808, Pte., k., 3/7/16, formerly 3/14642, West Riding Regt.
Fraser, John Tindall, 2164, Pte., k., 20/7/15.
Fryer, Smith, 2200, Pte., d.h., 7/4/15.
Gibson, Ronald, 3814, Pte., k., 15/8/16.
Gomersall, Ernest Herbert, 2190, Pte., d., 1/1/16.
Goodwin, Eric Benjamin, 202259, Pte., k., 3/9/16.
Gouch, Norman, 5970, Pte., k., 28/9/16 formerly 5660, Northumbrian Cycle Corps.
Graham, Nathan, 202524, Pte., 16/8/16.
Graves, Charles Robert, 4647, Pte., k., 3/9/16.
Gray, Richard, 6441, Pte., k., 28/9/16.
Gubbings, Alfred Ernest, 6507, L/Cpl., k., 3/9/16.
Haigh, Ernest, 1411, Pte., d.h., 11/10/16.
Haley, William Austin, 2194, Pte., k., 11/7/15.
Hall, Arthur Herbert, 3316, Pte., k., 3/9/16.
Haney, John, 6509, Cpl., d., 28/9/16.
Hardwick, Frank, 1812, Pte., d., 27/9/15.
Harrison, Ernest, 2754, Pte., k., 26/5/15.
Harrison, Frederick, 202798, L/Cpl., k., 28/9/16.
Harrison, William, 1283, Sgt., k., 29/9/16.
Harvey, Edward, 6450, Pte., d., 4/12/16, formerly 21642, 14th Res. Cav. Regt.

The Prince of Wales's Own (West Yorks. Regt.)—Casualties 321

Heavisides, John, 1723, Pte., k., 19/12/15.
Henderson, Francis John, 2296, Pte., k., 2/7/16.
Heslop, Henry, 5511, Pte., k., 2/7/16, formerly 15961, East Yorks Regt.
Hesselden, Arthur, 5845, Pte., k., 27/9/16, formerly 5079, West Riding Regt.
Hewson, Frank, 202341, Pte., k., 3/9/16.
Hick, George, 2507, Pte., d., 3/8/16.
Hingley, Frank, 5978, Pte., k., 26/11/16, formerly 154, Northumbrian Cycle Corps.
Holden, Samuel, 202220, Pte., k., 28/9/16.
Holgate, Edward, 202574, Pte., k., 1/7/16.
Holland, Leonard, 2523, Pte., d., 21/12/15.
Holmes, Harry Beetham, 200603, Cpl., k., 28/9/16.
Holmes, John, 2336, Pte., k., 29/12/15.
Holmes, John Henry, 3871, Pte., k., 9/8/16.
Holmes, Sydney Roy, 2181, Pte., d., 15/8/16.
Homer, John Wilfred, 202807, Pte., k., 28/9/16, formerly 4776, Durham L.I.
Hopkins, Arthur, 202334, Pte., k., 3/9/16.
Horsfield, Harold, 1356, Pte., k., 23/2/16.
Howard, Percy, 3895, Pte., k., 3/9/16.
Hudson, Arthur, 1288, Pte., d., 11/9/16.
Inman, Charles, 1476, Pte., k., 3/9/16.
Iredale, Edward Elisha, 1588, C.S.M., k., 29/8/16, M.M.
Jackson, Michael, 6508, L/Cpl., k., 3/9/16.
Jennings, William, 2665, Pte., k., 25/7/15.
Johnson, Arnell, 2757, Pte., k., 26/5/15.
Johnson, Gilbert, 1700, Pte., k., 28/9/15.
Johnson, William, 1630, Pte., k., 27/9/16.
Jordan, Reuben Frederick, 5527, Pte., k., 20/7/16.
Kelly, Fred, 2012, L/Cpl., d., 15/7/15.
Kendall, Charles James Lucas, 2365, Pte., d., 25/9/16.
Kilvington, Charles E., 2729, Pte., k., 19/12/15.
Kitson, Frank Percy, 2288, Pte., k., 2/8/15.
Knowles, John Henry, 2313, Pte., d., 23/11/15.
Large, George, 200151, Cpl., k., 28/9/16.
Lawson, Allan, 4924, Pte., k., 3/9/16.
Lea, Walter, 988, L/Cpl., k., 11/7/15.
Leaning, Fanthorpe, 202332, Pte., k., 3/9/16.
Lee, Fred, 202310, Pte., k., 3/9/16.
Levitt, Harold, 202757, Pte., k., 28/9/16.
Leyland, John Harold, 2590, Pte., d., 20/12/15.
Lickley, Frederick Snowden, 3330, Pte., k., 3/9/16.
Lickley, George Henry, 201371, L/Cpl., k., 1/7/16.
Lickley, James, 2304, Pte., k., 30/5/15.
Liddle, John, 202882, Pte., k., 28/9/16.
Loftus, John, 5496, Pte., k., 10/7/16.
Long, Edward, 2388, Pte., d., 13/8/15.
Long, Fred, 1290, Pte., k., 23/6/15.
Lowe, Edward, 202231, Pte., k., 3/9/16.
Lucas, Walter, 202229, Pte., k., 3/9/16.
Lund, Gordon, 200435, C.S.M., k., 1/7/16, D.C.M.
Lund, Henry Walker, 2480, Pte., k., 11/7/16.
Lupton, Selwyn, 1380, Pte., d.h., 10/1/16.
Macey, George, 1517, Drmr., k., 11/7/15, formerly 1549, Yorks Regt.
Mackridge, George Ishmael, 2461, Pte., k., 20/7/16.
Malthouse, Walter, 1363, Pte., k., 9/5/15.
Marshall, Ronald, 2094, L/Cpl., k., 20/12/15.
Mason, James, 202227, Pte., k., 3/9/16.
Mason, Percy, 2435, Pte., k., 19/12/15.
Melvin, John, 5515, Pte., k., 2/7/16.
Miller, Herbert, 6380, Pte., k., 3/9/16.
Millins, John Thomas, 201624, Pte., k., 28/9/16.
Milner, James William, 677, Drmr., k., 21/5/15.
Mitchell, John, 1436, Pte., d., 3/7/16.

Mosley, Thomas, 5542, L/Cpl., k., 15/7/16.
Moxon, Victor, 5539, Pte., d., 10/8/16.
Moyser, Hubert Henry, 2320, Pte., k., 20/2/16.
Mumford, William, 1562, Pte., k., 13/10/15.
Munday, Herbert, 2332, Pte., k., 20/2/16.
McGregor, Donald, 203099, Pte., k., 29/9/16.
McNichol, Daniel, 1572, Pte., d., 18/11/15.
McTierman, James, 2926, Pte., k., 21/11/15.
Naylor, Arthur, 4011, Pte., k., 7/8/16.
Newton, Thomas, 5487, Pte., d., 5/9/16, formerly 20582, K.O.Y.L.I.
Oliver, John Thomas, 3537, Pte., k., 28/9/16.
Parker, Henry, 2338, Pte., k., 21/7/15.
Peacock, Alec, 3259, Pte., d., 15/6/16.
Peacock, Francis William, 1477, Pte., k., 7/9/15.
Pearson, Dick, 202321, Pte., k., 3/9/16.
Peet, George, 4621, Pte., d., 22/7/16.
Pennington, Frank, 1125, L/Cpl., d., 6/8/15.
Penrose, Samuel, 1218, Pte., k., 20/12/15.
Pheasey, Ernest, 2340, Pte., d., 17/8/15.
Pickard, Victor, 2780, Pte., k., 3/9/16.
Pickles, Joseph, 1304, Sgt., k., 1/7/16.
Pickles, Joseph Leonard, 202769, Pte., k., 28/9/16, formerly 5862, West Riding Regt.
Pink, George, 1573, Pte., d., 22/12/15.
Pounder, Alfred William, 1707, L/Cpl., d. 27/12/15.
Pounder, George, 2205, Cpl., d., 4/10/16.
Pryor, Harold, 3930, Pte., k., 17/7/16.
Pybus, William Hutchinson, 1785, Pte., d. 19/12/15.
Ramsden, James Frederick, 5536, Pte., d., 23/7/16, formerly 13899, West Riding Regt.
Ramsey, Edward, 2431, Pte., k., 18/6/15.
Rands, Charles, 202228, Pte., k., 3/9/16.
Raw, George, 1154, L/Cpl., k., 11/10/15.
Rennie, Wallace Stanley, 1777, L/Cpl., k., 15/7/16.
Richardson, Norman, 2930, Pte., d., 16/9/16.
Robinson, Edward Alexander, 2415, Pte., k., 3/9/16.
Robinson, Ernest, 6471, Pte., k., 28/9/16.
Robinson, James, 2458, Pte., k., 29/9/16.
Robinson, John Cheer, 1797, Pte., k., 1/2/16.
Robinson, Richard, 2330, Pte., k., 20/2/16.
Rodgers, Stephen, 1763, Pte., d., 16/7/16.
Royce, Stephen, 2145, Pte., d., 3/9/15.
Rymer, Horace William, 2154, Pte., d., 29/7/16.
Sandbrook, Bertram William, 2095, Pte., k., 8/7/16.
Seal, Albert, 1838, Pte., d., 23/7/15.
Sharp, William, 1598, Pte., d., 21/8/16.
Simpson, Charles, 2335, L/Cpl., k., 28/7/16.
Skinner, George Herbert, 201090, Pte., k., 1/7/16.
Smith, Percy, 3829, Pte., d., 12/7/16.
Smith, William, 1599, L/Cpl., d., 31/10/15.
Spinks, William, 2677, Pte., k., 3/9/16.
Stead, Frank, 2261, Pte., d., 18/8/15.
Street, Arthur, 201572, Pte., k., 3/9/16.
Strudwick, Harry John, 6503, Sgt., k., 28/9/16.
Sunley, James, 3704, Pte., k., 20/7/16.
Swale, Charles Leopold, 202281, Pte., k., 3/9/16.
Swales, Leonard, 3638, Pte., d., 7/8/16.
Tate, Dennis, 2285, Pte., k., 20/2/16.
Taylor, Joseph, 3253, Pte., k., 3/9/16.
Taylor, Samuel, 202780, Pte., k., 27/9/16 formerly 5015, West Riding Regt.
Terry, Frederick, 2503, Sgt., k., 29/9/16.
Thirkell, Alfred, 202555, Pte., k., 1/7/16.
Thompson, George Ransom, 1239, L/Cpl., d. 31/5/15.

Thompson, Thomas William Wright, 202335, Pte., k., 3/9/16.
Thornton, Alfred H., 2693, Pte., k., 11/7/15.
Thornton, William, 202304, Pte., k., 3/9/16.
Tiffney, Edwin, 201031, Pte., k , 27/9/16.
Timmins, George, 1336, Pte., k., 23/7/15.
Townend, Albert, 2403, Pte., d., 1/9/16.
Triffit, Thomas, 2469, Pte., d., 2/7/16.
Tuppen, Alexander David, 1284, Cpl., k. 1/8/15.
Tute, Richard, 1452, Pte., k., 20/12/15.
Wailes, Gilbert, 5877, Pte., d.h., 8/10/16 formerly 4978,, West Riding Regt.
Waine, John Robert, 1662, Pte., k., 10/5/15.
Waite, Wilson, 5540, L/Cpl., k., 1/7/16.
Walker, Alan, 2252, Cpl., k., 28/9/16.
Walker, Ernest, 1490, Pte., k., 1/7/16.
Walker, Frederick George, 864, Cpl. k., 20/7/15.
Walker, Henry, 1737, Pte., k., 15/7/16.
Walker, Thomas, 2360, Pte., k., 1/7/16.
Watson, Thomas, 2645, Pte., k , 4/9/16.
Weatherhead, Arthur, 200516, L/Cpl., k., 28/9/16.

Webster, Frank, 2141, Pte., d., 11/7/16.
Wells, Charles William, 1842, Pte., k., 28/7/16.
West, Harry, 1611, Pte., k., 26/5/15.
Wetherill, Henry, 2489, L/Cpl., d., 24/9/16.
Wetherill, John, 1854, Pte., k., 11/7/15.
Wharton, Fred, 201454, Pte., k., 1/7/16.
White, James Arthur, 1242, Pte., k., 3/9/16.
Wilde, Arthur Hirst, 2424, Pte., d., 11/5/15.
Wilcock, Henry, 2355, Pte., k., 20/8/15.
Wilmot, Robert, 1330, Pte., k., 19/12/15.
Wilson, Albert, 202292, Pte., k., 3/9/16.
Wilson, George Frederick, 3332, Pte., k., 27/9/16.
Wilson, Richard, 2466, Pte., d., 19/12/15.
Wilson, Robert, 5537, Sgt., k., 15/7/16, formerly 11/279, East Yorks Regt.
Wilson, William Watts, 5892, Pte., k., 28/9/16, formerly 244, Northumbrian Division Cyclist Corps.
Worth, Harold, 3857, Pte., k., 3/9/16.
Wrather, Joseph, 200843, Pte., k., 27/9/16.
Wray, Harold, 2967, Pte., k., 20/9/16.
Yates, Francis Cecil, 2093, Pte., k., 28/9/15.

2/5th BATTALION

Donaldson, John, 3111, Pte., d.h., 9/7/16.

3/5th BATTALION

Southward, Charles, 3492, Pte., d.h., 18/7/16.
Symonds, John 3877, Pte., d.h., 9/3/16.

1/6th BATTALION

Ackroyd, Arthur, 5481, L/Cpl., k., 3/9/16.
Aikman, William, 240797, Pte., k., 1/7/16.
Allan, Harry, 3267, Pte., d., 15/7/15.
Allum, William Gilbert, 2426, L/Cpl., k., 1/7/16.
Alston, Robert R., 3313, Cpl., k., 20/12/15.
Anderton, Tobias Copley, 4156, Pte., k., 20/12/15.
Andrews, Fred, 1874, Pte., d., 7/7/16.
Ankers, Bertram, 7155, Pte., k., 3/9/16.
Arrowsmith, Robert Chandler, 7040, Pte., k., 23/11/16, formerly 30678, Durham L. I.
Ashley, Clarence, 1226, Pte., k., 12/7/16.
Attwood, Jesse, 4677, Pte., k., 7/7/16.
Bailey, Arthur, 2104, Pte., k., 31/5/15.
Bailey, Frank, 4491, Pte., k., 14/8/16.
Bairstow, James, 1934, L/Cpl., k., 9/5/15.
Banks, John William, 1751, Pte., k., 1/7/16.
Bannister, John William, 1126, Pte., k., 3/9/16.
Barber, Walter, 3560, Pte., k., 19/12/15.
Barker, Stephen, 1483, L/Cpl., k., 1/7/16.
Barnett, William, 2789, L/Cpl., k., 3/9/16.
Barraclough, Fred, 241606, Pte., k., 3/9/16.
Barrett, Alfred Cecil, 3398, Pte., k., 24/8/15.
Baxter, Ernest, 2990, Pte., d., 5/9/16.
Baxter, William, 834, Pte., k., 1/7/16.
Beckett, John, 4937, Pte., k., 11/7/16.
Beecroft, Thomas, 4239, Pte., k., 17/2/16.
Bell, Frederick, 241236, Pte., k., 3/9/16.
Birch, Ernest, 4775, Pte., k., 9/8/16.
Bird, John, 1567, Pte., d., 27/10/15.
Blackburn, Percy, 2944, Pte., k., 20/12/15.
Blakey, Frederick, 4481, Pte., k., 20/7/16.
Blaydes, Charles Henry, 3479, Pte., k., 3/11/15.
Bloomer, Arthur Kenneth, 2070, Pte., k., 1/7/16.

Booth, Haydon, 3936, Pte., d., 21/8/15.
Booth, Herbert, 3048, Pte., k., 2/7/16.
Bottomley, Herbert Cecil, 2660, Pte., k., 19/12/15.
Bowers, Stanley, 3475, Pte., d., 2/8/15.
Boyle, Edgar, 526, Pte., d., 5/9/16.
Bracewell, John William, 2585, Pte., k., 10/8/16.
Bradley, Thomas, 1756, Pte., k., 3/9/16, M.M.
Broadley, John Henry, 2733, Cpl., k., 9/8/16.
Brogden, Albert Percy, 240732, Pte., k., 3/9/16.
Brook, Arnold, 3071, Pte., k., 17/2/16.
Brookes, Frank, 240502, Pte., k., 3/9/16.
Brown, Harry, 4265, Pte., k., 13/8/16.
Buckley, Edward, 61, Sgt., k., 21/12/15.
Buckley, Frank, 3441, Pte., k., 1/7/16.
Burd, Albert Harry, 2793, L/Cpl., k., 3/9/16.
Burgess, Harold, 2735, Pte., k., 30/4/15
Burgess, John Henry, 1846, Pte., k., 25/5/15.
Butler, Henry, 240147, Pte., k., 3/9/16.
Cafferty, James, 4524, Pte., d., 10/7/16.
Caine, Frederick, 4405, Pte., k., 1/7/16.
Carr, William Benjamin, 4251, Pte., k., 3/9/16.
Carradice, Ramsey, 743, L/Cpl., k., 1/7/16.
Cawthron, George, 1282, Cpl., d., 19/1/16.
Chaffer, George, 2431, Pte., k., 23/11/15.
Child, John, 4217, Pte., k., 25/7/16.
Clarey, William, 4215, Pte., d., 25/7/16.
Clark, Edward, 1613, Pte., k., 1/7/16.
Clark, Samuel, 241162, Pte., k., 3/9/16.
Clark, Samuel, 241162, Pte., k., 3/9/16.
Claven, John, 4575, Pte., k., 7/7/16.
Clayton, Arthur, 2172, Pte., k., 24/9/15.
Close, Harold, 4734, Pte., k., 3/9/16.
Clough, Herbert, 3396, Pte., k , 9/8/15.
Cohen Arthur Gordon, 2338, Pte., k., 19/12/15

Conder, George William, 2006, L/Cpl., k., 11/10/15.
Cook, Harry, 4286, Pte., k., 20/12/15.
Coope, William, 4499, Pte., d., 7/7/16.
Cousins, Frederick, 6545, Pte., k., 22/10/16.
Cousins, Stanley, 3004, Drmr., d., 2/7/16.
Coyne, Bernard, 4592, Pte., k., 1/7/16.
Crabtree, Ede, 4931, Pte., k., 3/9/16.
Craven, William, 1651, Pte., k., 3/9/16.
Cryer, Harry, 1962, L/Cpl., k., 19/8/15.
Cure, George, 1543, Pte., k., 29/7/15.
Curtis, Asa, 4946, Pte., k., 14/7/16.
Dale, Frank, 2647, Pte., k., 25/7/16.
Dawson, Henry, 1516, C.Q.M.S., d., 3/6/15.
Dennison, Lawrence, 2428, Pte., d., 18/12/15.
Dobson, Stephen, 3804, Pte., d., 5/7/16.
Dooley, Edward Patrick, 2329, Pte., k., 4/8/16.
Duckworth, James, 4427, Pte., d., 4/9/16.
Dunn, Frank, 4546, Pte., k., 9/8/16.
Dunn, Joseph, 2853, Pte., k., 1/7/16.
Dyson, Frederick, 2589, Pte., k., 25/7/16.
Earnshaw, Willie, 3325, Pte., d., 23/9/16.
Easton, James Henry, 3594, Pte., k, 19/12/15.
Edmondson, George, 2532, L/Cpl., k., 1/7/16.
Edmondson, Joseph Bernard, 3221, Pte., k., 1/7/16.
Ellerton, John Willy, 1755, Pte., k., 16/5/15.
Farnish, Leonard, 241648, Pte., k., 3/9/16.
Farrar, Thomas, 3307, Pte., k., 2/7/16
Feather, Ernest, 242181, Pte., k., 3/9/16.
Featherstone, Sidney, 2403, Sgt., k., 3/9/16.
Fell, Thomas, 3508, Pte., k., 1/7/16.
Ferigan, William, 3094, Pte., k., 20/12/15.
Fieldhouse, Robert, 241516, Pte., k., 2/7/16.
Firth, Charles, 3143, Pte., k., 15/6/15.
Firth, Gilbert, 1833, Pte., d., 12/5/15.
Firth, Joel, 1379, Pte., d., 23/3/16.
Forbes, Robert, 2691, L/Cpl., k., 12/7/16.
Foster, Harold, 1744, Cpl., k., 19/11/15.
Frost, Frederick Daniel, 1430, Pte., d., 21/12/15
Fryer, James Mitchell, 240123, L/Cpl., k., 3/9/16.
Fuller, Raistrick, 4047, L/Cpl., k., 14/8/16.
Furniss, George, 2125, Pte., k., 10/6/15.
Gawthorpe, Alfred, 3176, Pte., k., 1/7/16.
Gellert, Edward, 2353, Pte., k., 19/12/15.
Gilbert, Patrick, 2975, Pte., k., 12/11/15.
Gill, Arthur, 4564, Pte., k., 3/9/16.
Gill, John, 1877, Pte., k., 24/9/15.
Gill, Norman, 240067, Sgt., k., 3/9/16.
Goodrick, Stephen, 7312, Pte., d.h., 12/10/16.
Goodwin, Ernest, 1274, Sgt., d., 16/12/15.
Greenwood, Fred Clarkson, 3136, Pte., k., 19/12/15.
Greenwood, Lancelot, 2305, Cpl., k., 14/7/16.
Haigh, Ernest, 4235, Pte., k., 14/8/16.
Haigh, William, 3344, Pte., k., 4/8/16.
Haley, Edmund, 3796, Pte., d., 18/8/16.
Hall, Arthur, 3627, A/Cpl., k., 23/11/16.
Hall, Harry, 4310, Pte., k., 20/12/15.
Hall, William Frederick, 2844, Cpl., k., 26/8/16.
Halliday, Joseph, 3562, Pte , k., 22/10/16.
Hammond, John, 264, Sgt., k., 16/5/15.
Harper, Miles, 242184, Pte., k., 3/9/16.
Hartley, John William, 4715, Pte., k., 26/8/16.
Harvey, Willie, 5611, Pte., k., 3/9/16.
Haste, Walter Bottomley, 4884, Pte., k., 3/9/16.
Hearn, Donald Henry, 1399, Pte., k., 25/7/16.
Helliwell, Alfred, 1752, L/Cpl., k., 14/8/16.
Helliwell, Robert, 1158, L/Cpl., k., 1/7/16.
Hemsley, Arthur, 2584, Cpl., d., 8/9/16.
Higgins, Edward, 1876, Pte., k., 12/7/16.
Holgate, Harry, 2858, Pte., k., 1/7/16.
Holgate, Richard, 1471, Pte., k., 29/8/16.

Holmes, Edgar Stephenson, 3940, Pte., k., 30/8/16.
Holmes, Harry, 4226, Pte., k., 26/9/16.
Holmes, Joseph, 1321, Pte., d., 14/7/15.
Holt, Joseph Alfred, 1727, L/Cpl., k., 31/10/15.
Hopwood, Arthur, 4201, Pte., k., 28/8/16.
Horgan, William, 241841, Pte., k., 3/9/16.
Horne, Fred, 1530, Pte., d., 22/7/16.
Hornsby, Charlie, 4754, Pte., k., 1/7/16.
Horsfield, Harry, 4615, Pte., k., 3/9/16.
Howker, Joseph William, 2618, Pte., k., 10/9/16.
Howlett, Thomas Edward, 185, Cpl., k., 27/9/15.
Hudson, James Henry, 4408, Pte., k., 3/9/16.
Humphreys, Sydney, 3461, Pte., k., 2/10/15.
Humpleby, Thomas, 4252, Pte., d., 13/7/16.
Huntington, George Edward, 7121, Pte., k., 22/10/16, formerly 31590, 3rd Durham L.I.
Hustwick, Percy, 1155, Pte., k., 1/7/16.
Hutchinson, Horace, 4285, Pte , d., 11/7/16.
Ingham, Jack, 3005, Sgt., k., 18/7/16.
Ingleson, Ronald, 1623, Pte., k., 24/9/15.
Imeson, Albert, 4470, Pte., k., 14/8/16.
Jackson, Arthur, 240552, Pte., k., 1/7/16.
Jackson, Vernon, 240182, Pte., k., 3/9/16.
Jagger, Sylvester, 241732, Pte., k., 2/7/16.
Jarvis, Isaac, 3424, Pte., k., 9/10/15.
Jenkins, George, 5523, Pte., k., 3/9/16.
Jennings, William, 98, Cpl., k., 3/6/15.
Johnson, Alfred, 4505, Pte., k., 9/7/16.
Johnson, Edward, 2240, Pte., k., 1/7/16.
Jones, William Henry, 1866, L/Cpl., k., 9/7/16.
Jordon, Frank, 1473, Pte., k., 1/7/16.
Kalaher, Daniel, 2693, Pte., k., 15/7/16.
Kaye, George, 3933, Pte., k., 2/7/16.
Kaye, John, 4182, Pte., k., 9/7/16.
Keighley, Philip, 2469, Pte., d., 24/12/15.
Kenworthy, Fred, 4789, Pte., k., 2/7/16.
Kettlewell, Albert, 1980, Pte., d.h., 20/10/14.
King, James, 2300, Pte., k., 3/9/16.
King, Walter, 4526, Pte., d., 7/8/16.
Knowles, Jarvill, 3948, L/Cpl., k., 1/10/15.
Lambert, Percy, 1672, Pte., k., 7/7/16.
Laycock, Alfred, 2668, L/Cpl., k., 16/8/16.
Laycock, Harry, 1453, Pte., k., 11/8/15.
Lee, Anthony, 2763, Pte., k., 1/7/16.
Lee, Samuel, 2281, L/Cpl., d., 8/9/16.
Lennon, Albert Edward, 2468, Cpl., k., 26/8/16.
Lightowler, Allen, 3323, Pte., d., 14/9/16.
Lister, John, 1429, Pte., k., 11/8/15.
Loftus, Mark, 1700, Pte., k., 13/10/15.
Loftus, Mark, 1700, Pte., k., 13/10/15.
Longstaff, Fred, 4940, Pte., k., 21/7/16.
Lord, Alfred Clifford, 2384, Pte., d., 21/10/15.
Lord, Richard, 1697, Pte., k., 16/5/15.
Mansfield, Will, 51296, Pte., k., 11/10/15, formerly G/29549, Royal Fusiliers.
Margerison, Albert, 2437, Pte., d., 17/7/15.
Margetts, John T. C., 2220, Pte., d., 14/12/15.
Martin, John, 4654, Pte., k., 14/7/16.
Matthewman, Charles, 2297, Pte., k, 15/7/16.
Matthewman, Frank, 1277, Cpl., k., 21/7/16.
Mawson, Samuel, 5506, Pte., k., 15/8/16.
Metcalfe, Joseph William, 2969, Pte., k., 22/5/15.
Midgley, Walter, 1171, Drmr., k., 19/11/15.
Milnes, Frederick Charles, 2408, Pte., d., 17/11/15.
Mitchell, Joseph, 2573, Pte., d., 4/9/16.
Modley, Samuel, 3736, Pte., k., 12/7/16.
Moore, Avon, 1630, Pte., k., 1/7/16.
Moore, Norman, 2480, Pte., k., 17/11/15.
Moore, Percy, 7292, Pte., d., 8/11/16.
Moran, Francis, 1614, Pte., k., 28/8/16.
Morgan, Fred, 5077, Pte., d., 15/7/16.

Morland, Matthew, 242754, Pte., k., 3/9/16, formerly 28412, Durham L.I.
Morton, John William, 4409, Pte., k., 3/9/16.
Musham, Wilfred, 5550, Pte., k., 15/8/16.
Myers, Jos., 1289, Pte., k., 23/11/16.
McGrath, John William, 2077, L/Cpl., k., 1/7/16.
McPhail, William, 1689, Pte., k., 6/10/15.
Naiswith, John William, 1026, Cpl., d., 8/5/15.
Naylor, Harry, 4376, Pte., d., 29/8/16.
Newby, Charles Allan, 2505, Pte., k., 19/8/15.
Nicholson, Ernest, 3902, Pte., k., 1/7/16.
Nicholson, Stewart, 3691, L/Cpl., k., 25/7/16.
Nightingale, Andrew, 2373, L/Cpl., k., 19/12/15.
Nolan, Francis, 7298, Pte., k., 23/11/16.
Normington, Fred, 2534, Pte., k., 23/5/15.
Northend, William, 3183, Pte., k., 16/12/15.
O'Brien, John, 7150, Pte., k., 23/11/16, formerly 9052, Durham L.I.
O'Grady, Edward, 2946, Pte., k., 19/11/15.
Onion, John Bradford, 1704, Pte., d., 11/9/16.
Overton, George Frederick, 681, Sgt., k., 7/9/15.
Padley, George, 4623, Pte., k., 3/9/16.
Paley, Benjamin James, 2088, Pte., k., 24/6/15.
Parker, George, 2344, Pte., k., 5/9/15.
Parkinson, Albert, 3503, Pte., k., 1/7/16.
Parkinson, Henry, 3455, Pte., k., 7/11/15.
Parkinson, Robert, 1659, Pte., k., 21/7/16.
Parkinson, William, 3171, Pte., k., 1/7/16.
Parratt, Edwin, 240482, Pte., k., 3/9/16.
Patefield, Ernest Edward, 2830, L/Cpl., d., 20/7/16.
Payton, James, 3374, Pte., k., 25/5/15.
Pearce, Cyril, 241779, L/Cpl., k., 3/9/16.
Phelps, William Charles, 7131, Pte., k., 22/10/16 formerly 30927, Durham L.I.
Phillips, William, 3361, Pte., d., 17/8/16.
Pottage, John, 205, C.S.M., k., 12/8/15.
Powell, Richard, 2653, Cpl., d., 4/8/15.
Pritchard, James, 4402, Pte., k., 1/7/16.
Rain, Harry, 241763, Pte., k., 3/9/16.
Rawlings, Charles, 1145, Sgt., k., 3/9/16.
Rayner, James, 4458, Pte., k., 30/8/16.
Reece, Harold, 3117, Pte., k., 3/9/16.
Renney, Fred, 4269, Pte., d., 4/7/16.
Restall, Eldred, 4000, Pte., d., 29/8/16.
Reynolds, John William, 3100, Pte., d.h., 16/9/16.
Rhodes, Percy, 4588, Pte., d., 12/7/16.
Richardson, Albert, 7132, Pte., k., 23/11/16, formerly 30085 Durham L.I.
Riley, Ernest, 6558, Pte., k., 23/11/16.
Robertshaw, Simpson, 4672, Pte., d., 24/7/16.
Robinson, Charles, 3127, Pte., k., 19/11/15.
Robinson, Fred, 3474, Pte., k., 17/7/15.
Robinson, Harry, 3807, Pte., d. at sea, 17/11/15.
Robson, George William, 7076, Pte., k., 23/11/16, formerly 30868, Durham L.I.
Ross, Frederick Gilbert, 2766, Pte., d., 6/7/16.
Rudden, James, 241820, Pte., k., 3/9/16.
Rudolph, George, 1839, Pte., k., 19/12/15.
Rushton, Eric, 1880, Pte., d., 3/7/16.
Sawyer, Zeptha, 7259, Pte., k., 22/10/16.
Sayers, Joseph, 2626, Sgt., k., 15/7/16, D.C.M.

Scanlon, George William, 4381, Pte., d., 16/2/16.
Sharpe, William, 3831, Cpl., d., 6/12/16.
Silsby, Bernard, 1173, Pte., k., 12/7/16.
Simpson, Arthur, 1722, Pte., k., 19/11/15.
Simpson, George Cuthbert, 1773, C.Q.M.S., k., 3/9/16, D.C.M.
Smith, Albert Archer, 241237, Pte., k., 3/9/16.
Smith, Arthur, 2108, Pte., k., 3/6/15.
Smith, Harry, 2287, Pte., k., 12/10/15.
Smithies, Thomas, 3031, Cpl., k., 19/11/15.
Spencer, Wilson, 4899, Pte., k., 14/7/16.
Stansfield, John, 1626, Pte., k., 22/7/16.
Stanton, James, 2592, Pte., k., 19/12/15.
Stevenson, Edgar, 3619, Pte., k., 15/7/16.
Stott, Edgar, 4636, Pte., k., 17/2/16.
Stringer, Herbert George, 1412, Pte., k., 5/9/15.
Sutcliffe, Arnold, 240551, Pte., k., 3/9/16.
Sutcliffe, Joseph, 2806, Pte., k., 20/12/15.
Swan, Robert, 7184, Pte., k., 3/9/16, formerly 18/153, Durham L.I.
Swift, Joe Sykes, 5630, Pte., d., 22/8/16, formerly 4028, 3/1, Queen's Own Yorkshire Dragoons.
Taylor, Albert, 1906, Cpl., k., 11/10/15.
Thompson, Willie, 2316, Pte., k., 12/7/16.
Thornton, Sydney, 240272, Pte., k., 3/9/16.
Thornton, Willie, 2917, Cpl., k., 22/10/16.
Tindall, Frederick 2590, Pte., k., 1/7/16.
Tomlinson, James, 3657, L/Cpl., k., 15/7/16.
Tomlinson, John, 1593, L/Cpl., k., 3/9/16.
Tong, Edward, 1236, L/Cpl., k., 3/9/16.
Turner, George, 1468, L/Cpl., k., 2/8/16.
Turpin, Noah, 2115, L/Cpl., k., 1/7/16.
Turpin, Wilfred, 2596, Pte., k., 28/2/16.
Tuxford, Sam, 4697, Pte., d., 7/7/16.
Varley, Harry, 2306, Sgt., k., 14/8/16.
Ventress, Benjamin, 6600, Pte., k., 23/11/16.
Voinus, Samuel, 3185, L/Cpl., k., 12/7/16.
Wade, James Edward, 3789, Pte., k., 26/8/1
Waddington, Arthur, 4234, Pte., k., 7/8/16.
Walker, Fred, 1498, Pte., k., 10/8/15.
Walker, Gilbert, 2549, Pte., d., 12/5/15.
Walker, Richard, 4190, Pte., d., 15/7/16.
Wardell, John William, 1235, Pte., d., 3/7/16.
Warrener, George Arthur, 3113, L/Cpl., k., 19/12/15.
Wasteney, Walter, 1458, Sgt., d., 17/9/16.
Watkins, William, 1374, Pte., k., 29/8/15.
Watmough, Harold Rawnsley, 2460, Sgt., k., 1/7/16.
Watson, Eric Thomas, 904, Sgt., k., 23/11/16.
Wignall, George, 4559, Pte., k., 3/7/16.
Wild, George, 5484, Pte., k., 15/8/16.
Wilkinson, Edgar James, 1266, L/Cpl., k., 11/8/16.
Wilkinson, Joseph Ernest, 2449, Pte., d., 17/11/15.
Wilson, James, 242192, Pte., k., 3/9/16.
Wood, Harry, 2928, Pte., k., 3/9/16.
Wood, Joshua M., 2519, Pte., drowned at sea, 17/11/15.
Woodhouse, James, 24749, Pte., d., 19/7/16.
Yeadon, Victor, 1280, Pte., k., 12/10/15.
Young, George Shields, 4544, Pte., d., 29/11/16.

2/6th BATTALION

Ashcroft, Walter Herbert, 5211, Pte., d.h., 22/4/16.
Naylor, David, 2996, Cpl., d.h., 19/1/16.

Overend, George, 3034, Pte., d.h., (Accident). 12/11/15.

3/6th BATTALION

Roberts, Joseph William, 4638, Pte., d.h., 12/7/16.
Servant, William, 2183, Sgt., d.h., 4/8/16.
Tasker, John Henry, 3530, Pte., d.h., 14/2/16.
Ward, Fred, 4701, Pte., d.h., 1/9/15.
Wood, John Benjamin, 4467, Pte., d.h., 30/5/16,

7th RESERVE BATTALION

Hare, Joseph, 8072, Pte., d.h., 22/12/16.

1/7th BATTALION

Abbott, Thomas, 4318, Pte., k., 3/9/16.
Airey, George Armitage, 3221, Pte., d., 5/7/16.
Alderson, George, 2753, Pte., k., 18/12/15
Alderson, William, 4121, Pte., d., 3/7/16.
Ames, Charles William, 3090, Pte., k., 18/9/15.
Appleby, George, 2092, Pte., k., 22/5/15.
Appleton, Albert, 2666, Pte., k., 25/8/15.
Ashby, Thomas, 266222, Pte., k., 14/7/16.
Bailey, John William, 1667, Pte., drowned (accidentally), 29/4/15.
Bambrook, Wilfred, 1974, L/Cpl., d., 20/1/16.
Barker, Walter, 265560, Pte., k., 2/7/16.
Barnes, Harry, 4186, Pte., k., 8/7/16.
Bate, Harry, 1686, Pte., d., 23/12/15.
Beckwith, James Edwin, 3028, L/Cpl., k., 8/12/15.
Beckwith, Thomas, 1430, Pte., d.h., 12/8/14.
Bell, Ernest, 3324, Pte., k., 1/7/16.
Binns, Ernest, 2845, Pte., k., 15/8/15.
Birdsall, Harry, 1459, Pte., k., 10/11/15.
Bloomfield, Walter Edward, 6025, Pte., k., 24/9/16.
Bradstock, Harold, 265737, Cpl., k, 3/9/16
Brierley, Arthur, 1541, Pte., k., 2/7/16.
Brook, Henry, 2518, Pte., k., 22/6/15.
Brown, Arthur, 5300, Pte., k., 28/8/16.
Brown, Walter, 265828, Pte., k., 1/7/16.
Buckle, Albert, 4383, Pte., k., 8/7/16.
Buckley, Alfred, 1116, Pte., d., 21/12/15.
Burnett, Arthur, 1666, Pte., d.h., 19/5/16.
Cable, John, 3540, L/Cpl., k., 14/7/16.
Cantral, Edward, 5204, Pte., k., 3/7/16.
Carling, Harold, 4219, Pte., d.h., 11/10/16.
Carruthers, James Henry, 6138, Pte., k.,27/9/16.
Cathcart, Gavin Browning, 2724, Pte., k., 19/8/15.
Caufield, John, 2619, Pte., k., 2/7/16.
Chafer, Samuel, 4006, Pte., k., 5/8/16.
Chapman, Percy, 2116, Pte., k., 20/12/15.
Clapham, Rowland Hill, 3280, L/Cpl., k., 3/9/16.
Clark, John Dobson, 2234, L/Cpl., d., 15/7/15.
Clarke, Edward, 4309, Pte., k., 2/7/16.
Clarke, Ernest Albert, 2057, Rfln., k., 3/7/16.
Clarkson, John William, 2528, Pte., d., 3/7/16.
Connell, John, 6558, L/Cpl., k., 27/9/16.
Cooke, James Ephraim, 4419, Pte., d., 15/6/16.
Cooper, John William, 1512, L/Cpl., d.h., 27/9/16, M.M.
Cory, Harry, 5015, Pte., d., 16/7/16.
Cox, John, 3246, Pte., d., 23/2/16.
Coyle, Stephen, 6150, Pte., d., 27/9/16, formerly 5885, Northumberland Fusiliers.
Craven, James, 3150, Pte., d., 28/12/15.
Cumpson, Joseph, 6555, Pte., k., 26/9/16.
Dalby, Richard, 2937, Sgt., k., 24/11/15.
Davis, Walter, 4279, Pte., k., 2/7/16.
Dawes, Frederick, 4016, Pte., k., 1/7/16.
Day, Arthur, 2939, Pte., d., 29/7/15.
Dickinson, Leonard, 2526, Pte., k., 23/2/16.

Dods, Andrew, 2069, L/Cpl., k., 14/5/15
Doyle, Richard, 6028, Pte., k., 24/9/16.
Drake, Ernest, 2763, L/Sgt., k., 12/7/16.
Drury, Albert, 4501, L/Cpl. k., 3/9/16.
Dye, Frederick, 2235, Pte., k., 13/5/15.
Exley, Herbert, 2206, L/Cpl., k., 14/7/16.
Farrar, George William, 3756, Cpl., k., 1/7/16.
Farrell, John Edward, 265245, Cpl., k., 2/7/16.
Fisher, Edwin, 4578, Pte., k., 12/8/16.
Fitton, Lewis, 3264, Pte., d.h., 23/11/16.
Flint, George, 3601, Cpl., d., 28/9/16.
Flintham, Johnson Herbert, 2914, L/Cpl., k., 30/10/15.
Foggitt, Frank, 1660, L/Cpl., k., 14/7/16.
Ford, George, 3273, Pte., k., 4/11/15.
Fowler, George William, 2067, L/Cpl., d., 8/11/15.
Fox, Leonard, 2695, Pte., k., 15/5/15.
Frazer, Thomas, 1872, Pte., k., 20/7/15.
Gaunt, Herbert, 2329, Sgt., k., 1/7/16.
Gelderd, Walter, 266032, Pte., k., 3/9/16.
Godfrey, George Sidney, 6193, L/Cpl., k., 27/9/16.
Goldthorpe, Harry, 3311, Pte., k., 12/7/16.
Goodson, William, 3748, L/Cpl., k., 21/7/16.
Grant, John Waite, 3212, Pte., k., 8/12/15.
Grant, Squire, 3947, Pte., k., 14/7/16.
Grover, Thomas Henry, 4445, Pte., k., 2/7/16.
Haigh, Tom, 4389, Pte., d.h., 7/8/16.
Hampson, George, 2925, Pte., k., 3/9/16.
Hargreaves, George, 3987, Pte., k., 5/8/16.
Headlam, Harry, 4473, Pte., d., 18/7/16.
Heald, Arthur, 656, L/Sgt., d., 16/8/15.
Hitchen, Arthur Benjamin, 2804, Pte., k., 6/5/15.
Holmes, James Ernest, 5235, Rfln., d., 15/7/16
Holmes, Rowland Victor, 4288, Pte., d.h., 12/12/16.
Houston, James, 855, Sgt., k., 7/5/15.
Hudson, Harry, 2060, Pte., k., 15/8/15.
Hudson, John, 2148, Cpl., k., 27/9/16.
Ibbetson, Frank, 1972, Sgt., k., 21/7/16.
Ingleby, Harry, 2771, L/Sgt., d., 1/8/16.
Jackson, Walter, 4263, Pte., k., 14/7/16.
Jennings, John William, 1692, L/Cpl., k., 1/7/16.
Johnson, Frank, 2644, Pte., k., 2/7/16.
Johnson, Joseph, 4140, Pte., k., 28/8/16.
Jones, Ernest, 3400, Pte., k., 12/8/16.
Jones, William, 1682, Pte., d., 21/11/15.
Kellett, James, 2324, L/Cpl., k., 5/8/16.
Kendell, James, 2927, Pte., d., 11/7/16.
Kirk, Lawrence, 3000, L/Cpl., d., 21/7/16, M.M.
Lally, John, 3660, Pte., k., 8/7/16.
Lawrence, Harry, 2796, Pte., k., 3/9/16.
Lawrie, Robert, 6164, Pte., d., 2/7/16.
Lee, Arthur, 266302, Pte., k., 14/7/16.
Lee, George Henry Walmby, 2133, L/Cpl., k., 5/6/15.

Lee, James, 2986, L/Cpl., k., 14/7/16.
Lloyd, George, 3254, Pte., k., 10/5/15.
Lodge, Harry Watson, 2153, Pte., k., 22/5/15.
Lonsdale, Robinson, 3753, Pte., d., 16/11/15.
Lyon, Luke, 2273, Pte., k., 7/5/15.
Makin, Walter, 2625, L/Cpl., d., 16/7/16, D.C.M.
Malkin, Ernest, 3218, Pte., d., 12/5/15.
Maltby, Percy, 3305, Pte., d., 15/7/15.
Mann, Richard, 265092, Pte., k., 3/9/16.
Mann, Tom, 2809, Pte., k., 9/6/15.
Marsden, Ernest, 2127, L/Sgt., d., 20/9/16.
Marwood, George, 2716, L/Cpl., k., 14/7/16.
Mason, Farman, 2236, L/Cpl., k., 10/12/15.
Meek, Ernest, 2071, Pte., d., 5/9/16.
Merson, Harry, 2959, Pte., d., 2/7/16.
Metcalfe, Peter, 4476, Pte., k., 3/9/16.
Micklethwaite, Charles Arthur, 4090, Pte., k., 14/7/16.
Midgley, Benjamin Waller, 1925, Pte., k., 20/11/15.
Mole, George, 6136, Pte., k., 27/9/16, formerly 4199, Northumberland Fusiliers.
Moore, Clifford, 265543, Pte., k., 14/7/16.
McDonald, Thomas, 4453, Pte., d., 1/2/16.
Nowell, Walter, 3453, Pte., d., 5/8/16.
Oliver, Edward, 266965, Pte., k., 2/7/16.
Pearce, Edward, 2778, Pte., k., 7/5/15.
Penny, Christopher, 3571, Pte., d., 9/7/15.
Penny, Edward, 5011, Rfln., k., 28/8/16.
Petch, George, 3351, Pte., k., 14/7/16.
Phelan, Thomas, 5299, Pte., k., 3/9/16.
Pople, William Henry, 6174, Pte., k., 27/9/16.
Potter, Christopher, 4113, Pte., d., 6/9/16.
Powell, Walter, 2086, Sgt., k., 14/7/16.
Pritchard, Samuel Edward, 6035, Pte., k., 27/9/16.
Ramsden, Arthur, 3678, Pte., k., 1/7/16.
Ratcliffe, Charles, 2903, L/Cpl., d., 17/12/15.
Rawnsley, Fred, 2736, Pte., k., 2/7/16.
Redshaw, Robert, 1994, Pte., k., 8/12/15.
Ribchester, James, 1989, Pte., d., 6/8/15.
Robinson, George, 4724, Pte., d.h., 7/3/16.
Robson, Thomas William, 6135, Pte., k., 27/9/16, formerly 4202, 4th Northumberland Fusiliers.
Rose, Edward, 4795, Pte., d., 25/9/16.
Rosendale, Jacob, 3969, L/Cpl., d., 17/7/16.
Rothery, James, 1316, Pte., k., 12/12/15.
Ryall, Charles Robert, 2620, Pte., d., 14/7/16.
Saxton, George, 1336, Pte., d., 11/7/15.
Scatchard, Edward, 2731, Pte., k., 2/7/16.
Schofield, George, 1729, Pte., k., 2/7/16.
Scholey, James, 1823, Pte., k., 2/7/16.
Scholey, James, 5266, Pte., k., 27/9/16.
Schutz, Clarence, 43, Sgt., k., 8/12/15.
Scoffield, Freeman, 1636, Pte., k., 24/5/15.
Scott, William Edward, 590, C.S.M., k., 1/7/16.

Shepherd, George, 2077, Pte., drowned, at sea 17/11/15.
Shields, Horace, 5500, Pte., k., 19/11/16.
Simon, Charles, R., 193, Sgt., k., 9/10/15.
Smart, James, 1691, Bglr., d., 16/7/15.
Smith, Charles, 3047, L/Cpl., k., 3/9/16.
Smith, James, 4482, Pte., d., 13/7/16.
Smith, Joseph, 265638, Pte., k., 2/7/16.
Smith, Joseph Duncan, 3281, Pte., d., 28/5/15.
Smith, Norman, 2718, Pte., k., 26/5/15.
Smithson, Thomas Henry, 4550, Pte., k., 28/8/16.
Standage, Albert, 265246, L/Cpl., k., 3/9/16.
Stanley, George, 2861, Pte., k., 24/9/15.
Stead, Harold Kay, 5016, Pte., d., 30/10/16.
Stead, John, 1774, Pte., k., 24/5/15.
Stead, William Mallinson, 800, C.Q.M.S., d., 15/7/16.
Stephenson, Jeremiah, 3241, Cpl., k., 8/7/16.
Stevens, Ralph, 6132, Pte., k., 26/9/16.
Stockwell, Ernest, 1776, Pte., k., 29/9/15.
Summerscales, Harry, 4244, Pte., k., 14/7/16.
Tate, George, 4639, Pte., d., 15/7/16.
Teale, Sydney, 4596, Pte., k., 2/7/16.
Terry, Clifford, 3084, Pte., k., 3/9/16.
Thompson, Ernest, 5241, Rfn., d., 1/9/16.
Thompson, Sydney, 1571, L/Cpl., k., 14/7/16.
Tough, James, 1581, Cpl., k., 2/7/16.
Townend, John William, 4512, Pte., k., 28/8/16.
Turver, James, 2889, L/Cpl., k., 14/7/16.
Varley, Harry, 3942, Pte., k., 1/7/16.
Waddington, Harold, 3520, Pte., k., 2/7/16.
Walker, William, 4621, Pte., k., 1/7/16.
Wallis, Clifford, 2196, Pte., k., 4/8/16.
Walpole, Joe, 4248, Pte., k., 2/7/16.
Walsh, William Norman, 3219, Pte., d., 11/6/15.
Walton, Arthur, 3355, Pte., k., 9/5/15.
Walton, John Arthur, 3589, Pte., k., 2/7/16.
Wardale, Thomas, 1751, Pte., k., 20/9/15.
Waterworth, Richard, 5328, Pte., k., 23/10/16.
Watson, Arthur, 3011, Pte., k., 8/10/15.
Watson, William, 2848, Pte., d., 18/7/15.
Wesley, John Frederick, 2110, Pte., k., 3/9/16.
Wheelhouse, Arthur, 731, Sgt., k., 26/8/16.
Whiston, Samuel, 1703, Cpl., k., 28/8/16.
White, William, 2659, Pte., k., 1/7/16.
Wilkinson, Alfred, 4435, Pte., d., 3/7/16.
Wilkinson, Edmund, 2207, Pte., k., 8/12/15.
Wilkinson, William, 359, Sgt., d., 19/6/15.
Willians, Harold, 2867, Pte., d., 24/9/15.
Wilson, Arthur, 2612, Pte., k., 2/7/16.
Wilson, Clarence, 2742, Pte., k., 10/12/15.
Wilson, Herbert, 265344, Pte., k., 14/7/16.
Wood, George, 4436, Pte., k., 12/7/16.
Woodruff, William, 2176, Pte., d., 8/10/15.
Wormald, Alfred, 3899, Pte., k., 3/9/16.
Wrigglesworth, John Abson, 2714, L/Cpl., k., 14/7/16.

2/7th BATTALION

Ely, Fred, 3337, Pte., d.h., 14/7/15.

3/7th BATTALION

Chaplin, Arthur, 4716, Pte., d.h., 7/12/15.
Dains, Herbert Sanderson, 4989, Pte., d.h., 24/3/16.
Dodson, Walter, 4627, Pte., d.h., 17/3/16.

Eales, John Arthur White, 3989, Pte., d.h., 8/8/16.
Pullan, Joseph, 4506, Pte., drowned (accidental), h., 8/9/15.
Wallis, Arthur, 4513, Pte., d.h., 6/8/15.

The Prince of Wales's Own (West Yorks. Regt.)—Casualties

1/8th BATTALION

Adgie, Cecil, 305123, Pte., k., 3/9/16.
Akeroyd, Leonard, 1568, Pte., d., 9/5/15.
Allen, Fred, 1594, Pte., d., 21/9/16.
Almond, Francis, Edwin, 2718, Pte., k., 1/5/15.
Appleyard, Harry, 1564, L/Cpl., d., 1/6/15.
Arnold, Alfred Cecil, 1913, Cpl., d., 17/7/16.
Ashforth, Thomas James, 2041, L/Cpl., k., 14/6/15.
Bailey, Arthur Greenwood, 307087, Pte., k., 3/9/16.
Baldwin, Clifford, 1347, L/Sgt., k., 2/8/16.
Bannister, Albert, 305578, Cpl., k., 3/9/16.
Barclay, Arthur, 4505, Pte., d., 20/7/16.
Barker, Arthur John, 5387, Pte., k., 11/7/16.
Barker, Thomas, 306564, L/Cpl., k., 3/9/16.
Barnfather, Harry, 306364, Pte., k., 13/8/16.
Barran, Irwin, 2380, Pte., d., 29/12/15.
Bastide, Charley, 3827, Pte., d., 10/7/16.
Bastow, Charles Ratcliffe, 307086, Pte., d., 13/8/16.
Bean, Willie, 4418, Pte., d., 17/12/16.
Beardsley, Samuel, 6652, Pte., d., 20/9/16.
Beever, William, 3932, Pte., k., 13/8/16.
Bilton, Cephas, 2816, Pte., d., 7/8/16.
Boocock, William, 4959, Pte., k., 15/8/16.
Boshell, Irwin, 305769, Pte., k., 3/9/16.
Brady, Vincent, 4394, Pte., d., 16/7/16.
Briggs, James, 4743, Pte., k., 3/9/16.
Broadbent, Clifford, 5295, Pte., d., 12/9/16.
Brown, Martin Patrick, 4073, Pte., k., 3/9/16.
Bucktrout, Charles Albert, 4107, Pte., d., 8/8/16.
Butler, Thomas, 6529, Pte., k., 24/9/16.
Callis, Arthur, 4215, Pte., d., 24/7/16.
Calvert, James Arthur, 4758, Pte., k., 11/7/16.
Cameron, John, 2935, Pte., d., 8/8/15.
Chambers, Thomas, 3849, Pte., k., 3/9/16.
Chapman, Eric, 2209, Cpl., k., 22/9/15.
Chappelow, Tom Henry, 2233, Cpl., d., 17/7/16.
Charlesworth, Tom, 3173, L/Cpl., k., 3/9/16.
Clarkson, Joseph March, 6074, Pte., k., 27/9/16, formerly 4614, Durham L.I.
Clarkson, Walter, 53893, Pte., k., 20/7/18.
Clayton, Joel, 6090, Pte., d, 17/11/16.
Clayton, John William, 2198, Pte., k., 20/7/16.
Coates, Charles Edward, 1713, Pte., k., 3/9/16.
Collier, William, 2677, Pte., k., 3/9/16.
Collings, Arthur, 2509, Pte., d., 1/7/15.
Cooper, Wallace, 2795, Pte., d., 9/5/15.
Cousin, Sam, 2585, Sgt., d.h., 9/5/15.
Coville, Harry, 4798, Pte., k., 3/9/16.
Coward, John Willie, 4190, Pte., k., 3/9/16.
Crossland, Harry, 1321, Pte., k., 3/9/16.
Dacre, George, 1875, Cpl., k., 28/9/16.
Dalton, James Francis, 1527, Pte., k., 1/7/16.
Daly, Francis, 306439, Pte., k., 3/9/16.
Davidson, Charles, 4451, Pte., k., 20/9/16.
Dawkin, Charles, 2811, Pte., d., 8/6/15.
Day, Alfred, 4371, Pte., k., 13/8/16.
Denham, Frank, 4297, Pte., k., 11/7/16.
Denton, George, 1226, Sgt., k., 2/6/15.
Dickenson, Alfred, 1454, L/Cpl., k., 3/9/16.
Dickinson, William Alfred, 4607, Pte., k., 27/8/16.
Dobson, John Henry, 306592, Pte., k., 3/9/16.
Driffield, Richard, 1372, Pte., k., 8/10/15.
Dyer, Daniel, 3807, Pte., d., 3/7/16.
Eaton, Robert Ernest, 5026, Pte., k., 3/9/16.
Exley, Henry, 2469, Pte., d., 4/11/15.
Fear, William Henry, 3940, C.S.M., k., 14/7/16.
Fearnley, Levi, 2648, Pte., k., 21/2/16.
Featherstone, Alfred Charles, 2473, Pte., k., 12/5/15.

Ferguson, Thomas, 5257, Pte., d., 23/9/16.
Firth, Albert Edward, 2732, Pte., k., 2/7/16.
Fleming, Martin, 1893, L/Cpl., k., 3/9/16.
Flynn, John, 3804, Pte., k., 5/8/16.
Foster, Robert, 2295, Pte., k., 3/9/16.
Foster, Thomas, 3936, Pte., k., 2/7/16.
Fountain, Joe, 2318, Pte., d., 9/5/15.
Frankland, George William Frederick, 4920, Pte., k., 3/9/16.
Gerraghty, Alfred, 2991, L/Cpl., k., 1/7/16.
Gilchrist, John Anderson, 2182, Cpl., k., 14/8/15.
Gladstone, John Usher, 6105, Pte., k., 21/9/16, formerly 4649, Durham L.I.
Gooch, Wallace, 2672, Pte., k., 8/7/16.
Grant, Norman, 8204, Pte., k., 5/8/16.
Greatwich, Harry, 2622, L/Cpl., d., 3/7/16.
Greenhalgh, John, 2524, Cpl., d., 4/9/16.
Grimes, William, 4093, L/Cpl., d., 20/8/16.
Gudgeon, Alfred, 2367, Pte., k., 7/8/15.
Hanson, Owen Wright, 5380, Pte., k., 21/9/16.
Harding, Frederick William, 3239, L/Cpl., k., 2/8/16.
Harding, John Edward, 2901, Pte., k., 22/10/15.
Hardwick, John, 2366, L/Cpl., d., 3/7/16.
Hargrave, Hubert, 307553, Pte., k., 3/9/16.
Harkness, James, 3428, Pte., d., 6/9/16.
Harrison, Benjamin, 307145, Pte., k., 20/7/16.
Hart, Edward, 3963, Pte., k., 3/9/16.
Hartley, Reynard, 3887, Pte., k., 3/9/16.
Hawkesworth, David, 1919, Pte., d. (accident), 13/9/15.
Haxby, Robert, 2784, Pte., d., 20/7/16.
Hemingbrough, Alfred, 2911, Pte., k., 3/9/16.
Henry, Ernest Jules, 307133, Pte., k., 3/9/16.
Hey, Arthur, 4761, Pte., k., 5/8/16.
Hindle, Harry, 4980, Pte., k., 15/8/16.
Hirst, John Rowley, 4721, Pte., d., 14/9/16.
Hobson, George, 3934, Pte., k., 20/7/16.
Hodgson, Sam, 305139, Pte., k., 3/7/16.
Holliday, John, 2556, L/Cpl., d., 19/7/16.
Holmes, Fred, 4780, Pte., d., 4/9/16.
Hornby, Darius, 8/3945, Pte., k., 13/8/16.
Houlden, James Walter, 5044, Pte., k., 3/9/16.
Hudson, George Henry, 305460, Pte., k., 3/9/16.
Huffingley, Albert, 1669, Pte., d., 24/5/15.
Hurst, Charles Henry, 2439, Sgt., k., 3/9/16.
Illingworth, Sam, 3916, Pte., k., 2/7/16.
Illingworth, Willie, 6664, Pte., d., 5/10/16.
Jackson, Rolla Hirst, 4220, L/Cpl., k., 3/9/16.
Jeffs, Harry, 6112, Pte., d., 24/9/16.
Johnson, James Arthur, 5367, Pte., d., 23/9/16.
Johnson, Walter, 3885, Pte., k., 3/9/16.
Jones, Harold, 2231, Pte., k., 9/5/15.
Jordan, James, 4739, Pte., k., 3/9/16.
Jordan, James, 5040, Pte., d., 5/9/16.
Kearn, Sidney, 3080, Pte., d., 30/10/15.
Kell, Thomas Speight, 6513, Pte., d., 25/9/16.
Kelly, Joseph, 4028, Pte., k., 13/8/16.
Kerby, James John, 6507, Sgt., k., 28/9/16.
Kettlewell, William, 2176, L/Cpl., d., 6/9/16.
Kilburn, Percy, 1944, Pte., k., 16/7/15.
Kilby, Richard James, 531, Pte., k., 27/9/16.
Knott, Joe Sam, 6185, Pte., k., 27/9/16.
Laing, Edward, 3011, L/Cpl., d., 24/8/16.
Lawrence, Harry, 4197, Pte., k., 3/9/16.
Lawson, Willie, 1315, Pte., k., 18/7/15.
Layton, Ernest, 3356, Pte., k., 20/7/16.
Ledgard, Leonard, 3796, Pte., k., 2/7/16.
Leonard, Edward, 2202, Pte., k., 2/7/16.
Lewis, Albert Edward, 4301, Pte., d., 4/9/16.
Lewis, James, 4065, Pte., k., 20/7/16.
Lightfoot, Harry, 3915, Pte., k., 3/9/16.

Little, George Bond, 2515, Pte., k., 9/5/15.
Longbottam, Frederick, 2942, L/Cpl., k., 11/7/16.
Longfield, Percy, 1687, Sgt., d., 20/12/13.
Lye, Harry, 2519, Pte., k., 9/5/15.
Mann, Frank, 4772, Pte., k., 3/9/16.
Mann, Harold, 305528, L/Cpl., k., 3/9/16.
Marsland, Harold, 307542, Pte., k., 3/9/16.
Maude, John, 1787, Rfln., k., 24/10/15.
May, William, 3116, Pte., k., 3/2/16.
Mells, Harry, 4775, Pte., k., 3/9/16.
Mellor, Joe, 3799, L/Cpl., k., 20/7/16.
Mockford, William, 4164, Pte., k., 1/7/16.
Moore, John, 2451, L/Cpl., k., 9/5/15.
Morgan, Michael, 3972, Pte., d., 4/7/16.
Morley, Stewart, 2788, Pte., k., 1/7/16.
Morton, John, 1563, Pte., d., 14/6/15.
Morrell, James, 2276, Pte., k., 24/6/15.
Morris, Charles, 3052, Pte., k., 20/7/16.
Moss, Joe, 3387, Pte., k., 15/7/16.
Mottram, James, 1263, Pte., k., 21/2/16.
Mudd, Frank, 3485, Pte., k., 16/7/15.
Mullaney, Francis, 1608, Pte., d., 3/8/16.
Myers, David F., 499, C.S.M., k., 21/8/15.
McGuire, Joseph, 3276, Pte., d., 10/11/15.
McLoughlin, James, 2302, Pte., d., 15/7/16.
McMillan, Benjamin, 4345, Pte., k., 20/7/16.
Nicholls, Thomas, 2893, Pte., d., 15/7/16.
Nicholls, William Ewart, 306677, Pte., k., 3/9/16.
North, William, 1476, Sgt., k., 29/5/15.
Oddy, Benjamin, 3161, Pte., k., 5/8/16.
Overton, William, 343, L/Cpl., d.h., 28/8/14.
Pankhurst, Horace, 4272, Pte., d., 16/7/16.
Parker, Joseph, 244, Pte., k., 11/11/15.
Parr, Fred, 3507, Pte., k., 11/7/16.
Partridge, Henry, 1846, Pte., k., 2/7/16.
Pearson, Willie, 4169, Pte., d., 11/9/16.
Peck, William, 2193, Pte., k., 24/8/15.
Pemberton, George William, 1918, Sgt., k., 13/8/16, M.M.
Peniket, Edward, 1651, Pte., k., 2/7/16.
Perry, Ralph, 305008, C.S.M., k., 3/9/16.
Pickard, George, 3453, Pte., d., 20/7/16.
Pickard, Sam, 2226, Pte., k., 2/7/16.
Pickles, Thomas, 5365, Pte., k., 3/9/16.
Plowman, George Thomas, 4463, Pte., d., 24/7/16.
Pocklington, Herbert Charles, 2368, Pte., k., 19/11/15.
Pogson, John, 2872, Rflmn., k., 2/7/16.
Race, Thomas, 4903, Pte., d., 15/8/16.
Reason, Leonard, 2831, L/Cpl., k., 2/7/16.
Rhodes, Harry, 1547, Pte., k., 9/5/15.
Rhodes, Harry, 307119, Pte., k., 3/9/16.
Rhodes, Herbert, 1746, Sgt., d., 3/9/16.
Richardson, Harold, 2304, Pte., k., 8/12/15.
Riddell, Matthew, 6024, Pte., k., 27/9/16, formerly 53, Northumberland Cycle Corps.
Rigby, Alex, 3915, Pte., d., 4/9/16.
Riley, John, 1965, Pte., d.h., 10/6/15.
Robinson, James, 2412, L/Cpl., k., 2/7/16.
Robinson, Percy, 305364, Pte., k., 3/9/16.
Rodger, Herbert, 1924, Pte., k., 8/12/15.
Rogan, Hugh, 6022, Pte., k., 27/9/16, formerly 209, Northumberland Cycle Corps.
Rothwell, Arthur, 2560, Pte., d., 26/6/15.
Roundell, Arthur, 2292, Pte., k., 9/5/15.
Rowan, Andrew, 305860, Pte., k., 3/9/16.
Rowland, Thomas, 1324, Pte., k., 8/9/15.
Rushforth, John, 4099, Pte., d., 19/7/16.
Sanderson, George, 2207, Pte., k., 20/7/16.
Sanderson, John, 1709, Pte., k., 5/8/16.
Scarth, Garnet, 2428, Pte., k., 13/8/16.
Senior, Percy, 4827, Pte., d., 4/9/16.

Settle, William, 305101, Pte., k., 2/7/16.
Shaw, John Hanson, 1314, Cpl., k., 18/7/15.
Shepherd, John Henry, 6134, Pte., d., 25/9/16.
Shimeld, Thomas, 1187, Rflmn., k., 2/8/16.
Silcock, Fred, 2996, Pte., k., 3/9/16.
Simpson, Joseph Watson, 2323, Pte., k., 8/11/15
Slunker, John William, 1284, L/Cpl., k., 3/9/16
Smith, Charles, 2365, Pte., k., 6/5/15.
Smith, George, 1556, Pte., k., 8/10/15.
Smith, James, 1376, Cpl., k., 15/5/15.
Smith, Ralph, 2782, Pte., k., 27/9/16.
Smith, Sam, 305430, Sgt., k., 3/9/16.
Soar, Harry, 5070, Pte., k., 3/9/16.
Speed, William, 4435, Pte., k., 20/7/16.
Spencer, Fred, 4134, Pte., k., 20/7/16.
Spurr, John, 4417, L/Cpl., k., 3/9/16.
Stanley, Charles Ernest, 2637, Pte., k., 24/10/15.
Stansfield, Sidney, 4609, Pte., k., 3/9/16.
Stead, Charles, 306690, Pte., k., 3/9/16.
Steels, Thomas Robert, 2305, Pte., k., 8/12/15.
Stephenson, Joseph W., 1345, L/Cpl., d., 30/7/15.
Stone, William, 306615, Pte., k., 3/9/16.
Stones, Albert, 1740, Pte., k., 5/8/16.
Storey, James, 6030, Pte., k., 27/9/16.
Storr, Joseph, 306359, Pte., k., 2/7/16.
Strangeway, Joseph, 2219, Pte., k., 8/11/15.
Sugden, James, 3286, Pte., d., 16/7/16.
Taylor, Frederick William, 2228, Pte., d., 11/9/16.
Taylor, Gilbert, 5024, Pte., k., 3/9/16.
Taylor, Richard, 1988, Pte., d., 30/7/16.
Taylor, Wilfred, 1987, Pte., d., 19/8/15.
Taylor, William Hanson, 305780, L/Sgt., k., 3/9/16.
Thackray, Harry, 5004, Pte., d., 9/9/16.
Thackray, William, 2132, Cpl., k., 11/5/15.
Tindall, John Charles, 1888, Pte., k., 9/5/15.
Todd, Louis, 4353, Pte., k., 13/8/16.
Tonks, Amos, 4208, Pte., k., 1/7/16.
Topping, Frank, 306687, Pte., k., 3/9/16.
Turner, Albert Edward, 2335, L/Cpl., k., 4/10/15.
Vasey, William, 305108, L/Cpl., k., 3/9/16.
Wainwright, Willie, 5337, Rfln., k., 3/7/16.
Walker, Bert, 1945, Pte., d., 2/12/15.
Walker, Joseph, 1955, Pte., k., 2/7/16.
Wall, Ben, 6622, Pte., k., 24/9/16.
Ward, Sam, 1627, Pte., k., 2/7/16.
Ward, Stanley William, 6052, Pte., k., 27/9/16, formerly 62nd Div. Cyclist Company.
Ward, William, 306358, L/Cpl., k., 3/9/16.
Wardle, William Henry, 5058, Pte., k., 3/9/16.
Watson, Albert, 1730, Pte., k., 21/11/15.
Watson, Harry, 2853, Pte., k., 16/7/16.
Wells, William, 2863, Cpl., k., 9/3/16.
Wells, William, 2023, Pte., k., 9/5/15.
Westerley, Harold Oswald, 4777, Pte., k., 3/9/16.
White, Arthur, 2051, Sgt., k., 15/8/16.
Wilkinson, William, 4180, Pte., k., 20/7/16.
Williamson, Wilfred George, 1656, Pte., k., 11/7/16.
Wilson, Bernard, 2152, Pte., k., 30/11/15.
Wilson, Bernard, 4698, Pte., k., 3/9/16.
Wilson, John William, 2491, L/Cpl., d., 12/8/15.
Wilson, Robert, 6142, Pte., d., 8/10/16, formerly 4213, Durham L.I.
Wineley, Fred, 1832, Pte., k., 3/9/16.
Windsor, Arthur, 3766, Pte., k., 24/12/15.
Winduss, John William, 5027, Pte., k., 3/9/16.
Wise, Allan, 5351, Pte., k., 3/9/16.
Wolfe, Harry, 6647, Pte., d.h., 3/10/16.
Wright, Abram, 4968, Pte., k., 3/9/16.
Yarborough, Harry, 5353, Pte., k., 16/7/16.

The Prince of Wales's Own (West Yorks. Regt.)—Casualties

2/8th BATTALION

Dalton, Thomas, 2545, Pte., k., 2/6/16.
Dickinson, Harry, 3885, Pte., d.h., 18/7/15.
Good, Arthur, 4920, Pte., d.h., 20/11/16.
Harrison, George William, 3309, Pte., d., 20/11/16.
Hart, Martin, 3418, L/Cpl., d.h., 10/12/16.
Heaton, Simeon, 3610, Pte., d.h., 29/9/15.
Johnson, James William, 3073, Pte., d.h., 29/11/16.
Rodgers, Stephen, 2612, Pte., k., 18/8/15.

3/8th BATTALION

Holmes, Charles Henry, 4286, Sgt., d.h., 30/1/16.
Wilson, Arthur, 4585, Pte., d.h., 19/1/16.

9th BATTALION

Abbott, James, 17464, Pte., k., Gallipoli, 7/8/15.
Addle, Lewis Edward, 10834, Pte., k., Gallipoli, 9/8/15.
Aldous, Arthur, 15604, Pte., k., Gallipoli, 9/8/15.
Allan, Robert Hunter, 11282, Pte., d., Gallipoli, 14/8/15.
Allan, William, 3/8960, Pte., k., 14/9/16.
Allen, Francis, 15552, Pte., k., Gallipoli, 22/8/15.
Andrews, William James, 11816, Pte., k., Gallipoli, 22/8/15.
Appleby, Charles, 10872, Pte., d., Gallipoli, 7/8/15.
Archer, James William, 19467, d., 20/8/16.
Archer, Tom Burton, 15676, Pte., k., 14/9/16.
Armitage, George, 10331, Pte., k., Gallipoli, 21/8/15.
Atkinson, Harold, 18398, Pte., d., Gallipoli, 20/11/15.
Bailey, Joseph, 17682, Pte., d., at sea, 13/11/15.
Bailey, Charles Henry, 10624, Pte., k., Gallipoli, 7/8/15.
Bagley, Wilfred Arthur, 19032, Pte., d., 2/8/16.
Baines, George, 15442, L/Cpl., k., Gallipoli, 9/8/15.
Bampton, Samuel, 13229, Pte., k., Gallipoli, 9/8/15.
Barcroft, James Starkey, 3/8948, Sgt., k., 22/8/15.
Barker, Fred, 18593, Pte., k., 14/9/16.
Barnes, Stephen, 17984, Pte., k., Gallipoli, 22/8/15.
Barnes, Thomas, 15001, Pte., k., Gallipoli, 9/8/15.
Barrett, Sylvester, 19130, Pte., k., 27/9/16.
Bates, Alfred Christopher, 10407, Pte., k., Gallipoli, 9/8/15.
Baxter, William Henry, 15871, Pte., k., Gallipoli, 9/8/15.
Bayes, Harry, 10393, Pte., k., Gallipoli, 9/8/15.
Beanland, Walter, 10236, Pte., k., Gallipoli, 14/8/15.
Beard, Charles, 10551, Pte., k., Gallipoli, 7/8/15.
Beasley, Thomas, 11785, Pte., k., 30/11/16.
Beaumont, William, 19736, L/Cpl., d., 18/9/16.
Bedford Victor, 19042, L/Cpl., k., 14/9/16.
Beevers, George Henry, 40289, Pte., d., 18/12/16.
Bennett, Arthur John, 19284, L/Cpl., k., 14/9/16.
Bennington, John, 3/8670, Pte., d., 15/9/16.
Benson, John, 4/8342, Pte., d.h., 15/11/16.
Bentley, Lewis, 18771, Pte., k., Gallipoli, 25/10/15.
Binns, John, 21545, Pte., d., 2/10/16.
Bird, Albert, 15557, Pte., k., Gallipoli, 22/8/15.
Birtley, Charles Edwin, 25290, Pte., k., 27/9/16.
Bishop, Henry, 10766, Pte., k., Gallipoli, 9/8/15.
Blackburn, Fred, 10547, Pte., d.h., 25/9/15.
Blakeley, Herbert, 21513, Pte., k., 14/9/16.
Blandford, Albert Lionel, 20117, Pte., k., 14/9/16, formerly 13008, Hussars.
Bodman, William, 10887, Pte., k., Gallipoli, 9/8/15.
Bolton, James Popplewell, 15531, Pte., k., Gallipoli, 9/8/15.
Booth, Bernard, 10517, Pte., k., Gallipoli, 8/8/15.
Boothroyd, Percy, 40937, Pte., d., 7/12/16.
Botteril, Charles Thomas, 34942, Pte., k., 12/12/16.
Bowen, Francis John, 11875, Pte., k., Gallipoli, 9/8/15.
Bown, Ernest, 34311, Pte., k., 12/12/16.
Boyes, Joseph, 13592, L/Cpl., k., Gallipoli, 7/8/15.
Bradley, John, 11080, Pte., k., Gallipoli, 22/8/15.
Brannan, James, 3/10136, Pte., k., Gallipoli, 9/8/15.
Branton, Bob, 10387, Cpl., k., Gallipoli, 7/8/15.
Briggs, Henry Gelder, 32928, Pte., d., 13/12/16.
Briggs, Percy William, 18864, Pte., k., 14/9/16.
Broadley, James William, 17891, Pte., d., Egypt, 10/10/15.
Broadwith, Edgar, 17186, A/Cpl., k., 27/9/16.
Brodrick, James, 4/8491, Pte., d., Gallipoli, 17/9/15.
Brown, Cecil Geoffrey, 11820, L/Cpl., k., Gallipoli, 9/8/15.
Brown, Charles, 10350, Pte., k., Gallipoli, 9/8/15.
Brown, Norman, 12261, L/Cpl., d., 16/8/16.
Brown, Thompson, 17475, Pte., k., Gallipoli, 22/8/15.
Brown, William Bliss, 11837, L/Cpl., k., Gallipoli, 9/8/15.
Bunton, Frederick William, 19184, Pte., d., 16/9/16.
Burns, Frank William, 10424, Pte., k., Gallipoli, 7/8/15.
Burton, Oswald, 10288, Cpl., k., Gallipoli, 7/8/15.
Busfield, Percy, 17789, Pte., d., Gallipoli, 5/12/15.
Burrows, William, 18983, L/Cpl., d., Gallipoli, 3/12/15.
Byrom, Fred, 11878, Pte., k., Gallipoli, 9/8/15.
Calam, Edward Charles, 10434, L/Cpl., d., Gallipoli, 25/8/15.
Cameron, Matthew, 14829, Pte., d., 10/8/16.
Campbell, Peter, 10298, Pte., k., Gallipoli, 21/8/15.

Carroll, Edward, 11157, Pte., k., Gallipoli, 22/8/15.
Carter, John Edward, 15484, Pte., d., Gallipoli, 9/8/15.
Carthew, William, 11340, L/Sgt., k., Gallipoli, 15/8/15.
Chadwick, William, 3/9276, Pte., d., Egypt, 9/3/16.
Chambers, John, 10817, Pte., k., Gallipoli, 9/8/15.
Chapman, Ralph, 18604, Pte., k., 14/9/16.
Chappin, William, 19997, Pte., k., 27/9/16, formerly 13619, Hussars of the Line.
Charlton, Charles, 18090, Pte., k., 25/11/15.
Charlton, Thomas, 10322, Pte., k., Gallipoli, 9/8/15.
Chilton, Ernest, 10667, Pte., k., Gallipoli, 9/8/15.
Clark, Alfred, 10704, Pte., k., Gallipoli, 9/8/15.
Clark, David, 16021, Pte., d., Gallipoli, 21/8/15, formerly 12003, Northumberland Fusiliers.
Clark, Robert William, 11099, Pte., k., Gallipoli, 22/8/15.
Clarke, Charles Douglas, 11018, Pte., d., Mediterranean, 26/11/15.
Clarke, Frederick, 21536, Pte., k., 27/9/16.
Clayton, Charles, 8470, Sgt., k., Gallipoli, 22/8/15.
Clements, Fred, 19916, Pte., d.h., 18/12/16.
Clewes, John Edward, 12505, Pte., k., Gallipoli, 9/8/15.
Cloak, Ernest, 13242, Pte., k., Gallipoli, 22/8/15.
Clough, Albert Edward, 23967, Pte., k., 27/9/16.
Coates, Albert, 12074, Pte., k, Gallipoli, 9/8/15.
Coates, George Edward, 15755, Pte., k., Gallipoli, 9/8/15.
Coates, Harry, 15431, Pte., k., Gallipoli, 9/8/15.
Cobbledick, Thomas, 11063, Pte., k., Gallipoli, 9/8/15.
Collins, Michael, 15752, Pte., k., Gallipoli 9/8/15.
Condon, Henry, 10626, Pte., k., Gallipoli, 9/8/15.
Conlon, Anthony, 10922, Pte , k., Gallipoli, 9/8/15.
Connell, William, 40278, Pte., d., 13/12/16.
Conner, Richard, 10548, Pte., d., Gallipoli, 30/8/15.
Cook, George, 10453, Pte., k., Gallipoli, 9/8/15.
Cook, John William, 19465, Pte., k., 27/9/16.
Cooke, Joseph, 17487, Cpl., k., Gallipoli, 13/9/15.
Cooper, William, 4/8475, Sgt., k., Gallipoli, 22/8/15.
Copley, Reginald Kew, 18466, Pte., d., Malta, 4/12/15.
Corcoran, Martin, 10238, Pte., k., Gallipoli, 9/8/15.
Corner, Tom, 10937, Pte., k., Gallipoli, 9/8/15.
Coulson, George, 4/7886, L/Cpl., k., 14/9/16.
Coulson, William Sydney, 12518, Pte., k., Gallipoli, 8/8/15.
Covell, William Henry, 18901, Pte., k., 27/9/16.
Coxon, Thomas, 11092, L/Cpl., k., Gallipoli, 9/8/15.
Crabtree, John Rhodes, 10910, L/Sgt., k., Gallipoli, 9/8/15.
Craven, Marshall, 17970, Pte., k., Gallipoli, 9/8/15.
Crawford, John, 15868, Pte., k., Gallipoli, 9/8/15.
Crean, James, 17942, Pte., d., Malta, 10/11/15.
Creaser, Richard Johnson, 3/19885, Pte., k., 27/9/16.
Crofton, George, 3/8508, Pte., k., 14/9/16.

Cross, John, 10611, Pte., k.. 15/9/16.
Crossland, Alfred, 11896, Pte., k., Gallipoli, 9/8/15.
Crossland, Norman, 10207, Pte., k., Gallipoli, 7/8/15.
Crowther, Charles, 13000, Pte., k., 20/11/15.
Cruckshanks, Robert, 10686, Pte., k., Gallipoli, 8/8/15.
Cunningham, Joseph, 10488, Pte., d., Gallipoli, 7/8/15.
Cutts, James William, 18990, Pte., k., 27/9/16.
Cutts, Walter, 20060, Sgt., k , 14/9/16, formerly 22835, Hussars.
Dalby, Morris, 11988, Pte., k., Gallipoli, 9/8/15.
Daly, Peter, 11867, Pte., k., Gallipoli, 10/11/15.
Daniels, William, 19278, Pte., k., 27/9/16.
Darby, Philip, 21021, Pte., k., 14/9/16.
Davey, Francis, 3/9046, Pte., k., Gallipoli, 22/8/15.
Davidson, John, 10868, Pte., d.h., 11/10/14.
Davis, Joseph, 10208, Pte., k., Gallipoli, 9/8/15.
Davis, Richard, 18499, L/Cpl., d.h., 10/12/16.
Davison, Robert Liddell, 19046, Pte., d., Gallipoli, 30/10/15.
Day, George Alfred, 10456, Pte., k., Gallipoli, 21/8/15.
Daykin, Ernest, 13676, Pte., k., 14/9/16.
Dearden, Arthur, 21/966, Pte., d., 11/12/16.
Deilahunty, Richard, 18136, Pte., k., 27/9/16.
Dempster, Gilbert, 15436, Cpl., d.h., 14/10/16.
Dennehey, Charles, 15555, Pte., k., Gallipoli, 22/8/15.
Dixon, George, 10403, L, Sgt., k., Gallipoli, 9/8/15.
Dixon, Harold, 10554, Pte , k , Gallipoli, 9/8/15.
Dixon, Thomas, 11121, L/Cpl., k., Gallipoli, 22/8/15.
Dixon, William, 21060, Pte., k., 27/9/16.
Dobson, Albert, 10583, Pte., k.. Gallipoli, 9/8/15.
Door, John Charles, 20159, Pte., k., 14/7/16, formerly 15818, 12th Res. Cav. Regt.
Duffin, Thomas Howard, 18340, Pte., d., Gallipoli, 29/11/15.
Duffy, Clifford, 21147, Pte., k., 8/9/16.
Duffy, Robert William, 18284, L/Cpl., k., Gallipoli, 29/10/15.
Dunbar, Patrick, 10381, Pte., k., 15/9/16.
Dwyer, Daniel, 10651, Pte., k., Gallipoli, 9/8/15.
Dyson, Harry, 15835, Pte., k., Gallipoli, 9/8/15.
Edmondson, William, 11862, Pte., d., Gallipoli, 22/10/15.
Edwards, Walter, 21464, Pte., k., 14/9/16.
Edwards, Joseph, 11802, Cpl., k., Gallipoli, 8/8/15.
Ellis, Charley, 15758, Pte., k., Gallipoli, 9/8/15.
Emmerson, Samuel, 26272, Pte., k., 27/9/16.
England, Harry, 23049, Pte., k., 27/9/16, formerly 14587, East Yorks. Regt.
Errington, William, 12513, L/Cpl., k., Gallipoli, 9/8/15.
Eyre, Tom, 4/8238, Pte., k., 28/9/16.
Farr, Joseph, 10239, Pte., k., Gallipoli, 9/8/15.
Farrant, Harold, 15224, Pte., k., 14/9/16.
Fellows, Alfred J., 14825, L/Cpl., k., 7/8/15.
Fenwick, George, 11057, Pte., k., Gallipoli, 9/8/15.
Fenwick, William, 21026, Pte., k., Gallipoli, 31/10/15.
Ferguson, Christopher, 21231, Pte., d., Gallipoli, 12/12/15.
Fielding, Wilfred, 18245, L/Cpl., k., 14/9/16.
Finkle, Alfred, 11048, Pte., k., Gallipoli, 7/8/15.
Firth, James, 19330, Pte., k., 27/9/16.
Firth, John Richard, 19231, Pte., k., 25/9/16.

The Prince of Wales's Own (West Yorks. Regt.)—Casualties

Fisher, William Henry, 16006, Pte., k., 27/9/16.
Fletcher, James Coop, 10652, Sgt., k., Gallipoli, 9/8/15.
Fletcher, Robert, 11118, L/Cpl., d., Gallipoli, 31/8/15.
Fogherty, John, 19196, Pte., k., 28/9/16.
Foice, Fred, 15406, Pte., k., Gallipoli, 22/8/15.
Ford, William Frank, 15399, Pte., k., Gallipoli, 9/8/15.
Foster, Alma, 10452, Pte., k., Gallipoli, 9/8/15.
Foster, James, 18131, Pte., k., 28/9/16.
Foster, James, 21486, Pte., k., 28/9/16.
Foster, John, 21208, Pte., d., 10/8/16.
Foster, Robert, 21122, Pte., k., Gallipoli, 21/11/15.
Foster, Thomas William, 12521, Pte., k., Gallipoli, 9/10/15.
Foster, William, 15633, Pte., k., Gallipoli, 9/8/15.
Fountain, Alfred, 10804, Pte., k., Gallipoli, 9/8/15.
Fowler, Watkin Wynne, 8225, C.Q.M.S., d., at sea, 9/8/15.
Freeman, Thomas Flanders, 15587, L/Cpl., k., Gallipoli, 9/8/15.
Frost, Albert Edward, 11790, Pte., k., Gallipoli, 9/8/15.
Fuller, Jonathan, 10658, Pte., k., Gallipoli, 9/8/15.
Gale, Frank, 11798, Cpl., k., Gallipoli, 9/8/15.
Gallagher, Frank, 11470, Pte., k., 14/9/16.
Galloway, Sidney Ernest, 12696, L/Cpl., k., 27/9/16.
Galvin, John, 10277, Cpl., k., 27/9/16.
Ganning, Harry, 18471, Pte., k., 14/9/16.
Gant, Henry, 20126, Pte., k., Gallipoli, 9/11/15, formerly 24364, 12th Res. Cav. Regt.
Garbutt, Frederick, 21973, Pte., d., 16/9/16.
Gardner, Charles, 20005, Pte., d., Malta, 31/12/15, formerly 21194, Hussars.
Gardner, Matthew, 3/10204, Pte., d.h., 28/8/15.
Garforth, John Robert, 40948, Pte., k., 12/12/16.
Garland, John, 4/8515, L/Cpl., k., 15/12/16.
Gater, Herbert, 19926, Pte., d., 9/12/16.
Gaunt, Arthur, 24869, Pte., k., 27/9/16.
Geldart, William, 15716, Pte., k., Gallipoli, 7/8/15.
Germain, Joseph Henry, 10296, Pte., k., Gallipoli, 9/8/15.
Gibson, Horace, 18705, Pte., k., 14/9/16.
Gilchrist, Gordon Khartoum, 15038, L/Cpl., k., 14/9/16.
Gillis, Robert, 11291, L/Cpl., k., Gallipoli, 9/8/15.
Gillis, William, 16031, Pte., k., Gallipoli, 9/8/15.
Godbeer, William Frederick Richard, 10478, Pte., k., Gallipoli, 9/8/15.
Godbehere, William, 10482, Pte., k., Gallipoli, 9/8/15.
Godber, Harold Stanley, 10374, Pte., k., Gallipoli, 9/8/15.
Gold, John, 10608, Pte., k., Gallipoli, 9/8/15.
Goldsmith, Ernest, 17731, Pte., d., Gallipoli, 19/11/15.
Gollaglee, James, 17467, Pte., k., Gallipoli, 27/9/15.
Goode, William, 11866, Pte., d., 1/10/16.
Goodeve, Charles Alfred, 11032, Pte., k., Gallipoli, 9/8/15.
Goodwill, Francis, 33696, Pte., k., 12/12/16.
Goodwin, Thomas, 10858, Pte., k., Gallipoli, 9/8/15.
Gordon, Henry, 11732, L/Cpl., k., Gallipoli, 9/8/15.
Gould, Joseph, 3/8863, Pte., k., 14/9/16.

Graham, Henry, 11146, Sgt., k., Gallipoli, 7/8/15.
Graham, William, 10895, Pte., k., Gallipoli, 9/8/15.
Gratton, Walter, 11843, Pte., d., Gallipoli, 19/8/15.
Grayson, Ewart, 11977, Pte., k., Gallipoli, 20/11/15.
Griffiths, Ernest Henry, 19631, Pte., d., Gallipoli, 8/11/15.
Griffiths, John, 12567, Pte., k., 27/9/16.
Grimshaw, William, 10242, Pte., k., Gallipoli, 7/8/15.
Grocock, James Arthur, 19992, Pte., k., 27/9/16.
Gunby, Ernest, 15730, Pte., k., Gallipoli, 13/8/15.
Hadley, Edward Henry, 11924, Pte., k., Gallipoli, 7/8/15.
Haggarth, Elmer, 12524, L/Cpl., k., Gallipoli, 9/8/15.
Haigh, William, 3/9019, Pte., k., 14/9/16.
Hall, Frank, 13372, Pte., k., Gallipoli, 9/8/15.
Hall, Fred, 21/451, Pte., k., 27/9/16.
Hall, George, 10788, Pte., k., Gallipoli, 26/10/15.
Hall, James, 17445, Pte., k., Gallipoli, 21/8/15.
Hall, John, 19776, Pte., k., 14/9/16.
Hampshire, John William, 15439, Pte., k., Gallipoli, 9/8/15.
Handley, Tom, 33723, Pte., k., 10/12/16.
Hanson, Norman, 10669, Pte., d., at sea, 7/8/15.
Hardisty, Albert, 19842, Pte., k., 5/8/16.
Harling, William Henry, 10528, Pte., k., Gallipoli, 9/8/15.
Harn, James William, 21878, Pte., k., 14/9/16.
Harper, Joseph, 15429, Pte., k., 14/9/16.
Harris, Harry, 10711, L/Cpl., k., Gallipoli, 9/8/15.
Harris, Joseph, 10461, Pte., k., Gallipoli, 9/8/15.
Harrison, Fred, 21478, Pte., k., 14/9/16.
Harrison, Oliver, 15761, Pte., k., Gallipoli, 22/8/15.
Harsley, Ernest, 32205, Pte., k., 12/12/16.
Hawkes, Frederick 10479, Pte., k., Gallipoli, 9/8/15.
Hawkins, William, 18534, Pte., k., 27/9/16.
Hebden, Walter, 19172, Pte., d., Gallipoli, 14/11/15.
Heeley, James, 10497, Pte., k., Gallipoli, 22/8/15.
Hemsley, Hubert, 10053, L/Cpl., k., 7/9/16.
Hewson, Thomas, 10578, Pte., k., Gallipoli, 8/8/15.
Hezelgrave, Mark, 10590, d., at sea, 23/8/15.
Hick, Arthur, 10741, Pte., k., Gallipoli, 22/8/15.
Hill, William, 11880, Pte., k., Gallipoli, 21/8/15.
Hirst, Edward, 10038, Pte., k., Gallipoli, 9/8/15.
Hirst, James Welham, 21510, Pte., k., 27/9/16.
Hitching, Wilfred, 15372, Pte., k., Gallipoli, 8/8/15.
Hoad, Joseph William, 12349, Pte., k., 14/7/16
Hobman, Arthur, 11893, L/Cpl., k., Gallipoli, 7/8/15.
Hobson, Harvey, 10510, Pte., k., 27/9/16.
Hodgkinson, Henry, 18489, Pte., d., Gallipoli, 30/11/15.
Hodgson, Francis, 11876, Pte., k., 15/9/16.
Hodgson, William Henry, 10814, Pte., k., Gallipoli, 10/8/15.
Holden, Jonathan, 12506, Pte., k., Gallipoli, 10/8/15.
Holdsworth, James William, 10513, Pte., k., Gallipoli, 13/8/15.
Holland, Franklin, 10530, L/Cpl., k., Gallipoli, 6/8/15.
Holloway, John Lester, 19646, Pte., k., 29/9/16.

Holmes, Frank James, 20118, Pte., k., (accident), Gallipoli, 31/10/15, formerly 18171, 13th Hussars.
Holmes, Tom, 4/7766, Pte., k. (accident), Gallipoli, 29/10/15.
Holt, James, 15000, Pte., d., at sea, 24/9/15.
Holtby, Charles Ernest, 13526, Pte., k., 14/9/16.
Hopkins, George, 18746, Pte., k., Gallipoli, 5/8/16.
Hopkinson, John, 19718, Pte., d., Gallipoli, 10/11/15.
Horn, Fred, 11914, Pte., k., 14/9/16.
Horne, Frank, 21342, Pte., k., 27/9/16.
Horner, Charles Henry, 17822, Pte., k., 27/9/16.
Horner, Frederick William Charlton, 15228, Pte., k., Gallipoli, 9/8/15.
Horsley, Thomas, 32071, Pte., d., 4/12/16.
Horsman, Ernest, 13212, Pte., k., Gallipoli, 9/8/15.
Horsman, Thomas Albert, 21283, Pte., k., 27/9/16.
Houlison, Robert, 16025, Pte., k., Gallipoli, 9/8/15.
Howarth, Alfred, 12378, Pte., d., at sea, 9/11/15.
Howell, Francis, 15754, Pte., k., Gallipoli, 9/8/15.
Hudson, Thomas Ernest, 10813, Pte., k., Gallipoli, 7/8/15.
Hudson, William, 15729, Pte., d., at sea, 8/8/15.
Huggard, Henry, 10320, Sgt., k., Gallipoli, 9/8/15.
Hughes, Hugh, 3/9199, Sgt., k., Gallipoli, 9/8/15.
Hunton, John, 18486, L/Cpl., d., Gallipoli, 6/11/15.
Hurd, Harry, 10267, Cpl., k., Gallipoli, 7/8/15.
Hutcheson, William, 11046, Pte., k., Gallipoli, 22/8/15.
Hutchinson, George William, 12581, Pte., k., Gallipoli, 15/11/15.
I'Anson, Sydney, 18979, Pte., k., Gallipoli, 1/12/15.
Ibbetson, John, 3/8415, Pte., d., 29/7/16.
Ibbotson, Walter, 15305, Pte., d., at sea, 26/11/15.
Jackson, Richard, 10421, Pte., k., Gallipoli, 9/8/15.
Jacques, William, 17667, A/Cpl., d, 4/10/16.
Jenkinson, Joseph, 18924, Pte., k., 9/8/15.
Jennings, George, 19920, Pte., k., 8/9/16.
Jessop, Arthur, 10213, Pte., k., Gallipoli, 9/8/15.
Jewitt, Fred, 3/8940, Pte., k., 22/8/15.
Jewitt, Harold, 11792, L/Cpl., k., Gallipoli, 9/8/15.
Johnson, Charles, 21116, Pte., d., 11/12/16.
Johnson, William Herbert, 15002, Pte., k., Gallipoli, 7/8/15.
Johnson, William, 3/10232, Sgt., k., Gallipoli, 9/8/15.
Johnson, William Keeling, 15491, L/Cpl., k., Gallipoli, 9/8/15.
Jones, Lewis, 15789, Pte., k., Gallipoli, 22/8/15.
Joyce, Frederick, 3/8814, Pte., k., 11/12/15.
Jubb, William Cecil, 3/9668, Pte., k., 27/9/16.
Kay, Cyril, 19319, Pte., k., 6/6/16.
Kay, Frank, 4/8477, Pte., k., Gallipoli, 30/10/15.
Keith, Alfred, 11164, Pte., k., Gallipoli, 9/8/15.
Kelly, Charles, 11104, Pte., k., Gallipoli, 9/8/15.
Kelley, John, 21671, Pte., k., 14/9/16.
Kilbride, John, 10352, Pte., d., Egypt, 21/8/15.
Killingbreck, Thomas Holland, 17962, Pte., k., Gallipoli, 8/8/15.
King, Reuben, 11163, Pte., k., Gallipoli, 27/9/16.
King, Sidney, 11847, Pte., k., Gallipoli, 8/8/15.

Kingdom, Arthur, 10353, Pte., k., Gallipoli, 9/8/15.
Kirk, Henry, 15251, Pte., d., Gallipoli, 20/8/15
Kirk, Thomas, 10519, Pte., k., Gallipoli, 9/8/15.
Knight, Myles, 3/9321, Pte., k., 2/8/16.
Knowles, Herbert, 11794, Pte., k., Gallipoli, 9/8/15.
Larkin, Michael, 15717, Pte., k., Gallipoli, 22/8/15.
Law, Edward Charles, 11805, Pte., k., Gallipoli, 9/8/15.
Laws, Matthew, 11038, Pte., d., at sea, 10/8/15.
Lawson, Edward, 21111, Pte., k., 27/9/16.
Lawson, Harry, 12053, Pte., k., Gallipoli, 9/8/15.
Leather, Barrow William, 10260, L/Cpl., d., Gallipoli, 27/8/15.
Lee, Lawrence, 19182, Pte., d., at sea, 7/11/15.
Lees, Sam, 18186, Pte., k., Gallipoli, 6/12/15.
Leyden, Peter, 12269, Pte., k., 14/9/16.
Liegh, George Arthur, 15235, Pte., k., Gallipoli, 9/8/15.
Light, William, 11736, Pte., k., 27/9/16.
Linfoot, Ernest, 11877, Pte., k., Gallipoli, 9/8/15.
Linfoot, Guy, 10328, Pte., k., Gallipoli, 8/8/15.
Lloyd, Alfred Sydney, 10571, Pte., d., 29/9/16.
Lloyd, Michael, 10820, Pte., k., Gallipoli, 200
Loftus, Edward, 15742, Pte., d.h., 29/10/16.
Logan, Ernest, 15447, A/Cpl., d., Egypt, 26/5/16.
Long, Christopher, 10657, Pte., k., Gallipoli, 9/8/15.
Longbottom, Arthur Scholes, 15532, Pte., d., Gallipoli, 15/8/15.
Longbottom, Herbert, 21334, Pte., k., 27/9/16.
Lonsdale, Leonard Charles, 15147, Pte., d., Gallipoli, 23/8/15.
Low, Rufus Henry, 10328, Pte., k., 9/8/15.
Lowe, Reuben Wallis, 15296, Pte., k., Gallipoli, 9/8/15.
Mackenzie, Thomas, 12525, Pte., k., Gallipoli 7/8/15.
Maddison, Isaac, 16001, Pte., k., Gallipoli, 8/8/15.
Madgett, Samuel, 18231, Pte., k., 14/9/16.
Maloy, John, 10838, Pte., d., Egypt, 13/8/15.
Manaton, Fred Haslam, 20168, Pte., d., 17/9/16, formerly 13608, Hussars of the Line.
Mansfield, Henry James, 3/9413, Sgt., d., 30/9/16.
Markham, Ernest Albert, 10569, Pte., k., Gallipoli, 9/8/15.
Marriot, James William, 4/8301, Pte., k., 14/9/16.
Marsden, Ernest, 18722, Pte., k., 27/9/16.
Marshall, Frank, 10688, Pte., k., Gallipoli, 9/8/15.
Marshall, Harold, 19444, Pte., d., Gallipoli, 20/11/15.
Marshall, James, 11206, Pte., k., Gallipoli, 9/8/15.
Marshall, Robert, 19880, Pte., k., 27/9/16.
Martin, James Jonah, 15519, Pte., k., 25/9/16.
Martindale, George, 15636, Pte., k., Gallipoli, 9/8/15.
Marvell, Cyril, 15810, Pte., k., Gallipoli, 9/9/15.
Mason, Frederick, 11639, Pte., k., Gallipoli, 16/11/15.
Massheder, Arthur, 15547, Pte., k., Gallipoli 22/8/15.
Massheder, Harry, 17470, Pte., k., 27/9/16.
Mead, George Thomas, 11758, Pte., d.h. 21/12/15.

The Prince of Wales's Own (West Yorks. Regt.)—Casualties 333

Metcalfe, Alfred, 10451, Pte., k., Gallipoli, 22/8/15.
Middlemiss, Alfred, 10302, Sgt., k., Gallipoli, 9/8/15.
Middleton, Thomas, 3/9229, Pte., d.h., 14/9/15.
Miles, Percival, 11822, L/Cpl., k., Gallipoli, 9/8/15.
Miller, Robert, 17493, Pte., k., 27/9/16, formerly 4702, Northumberland Fusiliers.
Millican, John Thomas, 16028, Pte., k., Gallipoli, 8/8/15.
Minnithorpe, Charles Arthur, 10587, Pte., k., Gallipoli, 9/8/15.
Mison, Ernest George, 10562, Pte., k., Gallipoli, 9/8/15.
Moffitt, George Thomas, 19840, Pte., k., 14/9/16.
Monk, Walter George, 21047, Pte., k., Gallipoli, 21/11/15.
Monkley, Ambrose James, 13232, Pte., k., Gallipoli, 7/8/15.
Moody, John Allen, 11345, Pte., k., Gallipoli, 22/8/15.
Moore, William Steedman, 10577, L/Cpl., k., Gallipoli, 9/8/15.
Morrell, John, 21384, Pte., k., 14/9/16.
Morris, Horace John, 10570, L/Cpl., d., Gallipoli, 15/8/15.
Moss, George Henry, 8979, L/Cpl., k., Gallipoli, 7/8/15.
Moss, Percy, 19157, Pte., d., Gallipoli, 10/11/15.
Mower, Charles, 40925, Pte., k., 13/12/16.
Muir, Walter, 10867, Pte., k., Gallipoli, 9/8/15.
Muirhead, Alexander Hardy, 15632, Pte., k., Gallipoli, 13/8/15.
Mulcaster, Wilfred, 10617, Cpl., k., Gallipoli, 9/8/15.
Mullen, Frank, 11135, Pte., k., Gallipoli, 22/8/15.
Mullins, John, 4/7696, Pte., k., 27/9/16.
Mundell, William, 10787, Pte., k., Gallipoli, 9/8/15.
Murray, Thomas, 17431, Pte., k., Gallipoli, 22/8/15.
Mustard, George, 11304, Pte., k., Gallipoli, 9/8/15.
McAndrew, John, 10836, Pte., d., Gallipoli, 12/10/15.
McBeath, Samuel, 21874, Pte., k., 27/9/16.
McDonald, Thomas, 10280, Pte., k., Gallipoli, 9/8/15.
McFarlane, Francis, 13226, Pte., k., Gallipoli, 9/8/15.
McGarvey, Samuel, 10880, Pte., d., at sea, 23/8/15.
McKenzie, Albert, 10418, Pte., k., Gallipoli, 8/8/15.
McKinley, William Charles, 12514, Pte., d., Gallipoli, 14/8/15.
McLean, William, 15634, Pte., k., Gallipoli, 22/8/15.
McLoughlin, James, 21234, Pte., k., 27/9/16.
McNamee, William, 15628, Pte., k., Gallipoli, 9/8/15.
Nettleton, Harold, 15456, Pte., k., Gallipoli, 9/8/15.
Neve, William Maylam, 11801, Pte., k., Gallipoli, 21/8/15.
Newman, Walter, 18241, Pte., k., 14/9/16
Nicholds, Harry, 12382, Pte., d., 25/9/16.
Nicholson, Frederick Wardell, 22196, Pte., k., 27/9/16.
Nithsdale, John Quail, 12539, L/Cpl., k., Gallipoli, 9/8/15.

Nixon, Frederick Joseph, 4/8084, Pte., k., 14/9/16.
Northrop, Fred, 19237, Pte., k., 27/9/16.
Oakes, Thomas, 12508, Pte., k., Gallipoli, 9/8/15.
O'Brien, William, 10870, Pte., k., Gallipoli, 7/8/15.
O'Donnell, John, 11088, Pte., k., 27/9/16.
Officer, Samuel, 12438, Pte., d., 14/9/16.
Ogle, Thomas, 11256, L/Cpl., k., Gallipoli, 9/8/15.
Oldman, Robert, 11292, Pte., k., Gallipoli, 22/8/15.
Oram, Alfred, 15721, Pte., k., Gallipoli, 9/8/15.
Owen, William Michael, 10629, Pte., d.h., 9/10/16.
Padgett, Herbert, 3/9540, C.S.M., d., 30/9/16, D.C.M.
Pape, John Willie, 21563, Pte., k., 1/8/16.
Parker, John Alfred, 3/9034, Pte., k., 14/9/16.
Parker, Snowdon, 12044, Pte., k., 14/9/16.
Parkinson, James, 19125, Pte., k., 27/9/16.
Parkinson, Thomas, 12522, Pte., d., Gallipoli, 10/8/15.
Parry, Richard, 15482, Pte., k., Gallipoli, 9/8/15.
Pawson, William, 11889, Pte., k., Gallipoli, 9/8/15.
Peachey, Harry, 20109, L/Sgt., d., Gallipoli, 13/12/15, formerly 21157, Hussars.
Pearshouse, William, 15341, Pte., k., Gallipoli, 9/8/15.
Pearson, James, 17969, Pte., k., Gallipoli, 9/8/15.
Peel, John William, 11078, Pte., d., 3/8/16.
Petch, Edward, 19901, L/Cpl., k., 14/9/16.
Petherick, Thomas, 4/8659, Pte., k., 14/9/16.
Pickering, Gowan, 17457, L/Cpl., k., Gallipoli, 9/8/15.
Pinchbeck, David Herman, 4/7650, Pte., k., 14/9/16.
Pinder, Bertram, 15371, Pte., k., 27/9/16.
Pinder, Herbert, 45733, Pte., d., 4/12/16, formerly 12265, East Yorks. Regt.
Pitchers, William, 10450, Pte., d., Egypt, 24/8/15.
Plaster, Sydney Clifford, 17455, L/Cpl., k., Gallipoli, 7/8/15.
Pocklington, Louis, 17456, L/Cpl., k., Gallipoli, 9/8/15.
Poole, Benjamin, 18375, Pte., d.h., 30/9/16.
Porter, William, 15363, Pte., k., Gallipoli, 9/8/15.
Potter, Richard, 19564, Pte., k., 28/9/16.
Pounder, Joseph, 11555, Sgt., k., 14/9/16.
Precious, George, 11894, Pte., k., Gallipoli, 9/8/15.
Proctor, Horace, 33694, Pte., d., 30/11/16.
Quigley, John, 18947, Pte., k., 27/9/16.
Quinn, David, 4/8021, L/Cpl., k., 30/11/16.
Ramsay, Percival, 10460, Pte., k., Gallipoli, 9/8/15.
Rathmell, Ernest, 10290, Pte., k., Gallipoli, 22/8/15.
Raynor, William, 15728, A/Cpl., k., 13/9/16.
Render, Herbert, 15621, Pte., k., Gallipoli, 7/8/15.
Revitt, Matthew, 12287, Pte., d., 18/9/16.
Rhodes, Alfred Charles, 10618, Pte., k., Gallipoli, 9/8/15.
Rhodes, Harry, 15411, Pte., k., Gallipoli, 9/8/15.
Rhodes, Rowland Leonard Ambrose, 12112, Pte., k., 27/9/16.
Richardson, Fred, 10915, Pte., k., Gallipoli, 9/8/15.
Richardson, George Alfred, 15250, Pte., k., Gallipoli, 9/8/15.

Richmond, James, 21257, L/Cpl., d., 17/9/16.
Ridsdale, Fred, 11812, Pte., k., Gallipoli, 22/8/15.
Ringrose, Leonard, 12403, Pte., k., 14/9/16.
Ripley, William, 10283, Pte., d., at sea, 20/8/15.
Roan, James, 10446, Pte., k., Gallipoli, 9/8/15.
Roberts, Henry, 13224, Cpl., k., Gallipoli, 22/8/15.
Robinson, Harry, 19290, Pte., d., 12/9/16.
Robinson, Herbert, 19883, Pte., k., 27/9/16.
Robson, George, 10375, L/Cpl., k., Gallipoli, 9/8/15.
Roebuck, Herbert, 19616, L/Cpl., d., 17/9/16.
Rogers, John, 18114, Pte., k., 14/9/16.
Roll, Matthew, 10860, Pte., d., 17/9/16.
Rootkin, Fred, 10252, Pte., k., Gallipoli, 22/8/15.
Ross, Adam, 4/7419, Pte., d., Gallipoli, 31/10/15.
Ross, Fred Myles, 11763, Pte., k., Gallipoli, 27/10/15.
Ruffle, Charles, 8391, Sgt., k., Gallipoli, 9/8/15.
Rushworth, Frank Ewart, 202467, Pte., k., 28/5/16.
Russell, Ernest, 15347, Pte., k., Gallipoli, 10/8/15.
Russell, James William, 10725, Pte., d., 15/9/16.
Russell, John, 10270, Pte., k., 22/8/15.
Sadler, Lewis Henry, 11444, A/Cpl., d., 1/10/16.
Sawyer, Arthur, 10746, Pte., k., 27/9/16.
Sayers, Charles Edward, 10532, C.Q.M.S., d., Gallipoli, 10/11/15.
Sayner, William, 10947, Pte., k., Gallipoli, 9/8/15.
Scales, William, 18702, L/Cpl., k., 14/9/16.
Scott, Benjamin, 17472, L/Cpl., k., Gallipoli, 9/8/15, formerly 25557, Cavalry, Dragoons.
Scott, James Thomas, 7833, Sgt., k., Gallipoli, 9/8/15.
Scott, John, 3/10193, Sgt., k., Gallipoli, 9/8/15.
Scully, John, 10512, L/Cpl., d., Gallipoli, 23/8/15.
Sellers, Tom George, 8161, C.S.M., k., Gallipoli, 9/8/15.
Seyforth, Frederick Edward, 3/10205, Pte., d.h., 22/1/15.
Sharp, Lawrence Edgar, 17961, Pte., k., Gallipoli, 9/8/15.
Sharp, Reginald, 12203, L/Cpl., k., Gallipoli, 9/8/15.
Sharpe, James Arthur, 10549, Sgt., k., Gallipoli, 9/8/15.
Sherwood, Arthur Henry, 11799, Sgt., k., Gallipoli, 9/8/15.
Shevlin, William, 15551, Pte., k., Gallipoli, 9/8/15.
Shields, Percy, 14999, Pte., k., Gallipoli, 22/8/15.
Shortall, Edward, 10715, Pte., d., Gallipoli, 7/12/15.
Simmons, Harry, 20052, Pte., d., Gallipoli, 18/12/15, formerly 13649, Hussars.
Simmons, John, 8188 Pte., d., 18/12/16..
Simpson, Albert, 15317, Pte., k., 22/8/15.
Simpson, James William, 15592, Pte., k., Gallipoli, 9/8/15.
Slee, William, 15629, Pte., k., Gallipoli, 9/8/15.
Slimmon, Thomas, 3/9429, C.S.M., k., Gallipoli, 22/8/15.
Slingsby, John William, 40945, Pte., k., 30/11/16.
Smale, Leonard John, 20029, A/Sgt., k., 14/9/16, formerly 13602, Hussars of the Line.
Smart, Donald, 4/8156, Pte., d., 29/11/16.
Smith, Albert, 10399, Pte., k., Gallipoli, 8/8/15.
Smith, Frederick, 17477, L/Cpl., k., Gallipoli, 9/8/15.
Smith, John, 12519, Pte., d., at sea, 30/8/15.
Smith, John, 15998, Pte., k., Gallipoli, 9/8/15.
Smith, John Henry, 17482, Pte., d., Gallipoli, 31/8/15.
Smith, William, 10879, Pte., k., 15/9/16.
Sowrey, John Richard, 34578, Pte., k., 30/11/16.
Spence, Benjamin, 10344, Pte., k., Gallipoli, 22/8/15.
Spencer, Charles Thomas, 15799, Pte., k., Gallipoli, 9/8/15.
Spencer, George, 10881, Pte., k., 27/9/16.
Spencer, William, 4/7949, Pte., k., 14/9/16.
Spooner, James, 10431, Pte., k., Gallipoli, 9/8/15.
Squibb, George James, 10572, Cpl., k., Gallipoli, 9/8/15.
Stabler, Tom Alexander, 34068, Pte., k., 12/12/16.
Starkey, Fred, 10477, Sgt., k., Gallipoli, 9/8/15.
Stead, John Thomas, 19402, Pte., k., 27/9/16.
Stead, Thomas, 9518, Pte., d., 13/10/15.
Stephens, Charles, 15637, L/Cpl., k., 27/9/16.
Stephenson, Arthur, 15869, Pte., k., Gallipoli, 22/8/15.
Stephenson, George, 33441, Pte., d., 9/12/16.
Stephenson, John William, 33396, Pte., k., 8/12/16.
Stevens, Reginald William, 11489, Pte., k., 27/9/16
Stevenson, William, 9745, Cpl., d., 17/9/16.
Stewart, Charles, 10233, Pte., d.h., 8/11/15.
Stopper, Sydney, 18546, Pte., k., 27/9/16.
Stringer, Frank, 20032, Pte., k., 15/9/16, formerly 16420, 12th Res. Cav. Regt.
Strutt, Arthur, 10829, Cpl., k., 14/9/16.
Stubbs, Tom, 10371, Pte., k., Gallipoli, 22/8/15.
Suddards, Ellis, 10743, Pte., k., Gallipoli, 9/8/15.
Sugden, Lewis, 19947, Pte., d., 30/9/16.
Suggitt, William, 40283, Pte., k., 1/12/16.
Sunderland, Mawson, 3/9169, Pte., k., Gallipoli, 8/11/15.
Swain, Jack Charles, 20131, Pte., k., 27/9/16, formerly 13821, Hussars of the Line.
Swan, William, 16022, Pte., k., Gallipoli, 9/8/15, formerly 4558, Northumberland Fusiliers.
Swift, Albert Edward, 9145, Sgt., k., 14/9/16.
Sykes, Tom, 21162, Pte., k., 25/9/16.
Tarbottom, Richard, 10414, Pte., k., Gallipoli, 9/8/15.
Taylor, Arthur, 10595, Pte., k., Gallipoli, 9/8/15.
Taylor, Harry, 11882, Pte., k., Gallipoli, 9/8/15.
Taylor, Harry, 19670, Pte., k., 14/9/16.
Taylor, William Iveson, 3/9066, Pte., k., 27/9/16.
Terrey, Alfred John, 10527, Pte., d., 15/9/16.
Thackray, Charles, 21604, Pte., k., 27/9/16.
Thirkell, Edward, 15260, L/Cpl., d., Gallipoli, 10/8/15.
Thompson, James, 12423, Pte., d., at sea, 27/1/16.
Thompson, John Thomas, 10502, Cpl., k., Gallipoli, 9/8/15.
Thompson, Robert, 11079, L/Cpl., k., Gallipoli, 8/8/15.
Thompson, Samuel, 13260, Pte., k., 27/9/16.
Thorpe, William, 12183, Pte., k., Gallipoli, 18/10/15.
Threapleton, Joseph, 17979, Pte., k., Gallipoli, 20/8/15.

The Prince of Wales's Own (West Yorks. Regt.)—Casualties 335

Timlin, Edward, 10286, Pte., k., Gallipoli, 9/8/15.
Tingle, Walker, 4/7954, Pte., k., Gallipoli, 30/10/15.
Tinsley, Sidney Francis, 10297, Pte., k., Gallipoli, 8/8/15.
Towle, Joseph Henry, 10812, Pte , k., Gallipoli, 21/8/15.
Town, Sidney, 18490, Pte., k., 27/9/16.
Townsend, John, 4/7240, Pte., k., 18/10/15.
Tozer, Arthur Edward, 11396, Pte., k., Gallipoli, 22/8/15.
Trippitt, Joseph, 6778, Q.M.S., d., at sea, 27/10/15.
Trotter, William, 3/10384, Pte., k., 27/9/16.
Tucker, Charles Henry, 34215, A/Cpl., d., 28/12/16.
Turnbull, John William, 11422, Pte., d , Gallipoli, 1/11/15.
Turnbull, Ralph, 21843, Pte., k., 27/9/16.
Turner, Alexander, 3/8901, Pte., k., 6/11/15.
Turner, Alfred, 8975, Pte., k., 22/8/15.
Turner, George Edward, 3/8946, C.S.M., k., Gallipoli, 22/8/15.
Tuting, Harry, 10771, Pte., d., Gallipoli, 3/11/15.
Twineham, Fred, 4/7860, Pte., k., 14/9/16.
Varley, Frank, 7576, Sgt., k., 9/8/15.
Vasey, George, 19438, L/Cpl., k., 27/9/16.
Vater, William John, 12523, L/Sgt., k., Gallipoli, 9/8/15.
Vear, Henry, 40930, Pte., d., 19/12/16.
Venner, William, 17459, Pte., k., Gallipoli, 22/8/15.
Vevers, George, 9420, Pte., d.h., 15/9/14.
Wade, Frank Clifford, 19896, L/Cpl., k., 27/9/16.
Wadkin, Albert, 15759, Pte., k., Gallipoli, 9/8/15.
Wadkin, Arthur, 11883, Pte., k., Gallipoli, 9/8/15.
Wainfor, Nelson, 12198, Pte., k., 14/9/16.
Walder, Patrick, 19526, Pte., k., 27/9/16.
Wales, Harold, 19298, Pte., k., Gallipoli, 31/10/15.
Walker, Charles, 12104, Pte., d., Gallipoli, 21/11/15.
Walker, James, 33964, Pte., k., 4/12/16.
Waller, Samuel, 18390, Pte., d.h., 4/10/16.
Walls, John William, 19025, L/Cpl., k.,14/9/16.
Ward, Walter, 19286, Pte., k., Gallipoli, 7/11/15
Wardell, John, 10347, L/Cpl., k., Gallipoli, 9/8/15.
Warrilow, Henry, 17448, Sgt., d., Gallipoli, 23/8/15.
Waterman, Charles Leslie, 20141, Pte., k., 27/9/16, formerly 15776, Hussars.
Watkinson, John William, 11688, Pte., k., 27/9/16.
Watson, Fred Samuel, 21304, Pte., k., 27/9/16.
Watson, Harry, 10382, Pte., d.h., 27/8/15.
Watson, John Herbert, 33989, Pte., k., 12/12/16.
Watson, Joseph, 12507, L/Cpl., k., 14/9/16.
Watson, Richard, 21670, Pte., k., 8/9/16.
Watson, Thomas Edward, 21082, Pte., k , 27/9/16.
Webster, Albert Edward, 11899, L/Cpl., k., Gallipoli, 22/8/15.

Webster, Arthur, 6326, Pte., d.h., 28/10/16, formerly 22446, York and Lancs. Regt.
Webster, William Halder, 11654, L/Sgt., k., Gallipoli, 8/8/15.
Welch, Henry, 20043, Sgt., k., 27/9/16, formerly 5211, Devonshire Regt.
Welsh, Frank, 19418, L/Cpl., k., 17/11/16.
West, John Clayton, 10384, Pte., k., Gallipoli, 9/8/15.
Weston, Edmund Harold, 24841, Pte., k., 14/9/16.
Wetherill, John Joseph, 15232, Pte., k., Gallipoli, 9/8/15.
Wetherhill, Joseph, 15480, Pte., k., Gallipoli, 9/8/15.
Whitaker, John Stanley, 15432, Pte., d., Egypt, 2/10/15.
White, William Arthur, 11897, Pte., k., Gallipoli, 9/8/15.
Whitehead, Albert, 12826, Pte., k., 14/9/16.
Whittaker, Frank, 9577, Pte., k., 9/8/15.
Wiggins, Joseph, 17437, Pte., k., Gallipoli, 22/8/15.
Wilkinson, Harry, 19900, Pte., k., 27/9/16.
Wilkinson, Hugh, 11055, Pte., k., Gallipoli, 9/8/15.
Williams, Alfred, 20152, Sgt., k., 14/9/16, formerly 28072, Hussars of the Line
Williamson, Ambrose, 17806, Pte., k., Gallipoli, 24/11/15.
Wilson, Alfred, 21375, Pte., k., 28/9/16.
Wilson, Allan, 15004, Pte., k., Gallipoli, 28/11/15.
Wilson, John, 10940, Pte., k., 27/9/16.
Wilson, William, 17483, Pte., d., at sea, 13/8/15.
Wood, Arthur, 11873, Pte., k., Gallipoli, 8/8/15.
Wood, James Henry, 20999, Pte., k., 14/9/16.
Wood, William, 10999, Cpl., k., Gallipoli, 22/8/15.
Woodhead, Fred, 4/7658, Pte., d., at sea, 20/10/15.
Woolhouse, Booth, 12055, Pte., k., Gallipoli, 9/8/15.
Wooller, James Henry, 3/10236, Pte., k., 22/8/15.
Wooller, Thomas Mortimer, 3/9576, Sgt., k., Gallipoli, 9/8/15.
Wormald, George, 12019, Pte., k., 28/9/16.
Wormald, Willie, 17655, Pte., k., 7/12/16.
Worsnop, Tom, 21778, Pte., k., 9/8/15.
Wright, John, 19946, Pte., k., 27/9/16.
Yarwood, John, 10522, Sgt., d., Gallipoli, 10/9/15.
Yates, Samuel, 15390, L/Cpl., k., Gallipoli, 9/8/15.
York, Francis Stafford, 13219, Sgt., k., Gallipoli, 11/8/15.
Youds, Nicholas, 10810, L/Cpl., k., Gallipoli, 9/8/15.
Youles, Henry, 11818, Pte., k., Gallipoli, 9/8/15.
Young, Arthur Harold, 11016, Cpl., k., Gallipoli, 15/8/15.
Young, Herbert, 11795, Cpl., k., 14/9/16.
Young, John, 10822, Pte., k., Gallipoli, 9/8/15.
Young, Thomas, 11155, Pte., k., 14/9/16.

10th BATTALION

Alexander, Arthur, 13082, Pte., k., 3/3/16.
Anderson, William Francis, 13265, Pte., d., 3/3/16.
Argyle, Albert Victor, 24270, Pte., k., 1/7/16.
Armitage, Charles William, 13035, Pte., k., 1/7/16.
Armstrong, William, 11279, Pte., k., 1/7/16.
Ashley, John, 22003, Pte., k., 1/7/16.

Ashton, William, 43307, Pte., d., 31/10/16 formerly 18489, York and Lancs. Regt.
Atkin, Frederick George, 21216, Pte, k., 1/7/16.
Atkinson, Herbert, 21876, Pte., d., 2/11/16.
Atkinson, Samuel Smilley, 3/9642, L/Cpl., k., 31/10/16.
Atkinson, William, 12599, Pte., k., 1/7/16.
Atkinson, William, 43267, Pte., k., 30/10/16, formerly 30902, Durham L.I.
Baker, James Richard, 12209, Pte., k., 1/7/16.
Baker, John, 15465, L/Cpl., k., 4/5/16.
Ball, Sydney, 14275, Pte., k., 1/7/16.
Ball, Wilfred, 18041, Pte., k., 27/12/15.
Barker, Harry, 19797, Pte., k., 1/7/16.
Barraclough, Ellis, 18393, Pte., k, 1/7/16.
Barrett, John William, 21045, Pte., k., 20/4/16.
Barton, Harold, 13324, Cpl., k., 1/7/16.
Bean, Thomas, 21665, Pte., d.h., 25/8/16.
Beech, Frank, 24731, Pte., k., 1/7/16.
Bell, Charles, 13194, Pte., k., 1/7/16.
Bell, Watson, 10793, Pte., k., 1/7/16.
Bellwood, Robert Henry, 13029, Pte., k., 1/7/16.
Bennett, Forester, 15121, Pte., k., 30/7/15.
Bennett, William, 12341, Pte., k., 1/7/16.
Bennett, William, 11677, Pte., k., 1/7/16.
Bennitt, Lewis Henry, 15706, L/Cpl., k.,1/7/16
Bentley, Harold, 12238, Pte., k., 1/7/16.
Betts, Alma, 19194, Pte., k., 1/7/16.
Birdsall, Thomas, 24783, Pte., k., 1/7/16.
Blackburn, George, 21900, Pte., k., 1/7/16.
Blackwell, Alfred, 28745, Pte., k., 2/11/16.
Blanchard, Frederick, 18023, Pte., k., 1/7/16.
Bland, Thomas, 12016, L/Cpl., k., 27/12/15.
Blick, David, 11804, L/Sgt., k., 1/7/16.
Bloss, John, 15015, Pte., d., 28/7/16.
Bolton, Fred, 19/178, Pte., k., 1/7/16.
Bond, John James, 16172, Pte., k., 1/7/16.
Boocock, Harry, 13102, Pte., k., 1/7/16.
Boon, John George, 19874, Pte., k., 1/7/16.
Booth, Alan, 18057, Pte., d., 3/3/16.
Bovett, William George, 15331, L/Cpl., k., 1/7/16.
Bowers, Jack, 13106, Pte., k., 1/7/16.
Bradbury, William Henry, 11561, Pte., k., 1/7/16.
Bradley, John, 24113, Pte., k., 1/7/16.
Bramham, William, 13128, Pte., k., 4/9/16.
Brayshaw, Edward, 28637, Pte., k., 7/11/16.
Briggs, Elijah Samuel, 3/10078, Pte., k., 1/7/16.
Briggs, Willie, 21057, Pte., k., 1/7/16.
Briggs, William Arthur, 43071, Pte., k., 30/10/16.
Briscombe, Herbert, 43181, Pte., d., 16/11/16.
Britton, Charles Ernest, 12320, Pte., k., 1/7/16
Broadbelt, George, 13553, Pte., k., 1/7/16.
Brook, Rufus Lightowler, 15322, Pte., k., 3/10/15.
Brooke, George Edward, 23957, Pte., k., 11/8/16.
Brown, Andrew, 21944, Pte., k., 1/7/16.
Brown, Charley, 12765, L/Cpl., k., 1/7/16.
Brown, William, 12311, Pte., k., 1/7/16.
Brown, William Shackleton, 13075, Cpl., k., 1/7/16.
Brunskill, Thomas, 15151, Pte., k., 1/7/16.
Burdett, Harry, 12988, L/Cpl., k., 10/11/15.
Burgess, Lawrence, 14314, Pte., k., 1/7/16.
Burtoft, Thomas, 16062, Pte., k., 1/11/15.
Buxton, Frank, 10936, L/Cpl., k., 1/7/16.
Cable, Francis, 11189, Pte., k., 1/7/16.
Calvert, Frederick, 21901, Pte., k., 1/7/16.
Cambage, George Thomas, 17399, Pte., d. 30/4/16.
Cannell, Peter, 15679, Pte., k., 1/7/16.
Chambers, Albert, 14241, Pte., k., 1/7/16.

Chambers, Francis, Henry 18382, Pte., k. 1/7/16.
Chance, Alfred, 15453, Pte., k., 1/7/16.
Charlesworth, Joseph Henry, 43186, Pte., d., 1/11/16.
Clark, Edward, 12043, Cpl., d., 4/7/16.
Clark, John, 24271, Pte., k., 1/7/16.
Clarke, Harold, 11574, L/Cpl., k., 18/9/15.
Clarke, John, 12194, Pte., k., 1/7/16.
Clarkson, Frank, 24042, Pte., k., 1/7/16.
Clayton, Charles, 13606, L/Cpl., k., 1/7/16.
Clinton, Thomas, 11584, Pte., d., 14/11/15.
Coates, Horace Vernon, 23945, Pte., k., 1/7/16.
Cockroft, Harry, 18/726, Pte., k., 1/7/16.
Coggell, Tom, 33259, Pte., k., 11/11/16.
Collins, Edwin, 12094, Pte., k., 1/7/16.
Collins, Percy, 3/10126, Pte., k., 1/7/16.
Collis, George William, 13492, Pte., k., 15/2/16.
Cook, John William, 19791, Pte., k., 1/7/16.
Cook, William, 11987, Pte., k., 1/7/16.
Cooke, Walter, 11945, Pte., k., 1/7/16.
Cooper, George, 16587, Pte., k., 18/4/16.
Cooper, Harry, 13657, Pte., k., 1/7/16.
Cooper, John Edwin, 19808, Pte., k., 1/7/16.
Cooper, Percy, 16051, Pte., k., 2/11/16.
Copley, Ernest, 13367, Pte., k., 1/7/16.
Corker, James, 13503, Pte., k., 1/7/16.
Cox, Richard, 12116, L/Cpl., d.h., 16/7/16.
Crawshaw, William, 12323, Pte., k., 1/7/16.
Crockett, Joseph, 15188, Pte., d.h., 15/8/16
Croft, John, 11706, Pte., k., 1/7/16.
Crook, John, 12669, Pte., d., 8/7/16.
Crossling, John George, 3/10092, Sgt., k., 1/7/16.
Cullen, William, 14589, Pte., k., 4/4/16.
Curry, Oswald, 3/9858, Pte., d., 20/7/16.
Cushlow, Charles, 15156, Pte., k., 1/7/16.
Dale, Robert Henry, 12748, Pte., k., 1/7/16.
Davy, Charles, 18/1496, Pte., k., 1/7/16.
Dawson, David, 11671, Pte., d., 31/12/15.
Day, William George, 3/9827, Cpl., k., 5/5/16.
Dean, Thomas Clifford, 24094, Pte., k., 1/7/16.
Dillon, John, 11621, Pte., k., 15/2/16.
Dixon, Joseph, 15512, Pte., d., 5/7/16.
Dixon, Henry, 11017, L/Cpl., k., 1/7/16.
Dobson, Harry, 23838, Pte., d., 3/8/16.
Dobson, Herbert, 12734, Cpl., k., 1/7/16.
Dockray, Charles, 26327, L/Cpl., d., 14/9/16.
Doherty, Charles, 10/13326, Pte., k., 1/7/16.
Dow, James, 12769, Pte., k., 1/7/16.
Downey, Thomas Lawrence, 11930, Pte., k., 1/7/16.
Doyle, James, 18937, Pte., k., 1/7/16.
Draper, Allen, 12754, Pte., k., 1/7/16.
Draper, William, 15701, L/Cpl., k., 1/7/16.
Drury, Ernest, 13720, L/Cpl., k., 1/7/16.
Duffy, Peter, 3/9369, Sgt., d., 6/7/16, M.M.
Dunn, Ernest, 16/1363, Pte., d., 8/11/16.
Dunn, James, 17986, Pte., d., 19/2/16.
Earnshaw, Lewis, 11972, L/Cpl., k., 1/7/16.
Eden, Arthur, 12255, Pte., k., 3/3/16.
Edmonds, Benjamin, 18082, Pte., k., 3/3/16
Elkington, Robert Stanley, 12208, Pte., k., 1/7/16.
Evans, Alfred, 12132, Pte., k., 25/11/15.
Farr, Robert, 24102, Pte., k., 1/7/16.
Firn, Walter, 13202, Pte., d., 5/5/16.
Firth, John, 12913, Pte., k., 1/7/16.
Fishburn, John William, 19804, Pte., k., 1/7/16.
Fitzwater, George James, 12391, Cpl., k.,1/7/16.
Flanagan, Mark, 17442, L/Cpl., d., 5/4/16.
Fleetwood, Alfred, 12998, L/Cpl., k., 1/7/16.
Flockton, John William, 10636, Pte., k., 1/7/16.
Foster, Arthur, 19872, Pte., k., 1/7/16.
Foster, Edmund, 21065, L/Cpl., k., 1/7/16

The Prince of Wales's Own (West Yorks. Regt.)—Casualties 337

Fox, Richard, 12927, L/Cpl., k., 1/7/16.
Fox, Thomas, 15197, Pte., k., 5/5/16.
Frank, Maxwell, 18989, L/Cpl., k., 15/9/16.
Freer, Robert, 15711, Pte., k., 5/5/16.
Fryer, Ernest, 11519, Pte., k., 7/11/16.
Fryer, Thomas, 10717, Pte., k., 1/7/16.
Fuller, Robert, 13547, Cpl., k., 1/7/16.
Gaiety, Robert, 15510, Pte., k., 1/7/16.
Gamble, James, 12701, Pte., k., 1/7/16.
Garforth, Walter, 18299, Pte., d., 7/7/16.
Gascoigne, George William, 12822, L/Cpl., k., 1/7/16.
Gatenby, Albert, 19823, Pte., k., 30/12/15.
Gaunt, Samuel Driver, 23592, Pte., k., 1/7/16.
Gelder, James, 13013, C.S.M., k., 1/7/16.
Gibson, Sidney Charles, 11659, Pte., k., 1/7/16.
Gilbert, Claude Herbert Edwin, 16042, Pte., k., 1/7/16.
Gilder, John Young, 11026, Cpl., k., 1/7/16.
Gill, William, 11435, Cpl., k., 1/7/16.
Godfrey, Fred, 15693, Pte., k., 13/8/15.
Godwin, Joseph William, 19469, Cpl., k., 1/7/16.
Goode, Sydney, 14876, Pte., d., 2/7/16.
Gott, Fred, 28747, L/Cpl., k., 29/10/16.
Green, George, 24775, Pte., k., 1/7/16.
Green, Norris, 19939, Pte., k., 1/7/16.
Grey, Reginald, 11006, Cpl., k., 5/5/16.
Habgood, George Edward, 15324, Pte., d., 5/7/16.
Haley, Edmund, 8041, Sgt., k., 1/7/16.
Haley, John, 13459, Pte., k., 1/7/16.
Hall, Arthur William, 18027, Pte., d., 29/7/15.
Hall, Charles Arthur, 18/1283, Pte., k., 1/7/16.
Hall, George, 16209, Pte., k., 1/7/16.
Hall, Willie, 18/528, Pte., k., 1/7/16.
Hall, Willis, 13575, Pte., k., 1/7/16.
Halstead, Percy, 40106, Pte., d., 19/11/16.
Handley, Robert, 13816, Pte., k., 29/10/16.
Handley, Robert, 12677, Sgt., k., 3/4/16.
Hannington, Sidney, 15685, Sgt., k., 5/5/16.
Harding, Frank, 11813, Pte., k., 1/7/16.
Hardy, Ernest, 24778, Pte., k., 1/7/16.
Hargrave, Charles Edward, 22138, Pte., k., 1/7/15.
Harland, John, 13237, Pte., k., 1/7/16.
Harland, Maurice, 21007, Pte., d., 4/3/16.
Harmson, Ernest, 23855, Pte., k., 1/7/16.
Harris, Benjamin George, 15735, Pte., k., 1/7/16.
Harrison, Thomas, 3/8845, Pte., k., 1/7/16.
Hawkins, Alfred, 12101, Pte., d., 2/7/16.
Hawley, Ernest, 11925, Pte., k., 1/7/16.
Hayes, Charles, 13449, Pte., k., 1/7/16.
Hebden, Tom, 23906, Pte., k., 1/7/16.
Henderson, Frank, 12686, Pte., d., 8/7/16.
Henderson, Robert, 10904, Pte., k., 3/3/16.
Hewitson, George, 3/9992, L/Cpl., k., 1/7/16.
Hewitt, Bernard, 23949, Pte., k., 1/7/16.
Hewson, John, 24844, Pte., k., 1/7/16.
Hickey, William, 12174, Pte., k., 1/7/16.
Hickman, Edward, 12850, Pte., k., 1/7/16.
Hill, Albert, 13137, Pte., k., 1/7/16.
Hill, Charles, 15/459, Pte., k., 1/7/16.
Hines, Daniel, 11998, Pte., k., 1/7/16.
Hinton, Edward, 18053, Pte., k., 1/7/16.
Hodgson, Clifford, 25209, Pte., d., 8/11/16.
Hodgson, Henry, 12396, Pte., k., 1/7/16.
Holliday, Fred, 13139, Pte., d., 11/7/16.
Hollin, Hubert, 13653, Pte., k., 2/3/16.
Holmes, John Enoch, 15681, L/Cpl., k., 1/7/16.
Holt, William, 12433, Pte., k., 1/7/16.
Hood, Alfred, 23924, Pte., k., 1/7/16.
Hook, Harry, 17/75, Pte., k., 1/7/16.
Hope, John William, 3/9771, Pte., k., 1/7/16.
Hopkinson, Ernest George, 13692, Pte., k., 1/7/16.
Hopwood, Henry Frank, 18059, Pte., k., 1/7/16.
Horner, Francis, 21812, Pte., k., 1/7/16.
Hoyle, John, 19755, Pte., d., 4/7/16.
Huggins, William, 12342, Pte., k., 1/7/16.
Hull, John Murville, 11660, Pte., k., 1/7/16.
Hullah, Arthur, 19757, Pte., k., 1/7/16.
Hunter, Edward, 40129, Pte., k., 1/11/16.
Hyde, Tom, 3/9664, Pte., k., 1/7/16.
Ibbitson, John, 15/495, Pte., k., 14/7/16.
Ingram, John, 11615, Pte., k., 1/7/16.
Jackson, Albert, 3/9263, Pte., d., 5/7/16.
Jackson, Albert, 11287, Pte., k., 1/7/16.
Jackson, Fred, 11294, Pte., k., 1/7/16.
Jackson, Harold, 11683, Pte., k., 1/7/16.
Jackson, Thomas, 16045, Pte., k., 20/9/15.
Jackson, Wilfred, 19785, Pte., k., 1/7/16.
Jennings, Charles Harold, 15203, Pte., d. 27/11/15.
Jennings, Wilfred, 12249, Pte., d., 5/7/16.
Jessop, Frank, 21002, Pte., k., 21/2/16.
Jones, Charles, 13177, L/Cpl., k., 2/3/16.
Jones, Harry, 14600, Pte., k., 1/7/16.
Jones, Jesse, 13272, L/Cpl., k., 1/7/16.
Johnson, Benjamin, 3/10366, Sgt., k., 5/5/16.
Johnson, Ernest, 3/8627, Pte., k., 1/7/16.
Jordon, James, 14678, Cpl., k., 1/7/16.
Kavanagh, John, 13239, Pte., k., 1/7/16.
Kerrigan, Charles, 11631, Pte., k., 20/4/16.
Kershaw, Frederick William, 12444, Pte., k., 3/3/16.
Ketch, James, 43057, Pte., d., 7/11/16.
Kidger, Cornelius, 12914, Pte., k., 1/7/16.
King, Robert, 11628, Pte., k., 28/10/15.
Kingston, Joseph, 21815, Pte., k., 30/10/16.
Kirkbride, John William, 13555, Pte., d.h., 10/4/16.
Kirkwood, Clifford, 12844, Pte., k., 1/7/16.
Knighton, Harold, 11947, Pte., k., 5/5/16.
Lambert, Thomas, 11682, Pte., k., 1/7/16.
Langrick, Cyril Henry, 43408, Pte., k., 7/11/16, formerly 10250, East Yorks. Regt.
Langthorne, Frank, 13248, Pte., k., 4/4/16.
Lawrence, Leonard, 16066, Pte., k., 1/7/16.
Lea, Clarence, 23886, Pte., d., 3/7/16.
Leaf, Robert, 11503, Pte., k., 3/3/16.
Lee, Henry, 3/9316, Pte., k., 1/7/16.
Lee, Harry, 21449, Pte., k., 1/7/16.
Levi, Barnet, 25660, Pte., k., 30/10/16.
Levi, Louis, 24065, Pte., d., 5/7/16.
Livsey, Charles Sidney, 21085, Pte., k., 1/7/16.
Locker, John Edward, 15715, L/Cpl., d., 28/11/15.
Long, Thomas, 19517, Pte., k., 1/7/16.
Longbottom, Percy, 12810, Pte., k., 1/7/16.
Longbottom, William, 12751, Pte., k., 1/7/16.
Lowes, Harold, 12993, Pte., k., 1/7/16.
Lowes, John, 13016, Pte., k., 1/7/16.
Lowther, James, 13255, Pte., k., 1/7/16.
Ludlam, Albert, 16070, L/Cpl., k., 1/7/16.
Maccabe, Albert, 12729, Pte., k., 1/7/16.
Mainwaring, Henry, 12942, L/Cpl., k., 27/8/15.
Marr, James, 12746, Pte., k., 1/7/16.
Marr, William, 21657, Pte., k., 1/7/16.
Marsden, John, 23834, Pte., k., 7/7/16.
Mawhinney, George, 43251, Pte., k., 30/10/16, formerly 31784, 4th Durham L.I.
Medd, Tom, 12032, Pte., k., 1/7/16.
Mennell, Roy Walter, 43101, Pte., k., 2/11/16.
Merritt, Edwin James, 15420, Pte., k., 1/7/16.
Metcalfe, Henry Norris, 43285, Pte., k., 30/10/16, formerly 30876, Durham L.I.
Metcalfe, William, 16251, Pte., k., 1/7/16.
Miller, Richard, 10869, Cpl., drowned at sea, 17/11/15.
Minard, George, 11424, Pte., k., 1/7/16.

Mitchell, William, 12339, Sgt., k., 1/7/16.
Moody, John Watson, 11692, Sgt., k., 1/7/16, M.M.
Moorby, James Lambert, 18061, Pte., k., 1/7/16.
Moorhouse, William Henry, 18/661, Pte., k., 1/7/16.
Moran, John Edward, 13762, Pte., k., 1/7/16.
Morley, Edward, 21858, Pte., d., 12/3/16.
Morley, Fred, 16430, Pte., k., 20/4/16.
Morris, Frederick, 18040, Pte., k., 2/3/16.
Mortimer, George, 23862, Pte., k., 1/7/16.
Morton, Arthur, 10640, Pte., d., 21/2/16.
Moses, Edward Henry, 10729, Pte., k., 1/7/16.
Mudd, Thomas, 24952, Pte., k., 1/7/16.
Mulholland, Alex, 15986, Pte., k., 1/7/16.
Myco, Harry, 12771, Pte., k., 3/3/16.
Myers, Harry, 23964, Pte., k., 1/7/16.
McCarton, Edward, 43252, Pte., k., 8/11/16, formerly 31519, Durham L.I.
McDermott, Timothy, 21984, Pte., k., 1/7/16.
McIntosh, Harry, 12529, Pte., k., 1/7/16.
McKenzie, Frederick, 21785, Pte., k., 1/7/16.
McLoughlin, Michael, 13263, Pte., k., 1/7/16.
McLoughlin, Joseph, 13117, Pte., k., 1/7/16.
Nagle, Joseph, 18/1136, Pte., k., 1/7/16.
Naylor, Herbert, 12059, Pte., k., 1/7/16.
Neil, Thomas James, 43287, Pte., k., 3/11/16, formerly 30890, Durham L.I.
Newbold, James Neville, 16274, Pte., d., 3/3/16.
Newby, Ernest William, 19369, Pte., k., 1/7/16.
Newcombe, John, 11953, Pte., k., 5/5/16.
Nicholls, Robert Edgar, 43170, Pte., k., 30/10/16, formerly 1181, 3rd East Yorks. Regt.
Norman, John, 15054, Pte., k., 1/7/16.
Norman, William, 12227, Pte., k., 1/7/16.
North, John William, 12416, Pte., d., 6/7/16.
Nowell, Francis Arthur Grylls, 18351, Pte., k., 1/7/16.
Nunn, Charlie, 43198, Rfln., d.h., 30/11/16.
Nunn, Arthur, 17425, Pte., k., 1/7/16.
O'Brien, Luke Thomas, 13549, Sgt., k., 1/7/16.
O'Hare, John, 11072, Cpl., k., 4/5/16.
Oldroyd, Linley, 26356, L/Cpl., k., 1/7/16.
Oliver, Joseph, 15037, Pte., d.h., 16/7/16, M.M.
Ord, James, 11890, Pte., k., 1/7/16.
Ovenden, George, 5892, C.S.M., k., 5/5/16.
Palfreeman, Stead, 14/13306, Pte., k., 1/7/16.
Parker, Jim, 12142, Pte., k., 1/7/16.
Parry, Arthur, 13388, Pte., k., 1/7/16.
Patrick, George, 13178, Cpl., k., 1/7/16.
Patrick, Horatio, 19816, Pte., d., 5/7/16.
Patterson, James, 18559, Pte., k., 9/11/15, formerly B1740, 11th Rifle Brigade.
Pawson, Harry, 13011, Pte., d.h., 1/5/15.
Paylor, John William, 21457, Pte., k., 1/7/16.
Pearson, John, 19173, Pte., k., 9/11/15.
Pearson, Robert, 18458, Pte., k., 15/2/16.
Pearson, Thomas Henry, 13203, Pte., k., 3/3/16.
Peterson, Edward John, 18067, Pte., k., 22/2/16.
Pickersgill, Alfred, 3/10127, Pte., k., 30/12/15.
Pickersgill, Charles, 10971, Pte., k., 1/7/16.
Place, Willie, 25331, Pte., k., 1/7/16.
Platts, Ernest, 19087, Pte., k., 1/7/16.
Porritt, John Andrew, 12742, Pte., k., 1/7/16.
Porter, Robert, 13603, L/Sgt., k., 28/10/15.
Power, Leonard Anthony, 11012, Pte., k., 1/7/16.
Preston, Harry, 12728, Pte., k., 1/7/16.
Prouse, George, 9450, Pte., k., 1/7/16.
Pugh, Richard Henry, 15337, Pte., k., 3/3/16.
Purcell, Richard, 3/10301, Sgt., k., 1/7/16.
Quinn, James, 13908, L/Cpl., k., 1/7/16.
Raper, Mathew, 18/1177, k., 8/8/16.
Reed, Alfred, 3/9555, Pte., d., 9/7/16.

Rees, William, 11538, Pte., k., 3/3/16.
Reynolds, Thomas, 11905, L/Cpl., k., 1/7/16.
Richmond, John, 14712, Pte., k., 1/7/16.
Richmond, Joseph William, 13278, Pte., k., 1/7/16.
Richmond, Wilfred Norburn, 43129, Pte., k., 7/11/16, formerly 790, East Yorks. Regt.
Ridley, Tom, 28601, Pte., k, 1/11/16.
Riley, Wilfred, 10633, Pte., k., 1/7/16.
Robertshaw, John Edward, 14161, Pte., k., 1/7/16.
Robertshaw, William, 12361, Pte., k., 1/7/16.
Robinson, Edwin, 12936, Pte., k., 1/7/16.
Robinson, Lawrence, 43131, L/Cpl., d., 25/12/16, formerly 708, East Yorks. Regt.
Robinson, William, 19661, Sgt., k., 1/7/16.
Robinson, Walter, 11589, Pte., k., 1/7/16.
Roddy, John Edward, 12502, Pte., k., 1/7/16.
Rose, William, 12952, Pte., d., 15/11/15.
Russell, Arthur Charles, 12383, L/Cpl., k., 2/3/16.
Ryott, Leonard Gordon, Pte., k., 3/3/16.
Sadler, Thomas, 12121, Pte., d., 29/12/15.
Saville, James Hood, 19805, Pte., k., 4/5/16.
Schofield, Harry, 10972, L/Cpl., k., 1/7/16.
Schofield, Joseph Sam, 10973, Pte., k., 1/7/16.
Scott, Arthur Irwin, 19/116, Pte., k., 1/7/16.
Scott, William, 19801, Pte., k., 1/7/16.
Seage, William Samuel, 19815, Pte., k, 1/7/16.
Sedgwick, Leonard, 16432, Pte., d., 13/7/16.
Severn, John, 10/12374, L/Cpl., k., 1/7/16.
Seymour, Frank, 13659, Cpl., k., 1/7/16, D.C.M.
Shannon, John, 19978, L/Cpl., k., 1/7/16.
Sharp, Albert Edward, 12334, Pte., k., 1/7/16.
Sharp, George, 24752, Pte., d., 2/7/16.
Sharp, Harry Leonard, 43138, Pte., k., 11/11/16.
Shaw, George Herbert, 13756, L/Cpl., d., 6/5/16.
Sheldrake, John, 12915, Pte., d., 3/7/16.
Shipman, Edward, 10362, Pte., k., 1/7/16.
Shipman, Lawrence, 25709, Pte., k., 1/7/16.
Shippen, Albert, 24243, Pte., k., 1/7/16.
Shoesmith, Fred, 18/1452, Pte., d., 12/7/16.
Showell, Bertie, 15695, Pte., k., 1/7/16.
Shuttleworth, Squire, 12761, Pte., k., 1/7/16.
Siddaway, James, 18020, Pte., k., 1/7/16.
Simms, George Francis, 16057, Pte., k., 2/3/16.
Sims, Charles Angus, 18096, Pte., k., 4/5/16.
Smallwood, Tom, 11934, Pte., k., 22/2/16.
Smith, Arthur, 18/1600, Pte., k., 1/7/16.
Smith, Frank, 17/1590, Pte., k., 1/7/16.
Smith, Frederick William John, 12219, Sgt., k., 1/7/16.
Smith, George, 18/1067, Pte., d., 23/7/16.
Smith, James Arthur, 21041, Pte., d., 23/7/16.
Smith, Joseph, 43421, L/Cpl., k., 25/12/16, formerly 15602, York and Lancs. Regt.
Smith, John Edward, 12220, L/Cpl., d., 2/7/16
Smith, John Norris, 19/135, Pte., k., 1/7/16
Smith, Stephen, 6261, C.S.M., k., 1/7/16.
Smith, Thomas, 18553, Pte , d., 23/2/16.
Smyth, Albert Edward, 24068, Pte., d., 5/7/16
Spence, Ernest, 18/1468, Pte., k., 1/7/16.
Spooner, Wilfred John, 14886, Pte., d., 6/5/16.
Stansfield, Thomas, 43202, Pte., k., 30/10/16.
Stark, William Raymond, 43145, Pte., d., 5/11/16, formerly 1259, East Yorks. Regt.
Starr, Henry, 12693, L/Cpl., k., 28/10/15.
Stead, John, 18/1598, Pte., d., 1/7/16.
Stead, Laurence, 24244, Pte., k., 1/7/16.
Steer, Percy, 18026, Pte., k., 14/2/16.
Stevens, Charles Ernest, 3/9231, Sgt., d.h. 7/3/15.
Stevens, Ernest, 13162, Pte., k., 1/7/16.

Stockdale, David, 18/1457, Pte., k., 1/7/16.
Stonehouse, Samuel Dickson, 19166, Pte., k., 1/7/16.
Stowe, Ernest, 10772, Pte., k., 1/7/16.
Street, Leonard, 19479, Pte., k., 1/7/16.
Sullivan, Francis, 23284, Pte., k., 1/11/16.
Summers, John, 15314, L/Cpl., k., 1/7/16.
Summersgill, James Arthur, 18/863, Pte., k, 1/7/16.
Sutton, John, 11765, Pte., k., 1/7/16.
Swann, Everett George, 11675, Pte., d., 12/7/16.
Swift, James, 21018, Pte., d.h., 9/10/16.
Tattersall, George Robert, 11513, Pte., k., 1/7/16
Taylor, Charles, 17/161, Pte., k., 1/7/16.
Taylor, Charles, 18025, L/Cpl., k., 2/3/16.
Taylor, George Edward, 43148, Pte., k., 30/10/16, formerly 941, 5th East Yorks. Cycle Corps.
Taylor, George Henry, 43299, Pte., d., 31/10/16 formerly 13/1117, East Yorks. Regt.
Taylor, Oliver, 23874, Pte., k., 1/7/16.
Taylor, William Edward, 33497, Pte., d., 8/11/16.
Thompson, George Edward, 19862, Pte., k., 1/7/16.
Thompson, Herbert, 15193, Pte., k., 1/7/16.
Thompson, Joseph, 12858, L/Sgt., k., M.M.
Thompson, Joseph Harold, 20/42, Pte., k., 1/7/16.
Tindale, Edwin, T.R./5/20057, Pte., d.h., 10/11/16.
Tomlinson, Samuel, 11730, Pte., k., 1/7/16.
Tonge, William, 10/13376, L/Cpl., k., 1/7/16.
Toulson, William, 12762, Pte., d., 1/11/16.
Towler, John Albert, 15694, Pte., k., 1/7/16.
Townend, David, 13019, Pte., k., 1/7/16.
Turner, John, 16055, Pte., k, 1/7/16.
Turner, John, 19/72, Pte., k., 1/7/16.
Turner, Robert Henry, 13103, Pte., k. 5/5/16
Tuttle, John Thomas Rushbrook, 12036, L/Cpl., k., 1/7/16.
Tyler, Percy, 11853, Pte., k., 1/7/16.
Upton, Harry George, 16343, L/Cpl., k.,1/7/16.
Varley, Harold, 13031, Pte., k., 1/7/16.
Veal, James, 13133, Pte., k., 1/7/16.
Waddington, Herbert, 13152, Pte., k., 1/7/16.
Waddington, Harry, 22380, Pte., k., 1/7/16.
Walker, Clifford, 12992, Cpl., k., 1/7/16.

Walker, John Henry, 11761, Pte., k., 1/7/16.
Walker, William, 9713, Sgt., k., 1/7/16.
Wall, Frederick Arthur, 18052, Pte., k., 1/7/16.
Ward, Richard, 23912, Pte., k., 1/7/16.
Warringham, Andrew, 43332, Pte., k., 31/10/16, formerly 4631, York and Lancs. Regt.
Warrington, Arthur, 28752, L/Cpl., k., 30/10/16.
Warriss, William, 12500, Pte., k., 1/7/16.
Waterfall, Arthur, 17098, Pte., d.h., 26/7/16.
Watkinson, James, 19971, Pte., k., 1/7/16.
Watson, Leonard, 28786, Pte., k., 1/11/16.
Watts, Enoch, 17374, Pte., k., 1/11/16, formerly W 15182, East Yorks. Regt.
Waudby, Frank, 12179, Pte., k., 1/7/16.
Weatherill, Clarence, 11588, L/Cpl., k., 2/3/16
Wharton, Percy, 11623, L/Cpl., k., 1/7/16.
Whelan, James, 11134, Pte., k., 1/7/16.
Whitaker, John William, 19943, Pte., k., 1/7/16.
White, Edward, 12855, Pte., k., 1/7/16.
White, George Robert, 13423, Pte., k., 1/7/16.
Whitehead, Arthur, 11935, L/Cpl., k., 1/7/16.
Whitehead, James, 15578, Pte., k., 1/7/16.
Whiteley, Charles, 23896, Pte., k., 1/7/16.
Wigglesworth, James, 12293, Pte., d., 27/12/15.
Wildman, Joseph Constantine, 24237, Pte., k., 1/7/16.
Wilkins, Charles, 12373, Pte., k., 1/7/16.
Willford, Arthur Chester, 43160, Pte., k., 31/10/16, formerly 5421, East Yorks. Regt.
Williams, William, 22014, L/Cpl., k., 1/7/16.
Williamson, Thomas, 13607, Pte., k., 1/7/16.
Wilson, Harold, 18054, Pte., d., 7/7/16.
Wilson, James, 11902, Pte., k., 1/7/16.
Wilson, John William Hayes, 12310, Pte., d., 3/7/16.
Winn, Richard, 13247, Pte., k., 1/7/16.
Winson, Edgar, 11024, Pte., k., 11/12/15.
Wombwell, Fred, 13681, Pte., k., 1/7/16.
Wood, Alfred William, 43265, Pte., d.,30/10/16, formerly 31554, Durham L.I.
Woodhead, Squire, 10917, Pte., k., 5/5/16.
Woodward, William Robinson, 24683, Pte., k., 2/11/16.
Worsman, Fred, 3/9982, Pte, d., 27/3/16.
Worth. John William, 12974, Pte., d., 1/7/16.
Wray, Henry Ernest, 21825, Pte., d., 4/7/16.
Younger, Alfred, 18036, Pte., k., 1/7/16.

11th BATTALION

Allison, Cyril, 19/154, Pte., d., 24/8/16.
Appleyard, Wilfred, 26905, Pte., k., 7/10/16.
Ashforth, William Henry, 13699, Pte., k., 10/7/16.
Ashmell, Arthur Edward, 24537, L/Cpl., k., 7/10/16.
Atkinson, Albert, 15/1807, Pte., k., 10/7/16.
Atkinson, Ernest, 15929, L/Cpl., d., 11/7/16.
Atkinson, John, 12838, Pte., d.h., 27/10/16.
Atkinson, Walter, 22405, Pte., d., 1/6/16.
Baker, Walter, 15896, Pte., k., 7/10/16.
Barron, John William, 14182, Pte., k., 4/7/16.
Bartle, Ernest, 24152, Pte., k., 20/7/16.
Battle, John Patrick, 4/8557, Pte., k., 14/11/16.
Batty, Percival, 36580, Pte., k., 20/11/16.
Baxter, Thomas, 4/8250, Pte., k., 4/7/16.
Bell, Albert Horace, 24049, Pte., k., 7/10/16
Berry, Albert, 12710, Pte., k., 30/1/16.
Binns, Arnold, 13109, Pte , k., 30/1/16.
Blackburn, Wilfred, 13927, Pte., k., 7/10/16.
Briggs, Harold Archibald, 15132, Pte., k., 10/7/16.

Britton, Harry, 27773, Pte., k., 7/10/16.
Brown, William Henry, 13845, A/C.Q.M.S., k., 27/9/16.
Burns, Robert, 14761, L/Cpl., k., 4/7/16, M.M.
Burrows, Cyril, 23783, Pte., k., 16/7/16.
Burton, William, 13680, Pte., k., 7/10/16.
Calpin, Joseph Farrell, 14073, Pte., d., 19/5/16.
Calvert, Thomas, 14215, Pte., k., 8/1/16.
Carlton, Samuel Senior, 13034, Pte., d.,22/5/16.
Chapman, Lewis, 14017, Pte., k., 27/1/16.
Clay, Arthur, 14499, Pte., k., 7/10/16.
Cockayne, John, 21322, Pte., k., 10/7/16.
Coffin, Harold William, 15662, L/Cpl., d., 23/8/16.
Cole, Albert, 15939, Pte., d.h., 7/8/16.
Collins, Richard, 4/6645, Sgt., d., 1/8/16.
Connor, Thomas, 15845, Pte., k., 4/7/16.
Cowlishaw, Walter, 12543, Pte., d., 28/1/16.
Cox, John, 14605, Pte., k., 7/10/16.
Crane, Robert, 21556, Pte., d.h., 15/10/16.
Craven, John, 13147, Pte., k , 29/7/16.
Craven, Willie, 13062, Pte., k., 16/4/16.

Creswick, James, 14498, Pte., k., 7/10/16.
Crowther, Maurice, 43751, Pte., d., 21/10/16, formerly 28252, K.O.Y.L.I.
Cuff, William Henry, 8836, Pte., k., 5/7/16.
Davies, John, 15663, Pte., k., 5/7/16.
Davis, Arthur James, 15138, Pte., k., 7/10/16.
Davis, Charlie, 14347, Pte., k., 4/7/16.
Derry, Willis, 22448, Pte., k., 4/7/16.
Dews, Frederick, 5299, A/R.S.M., k., 21/9/16.
Dixon, James, 43761, Pte., k., 7/10/16, formerly 28235, K.O.Y.L.I.
Dyer, Harry, 14316, Pte., d., 3/8/16.
Dykes, William Henry, 13377, Sgt., d., 8/10/16.
Eaton, George, 13567, Pte., k., 10/7/16.
Eddison, James, 15/1025, Pte., d., 13/7/16.
Edmondson, James, 13642, Pte., k., 22/9/16.
Ellt, Horace, 14531, Pte., k., 10/7/16.
Eshelby, Herbert, 13535, Pte., k., 5/7/16.
Flynn, Peter, 13482, Cpl., k., 7/10/16.
Frankland, Arthur, 13079, Pte., d., at sea, 17/11/15.
Fretwell, Fred Valentine, 22465, Pte., d., 14/10/16.
Furness, James, 14238, Pte., k., 5/7/16.
Gibson, Ernest, 13780, Pte., k., 10/7/16.
Gladwin, Harry, 43718, Pte., k., 7/10/16, formerly 15083, West Riding Regt.
Golding, Charles, 23302, Pte., k., 7/8/16.
Goodall, Fred, 4/8547, Pte., d., 9/7/16.
Gorman, Thomas, 16/23, Sgt., d., 13/7/16.
Gray, Joseph, 13970, L/Cpl., k., 29/9/16.
Guyll, Percy, 12/16521, Pte., k., 7/10/16, formerly 18615, Yorks. Regt.
Hague, George Harry, 43757, L/Cpl., k., 7/10/16, formerly 9/12213, West Riding Regt.
Hague, Stamford, 3/10338, L/Cpl., k., 5/7/16.
Hales, William Richard, 14339, Pte., k., 4/7/16.
Hall, John, 13295, Cpl., k., 2/9/16.
Hall, Stanley, 13988, Pte., k., 5/7/16.
Hardcastle, Edwin, 23807, Pte., d., 12/7/16.
Harland, Roland, 13838, Pte., k., 3/2/16.
Harper, Bert, 14540, Sgt., d., 21/9/16.
Harris, William Henry, 19734, Pte., k., 5/7/16.
Hartley, Ernest, 16/372, L/Cpl., k., 7/10/16.
Hartley, Lorrie, 12013, L/Cpl., k., 20/9/16.
Hastings, George, 15823, Pte., k., 7/10/16.
Havelock, Frank, 14508, Pte., k., 7/10/16.
Hearon, Thomas, 4/8670, Pte., k., 2/9/16.
Hobson, Ernest, 24925, Pte., d.h., 27/7/16.
Hogg, Richard Warmsley, 13829, A/Sgt., k., 7/10/16.
Holdsworth, Herbert, 10984, Pte., d., 4/10/15.
Hudson, James Arthur, 19636, Pte., d.h., 6/8/16.
Hutton, Henry, 4/8641, Pte. d., 8/10/16.
Ismay, William, 14/12012, L/Cpl., d., 30/5/16.
Jackson, John, 18/217, Pte., k., 7/10/16.
Jackson, Harry, 12750, Pte., k., 4/7/16.
Jewitt, Reginald, 15891, Pte., d., 12/10/15.
Johnson, Robert, 15903, Pte., k., 7/10/16.
Jones, Henry, 14022, Pte., k., 7/10/16.
Kendall, John Edward, 23288, Pte., k., 4/7/16.
King, William, 28869, Pte., k., 7/10/16.
Lane, Leonard Wilson, 14335, L/Cpl., k., 6/10/16, M.M.
Langham, George, 12584, Pte., k., 7/10/16.
Lansdown, James, 15273, Cpl., d., 8/10/16.
Lavin, Michael, 14587, Pte., k., 7/10/16.
Leonard, Samuel, 21421, Pte., d., 7/7/16.
Leuchters, Douglas, 15/1616, Pte., k., 10/7/16.
Lewis, Joseph, 43723, Pte., k., 7/10/16, formerly 18503, West Riding Regt.
Lobley, Alfred, 15919, Pte., d.h., 10/11/16, M.M
Lockett, Thomas James, 18439, Pte., d., 1/1/16.

Lund, Norman, 18/1526, Pte., k., 7/10/16.
Manley, Joseph, 13300, Pte., k., 1/1/16.
Marples, John William, 11537, Pte., k., 4/7/16.
Marsden, Arthur, 18/1270, Pte., d., 18/7/16.
Marshall, Norman Dale, 13512, Pte., k.,28/1/16.
Massey, William, 14139, Pte., k., 7/10/16.
Maybury, Arthur, 15732, Pte., k., 7/10/16.
Metcalfe, Aaron, 13302, Pte., d., 2/1/16.
Midgley, Frank, 43728, Pte., k., 7/10/16, formerly 11/18106, West Riding Regt.
Monson, Alfred, 22467, Pte., k., 4/7/16.
Moorby, John Wilkinson, 14214, Pte., k., 3/9/16.
Morley, Austin, 14131, Pte., k., 5/7/16.
Morris, Allen, 14154, Cpl., k., 28/7/16.
Mullins, Daniel, 18/1033, Pte., k., 7/8/16.
Myers, Martin, 13811, Pte., k , 2/4/16.
Nester, Walter, 13767, A/Cpl., d., 19/10/16.
Nelson, William, 18/1137, Pte., d., 10/10/16.
Nightingale, Arthur, 43756, Pte., k., 7/10/16, formerly 28243, K.O.Y.L.I.
Noble, Harry, 43730, Pte., k., 7/10/16, formerly 11/19162, West Riding Regt.
Oliver, William, 13513, Pte., 13/11/15.
Osborne, Ernest William, 11/13360, Pte., k., 9/1/16.
Otway, Joseph, 14443, Cpl., d., 29/9/16.
Overton, Joseph, 12712, Pte., k., 20/9/16.
Parker, William, 18/1175, Pte., k., 7/10/16.
Parsons, William, 14742, Pte., k., 7/10/16.
Pearson, William, 16/714, L/Cpl., k., 7/10/16.
Pennistone, Herbert, 4/8331, Pte., d., 5/9/16.
Petty, Sylvester, 18/39, Pte., k., 7/10/16.
Phillips, William Henry, 15/1466, Pte., k., 7/10/16.
Pilley, George Richard, 43734, Pte., k., 7/10/16, formerly 11/18238, West Riding Regt.
Pitts, Louis, 43735, Pte., k., 20/9/16, formerly 11/18122, West Riding Regt.
Ratcliffe, John William, 21928, Pte., d., 9/10/16.
Reay, John, 15900, Pte., d.h., 30/12/16.
Redhead, Robert, 15/1543, Pte., k., 4/7/16.
Renton, Henry Morris, 21988, Pte., k., 5/7/16.
Rhodes, James Henry, 24810, Pte., d., 11/7/16.
Rider, Thomas, 41211, Pte., k., 29/12/16.
Roach, Thomas, 14533, Pte., k., 1/1/16.
Roberts, William Ernest, 14019, Pte., k., 10/7/16.
Robertshaw, Frank, 29328, Cpl., k., 7/10/16.
Robinson, George, 13810, Pte., k., 4/7/16.
Rodgers, Herbert, 13068, Pte., k., 10/7/16.
Roper, Herbert, 22370, Pte., d., 8/7/16.
Russell, Frank, 24285, Pte., d., 11/7/16.
Salvidge, Edmund, 13520, Pte., 13/11/15.
Sarginson, John, 11505, Cpl., k., 7/10/16.
Sarson, George, 12603, Pte., k., 26/3/16.
Senior, Hilbert, 43736, Pte., k., 7/10/16, formerly 17315, West Riding Regt.
Shakespeare, Fred, 15906, A/Cpl., k., 7/10/16.
Sharp, Fred, 43737, Pte., k., 7/10/16, formerly 11/18511, West Riding Regt.
Short, Frederick John, 16113, Pte., k., 4/7/16.
Singleton, Fred, 43740, Pte., k., 4/7/16, formerly 12066, West Riding Regt.
Sleight, John William, 13782, Cpl., k., 7/10/16.
Smith, Albert, 22311, Pte., k., 3/4/16.
Smith, Robert, 4/8295, Pte., d., 29/3/16.
Smith, William, 13486, L/Cpl., k., 5/7/16.
Smith, William, 15654, Pte., k., 7/10/16.
Southwort, Thomas, 15847, Pte., d., 11/7/16.
Spencer, William Lewis, 14580, Pte., k.,4/10/16.
Spofforth, Francis Page, 3/10124, Pte., k., 29/3/16.
Stephenson, Ernest, 13505, Pte., d., 8/10/16.
Stevens, Albert John, 14820, Pte., k., 7/10/16.

Stone, John, 14774, Pte., k., 7/10/16.
Straw John, 10345, Pte., k., 5/7/16.
Summers, William Henry, 13600, Pte., k., 23/9/15.
Swain, Albert, 12758, L/Cpl., k., 4/7/16.
Swinburn, John Ernest, 11529, Pte., k., 7/10/16.
Teakle, Harry Albert, 17361, Pte., d.h., 3/8/16, formerly 15291, East Yorks. Regt.
Teal, William, 17411, Pte., k., 7/10/16.
Tate, John Edmund, 24542, Pte., d., 18/7/16.
Taylor, William, 22149, Pte., k., 22/9/16.
Tetley, Wilfred, 43750, Pte., k., 7/10/16, formerly 11/17975, West Riding Regt.
Thomas, Harold, 14009, Pte., d., 1/8/16.
Thompson, William, 12678, Pte., d., 20/11/15.
Thornton, Henry, 4/8638, Pte., d., 3/12/15.
Thurnell, William, 4/8392, Pte., k., 2/4/16.
Timmings, Albert James, 11/13270, Pte., d., 3/1/16.
Trousdale, Fred, 41194, Pte., k., 20/11/16.
Urwin, Christopher, 18255, Pte., k., 4/7/16.
Vyner, George, 4/8364, Pte., d., 18/7/16.
Waite, Fred, 13942, Sgt., k., 7/8/16

Walker, Albert Edward, 13628, Pte., d., 7/10/16.
Walker, Frank, 13921, Pte., k., 7/10/16.
Walton, Fred, 15768, Pte., k., 5/7/16.
Walton, John Luther, 17407, Pte., k., 19/5/15.
Walton, Harry, 19265, Pte., d., 11/10/16.
Waterton, William, 24563, Pte., d., 21/9/16.
Watson, James, 19775, Pte., k., 5/7/16.
Welsh, John, 14089, Pte., d., 21/9/16.
West, Robert, 41220, Pte., d., 4/12/16.
Whaley, Henry Harold, 3/9261, Pte., k., 4/7/16.
Wilkinson, Robert, 15036, Pte., d., 22/9/16.
Williams, George Henry, 11/13353, Pte., k., 4/7/16.
Williams, Robert Alfred, 22331. Sgt., k., 7/10/16.
Wilson, Henry, 18/1307, Pte., k., 7/10/16.
Wood, George, 12860, L/Cpl., d., 25/10/16.
Woodhead, Norman, 43748, Pte., k., 20/9/16, formerly 17974, West Riding Regt.
Wright, Ernest, 21514, Pte., k., 7/10/16.
Yeats, Albert Marshall, 24959, Pte., k., 7/10/16.
Youll, William, 11085, L/Cpl., d.h., 18/10/16

12th BATTALION

Abbott, Harry, 18/1223, A/Sgt., k., 23/7/16.
Abbott, Harry, 27996, Pte., k., 17/8/16.
Aked, Henry, 15523, Pte., k., 14/7/16.
Alderson, Mark, 12158, L/Cpl., k., 10/10/16.
Allcock, Edgar Herbert, 15476, Pte., k., 27/9/15.
Allcock, James, 13443, Pte., d., 14/7/16.
Allen, Frank, 40609, Pte., k., 9/11/16, formerly 18640, North Staffs. Regt.
Alred, James Arthur, 20/13, L/Cpl., d.,22/8/16.
Anderson, John Thomas, 26216, Pte., d., 28/8/16.
Ankers, John, 14421, Pte., k., 14/7/16.
Arnott, Harold, 16/594, Pte., k., 14/7/16.
Arthurs, John Alfred, 13185, Pte., k., 24/7/16.
Ashbridge, Percy, 18233, Pte., k., 14/7/16.
Ashmore, George, 16107, Pte., k., 14/7/16.
Asquith, Sam, 28072, Pte., k., 17/8/16.
Bainbridge, Percy, 14382, Pte., k., 28/7/15.
Baker, Walter John, 15423, L/Cpl., d., 24/7/16.
Balmforth, Willie, 18/759, Pte., k., 17/8/16.
Banks, George Walter, 40552, Pte., d., 3/11/16, formerly 6103, Leicestershire Regt.
Barker, Harold Marshall, 13790, Pte., k., 19/5/16.
Barnes, Fred, 14191, Pte., k., 26/9/15.
Barratt, William, 12676, Pte., k., 14/7/16.
Bartle, George, 21074, Pte., k. (accident), 24/11/16.
Bashforth, Willie, 14457, Pte., d., 27/3/16.
Bates, Mark Parkinson, 13586, Pte., d.,25/11/15.
Baxter, Ernest, 19991, Pte., k., 14/7/16.
Bayes, Cyril, 18304, Pte., k., 3/4/16.
Bayles, Henry, 15069, Pte., k., 23/7/16.
Bean, Edward Wilkinson, 19185, Pte., k., 14/7/16.
Beaumont, Jonah, 16/981, Pte., k., 18/8/16.
Beevers, Albert Arthur, 28175, Pte., k., 11/10/16.
Benson, George, 15080, L/Cpl., k., 17/8/15.
Benson, Thomas, 14413, Pte., k., 14/7/16.
Bentley, Clifford, 14802, Pte., d., 30/9/15.
Bentley, John, 18/1041, Pte., k., 14/7/16.
Berry, Alfred, 28074, Pte., d., 18/8/16.
Bickerdyke, Arthur, 14232, Pte., k., 27/9/15.
Biltcliffe, Joe Willie, 27195, Pte., k., 17/8/16.
Binns, Albert, 18/1222, Pte., d., 26/9/16.
Birrell, James, 4/6818, L/Sgt, k., 22/12/16.
Blakeborough, Frederick, 18/45, Pte., k., 17/8/16.

Boden, William, 18286, Pte., d.h., 21/7/16.
Boland, William, 13744, Pte., k., 16/10/16.
Bolton, Joseph, 3/10110, Cpl., k., 26/9/15.
Bond, George, 18/1337, Pte., k., 9/5/16.
Boocock, George, 3/9996, Sgt., d., 4/10/15.
Booth, Charles, 16246, Pte., k., 14/7/16.
Bouncer, Joseph, 11527, Pte., k., 23/11/15.
Bowen, Edward, 15198, Pte., k., 5/7/16.
Bradd, George Simpson Frankish, 14710, Pte., k., 27/9/15.
Brady, Alfred, 28019, Pte., k., 17/8/16.
Braithwaite, Charles, 27998, Pte., k., 17/8/16.
Briggs, Alfred, 27852, Pte., k., 18/8/16.
Broadbent, Herbert, 20/65, Pte., d., 9/5/16.
Broadbent, Leonard, 27202, Pte., k., 17/8/16.
Broadfield, John Henry, 15468, Pte., k.,17/5/16.
Bromley, Charles Ernest, 16491, Pte., k., 28/3/16.
Brook, Willie, 16512, Pte., k., 27/9/15.
Brown, James, 19715, Pte., k., 23/12/15.
Bryan, Frederick Charles, 15052, Pte., d., 19/11/15.
Bullen, John Robert, 45926, Pte., k., 7/12/16.
Bullock, Thomas, 16/1621, Pte., d., 12/10/16.
Burnell, Henry, 15301, Pte., k., 23/7/16.
Burnett, Edward, 18568, Pte., k., 10/1/16.
Burns, John, 17432, Pte., k., 13/7/16.
Butler, Robert, 10625, Pte., k., 23/7/16.
Butterworth, Sam, 16/1650, Pte., d.h., 16/9/16.
Cahill, Sydney, 12180, Pte., k., 14/7/16.
Cameron, Thomas, 14240, Pte., d., 7/10/15.
Cammidge, Charles William, 19696, Pte., k., 23/7/16.
Campbell, William, 16182, Pte., k., 26/9/15.
Canham, Herbert, 9265, A/Cpl., k., 14/7/16
Carlton, Percival, 14362, L/Cpl., k., 27/9/15.
Carney, Martin, 16233, Pte., k., 23/7/16.
Carney, Martin, 19706, Pte., k., 17/8/16.
Caulkin, Alfred, 13562, Pte., k., 6/5/16.
Chambers, John, 15026, Cpl., k., 23/7/16.
Chambers, Samuel, 28243, Pte., k., 7/11/16.
Champlin, Henry, 27197, Pte., k., 7/8/16.
Chaplin, Charles Frederick, 18/1493, L/Cpl., d., 25/7/16.
Chapman, Thomas, 21228, Pte., d., 27/7/16.
Chapman, Thomas William, 22219, Pte., k., 23/7/16.
Child, Charles William, 14228, Pte., d., 1/4/16.

The Prince of Wales's Own (West Yorks. Regt.)—Casualties

Chipperton, William John, 4/8028, Pte., k., 3/5/16.
Chorley, Harold, 19063, Cpl., k., 18/7/16.
Clark, Walter, 3/9869, Pte., k., 14/7/16.
Clarke, Charles, 16421, Pte., k., 27/9/15.
Clarke, John, 16505, Pte., d., 27/9/15.
Clarkson, Alfred, 17071, Pte., k., 14/7/16.
Claxton, Ernest, 14655, Pte., k., 14/7/16.
Clayton, Harry, 24782, Pte., k., 17/8/16.
Clayton, Percy, 26176, Pte., d., 18/10/16.
Coates, Arthur, 19/90, Pte., k., 14/7/16.
Cochrane, James, 21758, Pte., k, 18/8/16.
Cockcroft, Herbert, 20/55, Pte., k., 22/12/16.
Cockcroft, Wilfred, 20/54, Pte., k., 24/7/16.
Coleman, Fred, 28015, Pte., k., 11/10/16.
Colohan, James, 22340, Cpl., k., 10/10/16.
Condron, Arthur, 4/8173, Pte., k., 18/8/16.
Connor, James, 16436, Pte., k., 26/9/15.
Conway, Louis Wright, 3/8542, Pte., k., 11/7/16.
Cook, Martin, 3/9601, L/Cpl., k., 12/10/16.
Cook, William Arnott, 19288, L/Cpl., k., 27/9/16.
Cooper, John, 13054, Pte., k., 3/4/16.
Copeman, Alfred, 19650, Pte., k., 23/7/16.
Coulthirst, Gordon, 14459, L/Cpl., k., 26/9/15.
Cowell, Jacob, 19592, Pte., k., 24/7/16.
Coyne, William, 13797, Pte., d.h., 11/8/16.
Cragg, Leonard, 18/1210, Pte., k., 14/7/16.
Cundall, James Arthur, 19728, Pte., k., 14/7/16.
Cushions, Joseph Wilfred, 16/1693, Sgt., k., 23/7/16.
Dale, Leo Peacock, 13047, L/Sgt., k., 14/7/16.
Davey, Walter James, 21501, Pte., k., 24/12/15.
Davies, John Thomas, 13656, Pte., k., 27/9/15.
Davies, Joseph William, 12399, Sgt., k., 4/5/16.
Davis, Richard Petty, 16287, Pte., k., 27/9/15.
Davison, Mark, 19357, Pte., k., 14/7/16.
Deacon, William, 13987, Pte., k., 27/9/15.
Delaney, Frederick, 14662, Pte., k., 25/9/15.
Devaney, John, 3/9883, Pte., k., 27/9/15.
Devine, Francis, 4/8584, Pte., k., 14/7/16.
Dixon, John Edward, 19015, Pte., d., 16/11/16.
Dixon, Ralph, 28218, Pte., k., 17/8/16.
Dobson, Stanley, 16278, Pte., k., 14/7/16.
Dobson, Thomas Temple, 14300, Pte., k., 12/10/16.
Dobson, William, 13841, Pte., k., 3/4/16.
Dodds, Fred, 15947, L/Cpl., k., 26/9/15.
Dodson, Willie, 17077, Pte., k., 14/7/16.
Drennen, John Henry, 16192, Pte., k., 27/9/15.
Driver, George, 14691, Pte., d., 25/11/15.
Dunweil, Richard, 14469, Sgt., k., 27/9/15.
Durrant, George, 12579, Pte., d., 29/11/15.
Eaddie, John Edward, 11476, L/Cpl., k.,3/4/16.
Earle, Frederick, 12866, Pte., k., 9/10/16.
Eliassen, George, 13522, Pte., k., 27/9/15.
Ellerker, George, 28206, Pte., d., 20/8/16.
Ellis, John Leonard, 14291, Pte., k., 3/4/16.
Ellis, Thomas Henlock, 28759, Pte., k., 17/8/16.
Ellison, George, 14002, Pte., k., 14/7/16.
Emsley, George Henry, 19677, Pte., k., 28/3/16.
Farrand, Herbert, 16252, Pte., k., 14/7/16.
Farrar, James, 20/32, L/Cpl., k., 23/7/16.
Farrar, Thomas Edwin, 14996, Pte, k., 3/4/16.
Fearn, Benn, 12297, Pte., d., 19/7/16.
Fielder, Thomas Godfrey, 14857, Pte., k., 27/9/15.
Firth, Arthur, 11700, Pte., k., 22/7/16.
Firth, Thomas, 16/1681, Pte., k., 14/7/16.
Flannagan, William, 13747, Pte., k, 26/9/15.
Ford, Edward, 3/9889, Sgt., k., 14/7/16.
Foster, Riley, 16/1377, Pte., d., 16/8/16.
Garnham, James Albert, 17403, Pte., k.,27/9/15.
Gaunt, Morris, 28032, Pte., k., 17/8/16.

Geldart, William, 12245, Pte., d., 1/12/15.
Goodwill, Stanley, 28067, Pte., d., 23/8/16.
Gover, Edward James, 13994, Pte., d., 31/3/16.
Gowland, John William, 15921, Pte., d.,1/10/15.
Grant, Albert, 13748, Pte., k., 23/7/16.
Greaves, Harry, 12547, Pte., k., 26/9/15.
Green, John, 4/7777, Pte., k., 14/7/16.
Greenfield, Benjamin, 14287, Pte., k., 27/9/15.
Greville, Peter, 28756, Pte., k., 17/8/16.
Hall, Harold, 16473, Pte., d., 15/12/15, formerly 10172, Northumberland Fusiliers.
Hammond, James, 15969, Pte., k., 27/9/15.
Harding, Arthur, 15536, Pte., k., 24/7/16.
Hardman, William John, 23395, Pte., k., 14/7/16.
Hardy, Walter Bertram, 3/10112, Pte., k., 23/7/16.
Harris, William, 15163, Pte., k., 14/7/16.
Harrison, Jesper, 16495, Pte., k., 23/7/16.
Havenhand, James, 3/9528, Pte., k., 28/3/16.
Haw, Harry, 16/1682, Pte., k., 23/7/16.
Head, Reece, 14640, Pte., k., 16/8/16.
Heaton, Joseph Copley, 15/1681, Pte., k., 11/7/16.
Hempsall, Edgar, 27863, Pte., k., 7/8/16.
Herringshaw, Cecil, 26154, Pte., k., 10/10/16.
Higginbottom, William, 16208, Pte., k., 27/9/15, formerly 15189, East Yorks. Regt.
Hind, Horace, 16526, Pte., k., 17/8/16.
Hobson, John Robert, 19349, Pte., k., 12/10/16.
Holdsworth, Sydney, 20/11, Pte., d., 23/7/16.
Holland, Benjamin, 3/9603, Pte., k., 27/9/15.
Holland, Herbert, 18/1226, A/Sgt., k., 23/7/16
Holmes, Harry, 16/1618, Pte., k., 23/7/16.
Holmes, Herbert, 16/1598, Pte., k., 12/7/16.
Horsfall, John William, 16/1642, Pte., d., 17/7/16.
Hutchinson, George Williamson, 19820, Pte., k., 23/7/16.
I'anson, Leonard Thomas, 3/9377, Pte., k., 27/9/15.
Ibbotson, Alwyn, 12491, L/Cpl., d., 19/7/16.
Ibbotson, Charles Percy, 14024, Pte., k., 27/9/15
Illingworth, Sam, 18/749, Pte., k., 18/8/16.
Jack, Robert, 20/71, L/Cpl., d., 24/7/16.
Jackson, Joseph Henry, 16221, Pte., d., 14/9/16, M.M.
Johnson, Mark, 17072, L/Cpl., k., 20/7/16.
Johnson, Raymond, 13843, Pte., k., 14/7/16.
Johnson, Sydney, 14982, Pte., d., 19/8/16.
Johnston, David, 14657, Pte., k., 27/9/15.
Kay, Henry, 22131, Pte., k., 23/7/16.
Kell, William, 19634, Pte., d., 18/8/16.
Kelly, John, 14948, Pte., k., 21/5/16.
Kendall, James Thompson, 25511, Pte , k., 6/9/16.
Kendrew, James, 15082, Pte., k., 28/3/16.
Kennedy, Patrick, 16488, Sgt., k., 26/9/15.
Kenny, John, 14254, Pte., k., 23/7/16.
Kerry, Samuel, 14672, Pte., k., 13/7/16.
Ketteridge, Edward, 28366, Pte., k., 18/8/16.
Kilner, Herbert, 28562, Pte., k., 17/8/16.
Kirkbride, Frederick, 26209, Pte., k., 3/9/16.
Kirlew, Harry, 14020, Pte., k., 3/4/16.
Kirton, John William, 17305, L/Cpl., k., 14/7/16.
Laccohee, Edward Jacob, 19839, Pte., k., 27/9/15.
Lang, Patrick, 16/1626, Pte., k., 14/7/16.
Langdale, Fred, 15959, A/Sgt., k., 14/7/16.
Langley, Tom, 3/10068, Sgt., k., 26/9/15.
Law, Kenneth, 23844, Pte., k., 3/9/16.
Law, Sydney, 16289, Pte., d., 13/10/16.
Lawn, James, 13432, Pte., d., 25/7/16.
Lazenby, Robert, 15938, Pte., k., 27/9/15.

The Prince of Wales's Own (West Yorks. Regt.)—Casualties 343

Ledgard, Arthur, 26210, Pte., k., 3/9/16.
Lindley, Maurice, 11637, Pte., k., 14/7/16.
Littleboy, Edward, 18001, Pte., d., 13/7/16.
Lockwood, Harold, 18840, Pte., k., 17/8/16, M.M.
Long, Alfred, 18364, Pte., k., 10/10/16.
Loomes, Arthur, 28268, Pte., k., 16/8/16.
Loughborough, Edward, 13005, Pte., k., 14/7/16.
Lovatt, John, 16475, Pte., k., 3/4/16.
Lowrey, James, 27938, Pte., k., 17/8/16.
Lumb, John, 18402, Pte., k., 12/5/16.
Lumby, George Arthur, 27916, Pte., k.,17/8/16.
Lund, Lawrence, 20/40, Pte., d., 29/9/16.
Mackin, Thomas, 11281 Pte., k., 22/12/16.
Magee, Joseph, 11681, Pte., k., 14/7/16.
Malkin, Willie Ross, 20/88, Pte., k., 24/7/16.
Mallin, Edwin George, 13250, Pte., k., 27/9/15.
Marshall, John, 3/9456, Pte., k., 23/7/16.
Matthews, Frank, 18267, Pte., k., 27/9/15.
Maw, Frank, 14005, Pte., k., 27/9/15.
Mawson, Charles, 24956, Pte., k., 24/7/16.
May, George, 3/9431, Pte., k., 27/9/15.
May, Thomas, 13755, Pte., d., 27/9/15.
Meakin, John Thomas, 19450, Pte., k., 14/7/16.
Mercer, Albert, 12186, Pte., k., 3/4/16.
Merritt, George, 27905, Pte., d., 20/10/16.
Metcalfe, James, 14652, Pte., k., 27/9/15.
Metcalfe, Walter Holden, 13763, A/Cpl., d., 1/4/16, M.M.
Middleton, Jonathan Lester, 16/1375, Pte., d., 31/7/16.
Middleton, William Newstead, 14388, Pte., k., 14/7/16.
Mitchell, Harry, 18129, Pte., k., 3/4/16.
Moles, James, 28315, Pte, k., 18/8/16.
Moore, George William, 14888, Pte., k.,17/8/16.
Moran, Thomas, 13898, Pte., k., 27/9/15.
Moran, Thomas, 19155, Pte., k., 14/7/16.
Moule, Harry, 14842, Pte., k., 28/3/16.
Murray, Edwin Sinclair, 17401, Pte., k., 3/4/16, formerly 14666, East Yorks. Regt.
Murray, James, 27933, Pte., k., 17/8/16.
Myers, James, 18383, Pte., d., 15/7/16.
McCarroll, Patrick, 19719, Pte., d., 21/8/16.
McCready, William, 3/9464, Pte., k., 27/9/15.
McDermott, Michael, 14283, Pte., d.h., 2/8/16.
McGuire, John, 17078, Pte., k., 27/9/15.
McGuire, William, 18358, Pte., d.h., 7/8/16.
McKay, Thomas, 14894, Pte., d.h., 28/4/16.
McMahon, John, 12120, L/Sgt., k., 3/5/16.
McMain, John William, 16/1615, Pte. d., 30/7/16.
McMann, William Andrew, 16/288, Sgt., d., 27/10/16.
Nadin, Albert, 20/135, Pte., k., 18/7/16.
Newham, Thomas, 14912, Pte., k., 27/9/15.
Nicholl, Abraham, 16/1597, Pte., k., 23/7/16.
Nicholson, Joseph, 12730, Pte., d., 12/7/16.
Nutter, James Milton, 18/184, L/Cpl., k., 10/10/16.
O'Donnell, Samuel, 10357, Pte., k. 14/7/16.
Oldroyd, Joseph, 14277, Pte., k., 27/9/15.
Owston, Henry Thomas, 17413, Pte., k., 9/8/16
Oxley, Ernest, 15937, Pte., d., 9/5/16.
Parker, Arthur Yeoman, 21218, Pte., k.,28/3/16.
Parker, Frank, 14661, Pte., k., 27/9/15.
Parker, Norman, 14251, Pte., k., 27/9/15.
Parker, Sydney, 23876, Pte., k., 14/7/16.
Parkinson, Alfred, 13552, Pte., k., 10/10/16.
Parrish, Harold Wheelhouse, 16/1542, L/Cpl., k., 18/7/16.
Patterson, John, 3/9301, Pte., d., 3/5/16.
Pattison, George Askew, 17336, L/Cpl., k., 28/3/16.

Pawson, George Ernest, 28053, Pte., k., 17/8/16.
Paylor, Matthew, 14492, Pte., k., 27/9/15.
Peacock, Thomas, 18354, Pte., k., 27/9/15.
Pearson, Henry, 14946, Pte., d., 5/5/16.
Penrose, Richard, 20/75, Pte., d., 13/7/16.
Phillips, Frank, 15559, Pte., k., 23/7/16.
Powell, Duncan, 14663, Pte., k., 14/7/16.
Prendergast, Michael, 14486, Pte., d., 4/4/16.
Preston, William Henry, 18/1429, Cpl., k., 14/7/16.
Price, Charles Harry, 16/1370, Pte., k., 14/7/16.
Price, John, 3/10113, Sgt., d , 29/9/15.
Proctor, Thomas, 14700, Pte., k., 19/5/16.
Quigley, Christopher, 14676, Pte., k., 26/9/15.
Reddington, Thomas, 13799, Pte., k., 27/9/15.
Render, Cyril, 14654, Pte., d.h., 10/10/14.
Render, Henry, 14658, Pte , k., 14/7/16.
Rhodes, Malcolm Ernest, 20/141, Pte., k., 23/7/16.
Richardson, Abraham, 13257, Pte., k., 3/5/16.
Richardson, Tom, 27917, Pte., d., 9/10/16.
Riley, Michael, 17339, Pte., k., 28/3/16, formerly 15323, East Yorks. Regt.
Riley, Philip, 17344, Pte., k., 14/7/16, formerly 15159, East Yorks. Regt.
Robinson, Alfred, 21034, Pte., k.,14/7/16, M.M.
Robinson, Alfred James, 16517, Pte., k.,27/9/15.
Robinson, Robert, 15603, A/Sgt., k., 14/7/16.
Rodgers, Philip, 14437, Pte., k., 27/9/15.
Rooke, Albert, 16519, Pte., k., 24/7/16.
Rowley, Harry, 14835, Pte., k., 27/9/15.
Ruff, George Herbert, 19717, Pte., k., 23/7/16
Rushforth, Gilbert, 14914, Pte., k., 27/9/15.
Rushworth, Arthur, 27713, Pte., k., 17/8/16.
Scott, Edward, 14375, L/Cpl., d., 24/7/16, M.M.
Scott, George, 19584, Pte., k., 19/7/16.
Sephton, Frederick, 14765, Pte., k., 27/9/15.
Sharp, James, 3/9962, Pte., k., 27/9/15.
Shaw, George, 23978, Pte., k., 14/7/16.
Shevill, Edward, 19937, Pte., k., 3/5/16.
Skirrow, Harry, 18/1178, A/Cpl., k, 4/5/16.
Slack, James Ernest, 11764, Pte., d., 28/12/16.
Slawson, Clifford, 13938, Pte., k., 14/7/16.
Sleigh, John, 3/9611, Pte., k., 27/9/15.
Smith, Charles Stanley, 15963, Pte., k., 27/9/15.
Smith, George, 14757, Pte., k., 14/7/16.
Smith, George, 16345, Pte., k., 3/4/16.
Smith, George Arthur, 16278, Pte., k., 27/9/15.
Smith, Herbert, 10761, Pte., k., 3/4/16.
Smith, James, 16498, Pte., k., 3/4/16.
Snooks, James, 12221, Pte., d., 4/4/16.
Spilsbury, William, 16288, L/Cpl., k., 3/4/16.
Stanyer, John Francis, 40719, Pte., d., 29/12/16, formerly 5557, 3/5th North Staffs. Regt.
Stares, Reginald, 14809, Pte., k., 26/9/15.
Steele, William, 16462, Cpl., d., 2/10/15.
Stevens, William, 20/258, Pte., k., 25/10/16.
Stringer, Clarence, 28090, Pte., k., 3/9/16.
Sullivan, Michael, 14096, Pte., k., 27/9/15.
Suthern, Robert, 3/9610, Pte., d., 9/5/16.
Tankard, George, 14933, Pte., d., 10/12/15.
Tantram, John William, 14258, C.S.M., k., 14/7/16.
Tarpey, Michael, 14739, Pte., k., 27/9/15.
Taylor, Alwyn, 18331, Pte., k., 10/5/16.
Taylor, Fred, 16518, Pte., k., 21/1/16, formerly G/18137, Royal Fusiliers.
Taylor, Gilbert, 21292, Pte., k., 28/3/16.
Taylor, Harold, 16/1327, Cpl., k., 23/7/16.
Taylor, Harold, 13089, Cpl., k., 27/9/15.
Taylor, Harold, 16511, Pte., k., 27/9/15.
Taylor, John William, 12679, Pte., k., 10/10/16.
Taylor, Walter, 16/1403, Pte., d., 21/5/16.

Tebbett, George William, 13634, Pte., k., 24/7/16.
Terrey, Leonard Phillip, 15470, Pte., k.,27/9/15.
Thomas, Arthur, 24976, Pte., k., 14/7/16.
Thompson, Atkinson, 14110, Pte., k., 27/9/15.
Thompson, Joseph, 15922, Pte., k., 14/7/16.
Thompson, Percy, 24950, Pte., k., 23/7/16.
Thornton, Walter Henry, 12921, Pte., k., 14/7/16.
Thorpe, Walter William, 18/1603, A/Sgt., k., 17/8/16.
Tinsley, John William, 19073, Pte., k., 5/2/16.
Topham, Henry, 18460, Pte., d.h., 17/6/16.
Toulman, Martin Luther, 18526, Pte., k., 23/7/16.
Townend, Walter, 13834, Pte., k., 27/9/16.
Townsley, Ernest Arthur, 13930, Pte., k., 10/10/16.
Turnbull, Henry, 19586, Pte., d., 23/7/16
Turner, Albert, 22431, Pte., d., 22/7/16.
Turner, Albert, 14471, Sgt., k., 13/5/16.
Turton, John, 14574, Pte., k., 3/5/16.
Waddle, George William, 23980, Pte., k., 14/7/16.
Waddington, George, 18295, Pte., k., 18/7/16.
Waddington, William, 20/64, Pte., k., 14/7/16.
Walker, Albert, 14217, Pte., k., 27/9/15.
Walker, Charles James, 16/1714, Pte., k., 13/7/16.
Walker, Harry, 18303, Pte., d., 16/8/16.
Walls, William, 14646, Pte., k., 27/9/15.
Ward, William Edward, 16580, Pte., k., 27/9/15.
Ware, George, 14890, Pte., d., 10/1/16.
Warner, John, 13171, Pte., k., 26/9/15.

Warriner, William, 10372, Pte., d., 1/9/16.
Whatmough, Albert, 18/866, Pte., k., 12/10/16.
Watson, Alfred Ferrier, 14819, Pte., d.h., 21/7/15.
Watson, Frank, 25534, Pte., k., 5/9/16.
Watson, William, 13742, Pte., k., 14/7/16.
Watts, Vincent, 28062, L/Cpl., k., 17/8/16.
Weatherill, Alfred, 19055, Pte., k., 23/7/16.
Webster, George, 19/127, Pte., k., 14/7/16.
West, Jeffrey Willock, 28134, Pte., k., 3/9/16
Whalley, James Arthur, 16/322, Pte., d., 21/10/16.
Whisson, William Flaxman, 16429, Pte., k., 14/7/16.
White, John William, 21149, Pte., k., 16/8/16.
Wigglesworth, Lewis James, 18/1368, Pte., k., 14/7/16.
Wilde, Joseph, 19555, Pte., d., 28/3/16.
Wildman, John Thomas, 15102, Pte., k., 14/7/16.
Wilkinson, Arnold, 18/1455, Pte., k., 14/7/16.
Williamson, Robert Edward, 25508, Pte., k., 6/9/16.
Wilson, Alfred, 14051, Pte., k., 28/3/16.
Wilson, George, 14855, Pte., k., 18/8/16.
Winter, Thomas Henry, 18164, Pte., k.,23/7/16.
Wood, Alexander, 16266, Pte., d., 19/7/16.
Wood, George Alfred, 26069, Pte., k., 10/10/16.
Wood, Willie, 28281, Pte., k., 17/8/16.
Woodhead, William, 28114, Pte., k., 3/9/16.
Yates, Reginald, 24115, Pte., k., 23/7/16.
Young, John Edgar, 3/9987, Pte., d., 24/7/16.
Young, Sidney, 12411, Pte., k., 3/4/16.

13th BATTALION

Cuddy, Joseph, 26628, Pte., d.h., 12/4/16.
Doherty, Thomas Thompson, 3/9880, Sgt., d.h., 3/9/15.
Drury, Richard, T.R.6/20436, Pte., d.h., 15/9/16.
Hall, Herbert, 15114, Pte., d.h., 14/2/16.
Johnson, Harry, 21856, Pte., d.h., 26/7/16.

Leach, George, 3/9922, Pte., d.h., 27/5/15.
Middleton, Harry, 3/9324, Pte., d h., 21/4/15.
Pillinger, Harold, 21929, Pte., d.h., 28/3/16.
Prevost, Harold Edwin, 16524, Pte., d.h., 20/3/16, formerly 8/13291, 8th Lincoln Regt.

14th BATTALION

Adams, Thomas, 23749, Pte., d.h., 21/3/16.
Cuss, Randall, 12021, Pte., d.h., 24/3/15.

Parnaby, William Usher, 35256, Pte., d.h., 12/7/16.

15th BATTALION

Abbott, George, 15/1385, Pte., d., 9/7/16.
Allen, Harold, 15/1570, Pte., k., 1/7/16.
Alnwick, George, 15/1417, Pte., k., 1/7/16.
Althorp, Albert, 15/15, L/Cpl., k., 14/9/16.
Armitage, Ernest, 33041, Pte., k., 8/11/16.
Ashworth, Herbert, 15/1313, Pte., k., 1/7/16.
Aspinall, John Franklin, 15/34, Pte., d.h., 15/7/16.
Atkinson, George William, 15/1059, L/Cpl., k., 1/7/16.
Atkinson, William Alfred, 26286, Pte., k., 20/8/16.
Axe, Arthur Cecil, 15/1282, Pte., k., 1/7/16.
Balme, John Edwin, 15/1093, Pte., d.h., 8/7/16.
Bannister, Charles, 15/150, Pte., d., 4/7/16.
Barker, Sydney, 15/1236, Pte., k., 1/7/16.
Batty, Samuel Thomas Duncan, 15/126, Pte., k., 1/7/16.

Beard, Harold, 15/91, Pte., k., 28/4/16.
Beckton, John, 15/1674, Pte., k., 22/5/16.
Bennett, Frederick George, 15/1201, Pte., k., 1/7/16.
Beverley, Bernard, 15/46, Pte., k., 1/7/16.
Bland, Benjamin Clifford Wadsworth, 15/93, Cpl., k., 1/7/16.
Bland, Robert, 15/1045, A/Sgt., k., 1/7/16.
Bleksley, Francis Gilbert, 15/83, Sgt., k.,1/7/16
Bond, Percy Gibson, 15/159, Pte., k., 1/7/16.
Bowman, David, 15/76, Pte., k., 1/7/16.
Bradfield, Walter Lanning, 15/54, Pte., k., 5/12/16.
Briggs, William Henry, 15/139, Cpl., k., 1/7/16.
Brook, Clifford, 15/163, Sgt., k., 1/7/16.
Brook, Herbert, 15/145, Pte., k., 1/7/16.
Brook, John George, 15/1271, Pte., k., 1/7/16.
Brook, Samuel, 15/1581, Pte., k., 1/7/16.

The Prince of Wales's Own (West Yorks. Regt.)—Casualties 345

Brooke, John James, 15/114, Pte., k., 1/7/16.
Broomhead, Robert, 15/128, Pte., k., 1/7/16.
Brown, Lawrence, 15/1444, Pte., k., 1/7/16.
Brown, Walter, 15/1291, Pte., k., 19/5/16, formerly 20124, K.O.Y.L.I.
Bullimore, James William, 15/57, Cpl., k., 1/7/16.
Burnley, Herbert, 15/160, L/Cpl., k., 1/7/16.
Burniston, Harry, 15/64, Pte., k., 1/7/16.
Burrow, Wilfred, 15/1317, Pte., k., 1/7/16.
Buxton, Samuel Lawrence, 15/1337, Pte., k., 1/7/16.
Bygott, Frank, 15/74, Cpl., k., 30/3/16.
Calderhead, Clifford, 15/1584, Pte., k., 1/7/16.
Calverley, Tom, 15/1086, Pte., k., 1/7/16.
Campleman, Charles, 15/1331, Pte., k., 1/7/16.
Casling, Stanley, 24225, Pte., k., 21/9/16.
Casson, Harry Stuart, 15/180, Pte., k., 1/7/16.
Cathrick, Harry Raine, 15/181, Pte., k., 1/7/16.
Cawood, Fred, 15/1121, Pte., k., 1/7/16.
Chambers, Herbert John, 15/187, Pte., k., 1/7/16.
Chapman, Herbert, 15/191, Pte., k., 1/7/16.
Chapman, William Foster, 15/192, Pte., k., 1/7/16.
Clarke, Robert Little, 15/1180, Pte., k., 1/7/16.
Clarke, Frank, 15/202, Pte., d., 4/7/16.
Clarkson, Thomas, 15/1898, Pte., d., 12/7/16.
Clayton, Edwin, 40527, Pte., k., 3/11/16.
Clayton, Frank, 15/209, Sgt., k., 1/7/16.
Coggill, Harold, 15/215, Cpl., k., 1/7/16.
Colcroft, George William, 15/216, Pte., d.h., 19/11/14.
Cole, George Clifford, 15/1185, Pte., k., 1/7/16.
Colquhoun, William Campbell, 15/219, Cpl., k., 1/7/16.
Conyers, William, 15/222, L/Sgt., k., 1/7/16.
Cook, Percy, 15/1141, Cpl., k., 1/7/16.
Cowling, William, 15/1184, Pte., k., 1/7/16.
Cox, Charles Francis Alexander, 15/237, L/Cpl. k., 1/7/16.
Craven, Ernest, 33368, Pte., d., 27/10/16.
Craven, Ernest, 15/242, Pte., k., 1/7/16.
Crossley, Wilfred, 15/249, Pte., k., 1/7/16.
Crowther, Maurice Robinson, 15/252, Pte., k. 1/7/16.
Curphey, Albert Edward, 15/255, Pte., k., 1/7/16.
Davis, William Creswell, 15/267, Pte., k., 1/7/16.
Davison, Christopher, 15/1592, Pte., k., 1/7/16.
Dennison, Austin William, 15/1374, Pte., k., 5/12/16.
Dent, William, 15/1593, Pte., d.h., 9/7/16.
Dobson, Arthur Spencer, 15/281, Pte., k., 1/7/16.
Dodgson, John Ernest, 15/283, Pte., d., 9/7/16.
Dolben, John Alfred, 3/10376, Pte., d., 22/8/16.
Donnelly, Stephen, 15/285, Pte., k., 1/7/16.
Doughty, John Cecil, 15/286, Pte., k., 1/7/16.
Drewry, George, 15/287, Pte., k., 10/6/16.
Drewry, Robert, 15/288, Pte., k., 1/7/16.
Dykes, Harry, 40151, Pte., d., 5/12/16.
Easy, George Fison, 15/302, Sgt., k., 1/7/16.
Elsegood, Stanley Francis, 23483, Sgt., d., 21/9/16, formerly 7185, Royal Fusiliers
Eschle, Arthur Bertrand, 15/312, Pte., k., 1/7/16, M.M.
Ewart, John Sydney, 15/314, Cpl., k., 20/8/19.
Fairburn-Hart, George Stanley, 15/317, Cpl., d., 27/4/16.
Fillingham, Arthur Edwin, 15/327, Pte., k., 1/7/16.

Fletcher, Stanley Pickup, 15/1275, Pte., k., 1/7/16.
Flint, John, 15/340, Pte., k., 1/7/16.
Flockton, Fred, 15/341, Pte., k., 1/7/16.
Ford, Charles Henry, 28777, Pte., k., 26/10/16.
Foskett, Arthur Ernest, 15/1519, Pte., k., 1/7/16.
Fotherby, Alfred, 36774, Pte., k., 16/12/16.
Foxcroft, John, 15/349, Pte., k., 1/7/16.
Frobisher, Albert, 15/1786, Cpl., d., 22/8/16.
Garbutt, John William, 15/357, Pte., k., 9/6/16.
Gill, Harry, 15/374, C.S.M., d., 3/7/16.
Gittus, William, 15/1144, Pte., d., 11/7/16.
Glew, Frank, 15/572, Pte., k., 1/7/16.
Goldsborough, Wilfred, 15/1332, Pte., k., 1/7/16.
Gott, Howard, 15/386, Pte., d.h., 14/7/16.
Gough, Norman, 15/1802, Pte., k., 1/7/16.
Gower, Sidney, 15/1333, Pte., k., 1/7/16.
Grassby, William Henry, 15/1671, Pte., k., 1/7/16.
Greasley, Alfred Reginald, 15/371, L/Sgt., k., 1/7/16.
Greaves, Charles Galloway, 15/1601, Pte., k., 1/7/16.
Griffiths, Harold, 15/1425, Pte., k., 20/8/16.
Gurmin, George Thomas, 15/405, Sgt., k., 1/7/16.
Guttridge, Albert, 15/407, L/Sgt., d.h., 30/7/16.
Hall, William, 15/1161, Pte., k., 1/7/16.
Hamilton, Gavin Park, 15/419, Pte., k., 1/7/16.
Hampshire, Joseph, 15/421, Pte., k., 1/7/16.
Hancock, Geoffrey, 15/422, L/Cpl., k., 9/6/16.
Hardcastle, John Thomas, 15/1372, Pte., d., 26/5/16.
Hardy, Frank, 15/428, Pte., k., 1/7/16.
Harlow, Edward Cecil, 15/432, Pte., k., 1/7/16.
Harrison, Charles William, 15/1754, Pte., k., 1/7/16.
Harrison, Evelyn Clifford, 15/1415, Pte., k., 22/5/16.
Hayhurst, John, 15/1281, Pte., k., 22/5/16.
Healy, Edward, 15/442, Cpl., k., 1/7/16.
Heaton, Thomas Herbert, 15/441, Pte., k., 1/7/16.
Hemingbrough, Charles Arthur 15/444, Pte., k., 1/7/16.
Henderson, Robert, 19704, Pte., 30/6/16.
Herson, George William, 21044, Pte., k., 1/7/16.
Hewitt, Herbert, 15/449, L/Sgt., k., 1/7/16.
Hickson, Lawrence, 15/457, Pte., k., 1/7/16.
Higginbottom, Joseph Frederick, 15/1805, Pte., k., 1/7/16.
Hill, Claude Scott, 15/460, Pte., d., 24/10/16
Hill, Herbert Archer, 15/1489, L/Cpl., d., 24/9/16.
Hill, John Richard, 15/1524, Pte., k., 1/7/16.
Hirley, John William, 15/447, Pte., k., 1/7/16.
Hirst, Clifford. 15/1088, Pte., d.h., 8/7/16.
Hirst, George, 15/1490, Pte., k., 1/7/16.
Hirst, Oswald, 15/405, Pte., k., 1/7/16.
Hitchen, George Henry, 15/1772, Pte., k., 1/7/16.
Holliday, Arthur, 15/1285, Pte., k., 1/7/16.
Hollis, George Worthington, 15/472, L/Cpl., k., 1/7/16.
Holmes, Rennard Lenty, 15/1122, Pte., k., 1/7/16.
Hopkin, Edward, 15/475, Pte., d., 29/5/16.
Hunter, John Henry, 15/488, Pte., k., 1/7/16.
Hutchinson, Tom, 15/1264, Pte., k., 1/7/16.
Hutton, George Arthur, 15/492, Pte., k., 9/6/16.
Iles, Horace, 15/1784, Pte., k., 1/7/16.
Iley, Charles, 18285, Pte., k., 1/7/16.
Ingleson, Ernest, 15/501, Pte., k., 1/7/16.
Jackson, Arthur, 15/503, Cpl., d.h., 20/7/16.

Jackson, Fred, 15/1204, Pte., k., 1/7/16.
Jackson, Norman, 15/509, Sgt., k., 1/7/16.
James, Thomas Galloway, 15/514, Sgt., k., 1/7/16.
Jenkinson, Sydney, 15/522, Pte., k., 1/7/16
Jessop, John William, 15/1530, Pte., k., 1/7/16.
Johnson, Charles Howard, 15/1058, Pte., k., 1/7/16.
Johnson, Vernon, 15/1366, Pte., k., 1/7/16.
Jones, Reginald, 15/533, Pte., k., 1/7/16.
Jubb, Joseph Sheard, 15/1612, Pte., d., 2/8/16.
Kerton, Sydney, 15/548, Sgt., k., 22/5/16.
Killen, Horace Hugh, 15/549, Pte., d., 30/8/16.
Killen, John, 15/550, Pte., k., 1/7/16.
King, Willie, 15/1365, Pte., k., 1/7/16.
Kirk, Alfred Edward Morgan, 15/557, L/Cpl., k., 1/7/16.
Klouman, Gerhard Arnulf, 15/1215, Pte., k., 1/7/16.
Lake, Thomas William, 15/565, Pte., k., 1/7/16.
Lancaster, Frederick, 15/567, Pte., d , 21/8/16
Langstaff, Clifford, 15/1237, Pte., k., 1/7/16
Lee, Albert, 15/582, Pte., k., 1/7/16.
Lennox, Francis William, 15/586, Pte., d., 18/11/16.
Lewis, Frederick Richard, 15/587, Pte., d., at sea, 5/7/16.
Longley, Ernest, 15/601, Pte., k., 1/7/16.
Loughton, George William, 15/1323, Pte., k., 1/7/16.
Lumb, Wilfred Denison, 15/603, Pte., d., 3/7/16.
Mason, Herbert Harry Jagger, 15/621, L/Cpl., k., 1/7/16.
Matthews, Richard, 15/1620, Pte., k., 1/7/16.
Maude, Donald Charles, 15/1930, Pte., k., 1/7/16.
Meades, James Edward, 18899, Pte., k., 10/6/16.
Meeks, John, 4/8286, L/Cpl., d., 5/12/16.
Meeson, Arthur, 15/633, L/Cpl., k., 1/7/16.
Mellard, Richard Lawrence, 15/1881, A/Sgt., k., 1/7/16.
Metcalfe, Walter, 15/642, Pte., d.h., 9/7/16.
Miller, John Anderson, 15/647, L/Cpl., k., 1/7/16.
Miller, Mark, 14966, L/Cpl., k., 22/5/16.
Millns, Harold, 40365, Pte., d.h., 15/12/16, formerly 53617, Lincolnshire Regt.
Milner, John William, 15/1785, Pte., k., 1/7/16.
Milnes, Fred, 15/651, Pte., k., 1/7/16.
Milnes, George, 40174, Pte., d., 21/11/16.
Moore, Clifford, 15/1897, Pte., k., 1/7/16.
Moore, Edgar, 15/633, L/Cpl., k., 1/7/16.
Morley, William Foster, 15/780, Pte., k., 1/7/16.
Mortimer, George Francis Beaumont, 15/657, Pte., k., 1/7/16.
Mortimer, George Harold, 15/658, Pte., k., 1/7/16.
Mortimer, William, 40184, Pte., d., 26/11/16.
Morton, John Stewart, 15/664, Cpl., k., 1/7/16.
Mossop, Matthew Hudson, 15/1027, Sgt., k., 1/7/16, M.M.
Musgrave, Joe, 15/667, Pte., k., 1/7/16.
McEwan, Robert Watt, 15/629, Pte., k., 1/7/16.
McKill, Henry, 40508, Pte., d., 24/12/16.
Naylor, Frank, 15/671, Pte., k., 1/7/16.
Newborn, Percy George, 15/679, Sgt., d., 23/5/16.
Newell, Sam, 15/680, L/Cpl., d., 12/11/16.
Newton, Thomas, 15/1906, Pte., k., 1/7/16.
Odgers, Hugh Bearne, 15/691, Sgt., k., 1/7/16.
Oyston, Tom, 15/1113, Pte., k., 1/7/16.
Palliser, Arnold, 15/696, Pte., k., 1/7/16.
Panther, Horace, 15/1115, Pte., k., 1/7/16.
Pape, James, 15/699, Pte., k., 21/9/16.

Parker, Ben Thornton, 15/1210, Pte., k., 1/7/16.
Paul, Alfred, 15/708, Pte., d.h., 24/7/16.
Payne, James Victor, 15/1355, Pte., k., 1/9/16.
Peel, Clifford Fred, 15/1309, L/Cpl., k., 1/7/16.
Perkins, Frederick Bonner, 40374, Pte., d., 12/11/16, formerly 53751, 5th Lincolnshire Regt.
Phillips, George Geoffrey, 15/1273, Pte., k., 1/7/16.
Pickup, Fred Herbert, 15/1094, Pte., k., 10/6/16.
Plowman, Arthur, 15/1540, Pte., k., 1/7/16.
Poskitt, John Roland, 15/1107, Pte., d., 6/7/16.
Power, Alan Maynard, 15/732, Pte., k., 28/4/16.
Preston, Arthur, 15/1563, Pte., k., 21/9/16.
Preston, Henry, 15/1071, R.S.M., k., 1/7/16.
Priestley, William Robert, 15/735, Pte., k., 1/7/16.
Proctor, Ralph Victor, 15/737, L/Cpl., k., 1/7/16.
Quigley, Isaac, 15/1106, Cpl., k., 1/7/16.
Ramsden, Harold, 15/1102, Pte., k., 20/8/16
Rayfield, Sydney Marshall, 15/745, Pte., k., 1/7/16.
Rayner, Frederick, 15/746, Pte., k., 1/7/16.
Redfern, Harry, 15/748, L/Cpl., k., 1/7/16.
Redshaw, Leonard, 15/749, L/Cpl., k., 25/9/16.
Reyner, Burnett, 15/754, Pte., k., 1/7/16.
Reyner, Percival, 33943, Pte., k., 13/11/16.
Rhodes, Herbert Walker, 15/757, Cpl., k., 22/5/16.
Richardson, Edwin, 40378, Pte., k., 5/11/16, formerly 53763, Lincolnshire Regt.
Richardson, Sidney Brown, 15/760, Pte., k., 1/7/16.
Robinson, Ernest Leslie, 15/769, Pte., k., 1/7/16.
Robson, George, 15/1300, Pte., k., 23/11/16, M.M.
Rogers, Arthur Denton, 15/772, Pte., k., 1/7/16
Salvin, Charles William, 14515, Pte., k., 20/8/16
Saxby, Frank, 15/784, Pte., k., 20/8/16.
Saynor, William, 15/1351, L/Cpl., k., 1/7/16.
Scawbord, Tom, 15/1545, Pte., k., 1/7/16.
Scott, Fred, 15/792, Pte., k., 1/7/16.
Scott, John Edwin, 15/1070, L/Cpl., k., 1/7/16.
Selby, Charles Ernest, 15/793, Pte., k., 1/7/16.
Sen, Jogendra, 15/795, Pte., k., 22/5/16.
Sewell, Wilfred, 15/800, Sgt., d.h., 8/7/16.
Sharp, Frank, 15/1039, Pte., k., 1/7/16.
Sharpe, John Thomas, 40384, Pte., k., 8/11/16 formerly 53761, 4th Lincolnshire Regt.
Sharples, James, 15/804, Cpl., k., 1/7/16.
Shaw, Alfred Houlden, 15/1568, Pte., k., 1/7/16.
Shaw, Horatio, 15/1326, Pte., k., 1/7/16.
Shaw, Walter Clifford, 15/806, Pte., k., 1/7/16.
Shaw, William, 15/1306, Pte., k., 1/7/16.
Sheard, John Lindley, 15/809, Pte., d., 26/5/16.
Simpson, Horace Cumberland, 15/812, Pte., k., 1/7/16.
Smith, Edward, 33170, Pte., k., 8/11/16.
Southward, Edward, 15/834, Pte., k., 1/7/16.
Stainforth, Sydney, 15/1693, Pte., d., 11/6/16.
Stansfield, Allen Firth, 15/1842, Pte., k., 1/7/16.
Steel, John Robert Arthur, 15/1181, Pte., k., 1/7/16.
Stendell, George Frederick, 15/1270, Pte., k., 1/7/16.
Stephenson, Percy, 15/851, Pte., k., 1/7/16.
Stewart, William, 15/1327, Pte., k., 1/7/16.
Stillwell, Clifford, 15/1225, Pte., k., 6/6/16.
Stockwell, Albert Edward, 15/1171, Pte., k., 1/7/16.
Stokoe, Crawford, 15/855, Pte., k., 1/7/16.
Summerscale, Norman, 15/861, Pte., k., 1/7/16.
Summerscale, Stanley, 15/862, Pte., k., 1/7/16.

The Prince of Wales's Own (West Yorks. Regt.)—Casualties

Sunderland, Herbert William, 15/864, Pte., k., 1/7/16.
Sutcliffe, Fred, 15/865, Pte., k., 1/7/16.
Swindells, Thomas, 15/1278, Pte., k., 1/7/16
Taylor, Frederick William, 15/878, Pte., k., 1/7/16.
Tennant, Percy Herbert, 15/881, Pte., d., 28/7/16.
Thompson, Arthur Norman, 15/885, Pte., k., 1/7/16.
Thompson, James Donald, 15/890, Pte., k., 1/7/16.
Tillotson, Thomas Weeks, 15/897, Pte., k., 1/7/16.
Timms, Robert Evans, 15/899, Pte., k., 22/5/16.
Titchener, Charles Frederick, 40397, Pte., k., 13/11/16.
Townend, George Priestley, 15/911, Pte., k., 1/7/16.
Trueman, Cyril, 15/1656, Pte., k., 1/7/16.
Tucker, Frederick Edmundson, 15/1064, Pte., k., 1/7/16
Turner, Bert, 15/1790, Pte., k., 1/7/16.
Vaile, Joseph, 15/1272, A/C.S.M., d., 5/7/16, formerly 7681, 1st Grenadier Guards.
Vince, Walker William, 15/918, C.S.M., k., 1/7/16.
Wait, Thomas, 15/1214, Pte., k., 21/7/16.
Walker, Ernest, 15/930, Pte., k., 22/5/16.
Walker, Oliver Benson, 15/1860, Pte., k.,1/7/16.
Walton, Sydney, 15/948, Cpl., k., 1/7/16.
Waring, Horace, 15/942, Pte., k., 1/7/16.
Warren, Arthur, 15/1857, Pte., k., 1/7/16.
Watson, Harry, 15/949, L/Cpl., k., 22/5/16.
West, Norman, 15/965, L/Cpl., k., 1/7/16.
Wheatley, Harold, 15/1336, Pte., k., 1/7/16.
White, Walter, 15/959, A/Cpl., k., 1/7/16.
Whitehead, Sydney, 15/960, Pte., k., 1/7/16
Whiteley, Leonard, 15/975, L/Cpl., k., 1/7/16.
Whitley, George Arthur, 15/1493, Pte., k., 1/7/16.
Wilkes, Fred, 15/1440, Pte., k., 1/7/16.
Wilkinson, Gerald, 15/982, L/Cpl., k., 1/7/16.
Wilkinson, Reginald, 15/984, Pte., k., 1/7/16.
Wilkinson, William, 15/1194, L/Cpl., d., 22/5/16.
Wilson, Frank Norman Emmott, 15/988, Pte., k., 1/7/16.
Wilson, Herbert, 15/992, Pte., k., 22/5/16.
Winch, Arthur, 15/997, L/Cpl., k., 1/7/16.
Wintle, Edward Collingwood, 15/999, Pte., Egypt, 9/2/16.
Wissler, Max Taylor, 15/1000, L/Cpl., k., 1/7/16.
Wood, Bertram, 15/1009, Pte., k., 1/7/16.
Wood, Benjamin Frederick, 15/1011, Pte., k., 1/7/16.
Wood, Frederick, 18/471, Pte., d., 14/9/16.
Wood, Frederick William, 15/1013, Pte., k., 1/7/16.
Wood, Geoffrey, 15/1414, Pte., k., 1/7/16.
Woods, Hugh, 15/1261, Pte., k., 1/7/16.
Wood, Percy, 15/1328, Pte., k., 1/7/16.
Wood, Robert, 15/1017, Pte., d., 2/7/16.

16th BATTALION

Ackroyd, Willie, 16/682, Pte., k., 27/7/16.
Airton, George Beecroft, 16/1343, Sgt., k., 1/7/16.
Aked, Clement, 16/858, Pte., k., 1/7/16.
Ambler, Victor, 16/739, Sgt., k., 1/7/16.
Arnold, Edmund Gilyard, 16/1264, Pte., k., 1/7/16.
Arthington, Ernest Harry, 16/1141, Pte., k., 1/7/16.
Aveyard, John Hodgson, 16/1140, k., 1/7/16.
Backhouse, Sidney, 31999, Pte., k., 13/11/16.
Balme, Benjamin, 16/736, Pte., k., 1/7/16.
Bannister, William, 16/438, Pte., k., 24/4/16.
Barker, Alfred, 16/188, Pte., k., 1/7/16.
Barker, Herbert, 16/543, Pte., k., 1/7/16.
Barstow, Rawden, 16/1547, Pte., d.h., 13/12/16.
Bastow, Frank, 16/1244, Pte., k., 1/7/16.
Batley, Bernard Walton, 16/1228, Pte., d.h., 8/8/16.
Beard, Joseph, 11981, Pte., d., 10/11/16.
Bell, Edward, 16/1065, Cpl., k., 1/7/16.
Bentley, Sargent, 16/312, Pte., k., 4/7/16.
Blackwell, Arthur, 16/1147, Pte., d., 9/8/16.
Blakeborough, William Herbert, 16/369, Pte., d.h., 14/5/15.
Blakey, Percy, 16/820, Pte., d., 24/4/16.
Booth, William Crane, 16/1029, Pte., d., 6/7/16.
Bower, John Arthur, 16/263, k., 1/7/16
Brayshaw, William Alan, 16/1391, Pte., d.h., 20/10/15.
Briggs, Albert, 16/1040, Pte., k., 1/7/16.
Broady, Michael, 16/1628, Pte., k., 1/7/16.
Brook, James, 40194, Pte., k., 13/11/16.
Buckborough, James Ernest, 16/104, Pte., k., 1/7/16.
Buckley, Albert, 16/410, Pte., k., 1/7/16.
Burnley, Arthur, 16/1585, Pte., k., 1/7/16.
Burrows, John, 16/920, Sgt., d., 7/5/16.
Busfield, Whitehead, 32002, Pte., k., 13/11/16.
Cawthra, Arthur, 26102, Pte., k., 9/11/16.
Clement, John Henry, 24533, Pte., k., 13/11/16.
Clough, Squire, 16/707, Cpl., k., 1/7/16.
Cockroft, William, 16/1170, Pte., k., 1/7/16.
Coe, Harold Glover, 16/130, Pte., k., 1/7/16.
Constable, Alfred, 16/514, L/Cpl., d., 27/6/16.
Cooper, George, 16/1443, Pte., k., 1/7/16.
Cousins, Arthur, 19212, Pte., k., 27/7/16.
Crabtree, Leonard, 16/609, Pte., k., 1/7/16.
Craven, George Willie, 16/806, Pte., k., 1/7/16.
Creek, Luther, 16/1240, Pte., d., 7/7/16.
Cromwell, Garfield, 16/475, Pte., k., 1/7/16.
Cryer, John Henry Ernest, 16/863, Pte., k., 1/7/16.
Culling, William Alfred, 16/904, Sgt., k., 27/7/16.
Dadswell, Hugh Cecil, 16/397, Sgt., k., 1/7/16.
Davies, Ernest Jones, 16/177, Pte., k., 13/8/16.
Dearden, Ernest, 16/283, Pte., d., 21/8/16.
Dixon, Parrington, 16/391, Pte., k., 1/7/16.
Dowson, John, 16/1198, Pte., k., 1/7/16.
Duce, Walter, 16/1084, Pte., k., 1/7/16.
Duncan, Thomas Thompson, 16/462, Pte., k., 1/7/16.
Durkin, Martin, 20/219, Pte., d., 29/7/16.
Easterby, Albert, 16/745, Pte., k., 1/7/16.
Edmondson, Willie, 16/902, Pte., k., 11/11/16.
Ellis, Francis Wilfred, 16/1591, Pte., k.,27/6/16.
Ellis, John Cyril, 16/954, Pte., d., 5/7/16.
Elson, Charles Robert, 16/1484, Pte., d., 12/6/16.
Essex, Henry, 31963, Pte., k., 10/11/16.
Fawthorpe, Harold, 16/642, Pte., k., 1/7/16.
Fenton, Arthur, 16/239, Pte., k., 1/7/16.
Fethney, Harry, 18/1420, L/Cpl., k., 1/7/16.
Forder, Alfred, 16/921, Pte., k., 1/7/16.
Foster, Edwin, 16/530, Pte., k., 1/7/16.
Fowler, George Haughton, 16/1354, Pte., k., 1/7/16.

Frost, James William, 16/1666, Pte., k., 1/7/16.
Fuller, George, 16/1434, Pte., k., 1/7/16.
Garbutt, William, 16/1629, Pte., k., 2/12/16.
Gatehouse, Fred, 16/1577, Pte., d., 3/7/16.
Gee, Fred, 16/674, L/Cpl., k., 1/7/16.
Gibson, John Robert, 31965, Pte., k., 13/11/16.
Gilgan, James, 16/947, Pte., d., 3/11/16.
Grainge, Edmund, 16/834, Pte., d., 13/6/16.
Gray, Gerald, 16/886, Pte., d.h., 18/1/15.
Greenwood, Arthur, 16/953, Pte., k., 1/7/16.
Hall, Joseph, 16/1684, Pte., k., 1/7/16.
Halmshaw, Joseph, 16/1474, Pte., k., 1/7/16.
Hand, Edgar, 16/868, Pte., k., 3/7/16.
Hanson, Albert, 16/1490, Pte., k., 1/7/16.
Hanson, Brinton, 16/824, Sgt., k., 9/11/16.
Harbron, Albert, 16/1145, Pte., k., 1/7/16.
Hargreaves, Thomas Edward, 16/1568, Pte., k., 1/7/16.
Harris, Frederick, 35957, Pte., d.h., 29/12/16.
Harrison, George Tate, 16/1233, L/Cpl., k., 13/11/16.
Harrison, Philip James, 16/1001, Pte., k.,1/7/16.
Hartley, Walter, 16/232, Pte., k., 1/7/16.
Hawkesworth, Richard, 16/167, Sgt., k., 1/7/16.
Hirst, John Wade, 16/1452, Pte., d., 5/7/16.
Hodgson, Alfred, 16/926, Pte., k., 1/7/16.
Hodgson, James Frederick, 16/733, Pte., k., 11/8/16.
Holmes, Clough, 16/1121, Pte., k., 1/7/16.
Holmes, Wilfred, 16/713, Pte., k., 1/7/16.
Horn, Dawson, 16/865, Pte., k., 1/7/16.
Horsfall, Tom, 16/535, Pte, k., 1/7/16.
Howard, Ernest, 16/998, L/Cpl., k., 1/7/16.
Howarth, George, 16/1016, Pte., k., 1/7/16.
Hunt, William Denis, 16/420, Pte., d.,13/11/16.
Hutchison, Louis, 24815, Pte., d., 16/11/16.
Illingworth, Henry, 16/95, Pte., d.h., 30/12/14.
Irving, Frank, 16/152, Pte., d., 10/11/16.
Irving, Wilfred, 40215, Pte., k., 9/11/16.
Jackson, Wilfred, 16/195, Pte., d., 12/7/16.
Johnson, Alfred, 16/217, Pte., k., 1/7/16.
Johnson, Henry Martin Finch, 16/362, Cpl., k., 1/7/16.
Jones, George, 10193, L/Cpl., k., 27/10/16.
Jordan, Walter, 16/1186, Pte., k., 1/7/16.
Jowett, Harry, 16/1368, Pte., k., 1/7/16.
Kendrick, Fred, 16/1262, Pte., k., 1/7/16.
Kenningham, Edgar, 18/771, L/Cpl, k.,1/7/16.
Kenny, William, 16/336, Pte., d., 7/7/16.
Kershaw, Frederick Percy, 16/415, Pte., k., 1/7/16.
King, Herbert, 32307, Pte., k., 9/11/16.
Kirkman, Harry, 16/1189, Pte., d., 20/11/16.
Kitchingman, Norris, 16/248, Pte., k., 19/5/16.
Knight, Rowland Hebden, 16/737, Pte., k., 1/7/16.
Lassey, Willie, 16/29, Pte., d., 16/5/16.
Latham, Percy George, 16/156, C.S.M., k., 1/7/16.
Leach, Ernest, 16/198, Pte., k., 1/7/16.
Leach, Eddy, 16/531, Pte., k., 1/7/16.
Ledger, Joseph Henry, 22587, Pte., k., 1/7/16, formerly 24906, K.O.Y.L.I.
Leech, George Edward, 16/749, Pte., k., 1/7/16.
Leeming, Henry Richard, 20/146, Pte., k., 29/7/16.
Leeming, Jonas Manasseh, 16/1511, Pte., k., 1/7/16.
Leigh, Ernest Kirkham, 20/188, Pte., k., 29/7/16
Lightowler, Willie, 20/24, Pte., k., 1/7/16.
Lingard, Thomas, 16/175, Pte., k., 1/7/16.
Linley, Abraham, 16/1677, Pte., k., 1/7/16.
Lockett, John, 16/199, Pte., k., 1/7/16.
Lowe, Bertie, 16/1673, Pte., k., 1/7/16.

McConnell, William, 16357, L/Cpl., k.,27/7/16.
McDermott, Frederick, 16/560, Pte., k., 1/7/16
McMahon, John Thomas, 16/1509, Pte., k., 1/7/16.
Mackay, Edford, 16/908, Pte., d., 10/5/16.
Mallinson, Albert, 16/704, Pte., k., 1/7/16.
Marsden, Ben, 16/1241, Pte., k., 1/7/16.
Marston, James, 16/1277, L/Cpl., k., 1/7/16.
Martindale, Irvin, 16/1297, Pte., k., 1/7/16.
Martindale, Maurice, 16/319, Pte., k., 1/7/16
May, Clement, 32857, Pte., d., 13/11/16.
May, William, 16/1437, Pte., d.h., 9/7/16.
Midgley, Verity, 16/518, L/Cpl., k., 1/7/16.
Mills, John William, 16/399, Pte., k., 1/7/16.
Mooney, Joseph, 16/735, Sgt., k., 13/11/16
Moore, John, 16/1423, Pte., k., 1/7/16.
Moore, Joe, 16/892, Pte., k., 27/7/16.
Morgan, William, 16/8, Sgt., k., 1/7/16.
Mosley, William Arthur, 16/133, Cpl., k, 1/7/16.
Muff, Herbert, 16/1291, Pte., k., 28/8/16.
Musgrave, Frank, 16/762, Pte., k., 1/7/16.
Newman, Herbert Beaumont, 16/1100, Pte., k., 1/7/16.
Newton, Alfred Ernest, 16/524, Cpl., k., 1/7/16
Packett, Donald, 16/659, Cpl., k., 1/7/16.
Parker, Tom, 16/1258, Pte., k., 1/7/16.
Parker, Willie. 16/725, Pte., k., 1/7/16.
Parkinson, Walter, 19249, Pte., k., 2/12/16.
Paterson, Malcolm Bruce, 16/687, Pte., k., 1/7/16.
Pearson, James Arthur, 20/131, Pte., k.,29/7/16.
Pearson, Maurice, 16/1433, Pte., k., 1/7/16.
Pearson, Stephen, 16/1420, Pte., k., 1/7/16.
Perray, Percy, 27850, Pte., k., 2/12/16.
Pickup, James Edwin, 16/521, L/Cpl., k., 1/7/16.
Poole, Samuel, 16/1037, L/Cpl., k., 1/7/16.
Porter, Fred, 16/632, Pte., k., 1/7/16.
Potts, Joseph, 16/1336, Pte., k., 1/7/16.
Quirk, Thomas, 20/114, Pte., d., 1/8/16.
Raine, George, 16/691, Pte., k., 1/7/16.
Ramsden, Herbert, 16/731, Pte., k., 1/7/16.
Rawnsley, Herbert Vincent, 16/1133, Pte., k., 1/7/16.
Renshaw, Ernest, 16/513, Pte., k., 1/7/16.
Reveley, Gordon Reginald, 16/837, Pte., k., 18/5/16.
Rhodes, Charles, 16/964, Pte., k., 1/7/16.
Rhodes, Thomas, 16/1247, Pte., k., 1/7/16
Rice, Lawrence, 16/1344, Pte., k., 1/7/16.
Ridley, Fred, 16/1428, Pte., k., 1/7/16.
Robertson, John Bright, 16/123, Pte., d.,3/7/16
Robinson, Frederick William, 16/1326, Pte., d., 10/7/16.
Rogers, Henry Lawrence, 16/340, Pte., k., 1/7/16.
Rowland, Robert, 16/1398, Pte., k., 1/7/16.
Rudd, Joseph, 16/663, Pte., k., 2/12/16.
Rushworth, William, 16/246, Pte., k., 15/8/16.
Rust, Walter, 19/130, Pte., d., 9/11/16.
Ryan, Bernard, 14980, Pte., k., 3/9/16.
Saunders, James Henry, 16/701, Pte., d.,7/8/16.
Sayers, John James, 16/1293, Pte., k., 1/7/16.
Scott, Harry, 16/1289, Pte., k., 1/7/16.
Selby, Christopher, 16/1399, Pte., d., 5/7/16.
Shackleton, Ernest, 16/825, Pte., k., 1/7/16.
Sharman, Charles Victor, 16/370, Pte., d., 1/8/16.
Shaw, Albert, 16/879, Pte., d., 4/9/16.
Shooter, James Robert, 16/1048, Pte., k.,1/7/16.
Sircom, Harry Innerdale, 16/732, Pte., d., 19/6/16.
Skirrow, Harry Edmundson, 16/914, Pte., d., 13/12/16.

The Prince of Wales's Own (West Yorks. Regt.)—Casualties

Slingsby, Fred, 16/350, Pte., k., 23/4/16.
Smith, Frederick Arthur, 16/1416, Pte., k., 1/7/16.
Smith, Raymond, 16/21, Pte., k., 1/7/16.
Smith, Victor, 16/269, Pte., k., 23/4/16.
Smith, Walter, 16/451, Pte., d., 9/7/16.
Smith, Willie, 24153, Pte., k., 28/10/16.
Speight, Albert, 16/1430, Pte., k., 1/7/16.
Spence, Alfred Brightrick, 16/823, Sgt., k., 1/7/16.
Spence, Eric, 16/466, L/Cpl., k., 1/7/16.
Spire, Henry Osbourne, 16/726, L/Cpl., k. 1/7/16.
Stamp, Edward John, 17198, A/Cpl., k., 1/7/16.
Stell, Joseph, 18/1046, L/Cpl., k., 1/7/16.
Stephenson, William David, 4/8430, L/Cpl., k., 9/11/16.
Sugden, Arnold, 28324, Pte., d., 22/11/16.
Sutcliffe, Herbert, 32422, Pte., k., 9/11/16.
Swinbank, James Allan, 16/314, Pte., k., 9/11/16.
Sykes, Arthur, 16/1706, Pte., d., 1/8/16.
Sykes, Arthur Edward, 16/1448, L/Cpl., k., 1/7/16.
Tarrant, George, 16/455, L/Cpl., d., 12/6/10.
Tasker, Douglas, 16/1274, Pte., k., 1/7/16.
Taylor, George Stead, 16/505, Pte., k., 1/7/16.

Thackray, Thomas, 26127, Pte., k., 29/7/16.
Thrippleton, Austin, 16/1266, Pte., k., 1/7/16.
Tolson, Percy, 16/1024, Pte., d., 29/9/16.
Tomlinson, Denis, 16/734, Pte., k., 1/7/16.
Townend, James Arthur, 16/120, L/Cpl., k., 1/7/16.
Underwood, Harry, 16/31, Cpl., k., 1/7/16.
Waddilove, Norman, 16/313, Pte., k., 1/7/16.
Walker, Percy, 16/169, L/Sgt., k., 1/7/16.
Walmsley, Arthur, 16/380, L/Cpl., k., 1/7/16.
Watson, Charles Arthur, 16/73, C.S.M., k., 1/7/16.
Weaver, Charles, 16/1631, Pte., k., 1/7/16.
Williams, William, 28726, Pte., k., 2/12/16.
Willis, Edgar, 16/614, Pte., k., 1/7/16.
Wilson, George, 16/82, L/Cpl., k., 1/7/16.
Wilson, Norris, 31986, Pte., k., 9/11/16.
Wood, James Preston, 19983, Pte., d., 10/11/16.
Wood, Thomas Stanley, 16/355, Pte., k., 1/7/16.
Woodhead, Ernest, 16/469, Pte., k., 26/6/16.
Woodhouse, Francis John, 16/106, L/Sgt., d., 22/7/16.
Woodhouse, Norman, 16/1435, Pte., k., 1/7/16.
Woodhouse, Walter, 16/69, Pte., k., 1/7/16.
Woodrow, William, 16/1397, Pte., k., 1/7/16.
Woods, Gilbert, 13968, Pte., k., 10/11/16.

17th BATTALION

Allen, Richard, 17/13, Pte., k., 10/6/16.
Ashworth, Walter, 17/1379, L/Cpl., d.,20/5/16.
Baines, Matthew, 17/1387, Pte., d., 7/6/16.
Baldwin, William, 17/1523, Pte., k., 28/3/16.
Beaufoy, Horace, 17/1529, Pte., k., 30/7/16.
Bernard, Benjamin, 17/1308, Cpl., d., 31/7/16.
Berry, Dixon, 43566, Pte., k., 2/11/16, formerly 29082, Yorks. Regt.
Berry, Walter, 17/1703, Pte., d., 28/8/16.
Boot, George Henry, 17/512, Pte., k., 14/9/16.
Brockbank, Sidney, 17/601, Sgt., k., 25/8/16.
Brown, Alfred, 17/747, Pte., k., 6/6/16.
Brookes, Ernest, 17/600, Pte., d., 8/5/16.
Cafferty, Michael, 17/1039, Pte., d., 1/8/16.
Caine, David, 17/940, Pte., k., 30/7/16.
Carruthers, William George, 17/1541, Pte., k., 17/7/16.
Catton, William, 17/1352, Pte., k., 20/2/16.
Cavenagh, Frank Richard, 17/305, Pte., d.h., 22/8/16.
Chadwick, Herbert, 19/34, Pte., d., 31/8/16.
Clark, Herbert, 25937, Pte., k., 14/7/16.
Constive, Percy, 25857, Pte., k., 14/7/16.
Cookson, Joseph, 17/1663, Pte., k., 30/7/16.
Coulter, Henry, 17/1570, A/Cpl., d., 19/10/16.
Croft, William, 17/51, Pte., d., 26/8/16.
Crombie, Thomas, 17/1589, Pte., k., 24/7/16.
Culley, Thomas Edward, 19/28, Pte., k., 23/7/16.
Dalton, Herbert, 17/1259, Pte., d., 5/6/16.
Doolan, John, 17/1007, Sgt., k., 8/6/16.
Doyle, Charles, 17/1194, Pte., d., 28/11/16.
Drake, Clement, 25925, Pte., d., 23/10/16.
Duffy, Timothy, 17/604, Pte., k., 21/10/16.
Dunn, John, 17/1621, L/Cpl., d., 24/7/16.
Dykes, Edward, 17/56, Sgt., k., 29/7/16.
Edon, Cecil, 28224, Pte., k., 25/8/16.
Emmonds, Alfred, 17/1682, Pte., k., 23/7/16.
Emsley, William, 17/1593, Pte., k., 17/7/16.
Eve, Richard, 17/463, Pte., d., 30/7/16.
Fleming, John William, 17/561, Pte., k., 26/8/16.
France, Archer, 17/1037, Pte., k., 24/7/16.

France, Baldwin, 17/1600, Sgt., k., 30/7/16.
Gallagher, Edward, 17/1392, Sgt., k., 24/7/16.
Gavaghan, Joseph, 17/1018, L/Sgt., k.,25/8/16.
Gavins, Joe, 17/715, L/Cpl., d., 22/10/16.
Glover, Percy, 17/648, Pte., k., 17/7/16.
Gray, Christian, 17/649, Pte., d.h., 4/11/16
Gregory, James, 17/1647, Pte., d.h., 23/11/15.
Greenwood, John Robert, 28449, Pte., k., 26/8/16.
Guthrie, George Gilbert, 17/65, Pte., d.h., 11/12/15.
Haigh, Alfred, 17/1140, Pte., d., 18/7/16.
Haggerty, Thomas, 17/378, Pte., k., 10/10/16.
Hancock, Dennis, 17/1074, Pte., k., 30/7/16.
Hardy, Thorpe, 17/1047, Pte., d.h., 24/8/16.
Harrison, Robert, 17/548, Pte., d., 31/7/16.
Harvey, Ernest Nigel, 25984, Pte., k., 28/8/16.
Haswell, John Charles, 17/84, Pte., k., 30/7/16.
Hayton, Walter, 17/885, Sgt., k., 25/7/16.
Healey, Frederick, 17/425, A/Cpl., k., 25/8/16
Hemingway, Alfred, 17/1331, Pte., k., 30/7/16.
Hepworth, Harold, 17/1266, L/Cpl., d., 26/8/16.
Hill, John William, 26065, Pte., k., 10/10/16.
Hodgkin, Harry, 25843, Pte., k., 14/7/16.
Holmes, Albert, 17/1000, Pte., k., 30/7/16.
Horner, William, 17/1068, L/Cpl., k., 25/8/16.
Hotter, John Thomas, 17/1697, Pte., d. 10/6/16.
Hurst, John Allison, 17/1619, Sgt., k., 24/7/16.
Hurst, Robert, 17/1700, Pte., k., 29/5/16.
Ineson, Herbert, 17/1012, Pte., k., 30/7/16.
Jackson, Walter, 17/615, Pte., k., 24/7/16.
Jarrat, William, 19/31, Pte., k., 30/7/16.
Jenkinson, Frederick William, 17/1054, Pte., k., 8/6/16.
Johnson, Edward, 17/884, Pte., k., 30/7/16.
Jones, Horace, 17/1629, Pte., k., 30/7/16.
Judson, Frederick Wilkinson, 19/119, Pte., d., 25/8/16.
Kavanagh, Clifford, 17/90, Pte., k., 6/6/16.
Keedy, John Robert, 17/89, Sgt., k., 13/4/16.
Killeen, William Lee, 17/1471, Pte, k.., 23/7/16

350 The Prince of Wales's Own (West Yorks. Regt.)—Casualties

Lee, Thomas, 17/96, Pte., d., 25/7/16.
Linn, Walter Henry, 17/1611, Pte., k., 9/5/16, formerly 20159, K.O.Y.L.I.
Lobley, John William, 17/1235, Cpl., k., 30/7/16.
Lockwood, Harry, 17/1644, Pte., k., 16/5/16.
Lowe, Richard, 17/1699, Pte., d., 31/5/16.
Marsden, John, 17/429, Pte., k., 30/7/16.
Marsden, Joseph, 17/385, Pte., k., 30/7/16.
Marshall, Edward, 17/982, C/Q.M.Sgt., 19/9/16.
Marshall, Ernest, 17/917, Pte., d., 31/7/16.
Mason, Willie, 17/1579, Pte., k., 24/7/16.
Matthew, James, 17/1077, Pte., k., 30/7/16.
Matthewman, Willie, 17/569, Pte., k., 26/8/16.
Mellor, Lindley, 17/450, Pte., d., 5/12/16.
Midgley, Alfred, 17/844, Pte., k., 30/7/16.
Miller, Albert, 17/467, Pte., 16/9/16.
Moran, John, 17/1576, Pte., d., 25/7/16.
Morrell, Ernest, 17/274, Pte., k., 30/7/16.
Morton, Richard, 17/658, Pte., k., 10/10/16.
Munro, James, 17/117, Pte., d.h., 30/8/16.
McManus, Francis, 17/105, Pte., 29/3/16.
Nason, James, 25974, Pte., k., 22/10/16.
Naylor, Wilfred, 17/575, Pte., k., 1/11/16.
Nowland, George, 17/1353, A/Cpl., k., 25/8/16.
Oldfield, Harry, 17/881, Pte., k., 30/7/16.
Parker, Charles Alfred, 25837, Pte., k., 23/9/16.
Parker, Harold George, 17/1456, Pte., k., 17/7/16.
Parkin, John Simpson, 17/320, Pte., k., 24/7/16.
Pickles, Sam, 17/1058, L/Cpl., k., 8/10/16.
Platts, James Arthur, 17/491, Pte., k., 30/7/16.
Prentice, Willie, 28425, Pte., d., 23/11/16.
Pursglove, George, 17/1317, Pte., k., 30/7/16.
Reveley, William, 17/1606, A/C.S.M., k., 22/10/16.
Richardson, Matthew, 17/136, Pte., k., 1/11/16.
Richardson, Walter, 77/458, L/Cpl., d., 27/9/16.
Riley, Frederick, 19/40, Pte., d., 26/7/16.
Robinson, Fred, 17/530, A/Cpl., d., 25/8/16.
Robinson, Newton, 28438, Pte., k., 10/10/16.
Robinson, Percival, 17/1267, Cpl., k., 30/7/16.
Roberts, Arthur, 17/531, Pte., d.h., 29/3/15.

Sallis, James, 17/850, Pte., k., 25/8/16.
Sharp, Albert, 17/854, Pte., d., 8/4/16.
Sherwin, Hugh, 17/781, Pte., k., 25/7/16.
Smickersgill, George Arthur, 17/919, Pte., k., 30/7/16.
Smith, Joseph, 17/588, Pte., k., 10/10/16.
Sorfleet, Willie, 17/1499, Sgt., k., 24/7/16.
Speight, Charles Alfred, 17/584, Pte., k., 17/5/16.
Steele, Laurence, 11460, Sgt., d., 25/4/16.
Stevens, Amos, 17/953, Pte., k., 18/5/16.
Stocks, Walter James, 17/144, Pte., k., 24/2/16.
Stretton, George, 17/701, Pte., d., 25/7/16.
Stych, Samuel Henry, 17/1041, Pte., k., 9/3/16.
Sykes, Harold, 28335, Pte., k., 25/8/16.
Taylor, Jesse, 17/1395, L/Cpl., k., 30/7/16.
Thompson, Harry, 17/249, Pte., k., 30/7/16.
Thompson, Harry, 17/413, Pte., k., 18/5/16.
Thompson, Reginald, 25861, Pte., k., 14/7/16.
Towers, Ernest, 17/703, L/Cpl., k., 30/7/16.
Towns, James Henry, 17/158, L/Cpl., k., 24/8/16.
Turner, Herbert, 17/289, Pte., k., 23/7/16.
Wadd, Ernest, 17/1303, Pte., k., 30/6/17.
Wainwright, Ernest, 17/1332, L/Cpl., k., 30/7/16.
Walder, Michael, 17/175, Pte., d., 17/6/16.
Walker, Herbert, 17/498, Pte., k., 30/7/16.
Warrener, William, 17/539, Pte., d., 20/4/16.
Webb, Charles, 17/861, Pte., k., 30/7/16.
Welsh, Thomas Patrick, 17/1641, Pte., k., 30/7/16.
Whitaker, Christopher, 17/297, L/Cpl., d., 22/11/16.
Whitehead, Robert, 17/290, A/Cpl., k., 30/7/16.
Whiteley, Harry, 25946, Pte., k., 14/7/16.
Whitworth, George, 17/591, Pte., k., 26/8/16.
Widdop, Joseph, 17/199, Pte., k., 31/7/16.
Wilby, William Cooper, 17/632, Pte., k., 31/7/16
Wilcock, Arthur Buckley, 19/35, Pte., k. 25/8/16.
Williams, Harry, 17/927, Pte., d., 19/7/16.
Williamson, Wilfred, 17/359, Pte., d., 30/7/16.
Windsor, Arthur, 17/1425, Pte., k., 30/7/16.

18th BATTALION

Abbott, William Edwin, 18/625, A/Sgt., k., 30/6/16.
Alderton, Harry, 18/454, Pte., k., 1/7/16.
Allatt, Thomas Henry, 18/248, Pte., k., 16/9/16.
Allott, James, 33101, Pte., d., 25/10/16.
Ambler, Frederick Brammer, 18/1409, Pte., d., 22/4/16.
Applin, Harry Warren, 18/1410, Pte., d., 15/7/16.
Atkinson, William, 18/1458, Pte., d., 25/10/16.
Auker, Frank, 18/1569, Pte., k., 30/6/16.
Austin, William, 22677, Pte., d., 24/5/16, formerly 23, York and Lancs. Regt
Barber, Edward, 18/744, Pte., k., 1/7/16.
Barber, George Arthur, 18/876, L/Sgt., d., 1/7/16.
Barker, Willie, 18/1164, Pte., d., 27/7/16.
Barnes, Charlie, 18/1391, Pte., k., 1/7/16.
Barraclough, Norman, 18/1097, Pte., d. 25/10/16.
Barraclough, William, 18/123, Pte., k., 24/4/16.
Barran, Morris, 20/136, Pte., k., 1/7/16.
Bateman, Percy, 18/104, Cpl. d h., 8/7/16
Beck, Harry, 18/81, Pte., k., 1/7/16.
Betts, Ross, 10375, Pte., 27/7/16.

Biggins, Laurence Lyons, 18/71, L/Cpl., k., 27/5/16.
Binns, Thomas, 18/874, Pte., k., 30/6/16.
Booth, Edmund, 18/190, Pte., k., 1/7/16.
Booth, George Herbert, 18/296, Pte., k., 1/7/16.
Bowskill, Arthur William, 18/1119, Pte., d., 1/7/16.
Brewer, Albert, 20/155, Pte., k., 1/7/16.
Briggs, Arthur, 18/456, Pte., k., 24/4/16.
Brock, James Edgar, 18/993, Pte., k., 1/7/16.
Brogden, Thomas Blakey, 18/950, Pte., k., 1/7/16.
Brown, Alfred, 18/431, Pte., d., 3/7/16.
Brown, John, 18/1487, Pte., k., 1/7/16.
Burton, Norman, 18/378, Pte., k., 1/7/16.
Caley, Ernest William, 40329, Pte., d., 25/10/16.
Carter, Guy Ripley, 40327, Pte., k., 13/11/16.
Cawthorne, Herbert, 18/449, Pte., k., 1/7/16.
Chambers, Arthur, 40252, Pte., d., 25/10/16.
Cheshire, Norman, 18/697, Pte., k., 1/7/16.
Clayton, Horace, 18/844, Pte., k., 1/7/16.
Clegg, Joseph, 18/879, Cpl., d., 1/7/16.
Clough, George, 18/507, Pte., k., 1/7/16.
Cockshott, Frank, 18/902, Pte., k., 30/7/16.
Coulson, George, 26275, Pte., d., 15/9/16.

The Prince of Wales's Own (West Yorks. Regt.)—Casualties 351

Craven, James, 18/152, Pte., k., 1/7/16.
Craven, Wilfred, 18/878, Pte., k., 30/6/16.
Craven, William Allen, 18/667, Pte., k., 1/7/16
Crerar, John, 18/997, Pte., d., 29/9/16.
Croft, Stanley, 18/35, L/Cpl., k., 27/7/16.
Crossley, Herbert, 18/683, Pte., k., 13/11/16.
Crossley, John William, 18/17, Pte., d., 19/5/16.
Crotch, Ernest, 18/525, Pte., k., 1/7/16.
Crowe, Norman, 40269, Pte., k., 13/11/16.
Crowther, Clarance, 18/672, Pte., k., 1/7/16.
Cullum, Harold, 18/1055, Pte., k., 18/8/16.
Cure, Vincent, 18/1211, Pte., d., 3/7/16.
Darling, Horace, 18/1264, Pte., k., 13/11/16.
Daybell, Arthur, 18/187, Pte., k., 1/7/16.
Dixon, Fred, 18/479, Pte., k., 1/7/16.
Dixon, Wilfred, 18/375, Pte., d., 20/5/16.
Driver, Herbert, 18/1480, L/Cpl., k., 27/9/16.
Duggan, John, 18/624, Pte., d., 30/9/16.
Dutton, Henry Frederick, 40462, Pte., d. 26/11/16, formerly 31024, Leicestershire Regt.
Dyson, Herbert, 18/261, Sgt., k., 1/7/16, M.M.
Eccles, Harry, 18/1463, Pte., k., 10/6/16.
Fawcett, Joseph Robert, 18/176, Pte., k.,1/7/16.
Ferrand, Claude Ernest, 18/252, Pte., k, 22/5/16.
Firth, Arthur, 18/1076, Pte., k., 30/6/16.
Firth, Joseph, 20/169, Pte., d., 1/7/16.
Firth, Lewis, 18/1167, Pte., d., 1/7/16.
Fry, James, 18/68, Pte., k., 28/4/16.
Garbutt, John, 18/638, L/Cpl., k., 1/7/16.
Garside, Ratcliffe, 18/882, Pte., k., 27/8/16.
Gaunt, Leonard, 18/405, Pte., k., 1/7/16.
Gill, John, 18/836, Pte., d., 1/7/16.
Gill, Sam, 18/783, Pte., d., 3/7/16.
Gillett, Herbert Elijah, 20/26, Pte., k., 30/6/16.
Gledhill, Herbert, 18/614, Pte., k., 1/7/16.
Goldthorpe, Walter, 18/784, Pte., d., 1/7/16.
Gough, George Albert, 18/555, Pte., d., 15/11/16.
Grant, Albert, 33377, Pte., d., 11/12/16.
Grayson, Randolph, 40302, Pte., k., 24/10/16.
Green, Harry Charles, 18/193, Sgt., d., 22/6/16.
Green, Walter, 32178, Pte., k., 13/11/16.
Greenwood, Henry Bernal, 18/9, Sgt., k., 30/6/16.
Gresswell, William Wood, 16/1728, Pte., k., 26/10/16.
Hackford, Frank, 18/413, Pte., d., 6/7/16.
Hague, Harold, 9071, Pte., k., 1/7/16.
Haigh, Morris, 18/1105, Pte., k., 27/7/16.
Halliday, Samuel, 18/80, L/Cpl., d.h.,10/11/15.
Hamblin, Hubert Charles, 18/196, C.S.M., k., 1/7/16.
Hammond, Percy, 18/206, Pte., k., 1/7/16.
Hargreaves, Richard, 18/1107, Pte., d., 17/5/16.
Harper, John Abbotson, 20/145, Pte., k.,1/7/16.
Hayes, Walter, 24254, L/Cpl., d., 27/10/16.
Haylock, Arthur, 40303, Pte., k., 13/11/16.
Haynes, John Edward, 18/940, Pte., k., 1/7/16.
Haywood, Bertie, 40258, L/Cpl., k., 26/10/16.
Hazlewood, Harry, 18/25, Pte., k., 3/9/16.
Helliwell, Albert, 18/1475, Pte., d., 6/7/16.
Helliwell, Maurice, 18/279, Pte., k., 1/7/16.
Hill, Harry, 18/1424, Cpl., k., 1/7/16.
Hill, John Henry, 18/95, Pte., d., 27/4/16.
Hill, Norman, 19/98, Pte., d., 6/7/16.
Hill, Thomas, 18/1106, Pte., k., 1/7/16.
Hills, Harry, 18/295, Pte., k., 1/7/16.
Hodgson, Joseph, 18/1498, Pte., k., 1/7/16.
Holdsworth, Harry, 18/126, Cpl., k., 1/7/16.
Holmes, John, 18/1625, Pte., k., 1/7/16.
Horrocks, George, 18/374, Pte., k., 1/7/16.
Hughes, Hughie, 20012, Cpl., k., 1/7/16, formerly 25081, 10th Hussars.

Humphreys, Stanley, 18/1132, Pte., k., 1/7/16.
Hutchinson, Harrison, 18/1594, Pte., d., 27/7/16.
Jackson, Fred, 18/1427, Pte., k., 1/7/16.
Jagger, George William, 18/942, Pte., d.,1/7/16
Johnson, Arthur, 18/975, L/Cpl., k., 1/7/16.
Johnson, Herbert, 18/838, L/Cpl., k., 1/7/16.
Jones, William Harold, 18/1269, Pte., k.,1/7/16
Jordan, Arthur, 18/1585, Pte., k., 1/7/16.
Jowett, Frederick, 18/450, Pte., d., 27/7/16.
Jowett, Thomas Lund, 18/943, Pte., k., 1/7/16.
Joyce, Michael Henry, 18/1523, L/Cpl., d., 3/7/16.
Kendall, Harry, 18/634, Drmr., k., 1/7/16.
Lapish, Fred, 19/103, Pte., k., 13/11/16.
Lister, William Edward, 18/1300, Pte., k., 1/7/16.
Lowndes, Sam, 18/713, L/Cpl., k., 1/7/16.
McCaffrey, James, 19/229, Pte., d., 25/10/16
McDonald, Joseph, 18/1346, Pte., k., 1/7/16.
Macaulay, Kenneth, 18/835, Pte., k., 30/6/16.
Margerison, John, 18/49, Drmr., k., 1/7/16.
Marsden, Charles, 18/1271, Pte., k., 1/7/16.
Massen, Thomas, 18/1010, Cpl., k., 1/7/16.
Mayne, John George, 18/700, Sgt., d., 5/7/16.
Meays, Harry, 18/650, Pte., k., 30/6/16.
Melia, Patrick Franice, 21330, Pte., d., 22/8/16
Metcalfe, Willie, 18/446, Ptc., k., 1/7/16.
Milner, Herbert, 18/237, Pte., k., 1/7/16.
Milnes, Richard, 18/474, Sgt., d.h., 29/6/15.
Mitchell, William Henry, 29264, Pte., d., 25/10/16
Morris, Edwin, 18/271, Pte., d., 25/5/16.
Murgatroyd, Arthur Edgar, 18/13, Pte., k., 1/7/16.
Muscroft, Lorry, 18/1112, Pte., k., 1/7/16.
Newton, John, 18/1160, Pte, k., 14/7/16.
Normington, Arthur, 18/1374, Pte., d., 1/7/16.
Normington, Joseph, 18/373, Sgt., k., 1/7/16.
North, John Richard, 18/31, Pte., k., 1/7/16.
North, Reginald, 18/40, Pte., k., 1/7/16.
Nuttall, Leonard, 18/202, Pte., d., 27/4/16.
Oates, John Joseph, 40797, Pte., d., 24/11/16, formerly 28982, K.R.R.
O'Brien, James Hadcock, 40315, Pte., k., 13/11/16.
Palframan, Gordon, 40246, Pte., k., 13/11/16.
Pape, Charles, 18/860, Pte., k., 1/7/16.
Parkin, Charles, 40245, Pte., d., 16/11/16.
Pass, Harry, 18/626, C.S.M., d., 5/7/16.
Pennett, William, 18/358, Pte., k., 1/7/16.
Plows, Richard, 18/1381, L/Cpl., d., 27/5/16.
Powell, Albert Edward, 23061, Pte., d., 9/7/16, formerly 9/14511, East Yorks. Regt.
Presland, Albert Maltman, 18/912, Pte., d.h., 30/11/16
Preston, Robert, 40307, Pte., k., 13/11/16.
Pullan, Edgar, 18/619, Pte., k., 13/11/16.
Redman, Harry, 18/890, Pte., k., 1/7/16.
Reynolds, Arthur, 18/1084, Pte., k., 1/7/16.
Riley, Ralph, 18/1085, Pte., d., 19/5/16.
Robinson, Frank, 18/493, Pte., k., 16/9/16.
Robinson, Thomas Henry, 18/195, Pte., k., 1/7/16.
Robson, Ernest, 18/151, Pte., k., 1/7/16.
Rumbold, William Edgar, 23940, Pte., k., 27/7/16.
Rushworth, Charles, 18/1205, Pte., k., 1/7/16.
Sansome, Frank, 18/945, Pte., d., 4/7/16.
Saville, James William, 18/776, Pte., k.,30/6/16.
Schofield, Percy, 18/2, L/Cpl., k., 19/5/16.
Shuttleworth, Thomas Whitaker, 18/1045, Pte., k., 1/5/16.
Skirrow, Joe Forrest, 18/1185, Pte., k., 1/7/16.
Smith, Fred, 25035, Pte., k., 25/10/16.

352 The Prince of Wales's Own (West Yorks. Regt.)—Casualties

Smith, Harold Howard, 18/544, Pte., k., 1/7/16.
Smith, John Edward, 18/870, Pte., d.h.,7/10/16.
Stenhouse, James Thomas, 18/1325, L/Cpl., k., 27/9/16.
Sunderland, Joseph, 18/385, Pte., d., 11/10/16.
Sutcliffe, Frank, 18/1196, Pte., k., 3/9/16.
Swaine, George Albert, 18/1333, Pte., k.,1/7/16.
Tarran, Arthur, 18/790, Pte., k., 1/7/16.
Tate, Joseph, 18/89, Pte., d., 30/6/16.
Thompson, Ernest, 18/893, Pte., k., 1/7/16.
Thompson, Horace, 18/342, Pte., k., 1/7/16.
Tidswell, Herbert Bedford, 40233, Pte., d., 13/11/16.
Topham, George Henry, 18/984, Pte., k., 1/7/16.
Upton, George Henry, 18/140, Sgt., k., 27/7/16.
Vickerman, William, 21159, L/Cpl., d., 25/10/16.
Waddington, John, 18/896, Pte., k., 1/7/16, D.C.M.

Walden, Ernest, 18/357, A/Cpl., k., 22/5/16.
Walker, Harry, 19559, Pte., k., 1/7/16.
Walker, Stanley, 20/191, Pte., k., 1/7/16.
Whitaker, Charles Gordon, 18/245, L/Cpl., k., 27/7/16.
Whittaker, Harold, 18/541, Pte., k., 1/7/16.
Whitaker, James, 18/1277, Pte., k., 1/7/16.
Whitaker, Willie, 18/596, Pte., k., 1/7/16.
White, Eric, 18/1039, Pte., d., 8/7/16.
Widdop, Edwin, 18/1186, Pte., k., 1/7/16.
Wilkinson, Edgar, 18/1127, Pte., k., 27/7/16.
Wilks, Francis William, 18/467, Pte., k., 1/7/16.
Willan, John, 18/1197, Pte., k., 15/8/16.
Wise, Thomas, 18/1128, L/Sgt., k., 13/11/16.
Wood, Edward, 40342, Pte., k., 13/11/16.
Wood, John William, 18/274, Pte., d., 28/4/16.
Wood, Peter Barrett, 18/564, Pte., d., 18/8/16.
Wright, Harold, 18/189, L/Cpl., d.h., 15/7/16.

19th BATTALION

Kaberry, Walter, 27994, Pte., d.h., 6/12/16.
Mahoney, Joseph, 17/1521, Pte., d.h., 10/3/16

Tottie, Robert, 15/1636, Pte., d.h., 3/3/16

20th BATTALION

Dodgson, Walter, 19/118 Pte., d.h., 13/12/15.

Hirst, Frank, 20/81, Pte., d.h., 17/12/15.

21st BATTALION

Brooke, Joshua, 21/409, Pte., d., 2/12/16.
Bush, Walter George, 23517, A/Sgt., d., 25/10/16.
Chadwick, George Arthur, 21/25, Pte., k., 1/7/16.
Davies, Fred, 21/784, Pte., d.h., 10/3/16.
Dean, Reginald, 21/185, Pte., k., 1/7/16.
Dyson, Thomas Asquith, 21/520, Pte., k., 21/12/16.
Earnshaw, Leonard, 21/728, Pte., k., 19/10/16.
Edmondson, Benjamin, 21/971, Pte., k. 19/10/16.
Ellis, Smith, 21/537, Pte., d., 29/12/16.
Firth, John Willie, 21/693, Pte., k., 11/12/16.
Foster, Fred, 21/776, Pte., k., 26/8/16.
France, Gordon, 21/243, Sgt., k., 17/12/16.
Gatehouse, Harold, 27969, Pte., 29/11/16.
Hainsworth, Robert, 21/885, Pte., k., 26/8/16.
Hartley, Richard H. H., 29315, Pte., k., 17/12/16.
Haworth, Ernest Vincent, 21/851, Cpl., k., 19/10/16.

Helliwell, Frank, 27979, Pte., k., 12/10/16.
Horsley, Joseph, 21/234, C.Q.M.S., k., 17/12/16.
Hughes, Edgar, 21/843, Pte., k., 19/10/16.
Hume, Robert, 21/675, Pte., k., 31/7/16.
Hutton, Arthur, 21/239, Pte., d., 14/10/16.
Kerbotson, Joe, 21/663, Pte., k., 3/7/16.
Newsome, Harry, 21/651, Pte., k., 3/7/16.
Oddy, James, 21/856, Pte., k., 19/10/16.
Pearce, Charles Edward, 27977, Pte., d.,26/6/16.
Pearson, Arthur, 21/618, Pte., d., 18/12/16.
Platt, Brandon, 21/727, Pte., k., 8/7/16.
Richardson, Joseph, 21/741, Pte., k., 21/10/16.
Ringwood, William Alfred, 43469, Pte., k., 12/10/16, formerly 28/535, Northumberland Fusiliers.
Roseberry, William Thompson, 21/769, Pte., d., 18/7/16.
Singleton, Thomas, 21/629, Pte., d., 19/12/16.
Taylor, Ben, 21/903, Pte., k., 19/10/16.
Thorsby, Harry, 21089, Pte., d., 14/12/16.

22nd BATTALION

Arthur, James, 30593, L/Cpl., d., 14/7/16, formerly 22178, Lincolnshire Regt.
Ashton, William, 30002, Pte., d., 12/9/16, formerly 24579, York and Lancaster Regt.
Cowling, Allen, 30026, Pte., k., 12/9/16 formerly 24610, York and Lancaster Regt.
Dodds, Herbert, 30036, Pte., k., 12/9/16, formerly 24590, York and Lancaster Regt.
Drury, James, 30167, Pte., d., 12/9/16, formerly 24978, York and Lancaster Regt.

Harrison, William Henry, 30065, Pte., d., 9/6/16, formerly 24619, York and Lancaster Regt.
Hayes, Alfred, 30076, Pte., d., 14/12/16, formerly 24527, York and Lancaster Regt.
Headley, James, 29789, Pte., k., 28/10/16.
Lee, Thomas Henry, 31443, Pte., k., 12/9/16, Martin, Mark, 31403, L/Sgt., k., 12/9/16, formerly 15662, South Staffs. Regt.

26th PROVISIONAL BATTALION

Kilkenny, James, 3329, Pte., d.h., 3/8/16.

Rumfitt, Thomas, 1912, Pte., d.h., 5/3/16.

INDEX

Aisne, Battle of the, 9; Disposition of the opposing forces ... 10
Alexander, Lieut-Col. J. W. 52, 199, 218
Atkinson, Lieut.-Col. F. N. J. 180, 246
Atkinson, Lieut.-Col. H. S. ... 303
Armentières, Battle of, 15; Disposition of opposing forces, 15, 16; Bleu captured, 16; Meteren captured, 17; Disposition of opposing forces 18th Oct., 18, 19; Ennetieres captured, 19; Premesques captured, 20; How the 1st Battalion held the line, 21
Barker, Lieut.-Col. 227, 230, 250, 283, 284

Battalions :
1st : 1, 11, 12, 13, 14, 16, 17, 19, 21, 22, 23, 29, 32, 36, 49, 51, 55, 56, 57, 61, 64, 97, 102, 103, 107, 108, 109, 110, 111, 130, 133, 134, 137, 138, 142, 164, 165, 166, 183, 184, 262, 263, 264, 265, 267, 268, 269, 270, 285, 286, 287, 288

2nd : 30, 31, 32, 33, 34, 35, 36, 38, 40, 41, 42, 43, 46, 47, 48, 49, 51, 55, 57, 63, 101, 115, 129, 133, 146, 147, 163, 166, 167, 168, 199, 204, 205, 206, 207, 208, 209, 215, 224, 290, 291, 292, 293, 294, 295, 296, 297

3rd : 1
4th : 1

1/5th : 52, 53, 55, 58, 63, 98, 99, 103, 104, 105, 113, 118, 131, 133, 134, 138, 140, 163, 168, 169, 170, 171, 199, 215, 217, 218, 219, 221, 224, 225, 231, 232, 233, 253, 254, 255, 256, 257, 278, 279, 280, 300

1/6th : 52, 53, 55, 58, 59, 63, 98, 99, 103, 104, 105, 113, 118, 133, 134, 135, 136, 138, 139, 141, 163, 168, 169, 170, 171, 199, 215, 217, 218, 219, 220, 221, 224, 225, 226, 231, 232, 233, 253, 254, 255, 256, 257, 278, 300

Battalions—contd.

1/7th : 52, 53, 55, 59, 64, 98, 99, 103, 104, 105, 118, 133, 134, 138, 142, 163, 168, 169, 170, 171, 199, 215, 218, 219, 221, 224, 226, 231, 232, 233, 253, 254, 255, 256, 278, 300

1/8th : 52, 53, 55, 59, 64, 65, 97, 99, 103, 104, 105, 118, 133, 134, 138, 163, 168, 169, 170, 171, 215, 218, 219, 221, 224, 226, 231, 232, 233, 253, 254, 255, 256, 257, 278, 300

9th : 71, 72, 73, 74, 75, 76, 77, 78, 79, 80, 82, 84, 87, 88, 91, 93, 133, 134, 151, 153, 154, 155, 163, 171, 257, 258, 259, 260, 261, 274, 275, 276, 277, 278, 300, 301

10th : 100, 114, 130, 133, 134, 143, 163, 172, 173, 174, 193, 199, 200, 201, 202, 215, 224, 226, 295, 301, 302

11th : 117, 133, 134, 163, 174, 175, 176, 227, 228, 229, 230, 231, 249, 250, 266, 281, 282, 283, 284

12th : 121, 124, 125, 126, 127, 128, 133, 134, 143, 144, 145, 146, 163, 176, 177, 178, 179, 236, 237, 238, 239, 240, 241, 244, 245, 251, 252, 253, 297, 298

15th (Leeds Pals) : 164, 182, 199, 209, 210, 211, 212, 213, 214, 215, 225, 297, 298, 299

16th (1st Bradford Pals) : 104, 182, 199, 209, 210, 211, 212, 213, 214, 215, 297, 298, 299

17th : 180, 181, 244, 245, 246, 247, 248, 302

18th (2nd Bradford Pals) : 164, 182, 199, 210, 211, 213, 214, 215, 225, 297, 298, 299

21st (Pioneer) : 199, 214, 215, 288, 289, 290

INDEX—Continued.

22nd (Labour): 302, 303
Barrington, Lieut.-Col. T. P. 23, 163
Bellewaerde, First Attack on, 61;
  Casualties of 1st Bn. 62; Second
  Attack on 130,
Bousfield, Col. 279, 280
Boyall, Major A. M. 204
Bullock, Major 126, 127
Campbell, Lieut.-Col. C. H. 144, 163
Carter, Major H. F. C. 214
Clark, Lieut.-Col. E. K. 163
Clarke, Lieut.-Col. Sir E. H. St. L.
  199, 214
Cliffe, Major H. T.... ... 14, 17
Cooper-King, Major R. G. ... 34
Cuthell, Major A. H. ... 87, 92
Dardenelles: Battles of Suvla,
  6-21 Aug., 1915, 71; Introduction, 72; Plan of Attack,
  73; Landing, 77; Capture of
  Lala Baba, 77; Heavy losses in
  officers 9th Bn., 83; Total
  casualties 9th Bn., 85; Battle of
  Scimitar Hill, 87; Scheme of
  operations, 89; 9th Bn. held up,
  91; Losses of 9th Bn., 92;
  Trench Warfare at Suvla and
  the evacuation, 19-20 Dec.,
  1915, 151; 9th Bn. leaves, 154
Dickson, Lieut.-Col. A. 199, 202, 203
Dillon, Major H. M. 265
Edwards, Lieut.-Col. W. M. ... 163
Estridge, Major C. L. ... 258, 301
Evatt, Lieut.-Col. F. W.... ... 163
Goodwyn, Lieut.-Col. W. M. ... 164
Guyon, Major G. S. ... 199, 213
Hartley, Major J. C. 214
Hooge, Actions of 1st Aug., 1915,
  107; Attack launched... ... 109
Hudson, Major 231
Hume-Spry, Lieut.-Col. 199, 204, 292
Ingles, Major A. W. ... 11, 12
Isacke, Major R. 92, 153, 163
Jack, Major, J. L. 292, 294, 296
Jacques, Major, J. H. ... 125, 127
Kennard, Lieut.-Col. E. C. H.,
  164, 182, 210, 213
Kennard, Lieut.-Col. M. N. ... 199
Kennedy, Major H. H. ... 182, 209
Kirk, Lieut.-Col. A. E. 52, 163, 199, 218
Knott, Major J. 202, 203
Knowles, Lieut.-Col G. W. ... 163
Lang, Lieut.-Col. G. G., 12, 13,
  20, 22, 108, 163, 183, 264, 265
Leggett, Lieut.-Col. R. A. C. L. 122, 127

Loos, The Battle of, 25th Sept.—
  8th Oct., 1915, 119; Disposition of opposing forces, 120;
  Allies' first use gas, 120; 12th
  Bn. moves up, 123; Bn. held
  up, 125; Casualties, 127; Subsidiary Actions, 129; Action of
  Pietre and Bois Grenier, 129
Mathews, Major A. S. 179
Meekosha, V.C., Corporal S. ... 138
Minogue, Lieut.-Col. J. O. B., 71,
  87, 92, 257, 258
Neill, Major R. B. ... 199, 209, 212
Neuve Chapelle, Battle of, 37;
  Operation Order No. 12, 38, 39,
  40; Casualties of 2nd Bn. 49
Oswald, Major W.O., 227, 236, 239,
  240, 241
Phillips, Lieut.-Col. G. F. 30, 33, 35
Sanders, V.C., Corporal G. 221, 222
Scott, Lieut.-Col. C. E. 220
Soames, Lieut.-Col. G. H.... ... 302
Somme, Battles of the, 1st July—
  18th Nov., 1916. Enemy's defences, 191; Disposition of
  British Forces, 192, 193; General attack, 195; Battle of Albert
  1st-13th July, 199; Capture of
  Fricourt, 199, 200; Attack on
  Ovillers-la-Boisselle, 203; Attack on Serre and Pendent Copse
  208, 209; Attack on Thiepval,
  216; Cpl. G. Sanders, 1/7th Bn.
  wins second V.C. for Regt., 221,
  222; Capture of Horseshoe
  Trench, 227; Capture of Bailiff
  Wood and Contalmaison, 229;
  Leipzig Salient, 231; Battle of
  Bazentin Ridge, 235; Battle of
  Delville Wood, 243; Attack on
  Munster Alley, 249; Attack on
  Lonely Trench, 251; Attack on
  Thiepval, 2nd-3rd Sept., 255;
  Attack on Wundt Werk, 259;
  Tanks first used, 261; Capture
  of the Quadrilateral, 264;
  Battle of Morval, 267; Capture
  Lesbœufs, 269; Battle of
  Thiepval Ridge, 273; Attack
  on Schwaben Redoubt, 279;
  Battle of Transloy Ridge, 281;
  Attack on Mild and Cloudy
  Trenches, 284; Attack on Zenith Trench, 290

INDEX—Continued.

	Page
Stewart, Lieut.-Col. J. S. S.	... 303
Taylor, Lieut.-Col. S. C. ...	164, 182
Thompson, Major F.C. ...	221, 225
Thomson, Major ...	240, 251, 252
Towsey, Lieut.-Col. F. W., 1, 11, 12, 17, 20, 54, 108, 111	
Trench Warfare :	
Nov., 1914—Mar., 1915, 29, 30, 31 ; Visit of H.M. the King and H.R.H. Prince of Wales, 32 ; Bombers do well, 33	
15th Mar.—15th June, 1915 ...	51
18th—30th June, 1915... ...	63
1st—31st July, 1915, 97 ; Five Battalions meet...	99
Trench Mortar Battery introduced	101
1st—31st Aug., 1915 ...	113
Visit of H.R.H. Prince of Wales	116
1st Oct.—31st Dec., 1915 ...	133
Visit of H.M. the King, ...	137

	Page
Cpl. Meekosha, 1/6th Bn. wins first V.C. for West Yorks Regt., 138 ; A gas mask story, 139 ; Gas attack on 1/5th Bn. 140 ; 1st Jan.—31st March, 1916, 163; Disposition of West Yorkshire Battalions, 163, 164 ; Attack on the Bluff and St. Eloi, 165 ; The Unwanted Trench Mortar, 171 ; The Bluff again, 173 ; Raid by 12th Bn., 177 ; 12th Bn. commended, 179 ; A minor enterprise, 183	
Umfreville, Lieut.-Col. H. K. ...	100
Vaughan, Major A. O.	128
Wade, Lieut.-Col. H. O., 52, 199, 217, 220	
Wood, Lieut.-Col. C. E., 52, 163, 199, 217, 221, 225	
Wood, Major M. D.	92
Worsley, Major F. P.	301

www.ingramcontent.com/pod-product-compliance
Lightning Source LLC
Chambersburg PA
CBHW052132010526
44113CB00035B/1959